THE SCIENCE OF COGNITIVE BEHAVIORAL THERAPY

THE SCIENCE OF COGNITIVE BEHAVIORAL THERAPY

Edited by

STEFAN G. HOFMANN
Boston University, Boston, MA, United States

GORDON J.G. ASMUNDSON
University of Regina, Regina, SK, Canada

ACADEMIC PRESS
An imprint of Elsevier

Academic Press is an imprint of Elsevier
125 London Wall, London EC2Y 5AS, United Kingdom
525 B Street, Suite 1800, San Diego, CA 92101-4495, United States
50 Hampshire Street, 5th Floor, Cambridge, MA 02139, United States
The Boulevard, Langford Lane, Kidlington, Oxford OX5 1GB, United Kingdom

Notices
Knowledge and best practice in this field are constantly changing. As new research and experience
broaden our understanding, changes in research methods, professional practices, or medical treatment
may become necessary.

Practitioners and researchers must always rely on their own experience and knowledge in evaluating
and using any information, methods, compounds, or experiments described herein. In using such
information or methods they should be mindful of their own safety and the safety of others, including
parties for whom they have a professional responsibility.

To the fullest extent of the law, neither the Publisher nor the authors, contributors, or editors,
assume any liability for any injury and/or damage to persons or property as a matter of products
liability, negligence or otherwise, or from any use or operation of any methods, products, instructions,
or ideas contained in the material herein.

British Library Cataloguing-in-Publication Data
A catalogue record for this book is available from the British Library

Library of Congress Cataloging-in-Publication Data
A catalog record for this book is available from the Library of Congress

ISBN: 978-0-12-803457-6

For Information on all Academic Press publications
visit our website at https://www.elsevier.com/books-and-journals

Working together
to grow libraries in
developing countries

www.elsevier.com • www.bookaid.org

Publisher: Nikki Levy
Acquisition Editor: Nikki Levy
Editorial Project Manager: Barbara Makinster
Production Project Manager: Nicky Carter
Cover Designer: Matthew Limbert

Typeset by MPS Limited, Chennai, India

Contents

I

SCIENTIFIC FOUNDATIONS

II

EXTENSIONS, INNOVATIONS, AND MODIFICATIONS OF TREATMENT STRATEGIES

III

PROBLEM-FOCUSED APPROACHES

IV

COMPUTER-ASSISTED APPLICATIONS

21. Internet-Based Cognitive Behavior Therapy 531

GERHARD ANDERSSON, PER CARLBRING AND HEATHER D. HADJISTAVROPOULOS

22. Virtual Reality and Other Realities 551

CRISTINA BOTELLA, ROSA M. BAÑOS, AZUCENA GARCÍA-PALACIOS AND SOLEDAD QUERO

Index 591

List of Contributors

Amelia Aldao The Ohio State University, Columbus, OH, United States

Nader Amir San Diego State University/University of California San Diego, San Diego, CA, United States

Gerhard Andersson Linköping University, Linköping, Sweden; Karolinska Institute, Stockholm, Sweden

Natalie Arbid University of Massachusetts Boston, Boston, MA, United States

Scarlett O. Baird The University of Texas at Austin, Austin, TX, United States

Rosa M. Baños Universitat de Valencia, Valencia, Spain

Eni S. Becker Radboud University Nijmegen, Nijmegen, The Netherlands

Hannah Boettcher Boston University, Boston, MA, United States

Cristina Botella Universitat Jaume I, Castellón, Spain

Richard A. Bryant University of New South Wales, Sydney, NSW, Australia

Per Carlbring Stockholm University, Stockholm, Sweden

Fredrick Chin University of Nevada, Reno, NV, United States

Tommy Chou Florida International University, Miami, FL, United States

Jonathan S. Comer Florida International University, Miami, FL, United States

Laren R. Conklin Chalmers P. Wylie VA Ambulatory Care Center, Columbus, OH, United States

Elizabeth C. Conti Baylor College of Medicine, Houston, TX, United States

Zafra Cooper University of Oxford, Oxford, United Kingdom; Yale University Medical School, New Haven, CT, United States

Danielle Cornacchio Florida International University, Miami, FL, United States

Michelle L. Davis The University of Texas at Austin, Austin, TX, United States

Keith S. Dobson University of Calgary, Calgary, AB, Canada

Michael R. Dolsen University of California, Berkeley, CA, United States

David J.A. Dozois The University of Western Ontario, London, ON, Canada

Azucena García-Palacios Universitat Jaume I, Castellón, Spain

Caitlin E. Gasperetti University of California, Berkeley, CA, United States

Riccardo D. Grave Villa Garda Hospital, Garda, Italy

Heather D. Hadjistavropoulos University of Regina, Regina, Canada

Allison G. Harvey University of California, Berkeley, CA, United States

Kristen M. Haut   Rush University Medical Center, Chicago, IL, United States

Steven C. Hayes   University of Nevada, Reno, NV, United States

Bridget A. Hearon   Albright College, Reading, PA, United States

Devon Hinton   Arbour Counseling Services, Lowell, MA, United States; Massachusetts General Hospital and Harvard Medical School, Boston, MA, United States

Christine I. Hooker   Rush University Medical Center, Chicago, IL, United States

Maria Kleinstäuber   Philipps-University, Marburg, Germany

Cynthia Kraus-Schuman   Baylor College of Medicine, Houston, TX, United States

Jennie M. Kuckertz   San Diego State University/University of California San Diego, San Diego, CA, United States

Josie Lee   Boston University, Boston, MA, United States

Marsha M. Linehan   University of Washington, Seattle, WA, United States

Anita Lungu   Lyra Health, Burlingame, CA, United States

Jennifer H. Martinez   University of Massachusetts Boston, Boston, MA, United States

Vijay A. Mittal   Northwestern University, Evanston, IL, United States

Susan M. Orsillo   Suffolk University, Boston, MA, United States

Michael W. Otto   Boston University, Boston, MA, United States

Anushka Patel   The University of Tulsa, Tulsa, OK, United States

Andre J. Plate   The Ohio State University, Columbus, OH, United States

Soledad Quero   Universitat Jaume I, Castellón, Spain

Leanne Quigley   University of Calgary, Calgary, AB, Canada

Winfried Rief   Philipps-University, Marburg, Germany

Katerina Rnic   The University of Western Ontario, London, ON, Canada

Lizabeth Roemer   University of Massachusetts Boston, Boston, MA, United States

Amanda L. Sanchez   Florida International University, Miami, FL, United States

Stewart A. Shankman   University of Illinois at Chicago, Philadelphia, IL, United States

Jasper A.J. Smits   The University of Texas at Austin, Austin, TX, United States

Leslie Sokol   Academy of Cognitive Therapy, Philadelphia, PA, United States

Melinda A. Stanley   Baylor College of Medicine, Houston, TX, United States

Janna N. Vrijsen   Radboud University Medical Center, Nijmegen, The Netherlands; Pro Persona Mental Health Care, Nijmegen, The Netherlands

Scott H. Waltman   University of Pennsylvania, Philadelphia, PA, United States

Sara M. Witcraft   The University of Texas at Austin, Austin, TX, United States

Preface

In 2013, we published a target article entitled, *The Science of Cognitive Therapy* in the journal *Behavior Therapy* (Hofmann, Asmundson, & Beck, 2013) as a follow-up to a 2008 article published in *Clinical Psychology Review* (Hofmann & Asmundson, 2008). These articles have become two of the most downloaded and frequently cited articles in the clinical field. Soon after publication of the 2013 article, Elsevier approached us with the idea to turn it into a book. The book you are reading now is the result of this.

In this text, we focus on contemporary scientific models that fall under the general term, cognitive behavioral therapy (CBT). CBT is not a single treatment protocol. Instead, it refers to a family of interventions, as well as a scientific approach toward understanding and treating psychiatric disorders and human suffering. It includes a family of interventions that share the same basic elements of the CBT model that focus on the importance of cognitive and behavioral processes. This family has evolved from a specific treatment model into a scientific approach that incorporates a wide variety of disorder-specific interventions and treatment techniques as well as several unified or transdiagnostic protocols.

CBT is undoubtedly one of the big success stories of contemporary psychology and psychiatry. Soon after the generic CBT model was formulated by Aaron T. Beck and others (e.g., Beck, 1975) it revolutionized the field of clinical psychology and psychiatry. In recognition of his contribution, Beck received the Lasker Award in 2006, a highly prestigious medical prize. The chairman of the Lasker jury noted that "cognitive therapy is one of the most important advances—if not the most important advance—in the treatment of mental diseases in the last 50 years" (Altman, 2006).

Since then, an overwhelming number of effective CBT protocols have been developed for specific mental disorders. A review of the empirical literature identified 269 metaanalytic studies examining CBT for nearly every psychiatric problem (Hofmann, Asnaani, Vonk, Sawyer, & Fang, 2012). A description of the various CBT protocols easily fills a 3-volume text book series (Hofmann, 2014).

Not surprisingly, many countries around the world have invested greatly in the training and dissemination of CBT, recognizing the enormous value of this family of effective short-term treatments. Economic data consistently show that the provision of CBT for common mental disorders is more cost-efficient than pharmacotherapy or other interventions, such as psychodynamic therapies. Unfortunately, the United States, Canada, and other developed countries are still lagging behind other nations, such as the United Kingdom and Australia, in necessary dissemination efforts of CBT. Therefore, wider dissemination of CBT should be a priority for future research. More recently, some authors have begun to develop unified CBT protocols that cut across diagnostic categories in order to facilitate dissemination (e.g., Barlow et al., 2010). Books such as this will further facilitate recognition and dissemination of CBT worldwide.

This book is particularly relevant for graduate and advanced undergraduate students. It can be used as a supplement for classes in abnormal psychology, social psychology, and related courses. The text may also be applicable to clinical psychology and psychiatry residency programs and may be of great interest to researchers and CBT scholars. Written by some of the foremost experts and developers of these models and related interventions and treatment techniques, this text will fill a void in the literature by assembling seemingly diverse models, all of which belong to the same CBT family.

This book, which provides a cross-sectional view of some of the exciting new developments in the field of CBT, is organized into four broad sections. Section 1 covers scientific foundations and includes chapters on the generic model of CBT (Chapter 1: The Generic Model of Cognitive Behavioral Therapy: A Case Conceptualization-Driven Approach by Scott Waltman and Leslie Sokol), the basics of treatment-relevant assessments (Chapter 2: Treatment-Relevant Assessment in Cognitive Behavioral Therapy by Katerina Rnic and David Dozois), learning principles in CBT (Chapter 3: Learning Principles in CBT by Michelle Davis, Sara Witcraft, Scarlett O. Baird, and Jasper Smits), cognitive processes (Chapter 4: Cognitive Processes in CBT by Eni Becker and Janna Vrijsen), emotion regulation in CBT (Chapter 5: Emotion Regulation in Cognitive Behavioral Therapy: Bridging the Gap Between Treatment Studies and Laboratory Experiments by Andre Plate and Amelia Aldao).

Section 2 focuses on extensions, innovations, and modifications of CBT strategies, including adding pharmacotherapy to CBT (Chapter 6: Combined Treatment With CBT and Psychopharmacology by Josie Lee, Bridget Hearon, and Michael Otto), Acceptance and Commitment Therapy (Chapter 7: Acceptance and Commitment Therapy and the Cognitive Behavioral Tradition: Assumptions, Model, Methods, and Outcomes by Fredrich Chin and Steven Hayes), mindfulness-based treatments (Chapter 8: Mindfulness-Based Cognitive Behavioral Treatments by Lizabeth Roemer, Natalie Arbid, Jennifer Martinez, and Susan Orsillo), cultural adaptations (Chapter 9: Global to Local: Adapting CBT for Cross-Cultural Expressions of Psychopathology by Anushka Patel and Devon Hinton), adaptations for older adults (Chapter 10: Cognitive Behavioral Therapy in Older Adults by Elizabeth Price, Cynthia Kraus-Schuman, and Melinda Stanley), and adaptations for children and adolescents (Chapter 11: Cognitive Behavioral Therapy for Children and Adolescents by Danielle Cornacchio, Amanda Sanchez, Tommy Chou, and Jonathan Comer).

Section 3 covers problem-focused approaches, including behavioral activation for depression (Chapter 12: Behavioral Activation Treatments for Depression by Leanne Quigley and Keith Dobson), PTSD (Chapter 13: Posttraumatic Stress Disorder by Richard Bryant), eating disorders (Chapter 14: Eating Disorders: Transdiagnostic Theory and Treatment by Zafra Cooper and Ricardo Dalle Grave), anxiety disorders (Chapter 15: Transdiagnostic Treatment for Anxiety Disorders by Laren Conklin and Hannah Boettcher), sleep problems (Chapter 16: Cognitive Behavioral Therapy for Sleep Disorders by Caitlin Eggleston, Michael Dolsen, and Allison Harvey), somatoform disorders and pain (Chapter 17: Cognitive Behavioral Therapy for Somatoform Disorders and

Pain by Maria Kleinstäuber and Winfried Rief), and dialectic behavior therapy for borderline personality disorder, suicidality, and other emotion dysregulation disorders (Chapter 18: Dialectical Behavior Therapy: Overview, Characteristics, and Future Directions by Anita Lungu and Marsha Linehan).

The fourth and final section covers computer-assisted applications, including cognitive bias modification training (Chapter 19: Cognitive Bias Modification by Jennie Kuckertz and Nader Amir), cognitive remediation training (Chapter 20: Cognitive Training in Schizophrenia by Kristen Haut, Vijay Mittal, Stewart Shankman, and Christine Hooker), internet-based CBT (Chapter 21: Internet-Based Cognitive Behavior Therapy by Gerhard Andersson, Per Carlbring, and Heather Hadjistavropoulos), and virtual reality (Chapter 22: Virtual Reality and Other Realities by Cristina Botella, Rosa Baños, Azucena García-Palacios, and Soledad Quero).

The selection of these chapters illustrates that the particular CBT approach needs to be tailored to the particular presenting problems, the context, and the particular person. Therefore, in order to maximize the efficacy of treatment, the CBT therapist has to understand the patient's psychological problems within the CBT framework and then identify the appropriate therapeutic targets and select the most effective treatment strategies. This directly links the theory to the techniques. We hope that this book will assist clinicians to deliver these highly effective evidence-based treatments to reduce human suffering and enhance quality of life.

Stefan G. Hofmann[1] and Gordon J.G. Asmundson[2]
[1]Boston University, Boston, MA, United States
[2]University of Regina, Regina, SK, Canada

References

Altman, L.K. (2006, September 17). *Psychiatrist is among five chosen for medical award.* New York Times, <http://www.nytimes.com/2006/09/17/health/17lasker.html>.

Barlow, D. H., Ellard, K. K., Fairholm, C., Farchione, T. J., Boisseau, C. L., Ehrenreich-May, J. T., & Allen, L. B. (2010). *Unified protocol for transdiagnostic treatment of emotional disorders (treatments that work series).* New York, NY: Oxford University Press.

Beck, A. T. (1975). *Cognitive therapy and the emotional disorders.* New York, NY: Guilford University Press.

Hofmann, S. G., & Asmundson, G. J. G. (2008). Acceptance and mindfulness-based therapy: New wave or old hat? *Clinical Psychology Review, 28,* 1—16.

Hofmann, S. G., Asmundson, G. J., & Beck, A. T. (2013). The science of cognitive therapy. *Behavior Therapy, 44,* 199—212.

Hofmann, S. G., Asnaani, A., Vonk, J. J., Sawyer, A. T., & Fang, A. (2012). The efficacy of cognitive behavioral therapy: A review of meta-analyses. *Cognitive Therapy and Research, 36,* 427—440.

Hofmann, S. G. (Ed.), (2014). *The Wiley handbook of cognitive behavioral therapy* (Vols. I—III). Chichester, UK: John Wiley & Sons, Ltd.

SCIENTIFIC FOUNDATIONS

1

The Generic Model of Cognitive Behavioral Therapy: A Case Conceptualization-Driven Approach

Scott H. Waltman[1] and Leslie Sokol[2]

[1]University of Pennsylvania, Philadelphia, PA, United States
[2]Academy of Cognitive Therapy, Philadelphia, PA, United States

Cognitive Behavioral Therapy (CBT) is among the most studied forms of psychotherapy, with hundreds of outcome trials demonstrating the clinical efficacy and effectiveness (Clark & Taylor, 2009; Hofman, Asnaani, Vonk, Sawyer, & Fang, 2012). These clinical trials are mostly based on the use of single-diagnosis protocols, which are facilitative to highly controlled internally valid studies. Persons (1991, 2013) was an early voice in highlighting the potential disconnect between the manner in which CBT was studied and practiced. Although CBT may sometimes be inaccurately conceptualized as a collection of interventions and strategies, the model is better characterized as a way of thinking, or a theory-driven philosophy (Beck & Dozois, 2011; Waltman, Creed, & Beck, 2016), which can be used to guide the selection of interventions (Rosenbaum & Ronen, 1998). This working formulation (i.e., the cognitive case conceptualization) evolves over the course of treatment, serving as a guide for treatment and a lens for understanding the client (Beck, 2011). Researchers refer to the Generic Cognitive Model of CBT as the case formulation-driven or case

The Science of Cognitive Behavioral Therapy.
DOI: http://dx.doi.org/10.1016/B978-0-12-803457-6.00001-5

conceptualization-driven approach to CBT (Persons, 2008) or transdiagnostic CBT (Creed et al., 2016); whereas, practitioners would self-identify as practicing cognitive therapy, Beckian CBT, or formulation-driven CBT. This approach was first developed to treat depression (Beck, Rush, Shaw, & Emery, 1979) and has expanded over the past 40 + years to represent a set of shared evidence-based principles for a wide range of presenting problems and stressors (Beck & Haigh, 2014).

Transdiagnostic CBT for anxiety disorders is a protocol that has been developed to target common mechanisms across anxiety disorders. Although there exists promising research about the effectiveness of this approach (Craske, 2012; Norton, 2012; Norton & Barrera, 2012; Norton et al., 2012; Rector, Man, and Lerman, 2014; Reinholt & Krogh, 2014), this protocol is manualized and not case-conceptualization driven; therefore, this chapter will not focus on transdiagnostic CBT for anxiety disorders.

When working with multiproblem populations, a course of case conceptualization-driven CBT is recommended over several courses of single-diagnosis protocols (Persons, 2006). This approach involves forming an individualized conceptualization of the precipitants leading to the client's problems and the contingencies and maladaptive behaviors maintaining them (Waltman, 2015). A cognitive case conceptualization-driven approach to therapy essentially means treating each individual as a single-case study design, where the clinician, in collaboration with the client, forms testable hypotheses about the psychological mechanisms that cause and maintain the client's difficulties (Eells, 2009; Persons, 2008). The case conceptualization-driven approach to CBT is not a rejection of single-diagnosis protocols, but rather a strategic approach where interventions from single-diagnosis protocols are selected to target the hypothesized underlying mechanisms in the individual's presentation. Over the course of treatment, data are gathered to assess the accuracy of the hypotheses and the effects of treatment, and correspondingly the case conceptualization is revised as treatment progresses. Thus, two main advantages to the case conceptualization-driven approach are that it allows for flexibility when working with people with cooccurring problems and that it allows for course corrections as the clinician's understanding of the case evolves.

EMPIRICAL SUPPORT

As stated above, a majority of the CBT outcome studies have been conducted on single-disorder protocols. The Generic Cognitive Model of CBT is an approach that relies on the evidence-based principles derived from that research. Nonetheless, a number of randomized controlled trials (RCTs) have demonstrated that a case conceptualization-based approach produces outcomes equivalent to those observed in RCTs of single-disorder protocols (Eells, 2013; Ghaderi, 2006; Jacobson et al., 1989; Kuyken, Padesky, & Dudley, 2008; Schneider & Byrne, 1987). For example, a trial ($n = 58$) of a case conceptualization-driven approach to CBT for anxious and depressed clients in a private practice setting showed clinically significant changes in symptoms at rates similar to those found in RCTs of CBT protocols designed to treat clients with a single diagnosis (Persons, Roberts, Zalecki, & Brechwald, 2006). In another study comparing manualized approaches to CBT with case conceptualization-driven CBT in treating patients with bulimia nervosa ($n = 50$), the case-formulation approach slightly outperformed the manual at posttreatment, but at follow-up treatment, outcomes were equivalent (Ghaderi, 2006).

Clients who present to treatment meeting diagnostic criteria for several diagnoses may benefit from receiving one course of a case conceptualization-driven approach to CBT as opposed to receiving several courses of treatment from different treatment protocols (Persons et al., 2006). As comorbidity is such a common concern, it is prudent to train clinicians working within a managed care setting to use this efficient approach to therapy. Notably, a recent review (Kuyken et al., 2008) highlighted that while there is promising evidence to suggest the clinical utility of using a case conceptualization-driven approach to CBT, it remains unclear whether this uniformly enhances the therapeutic process.

One area where the use of a case conceptualization-driven approach seems to enhance the therapeutic process is in working with clients who have not demonstrated the expected improvements following a course of CBT treatment with a manualized single-disorder protocol. A few case studies have shown promising results regarding the use of the case conceptualization to address treatment failures and nonresponders to improve clinical outcomes (Persons, Beckner, & Tompkins, 2013; Persons & Mikami, 2002). As single-disorder protocols work well with clients who have straightforward single problem presentations, the prospect of having an approach to improve clinical outcomes with more difficult presentations is a current need in the field.

APPLYING THE GENERIC COGNITIVE MODEL OF CBT TO TRAINING AND SUPERVISION

Training and supervision in CBT is modeled after what CBT looks like in practice (Sudak et al., 2016). Model-consistent CBT supervision and training is a psychotherapy-based approach that incorporates components of CBT in the process to facilitate experiential learning (Beck, Sarnat, & Barenstein, 2008; McFarr et al., 2014; Padesky, 1996; Sudak et al., 2016; Waltman, 2016). This involves adhering to CBT session structure, maintaining an empathic and validating stance, and demonstrating/role-playing CBT interventions and strategies. This practice can also include using a cognitive and behavioral framework to conceptualize supervisees and trainees, which is well illustrated in a case example by Waltman (2016).

A social worker with much experience in the field was taking part in a CBT implementation program and was having difficulty learning and demonstrating the competencies associated with CBT practice, falling into a habit of solely doing case management. As this was empathically addressed by the trainer, it became evident that this social worker had early experiences in her career where she felt therapeutically ineffective and that she had learned to focus on doing what she did well—case management. Over the years, this avoidance of therapy led to strong underlying beliefs about her therapeutic incompetence, and she developed the following intermediate assumption, "If I do therapy it won't help, but if I do case management I can help improve people's lives." Identifying this assumption allowed the trainer to strategize a two pronged approach of skills training, where the standard CBT training was supplemented with cognitive strategies to help this social worker test out her assumptions and come to form more balanced beliefs about her therapeutic effectiveness, which ultimately led to improved training and clinical outcomes. This level of attention and conceptualization may not be necessary for every supervisee/trainee, but for those that struggle, this strategy of using a hypothesis-driven approach to conceptualizing and addressing the problem can be invaluable (Waltman, 2016).

The case conceptualization-driven approach to CBT is not without disadvantages; it relies on the clinician being able to form an accurate cognitive formulation, which is one of the main critiques of this approach (Wilson, 1996). Learning how to form cognitive case conceptualizations can be difficult, with a recent qualitative survey of CBT trainers reporting the perception that perhaps the intermediate beliefs (i.e., conditional assumptions) are the hardest component of the cognitive conceptualization to learn (Waltman, Hall, McFarr, Beck, & Creed, 2017). Therapists typically need to be trained in how to create, test, and revise the formulation (Dudley, Kuyken, & Padesky, 2011; Waltman, 2016); even still, after training not all therapists produce good quality case conceptualizations (Kuyken, Fothergill, Musa, & Chadwick, 2005). For example, as part of a continuing education training, therapists (n = 115) were presented with the same case information and asked to fill out a case conceptualization diagram (see Beck, 2011). The clinicians' written case conceptualizations were compared to the prototype provided by Beck (2011) and rated for parsimony, coherence, and meaningful account of the client's presenting problem. Responses were rated as being "good," "good enough," "poor," or "very poor," by the researchers with an acceptable rate of interrater agreement (k = 0.85; Kuyken et al., 2005). Altogether, only 44% of the formulations were judged to be of an adequate quality.

Although case conceptualization is a foundational skill in the Generic Cognitive Model of CBT, only recently has a psychometrically sound tool been developed to measure the accuracy and quality of a CBT case conceptualization. Kuyken et al. (2015) developed the Case Conceptualization Rating Scale as a useful tool for assessing and refining the case formulation. Standardization data demonstrated impressive reliability with high internal consistency (α = 0.94) and adequate interrater reliability (ICC = 0.84). Controlled studies on the effects of using this rating scale are needed; correspondingly, it is too early to tell if using this measure leads to improved training or clinical outcomes. It might be that expecting all therapists to learn how to form high-quality and accurate case conceptualizations is a lofty goal; thus, manualized-approaches to treatment remain necessary and valuable (Wilson, 1996).

Rogers, Reinecke, and Curry (2005) conducted a study on the use of a case conceptualization-driven approach to CBT for treating adolescents with depression. The researchers presented a case study that helped to illustrate how this case conceptualization-driven approach allowed for flexibility and personalization within the treatment model. Thus manualized-based approaches to care and individualizing treatment through the use of cognitive case conceptualization are not mutually exclusive practices (Rogers et al., 2005). Notably, the larger Treatment for Adolescents with Depression Study (TADS; The TADS Team, 2007) used a modular approach to personalization; that is, based upon the case conceptualization, treatment targets are identified and specific relevant treatment modules are selected from a manual. Evidence for the effectiveness of this approach is demonstrated by the 81% treatment response rate of adolescents in the CBT condition of the TADS study (see The TADS Team, 2007). This approach to personalization of treatment is similar to the proposal of Thompson-Hollands, Sauer-Zavala, and Barlow (2014) regarding the future directions for The Unified Protocol for Transdiagnostic Treatment of Emotional Disorders (UP).

COMPARING THE GENERIC COGNITIVE MODEL OF CBT TO THE UNIFIED PROTOCOL

The UP was originally developed as a single protocol that could be administered to most clients regardless of diagnosis or presenting problem, similar to the transdiagnostic CBT for anxiety disorders protocol (Norton et al., 2012; Reinholt & Krogh, 2014). It was noted that many diagnoses have similar underlying mechanisms and that a single protocol could be developed to treat a host of problems. An additional consideration in the development of the UP was the large amount of time required to learn several problem-specific treatment protocols (e.g., Exposure and Response Prevention for Obsessive-Compulsive Disorder). The treatment developers argued that it was too difficult for community providers to learn all the different treatment protocols and that using the UP would be easier for clinicians working in the community behavioral health systems to learn (Barlow, Farchione, Fairholme, & Ellard, 2011). Practically speaking, the UP was to work like a Swiss Army Knife, having multiple uses. Since that time, Barlow's lab has shifted their focus from having a single protocol to use with most clients to personalizing treatment (see Thompson-Hollands et al., 2014). Their proposal is to base the ordering and selection of modules from the UP for a specific client based upon a personalized assessment, including an interpretation of the client's responses to a dimensional classification system for emotional disorders (Rosellini, 2013). Notably, the cognitive case conceptualization-driven approach to CBT and the proposed methods of personalizing the application of the UP are similar yet distinct approaches to idiographic transdiagnostic client care. The comparative effectiveness, utility, and acceptability of these two different approaches is an empirical question that future studies will have to investigate.

DESCRIPTION OF GENERIC COGNITIVE MODEL OF CBT

The Generic Cognitive Model stipulates that perceptions of situations, rather than the situation itself, directly influence emotion, physiology, and behavior (Beck, 1963, 1964). Situation-specific thoughts or automatic thoughts typically arise spontaneously are often brief and fleeting, take the form of a thought or image, and are regarded as true without reflection or evaluation. The Generic Cognitive Model proposes that all psychological problems, regardless of their etiology, result in problems in thinking (Beck, 1963, 1964; Beck & Haigh, 2014). In CBT, identifying and correcting these biases and distorted errors in thinking are the key to reducing client distress. As CBT holds a robust tradition of research and scientific inquiry, the Generic Cognitive Model of CBT has been revised and refined over the years with additions including the continuity between adaptive and maladaptive functioning, schemas, and the role of attentional focus (Beck & Haigh, 2014)—all of which will be elaborated below in the following examples.

EXAMPLE: THE COGNITIVE MODEL

Situation: A person sends a text to a friend. Although the friend typically responds right away, many hours have passed without a response.

Here are some examples of how one might think, feel emotionally and physiologically, and behave:

Person 1 thinks, "They are purposely ignoring me," feels angry and aroused, and repeatedly sends the same text message demanding an answer.

Person 2 thinks, "They are mad at me, I must have done something wrong." They feel sad and lethargic and give up trying to reach the person.

Person 3 thinks, "Something bad must have happened to them." They feel anxious, their heart starts racing, and they start calling everyone they know in an effort to find out what happened.

Person 4 thinks, "They are probably too busy to respond or more likely their phone is dead." They feel neutral, remain calm, and wait patiently for a response.

Apparent across these examples is that the content of one's thinking directly influences the affect, physiological response, and one's consequent behavior. Formulating a cognitive conceptualization of a client requires understanding their situation-specific thoughts, feelings, and behaviors across upsetting situations. Cognitive change can be produced through cognitive, behavioral, and emotive strategies (Lorenzo-Luaces, German, & Derubeis, 2015); however, identifying, evaluating, and modifying these situation-specific perceptions is only the first step in reducing distress. Identifying and evaluating the pervasive negative core beliefs that influence those situation-specific perceptions is hypothesized to produce more enduring symptom relief (Safran, Vallis, Segal, & Shaw, 1986) and to be a crucial step in bolstering adaptive competing schema and core beliefs (Dozois et al., 2014). For example, in a study of CBT treating individuals with social anxiety disorder, it was found that changes in maladaptive interpersonal beliefs (i.e., core beliefs) fully accounted for reductions in social anxiety following a course of CBT (Boden et al., 2012).

Core beliefs are the ideas we formulate about others, the world, and ourselves over the course of time. These ideas can be positive and negative and typically are accepted as absolute truths regardless of their validity. Often negative core beliefs are actually overgeneralizations of partial truths; but, sometimes they are actually a reflection of the complete opposite of the actual truth. Although automatic thoughts reflect the view of a given situation, core beliefs are more global ideas that exist independent of any given situation. In the texting example above, the question arises as to what lead one person to see an angry viewpoint, another a negative viewpoint, another danger, and the last a neutral perspective. Typically our negatively biased core beliefs about ourselves are what lead to the biased view rather than the more neutral or reasonable viewpoint.

Negative core beliefs about one's self often fall into two major themes, competency or desirability (Dozois & Beck, 2008). A person may have doubt in both domains or may more strongly endorse negative views about themselves in only one domain. Examples of core belief labels reflective of incompetence are I am incompetent, I am a failure, I am weak, I am not good enough, I am inferior, and I am dumb. Examples of core belief labels reflective of undesirability are I am undesirable, I am unattractive, I am unlovable, I am unlikable, I am bad, and I am worthless. It is possible to embrace one global negative belief about one self or many. These core beliefs may always prevail, biasing every situation the person faces, or only rule when the person is facing a difficult or challenging situation or struggling with a psychological disorder such as depression or anxiety. Commonly, clients with chronic or reoccurring psychological problems and personality disorders, have pervasive negative beliefs that are always yelling in their ear and distorting almost all interpretations of every situation (Beck, 1963, 1964). Imagine the client who believes they are undesirable so they get mad when you are looking at them and smiling, thinking you are making fun of them and when you turn your glance away, they get even angrier thinking you don't care about them and are no longer paying attention. Similarly, when you fail to immediately respond to their text message, their first conclusion is that you are ignoring them on purpose. On the other hand, the client who believes they are a failure thinks you are not responding to their text messages because they must have done something to ruin the relationship. In work settings, these individuals might think that they must have done a horrible job on something when their manager asks for a meeting or they don't bother trying to make a sale, believing it will never work out anyway.

The question arises as to where do these beliefs come from and what perpetuates them? Core beliefs are shaped by biology and environment (Beck & Haigh, 2014). Temperament and biological predisposition is impacted by the social world we are a part of. The baby who prefers to be held when falling asleep versus the one who falls asleep in their crib or the child who startles easily versus the one who can sleep through anything reflects preference, sensitivity, and temperament. The social world then impacts this predisposition. Sometimes the social world is harsh, abusive, negligent, or aversive. However, a trauma history is not a determination of negative self-views (Sobel, Resick, & Rabalais, 2009). When the trauma history is interpreted in a personal way, meaning the person takes blame and responsibility for the adversity, then negative core beliefs are more likely (Ehlers & Clark, 2000). But, when the trauma is seen as an external event independent of the recipient, then negative core beliefs may stay at bay. In additionally, trauma or adversity is not a requirement for the development of negative core beliefs. Benign histories can also have a significant impact on the developing child. It is not the history itself that grows the negative core beliefs, but the person's interpretation of those events (Beck & Haigh, 2014). The development of negative core beliefs may begin early in life and experiences throughout our lives continue to reinforce or discount those views (Beck, 2011).

In between situation-specific automatic thoughts and more pervasive core beliefs are what is referred to as rules or assumptions. Rules are universal ideas that people believe about themselves, others, or the world, such as things will never work out for me, everyone else is capable, or the world is a dangerous place. Assumptions are conditional statements that link behavioral strategies with core beliefs. For example, the person who believes they are undesirable may hold the following assumptions: "If I always acquiesce and say yes, then people will like me" or "If I put on a façade and pretend everything is okay then I won't be rejected." Similarly, a client who believes they are a failure might have the following assumptions: "If I am perfect, then I won't be a failure" or "If I don't try, then I cannot fail." In these examples the behavioral strategy was believed to be a coping strategy on the part of the client as it served a protective role. These are positively stated assumptions. Assumptions can be both positive and negative. Negative assumptions simply result in a negative result. For example, "If I say no, they won't like me" or "If I make a mistake, I am a failure."

In understanding individuals through the lens of the Generic Cognitive Model, it is essential to identify both their thinking and their behavior. Like automatic thoughts, there are behaviors that take place in a specific situation. Similarly, like prevalent core beliefs, there are behavioral strategies that people use across situations. In CBT, the key to behavioral strategies is to examine their effectiveness and help people consider alternative behavioral strategies when the strategy they are using is not working; for example, replacing perfectionism with trying your best, assertiveness for ineffective communication, or avoidance with facing the situation. Often what is initially observed is a behavior pattern of short-term coping/relief leading to long-term distress, and the work of CBT involves helping people to tolerate temporary distress in the service of long-term gains.

Understanding the Generic Cognitive Model is essential in formulating a cognitive conceptualization of the individual and their problem. The cognitive conceptualization of the individual is simply identifying the situation-specific thoughts, emotions, and behaviors across specific situations and using that information to identify the more pervasive beliefs, assumptions, and compensatory strategies. Ascertaining the history is an important piece in understanding the individual. Understanding the problem through the lens of the cognitive model then simply involves identifying the problems in thinking at all levels of thinking: automatic thoughts, assumptions, and beliefs.

A number of different methods to form case conceptualization have been developed. Judy Beck's Cognitive Conceptualization Diagram (CCD) is among the most popular (see Beck, 2011). Other commonly used methods include one developed by Persons (2008) that is similar to the CCD; Persons's model is cognitive-behavioral, so in addition to key cognitions, her form also focuses on the hypothesized mechanism that is maintaining the difficulties (similar to a functional analysis). Padesky and Mooney (2012) have modified the CCD (Beck, 2011) to incorporate strength and resiliency factors, and Moorey (2010) developed a "vicious flower" conceptualization format that is used to draw out the cycle of thoughts, beliefs, behavior, and interactions involved in maintaining a client's difficulties.

FORMING AND USING THE CBT CASE CONCEPTUALIZATION TO INFORM TREATMENT

Regardless of the specific format used to help construct a cognitive case conceptualization, there are a number of common elements that comprise the individual's current problematic situations, their corresponding thoughts, feelings, and behaviors, and the underlying beliefs that are driving these current thoughts, feelings, and behaviors. The CBT therapist employs a strategic approach and is most interested in what is maintaining these belief sets; therefore, a main objective of the case conceptualization is to draw out how the underlying beliefs are impacting current thoughts and behaviors and how current cognitive styles and behaviors strengthen and reaffirm strongly held core beliefs and underlying assumptions. For example, consider the assumption (i.e., intermediate belief), "If I try then I'll fail, but if I don't try then I can't fail." This type of assumption would likely correspond to core beliefs of incompetence and behavioral strategies of avoiding difficult tasks and bailing out at the first sign of failure. This type of pattern tends to get stronger and stronger over time. This individual likely feels shame and sadness when having thoughts about their inadequacy. "I'm such a failure." "I can't do anything right." "I have nothing to show for my life." Consequently, they do not take a lot risks in their life—why try if you're sure you'll fail? Therefore, they have a low level of accomplishment in their life, which they construe as evidence that they are incompetent. "Of course I'm a failure; I have accomplished nothing with my life." This leads to more thoughts about their inadequacy and further behavioral avoidance. Thus, it is a cycle and a CBT therapist would seek to break up this pattern using cognitive strategies and behavioral experiments.

Sometimes the pattern is less obvious. Consider the high-achieving professional with a constant fear of failure. She has accomplished much in her personal and professional life and yet why is she plagued with thoughts and predictions of failure? It is because her information processing style does not allow her to form more balanced beliefs about her competency or successfulness. Growing up, high expectations were placed upon her and she learned that even small mistakes could be met with criticism, which lead to the development of a rigid assumption that, "If I make a mistake, then others will see how incompetent I am, but if I work as hard as I can, harder than anyone else, maybe people won't notice that I'm incompetent and they'll keep me around for now." This thought process led to great productivity and accomplishments, none of which she was able to enjoy, as she was constantly worried about being found out as the failure she was sure that she was. This attentional bias led to her fixating on minute missteps, causing her to miss the big picture. An unsophisticated cognitive therapist may try to address her beliefs about incompetency by focusing on her accomplishments. A more nuanced approach would be to ask, "Why does she still have thoughts of being a failure given her success?" In other words, "Why hasn't this problem resolved on its own?" This is the key treatment target. In this case, the key cognitive structure to target is her all-or-nothing thinking related to how she defines success, and how human she is allowed to be before she becomes a failure. Therefore, the recommended strategy is to first seek to understand the client's patterns as they are before rushing in with interventions; this can be done by drawing out the conditional assumptions (Beck, 2011), vicious cycles (Moorey, 2010), maintaining factors (Persons, 2008, 2013), or attentional biases (Beck & Haigh, 2014).

SUMMARY

The Generic Cognitive Model both predates and relies on the vast research on single-diagnosis CBT protocols. In practice, CBT is a way of thinking that is driven by hypothesis testing and case formulation.

Research has demonstrated that a case conceptualization-driven approach to CBT generally produces outcomes equivalent to single-diagnosis protocols. This formulation-driven approach may be most valuable when working with individuals who are not making the expected progress in response to standard protocols. Future research on training clinicians in how to develop adequate case formulations and comparing methods of transdiagnostic care, including the case conceptualization-driven approaches, such as the UP are warranted.

References

Barlow, D. H., Farchione, T. J., Fairholme, C. P., & Ellard, K. K. (2011). *The unified protocol for transdiagnostic treatment of emotional disorders: Therapist guide*. New York, NY: Oxford University Press.

Beck, A. T. (1963). Thinking and depression I. Idiosyncratic content and cognitive distortions. *Archives of General Psychiatry, 9*, 324–333.

Beck, A. T. (1964). Thinking and depression II. Theory and therapy. *Archives of General Psychiatry, 10*(6), 561–571.

Beck, A. T., & Dozois, D. J. A. (2011). Cognitive therapy: Current status and future directions. *Annual Review of Medicine, 62*, 397–409.

Beck, A. T., & Haigh, E. A. P. (2014). Advances in cognitive theory and therapy: The Generic Cognitive Model. *Annual Review of Clinical Psychology, 10*, 1–24.

Beck, A. T., Rush, A. J., Shaw, B. F., & Emery, G. (1979). *Cognitive therapy of depression*. New York, NY: Guilford.

Beck, J., Sarnat, J. E., & Barenstein, V. (2008). Psychotherapy-based approaches to supervision. In C. Falendar, & E. Shafranske (Eds.), *Casebook for clinical supervision: A competency-based approach*. Washington, DC: American Psychological Association.

Beck, J. S. (2011). *Cognitive behavior therapy: Basics and beyond* (2nd Ed.). New York: The Guilford Press.

Boden, M. T., John, O. P., Goldin, P. R., Werner, K., Heimberg, R. G., & Gross, J. J. (2012). The role of maladaptive beliefs in cognitive-behavioral therapy: Evidence from social anxiety disorder. *Behaviour Research and Therapy, 50*(5), 287–291.

Clark, D. A., & Taylor, S. (2009). The transdiagnostic perspective on cognitive-behavioral therapy for anxiety and depression: New wine for old wineskins? *Journal of Cognitive Psychotherapy, 23*(1), 60–66.

Craske, M. G. (2012). Transdiagnostic treatment for anxiety and depression. *Depression and Anxiety, 29*(9), 749–753.

Creed, T. A., Frankel, S., German, R., Green, K., Jager-Hyman, S., Pontoski, K., ... Beck, A. T. (2016). Implementation of transdiagnostic cognitive therapy in community behavioral health: The beck community initiative. *Journal of Consulting and Clinical Psychology, 84*(12), 1116–1126.

Dozois, D. J., & Beck, A. T. (2008). Cognitive schema, beliefs, and assumptions. In K. S. Dobson, & D. J. Dozois (Eds.), *Risk factors in depression* (pp. 122–144). Amsterdam: Elsevier/Academic.

Dozois, D. J., Bieling, P. J., Evraire, L. E., Patelis-Siotis, I., Hoar, L., Chudzik, S., ... Westra, H. A. (2014). Changes in core beliefs (early maladaptive schemas) and self-representation in cognitive therapy and pharmacotherapy for depression. *International Journal of Cognitive Therapy, 7*(3), 217–234.

Dudley, R., Kuyken, W., & Padesky, C. A. (2011). Disorder specific and trans-diagnostic case conceptualisation. *Clinical Psychology Review, 31*(2), 213–224.

Eells, T. D. (2009). Review of The case formulation approach to cognitive-behavior therapy. *Psychotherapy: Theory, Research, Practice, Training, 46*(3), 400−401.

Eells, T. D. (2013). The Case formulation approach to psychotherapy research revisited. *Pragmatic Case Studies in Psychotherapy, 9*(4), 426−447.

Ehlers, A., & Clark, D. M. (2000). A cognitive model of posttraumatic stress disorder. *Behaviour Research and Therapy, 38*(4), 319−345, doi:10.1016/s0005-7967(99)00123-0.

Ghaderi, A. (2006). Does individualisation matter? A randomised trial of standardised (focused) versus individualized (broad) cognitive behaviour therapy for bulimia nervosa. *Behaviour, Research and Therapy, 44*, 273−288.

Hofmann, S. G., Asnaani, A., Vonk, I. J., Sawyer, A. T., & Fang, A. (2012). The efficacy of cognitive behavioral therapy: A review of meta-analyses. *Cognitive Therapy and Research, 36*(5), 427−440.

Jacobson, N. S., Schmaling, K. B., Holtzworth-Munroe, A., Katt, J. L., Wood, L. F., & Follette, V. M. (1989). Research-structured vs clinically flexible versions of social learning-based marital therapy. *Behaviour Research and Therapy, 27*(2), 173−180.

Kuyken, W., Beshai, S., Dudley, R., Abel, A., Görg, N., Gower, P., & Padesky, C. A. (2015). Assessing competence in collaborative case conceptualization: Development and preliminary psychometric properties of the collaborative case conceptualization rating scale (CCC-RS). *Behavioural and Cognitive Psychotherapy, 44*(02), 179−192. Available from http://dx.doi.org/10.1017/s1352465814000691.

Kuyken, W., Fothergill, C. D., Musa, M., & Chadwick, P. (2005). The reliability and quality of cognitive case formulation. *Behaviour Research and Therapy, 43*(9), 1187−1201.

Kuyken, W., Padesky, C. A., & Dudley, R. (2008). The science and practice of case conceptualization. *Behavioural and Cognitive Psychotherapy, 36*(06), 757−768.

Lorenzo-Luaces, L., German, R. E., & Derubeis, R. J. (2015). It's complicated: The relation between cognitive change procedures, cognitive change, and symptom change in cognitive therapy for depression. *Clinical Psychology Review, 41*, 3−15.

McFarr, L., Brown, L. A., Holler, R., Jackson, L., Ramirez, U., & Morgan, W. (2014). Cognitive behavior therapies in Southern California. *The Behavior Therapist, 37*, 117−121.

Moorey, S. (2010). The six cycles maintenance model: Growing a "vicious flower" for depression. *Behavioural and Cognitive Psychotherapy, 38*(2), 173−184.

Norton, P. J., & Barrera, T. L. (2012). Transdiagnostic versus diagnosis-specific CBT for anxiety disorders: A preliminary randomized controlled noninferiority trial. *Depression and Anxiety, 29*(10), 874−882.

Norton, P. J., Barrera, T. L., Mathew, A. R., Chamberlain, L. D., Szafranski, D. D., Reddy, R., & Smith, A. H. (2012). Effect of transdiagnostic CBT for anxiety disorders on comorbid diagnoses. *Depression and Anxiety, 30*(2), 168−173.

Norton, P. J. (2012). A randomized clinical trial of transdiagnostic cognitive-behavioral treatments for anxiety disorder by comparison to relaxation training. *Behavior Therapy, 43*(3), 506−517.

Padesky, C. A. (1996). Developing cognitive therapist competency: Teaching and supervision models. In P. Salkoskis (Ed.), *Frontiers of cognitive therapy* (pp. 266−292). New York: Guilford Press.

Padesky, C. A., & Mooney, K. A. (2012). Strengths-based cognitive-behavioural therapy: A four-step model to build resilience. *Clinical Psychology & Psychotherapy, 19*(4), 283−290.

Persons, J. B. (1991). Psychotherapy outcome studies do not accurately represent current models of psychotherapy: A proposed remedy. *American Psychologist, 46*(2), 99−106.

Persons, J. B. (2006). Case formulation-driven psychotherapy. *Clinical Psychology: Science and Practice, 13*(2), 167−170.

Persons, J. B. (2008). *The case formulation approach to cognitive-behavior therapy*. New York: Guilford Press.

Persons, J. B. (2013). Who needs a case formulation and why: Clinicians use the case formulation to guide decision-making. *Pragmatic Case Studies in Psychotherapy, 9*(4), 448–456.

Persons, J. B., Beckner, V. L., & Tompkins, M. A. (2013). Testing case formulation hypotheses in psychotherapy: Two case examples. *Cognitive and Behavioral Practice, 20*(4), 399–409.

Persons, J. B., & Mikami, A. Y. (2002). Strategies for handling treatment failure successfully. *Psychotherapy: Theory, Research, Practice, Training, 39*, 139–151.

Persons, J. B., Roberts, N. A., Zalecki, C. A., & Brechwald, W. A. (2006). Naturalistic outcome of case formulation-driven cognitive-behavior therapy for anxious depressed outpatients. *Behaviour Research and Therapy, 44*(7), 1041–1051.

Rector, N. A., Man, V., & Lerman, B. (2014). The expanding cognitive-behavioural therapy treatment umbrella for the anxiety disorders: Disorder-specific and transdiagnostic approaches. *Canadian Journal of Psychiatry. Revue Canadienne de Psychiatrie, 59*(6), 301–309.

Reinholt, N., & Krogh, J. (2014). Efficacy of transdiagnostic cognitive behaviour therapy for anxiety disorders: A systematic review and meta-analysis of published outcome studies. *Cognitive Behaviour Therapy, 43*(3), 171–184.

Rogers, G. M., Reinecke, M. A., & Curry, J. F. (2005). Case formulation in TADS CBT. *Cognitive and Behavioral Practice, 12*(2), 198–208.

Rosellini, A. J. (2013). *Initial development and validation of a dimensional classification system for the emotional disorders.* Unpublished Doctoral Dissertation. Boston, MA: Boston University.

Rosenbaum, M., & Ronen, T. (1998). Clinical supervision from the standpoint of cognitive-behavior therapy. *Psychotherapy: Theory, Research, Practice, Training, 35*(2), 220–230.

Safran, J. D., Vallis, M., Segal, Z. V., & Shaw, B. F. (1986). Assessment of core cognitive processes in cognitive therapy. *Cognitive Therapy and Research, 10*(5), 509–526.

Schneider, B. H., & Bryne, B. M. (1987). Individualizing social skills training for behavior-disordered children. *Journal of Consulting and Clinical Psychology, 55*(3), 444–445.

Sobel, A. A., Resick, P. A., & Rabalais, A. E. (2009). The effect of cognitive processing therapy on cognitions: Impact statement coding. *Journal of Traumatic Stress, 22*(3), 205–211. Available from http://dx.doi.org/10.1002/jts.20408.

Sudak, D. M., Codd, R. T., III, Ludgate, J. W., Sokol, L., Fox, M., Reiser, R. P., & Milne, D. L. (2016). *Teaching and supervising cognitive behavioral therapy.* Hoboken, NJ: Wiley & Sons, Inc.

The TADS Team (2007). The Treatment for Adolescents with Depression Study (TADS). *Archives of General Psychiatry, 64*(10), 1132–1144. Available from http://dx.doi.org/10.1001/archpsyc.64.10.1132.

Thompson-Hollands, J., Sauer-Zavala, S., & Barlow, D. H. (2014). CBT and the future of personalized treatment: A proposal. *Depression and Anxiety, 31*(11), 909–911.

Waltman, S. H. (2016). Model-consistent CBT supervision: A case-study of a psychotherapy-based approach. *Journal of Cognitive Psychotherapy, 30*(2), 120–130.

Waltman, S. H. (2015). Functional analysis in differential diagnosis: Using cognitive processing therapy to treat PTSD. *Clinical Case Studies, 14*(6), 422–433. Available from http://dx.doi.org/10.1177/1534650115571003.

Waltman, S. H., Creed, T. A., & Beck, A. T. (2016). Are the effects of cognitive behavior therapy for depression falling? Review and critique of the evidence. *Clinical Psychology: Science and Practice, 23*, 113–122.

Waltman, S. H., Hall, B. C., McFarr, L. M., Beck, A. T., & Creed, T. A. (2017). In-session stuck points and pitfalls of community clinicians learning CBT: Qualitative investigation. *Cognitive and Behavioral Practice.* Available from http://dx.doi.org/10.1016/j.cbpra.2016.04.002.

Wilson, G. T. (1996). Manual-based treatments: The clinical application of research findings. *Behaviour, Research and Therapy, 34*, 295–314.

Further Reading

Chadwick, P., Williams, C., & Mackenzie, J. (2003). Impact of case formulation in cognitive behaviour therapy for psychosis. *Behaviour Research and Therapy, 41*(6), 671−680.

Johansson, R., Sjöberg, E., Sjögren, M., Johnsson, E., Carlbring, P., Andersson, T., Rousseau, A., & Andersson, G. (2012). Tailored vs. standardized internet-based cognitive behavior therapy for depression and comorbid symptoms: A randomized controlled trial. *PLoS Clinical Trials, 7*(5), e36905.

Mansell, W., Harvey, A., Watkins, E., & Shafran, R. (2009). Conceptual foundations of the transdiagnostic approach to CBT. *Journal of Cognitive Psychotherapy, 23*(1), 6−19.

Rainforth, M., & Laurenson, M. (2013). A literature review of case formulation to inform mental health practice. *Journal of Psychiatric and Mental Health Nursing, 21*(3), 206−213.

2

Treatment-Relevant Assessment in Cognitive-Behavioral Therapy

Katerina Rnic and David J.A. Dozois

The University of Western Ontario, London, ON, Canada

TREATMENT-RELEVANT ASSESSMENT IN COGNITIVE-BEHAVIORAL THERAPY

Cognitive behavioral therapy (CBT) has proliferated over the past several decades. CBT is now widely disseminated by academic training programs (Heatherington et al., 2012) and through workshops, and is the preferred mode of therapy for many clinicians and organizations (see Prochaska & Norcross, 2013). Hundreds of CBT-oriented self-help books, therapy manuals, and textbooks are available for the public, practitioner, student, and researcher. The efficacy, effectiveness, and mechanisms of action of CBT have been researched comprehensively across various psychiatric and medical disorders (cf. Beck & Dozois, 2011; Epp & Dobson, 2010; Hofmann, 2013; Hofmann, Asnaani, Vonk, Sawyet, & Fang, 2012), and CBT has been adapted successfully to a variety of client populations, including adults, children, couples, and families.

In contrast to the wide-spread training of therapists, dissemination of knowledge to the psychology community and public, and research on therapy outcome and mechanisms of change, the science and practice of evidence-based cognitive behavioral assessment has remained relatively neglected by both clinicians and researchers. This lag in the research and application of assessment is striking, particularly given

The Science of Cognitive Behavioral Therapy.
DOI: http://dx.doi.org/10.1016/B978-0-12-803457-6.00002-7

19

the recent advancements in psychometric research (e.g., Dobson & Dobson, 2009; Guller & Smith, 2015; Hawkes & Brown, 2015). For example, the Psychological Assessment Work Group, commissioned by the American Psychological Association, reported that psychological test validity is strong, compelling, and comparable to medical test validity (Meyer et al., 2001). Evidence-based assessment (EBA), however, is comprised not only of the reliability and validity of various individual assessment tools, but also the selection of constructs to be assessed, the methods and measures used, and their combined utility for improving decision making, diagnosis, and treatment. The process of assessment is important to attend to carefully. Controlled test administration, appropriate data synthesis and interpretation, and a balancing of costs and resources with the potential value of clinical data to be acquired are all important features to consider when conducting assessments (Hunsley & Elliot, 2015; Hunsley & Mash, 2007; Mash & Hunsley, 2005; McLeod, Jensen-Doss, & Ollendick, 2013). The practice of EBA requires scientific thinking and hypothesis testing, and the process of EBA must be informed by scientific evidence (Hunsley & Elliot, 2015).

EBA is critical for making a differential diagnosis and for understanding the patient's presenting problems. EBA utilizes multiple sources of information that the clinician must integrate and interpret to make optimal recommendations or decisions. The use of distinct assessment methods provides unique information, whereas clinical interviews alone deliver an incomplete understanding of the patient (Hunsley & Meyer, 2003; Meyer et al., 2001). EBA is also necessary for initial as well as ongoing case conceptualization and treatment planning, such that clinicians may target interventions based on both nomothetic and idiographic information. A comprehensive assessment conducted using scientific principles provides clinicians with an accurate description of a patient's functioning, informs treatment decisions in a way that is less clouded by confirmation biases and other heuristics, and helps clinicians to optimally test clinical hypotheses.

In addition to deriving an accurate diagnosis and comprehensive understanding of a patient's concerns are a number of other important functions of the assessment. The intake interview, for instance, provides an opportunity for the clinician to orient the patient to the cognitive model and to establish rapport. Jointly developing a problem list and setting treatment goals socializes the patient to collaborative empiricism. Assessment is also necessary for monitoring progress and change during therapy, for deciding when to shift focus from change to relapse prevention, and for determining when to terminate treatment. Assessment can also be used to evaluate outcomes at both termination and at follow-up, which increases the clinician's ability to demonstrate treatment efficacy and cost effectiveness. Moreover, assessing vulnerability factors and risk for relapse improves prevention efforts. Finally, assessment allows the clinician to better respond to external pressures by third party payers or managed care providers, among others.

Although CBT is an effective treatment with medium to large effect sizes (e.g., 0.73 in anxiety disorders; Hofmann & Smits, 2008; see Butler, Chapman, Forman, & Beck, 2006 for review), there is evidently room for improvement. Use of EBA may be one method of enhancing existing interventions. The promotion of evidence-based therapy without attention to EBA has been compared to building a beautiful house without constructing a foundation (Achenbach, 2005); CBT may have stronger and more enduring effects if treatment is individualized by the use of scientific, objective data.

Research on EBA may provide clinicians with more specific recommendations to better utilize assessment data to select and time specific treatment strategies for particular patients and to generate informed clinical decisions. Regardless of their scientific validity, assessment instruments will only be endorsed and used by practitioners if they also have strong clinical utility, including cost and ease of administration. For this reason, we emphasize the importance of both evidence-based practice and practice-based evidence, which should be mutually influential in order to minimize the research-practice gap (see Dozois, 2013; Kazdin, 2008).

The purpose of this chapter is to discuss empirically supported assessment in the context of CBT and to demonstrate how assessment can be effectively used across all phases of treatment. The importance of the mutual influence of evidence-based practice and practice-based evidence is emphasized. Strategies and issues for the selection, use, interpretation, and evaluation of assessment measures for symptom-, behavioral-, and cognitive-based assessment are highlighted, and ongoing challenges and future directions for the science of cognitive behavioral assessment discussed.

PHASES OF ASSESSMENT IN CBT

The historical distinction between assessment and therapy is somewhat artificial, owing to the dynamic interplay between the two. Assessment continually informs treatment and, as treatment progresses, there is a persistent need to reassess and supplement or update existing information (Persons & Davidson, 2010). Assessment should not only occur at the beginning of therapy, but continue to be an ongoing priority. Following intake, assessment can be used to monitor treatment, develop and revise the case conceptualization, determine when and how to shift focus to relapse prevention, and decide when treatment termination is appropriate.

Intake Assessment

Assessment in CBT typically begins with an intake interview. This interview should collect information relevant to diagnosis as well as to cognitive and behavioral variables that are pertinent for CBT case conceptualization. On the contrary, no standardized interview or format exists for empirically based cognitive behavioral assessment. However, Dobson and Dobson (2009) introduced a semistructured cognitive behavioral assessment interview, the domains of which are summarized below.

At the outset, it is essential that the therapist determine the main presenting problem(s), assess the appropriateness of CBT for a patient's stated goals and determine whether the patient is a suitable candidate for this intervention. The therapist may work with the patient to assess current functioning and to generate a problem list, including domains such as relationship issues, employment, education, finances, sleep, and health and to begin to assess how these variables may interact with the patient's symptoms. The clinician should also ask about antecedents and consequences of the presenting problem(s) that relate to maladaptive responses, including dysfunctional cognitions, maladaptive behaviors, or negative emotions, to begin to ascertain the functional relationships between the patient and events, situations, and individuals in his or her life. Furthermore, clinicians should assess for affective, physiological, cognitive (including thoughts and images), and behavioral (including actions and action tendencies) responses the patient tends to experience when he or she is symptomatic. Assessment of these variables provides an opportunity for the practitioner to begin to orient the patient to the CBT model. Individuals who have difficulty noticing and stating their thoughts may benefit from role plays or imaginal techniques to aid with recall. Patients who lack the vocabulary to express feelings or who conflate them with thoughts may be provided with a feelings and emotions list (Dobson & Dobson, 2009).

A further aim of the intake interview is to assess for maladaptive and adaptive coping and approach/avoidance patterns. There are a number of maladaptive behaviors that clinicians should be attentive to, including excessive reassurance seeking, compulsive checking, use of drugs and/or alcohol, withdrawal, passivity, and use of safety behaviors. A risk assessment for suicidal ideation, plans, and self-harm must also be conducted. Assessing for skills and knowledge deficits to ensure that they are not confused with symptomatology (e.g., depressed mood or social anxiety may be mistaken for poor interpersonal skills) is also beneficial.

An additional domain to evaluate during the intake assessment is the patient's social support networks, concerns pertaining to family, friends, or professional relationships, and other interpersonal problems. Social support can be a protective factor and a buffer against stress (see Uchino, Cacioppo, & Kiecolt-Glaser, 1996); but, interpersonal conflict and poor social functioning can cause, maintain, or exacerbate problems (e.g., Hammen & Shih, 2014). Interpersonal functioning is, therefore, a key domain that is highly informative for treatment planning.

Furthermore, as part of the intake interview the clinician should determine the developmental course and timeline of the patient's major presenting problem(s). This helps us to establish which problem to focus on first (typically the most severe and long-standing; Dozois & Dobson, 2010). The patient's response can also help to ascertain whether his or her own causal theory is congruent with a CBT conceptualization that can be emphasized over the course of treatment (e.g., the patient refers to life stressors that were triggering events and/or personal vulnerabilities that were exacerbated, as in a diathesis-stress model) or whether the patient may benefit from psychoeducation and reorientation (e.g., the patient views his or her problem as a disease that is inherited or caused by a "chemical imbalance").

Finally, it is also helpful to discuss any history of psychotherapy or pharmacotherapy (and the nature of the service that the patient received) to ascertain patient preferences, aspects of treatment that the patient did not like or did not find helpful, his or her use of problem solving and coping strategies during therapy, how he or she handled setbacks, and motivation to change. During the intake assessment, it is also useful to collect data on symptoms and functioning using self-report measures, as well as data from multiple informants (e.g., partner, parent, and teacher) and sources (e.g., previous assessment reports), when possible.

Treatment Monitoring

Over the course of therapy, the clinician should engage in ongoing treatment monitoring to assess the patient's progress toward collaboratively set goals, to revise the case formulation, and, if necessary, the goals and treatment plan, and to adapt treatment to target the patient's current needs. Ideally, there is an ongoing transaction between assessment, case formulation, and treatment (cf. Dozois et al., 2014b; Persons & Davidson, 2010). Although many clinicians emphasize the importance of assessment at intake, ongoing and repeated assessment during treatment and again at termination is much less common (Dobson & Dobson, 2009). This neglect of ongoing evaluation is especially problematic given that evidence-based treatments, including CBT, may be successful in large measure due to the practice of treatment monitoring, which is routinely employed in clinical trials (Hunsley & Mash, 2010).

Clinicians should evaluate variables that comprise specific problems that are the focus of treatment (e.g., symptoms), as well as those that are theoretically applicable. This allows the clinician to assess the effects of treatment on both outcome and potential causal variables (Dozois & Dobson, 2010). Variables should be theoretically and empirically expected to change at a rate that justifies the regularity of assessment of that variable. For example, it would make sense to assess for changes in cognitive distortions every few sessions, but not to assess schema content or organization at that same frequency, as these constructs are hypothesized to change much more slowly. Furthermore, clinicians must select measures that are validated for repeated administration and that have documented sensitivity to detect meaningful change (Hunsley & Elliot, 2015). Such measures tend to be shorter in length and relatively specific (Dobson & Dobson, 2009). When interpreting results, clinicians must also be mindful of regression to the mean (i.e., extreme scorers tend to score closer to the mean on subsequent administrations; see Barnett, Van Der Pols, & Dobson, 2005).

Beidas et al. (2015) provide a list of well-validated, brief measures for the most common mental health disorders in youth and adults that are available at no cost, thereby reducing the resource barriers to implementation of EBA (also see Antony, Orsillo, & Roemer, 2001; Nezu, Ronan, Meadows, & McClure, 2000). Beidas et al. (2015) also underscored the importance of making additional instruments available for treatment monitoring.

Compelling evidence indicates that therapists should assess symptom, behavioral, and cognitive outcomes regularly. A meta-analysis of large-scale randomized trials indicated that when treatment is monitored and therapists receive patient progress data, patients have 3.5 times higher odds of making reliable clinical changes over the course of therapy, as well as less than half the odds of deteriorating (Lambert & Shimokawa, 2011). Progress data allow the clinician to monitor and determine his or her efficacy and explore whether there are issues in case conceptualization or treatment administration (Dozois & Dobson, 2010).

Progress data can also have direct benefits for the patient and the therapeutic alliance. Treatment progress can be measured using self-report questionnaires or self-monitoring records and tends to be most useful when therapists graph the results and share them with patients (Harkin et al., 2016). Providing feedback keeps the patient involved in treatment and treatment planning, consistent with the emphasis of CBT on collaborative empiricism. Ongoing feedback also allows the therapist–patient dyad to examine whether the patient's perceptions of progress match the outcome data and to explore the patient's understanding of why therapy may or may not be proceeding well. This interchange demonstrates accountability and stimulates discussion of speed of progress, stability of treatment response, obstacles that need to be addressed (e.g., interpersonal process issues, external stressors), patient expectations (e.g., pessimistic or optimistic) which may require modification, and the need for ongoing treatment. When progress toward treatment goals has been made, providing objective feedback and evidence of change can be highly reinforcing and motivating for patients.

Informal, within-session evaluations can be an additional source of information. These evaluations can provide a useful springboard for discussion of interpersonal processes in therapy and can enhance rapport and prevent ruptures in the therapeutic alliance. However, clinicians must be aware that such evaluations place large demand characteristics on patients, who may be wary of providing the therapist with honest and potentially critical feedback.

Relapse Prevention and Treatment Termination

Assessment is also important to help clinicians decide when to transition toward relapse prevention and to determine the timing of treatment termination. When cognitive change and symptom amelioration have been achieved (as best determined using normative data, discussed in detail below), therapy may shift focus to maintaining and consolidating gains and preventing relapse. For example, patients are at elevated risk of relapse for depression when they continue to demonstrate cognitive reactivity; that is, when primed by a negative mood induction, these individuals demonstrate a reinstatement of negative thinking that is not evident in individuals less vulnerable to relapse (Segal et al., 2006; Segal, Gemar, & Williams, 1999). Toward the end of treatment, individuals who exhibit depressive symptomatology that is mild or higher in severity should also be considered for additional sessions (Jarrett & Vittengl, 2016). Assessing for cognitive reactivity and unstable remission may allow clinicians to determine how much emphasis and time should be placed on relapse prevention.

Once the patient and therapist have agreed to terminate therapy, it is useful to provide a clear summary of outcomes and results to the patient. This information can be reinforcing for patients and may encourage them to maintain gains. Given that various symptoms and problems in functioning may change at different rates, outcome assessment should be multidimensional (Dozois & Dobson, 2010). For example, a clinician may assess a patient treated for depression by examining symptoms (e.g., depressive and comorbid symptoms), behaviors (e.g., engagement in activities that give the patient a sense of pleasure or mastery), and cognitions (e.g., negative automatic thoughts, cognitive distortions, schemas) that were targeted over the course of therapy. Outcome assessment can similarly be conducted at booster sessions to quantify change in symptoms, functioning, and cognitive/behavioral vulnerability. This information could then be utilized to determine what skills and strategies the patient may need to reinstate or develop further.

Summary

Assessment should be an ongoing process that continuously informs case conceptualization and treatment. At intake, the clinician establishes what the major presenting problem is and its developmental course, as well as the patient's causal theory of the problem. The clinician should also evaluate other problems as well as the patient's social support, coping styles, and treatment preferences. Over the course of therapy, the clinician should monitor patient progress in terms of not only symptomatology, but also theoretically applicable cognitive and behavioral variables. These data help the clinician assess efficacy and update his or her case conceptualizations and, when shared with the patient, reinforces collaborative empiricism and may strengthen the therapeutic alliance. Assessment also aids the clinician in deciding when the patient is ready to shift from active treatment to relapse prevention, and when to terminate therapy. Outcome assessment can motivate patients to maintain gains while also highlighting what areas the patient still needs to work on.

Regardless of the timing or purpose of an assessment, the tools used should have strong psychometric properties and, if possible, be validated in a population that the patient belongs to (cf. Therrien & Hunsley, 2012). Research refining the validity and utility of measurement at each phase of assessment is needed, particularly because the psychometric properties of an instrument are conditional on the purpose (e.g., screening, treatment evaluation) for which the tool was developed and validated (Haynes, Smith, & Hunsley, 2011).

TARGETS OF ASSESSMENT

Use of multiple strategies and modes of assessment are recommended to gain a comprehensive and complete understanding of the patient and to enhance the validity of the assessment findings. Assessment includes evaluation of symptoms and their severity, diagnostic criteria, behaviors, and cognitive mechanisms of change theorized by the cognitive model. The latter are important for cognitive behavioral assessment given the emphasis placed on cognitive restructuring as a mediator of symptom change (Clark, 2014) and a protective factor from relapse and recurrence (e.g., Segal et al., 2006). These variables include cognitive products (conscious automatic thoughts or images), processes (operations that are used to infer meaning from environmental input), and deeper structures, which consist of both the content (core beliefs) and organization or architecture of self-schemas and serve to guide subsequent information processing (see Dozois & Beck, 2008).

Targeting theory-specific variables in assessment may actually improve treatment efficacy, as it provides the therapist with direction regarding what areas still need further intervention. For example, a patient with depression may show decreases in negative thinking but continue to demonstrate deficits in positive cognition. This information would allow the therapist to tailor treatment to focus on increasing positive thinking, possibly by increasing reinforcers via behavioral activation. To be included in an assessment battery, each measure should add sufficient information (i.e., incremental validity, clinical utility) to justify the administration. Beyond psychometric characteristics, clinicians must also consider the cost of measures, availability, language level and readability, ease of administration and scoring, cultural relevance and appropriateness, and acceptability to clients. If measures do not satisfy these indicators of clinical utility, they are likely to be underutilized.

Symptom-Based Assessment

Clinicians typically conduct diagnostic evaluations to determine what cognitive constructs to assess, which treatment literature to consult, as well as what type of CBT treatment to offer the patient. When assessing symptoms, clinicians typically use a combination of interview and self-report or clinician-administered measures. Many structured and semistructured interviews are available to collect diagnostic information (see Antony & Barlow, 2010). These include the Structured Clinical Interview for DSM-5 (First, Williams, Karg, & Spitzer, 2015), the Schedule for Affective Disorders and Schizophrenia (Endicott & Spitzer, 1978), the Diagnostic Interview Schedule (Robins, Cottler, Bucholz, & Compton, 1995), and the Anxiety Disorders Interview Schedule for DSM-IV (ADIS-IV; Brown, DiNardo, & Barlow, 1994). Such interviews typically take 45–120 minutes to administer, although shorter options exist, such as the Mini-International Neuropsychiatric

Interview version 5.0 (Sheehan et al., 1998). These instruments are standardized, require training in proper administration, are predominantly used in research settings, and are less useful in the context of CBT as they do not query for patterns of cognitions or functionality of behavior. However, of these, the ADIS is arguably the most useful for determining problematic situations and reactions in the patient's life because it queries for examples that are relevant for beginning to conceptualize a case.

Several compendia of psychometrically sound self-report symptom measures exist, including those for anxiety (Antony et al., 2001) and depression (Nezu et al., 2000), both of which include reprints of a number of scales for clinical use. Furthermore, Antony and Barlow (2010) reviewed assessment approaches and measures for a range of disorders, and the Nineteenth Mental Measurements Yearbook provides a complete list of all psychological tests along with references to relevant research (Carlson, Geisinger, & Jonson, 2014). When selecting measures, clinicians should be mindful that they choose instruments that are suitable for repeated use so that they can be administered on multiple occasions throughout the course of treatment and/or at booster sessions as an index of treatment success.

The importance of accurate diagnostic and symptom assessment should not be understated. Jensen-Doss and Weisz (2008) found that when clinician-generated diagnoses were divergent with research-based diagnoses, there were more "no-shows," canceled appointments, treatment dropouts, and smaller treatment gains as compared to when clinician- and research-generated diagnoses matched. Although more research in this area is needed, these findings suggest that accurate diagnosis has an effect on treatment implementation, engagement, and outcome.

Behavioral Assessment

As part of cognitive behavioral assessment, the clinician should also assess relevant behaviors that serve to cause or reinforce a patient's problems. These behaviors can be assessed using self-report measures, self-monitoring, and observation. Numerous self-report measures can be used for behavioral assessment (cf. Antony & Barlow, 2010). For instance, there are self-report measures of avoidance (e.g., the Cognitive-Behavioral Avoidance Scale; Ottenbreit & Dobson, 2004; the Fear Questionnaire; Marks & Matthews, 1979), mobility (e.g., the Mobility Inventory for Agoraphobia; Chambless, Caputo, Gracely, Jasin, & Williams, 1985), and excessive reassurance seeking (the Depressive Interpersonal Relationships Inventory-Reassurance Seeking Subscale;

Joiner, Alfano, & Metalsky, 1992), among others. These measures are useful because they provide quantitative data on a patient's behavior, making assessment of change over time straightforward. Such indices are also easy to administer, and probe for specific information that could be missed by other methods of behavioral assessment.

Self-monitoring is another method for collecting behavioral or cognitive data and involves the patient systematically observing specified behaviors or dysfunctional cognitions and recording their occurrence or nonoccurrence. This method has high ecological validity. Examples frequently used in CBT include Activity Schedules, Panic Attack Logs, Thought Records, and Activity Logs (see Brown & Clark, 2015; Dobson & Dobson, 2009). When using Activity Logs, the patient records the number of times or amount of time he or she spent engaging in a particular behavior. Information may be sampled only during particular times of day, or throughout the day. Some paradigms use an experience sampling method, whereby patients record behaviors or cognitions when cued with a device that beeps at random or quasi-random intervals. This strategy can be useful for collecting information that is not contingent on the occurrence of specific events. Monitored behaviors may include those that the patient is trying to engage in less (e.g., hair pulling, smoking, reassurance seeking) or more (e.g., initiating conversations, exercise) frequently.

Self-monitoring can be conducted using a variety of methods, including unstructured, free form journals, structured forms or questionnaires, and apps for smart phones or tablets. Like all CBT homework, it is important that the therapist discuss with the patient what format he or she prefers to use, as well as potential obstacles to completing self-monitoring in order to increase his or her adherence and successful completion. Self-monitoring is likely associated with less bias and more accurate reporting than retrospective measures, which are vulnerable to recall biases. Furthermore, the very act of self-monitoring can have beneficial impacts on behavioral change as the patient becomes more aware of his or her behaviors and develops a sense of accountability (Karoly, 2005). A recent meta-analysis found that across various problems, patients who self-monitor behavior or progress toward a goal achieve better outcomes, with an effect size of .40. Outcomes are best when self-monitoring is recorded and discussed (e.g., with a therapist; Harkin et al., 2016).

Observational methods, both formal and informal, entail another useful assessment strategy. The clinician should always be observing the patient for verbal and nonverbal behavior and communication that may inform hypotheses. The patient's manner of presenting and behaving with the clinician is a useful sample of his or her typical behavior across various situations. Clinicians should be attentive to patients' manner of dress and grooming, use of eye contact (e.g., fixed, fleeting), posture, psychomotor agitation or retardation, affective quality (dysphoric, neutral, euthymic, irritable, anxious) and intensity (e.g., exaggerated, restricted, blunted, flat), use of language (e.g., tendency to use second person when describing problems, tendency to use passive grammatical structure), thought content (goal-directed, logical, linear, tangential, circumstantial, overinclusive, delusional), speech (volume, rate, rhythm, prosody), and whether the patient responds to redirection. Clinicians should also note patient behaviors during administration of assessment measures and their completion time. Furthermore, these observations should be documented on an ongoing basis to track any changes in the patient's presentation across sessions and over the duration of therapy.

More formal observational methods may also be used to assess patient's skills deficits and abilities, such as the Inventory of Interpersonal Problems (Horowitz, Rosenberg, Baer, Ureño, & Vallaseñor, 1988). Clinicians may also find it helpful to use tools such as stopwatches to measure the duration of behaviors, golf counters to assess frequency, and audio-taping or video recording, which can subsequently be reviewed with the patient.

Cognitive Assessment

Cognitive theory posits that an extensive cognitive system exists that has a taxonomical structure, varying from surface level thoughts (products), to mechanisms that operate on information (processes), and deep structures (schemas). Cognitive structures drive the manner in which information is processed which, in turn, manifest as cognitive products (see Beck & Dozois, 2014; Dozois & Beck, 2008). Each level of this taxonomy is assumed to be relevant to risk for disorder, although it is not currently known which has the most relevance to negative outcomes and, therefore, to assessment. Cognitive clinical assessment is defined as "systematic empirically derived protocols, procedures, or instruments intended to measure the frequency, intensity, and salience of meaningful information comprising the thoughts, images, and beliefs that characterize psychopathological states" (Brown & Clark, 2015, p. 5). Cognitive assessment poses particular challenges to researchers and clinicians due to the private, internal, and unobservable nature of cognitive content, making it difficult for patients to access and accurately report on their cognitions (Kendall, 1981).

Cognitive Products

To assess cognitive products (i.e., automatic thoughts, self-talk, private speech) clinicians may ask patients to "think aloud," whereas they are engaged in a task or are role-playing, or to engage in "thought listing" before and after completing a task. These techniques may also be used when the patient is imagining a prior experience and reconstructing his or her inner dialogue. Clinicians may audiorecord the patient's verbalizations, which can subsequently be transcribed and coded into relevant categories (see Kendall & Hollon, 1981). The Articulated Thoughts in Simulated Situations (Davison, Robins, & Johnson, 1983; Davison, Vogel, & Coffman, 1997) is a more formal method of obtaining samples of a patients' inner monologue. After listening to a 2−3 minutes stimulus of a situation presented on audiotape while imagining being in that situation, the patient has 10−15 seconds to think out loud. Trained raters and judges make inferences on the patient's cognitive style on varying categories of interest. These open response, "production" measures have limitations, however; the clinician is limited to what the patient is able or willing to verbalize, and it is unclear whether pauses or silence are indicative of a lack of cognitive processing (which appears unlikely). The instructions that are provided can also result in varying reporting styles and content (see Dunkley, Blankstein, & Segal, 2010). Notwithstanding these issues, "think aloud" and "thought listing" approaches are appealing because one can obtain highly individualized information that might not be predicted or ascertained using self-report measures.

Cognitive products are more typically assessed using self-report measures, which request that the patient endorse statements of self-verbalizations, thoughts, attributions, attitudes, and related cognitive activity. Advantages of self-report, endorsement measures include their economy, ease of scoring and administration, standardization, and availability of normative and psychometric data, all of which make them appealing for use in clinical research and practice. Measures may instruct patients to rate whether or not they experience a thought, their degree of belief in the thought, and the frequency with which they experience it. For example, a commonly used measure that is relevant to cognitive behavioral assessment is the Dysfunctional Attitudes Scale (DAS; Weissman & Beck, 1978), a 40-item self-report questionnaire. Two parallel 9-item short forms developed using item response theory (IRT) are also available for use in pre- and postpriming assessments (Beevers, Strong, Meyer, Pilkonis, & Miller, 2007). The DAS is content valid as it is associated with dysphoric mood (see Scher, Ingram, & Segal, 2005) and sensitive to the effects of priming in individuals with remitted depression (Lau, Haigh, Christensen, Segal, & Taube-Schiff, 2012). Individuals with past depression who responded to therapy, however, did not report elevated DAS scores (Jarrett et al., 2012), suggesting that cognitive change may have mediated recovery. Similar findings have been reported in individuals with depression who responded to therapy versus those who responded to pharmacotherapy, whereby only individuals treated with CBT were not cognitively reactive, as indicated by the DAS, to priming (Segal et al., 1999, 2006). The DAS is, therefore, sensitive to changes resulting from psychotherapy. The DAS also has demonstrated good predictive validity for clinical outcomes. Using primes, the DAS can identify individuals who are vulnerable to an initial episode of depression and can predict who will have greater symptom severity and more frequent and chronic depressive episodes (Alloy, Abramson, Walshaw, & Neeren, 2006; Iacoviello, Alloy, Abramson, Whitehouse, & Hogan, 2006). In addition to assessing individuals at risk for or with current or past depression, the DAS may also be useful for individuals with dysthymia, panic, generalized anxiety, anorexia nervosa, bipolar disorder, and schizophrenia (Dobson & Shaw, 1986; Horan et al., 2010; Reilly-Harrington et al., 2010).

There is consensus that convergent measures and formats of assessment should be used in an assessment battery, particularly since obtaining similar findings across measures is indicative of construct validity. However, open response production and endorsement measures tend to demonstrate low convergent validity (see Haaga & Solomon, 2015), which suggests that there may be psychometric issues with production methods, or that the two methods may be tapping different cognitive constructs.

Cognitive Processes

To assess for vulnerabilities in information processing, laboratory measures are necessary. Self-report measures, in contrast, are not capable of validly measuring processes, as individuals typically lack the knowledge and insight to report on their attention, memory, processing depth, and speed, or other operations. Laboratory measures assess for biases in these cognitive operations. Commonly used measures include the Emotional Stroop Task (Williams, Matthews, & MacLeod, 1996), the dot probe (MacLeod, Mathews, & Tata, 1986), and the Self-Referent Encoding Task (SRET; Kuiper & Derry, 1982).

The Emotional Stroop Task is a measure of attentional bias. Emotional stimuli are used to examine disruptions in performance on a color naming task, and this disruption is taken to have etiological significance for various forms of psychopathology (Williams et al. 1996). Delayed color-naming of affectively valenced words relative to the latency of color naming of neutral words reflects an attentional bias toward affective stimuli (Gotlib, Roberts, & Gilboa, 1996). Disorder-specific content (e.g., "threat" for anxiety, "sad" for depression) yields longer latencies than do control words matched for negativity, and several meta-analytic reviews report increased color-naming response latencies in patients versus healthy controls on the Emotional Stroop (anxiety: Bar-Haim, Lamy, Pergamin, Bakermans-Kranenburg, & IJzendoorn, 2007; posttraumatic stress disorder: Cisler et al., 2011; addictive disorders: Cox, Fadardi, & Pothos, 2006; eating disorders: Dobson & Dozois, 2004; depression: Epp, Dobson, Dozois, & Frewen, 2012; attention-deficit/hyperactivity: Lansbergen, Kenemans, & van Engeland, 2007; Schwartz & Verhaeghen, 2008; schizophrenia: Westerhausen, Kompus, & Hugdahl, 2011). The utility of assessment findings from the Emotional Stroop is unclear, as empirical findings have not yet determined whether cognitive interference on the task is reflective of the process of a cognitive vulnerability, or more accurately represents state variations in mood.

The dot-probe task is a computerized measure of attentional biases in the processing of affective information (e.g., MacLeod et al., 1986). Individuals are shown a series of stimuli (e.g., pairs of words or pictures); one stimulus is neutral, and the other is emotionally evocative (e.g., fear-eliciting, sad). Often faces are used as stimuli, which may have greater ecological validity for disorders with a marked interpersonal component (e.g., social anxiety, depression). At stimulus offset, one of the stimuli is replaced with a probe stimulus, which individuals are asked to identify as quickly as possible. Shorter response latencies for probes that replace the affectively valenced stimuli versus those that replaced neutral stimuli are posited to reflect an attentional bias for that valence of affect. Meta-analyses indicate that attentional biases as assessed using the dot-probe task are present in anxiety (Frewen, Dozois, Joanisse, & Neufeld, 2008), depression (Peckham, McHugh, & Otto, 2010), and disordered eating (Brooks, Prince, Stahl, Campbell, & Treasure, 2011). Furthermore, attentional biases assessed using the dot-probe paradigm occur at different stimulus exposure durations across different types of psychopathology. For clinical and subclinical depression, there is a bias toward negative stimuli at exposure durations of 1000 ms or longer (Gotlib, Krasnoperova, Yue, & Joormann, 2004; Joormann & Gotlib, 2007). In the context of anxiety, attentional biases to threatening stimuli occur at both the subliminal and supraliminal level, such that anxious individuals attend to threatening stimuli at short exposure durations, but avoid them at longer durations (Matthews & MacLeaod, 2005; Mogg & Bradley, 2005). Research investigating attentional biases at various exposure durations in other forms of psychopathology using the dot-probe task is needed. As well, research comparing attentional methods is necessary to determine which are the most valid and which best tap processing vulnerability. This research may inform why there are some inconsistencies in the literature. For example, research examining attentional biases using varied methods in individuals with remitted depression report mixed findings (Gilboa & Gotlib, 1997; Hedlund & Rude, 1995; Ingram & Ritter, 2000; see Scher et al., 2005 for review), even when primes are used.

The SRET (Kuiper & Derry, 1982) assesses memory biases for affectively valenced self-descriptive stimuli. Individuals are first presented with a series of positive and negative adjectives and are asked to indicate whether or not each adjective is self-descriptive. Following this task, participants are administered an unexpected free recall task. The outcomes of interest are positive schematic processing, or the proportion of positive words rated as self-descriptive that were recalled relative to all self-descriptive words, and negative schematic processing, or the proportion of negative words that were rated as self-descriptive and were recalled. Depressed individuals (including children and adolescents) and children of depressed mothers tend to obtain higher scores on negative than positive schematic processing, whereas the reverse is true for nondepressed individuals (see Scher et al., 2005 for a review).

Although these laboratory measures of information processing provide valuable information, they are not typically used in clinical settings and their external validity is, therefore, questionable (Glass & Arnkoff, 1997). Moreover, since these measures are not standardized, different stimuli and varying experimental procedures are used across studies. Greater standardization of these stimuli and tasks would permit more direct comparisons of results and would allow researchers to generate normative data for different phases of assessment (e.g., baseline, relapse prevention, termination). Normative data could be utilized by clinicians to determine the clinical significance of patients' performance on these tasks and to use processing measures as indices of cognitive reactivity. Consistent with this idea, recent advances in CBT have emphasized form of thought in addition to its content (e.g., Hayes, Strosahl, & Wilson, 2011; Watkins, 2016); however, because many CBT therapists tend to focus more on cognitive content than process, there may be less current interest in assessing change in operations compared to products and structures.

Cognitive Structures

Few approaches are available to assess the content and organization of schemas. Latent, structural aspects of cognition are, by definition, less accessible and often exert their effects outside of the individual's conscious awareness. However, assessment measures have been developed that assess the content and/or structure of schemas. These include the Young Schema Questionnaire (Young & Brown, 2003), a modified paradigm that uses the Emotional Stroop task (Segal, Gemar, Truchon, Guirguis, & Horowitz, 1995), and the Psychological Distance Scaling Task (Dozois & Dobson, 2001a,b).

The Young Schema Questionnaire (Young & Brown, 2003) is a 75-item self-report questionnaire that assesses for the content of early maladaptive schemas, or core beliefs. These early maladaptive schemas are rigid, pervasive beliefs about self that develop in childhood in response to problematic relational patterns and that are elaborated on throughout life, serving as templates for information processing (Dozois & Rnic, 2015). Early maladaptive schemas are organized into domains, including disconnection and rejection, impaired autonomy, impaired limits, other-directedness, and overvigilance and inhibition (Hoffart et al., 2005). These core beliefs predict depressive severity and episodes, and though they evince temporal stability (see Dozois & Rnic, 2015 for review), can be modified by CBT (Cruwys et al., 2014; Halford, Bernoth-Doolan, & Eadie, 2002).

Segal et al. (1995) used a priming paradigm as part of the Emotional Stroop task to examine organization of negative self-referent content. In this paradigm, each target word that the individual is asked to color name is relevant to the participant's self and is preceded by a prime word. The prime consists of a negatively valenced word that is either related or unrelated to that individual's self-concept. Segal et al. (1995) found greater interference in depressed patients for self-referent stimuli that were primed by negative self-referent adjectives than those primed by negative adjectives that were not relevant to the individual's sense of self. This finding is taken to indicate that negative self-referent adjectives are more highly organized in the individual's cognitive system when depressed. Priming self-referent words activates that element in the cognitive system which, in turn, activates interconnected elements and influences performance on tasks related to those cognitive elements.

The Psychological Distance Scaling Task (Dozois & Dobson, 2001a,b) is a computerized task whereby individuals place adjectives in two-dimensional space based on the degree of self-descriptiveness and valence of the word. The resulting clusters of adjectives are used to determine the degree of interconnectedness of both positive and negative self-referent content, which is considered to be an index of schema consolidation. Depressed and past-depressed individuals demonstrate a high degree of interconnectivity among negative interpersonal self-referent content, and greater dispersion of positive content (Dozois & Dobson, 2001a,b). Findings also suggest that cognitive organization may mediate the relation of early adversity with subsequent depression (Lumley & Harkness, 2009). Future research is needed to prospectively examine the associations between cognitive organization and first onset of depression (see Brown & Clark, 2015 for a comprehensive review of cognitive assessment in CBT).

Summary

To optimize comprehensiveness and validity of an assessment, the clinician should evaluate symptoms (including frequency and severity), diagnoses, and functionally- and theoretically relevant behaviors and cognitions (including products, processes, and the content and structure of schemas). Mixed methods, including self-report questionnaires, self-monitoring, observation, production measures (think aloud and thought listing), and laboratory measures (e.g., Emotional Stroop Task, dot probe, SRET, Psychological Distance Scaling Task) can provide rich data that goes beyond the information a clinician is able to gather in a typical intake or therapy session. These data may inform what areas are in most need of intervention or what areas continue to be problematic for a patient over time, which can enhance both the efficiency and effectiveness of therapy.

ISSUES IN COGNITIVE ASSESSMENT AND FUTURE DIRECTIONS

EBA is a research area that is still relatively underdeveloped; however, there are currently many ways in which clinicians can improve their assessment methods to better align with the evidence base, as well as a number of areas for further research that will better inform clinical practice. Relevant issues include the need to select measures that have good reliability as well as increasing the precision of measures, an overreliance on self-report measures and data, a need for greater use and development of normative data, and the need for increased use of priming techniques in both research and practice. Furthermore, although research examining the temporal stability of various cognitive constructs and the relation of cognitive systems with biological factors is burgeoning, further research is necessary.

Precision of Measurement

Many widely used assessment measures do not have adequate psychometric properties (Hunsley, Crabb, & Mash, 2004; Hunsley, Lee, Wood, & Taylor, 2015); so, it is vital that the clinician select measures that can provide good measurement precision. This is determined by reliability (e.g., inter-rater reliability, test—retest reliability, and internal consistency) and validity, including that the tool measures what it is supposed to measure (i.e., construct validity), convergence with measures assessing similar constructs (i.e., convergent validity), and divergence with measures assessing distinct constructs (i.e., divergent validity), as well as the ability to predict clinical outcomes (i.e., predictive validity). Self-report endorsement measures of cognitive products have been criticized on the basis of construct validity (Brown & Clark, 2015; Glass & Arnkoff, 1982; 1997). Although these measures may have high content validity in that they are representative of the themes that people generally think about, the idiographic meaning of endorsement of an item for a particular individual is less clear, particularly when individuals are asked to endorse thoughts based on their frequency. Glass and Arnkoff (1982, 1997) argued that individuals may endorse high frequency of a thought (1) when the thought matches with their self-view, regardless of whether they have actually experienced that particular thought, (2) when the thought represents an important idea to the patient, (3) when individuals have not experienced the thought but have translated fragmented or idiosyncratic thoughts to the thought presented on the inventory, and (4) when individuals translate an affective experience (e.g., physiological hyperarousal) to a thought listed on an inventory (e.g., "I'm worked up"). Despite these issues, many self-report measures have well-documented criterion and predictive validity and demonstrate sensitivity to treatment effects.

Glass and Arnkoff (1997) recommend that questionnaire developers supplement frequency scores with other rating scales that measure other aspects of cognition, such as intensity, salience, believability, controllability, impact, and importance. These factors may have greater veridicality as they assess more enduring constructs that rely less on episodic recall (Brown & Clark, 2015). Some existing questionnaires (e.g., the Automatic Thoughts Questionnaire: Hollon & Kendall, 1980; the Cognitive Distortions Scale: Covin, Dozois, Ogniewicz, & Seeds, 2011) include such scales. Clinicians might also want to inquire about the subjective meaning of endorsed thoughts with the client in order to more precisely understand the significance of the thought and whether or not the individual has experienced the thought per se, or related thoughts.

Advanced statistical techniques such as IRT, confirmatory factor analysis (CFA), and structural equation modeling (SEM) can be used to better develop and enhance measures (see Naragon-Gainey & Brown, 2015). IRT assumes that an individual's performance on an item is a function of his or her status with regard to the construct being measured and enables the researcher to select or delete items based on parameters such as item difficulty. CFA and SEM can be used to assess the underlying latent factor structure of a measure, which can be used to remove items or alter subscales for maximal validity and utility and to examine the relations of the resulting latent variables with other variables of interest. In terms of production measures of cognitive products (e.g., think aloud and thought listing), greater regularity in dimensions that are scored and scoring criteria would increase comparability across studies and would allow for normative and psychometric data to accrue. This consistency would also allow future research to better investigate the relations among cognitive structures, processes, and products, and to assess the convergent validity of measures designed to tap these constructs.

Overreliance on Self-Report

There tends to be an overreliance on self-report measures in both clinical practice and research. The overemphasis on self-report is not surprising given their ease of administration and the appeal of directly asking patients to provide information on their internal experiences. However, self-report measures are susceptible to a number of reporting problems, including mood-congruent biases, memory biases, and social desirability (Brown & Clark, 2015), and are insufficient in the context of cognitive behavioral assessment. Patients may sometimes lack the insight to accurately report on their experiences and, in the case of cognitive processes, which occur automatically, will not be able to articulate them. Moreover, many patients may not be aware of the content of their core beliefs. Experimental or process-based measures may provide more accurate information that can supplement information obtained using self-report indices. Alternative measures, such as behavioral challenges, observation, and self-monitoring can also help to fill in gaps. In all instances, the researcher or practitioner must ensure that the measure is reliable and construct valid.

Priming Techniques

Consistent with the diathesis-stress model of psychopathology, negative cognitions represent a vulnerability (i.e., diathesis) that is activated by stress. During times when symptoms are not clinically significant as a result of spontaneous remission or intervention, cognitive vulnerabilities are not activated, and are consequently more latent and less easily observed (Ingram & Price, 2010; Ingram, Miranda, & Segal, 1998), although they may still be present within the individual. This idea is in contrast to early research that concluded that since cognitive vulnerabilities appear to fluctuate alongside concomitant symptoms, they may represent merely epiphenomena of the disorder (e.g., Barnett & Gotlib, 1988). However, subsequent research has demonstrated that cognitive vulnerabilities are stable, trait-like, clinically meaningful, and measurable outside of highly symptomatic states (see Scher et al., 2005 for review). Although some cognitive structures, such as the organization of self-relevant information as measured by the Psychological Distance Scaling Task (Dozois, 2007), can be validly measured when these diatheses are not activated, the majority of cognitions should be activated prior to their assessment. This is achieved through the use of priming. When a negative mood is primed, cognitive vulnerabilities are more easily accessed, retrieved, and measured. This phenomenon can be accounted for by the mood-congruency hypothesis, which posits that when an individual is in a negative affective state, negative content regarding self is most likely to be activated (see Ingram et al., 1998; Segal, 1988). In this context, a negative mood prime is analogous to experiencing a naturalistic stressor (Persons & Miranda, 1992). Individuals with cognitive vulnerabilities who are primed have enhanced accessibility to cognitive structures and corresponding products and processes, thereby displaying maladaptive cognitions and information processing biases. In contrast, individuals without these risk factors do not display maladaptive cognition despite experiencing similar negative mood. Priming, therefore, allows the researcher or clinician to discriminate between individuals with and without cognitive vulnerability. Priming is also useful for assessing risk for relapse and recurrence, as reactivity to priming, even in the absence of current depression, is a predictor of future episodes (Segal et al., 1999, 2006) because the underlying vulnerability has not been successfully treated, leaving the individual vulnerable to be reactive to future stressors. Segal et al. (2006) found that past-depressed individuals who reported greater dysfunctional cognitions following a negative mood induction were at greater risk of relapse over the 18 months following treatment. The use of priming increases the time and resources spent on assessment but is recommended because doing so may enhance the validity of measures of cognitive vulnerability and provide rich clinical data. On the contrary, priming is rarely used in clinical practice despite its value for treatment planning.

Several techniques can be used for priming. In the context of cognitive behavioral assessment, priming negative mood states is most useful for assessing risk factors associated with psychopathology. Negative mood inductions include imaginal techniques, use of affect-inducing film clips, stories, or music, reading self-referent mood statements, false feedback on task performance, social interaction with a study confederate, and being asked to generate facial expressions consistent with the mood being induced. A meta-analysis indicated that film clips and stories, as well as combined approaches, produce the largest changes in affect (Westermann, Spies, Stahl, & Hesse, 1996). The remaining techniques are comparable and provide moderate changes in effect, with the exception of generation of facial expressions, which is the least effective mood induction. Further research is needed to characterize mood induction techniques in terms of how long a primed mood lasts and whether this varies across different mood states, as well as the optimal timing of cognitive assessment following the prime based on when negative cognitions are most activated and accessible. Potential moderators of response to priming, such as gender, age, and clinical status, should also be examined. The effectiveness of mood inductions is often assessed using self-reported mood, which may be influenced by demand characteristics; as such, other measures, such as facial affect coding and physiological measures, should be used to better validate priming techniques. Furthermore, when used in research or practice, manipulation checks should be used to ensure that the target mood was in fact induced. Procedures for negative mood reversal should also be investigated for their effectiveness.

Normative Data

When possible, clinicians should use measures that have normative data. Normative comparisons allow clinicians to assess the relative severity or frequency of symptoms and theoretically relevant measures as well as the clinical significance of observed change during and after treatment. For example, normative information may allow a clinician to determine if a patient's average functioning on a particular measure has shifted from the nomothetically clinical or dysfunctional range to the average or normal range, relative to a disordered and nondisordered sample, respectively (see Kendall & Sheldrick, 2000). This information is useful for case conceptualization, treatment planning, and deciding when to terminate treatment. Clinicians may also use tools specifically developed for progress-monitoring. These instruments provide session-by-session norms, which can be used to determine whether a patient's progress is consistent with likely treatment success or failure (Overington & Ionita, 2012). Norms are available from a test manual or in other publications (see Ingram, Nelson, Steidtmann, & Bistricky, 2007 for child measures of depression-related cognition; Dozois, Covin, & Brinker, 2003 for adult measures of depression-related cognition; Kendall & Sheldrick, 2000). It is essential that the clinician ensure that the patient being assessed is a member of the population from which the normative data were drawn, as indicated by characteristics such as age, gender, and ethnicity (Hunsley & Elliot, 2015). On the contrary, there is a paucity of normative data for process-based measures, making it difficult for clinicians to make nomothetic comparisons or to evaluate the clinical significance of changes.

Stability of Cognitive Constructs

Cognitive and behavioral vulnerabilities evince moderate temporal stability (e.g., Alloy et al., 2000; Dozois & Dobson, 2001a; Hankin, Fraley, & Abela, 2005; Zuroff, Blatt, Sanislow, Bondi, & Pilkonis, 1999). In essence, they are trait-like, and are present before the onset of a disorder and after episode remission (Ingram, Atchley, & Segal, 2011). It is important for future research to better assess the temporal stability of various cognitive vulnerabilities beyond their covariance with exacerbations and improvements of the disorder and associated symptomatology. Advancing the field in this respect will require multiple waves of prospective data collection (most extant studies are only comprised of two waves of data collection) and lengthier follow-up periods, as well as greater attention to laboratory measures of cognition. Research is also needed to assess cognitive stability across samples at various developmental stages. Burgeoning research supports moderate stability of cognitive risk (Hankin et al., 2009; Hankin, 2008), even in relatively young samples (Hayden et al., 2013b) and independent of change in depressive symptoms (Cole et al., 2009). There is also evidence of change in cognitive vulnerabilities (e.g., changes in cognitive organization following CBT and pharmacotherapy treatment; Dozois et al., 2009; Dozois et al., 2014a). Changes may result from maturation and developmental processes, life events (which, when consistent with negative views of the self, world, and future, may further consolidate those beliefs; Seeds & Dozois, 2010), and prevention and intervention. Changes in these underlying vulnerabilities over the course of therapy are indicative of decreased risk of relapse and recurrence as the individual is less vulnerable to future stressors and are, therefore, important to assess. If clinicians are aware of how long it typically takes for these constructs to change, they will also have a more solid basis on which to decide how often and when to assess these constructs. For example, deeper cognitive structures are theorized to be slower to change than more accessible cognitive processes and products; however, there are no data to indicate what rate of change clinicians can expect for various disorders. Furthermore, there is a need for the development or downward extension of assessment approaches to validly assess cognitive vulnerability in youth, which could have implications for improving early prevention and intervention efforts. Such research would also allow for multiwave longitudinal studies of vulnerability to be conducted.

Relations Among Cognitive and Biological Factors

Recent research has begun to explore biological correlates of cognitive vulnerability (Hayden et al., 2013a; Smoski, Keng, Schiller, Minkel, & Dichter, 2013). This research aims to uncover cognitive endophenotypes (Gottesman & Gould, 2003) that correspond to neural and genetic substrates of disorder and has potential value for informing what the mechanisms of action are for biological (e.g., pharmacotherapy, electroconvulsive therapy, transcranial magnetic stimulation) and combined biological and CBT treatment approaches. The interaction of these biological factors with various stressful life events to activate cognitive vulnerabilities is an area in need of further work.

CONCLUSION

It has long been established that advances in cognitive assessment are essential for research on the role of cognition in emotion and behavior and in the etiology and course of psychological disorders, the effects of treatment, and experimental research that aims to manipulate cognitive processes (Kendall, 1981). On the contrary, growth in the evidence base of cognitive behavioral assessment has been relatively stagnant, particularly in comparison to intervention research. It is essential that EBA is more formally examined. Studies examining outcomes, such as diagnostic status, symptomatology, and functional status in a group who received a diagnostic and/or cognitive behavioral assessment versus a group that did not (or a group whose therapists received assessment information versus a group whose therapists did not) would help clarify the importance of assessment. This research would also inform the incremental validity of assessment measures or batteries over unstructured intake interviews alone (Hunsley & Meyer, 2003). Furthermore, multimethod longitudinal studies assessing varied cognitive vulnerabilities are needed to determine which assessment measures have greatest predictive power for the development, maintenance, and relapse of psychopathology. Such studies could also examine the temporal patterns of stability and change across various cognitive constructs, both naturalistically and as potential mechanisms of change in CBT. Resultant findings would be highly informative for the practice of treatment monitoring and relapse prevention. By conducting research with a practice-based lens, and by assessing patients using an empirically based scientific approach, researchers and clinicians can better advance the field of cognitive behavioral assessment and, in turn, enhance treatment outcomes.

Acknowledgments

This research was supported in part by a Standard Research Grant from the Social Sciences and Humanities Research Council (SSHRC) and a SSHRC Vanier Canada Graduate Scholarship.

References

Achenbach, T. (2005). Advancing assessment of child and adolescent problems: Commentary on evidence based assessment of child and adolescent disorders. *Journal of Clinical Child and Adolescent Psychology, 34,* 542–547.

Alloy, L. B., Abramson, L. Y., Hogan, M. E., Whitehouse, W. G., Rose, D. T., Robinson, M. S., & Lapkin, J. B. (2000). The Temple–Wisconsin cognitive vulnerability to depression project: Lifetime history of Axis I psychopathology in individuals at high and low cognitive risk for depression. *Journal of Abnormal Psychology, 109,* 403–418.

Alloy, L. B., Abramson, L. Y., Walshaw, P. D., & Neeren, A. M. (2006). Cognitive vulnerability to unipolar and bipolar mood disorders. *Journal of Social and Clinical Psychology, 25,* 726–754.

Antony, M., & Barlow, D. (Eds.), (2010). *Handbook of assessment and treatment planning for psychological disorders* (2nd ed). New York: Guilford.

Antony, M., Orsillo, S., & Roemer, L. (Eds.), (2001). *Practitioner's guide to empirically based measures of anxiety.* New York: Springer.

Bar-Haim, Y., Lamy, D., Pergamin, L., Bakermans-Kranenburg, M. J., & IJzendoorn, M. H. (2007). Threat-related attentional bias in anxious and nonanxious individuals: a meta-analytic study. *Psychological Bulletin, 133,* 1–24.

Barnett, A. G., Van Der Pols, J. C., & Dobson, A. J. (2005). Regression to the mean: What it is and how to deal with it. *International Journal of Epidemiology, 34,* 215–220.

Barnett, P. A., & Gotlib, I. A. (1988). Psychosocial functioning and depression: Distinguishing among antecedents, concomitants, and consequences. *Psychological Bulletin, 104,* 97–126.

Beck, A. T., & Dozois, D. J. A. (2011). Cognitive therapy: Current status and future directions. *Annual Review of Medicine, 62,* 397–409.

Beck, A. T., & Dozois, D. J. A. (2014). Cognitive theory and therapy: Past, present and future. In S. Bloch, S. A. Green, & J. Holmes (Eds.), *Psychiatry – past, present and prospect* (pp. 366–382). Oxford: Oxford University Press.

Beevers, C. G., Strong, D. R., Meyer, B., Pilkonis, P. A., & Miller, I. W. (2007). Efficiently assessing negative cognition in depression: An item response theory analysis of the Dysfunctional Attitude Scale. *Psychological Assessment, 19,* 199–209.

Beidas, R. S., Stewart, R. E., Walsh, L., Lucas, S., Downey, M. M., Jackson, K., & Mandell, D. S. (2015). Free, brief, and validated: Standardized instruments for low-resource mental health settings. *Cognitive and Behavioral Practice, 22,* 5–19.

Brooks, S., Prince, A., Stahl, D., Campbell, I. C., & Treasure, J. (2011). A systematic review and meta-analysis of cognitive bias to food stimuli in people with disordered eating behaviour. *Clinical Psychology Review, 31,* 37–51.

Brown, G. P., & Clark, D. A. (2015). "Better the devil you know"? A conceptual critique of endorsement methods in cognitive therapy assessment. In G. P. Brown, & D. A. Clark (Eds.), *Assessment in cognitive therapy* (pp. 29–49). New York: Guilford.

Brown, G. P., & Clark, D. A. (2015). *Assessment in cognitive therapy.* New York: Guilford.

Brown, T., DiNardo, P., & Barlow, D. (1994). *Anxiety Disorders Interview Schedule for DSM-IV (ADIS-IV).* San Antonio, TX: Psychological Corporation.

Butler, A. C., Chapman, J. E., Forman, E. M., & Beck, A. T. (2006). The empirical status of cognitive-behavioral therapy: A review of meta-analyses. *Clinical Psychology Review, 26,* 17–31.

Carlson, J. F., Geisinger, K. F., & Jonson, J. L. (2014). *The nineteenth mental measurements yearbook.* Lincoln, NE: The Buros Center for Testing.

Chambless, D. L., Caputo, G. C., Jasin, S. E., Gracely, E. J., & Williams, C. (1985). The Mobility Inventory for Agoraphobia. *Behaviour Research and Therapy, 23,* 35–44.

Cisler, J. M., Wlitzky-Taylor, K. B., Adams, T. G., Babson, K. A., Badour, C. L., & Willems, J. L. (2011). The emotional Stroop task and posttraumatic stress disorder: a meta-analysis. *Clinical Psychology Review, 31,* 817–828.

Clark, D. A. (2014). Cognitive restructuring. In D.J.A. Dozois (Vol. Ed.), S.G. Hoffmann (Series Ed.). CBT: General Strategies. Volume 1. *The Wiley handbook of cognitive-behavioral therapy* (pp. 23–44). Oxford: Wiley-Blackwell.

Cole, D. A., Jacquez, F. M., Truss, A. E., Pineda, A. Q., Weitlauf, A. S., Tilghman-Osborne, C. E., & Maxwell, M. A. (2009). Gender differences in the longitudinal structure of cognitive diatheses for depression in children and adolescents. *Journal of Clinical Psychology, 65,* 1312–1326.

Covin, R., Dozois, D. J., Ogniewicz, A., & Seeds, P. M. (2011). Measuring cognitive errors: Initial development of the cognitive distortions scale (CDS). *International Journal of Cognitive Therapy, 4,* 297–322.

Cox, W. M., Fadardi, J. S., & Pothos, E. M. (2006). The addiction-Stroop test: Theoretical considerations and procedural recommendations. *Psychological Bulletin, 132,* 443–476.

Cruwys, T., Dingle, G. A., Hornsey, M. J., Jetten, J., Oei, T. P., & Walter, Z. C. (2014). Social isolation schema responds to positive social experiences: longitudinal evidence from vulnerable populations. *British Journal of Clinical Psychology, 53,* 265–280.

Davison, G. C., Robins, C., & Johnson, M. K. (1983). Articulated thoughts during simulated situations: a paradigm for studying cognition in emotion and behavior. *Cognitive Therapy and Research, 7,* 17–39.

Davison, G. C., Vogel, R. S., & Coffman, S. G. (1997). Think-aloud approaches to cognitive assessment and the articulated thoughts in simulated situations paradigm. *Journal of Consulting and Clinical Psychology, 65,* 950–958.

Dobson, D. J. G., & Dobson, K. S. (2009). *Evidence-based practice of cognitive-behavioral therapy.* New York: Guilford.

Dobson, K. S., & Dozois, D. J. A. (2004). Attentional biases in eating disorders: a meta-analytic review of Stroop performance. *Clinical Psychology Review, 23,* 1001–1022.

Dobson, K. S., & Shaw, B. F. (1986). Cognitive assessment with major depressive disorders. *Cognitive Therapy and Research, 10,* 13–29.

Dozois, D. J. A. (2007). Stability of negative self-structures: A longitudinal comparison of depressed, remitted, and nonpsychiatric controls. *Journal of Clinical Psychology, 63,* 319–338.

Dozois, D. J. A. (2013). Presidential address – Psychological treatments: Putting evidence into practice and practice into evidence. *Canadian Psychology, 54,* 1–11.

Dozois, D. J. A., & Beck, A. T. (2008). Cognitive schemas, beliefs and assumptions. In K. S. Dobson, & D. J. A. Dozois (Eds.), *Risk factors in depression* (pp. 121–144). Oxford: Elsevier.

Dozois, D. J. A., & Dobson, K. S. (2001a). A longitudinal investigation of information processing and cognitive organization in clinical depression: Stability of schematic interconectedness. *Journal of Consulting and Clinical Psychology, 69,* 914–925.

Dozois, D. J. A., & Dobson, K. S. (2001b). Information processing and cognitiveorganization in unipolar depression: Specificity and comorbidity issues. *Journal of Abnormal Psychology, 110,* 236–246.

Dozois, D. J. A., & Dobson, K. S. (2010). Depression. In M. M. Antony, & D. H. Barlow (Eds.), *Handbook of assessment and treatment planning for psychological disorders* (2nd ed., pp. 344–389). New York: Guilford.

Dozois, D. J. A., & Rnic, K. (2015). Core beliefs and self-schematic structure in depression. *Current Opinion in Psychology, 4*, 98–103.

Dozois, D. J. A., Bieling, P. J., Evraire, L. E., Patelis-Siotis, I., Hoar, L., Chudzik, S., & Westra, H. A. (2014a). Changes in core beliefs (early maladaptive schemas) and self-representation in cognitive therapy and pharmacotherapy for depression. *International Journal of Cognitive Therapy, 7*, 217–234.

Dozois, D. J. A., Bieling, P. J., Patelis-Siotis, I., Hoar, L., Chudzik, S., McCabe, K., & Westra, H. A. (2009). Changes in self-schema structure in cognitive therapy for major depressive disorder: a randomized clinical trail. *Journal of Consulting and Clinical Psychology, 77*, 1078–1088.

Dozois, D. J. A., Covin, R., & Brinker, J. K. (2003). Normative data on cognitive measures of depression. *Journal of Consulting and Clinical Psychology, 71*, 71–80.

Dozois, D. J. A., Mikail, S., Alden, L. E., Bieling, P. J., Bourgon, G., Clark, D. A., & Johnston, C. (2014b). The CPA Presidential Task Force on evidence-based practice of psychological treatments. *Canadian Psychology, 55*, 153–160.

Dunkley, D. M., Blankstein, K. R., & Segal, Z. V. (2010). Cognitive assessment: Issues and methods. In K. S. Dobson (Ed.), *The handbook of cognitive behavioral therapies* (3rd ed., pp. 133–171). New York: Guilford.

Endicott, J., & Spitzer, R. (1978). A diagnostic interview: The Schedule for Affective Disorders and Schizophrenia. *Archives of General Psychiatry, 35*, 837–844.

Epp, A. M., & Dobson, K. S. (2010). The evidence base for cognitive-behavioral therapy. In K. S. Dobson (Ed.), *Handbook of cognitive-behavioral therapies* (3rd ed., pp. 39–73). New York: Guilford.

Epp, A. M., Dobson, K. S., Dozois, D. J. A., & Frewen, P. A. (2012). A systematic meta-analysis of the Stroop task in depression. *Clinical Psychology Review, 32*, 316–328.

First, M. B., Williams, J. B. W., Karg, R. S., & Spitzer, R. L. (2015). *Structured clinical interview for DSM-5 disorders, clinician version (SCID-5-CV)*. Arlington, VA: American Psychiatric Publishing.

Frewen, P. A., Dozois, D. J. A., Joanisse, M. F., & Neufeld, R. W. J. (2008). Selective attention to threat versus reward: Meta-analysis and neural-network modeling of the dot-probe task. *Clinical Psychology Review, 28*, 307–337.

Gilboa, E., & Gotlib, I. H. (1997). Cognitive biases and affect persistence in previously dysphoric and never-dysphoric individuals. *Cognition and Emotion, 11*, 517–538.

Glass, C. R., & Arnkoff, D. B. (1982). Think cognitively: Selected issues in cognitive assessment and therapy. *Advances in Cognitive-Behavioral Research and Therapy, 1*, 35–71.

Glass, C. R., & Arnkoff, D. B. (1997). Questionnaire methods of cognitive self-statement assessment. *Journal of Consulting and Clinical Psychology, 65*, 911–927.

Gotlib, I. A., Krasnoperova, E., Yue, D. N., & Joormann, J. (2004). Attentional biases for negative interpersonal stimuli in clinical depression. *Journal of Abnormal Psychology, 113*, 127–135.

Gotlib, I. H., Roberts, J. E., & Gilboa, E. (1996). Cognitive interference in depression. In I. G. Sarason, G. R. Pierce, & B. R. Sarason (Eds.), *Cognitive interference: Theories, methods, and findings* (pp. 347–377). Mahwah, NJ: Erlbaum.

Gottesman, I. I., & Gould, T. D. (2003). The endophenotype concept in psychiatry: Etymology and strategic intentions. *The American Journal of Psychiatry, 160*, 636–645.

Guller, L., & Smith, G. T. (2015). Advances in construct validity theory: Implications for cognitive-behavioral assessment. In G. P. Brown, & D. A. Clark (Eds.), *Assessment in cognitive therapy* (pp. 316–336). New York: Guilford.

Haaga, D. A. F., & Solomon, A. (2015). Production-based assessment in cognitive-behavioral therapy. In G. P. Brown, & D. A. Clark (Eds.), *Assessment in cognitive therapy* (pp. 29–49). New York: Guilford.

Halford, W. K., Bernoth-Doolan, S., & Eadie, K. (2002). Schemata as moderators of clinical effectiveness of a comprehensive cognitive behavioral program for patients with depression or anxiety disorders. *Behavior Modification, 26*, 571–593.

Hammen, C. L., & Shih, J. (2014). Depression and interpersonal processes. In I. H. Gotlib, & C. L. Hammen (Eds.), *Handbook of depression* (pp. 277–295). New York: Guilford.

Hankin, B. L. (2008). Stability of cognitive vulnerabilities to depression: A short-term prospective multiwave study. *Journal of Abnormal Psychology, 117*, 324–333.

Hankin, B. L., Fraley, C. R., & Abela, J. R. Z. (2005). Daily depression and cognitions about stress: evidence for a trait-like depressogenic cognitive style and the prediction of depressive symptoms in a prospective daily diary study. *Journal of Personality and Social Psychology, 88*, 673–685.

Hankin, B. L., Oppenheimer, C., Jenness, J., Barrocas, A., Shapero, B. G., & Goldband, J. (2009). Developmental origins of cognitive vulnerabilities to depression: Review of processes contributing to stability and change across time. *Journal of Clinical Psychology, 65*, 1327–1338.

Harkin, B., Webb, T. L., Chang, B. P., Prestwich, A., Conner, M., Kellar, I., & Sheeran, P. (2016). Does monitoring goal progress promote goal attainment? A meta-analysis of the experimental evidence. *Psychological Bulletin, 142*, 198–229.

Hawkes, N., & Brown, G. P. (2015). Toward a validity framework for cognitive-behavioral therapy self-report assessment. In G. P. Brown, & D. A. Clark (Eds.), *Assessment in cognitive therapy* (pp. 243–267). New York: Guilford.

Hayden, E. P., Olino, T. M., Bufferd, S. J., Miller, A., Dougherty, L. R., Sheikh, H. I., & Klein, D. N. (2013a). The serotonin transporter linked polymorphic region and brain-derived neurotrophic factor valine to methionine at position 66 polymorphisms and maternal history of depression: Associations with cognitive vulnerability to depression in childhood. *Development and Psychopathology, 25*, 587–598.

Hayden, E. P., Olino, T. M., Mackrell, S. V., Jordan, P. L., Desjardins, J., & Katsiroumbas, P. (2013b). Cognitive vulnerability to depression during middle childhood: Stability and associations with maternal affective styles and parental depression. *Personality and Individual Differences, 55*, 892–897.

Hayes, S. C., Strosahl, K. D., & Wilson, K. G. (2011). *Acceptance and commitment therapy: The process and practice of mindful change.* New York: Guilford.

Haynes, S. N., Smith, G., & Hunsley, J. (2011). *Scientific foundations of clinical assessment.* New York: Taylor & Francis.

Heatherington, L., Messer, S. B., Angus, L., Strauman, T. J., Friedlander, M. L., & Kolden, G. G. (2012). The narrowing of theoretical orientations in clinical psychology doctoral training. *Clinical Psychology: Science and Practice, 19*, 364–374.

Hedlund, S., & Rude, S. S. (1995). Evidence of latent depressive schemas in formerly depressed individuals. *Journal of Abnormal Psychology, 104*, 517–525.

Hoffart, A., Sexton, H., Hedley, L. M., Wang, C. E., Holthe, H., Haugum, J. A., & Holte, A. (2005). The structure of maladaptive schemas: A confirmatory factor analysis and psychometric evaluation of factor-derived scales. *Cognitive Therapy and Research, 29*, 627–644.

Hofmann, S. G. (Ed.), (2013). *The Wiley handbook of cognitive behavioral therapy* (Vols. 1–3). Hoboken, NJ: Wiley.

Hofmann, S. G., Asnaani, A., Vonk, I. J. J., Sawyet, A. T., & Fang, A. (2012). The efficacy of cognitive behavioral therapy: A review of meta-analyses. *Cognitive Therapy and Research, 36*, 427–440.

Hofmann, S. G., & Smits, J. A. J. (2008). Cognitive-behavioral therapy for adult anxiety disorders: A meta-analysis of randomized placebo-controlled trials. *Journal of Clinical Psychiatry, 69*, 621–632.

Hollon, S. D., & Kendall, P. C. (1980). Cognitive self-statements in depression: Development of an automatic thoughts questionnaire. *Cognitive Therapy and Research, 4,* 383–396.

Horan, W. P., Rassovsky, Y., Kern, R. S., Lee, J., Wynn, J. K., & Green, M. F. (2010). Further support for the role of dysfunctional attitudes in models of real-world functioning in schizophrenia. *Journal of Psychiatric Research, 44,* 499–505.

Horowitz, L. M., Rosenberg, S. E., Baer, B. A., Ureño, G., & Villaseñor, V. S. (1988). Inventory of interpersonal problems: psychometric properties and clinical applications. *Journal of Consulting and Clinical Psychology, 56,* 885–892.

Hunsley, J., Crabb, R., & Mash, E. (2004). Evidence-based clinical assessment. *Clinical Psychologist, 57,* 25–32.

Hunsley, J., & Elliot, K. (2015). Implementing an evidence-based approach to cognitive-behavioral assessment. In G. P. Brown, & D. A. Clark (Eds.), *Assessment in cognitive therapy* (pp. 121–145). New York: Guilford.

Hunsley, J., & Mash, E. J. (2010). Role of assessment in evidence-based practice. In M. M. Antony, & D. H. Barlow (Eds.), *Handbook of assessment and treatment planning for psychological disorders* (2nd ed., pp. 3–22). New York: Guilford.

Hunsley, J., & Mash, E. J. (2007). Evidence-based assessment. *Annual Review of Clinical Psychology, 2,* 29–52.

Hunsley, J., & Meyer, G. J. (2003). The incremental validity of psychological testing and assessment: Conceptual, methodological, and statistical issues. *Psychological Assessment, 15,* 446–455.

Iacoviello, B. M., Alloy, L. B., Abramson, L. Y., Whitehouse, W. G., & Hogan, M. E. (2006). The course of depression in individuals at high and low cognitive risk for depression: A prospective study. *Journal of Affective Disorders, 93,* 61–69.

Ingram, R. E., & Price, J. M. (2010). Understanding psychopathology: The role of vulnerability. In R. E. Ingram, & J. M. Price (Eds.), *Vulnerability to psychopathology: Risk across the lifespan* (pp. 3–17). New York: Guilford.

Ingram, R. E., Atchley, R. A., & Segal, Z. V. (2011). *Vulnerability to depression: From cognitive neuroscience to prevention and treatment.* New York: Guildford.

Ingram, R. E., Miranda, J., & Segal, Z. V. (1998). *Cognitive vulnerability to depression.* New York: Guilford.

Ingram, R. E., Nelson, T., Steidtmann, D. K., & Bistricky, S. L. (2007). Comparative data on child and adolescent cognitive measures associated with depression. *Journal of Consulting and Clinical Psychology, 75,* 390–403.

Ingram, R. E., & Ritter, J. (2000). Vulnerability to depression: Cognitive reactivity and parental bonding in high-risk individuals. *Journal of Abnormal Psychology, 109,* 588–596.

Jarrett, R. B., Minhajuddin, A., Borman, P. D., Dunlap, L., Segal, Z. V., Kidner, C. L., & Thase, M. E. (2012). Cognitive reactivity, dysfunctional attitudes, and depressive relapse and recurrence in cognitive therapy responders. *Behaviour Research and Therapy, 50,* 280–286.

Jarrett, R. B., & Vittengl, J. R. (2016). The efficacy of cognitive behaviour therapy for depression. In A. Wells, & P. Fisher (Eds.), *Treating depression: MCT, CBT, and third wave therapies* (pp. 52–80). Chichester: Wiley.

Jensen-Doss, A., & Weisz, J. R. (2008). Diagnostic agreement predicts treatment process and outcomes in youth mental health clinics. *Journal of Consulting and Clinical Psychology, 76,* 711–722.

Joiner, T. E., Jr., Alfano, M. S., & Metalsky, G. I. (1992). When depression breeds contempt: Reassurance seeking, self-esteem, and rejection of depressed college students by their roommates. *Journal of Abnormal Psychology, 101,* 165–173.

Joormann, J., & Gotlib, I. H. (2007). Selective attention to emotional faces following recovery from depression. *Journal of Abnormal Psychology, 116,* 80–85.

Karoly, P. (2005). Self-monitoringIn M. Hersen, & J. Rosquist (Eds.), *Encyclopedia of behavior modification and cognitive behavior therapy* (Vol. 1, pp. 521–525). Thousand Oaks: Sage.

Kazdin, A. E. (2008). Evidence-based treatment and practice: new opportunities to bridge clinical research and practice, enhance the knowledge base, and improve patient care. *American Psychologist, 63,* 146–159.

Kendall, P. C. (1981). Assessment and cognitive-behavioral interventions: Purposes, proposals, and problems. In P. C. Kendall, & S. D. Hollon (Eds.), *Assessment strategies for cognitive-behavioral interventions* (pp. 1–12). New York: Academic Press.

Kendall, P. C., & Hollon, S. D. (1981). Assessing self-referent speech: methods in the measurement of self-statements. In P. C. Kendall, & S. D. Hollon (Eds.), *Assessment strategies for cognitive-behavioral interventions* (pp. 85–118). New York: Academic Press.

Kendall, P. C., & Sheldrick, R. C. (2000). Normative data for normative comparisons. *Journal of Consulting and Clinical Psychology, 68,* 767–773.

Kuiper, N. A., & Derry, P. A. (1982). Depressed and nondepressed content self-reference in mild depressives. *Journal of Personality, 50,* 67–80.

Lambert, M. J., & Shimokawa, K. (2011). Collecting client feedback. In J. C. Norcross (Ed.), *Psychotherapy relationships that work: Evidence-based responsiveness* (2nd ed., pp. 203–223). New York: Oxford University Press.

Lansbergen, M. M., Kenemans, J. L., & van Engeland, H. (2007). Stroop interference and attention-deficit/hyperactivity disorder: A review and meta-analysis. *Neuropsychology, 21,* 251–262.

Lau, M. A., Haigh, E. A. P., Christensen, B. K., Segal, Z. V., & Taube-Schiff, M. (2012). Evaluating the mood state dependence of automatic thoughts and dysfunctional attitudes in remitted versus never-depressed individuals. *Journal of Cognitive Psychotherapy: An International Quarterly, 26,* 381–389.

Lumley, M. N., & Harkness, K. L. (2009). Childhood maltreatment and depressotypic cognitive organization. *Cognitive Therapy and Research, 33,* 511–522.

MacLeod, C., Mathews, A., & Tata, P. (1986). Attentional bias in emotional disorders. *Journal of Abnormal Psychology, 95,* 15–20.

Marks, I., & Mathews, A. (1979). Brief standard self-rating scale for phobic patients. *Behavior Research and Therapy, 17,* 263–267.

Mash, E. J., & Hunsley, J. (2005). Evidence-based assessment of child and adolescent disorders: issues and challenges. *Journal of Clinical Child and Adolescent Psychology, 34,* 362–379.

Mathews, A., & MacLeod, C. (2005). Cognitive vulnerability to emotional disorders. *Annual Review of Clinical Psychology, 1,* 167–195.

McLeod, B. D., Jensen-Doss, A., & Ollendick, T. H. (Eds.), (2013). *Handbook of child and adolescent diagnostic and behavioral assessment.* New York: Guilford.

Meyer, G. J., Finn, S. E., Eyde, L. D., Kay, G. G., Moreland, K. L., Dies, R. R., & Reed, G. M. (2001). Psychological testing and psychological assessment: A review of evidence and issues. *American Psychologist, 56,* 128–165.

Mogg, K., & Bradley, B. P. (2005). Attentional bias in generalized anxiety disorder versus depressive disorder. *Cognitive Therapy and Research, 29,* 29–45.

Naragon-Gainey, K., & Brown, T. A. (2015). Enhancing measurement validation in cognitive clinical research with structural equation modeling and item response theory. In G. P. Brown, & D. A. Clark (Eds.), *Assessment in cognitive therapy* (pp. 268–290). New York: Guilford.

Nezu, A. M., Ronan, G. F., Meadows, E. A., & McClure, K. S. (Eds.), (2000). *Practitioner's guide to empirically based measures of depression*. Dordrecht, Netherlands: Kluwer Academic.

Ottenbreit, N. D., & Dobson, K. S. (2004). Avoidance and depression: The construction of the Cognitive-Behavioral Avoidance Scale. *Behaviour Research and Therapy*, *42*, 293–313.

Overington, L., & Ionita, G. (2012). Progress monitoring measures: A brief guide. *Canadian Psychology*, *53*, 82–92.

Peckham, A. D., McHugh, K. R., & Otto, M. W. (2010). A meta-analysis of the magnitude of biased attention in depression. *Depression and Anxiety*, *27*, 1135–1142.

Persons, J. B., & Davidson, J. (2010). Cognitive-behavioral case formulation. In K. S. Dobson (Ed.), *Handbook of cognitive–behavioral therapies* (3rd ed., pp. 172–193). New York: Guilford.

Persons, J. B., & Miranda, J. (1992). Cognitive theories of vulnerability to depression: Reconciling negative evidence. *Cognitive Therapy and Research*, *16*, 485–502.

Prochaska, J., & Norcross, J. (2013). *Systems of psychotherapy: A transtheoretical analysis* (8th ed.). Stamford, CT: Cengage.

Reilly-Harrington, N. A., Miklowitz, D. J., Otto, M. W., Frank, E., Wisniewski, S. R., Thase, M. E., & Sachs, G. S. (2010). Dysfunctional attitudes, attributional styles, and phase of illness in bipolar disorder. *Cognitive Therapy and Research*, *34*, 24–34.

Robins, L., Cottler, L., Bucholz, K., & Compton, W. (1995). *The diagnostic interview schedule, version IV*. St. Louis, MO: Washington University Medical School.

Scher, C. D., Ingram, R. E., & Segal, Z. V. (2005). Cognitive reactivity and vulnerability: Empirical evaluation of construct activation and cognitive diatheses in unipolar depression. *Clinical Psychology Review*, *25*, 487–510.

Schwartz, K., & Verhaeghen, P. (2008). ADHD and Stroop interference from age 9 to 41 years: A meta-analysis of developmental effects. *Psychology Medicine*, *38*, 1607–1616.

Seeds, P. M., & Dozois, D. J. A. (2010). Prospective evaluation of a cognitive vulnerability-stress model for depression: The interaction of schema self-structure and negative life events. *Journal of Clinical Psychology*, *66*, 1307–1323.

Segal, Z. V. (1988). Appraisal of the self-schema construct in cognitive models of depression. *Psychological Bulletin*, *103*, 147–162.

Segal, Z. V., Gemar, M., Truchon, C., Guirguis, M., & Horowitz, L. M. (1995). A priming methodology for studying self-representation in major depressive disorder. *Journal of Abnormal Psychology*, *104*, 205–213.

Segal, Z. V., Gemar, M., & Williams, S. (1999). Differential cognitive response to a mood challenge following successful cognitive therapy or pharmacotherapy for unipolar depression. *Journal of Abnormal Psychology*, *108*, 3–10.

Segal, Z. V., Kennedy, S., Gemar, M., Hood, K., Pedersen, R., & Buis, T. (2006). Cognitive reactivity to sad mood provocation and the prediction of depressive relapse. *Archives of General Psychiatry*, *63*, 749–755.

Sheehan, D. V., Lecrubier, Y., Sheehan, K. H., Amorim, P., Janavs, J., Weiller, E., & Dunbar, G. C. (1998). The Mini-International Neuropsychiatric Interview (MINI): The development and validation of a structured diagnostic psychiatric interview for DSM-IV and ICD-10. *Journal of Clinical Psychiatry*, *59*, 22–23.

Smoski, M. J., Keng, S. L., Schiller, C. E., Minkel, J., & Dichter, G. S. (2013). Neural mechanisms of cognitive reappraisal in remitted major depressive disorder. *Journal of Affective Disorders*, *151*, 171–177.

Therrien, Z., & Hunsley, J. (2012). Assessment of anxiety in older adults: A systematic review of commonly used measures. *Aging and Mental Health*, *16*, 1–16.

Uchino, B. N., Cacioppo, J. T., & Kiecolt-Glaser, J. (1996). The relationship between social support and physiological processes: A review with emphasis on underlying mechanisms and implications for health. *Psychological Bulletin, 119,* 488–531.

Watkins, E. R. (2016). *Rumination-focused cognitive-behavioral therapy for depression.* New York: Guilford.

Weissman, A. N., & Beck, A. T. (1978). Development and validation of the Dysfunctional Attitude Scale: A preliminary investigation. *Paper presented at the 86th annual meeting of the American Educational Research Association,* Toronto, Canada.

Westerhausen, R., Kompus, K., & Hugdahl, K. (2011). Impaired cognitive inhibition in schizophrenia: A meta-analysis of the Stroop interference effect. *Schizophrenia Research, 133,* 172–181.

Westermann, R., Spies, K., Stahl, G., & Hesse, F. W. (1996). Relative effectiveness and validity of mood induction procedures: A meta-analysis. *European Journal of Social Psychology, 26,* 557–580.

Williams, J. M. G., Mathews, A., & MacLeod, C. (1996). The emotional Stroop task and psychopathology. *Psychological Bulletin, 120,* 3–24.

Young, J.E., & Brown, G. (2003). *Young schema questionnaire: Short form.* Available from http://www.schemathearpy.com/id54.htm.

Zuroff, D. C., Blatt, S. J., Sanislow, C. A., Bondi, C. M., & Pilkonis, P. A. (1999). Vulnerability to depression: Re-examining state dependence and relative stability. *Journal of Abnormal Psychology, 108,* 76–89.

Further Reading

Kiresuk, T. J., Stelmachers, Z. T., & Schulz, S. K. (1982). Quality assurance and goal attainment scaling. *Professional Psychology, 13,* 145–152.

3

Learning Principles in CBT

Michelle L. Davis, Sara M. Witcraft,
Scarlett O. Baird and Jasper A.J. Smits

The University of Texas at Austin, Austin, TX, United States

LEARNING PRINCIPLES OF COGNITIVE BEHAVIORAL THERAPY

As the name suggests, cognitive behavioral therapy (CBT) is a psychotherapy with roots in both behavioral and cognitive learning theories. Behaviorist learning theories focus on how external stimuli affect behavior via reinforcement. Behaviorism was the predominant form of psychology throughout the 19th century. Soon after, social learning theorists expanded behavioral learning theory by describing how learning can take place in a social context regardless of direct reinforcement, via observation. In the 20th century, psychologists began to focus on cognitive learning theory, or how thoughts shape behavior and beliefs. These learning theories merge under the umbrella of CBT, which is now broadly recognized as an effective form of treatment for numerous mental health problems (Hofmann, Asnaani, Vonk, Sawyer, & Fang, 2012).

A recent meta-analysis (Hofmann et al., 2012) examined the efficacy of CBT across a broad array of mental health conditions and found that effect sizes for CBT were medium to large for anxiety disorders and somatoform disorders, and large for cannabis and nicotine use disorders. CBT was also found to be promising for positive symptoms of psychotic disorders and bulimia. However, the evidence base for CBT efficacy in the treatment of depression was mixed, with some studies showing large effects and other studies showing small effects, and treatments for bipolar disorder were small to medium. Similarly, CBT was less effective for both opioid and alcohol use disorders. Accordingly,

The Science of Cognitive Behavioral Therapy.
DOI: http://dx.doi.org/10.1016/B978-0-12-803457-6.00003-9

despite being a promising treatment for many problems, CBT still warrants improvement.

Current attempts to improve CBT outcomes focus on understanding the mechanisms involved in therapeutic change. Given that CBT was developed based on behavioral, cognitive, and social learning principles, understanding more about how specific techniques in CBT utilize aspects of various learning theories may shed light on potential areas for improvement or augmentation. This chapter provides an overview of numerous ways in which learning may occur within CBT, while also highlighting up-to-date research on how CBT therapists can maximize their clients' learning.

BEHAVIORAL LEARNING THEORIES: CLASSICAL CONDITIONING AND EXTINCTION

Classical conditioning, or respondent conditioning, is derived from Pavlov's famous dog experiment (Pavlov, 1927), in which he trained dogs to salivate when a tuning fork was presented in the absence of food. Pavlovian conditioning theory suggests that anxiety disorders are classically conditioned when pathological fear (e.g., fear of flying) is associated with an objectively innocuous stimulus (e.g., an airplane), which has been learned in association with a feared stimulus (e.g., death by plane crash). The fear structure is created and maintained when a fear response, or conditioned response (CR; e.g., fear of flying) to a conditioned stimulus (CS; e.g., an airplane) occurs in the absence of the unconditioned stimulus (US; death by plane crash). This erroneous association is what causes a specific phobia to develop, specifically, in this example, aerophobia (Moscovitch & Huyder, 2011). This theory of classical conditioning is one of the building blocks of behaviorism, and many novel interventions have been developed as a result. One of the most widely used and efficacious treatments for anxiety disorders is exposure therapy, which utilizes the idea of Pavlovian extinction.

Exposure Therapy

Exposure therapy, or the process of repeatedly exposing a client to a feared stimulus in the absence of a feared outcome, is based on the Pavlovian extinction principle that if a CS is repeatedly presented in the absence of the US, the CR will gradually stop. For example, Pavlov's dog eventually stopped salivating at the sound of a tuning fork once the sound no longer elicited food. This phenomenon is known as extinction learning. Anxiety disorders are thought to persist due to a failure to extinguish a CR, likely due to avoidance of the CS.

Exposure therapy reverses this habit of avoidance by having clients intentionally approach feared stimuli. Exposure therapy generally commences with the creation of a fear hierarchy, or a rank-ordered list of the clients feared stimuli and situations. Participants rate their anticipated anxiety and distress using a 0 to 100-point scale called the Subjective Units of Distress Scale (SUDS; Wolpe, 1958). Traditionally, exposures begin with the least feared item. Clients repeatedly approach the CS (in the absence of the US), rating their SUDS continually, until extinction learning takes place (i.e., until the client experiences a substantial reduction in fear, the CR). The end goal of each exposure should be such that the client can associate the previously feared stimulus with an environment that is now safe. The therapist and client gradually proceed up the hierarchy until extinction learning is achieved across a number of contexts (Yuksel, Marks, Ramm, & Ghosh, 1984).

Extinction Learning

Animal research has demonstrated how, during extinction, the original CS−US association learned during conditioning is not erased in one's memory but replaced by a novel memory (Bouton, 2002; Monfils, Cowansage, Klann, & LeDoux, 2009). This new learning, which has been coined "safety learning," results in the inhibition of the original learned (fear) memory (Otto, Smits, & Reese, 2005). This inhibitory learning is a fundamental feature of extinction learning and exposure therapy and can be explained using Pavlovian classical conditioning theory terminology.

Using the previous example of aerophobia, an individual with a fear of flying has formed an implicit association (e.g., CS−US) between the CS (plane) and the US (death by plane crash), which elicits fear (Craske, Treanor, Conway, Zbozinek, & Vervliet, 2014). The individual has erroneously learned that the CS is not safe, which creates a memory of fear. With inhibitory learning, the CS is repeatedly paired with a neutral stimulus (no-US; i.e., safety learning), which creates a new memory of safety. This safety memory then competes with the previous memory that the CS is dangerous (Craske, 2015). The original association between the CS and the US remains intact as the novel secondary, inhibitory learning about the CS−US link develops (Bouton & Swartzentruber, 1991). The CS−US association now holds two meanings: (1) The original association of CS−US (e.g., airplanes/death by plane), which elicits fear and (2) the new inhibitory meaning, CS−no US (e.g., airplane/safety), which implies no threat (Craske et al., 2014).

The inhibitory learning model posits that the original association is inhibited by novel information (rather than erased), which has the implication of spontaneous recovery (Bouton, 1993; Quirk, 2002) and reacquisition (Bouton, 1993). Therefore, the strength of the CR increases in proportion to the amount of time passed since extinction.

Through fear extinction the client does not "unlearn" the fear, but rather, attributes novel significance to the CS (e.g., airplanes are relatively safe) through safety learning (Otto et al., 2005). An integral component of safety learning is experiencing the anxiety and learning more about the feared stimuli (Rothbaum & Schwartz, 2002). For example, a client with social anxiety disorder has predictions (the US; i.e., "people will ridicule me") about what might happen during a public speaking situation (the CS). The client is unable to test or challenge this prediction without participating in the situation (i.e., not avoiding the CS). If the client engages in public speaking (CS) and the audience does not ridicule them (no US), the client has gained new safety learning related to social evaluative situations (CS–no US; e.g., "people are unlikely to ridicule me").

Extinction learning during exposure sessions generalizes to other feared stimuli and situations, which is another testament to its utility. For instance, social anxiety disorder treatment often consists of having clients deliver impromptu speeches to an audience. Clients frequently wonder how this will help them in their daily lives since they do not regularly give speeches. However, public speaking is typically the target as it is universally feared, easy to replicate in an outpatient setting, and is both time and cost efficient. Through the utilization of such an efficient and intensive exposure, the therapist can work to ensure that the extinction learning will generalize to other feared situations.

Maximizing CBT Outcomes: Enhancing Safety Learning

Given that old fear memories remain intact (i.e., original association of CS–US), the goal of the CBT therapist should be to maximize safety learning so that new, safe memories dominate older fear memories (Powers, Vervliet, Smits, & Otto, 2010). This can be accomplished by ensuring that the novel information from safety learning (CS–no US) overrides the old information, which underlies the disorder. Targeting a client's specific fears (e.g., "I will look stupid," "people will steal from me if I faint") will allow for the most relevant safety learning experience. By showing the client that even when his worst fears happen there is no real threat to his safety, he is able to learn unconditional safety (Powers et al., 2010). Additionally, therapists can utilize information gleaned from contemporary research on context-dependent learning, judicious safety behavior use, and expectancy violations to enhance safety learning (Hofmann, 2008).

Extending Safety Learning to Multiple Contexts

Even among those who benefit from CBT initially, not all maintain improvements over time. For example, Durham, Higgins, Chambers, Swan, and Dow (2012) followed 336 clients over the course of two to fourteen years after receiving CBT for anxiety disorders and found that only 38% experienced full recovery with little to no follow-up treatment. This is not a novel concept; Pavlov (1927) noted this "return of fear" when describing the phenomenon of spontaneous recovery after extinction learning. Animal research suggests that this may occur due to learning that takes place about the context, or cues, related to the feared stimulus (Bouton, 2002). For example, fear conditioning occurs in one context (e.g., a child develops a fear of bugs after observing his mother's exaggerated response to a spider in his childhood home), extinction or exposure occurs in a second context (e.g., a psychology laboratory), and the real-life test of whether extinction learning was successful takes place in a third context (e.g., on the playground when encountering an anthill). In order to maximize the effect of extinction learning, safety should be learned in a variety of contexts (e.g., locations, situations, internal states) so that a return of fear is not later stimulated by unextinguished fear cues. Accordingly, clinicians should work to ensure that the context of exposures varies, both in session and as part of home practice.

Monitoring and Reducing Safety Behaviors

Safety behaviors are forms of avoidance in which the client engages in to prevent a feared outcome (Wells, 2005). For example, a client with panic disorder may carry Xanax in her purse in case of a panic attack. Even though the client isn't actually taking the Xanax, the knowledge that it is there "in case of emergency" provides the client with a sense of safety. On the contrary, that safety behavior likely prevents the client from learning unconditional safety—that she is safe with or without medication, even if she has a panic attack. Powers, Smits, and Telch (2004) directly demonstrated that participants with access to safety behaviors during exposure therapy fared significantly worse than those without such access. Eliminating even subtle safety behaviors (e.g., mental distraction, avoiding eye contact) can help the client to immerse himself in the exposure, thereby learning unconditional safety and reducing the likelihood of relapse. Therapists should not only closely monitor potential safety behaviors but also educate clients on the potential negative effects of safety behaviors so that they can recognize and address them on their own.

Creating Expectancy Violations

Expectancy violation theory is a concept that accounts for how people respond to unanticipated violations of social norms and expectations (Boettcher, Brake, & Barlow, 2015; Hofmann, 2008; Mendes, Blascovich, Hunter, Lickel, & Jost, 2007). For instance, anxious individuals are more prone to developing rigid expectations within certain tasks, relationships, or performances as compared to nonanxious individuals (Compton et al., 2010). This rigid attribution style might lead anxious individuals to view things as very upsetting or anxiety provoking, which exacerbates symptoms. Compton et al. (2010) found that an exaggerated neural response (i.e., error related negativity, ERN) to violated expectancies (i.e., false-feedback) was related to individual differences in worry. This finding suggests that anxious individuals have an exaggerated negative reaction when receiving false-feedback information. An awareness of this exaggerated response can aid in planning a client's course of treatment.

Expectancy violations are advantageous to treatment outcomes when used as a component of exposure therapy to maximize inhibitory learning. This can be accomplished by designing an exposure that maximally violates an individual's expectations of the intensity of an aversive outcome (Craske et al., 2014; Davey, 1992; Gallistel & Gibbon, 2000; Hofmann, 2008; Rescorla & Wagner, 1972). By doing so, the client will certainly experience a high level of anxiety, which is important for safety learning. According to Rescorla and Wagner's (1972) hypothesis, new learning is heavily dependent upon the discrepancy between an individual's expectancy and an event's outcome, specifically when an outcome is far less anxiety provoking than the individual originally anticipated. A critical aspect of this approach to exposure therapy is to prolong the exposure until the conditions that violate expectancies are reduced—rather than the reduction of fear—as is typical to habituation trials (Craske et al., 2014). Importantly, after the expectation is violated (i.e., after the feared outcome did not occur), the client must recount his learning and account for the degree of surprise felt when the feared outcome did not happen, which then consolidates learning.

BEHAVIORAL LEARNING THEORIES: OPERANT CONDITIONING

Operant conditioning is a learning theory, which posits that behavior is determined largely by the ensuing consequences. Skinner (1937), often cited as the father of operant conditioning, first coined this term in the context of reflex physiology. However, Skinner's work was based largely on instrumental learning, an early derivative of operant conditioning that was originally studied by Edward Thorndike. Thorndike (1911) is most known for his law of effect, or the theory that behaviors following satisfying consequences tend to be repeated, whereas those with unpleasant consequences are less likely to be repeated. Skinner's work focused solely on observable behavior and resultant consequences, thereby rejecting Thorndike's notion of unobservable mental states (e.g., satisfaction).

Reinforcement

Some of Skinner's most notable work includes his experiments using the "Skinner Box," a chamber that was used to analyze animal behavior (most often rats and pigeons). Through experiments with this apparatus, four key concepts emerged to form the basis of operant conditioning: positive reinforcement, negative reinforcement, positive punishment, and negative punishment.

Reinforcement is any stimulus or event that increases, or strengthens, the frequency of a behavior. Positive reinforcement occurs when the addition of a positive stimulus or event strengthens a behavior and makes it more likely to occur in the future. Negative reinforcement occurs when a behavior is strengthened by the removal of an aversive event or stimulus. Conversely, punishment involves a stimulus or event that will decrease, or weaken, the likelihood of the behavior in the future. Positive punishment occurs when an aversive consequence is introduced to reduce a behavior. Negative punishment occurs when a positive stimuli or event is removed in order to decrease the frequency of a behavior. Taken together, these principles have a powerful effect on how psychologists view, and ultimately work to change, human behavior. Two examples of CBT applications of operant conditioning are the token economy and contingency management.

Token Economy

The token economy is a behavioral technique that utilizes positive reinforcement in order to increase the frequency of a desired behavior. The technique was first used among psychiatric patients during the 1960s (Atthowe & Krasner, 1968; Ayllon & Azrin, 1965, 1968). Since then, it has been applied across a diversity of populations, including intellectually disabled individuals, substance abusers, students, and outpatient adults (Kazdin & Bootzin, 1972; Matson & Boisjoli, 2009; McLaughlin & Williams, 1988).

The token economy is one of the more well-validated and effective behavioral treatments for severe psychiatric disorders (Glynn, 1990). Patients can earn tokens for events like participating in therapeutic activities, assessments, and individual target behaviors. In exchange, they can earn rewards such as extra smoke-breaks, television time, or snacks (LePage, 1999). Token economies have been shown to reduce the number of total assaults and staff injuries on an inpatient psychiatric unit (LePage, 1999; LePage et al., 2003). There is substantial support in the literature of the use of token economies for patients with schizophrenia; however, the token economy does hold a number of caveats (e.g., treatment gains may not be maintained once the contingencies are removed, there is a high degree of control given to staff members; for review see Dickerson, Tenhula, & Green-Paden, 2005). Despite its clinical success, use of token economies has decreased since the 1970s (Glynn, 1990; LePage et al., 2003).

Contingency Management

Contingency management is designed for clinical problems related to impulsivity; as such, its most common clinical application is among individuals with substance use problems (for a review, see Prendergast, Podus, Finney, Greenwell, & Roll, 2006; Sigmon, Dunn, & Higgins, 2007). The basics of contingency management rely on the premise that people's thoughts, feelings, and behaviors are related to the context in which they develop. Contingency is a description used to refer to the associations that develop among the target behavior, its antecedent, and its consequences. Contingency management relies on the assumption that the probability that a behavior will occur varies as a consequence of the context in which it occurs (Drossel, Garrison-Diehn, & Fisher, 2008). Some contexts may be reinforcing and others punishing. Thus, based on the impact of each behavior over time, some contexts will serve to maintain the behavior (i.e., increase its frequency), whereas others may mitigate the behavior (i.e., decrease its frequency). It is important to recognize that these contingencies may overlap and compete within the individual.

Budney, Bickel, and Hughes (1991) have developed a protocol called voucher-based reinforcement therapy (VBRT), in which clients earn vouchers for biological samples (urine or breath) that are tested negative for drugs. The vouchers typically represent a monetary amount but do not provide actual money, thereby enabling the client to acquire goods or facilitate activities conducive to a drug-free lifestyle with the long-term goal of continuous abstinence (Budney et al., 1991; Petry & Simcic, 2002). A review of the VBRT literature suggests that not only is

VBRT efficacious in the treatment of SUDs, but that VBRT may also yield improvements across other therapeutic behaviors (e.g., clinic attendance, medication compliance; Lussier, Heil, Mongeon, Badger, & Higgins, 2006).

Maximizing CBT Outcomes: Enhancing Learning via Reinforcement or Punishment

Clinicians can utilize functional analysis, or a careful analysis of the circumstances at play in a given situation, to identify various ways in which reinforcement may explain a client's behavior. Let us consider the example of an individual who is socially anxious and chooses to avoid going to a party. This individual will likely experience competing motivations for behavior: Reduction in anxious symptoms through the avoidance (reinforcement), but also a feeling of disapproval from their friends for avoiding yet another social activity (punishment). It is also important to consider that some contingencies may be immediate, whereas others may be more delayed and ambiguous. In the example above, the immediate reduction in anxiety through avoidance is significantly more powerful and rewarding than the long-term promise of a reduction in anxiety through exposure. As most individuals will likely experience these competing motivations, a therapist skilled in contingency management must then assign arbitrary, short-term reinforcements that serve to aid the individual in reaching the long-term goal. As a reward for attending the party for at least 1 hour, the individual could schedule an activity that would be immediately rewarding (e.g., going home to watch a favorite movie). Clinicians might also consider how they might adapt principles from the token economy (outlined in Ghezzi, Wilson, Tarbox, & MacAleese, 2008) to their practice by helping a client to set up his or her own system of rewards, tracking their progress, and providing accountability.

Punishment can also be effectively used as a means of decreasing the frequency of a behavior. It is important to note that novel behavior cannot be achieved through punishment. In this case, the therapist should work to reinforce the novel behavior so as to increase the frequency of recurrence. The therapist should have data from a functional assessment, which should serve to inform on current patterns of behavior as well as both immediate and remote contingencies (Drossel et al., 2008). The therapist can then establish a contract with the client. For instance, if a depressed client is having difficulty completing homework assignments (e.g., if he is unemployed and keeps procrastinating completing job applications), the therapist might offer to hold the client accountable to homework goals by collaboratively deciding on a punishment that can be implemented in the future if goals are not met. The client might provide the therapist with a check to a charity he doesn't support to be mailed if he doesn't apply for three jobs over the next two weeks. Clients can also involve their friends and family in holding them accountable via providing previously agreed-upon punishments.

COGNITIVE LEARNING THEORIES

Cognitive learning theories focus on how learning is derived via mental processes, including attention, perception, thought, language, and memory. CBT focuses heavily on the cognitive model, which was originally developed by Beck (1979) for the treatment of depression. Beck (2011) describes how individuals hold core beliefs about themselves, others, the world, and the future. These beliefs tend to be inflexible, absolute, and generalized and tend to be formed during childhood or times of significant stress. For example, a man who is abandoned by a parent at a young age may have a core belief that he is unlovable. In certain situations, these core beliefs can become activated and lead to automatic thoughts, which are situation-specific cognitions. The man in the previous example may find that in romantic situations, he is experiencing automatic thoughts (e.g., "she's going to leave me") triggered by his core belief of unlovability. Cognitive restructuring, a fundamental CBT technique for addressing these maladaptive automatic thoughts and core beliefs, is informed by the cognitive learning theories of constructivism, attribution, and metacognition.

Constructivism

Constructivism is a learning theory based on the assumption that humans learn via an interaction between their individual experiences and their ideas or beliefs. Jean Piaget, one of the fundamental researchers in constructivism, termed mental representations (i.e., thoughts and beliefs) as schema, and considered schemata to be the basic building blocks of thinking (Woolfolk, 1987). These schemata consist of categories or concepts relating information. Over time, schemata change and are refined with stimuli and experience. Piaget (1987) described the constructivist processes through which individuals learn: assimilation and accommodation. Assimilation is the incorporation of a new experience into schemata or belief systems, without changing the existing systems. For example, a child who sees a white dog for the first time (having previously been exposed to black or brown dogs) does not alter their existing schema defining what a dog is but, instead, adds new information (that dogs can also be white) to the existing schema. Assimilation can also involve dismissing information gleaned from experience in favor of stored schema. For example, if you have repeated experience with a coworker being friendly and polite, and one day you find them becoming short-tempered, you may dismiss this experience, attributing their behavior to stress or a bad day rather than revising your opinion of their character. Alternatively, accommodation involves the alteration of mental structures or beliefs due to new experiences. A young person who has grown up in a home in which a group of people are routinely stereotyped, but who later meets people belonging to this group and finds the stereotypes to be untrue, may revise their schema or belief system based on these interactions and experiences. According to constructivist theory, learning takes place via an interplay of human experience and schematic updating and revision.

Cognitive Restructuring

Cognitive restructuring, or the CBT practice of becoming aware of and subsequently revising maladaptive thoughts, is clearly derived from a constructivist framework. Ellis (2008), one of the founding fathers of cognitive therapy, pointed out the degree of choice involved in constructivism—individuals can choose to update their beliefs based on experiences, or not. Cognitive restructuring teaches clients how to elect to use experience as evidence to update or restructure unhelpful thoughts into more rational thoughts.

Cognitive restructuring involves first teaching clients to recognize automatic, maladaptive thoughts. By drawing links between thoughts, emotions, and behaviors, clients learn that certain thoughts can trigger negative consequences. Then, clients are shown how to evaluate the accuracy of their thoughts—certain thoughts, termed cognitive distortions, are inaccurate beliefs about the self or the world which tend to be negatively skewed. For example, a client with depression might have the thought, "no one cares about me." The CBT therapist would teach the client how to look at all the evidence related to this thought and evaluate whether or not it is accurate. In cases where the negative thought is inaccurate or distorted, which is most often the case, clients are taught to restructure the thought by replacing it with a more accurate thought; for example, "sometimes I feel like no one cares about me, but my wife and children do." Revised thoughts are not necessarily more positive, but more accurate.

From a constructivist perspective, cognitive restructuring is comparable to the process of accommodation. For example, if a client has the automatic thought, "I am a failure" (stemming from his negative self-related beliefs or schema) after getting a lower than expected grade on a test, the cognitive restructuring technique would be to gather all the evidence that this thought is true or untrue (e.g., Has the client failed in the past? Has the client succeeded in the past? How do others define failure?). The depressed client has likely not spent much time looking at evidence against the thought, "I am a failure," so participating in this exercise may allow him to gather evidence to the contrary, which then challenges his self-related schema. If the evidence is compelling enough, the client is then forced to adjust his schema to accommodate this new evidence.

Cognitive Processing Therapy

Cognitive processing therapy (CPT; Resick & Schnicke, 1993) is a CBT treatment for PTSD wherein clients process their traumatic experience, restructuring cognitive distortions as they arise. For example, some individuals with PTSD may erroneously believe they are responsible for the occurrence of their traumatic event that the world is an inherently unsafe place, or that others cannot be trusted. Resick and Schnicke (1993) explained how, from a constructivist perspective, clients receiving CPT are confronted with new information that is inconsistent with their schemas about themselves, the world, or others. Accordingly, they will either assimilate the information with their existing belief, or alter their existing belief to accommodate the new information. They also noted that some individuals with PTSD tend to over-accommodate information that is related to their traumatic event. To illustrate, a woman who was a victim of rape might believe that all men are either good or evil. Dismantling studies comparing the efficacy of CPT to prolonged exposure for PTSD treatment have demonstrated that both protocols are similar in efficacy (Powers, Halpern, Ferenschak, Gillihan, & Foa, 2010).

Attribution Theory

Attribution theory focuses on an individual's perception of the cause of events and behaviors. For example, in the aforementioned example of the short-tempered coworker, the individual's explanation of why the coworker is upset (e.g., they must be having a bad day) is an example of attribution—the bad mood is attributed to circumstances in the coworker's day. In his attributional theory, Weiner (1986) posited that there are four dimensions involved in making attributions regarding causality: internality (i.e., the perceived source of the cause, whether internal or external), stability (i.e., whether the cause is perceived to be permanent or transient), controllability (i.e., whether the cause is perceived to be controllable or not), and globality (i.e., whether the cause is perceived to affect many other situations or not). For example, individuals with low self-esteem tend to attribute failure to internal causal sources versus external occurrences (Fitch, 1970). Abramson, Seligman, and Teasdale (1978) suggested that individuals with a propensity toward depression may tend to have an attributional style that is internal, stable, uncontrollable, and global. In other words, individuals suffering from depression may view negative events as due to their own failings, as being permanent, out of their control, and a commonality in their life. A meta-analysis of approximately 15,000 individuals (Sweeney, Anderson, & Bailey, 1986) provided evidence of this, finding that attribution of negative events to internal, stable, and global causes was highly associated with depression. Accordingly, attributional style is a common target of cognitive restructuring (i.e., questioning the evidence of the source, stability, controllability, and globality of causal factors).

Metacognition

Metacognition, or the awareness of one's own thought processes, was defined by Flavell (1979) and is thought to be an important component of intelligence (Demetriou & Kazi, 2001). A psychopathology-related example of metacognition is an individual with GAD who worries that they worry too much. Metacognition not only plays a vital role in cognitive restructuring, as individuals have to first be aware of their own thought processes in order to successfully alter them, but also in defusing and regulating cognitions.

Cognitive Defusion

Rather than reacting or becoming overly involved in thoughts, cognitive defusion is a metacognitive strategy for distancing oneself from his own thought processes and viewing thoughts as simply thoughts, rather than truths or facts. Acceptance and commitment therapy (ACT; Hayes, Strosahl, & Wilson, 1999) is a third-wave cognitive-behavioral intervention which, rather than focusing on controlling or restructuring maladaptive thoughts, instructs clients to simply notice thoughts and accept them. Cognitive defusion techniques, however, have been around much longer than ACT or CBT. Titchener (1916) described a cognitive distancing exercise in which a word is rapidly repeated until it loses its meaning. Masuda et al. (2010) tested this exercise more recently, having participants rapidly repeat a self-generated, negative, self-referential thought (e.g., "I am stupid"), rating their emotional discomfort and believability of the statement before and after the exercise. Both emotional discomfort and believability of the negative thoughts decreased after cognitive defusion, compared to control conditions. A recent study directly compared the effects of a 60-minute intervention involving either cognitive restructuring or cognitive defusion on food craving among chocolate cravers (Moffitt, Brinkworth, Noakes, & Mohr, 2012). The authors found that individuals who received a cognitive defusion intervention were 3.26 times more likely than those who received a cognitive restructuring intervention to remain abstinent from a researcher-provided bag of chocolate over the course of a week, suggesting that cognitive defusion may be a useful tool for reducing appetitive urges.

Problem-Solving

Metacognitive control or regulation (i.e., controlling one's own thoughts or learning) is thought to involve three essential skills: planning, monitoring, and evaluating (Schraw, 1998). Though goal setting and problem-solving are fundamental to all CBT therapies, Problem-solving therapy (PST) is a cognitive-behavioral intervention which specifically focuses on adaptive problem-solving to reduce psychopathology. The basic PST strategy involves teaching clients to define a problem (e.g., "I am unhappy with my wife"), generate potential solutions (e.g., "I could leave her," "we could go to therapy," "I can try talking with her on my own"), decide on a solution, test the solution, monitor results, and then determine if they are satisfied with the outcomes or need to return to other potential solutions. PST has been successfully applied to a variety of mental health problems, including depression, suicidal ideation, social skills deficits, substance use disorders, and personality disorders (Malouff, Thorsteinsson, & Schutte, 2007).

Maximizing CBT Outcomes: Enhancing Cognitive Learning

One of the most important ways a clinician can aid a client in learning how his cognitions impact his symptoms and overall wellbeing is through self-monitoring (Jarrett & Nelson, 1987). Theory suggests that self-monitoring alone can have a powerful impact on an individual's self-efficacy, attributions, and motivation (Tee & Kazantzis, 2011). Cohen et al. (2013) describe various practical suggestions for implementing self-monitoring, including finding the best format (e.g., handwritten or using a mobile device), always remembering to discuss information gleaned from self-monitoring tasks, problem-solving regarding factors that interfere with completion, and utilizing insights gained from monitoring within in-session discussions and examples. Self-monitoring can also be utilized to assess progress and attributions as to the causes of progress, which are additional cognitive learning aspects to consider.

Utilization of Progress Monitoring

Progress monitoring, or measuring improvements and symptom reductions and providing feedback to the client, has been shown to reduce depressive symptoms (Newnham, Hooke, & Page, 2010). Additionally, a meta-analysis of 32 studies examining the effects of providing feedback within a variety of mental health conditions demonstrated that treatment outcomes tended to improve when participants were given feedback on their progress, particularly among participants who were "off-track," or not yet demonstrating progress in treatment (Gondek, Edbrooke-Childs, Fink, Deighton, & Wolpert, 2016). Soeken, Manderscheid, Flatter, and Silbergeld (1981) found that providing quantitative outcomes feedback to individuals receiving couples counseling also increased self-efficacy, pointing toward the potential usefulness of progress monitoring as a platform to discuss attribution of gains. However, a recent study found few clinicians (approximately 37% of those surveyed) reported assessing outcomes in their practices (Hatfield & Ogles, 2004). Further implementation of progress monitoring as a standard clinical practice may be a relatively cost- and time-effective way to improve cognitive-behavioral interventions. Additionally, research suggests that providing effort attributional feedback to students (e.g., providing feedback about gains and correlating these with the student's efforts) increases their perceived self-efficacy and achievement (Schunk, 1982). Highlighting correlations between homework completion and symptom reduction may be a powerful way to not only increase motivation, but also self-efficacy.

Assessing Attribution of Gains

Attributional style not only impacts the onset and maintenance of depression, but attribution of the cause of symptom reduction after successful treatment (i.e., attribution of gains) has been demonstrated to be important to treatment outcomes and risk for relapse. For example, individuals receiving alprazolam versus exposure therapy for panic disorder evidenced greater relapse due to their attribution of gains to the medication (Başoğlu et al., 1994). Powers, Smits, Whitley, Bystritsky, and Telch (2008) directly tested the prediction that attributions regarding medication would negatively impact anxiety treatment, hypothesizing that individuals who believed they had received a sedating medication during exposure treatment might evidence a poorer treatment outcome due to their attributions about why their fear declined during exposure. If an individual attributes a decline in fear to her own self-efficacy, or to the fact that fear simply goes away on its own, she may be less likely to fear similar future situations. If an individual attributes a decline in fear to the fact that she received a sedating medication, she may have lower expectations for a decline in fear without the presence of a sedating medication in similar future situations. Powers and colleagues found that individuals who believed they received a sedating medication (when they actually received placebo pills) evidenced significantly more return of fear than individuals receiving placebo pills who were not told that pills were sedating. This detrimental effect was also mediated by reduced self-efficacy, suggesting that individuals attributed their success to the medication, rather than their own self-efficacy. Conversely, individuals receiving PTSD treatment who attributed gains to their own personal efforts evidenced less relapse (Livanou et al., 2002). Accordingly, it is not only important to assess attributional style as a function of cognitive restructuring within treatment, but clinicians may also consider, when clients evidence improvement, assessing their attribution of gains. Clients attributing improvement to external sources may require cognitive restructuring or behavioral testing regarding this attribution.

SOCIAL LEARNING THEORIES

Social learning theories posit that learning occurs in a sociocultural context; as such, learning takes place in dyads or small groups rather than within the individual (Johnson & Bradbury, 2015). These theories tend to focus on learning in the context of interpersonal relationships, interactions, and observations. Three theories of social learning that are applicable to the learning that takes place within CBT are social constructivism, observational learning, and cognitive apprenticeship. Given the systematic nature of CBT (with many CBT applications manualized into disorder-specific protocols), the CBT therapist assumes a more directive, active role than many other types of therapy. Sessions are structured, beginning with agenda setting and homework review and ending with a review of the session and homework setting for the following session. Accordingly, a primary role of the CBT therapist is to structure the session so that there is adequate time for each component. The therapist also facilitates the implementation of specific strategies (e.g., cognitive restructuring, psychoeducation, exposures) tailored toward the needs of the client. In these ways, the relationship between therapist and client, and the learning that takes place as a function of this relationship, is distinctive from more psychodynamic therapies. This relationship can be explored as a function of the learning theories of social constructivism, observational learning, and cognitive apprenticeship.

Social Constructivism

Social constructivism, a social learning theory developed by Russian psychologist Lev Vygotsky, posits that individuals are active participants in the creation of their own knowledge (Schreiber & Valle, 2013). Vygotsky believed that learning takes place primarily in social and cultural settings, rather than solely within the individual (Schreiber & Valle, 2013). The social constructivism theory focuses heavily upon dyads (Johnson & Bradbury, 2015) and small groups. For instance, students learn primarily through interactions with their peers, teachers, and parents, whereas teachers stimulate and facilitate conversation through harnessing the natural flow of conversation in the classroom (Powell & Kalina, 2009). Social constructivism suggests that successful teaching and learning is heavily dependent on interpersonal interaction and discussion, with the primary focus on the students' understanding of the discussion (Prawat, 1992).

One of the core constructs of Vygotsky's theory of social constructivism is the zone of proximal development (ZPD), which emphasizes the role of the instructor in an individual's learning. The ZPD delineates the activities that a student can do without help, and the activities the student cannot do without the help of an instructor. The ZPD suggests that, with the help of an instructor, students are able to understand and master knowledge and skills that they would not be able to on their own (Schreiber & Valle, 2013). Once the students master a particular skill they are able to complete it independently. In this theory, the instructor plays an integral role in the students' acquisition of knowledge, rather than serving as a passive figure (Chen, 2012; Schreiber & Valle, 2013).

CBT can be viewed as a form of social constructivism: From the first session, an emphasis is placed not only on the active role of the client within therapy but also on the didactic nature of CBT (compared to other types of therapy in which the therapist takes on the role of an active listener; e.g., talk therapy). Though the client is ultimately in charge of his or her own outcomes, the therapist's initial role is that of an educator who provides the client with information about her disorder and its causes and instruction on how to engage in cognitive restructuring or behavioral exercises. A relevant example is the feedback session after the initial assessment visit, wherein the CBT therapist typically describes any relevant diagnoses to the client, explains what the treatment process will look like, and then begins describing the client's problems within the framework of a cognitive-behavioral model. Throughout treatment, the therapist helps the client become the expert on their own problems and how to "treat" these problems using CBT techniques.

Observational Learning

Albert Bandura's theory of observational learning and his famous Bobo doll experiment (Bandura, Ross, & Ross, 1963) are taught in many high school and college classrooms as an example of social learning. Bandura theorized that individuals learn social and trade skills, as well as their own behavioral responses, by observing the behavior of others (Bandura et al., 1963). For example, a child who witnesses his mother becoming extremely upset at the sight of a spider may learn to fear spiders himself, simply by observing her reaction. On the other hand, if the child sees his mother react calmly, he may learn that spiders are relatively innocuous.

An obvious application of observational learning to CBT is a group treatment format. For example, in group-based exposure therapy for social anxiety disorder, group members are not only able to participate in their own social exposures (with the economic benefit of group members as built-in confederate audience members), but they are also able to observe other group members engaging in exposure. This observation provides an opportunity for the other group members to objectively see and learn that: (1) Experiencing anxiety is not dangerous, (2) nothing objectively bad will occur if they engage in exposures, and (3) that their anxiety may decrease over time as well. Drossel (2008) outlines several factors to consider in the implementation of group therapy, including nonspecific group processes (e.g., group cohesiveness, ensuring confidentiality, the CBT therapist's role as group leader, and attrition).

Cognitive Apprenticeship

Cognitive apprenticeship refers to learning through guided experience via instructor modeling and scaffolding until the student is competent and able to work independently (Collins, Brown, & Newman, 1989). Cognitive apprenticeship is differentiated from social constructivism because instructors have a larger role when teaching the student. The instructor verbalizes his thoughts so the student can both hear and observe his instruction. The student then completes the task on his own and once he has completed it the instructor provides feedback (Stalmeijer, 2015). The instructor titrates his role in the student's learning, a process called scaffolding, until the student has completely mastered the task (Stalmeijer, 2015). Collins et al. (1989) suggest a variant, which is slightly more independent, to this method: instructors articulate their knowledge, students reflect on their own skills, and then they create their own learning goals. This alternative conceptualization of cognitive apprenticeship mirrors the cognitive restructuring method frequently used in CBT for anxiety and depressive disorders.

When employing cognitive restructuring, the therapist aims to actively dispute the client's irrational beliefs and teach the client to independently challenge his thoughts (Ellis, 2008). As mentioned previously as an example of an irrational thought, a depressed client may think that he is a failure because he failed a test. The therapist will vocalize the irrational nature of this belief, directly challenge the client's belief that he is always going to be a failure because he did poorly on one test, and cite an example of a different thought (e.g., "this particular test was especially difficult and the entire class did poorly"). Once the client understands the irrational nature of his belief, the therapist will work with him to challenge these thoughts (i.e., scaffolding), until the client is able to do this on his own. One of the fundamental goals of the CBT therapist should be to teach the client how to become his or her own therapist. This is accomplished through a repeated process of demonstrating, mirroring, and scaffolding, gradually reducing the role of the therapist.

Maximizing CBT Outcomes: Enhancing Social Learning

Piaget (1972) highlighted two principles for effective teaching—the instructor should ensure that learning is an active process (involving hands-on experience, independent problem-solving, and learning from errors) and that learning is "real" (i.e., pertaining to real-life, meaningful situations). One way to maximize learning within CBT is to rely on homework assignments. Homework assignments allow the client to learn how to apply what he has learned in therapy sessions to real world settings without the assistance of a therapist. For instance, someone with social anxiety disorder may watch the therapist demonstrate an in vivo exposure, then complete her own exposure with the therapist observing, and then complete exposures independently for homework. Assigning homework aids in consolidating what has been learned in session, increases the generalizability of the learning, and leads to an improvement in treatment outcomes (Kazantzis, Deane, & Ronan, 2000). It also allows the client to develop a sense of mastery and independence while still engaging in a social learning exercise with the therapist through discussions of homework at each session. Clinicians can utilize social learning strategies to increase homework compliance by reviewing homework and building credibility.

Reviewing Homework

Though the typical CBT session should begin with a review of homework, this practice can sometimes be overlooked if a client comes in very emotionally distressed. However, Bryant, Simons, and Thase (1999) empirically demonstrated the importance of this treatment component, finding that reviewing homework predicted future compliance. Neglecting to review homework may give the client the impression that home practice is not important or that, if he did complete the last assignment, this was time-wasted. Accordingly, the clinician should make a mental note to bring up homework at some point in the session if it is not feasible at the onset.

If a clinician finds that a client failed to complete an assignment, she should assess the reasons for noncompliance. For example, less difficult homework tasks are more likely to be completed than difficult ones (Conoley, Padula, Payton, & Daniels, 1994). If a client reports that a task was too time-consuming, the therapist should help him to break the task down into smaller, more manageable parts. Several studies (Kazantzis, Deane, Ronan, & L'Abate, 2005; Kazantzis & Shinkfield, 2007; Tompkins, 2002) describe how clients are more likely to comply with homework assignments when (1) assignments fit into the model of the client's problem formulation and treatment plan, (2) assignments fit their expectations regarding length and effort required, (3) assignments utilize particular strengths of the client, and (4) the therapist has a high level of social influence with the client. Accordingly, in reviewing homework, clinicians must routinely assess reasons for noncompliance. Future homework assignments should take previous noncompliance into account, tailoring assignments to the individual.

Building Credibility

Clients who have high expectations for change (i.e., those who believe that the treatment they are receiving will work) tend to participate more in the treatment process (Westra, Dozois, & Marcus, 2007). Clinicians should consider spending a significant amount of time in the first session discussing with the client the effectiveness of CBT, perhaps even providing them with research describing its efficacy in ameliorating specific conditions. Not only is belief in the credibility of the treatment important, this extends to the credibility of the practitioner. clients are more likely to comply with homework assignments when they perceive their therapist to be highly self-confident (Edelman & Chambless, 1993). Due to the social constructivist nature of the CBT relationship, clinicians should consider the impact their own beliefs about the effectiveness of both CBT and their own skills may be having on the client.

CONCLUSION

CBT is an integrated and dynamic treatment based on behavioral, cognitive, and social learning theories. By understanding how CBT works (i.e., how learning aids in reducing symptomatology), we may be able to enhance its efficacy. Recent attempts to augment CBT have followed this notion, focusing on pharmacotherapy that can consolidate or enhance the behavioral learning that takes place in exposure therapy. For example, numerous studies have suggested that d-cycloserine (DCS) may work as a cognitive enhancer through the augmentation of the learning processes underlying exposure therapy (Guastella et al., 2008; Hofmann et al., 2006; Otto et al., 2009; Ressler et al., 2004). However, in a recent review, Hofmann, Otto, Pollack, and Smits (2015) conclude that the effect is limited; DCS may indeed promote early treatment gains during CBT (and, specifically, exposure therapy) but only as long as it is administered in acute, small doses. Thus, the revised consensus is that DCS may serve to improve "good" exposures and have a detrimental effect on "bad" exposures (Hofmann, 2014; Smits et al., 2013a, 2013b). Although this is just one example of a pharmaceutical augmentative strategy, the DCS literature nicely illustrates the type of therapeutic gain we can obtain by studying learning processes and underlying learning theory. Although this chapter has predominantly provided suggestion for clinicians, the potential benefit derived from an understanding of learning principles is not specific to clinical work, and has the potential to generate further research opportunities. Future researchers may want to consider how the learning theories that have been delineated in this chapter may be useful to isolate and/or augment with pharmacological or behavioral strategies.

References

Abramson, L. Y., Seligman, M. E., & Teasdale, J. D. (1978). Learned helplessness in humans: Critique and reformulation. *Journal of Abnormal Psychology, 87*(1), 49.

Atthowe, J. M., Jr, & Krasner, L. (1968). Preliminary report on the application of contingent reinforcement procedures (token economy) on a "chronic" psychiatric ward. *Journal of Abnormal Psychology, 73*(1), 37.

Ayllon, T., & Azrin, N. H. (1965). The measurement and reinforcement of behavior of psychotics. *Journal of the Experimental Analysis of Behavior, 8*, 357–383.

Ayllon, T., & Azrin, N. H. (1968). *The token economy: A motivational system for therapy and rehabilitation.* New York: Appleton-Century-Crofts.

Bandura, A., Ross, D., & Ross, S. A. (1963). Imitation of film-mediated aggressive models. *The Journal of Abnormal and Social Psychology, 66*(1), 3–11. Available from http://dx.doi.org/10.1037/h0048687.

Başoğlu, M., Marks, I. M., Swinson, R. P., Noshirvani, H., O'Sullivan, G., & Kuch, K. (1994). Pre-treatment predictors of treatment outcome in panic disorder and agoraphobia treated with alprazolam and exposure. *Journal of Affective Disorders, 30*(2), 123–132.

Beck, A. T. (1979). *Cognitive therapy.* Westminster, London: Penguin.

Beck, J. S. (2011). *Cognitive behavior therapy: Basics and beyond.* New York, NY: Guilford Press.

Boettcher, H., Brake, C. A., & Barlow, D. H. (2015). Origins and outlook of interoceptive exposure. *Journal of Behavior Therapy and Experimental Psychiatry.* Available from http://dx.doi.org/10.1016/j.jbtep.2015.10.009.

Bouton, M. E. (1993). Context, time, and memory retrieval in the interference paradigms of Pavlovian learning. *Psychological Bulletin, 114*(1), 80–99.

Bouton, M. E. (2002). Context, ambiguity, and unlearning: sources of relapse after behavioral extinction. *Biological Psychiatry, 52*(10), 976–986.

Bouton, M. E., & Swartzentruber, D. (1991). Sources of relapse after extinction in Pavlovian and instrumental learning. *Clinical Psychology Review, 11*(2), 123–140. Available from http://dx.doi.org/10.1016/0272-7358(91)90091-8.

Bryant, M. J., Simons, A. D., & Thase, M. E. (1999). Therapist skill and patient variables in homework compliance: Controlling an uncontrolled variable in cognitive therapy outcome research. *Cognitive Therapy and Research, 23*(4), 381–399. Available from http://dx.doi.org/10.1023/A:1018703901116.

Budney, A. J., Bickel, W. K., & Hughes, J. R. (1991). A behavioral approach to achieving initial cocaine abstinence. *American Journal of Psychiatry, 148*, 1218–1224.

Chen. (2012). Cultural zone of proximal development: A construct to further our understanding of MI around the world. http://viking.coe.uh.edu/~ichen/ebook/et-it/social.htm.

Cohen, J. S., Edmunds, J. M., Brodman, D. M., Benjamin, C. L., & Kendall, P. C. (2013). Using self-monitoring: Implementation of collaborative empiricism in cognitive-behavioral therapy. *Cognitive and Behavioral Practice, 20*(4), 419–428.

Collins, A., Brown, J. S., & Newman, S. (1989). *Cognitive apprenticeship: Teaching the crafts of reading, writing, and mathematics. Knowing, learning, and instruction: Essays in honor of Robert Glaser* (pp. 32–42). Hove: United Kingdom: Psychology Press.

Compton, R. J., Dainer-Best, J., Fineman, S. L., Freedman, G., Mutso, A., & Rohwer, J. (2010). Anxiety and expectancy violations: Neural response to false feedback is exaggerated in worriers. *Cognition and Emotion, 24*(3), 465–479. Available from http://dx.doi.org/10.1080/02699930802696856.

Conoley, C. W., Padula, M. A., Payton, D. S., & Daniels, J. A. (1994). Predictors of client implementation of counselor recommendations: Match with problem, difficulty level, and building on client strengths. *Journal of Counseling Psychology, 41*(1), 3–7. Available from http://dx.doi.org/10.1037/0022-0167.41.1.3.

Craske, M. G. (2015). Optimizing exposure therapy for anxiety disorders: An inhibitory learning and inhibitory regulation approach. *Verhaltenstherapie, 25*(2), 134–143.

Craske, M. G., Treanor, M., Conway, C. C., Zbozinek, T., & Vervliet, B. (2014). Maximizing exposure therapy: An inhibitory learning approach. *Behaviour Research and Therapy, 58*, 10–23. Available from http://dx.doi.org/10.1016/j.brat.2014.04.006.

Davey, G. C. L. (1992). Classical conditioning and the acquisition of human fears and phobias: A review and synthesis of the literature. *Advances in Behaviour Research and Therapy, 14*(1), 29–66. Available from http://dx.doi.org/10.1016/0146-6402(92)90010-L.

Demetriou, A., & Kazi, S. (2001). *Unity and modularity in the mind and the self: Studies on the relationships between self-awareness, personality, and intellectual development from childhood to adolescence.* London: Routledge.

Dickerson, F. B., Tenhula, W. N., & Green-Paden, L. D. (2005). The token economy for schizophrenia: review of the literature and recommendations for future research. *Schizophrenia Research, 75*(2), 405–416.

Drossel, C. (2008). *Group interventions. Cognitive behavior therapy: applying empirically supported techniques in your practice.* New York: John Wiley & Sons.

Drossel, C., Garrison-Diehn, C. G., & Fisher, J. E. (2008). Contingency management interventions. In W. T. O'Donohue, & J. E. Fisher (Eds.), *Cognitive behavior therapy: Applying empirically supported techniques in your practice* (pp. 116–122). Hoboken, NJ: John Wiley & Sons.

Durham, R. C., Higgins, C., Chambers, J. A., Swan, J. S., & Dow, M. G. T. (2012). Long-term outcome of eight clinical trials of CBT for anxiety disorders: Symptom profile of sustained recovery and treatment-resistant groups. *Journal of Affective Disorders, 136*(3), 875–881. Available from http://dx.doi.org/10.1016/j.jad.2011.09.017.

Edelman, R. E., & Chambless, D. L. (1993). Compliance during sessions and homework in exposure-based treatment of agoraphobia. *Behaviour Research and Therapy*, 31(8), 767–773. Available from http://dx.doi.org/10.1016/0005-7967(93)90007-H.

Ellis, A. (2008). Cognitive restructuring of the disputing of irrational beliefs. In W. T. O'Donohue, & J. E. Fisher (Eds.), *Cognitive behavior therapy: Applying empirically supported techniques in your practice* (pp. 91–95). Hoboken, NJ: John Wiley & Sons.

Fitch, G. (1970). Effects of self-esteem, perceived performance, and choice on causal attributions. *Journal of Personality and Social Psychology*, 16(2), 311.

Flavell, J. H. (1979). Metacognition and cognitive monitoring: A new area of cognitive–developmental inquiry. *American Psychologist*, 34(10), 906.

Gallistel, C. R., & Gibbon, J. (2000). Time, rate, and conditioning. *Psychological Review*, 107 (2), 289–344.

Ghezzi, P. M., Wilson, G. R., Tarbox, R. S., & MacAleese, K. R. (2008). Guidelines for developing and managing a token economy. In W. T. O'Donohue, & J. E. Fisher (Eds.), *Cognitive behavior therapy: Applying empirically supported techniques in your practice* (p. 565). Hoboken, NJ: John Wiley & Sons.

Glynn, S. M. (1990). Token economy approaches for psychiatric patients: Progress and pitfalls over 25 years. *Behavior Modification*, 14(4), 383–407.

Gondek, D., Edbrooke-Childs, J., Fink, E., Deighton, J., & Wolpert, M. (2016). Feedback from outcome measures and treatment effectiveness, treatment efficiency, and collaborative practice: A systematic review. *Administration and Policy in Mental Health and Mental Health Services Research*, 43, 1–19.

Guastella, A. J., Richardson, R., Lovibond, P. F., Rapee, R. M., Gaston, J. E., Mitchell, P., & Dadds, M. R. (2008). A randomized controlled trial of D-cycloserine enhancement of exposure therapy for social anxiety disorder. *Biological Psychiatry*, 63(6), 544–549.

Hatfield, D. R., & Ogles, B. M. (2004). The use of outcome measures by psychologists in clinical practice. *Professional Psychology: Research and Practice*, 35(5), 485.

Hayes, S. C., Strosahl, K. D., & Wilson, K. G. (1999). *Acceptance and commitment therapy: An experiential approach to behavior change*. New York, NY: Guilford Press.

Hofmann, S. G. (2008). Cognitive processes during fear acquisition and extinction in animals and humans: Implications for exposure therapy of anxiety disorders. *Clinical Psychology Review*, 28(2), 199–210.

Hofmann, S. G. (2014). D-Cycloserine for treating anxiety disorders: Making good exposures better and bad exposures worse. *Depression and Anxiety*, 31(3), 175.

Hofmann, S. G., Asnaani, A., Vonk, I. J., Sawyer, A. T., & Fang, A. (2012). The efficacy of cognitive behavioral therapy: A review of meta-analyses. *Cognitive Therapy and Research*, 36(5), 427–440.

Hofmann, S. G., Meuret, A. E., Smits, J. A., Simon, N. M., Pollack, M. H., Eisenmenger, K., & Otto, M. W. (2006). Augmentation of exposure therapy with D-cycloserine for social anxiety disorder. *Archives of General Psychiatry*, 63(3), 298–304.

Hofmann, S. G., Otto, M. W., Pollack, M. H., & Smits, J. A. (2015). D-Cycloserine augmentation of cognitive behavioral therapy for anxiety disorders: An update. *Current Psychiatry Reports*, 17(1), 1–5.

Jarrett, R. B., & Nelson, R. O. (1987). Mechanisms of change in cognitive therapy of depression. *Behavior Therapy*, 18(3), 227–241.

Johnson, M. D., & Bradbury, T. N. (2015). Contributions of social learning theory to the promotion of healthy relationships: Asset or liability? *Journal of Family Theory & Review*, 7(1), 13–27. Available from http://dx.doi.org/10.1111/jftr.12057.

Kazantzis, N., Deane, F. P., & Ronan, K. R. (2000). Homework assignments in cognitive and behavioral therapy: A meta-analysis. *Clinical Psychology: Science and Practice*, 7(2), 189–202. Available from http://dx.doi.org/10.1093/clipsy/7.2.189.

Kazantzis, N., Deane, F. P., Ronan, K. R., & L'Abate, L. (2005). *Using homework assignments in cognitive behavior therapy.* London: United Kingdom: Routledge.

Kazantzis, N., & Shinkfield, G. (2007). Conceptualizing patient barriers to nonadherence with homework assignments. *Cognitive and Behavioral Practice, 14*(3), 317—324. Available from http://dx.doi.org/10.1016/j.cbpra.2006.08.003.

Kazdin, A. E., & Bootzin, R. R. (1972). The token economy: An evaluative review. *Journal of Applied Behavior Analysis, 5*(3), 343.

LePage, J. P. (1999). The impact of a token economy on injuries and negative events on an acute psychiatric unit. *Psychiatric Services, 50*(7), 941—944.

LePage, J. P., DelBen, K., Pollard, S., McGhee, M., VanHorn, L., Murphy, J., & Mogge, N. (2003). Reducing assaults on an acute psychiatric unit using a token economy: A 2-year follow-up. *Behavioral Interventions, 18*(3), 179—190.

Livanou, M., Baosglu, M., Marks, I. M., De Silva, P., Noshirvani, H., Lovell, K., & Thrasher, S. (2002). Beliefs, sense of control and treatment outcome in post-traumatic stress disorder. *Psychological Medicine, 32*(01), 157—165.

Lussier, J. P., Heil, S. H., Mongeon, J. A., Badger, G. J., & Higgins, S. T. (2006). A meta-analysis of voucher-based reinforcement therapy for substance use disorders. *Addiction, 101*(2), 192—203.

Malouff, J. M., Thorsteinsson, E. B., & Schutte, N. S. (2007). The efficacy of problem solving therapy in reducing mental and physical health problems: A meta-analysis. *Clinical Psychology Review, 27*(1), 46—57.

Masuda, A., Twohig, M. P., Stormo, A. R., Feinstein, A. B., Chou, Y. Y., & Wendell, J. W. (2010). The effects of cognitive defusion and thought distraction on emotional discomfort and believability of negative self-referential thoughts. *Journal of Behavior Therapy and Experimental Psychiatry, 41*(1), 11—17.

Matson, J. L., & Boisjoli, J. A. (2009). The token economy for children with intellectual disability and/or autism: A review. *Research in Developmental Disabilities, 30*(2), 240—248.

McLaughlin, T. F., & Williams, R. L. (1988). The token economy. In S. N. Elliott, F. Gresham, & J. C. Witt (Eds.), *Handbook of behavior therapy in education* (pp. 469—487). Heidelberg, NY: Springer.

Mendes, W. B., Blascovich, J., Hunter, S. B., Lickel, B., & Jost, J. T. (2007). Threatened by the unexpected: physiological responses during social interactions with expectancy-violating partners. *Journal of Personality and Social Psychology, 92*(4), 698—716. Available from http://dx.doi.org/10.1037/0022-3514.92.4.698.

Moffitt, R., Brinkworth, G., Noakes, M., & Mohr, P. (2012). A comparison of cognitive restructuring and cognitive defusion as strategies for resisting a craved food. *Psychology & Health, 27*(2), 74—90.

Monfils, M.-H., Cowansage, K. K., Klann, E., & LeDoux, J. E. (2009). Extinction-reconsolidation boundaries: Key to persistent attenuation of fear memories. *Science (New York, N.Y.), 324*(5929), 951—955. Available from http://dx.doi.org/10.1126/science.1167975.

Moscovitch, D. A., & Huyder, V. (2011). The negative self-portrayal scale: Development, validation, and application to social anxiety. *Behavior Therapy, 42*(2), 183—196. Available from http://dx.doi.org/10.1016/j.beth.2010.04.007.

Newnham, E. A., Hooke, G. R., & Page, A. C. (2010). Progress monitoring and feedback in psychiatric care reduces depressive symptoms. *Journal of Affective Disorders, 127*(1), 139—146.

Otto, M. W., Basden, S. L., McHugh, R. K., Kantak, K. M., Deckersbach, T., Cather, C., & Smits, J. A. (2009). Effects of D-cycloserine administration on weekly nonemotional memory tasks in healthy participants. *Psychotherapy and Psychosomatics, 78*(1), 49—54.

Otto, M. W., Smits, J. A. J., & Reese, H. E. (2005). Combined psychotherapy and pharmacotherapy for mood and anxiety disorders in adults: Review and analysis. *Clinical*

Psychology: Science and Practice, 12(1), 72−86. Available from http://dx.doi.org/10.1093/clipsy.bpi009.

Pavlov, I. (1927). *Conditioned Reflexes*. Oxford, England: Oxford University Press.

Petry, N. M., & Simcic, F. (2002). Recent advances in the dissemination of contingency management techniques: clinical and research perspectives. *Journal of Substance Abuse Treatment*, 23(2), 81−86.

Piaget, J. (1972). Development and learning. In C. S. Lavatelly, & F. Stendler (Eds.), *Reading in child behavior and development*. New York: Hartcourt Brace Janovich.

Piaget, J. (1987). *Possibility and necessity, volume* (p. 1). Minneapolis, MN: University of Minnesota Press.

Powell, K. C., & Kalina, C. J. (2009). Cognitive and social constructivism: Developing tools for an effective classroom. *Education*, 130(2), 241.

Powers, M. B., Halpern, J. M., Ferenschak, M. P., Gillihan, S. J., & Foa, E. B. (2010). A meta-analytic review of prolonged exposure for posttraumatic stress disorder. *Clinical Psychology Review*, 30(6), 635−641.

Powers, M. B., Smits, J. A. J., & Telch, M. J. (2004). Disentangling the effects of safety-behavior utilization and safety-behavior availability during exposure-based treatment: a placebo-controlled trial. *Journal of Consulting and Clinical Psychology*, 72(3), 448−454. Available from http://dx.doi.org/10.1037/0022-006X.72.3.448.

Powers, M. B., Smits, J. A. J., Whitley, D., Bystritsky, A., & Telch, M. J. (2008). The effect of attributional processes concerning medication taking on return of fear. *Journal of Consulting and Clinical Psychology*, 76(3), 478.

Powers, M. B., Vervliet, B., Smits, J. A. J., & Otto, M. W. (2010). Helping exposure succeed: Learning theory perspectives on treatment resistance and relapse. In M. Otto, & S. Hofmann (Eds.), *Avoiding treatment failures in the anxiety disorders* (pp. 31−49). New York: Springer. Retrieved from http://link.springer.com/chapter/10.1007/978-1-4419-0612-0_3.

Prawat, R. S. (1992). Teachers' beliefs about teaching and learning: A constructivist perspective. *American Journal of Education*, 100(3), 354−395.

Prendergast, M., Podus, D., Finney, J., Greenwell, L., & Roll, J. (2006). Contingency management for treatment of substance use disorders: A meta-analysis. *Addiction*, 101(11), 1546−1560.

Quirk, G. J. (2002). Memory for extinction of conditioned fear is long-lasting and persists following spontaneous recovery. *Learning & Memory (Cold Spring Harbor, N.Y.)*, 9(6), 402−407. Available from http://dx.doi.org/10.1101/lm.49602.

Rescorla, R.A., & Wagner, A.R. (1972). A theory of Pavlovian conditioning: Variations in the effectiveness of reinforcement and nonreinforcement. In *Classical conditioning: Current research and theory*.

Resick, P. A., & Schnicke, M. (1993). *Cognitive processing therapy for rape victims: A treatment manual* (Vol. 4Thousand Oaks, CA: Sage Publications Inc.

Ressler, K. J., Rothbaum, B. O., Tannenbaum, L., Anderson, P., Graap, K., Zimand, E., & Davis, M. (2004). Cognitive enhancers as adjuncts to psychotherapy: Use of D-cycloserine in phobic individuals to facilitate extinction of fear. *Archives of General Psychiatry*, 61(11), 1136−1144.

Rothbaum, B. O., & Schwartz, A. C. (2002). Exposure therapy for posttraumatic stress disorder. *American Journal of Psychotherapy*, 56(1), 59−75.

Schreiber, L. M., & Valle, B. E. (2013). Social constructivist teaching strategies in the small group classroom. *Small Group Research*, 44(4), 395−411. Available from http://dx.doi.org/10.1177/1046496413488422.

Schraw, G. (1998). Promoting general metacognitive awareness. *Instructional Science*, 26(1), 113−125.

Schunk, D. H. (1982). Effects of effort attributional feedback on children's perceived self-efficacy and achievement. *Journal of Educational Psychology*, 74(4), 548.

Sigmon, S. C., Dunn, K., & Higgins, S. T. (2007). Brief history of the contingency management working group. *Drug and Alcohol Dependence, 89,* 314–316.

Skinner, B. F. (1937). Two types of conditioned reflex: A reply to Konorski and Miller. *The Journal of General Psychology, 16*(1), 272–279.

Smits, J. A. J., Rosenfield, D., Otto, M. W., Marques, L., Davis, M. L., Meuret, A. E., & Hofmann, S. G. (2013a). D-Cycloserine enhancement of exposure therapy for social anxiety disorder depends on the success of exposure sessions. *Journal of Psychiatric Research, 47*(10), 1455–1461.

Smits, J. A. J., Rosenfield, D., Otto, M. W., Powers, M. B., Hofmann, S. G., Telch, M. J., & Tart, C. D. (2013b). D-Cycloserine enhancement of fear extinction is specific to successful exposure sessions: evidence from the treatment of height phobia. *Biological Psychiatry, 73*(11), 1054–1058.

Soeken, D. R., Manderscheid, R. W., Flatter, C. H., & Silbergeld, S. (1981). A controlled study of quantitative feedback in married-couples brief group psychotherapy. *Psychotherapy: Theory, Research & Practice, 18*(2), 204.

Stalmeijer, R. E. (2015). When I say ... cognitive apprenticeship. *Medical Education, 49*(4), 355–356. Available from http://dx.doi.org/10.1111/medu.12630.

Sweeney, P. D., Anderson, K., & Bailey, S. (1986). Attributional style in depression: A meta-analytic review. *Journal of Personality and Social Psychology, 50*(5), 974.

Tee, J., & Kazantzis, N. (2011). Collaborative empiricism in cognitive therapy: A definition and theory for the relationship construct. *Clinical Psychology: Science and Practice, 18*(1), 47–61.

Thorndike, E. L. (1911). *Animal intelligence: Experimental studies.* London, England: Macmillan.

Titchener, E. B. (1916). On ethnological tests of sensation and perception with special reference to tests of color vision and tactile discrimination described in the reports of the Cambridge anthropological expedition to Torres Straits. *Proceedings of the American Philosophical Society, 55,* 204–236.

Tompkins, M. A. (2002). Guidelines for enhancing homework compliance. *Journal of Clinical Psychology, 58*(5), 565–576. Available from http://dx.doi.org/10.1002/jclp.10033.

Weiner, B. (1986). Attribution, emotion, and action. In R. M. Sorrentino, & E. T. Higgins (Eds.), *Handbook of motivation and cognition: Foundations of social behavior* (pp. 281–312). New York, NY: Guilford Press.

Wells, A. (2005). Generalized anxiety disorder. In A. Freeman, S. H. Felgoise, C. M. Nezu, A. M. Nezu, & M. Reinecke (Eds.), *Encyclopedia of cognitive behavior therapy* (pp. 195–198). New York, NY: Springer.

Westra, H. A., Dozois, D. J. A., & Marcus, M. (2007). Expectancy, homework compliance, and initial change in cognitive-behavioral therapy for anxiety. *Journal of Consulting and Clinical Psychology, 75*(3), 363–373. Available from http://dx.doi.org/10.1037/0022-006X.75.3.363.

Wolpe, J. (1958). *Psychotherapy by reciprocal inhibition.* Stanford, CA: Stanford University Press.

Woolfolk, A. E. (1987). *Educational psychology* (3rd ed.). Englewood Cliffs, NJ: Prentice-Hall.

Yuksel, S., Marks, I., Ramm, E., & Ghosh, A. (1984). Slow versus Rapid Exposure in vivo of Phobics. *Behavioural and Cognitive Psychotherapy, 12*(03), 249–256. Available from http://dx.doi.org/10.1017/S0141347300010818.

Further Reading

Boulougouris, J. C., Marks, I. M., & Marset, P. (1971). Superiority of flooding (implosion) to desensitisation for reducing pathological fear. *Behaviour Research and Therapy, 9*(1), 7–16.

Cognitive Processes in CBT

Eni S. Becker[1] and Janna N. Vrijsen[2,3]

[1]Radboud University Nijmegen, Nijmegen, The Netherlands [2]Radboud University Medical Center, Nijmegen, The Netherlands [3]Pro Persona Mental Health Care, Nijmegen, The Netherlands

A BIT OF BACKGROUND: THE COGNITIVE MODEL

In order to successfully act and survive in the world and to respond to its challenges, we have to rapidly make sense of our fast changing environment. We have to perceive stimuli, attend to them, categorize them, connect them to our experience, evaluate and interpret them, and remember them. Our successful functioning in the world relies heavily on these cognitive processes. Some of them are unconscious or automatic, others we can influence directly with our conscious mind. Those cognitive processes are always biased, or skewed, due to our personality, experiences, and the environmental context. In mental disorders, those processes are systematically biased. Patients with an anxiety disorder allocate their attention to threat, and have a very hard time disengaging from threatening stimuli (e.g., Bar-Haim, Lamy, Pergamin, Bakermans-Kranenburg, & Van Ijzendoorn, 2007; Cisler & Koster, 2010). In an objectively threatening situation this is very useful, it would not do to ignore the lion that is out to get you. But to be constantly on the lookout for threat, or, for example, to worry about an acquaintance's remark, will not help in future social encounters and might eventually lead to avoidance and social isolation. The cognitive biases that should help us navigate our environment can become a hindrance. Not surprisingly the last decennia have seen a boom in research on cognitive processes in psychopathology. They have been identified as important causal and maintaining factors (Mathews & MacLeod, 2005) for many mental disorders and consequently, have become part of many

The Science of Cognitive Behavioral Therapy.
DOI: http://dx.doi.org/10.1016/B978-0-12-803457-6.00004-0

theoretical models of psychopathology (e.g., for panic disorder (Clark, 1986); for depression (De Raedt & Koster, 2010)). On one hand, our knowledge is increasing exponentially, but on the other hand we know little about how to influence biases via psychotherapy, or even how psychotherapy influences those biases. Nevertheless, some of those cognitive processes, like worrying or rumination, are foci of cognitive therapies (e.g., Wells, 2011; Segal, Williams, & Teasdale, 2012). A thorough theoretical understanding of the processes involved, and their interaction with emotion, personality, or the environmental context should help improve therapeutic interventions.

There are many cognitive processes to consider, such as perception, attention, working memory, associations, evaluation, interpretation, memory, rumination, and worry. Cognitive processes are all interconnected. Thus, our memories and experiences form the starting point of what to attend to and what will be allowed to pass the filter to be processed. Memories also help evaluate stimuli or situations. However, only what has passed the attentional threshold can be stored in memory and retrieved later. We usually study these processes in isolation, which results in a shortcoming of the field. Theories all point to interconnectedness (e.g., Clark & Beck, 1999; Bower, 1981, 1987), although it is difficult to illustrate interconnectedness in research (Everaert, Koster, & Derakshan, 2012).

The first step in cognitive processing is perception. Perception is the process of recognizing and interpreting sensory stimuli. It allows us to take the sensory information in and make it into something meaningful. In this way, perception is closely linked to categorization and association. Is the dot we see a spider or a dust speck? Is it threatening or harmless? Perception includes the five senses: sight, hearing, touch, smell and taste. It also includes what is known as proprioception, a set of senses involving the ability to detect changes in body positions, movements, or internal physiological changes, that play a major role e.g., in panic disorder. Perception is part of attention. According to psychologist and philosopher William James, attention "is the taking possession of the mind, in clear and vivid form, of one out of what may seem several simultaneously possible objects or trains of thoughts (...). It implies withdrawal from some things in order to deal effectively with others" (James, 1890). Thus, to stay with the spider example, attention means to pick the dot over other possible stimuli in a room (e.g., to notice it, and to attend to it, to make sure if this is really a spider). It is important to note that attention is limited in terms of both capacity and duration (e.g., Eriksen & James, 1986; Jersild, 1927; Pashler, 1994). As attention is a limited resource, we have to be choosy about what we decide to focus on; our attention is always selective.

Attention again is part of working memory. Working memory is a system for the transient storage and processing of information (Baddeley, 1992). There is a central executive that controls several "slave systems," as the visual spatial sketchpad or the phonological loop. The central executive is the part of the working memory that selects what we are attending too. Working memory is important for reasoning, comprehension and memory updating. The frontal cortex plays a major role in working memory. Working memory is closely linked to long-term memory, which can be considered as our knowledge storage. The speed and probability of accessing a memory is determined by the level of activation, which in turn is determined by how frequently and how recently we have used the memory (Anderson, 1990). Thus, remembering an encounter with a spider, whenever we see a dot, will keep the memory updated. It is the level of processing and not the intention of learning something that determines what and how easily we remember. It also has to be noted that memory is not static but rather a cognitive *process*. Thus, retrieving information from memory storage is not like replaying a video (Schacter, 2008). While we retrieve the memory we reconstruct it. How the memory is reconstructed depends on the context we are current in, our mood, our more recent experiences, and hints from the environment. When asking a person if he remembers, "If the big spider had hairy legs," the spider is likely to enlarge in memory because of the way the question was framed. This change in the memory happens without any awareness. We will confidently state that this is a correct memory, although, actually the memory might have changed dramatically while retrieving it. This way it is even possible to "remember" things that actually never happened (Loftus & Pickrell, 1995).

As previously mentioned, our memory is closely linked to associations, evaluations, appraisals and interpretation. Some of these processes are considered higher-level cognitive processes (i.e., part of reasoning), but many of them can be highly automatic or even unconscious. For example, if you hear the word "die"/"dye," which one of the version will you write down? Most likely, you will write down the one most relevant to you or more strongly cued by the context at the time. You will probably not be aware that there are two possible solutions, but you will interpret what you have heard. Ambiguity is part of our lives, and the resolution of ambiguity is our daily business. It is of crucial importance to be able to correctly identify ambiguous stimuli if there are signs of danger: was the sound we heard a firecracker or a gunshot?

All these processes differ in the amount of awareness that comes into play. Consciousness is defined as our moment-to-moment awareness of our environment and ourselves. Conscious and unconscious processes are seen as complementary forms of cognitive processing. Controlled, conscious processing requires effort and is slower than automatic processing, but it is more flexible and open to change. The conscious cognitive processes are the focus of cognitive therapy. Automatic processing is more rigid and more difficult to change. Nevertheless, most of our mental activity is unconscious and controls the greatest part of our behavior. We cannot clearly separate unconscious from conscious. Because we cannot clearly separate the different aspects of cognitive processing, like memory and interpretation, part of a process might be automatic and part might be under effortful control.

Cognitive processing is dynamic, ever-changing, and highly interactive. This makes cognitive processing a challenge not only for research, but also for treatment. How far do those biases play a role in the etiology of disorders? How can they be addressed in treatment? Can we change those biases, and in what way?

COGNITIVE PROCESSES IN MENTAL DISORDERS

Let us first have a closer look at the more dysfunctional forms of cognitive processes, as we see in mental disorders. Emotions influence our cognitive processing and vice versa. Emotions are affective states that involve cognitive, physiological, and behavioral patterns. They are almost always linked to motivations because we react emotionally if our motives or goals are gratified or threatened. Emotions are important adaptive functions, such as the fear response. In mental disorders emotions lose their adaptive value, e.g., the fear system is triggered way too easily. Thus the emotional and cognitive interplay becomes skewed, resulting in nonadaptive behaviors, such as avoidance behaviors in anxiety disorders that become a vicious circle.

This imbalance between the controlled cognitive and emotional system is reflected in the brain (Bishop, 2007). The prefrontal cortex is important for higher order cognitive processes and cognitive flexibility. Structures that lie deeper in the brain and are part of the limbic system, such as the amygdala, the hippocampus, and parts of the anterior cingulate cortex, are heavily involved in emotional responses. Emotional regulation depends on the interplay between the prefrontal cortex and the limbic system. The prefrontal cortex enacts top-down control on the amygdala and affects its firing patterns. In the mental disorders discussed in this chapter (e.g., depression, anxiety), the prefrontal areas fail to sufficiently control the activity of the emotional system, resulting in overly emotional, or biased, responses to emotional information (Blair et al., 2008; Hofmann, Ellard, & Siegle, 2012; Siegle, Thompson, Carter, Steinhauer, & Thase, 2007). This lack of control can come into existence because the amygdala response is especially strong, or the prefrontal areas too weak, or a combination of both.

For a long time, there was the question, "Do cognitive biases really play a causal role in disorders and thus warrant being addressed in treatment, or are they "mere" correlations?" The evidence suggests biases do play an important role in the development of disorders. There are few longitudinal studies on cognitive biases; however, there is some evidence from developmental studies that cognitive biases are a risk factor for mental disorders (Hadwin, Garner, & Perez-Olivas, 2006). For example, Schneider and Nündel (2002) found that children of parents with a panic disorder had similar interpretation biases and that those biases predicted later onset of anxiety problems in those children 7 years later. Other studies have found that biases mediate between genetic vulnerabilities and the later onset of disorders (Klumpp et al., 2014; Vrijsen et al., 2014, 2015). The strongest indicator for the causal nature of cognitive biases is manipulation of those cognitive biases and subsequent changed emotions (Mathews & MacLeod, 2002). Furthermore, changing those biases lessens psychopathology (e.g., Amir & Taylor, 2012). All in all, there is evidence that cognitive biases are more than a correlate, and addressing them in therapy might offer new treatment options.

Emotions influence all stages of processing; nevertheless there seem to be "prominent" biases for some mental disorders. Patients with anxiety disorders show strong attention and interpretation biases (e.g., Bar-Haim et al., 2010; Heinrichs & Hofmann, 2001), whereas in depression, memory seems to be changed, becomes overgeneralized, and patients prefer negative stimuli to positive ones (Matt, Vázquez, & Campbell, 1992). This does not mean we cannot find memory biases in anxiety or attentional biases in depression; however, the effects are much smaller (Dalgleish & Watts, 1990). Limited space prevents a discussion of all biases for all mental disorders; below we will provide examples of some biases in some disorders.

Attention Bias in Anxiety

Selection is perhaps the most central concept of attention when looking at the role of emotions. We are bombarded by a multitude of stimuli simultaneously, and we have to very quickly decide what information will pass our threshold to be processed in more depth. Not surprisingly, fear and anxiety play a major role here, because it is a central function of fear to allocate our attentional resources to threat in order to help us survive. Evolutionary theories play an important role in some models of anxiety. Thus, Öhman (1992, 1996) states that there are "threat feature detectors" operating at a very early stage of processing, before stimuli even enter awareness, that are sensitive to basic threat cues (e.g., a snake or an angry face). Öhman's idea was further elaborated on by LeDoux (1998), who provided the neurocognitive research actually showing fast pathways to the amygdala that allow for fast unconscious processing of biologically relevant threat cues. But how does attention change when an anxiety disorder develops? One of the first models, from Williams, Watts, MacLeod, and Mathews (1988), also poses this fast unconscious processing of threat cues but goes further. Williams et al. (1988) proposed that an anxiety prone individual has an enduring tendency to allocate attentional resource toward threat, thus stating for the first time that cognitive biases play a causal role. Mogg and Bradley (1998) build on this model, modifying and extending it. They conceptualize anxiety as an aversive motivational state, triggered by potential threat, which facilitates a rapid response to threat, including heightened attention. In both models, trait anxiety lowers the threshold of attention. However, according to Mogg and Bradley's model, it is the biases in evaluation of the stimuli as potentially threatening that underlies the vulnerability of anxiety. Most researchers see both processes working hand in hand.

Attention is usually measured with the help of reaction-time paradigms, sometimes in addition to eye movement measurements. There are two very prominent reaction-time paradigms: the emotional Stroop task (Williams, Mathews, & MacLeod, 1996) and the dot probe (MacLeod, Mathews, & Tata, 1986). In the emotional Stroop task, words (or pictures) are presented in different print colors. The participants' job is to disregard the content of the words and name the colors as fast as possible. Anxious participants, patients with an anxiety disorder, and children are consistently slower in naming the colors of threatening stimuli in comparison to neutral or positive ones (Homack & Riccio, 2004; MacLeod, 2005). In the dot probe task, participants are usually presented with two stimuli (words or pictures). They are asked to disregard the stimuli, but to react as fast as possible when a neutral probe (e.g., an arrow) replaces one of the pictures. The participants have to indicate in which direction the arrow points. Participants are faster to react to the probe if it replaces a picture they have just attended to. Anxious participants are faster reacting to probes that replace threatening pictures (Frewen, Dozois, Joanisse, & Neufeld, 2008). These are certainly not the only paradigms used, there are different versions of visual search paradigms, the Posner task and others, each of them looking at slightly different aspects of attention.

Numerous studies have shown that attentional biases are a reliable phenomenon in anxiety disorders across different paradigms and populations. This is true for conscious as well as subliminal processing of stimuli (Bar-Haim et al., 2007). Attentional biases also play a role, but to a lesser degree, in depression (Gibb, McGeary, & Beevers, 2015).

Interpretation Bias in Anxiety

Associations and interpretation bias also seem to play a major role in the development of anxiety disorders. Associations cannot always be clearly distinguished from attentional processes. To preferably attend to stimuli, the stimuli must have been appraised or categorized as emotional and important. There are different appraisal theories that state emotional processes are elicited, because stimuli are appraised on their relevance for goals (e.g., threat or general well-being; Ellsworth & Scherer, 2003). These processes are mainly unconscious and very fast. They are controlled partly by genetic patterns (e.g., in threat), but mostly guided by acquired values and experiences, thus, being part of a subjective evaluation process. This allows for much more flexibility, but also for the emergence of dysfunctional patterns (e.g., the very fast categorization of dots as spiders; Becker & Rinck, 2004). This also implies that the appraisal processes can be adjusted and influenced (Brosch, Pourtois, & Sander, 2010). Brosch et al. (2010) conclude that contextual top-down processes are extremely important for the categorization of stimuli as emotional and important, and impacts the most basic level of visual processing.

Interpretation processes take part at higher-level cognitive functions (Blanchette & Richards, 2010). Usually they have been studied using verbal material, from word recognition to reading whole ambiguous passages and resolving the ending. Ambiguity at the word level has been studied using homophones (e.g., "ails"/"ales") and homographs (e.g., "row"—a fight or "to row"). Those studies often found that patients with an anxiety disorder are more likely to come up with a negative meaning or interpretation (e.g., Eysenck, Mogg, May, Richards, & Mathews, 1991). Very often, ambiguous sentences or scenarios are applied, showing that anxious individuals make more negative interpretations and perceive themselves at higher risk of something bad happening. Interestingly, this bias is also apparent in children (e.g., Klein et al., 2014). Even more interesting, this bias is apparent in children without an acute anxiety problem, but whose parents have a panic disorder (Schneider, Unnewehr, Florin, & Margraf, 2002). Thus, these biases seem to be in existence in children vulnerable to developing an anxiety disorder.

In a review, Bishop (2007) comes to the conclusion that in neuroimaging studies that examine conditioned fear, attention to threat and interpretation of emotionally ambiguous stimuli indicate common amygdala–prefrontal circuitry underlying these processes. It seems that the balance of activity within this circuitry is altered by anxiety, creating a bias toward threat. Downregulation from the prefrontal cortex is weaker in anxiety, as well as a stronger amygdala reaction. The same circuit seems to be responsible for attention as well as interpretation biases. This means that for patients with anxiety disorders, the world seems a rather dangerous place. These patients will attend more to negative and threatening stimuli, will interpret ambiguity as more threatening, and thus, will subjectively have the feeling of being surrounded by threat, which becomes a vicious circle.

Recovered Memories—False Memories in Stress Disorders

For a long time now, there has been a discussion if it is possible to block memories—especially traumatic memories, or if it is possible to create false memories. The discussion started with Freud (1896), who first claimed that many of his patients had been sexually abused by their fathers or other family members, and finding this experience so awful they repressed it. Later Freud recounted his theory, claiming that the women actually wished for sexual intercourse with their fathers and made up the abuse stories (Freud, 1924). This second and more predominant version of the theory has been working against abused women for a very long time. Many therapists, family members and members of society, found incest so awful that they would rather not believe the victims. A tragedy, but when tides changed and child abuse was taken seriously, doubts arouse regarding some reports. Gruesome stories about satanic misuse or child abuse in childcare could not be confirmed and were refuted later. Some of those abuse stories, such as abuse by Martians (Clancy, McNally, Schacter, Lenzenweger, & Pitman, 2002), are rather unlikely. Discussions have been and still are very heated and bitter. It is of interest to see how research may help determine if we can block memories or have false memories.

The research has clear ethical limitations: one cannot induce a severe trauma to see if persons are able to repress it, and one cannot plant a truly traumatic memory. Case reports are also flawed. It is almost impossible to prove that something did not happen, although the research and case reports on Martian abductions or past lives (Meyersburg, Bogdan, Gallo, & McNally, 2009) do make a rather strong point for false memories. Case reports for repressed memories are somewhat difficult, because it is often difficult to "prove" that the abuse happened as reported (with one exception: Corwin & Olafson, 1997). It is clear that there are cases of amnesia after traumatic events, but in these cases usually there is more lost than just the traumatic event and memories tend to come back after a period of time. In other instances, victims of trauma usually try extremely hard to forget what happened and are unable to do so. Results of laboratory research on intentional forgetting are mixed, but some studies show that we can "intentionally forget" neutral stimuli (Gleaves, Smith, Butler, & Spiegel, 2004). Quite often we see the paradox of intentional forgetting; those stimuli we try to block are especially persistent in popping up in our conscious mind (Wegner, 1994). And there are doubts if we can forget horrific experiences at all. McNally and Geraerts (2009) go as far as proposing that if abuse is forgotten in some instances, it is probably because at the time it was not severe.

Planting false memories is rather easy because our memory is, as mentioned before, changed whenever we retain or retrieve a memory. There is an abundance of research showing that subtle changes of wording, like "How loud was the crash?" versus "Could you hear the noise?" will change the loudness of the remembered sound. There is also substantial research that we falsely remember highly emotional material. In an interesting experiment, researchers showed that it is possible to convince participants that they were lost in a mall when they were young. Participants elaborated on false memories and in some instances, it was extremely difficult to convince them after debriefing that the event never happened (Hyman, Husband, & Billings, 1995). Thus, clinical reports and studies on the rather unlikely memories of a Martian abduction or memories of past lives, together with laboratory research, shows it is possible to falsely remember a traumatic event. Tragically, this research is misused to also discredit memories of child abuse that never was repressed. In general, memories of child abuse are correct and the abuse did take place; usually these memories are not repressed and cannot be forgotten.

Memory Bias in Depression

Biased memory processing is most robust in depression (Matt et al., 1992). The types of memory biases discussed here are considered a rather stable trait (e.g., remaining after recovery from depression; Gotlib & Joormann, 2010; Peeters, Wessel, Merckelbach, & Boon-Vermeeren, 2002). In depression, memory processes are *negatively* biased (Gotlib & Joormann, 2010; Matt et al., 1992), which means negative material is more efficiently and frequently processed compared to neutral or positive material. We find memory bias at different stages of memory.

One of the earlier stages of memory processing happens in working memory. As with computers, working memory is the limited online storage of information that is relevant for the task at hand. Working memory capacity is higher for emotional rather than neutral information (Edelstein, 2006). Moreover, individuals differ in what type of information enters working memory and hence, is preferentially processed. In depression, the filter allows negative information to enter working memory more easily and it is removed less efficiently compared to positive information (Joormann & Gotlib, 2008).

Preferential processing of negative information in depression (and other disorders), promotes the encoding of negative material in long-term memory, resulting in enhanced recall of negative material. In depression, because of the negative ideas about oneself, memory bias is especially strong for information that is relevant to the self (Bradley & Mathews, 1983). This type of memory bias is generally measured with computerized verbal memory bias tasks, either with direct instructions to memorize words or without participants being aware of the later memory test (incidental recall). The Self-Referent Encoding Task (SRET; Klein, Loftus, & Burton, 1989) is the most frequently used task to assess verbal emotional memory bias. The SRET consists of three phases: an encoding phase, a brief distraction phase to allow for memory consolidation, and a recall phase. In most SRET versions, participants are instructed to indicate whether positive and negative adjectives describe them or not. After the distraction phase, participants are asked to type in the words they recall from the previous task (i.e., the encoding phase). The ratio of endorsed and correctly recalled positive and negative words reflects the memory bias.

Memory bias seems to strengthen over time (Sharot & Phelps, 2004). From a neurocognitive perspective, this is due to emotional information, rather than neutral information, activating brain areas. The hippocampus and the amygdala are both activated during encoding, consolidation, and retrieval of emotional information, whereas the hippocampus is especially active during encoding of neutral information (e.g., Buchanan, 2007; Cahill, Prins, Weber, & McGaugh, 1994; Dolcos, LaBar, & Cabeza, 2005; Hamann, Ely, Grafton, & Kilts, 1999). Information is encoded, consolidated, and retrieved congruent to the current mood state, called "mood-congruency" (Bower, 1981). Bower states that events are represented in memory based on associative networks of semantic concepts. Activation of an emotion "node," such as sadness in depression, results in spreading activation throughout the memory structures to which it is connected, like an electrical network, making negative memories more accessible. In addition, mood-congruent events are elaborated on more thoroughly, or ruminated over, and are thereby more easily recalled (Hertel, 2004).

Besides memory processes being negatively biased in depression, depressed individuals also have trouble recalling details, referred to as "overgeneral memory." It is common for a depressed patient to not be able to describe specific examples, but rather, seem to get "stuck" in categorical and schematic descriptions of past events (Williams & Dritschel, 1988). For example, in therapy if asked to remember a specific moment in life when one was very happy, a patient with depression often answers that his childhood was quite happy but cannot generate one specific event. Overgeneral recall is associated with persistence of depressive symptoms (Watkins, 2015); it remains after remission (Brittlebank, Scott, Williams, & Ferrier, 1993; Raes et al., 2006), and inhibits problem solving (Goddard, Dritschel, & Burton, 1996). A depressed person does not have sufficient information to generate solutions or coping options for current problems because of the lack of memory of details. Moreover, over-generality of the past impairs planning of future events (Williams et al., 1996). From a therapeutic stance, overgeneral memory can be problematic. For many models of therapy, retrieval of specific events is necessary for reordering, recoding, or reinterpreting (Williams, 2004).

Approach and Avoidance in Addiction

Approach tendencies are biased and cause dysfunctional behavior. Although approach, strictly speaking, is no "cognitive" bias, approach behavior is triggered automatically by the evaluation of stimuli. A pleasant stimulus triggers approach behavior and unpleasant stimuli trigger avoidance (Solarz, 1960). Thus approach can be seen as the output of an evaluation process; the behavior triggered by an emotion. There are many types of addictions: substance dependency, gambling addiction, shopping addiction, and overeating. In all types of addictions, the subject approaches a certain stimulus more than it should and has trouble avoiding it. Of course, we all have instances where we approach certain things more than we should, such as overeating during Christmas. We eat more than we should and more than we planned. Many individuals show an approach bias to alcohol from time to time, as occasional binge drinking is rather common in most parts of the world. However, for some people the approach of certain stimuli becomes problematic, resulting in an addiction disorder. Recent theories suggest that reward-related learning is important for the development of addiction (Hyman, Malenka, & Nestler, 2006; Wrase et al., 2002). Voluntary use changes; use becomes impulsive and easily triggered, resulting is approach responses (Robinson & Berridge, 1993, 2003).

Of course, the person is likely well aware of the over-approach of alcohol and alcohol-related contexts such as bars, liquor stores and friends who share the habit, as well as awareness of how unhealthy this behavior is (Stacy & Wiers, 2010). Nevertheless, an important part of the behavior is driven by unconscious and automatic processes (Barkby, Dickson, Roper, & Field, 2012). An imbalance between approach-oriented processes and cognitive control may explain this conflict between failing to control urges for the substance and an explicit desire to quit (Gladwin, Figner, Crone, & Wiers, 2011).

Similar to other types of biases, we can measure these automatic approach and avoidance tendencies using reaction-time tasks. The Approach-Avoidance Task (AAT; Rinck & Becker, 2007) is most frequently used. In the AAT, stimuli are presented on a computer screen, for example pictures of bottles and cans with alcoholic and nonalcoholic drinks when studying alcohol addiction. Participants respond to each stimulus by means of a joystick connected to the computer. They are instructed to pull the joystick toward themselves upon presentation of one type of stimuli and to push the joystick away from themselves whenever the other type is presented. Generally, a zoom-effect is used to create the visual impression of pulling something closer or of pushing the stimulus away. The reaction time of pulling and pushing the joystick gives an indication of the behavioral tendency. The Stimulus—Response Compatibility (SRC; De Houwer, Crombez, Baeyens, & Hermans, 2001) task is a slightly different approach-avoidance task. The SRC assesses the speed of categorization of disorder-related pictures by making symbolic approach and avoidance movements. To come back to our alcohol addiction example, the general finding is that alcohol abusers and addicted individuals are faster to approach alcohol-related pictures and avoid control (e.g., soda-related) pictures than vice versa. This approach bias seems to be related to high-risk genetic profiles for alcohol dependency (Wiers, Rinck, Dictus, & Van den Wildenberg, 2009). This heightened approach tendency is also reflected in the brain, as alcohol-dependent individuals show greater activation of prefrontal areas associated with impulsivity during approach on an AAT (Ernst et al., 2014). Studies on retraining these biases in alcohol dependency as an add-on treatment showed very reliably that relapse could be significantly reduced by 10% (Wiers, Eberl, Rinck, Becker, & Lindenmeyer, 2011; Eberl et al., 2013), providing support that these approach tendencies play a major role in maintaining alcohol dependency.

Summary

We have provided examples of skewed cognitive processing in mental disorders; however, this is by no means an exhaustive overview. As mentioned previously, many different stages of processing are impaired due to emotional or psychological problems. Although we described attentional biases within the context of anxiety disorders, we do find such biases in depression and substance abuse, as well as memory biases in anxiety disorders. Limited space prevents an overview of cognitive processes in other mental disorders. Eating disorders, schizophrenia, autism, and ADHD, for example, all show distortions in cognitive processing. It should be mentioned that persons without mental disorders also show biased processing. These individuals usually attend more to positive material, remember positive things better, and, in general, interpret ambiguous situations rather positively. There are studies that show information processing by patients with mental disorders is in fact more realistic than that of healthy controls (Alloy & Abramson, 1988). However, realism might be overrated; optimism is often quite helpful in life.

We have described the cognitive biases that influence therapy. Patients attend more to information that fits their schemata. Patients interpret what the therapist says in a way that fits with their worldview, and probably not as the therapist intended. It is important to know that these are mostly highly automatic processes, and not under voluntary control. Thus, can treatment change these crucial processes?

COGNITIVE BEHAVIORAL THERAPY AND COGNITIVE PROCESSES

Cognitive behavioral therapy (CBT) could change cognitive processes indirectly or directly. It is possible that successful classic CBT automatically influences cognitive processing. CBT is aimed at correcting habitual thinking errors and therefore, change basic (dysfunctional) beliefs. It is expected that in turn this will change the schemata, and thus, will also affect the way information is automatically processed. We expect cognitive preferential processing of disorder-relevant information to diminish. In short, CBT should affect cognitive biases. This can only happen if the new ways of thinking become truly automatic. New CBT approaches actually target cognitive processes directly. Cognitive Bias Modification (CBM), for example, uses computer programs to train attentional or interpretation biases. Other options, such as mindfulness-based interventions also target cognitive processes. We will first give a short overview of the indirect influences of CBT and then take a closer look at direct interventions.

Few studies have looked at the power of CBT to change cognitive processes. The vast majority of research on CBT and cognitive processes has been done in subclinical anxiety: mainly social anxiety and generalized anxiety disorder, and some studies in panic disorder and specific phobia. Most of the available studies looked at changes in attentional biases. The results show that biases can be changed, but also that the pattern is rather complex. In a pilot study, a sample of individuals diagnosed with social anxiety disorder underwent an 8-week CBT treatment (Calamaras, Tone, & Anderson, 2012). Attentional bias for threatening faces was measured before and after CBT. Socially anxious patients showed less attentional avoidance of threatening faces after CBT. But this was not true for all patients. In contrast to patients with an avoidant attentional bias, CBT did not affect bias in patients with attentional vigilance pattern. This subdivision in attentional bias toward and away from threat in social anxiety disorder was substantiated by the results of Boettcher, Hasselrot, Sund, Andersson, and Carlbring (2014), who showed that avoiding patients became more vigilant and initially vigilant patients more attentionally avoidant of negative information. However, there was no difference in the success of treatment between patients with the two different styles of attentional bias. These results leave us wondering what the interaction of CBT and cognitive processes really looks like. How individuals tend to focus their attention on emotional information may be very important for how CBT works. More research is needed; in the future it might be beneficial to tailor CBT approaches to anxious patients' type of automatic attentional biases.

Besides attentional bias, CBT also affects biased interpretations. Positive effects on attentional bias, as well as interpretations of ambiguous scenarios, were found immediately and 1 week after a computerized CBT session in socially anxious individuals (Mobini et al., 2014). Bowler and colleagues found similar results (Bowler et al., 2012). In their study, the effect of CBT on bias explained part of the effect of CBT on affective symptoms. Hence, there is limited evidence that change in interpretation bias moderates the effect of CBT on symptoms of anxiety, indicating biased processing as a working mechanism of CBT.

CBT also appears to influence biased processing in Generalized Anxiety Disorder (GAD) and hypochondria. In a sample of GAD patients, the original negative worry-related associations became more positive after 15 weekly sessions of CBT, and GAD patients showed less worry-related intrusive thoughts after CBT (Reinecke, Hoyer, Rinck, & Becker, 2013; Reinecke, Rinck, Becker, & Hoyer, 2013). Interestingly, only CBT effects on *disorder-specific* worry-thoughts were found; this effect did not generalize to worry-unrelated negative thoughts (Reinecke, Hoyer, et al., 2013). Thus, the disorder-specific bias was changed but CBT did not induce a general positive bias. Pretreatment cognitive bias, as well as change in bias did modulate CBT effects on worry, again implicating biased processing as a working mechanism.

In a sample of subclinical specific phobia (i.e., spider anxiety), the effect of brief group-based CBT on an array of cognitive processes was measured (Reinecke, Soltau, Hoyer, Becker, & Rinck, 2012): implicit associations, approach-avoidance tendencies, and emotional working memory. Reinecke et al. (2012) found that after CBT, implicit threat associations and threat avoidance were diminished. This was not true with regard to working memory. In this study, the evidence for moderation of treatment effect by cognitive processing was weak at most.

The effect of CBT on attentional bias in depression has been studied, but far less frequently. Moreover, the results are not clear-cut. For instance, Pearson et al. (2013) found that after a 9-to-12 week CBT program, depressed pregnant women showed more distraction by pictures of distressed infants, compared to a group of depressed pregnant women who received treatment as usual. The authors interpret this finding as a CBT-induced functional bias because the mothers showed more attention to distressed children; however, it might also reflect an increase in focus on the negative. It is unclear whether this change in attentional bias moderated symptom change.

Regardless of the key role distorted memory processes seem to play in depression, the effect of CBT on memory has been given little attention in research so far. There is evidence for CBT reducing overgeneral memory in depressed patients (McBride, Segal, Kennedy, & Gemar, 2007). After CBT, the proportion of categorical memories decreased and the proportion of specific memories increased. One study in a sample of patients with euthymic bipolar I disorder showed decreased memory for negative, and increased memory for positive and neutral words after 6 months of group-CBT compared to a waitlist condition (Docteur, Mirabel-Sarron, Guelfi, Rouillon, & Gorwood, 2013). Although interesting, we do not know the effect of CBT on memory bias. Due to limited research, we also know very little about the effect of CBT on biases in disorders other than anxiety and depression.

To summarize the results, CBT affects not only symptoms, it also appears to change the way individuals *automatically* process emotional information. For attentional processing, this effect may depend on the type of bias (vigilant or avoidant) patients have pretreatment. How long lasting those effects are is not known. The effect of CBT on symptoms might be partly explained by change in cognitive processes. As explained above, cognitive theories assume that CBT works through conscious thought processes, changing the underlying schemata, and in turn affecting the automatic information processing style. There is compelling evidence in panic disorder patients that CBT rapidly affects automatic cognitive processes, specifically implicit associations and attentional bias, and that this change is an early marker for treatment response (Reinecke, Waldenmaier, Cooper, & Harmer, 2013; Teachman, Marker, & Smith-Janik, 2008). In other words, mediation of automatic cognitive processes on treatment effect means that change in cognitive processing is part of the treatment effect and hence a working mechanism of CBT. Changing the automatic processes positively influences the course of treatment. Based on cognitive theories, it is assumed that this is the case for many mental disorders. However, we have seen that the evidence in disorders other than anxiety disorders is sparse to nonexisting. Looking at what has not been studied is also telling. For example, few studies have focused on change in biases in memory, interpretation, and working memory. Whether change in biased processing in these cognitive domains is also involved in CBT is not known at this point. Moreover, comparing the different studies raises the question of whether the working mechanism of CBT is the same across mental disorders and across cognitive processes (e.g., attention, associations, memory). A strong interplay between cognitive biases is assumed in the cognitive theories (e.g., Clark & Beck, 1999; Bower, 1981, 1987). Or are there, in line with what has been discussed above, specific cognitive processes that change during CBT in specific disorders while other processes are not or less affected? Again, we currently do not know.

Treatments That Directly Target Cognitive Processes

As these automatic processes are important in guiding our behavior, are there ways to influence them more directly than changing cognitions? The most direct approach is Cognitive Bias Modification, CBM. CBM uses computerized training procedures to change automatic processing of emotional material. By changing automatic dysfunctional cognitive processes, CBM compliments processes central to CBT. Hence, CBM can be used as an add-on tool in the treatment of mental-disorders (e.g., Wiers et al., 2011; and see editorial by Woud & Becker, 2014), but CBM has also been used with surprising results as a stand-alone intervention (e.g., Amir et al., 2009). Several meta-analyses provide an overview of the work on CBM (see Beard, Sawyer, & Hofmann, 2012; Hakamata et al., 2010; Hallion & Ruscio, 2011). There are several other cognitive interventions that target the change of cognitive processes, such as mindfulness-based interventions [e.g., mindfulness based cognitive therapy (MBCT); Teasdale, Segal, & Williams, 1995], competitive memory training (COMET; Korrelboom, 2011), metacognitive therapy (Wells, 2008), trauma treatment, or memory specificity training (MEST; Raes, Williams, & Hermans, 2009) that we will describe in more detail, specifically their influence on the cognitive biases.

Cognitive Processes in Mindfulness

MBCT is a so-called third-wave psychological treatment: a group of psychological therapies that target the process of thoughts to help people become aware of their thinking patterns and accept their thoughts in a nonjudgmental way (Hunot et al., 2013). MBCT combines mindfulness with elements of CBT, such as activation and psychoeducation. As CBT, MBCT is based on the assumption that patients with mental disorders differ from healthy individuals in cognitive processing (Teasdale et al., 1995; Ma & Teasdale, 2004).

Mindfulness stems from Buddhist meditation practice and is described as attending to and being in the present moment, with a nonjudgmental attitude toward all things including yourself, and being open and accepting to all experiences (Kabat-Zinn, 1994). Although there is an overlap in the structure and working mechanisms of CBT and MBCT, they differ in their aim: CBT aims to change dysfunctional thinking, whereas MBCT teaches individuals to be open to experiences and to be accepting of negative thoughts and feelings. Instead of worrying about the future or ruminating about the past, participants are taught to control their attention and keep it firmly on the present moment, feelings, and thoughts.

In recent years, efforts have been made to test if cognitive processes are really changed by MBCT and if so, in what way. Because attentional processes are key to mindfulness practice, the cognitive attentional domain has been studied most in association with MBCT treatment outcome effects. More specifically, studies have focused mainly on sustained attention, attention switching (or shifting), selective attention, attention interference, and other inhibitory processes. Other cognitive domains such as memory have also been associated with MBCT effects but are not as well researched.

Studies in healthy samples provide first evidence for the change of cognitive processes as a working mechanism of MBCT. Participation in a 10-day mindfulness retreat resulted in improved performance of working memory and sustained attention (Chambers, Lo, & Allen, 2008). The improvement in sustained attention was in turn associated with a decrease in depressive symptoms in this healthy sample. However, results are mixed. Although it was found that mindfulness practice increased positive memory bias (Roberts-Wolfe, Sacchet, Hastings, Roth, & Britton, 2012), attentional processes may not change (Anderson, Lau, Segal, & Bishop, 2007).

Most of the clinical studies of cognitive processes as a working mechanism of MBCT have examined remitted depressed samples, mainly because MBCT was first proven effective as depression relapse prevention. De Raedt et al. (2012) studied changes in attentional processing of emotional information in remitted depressed patients before and after an 8-week MBCT training, in comparison to a no-intervention group. Attentional inhibition of pictures of emotional faces was measured. Participation in the MBCT training changed the initial bias toward negative and away from positive information. After MBCT, participants had more attention for positive and less attention for negative faces, making attentional processing of positive and negative information more equal and less bias. Verhoeven, Vrijsen, van Oostrom, Speckens, and Rinck (2014) found similar effects on attentional bias in a remitted depressed sample. They used the emotional Stroop task to measure attention interference (or, alternatively, emotional working memory). The remitted depressed patients who participated in the MBCT showed less distraction by task-irrelevant neutral and negative words after the MBCT, compared to before and compared a no-training control group. However, no evidence for MBCT effects on nonemotional attention processes, such as subjective attentional control or sustained attention, were found.

The cognitive and clinical effects of mindfulness are associated with changes in brain activity. Evidence for the neural effect of mindfulness was found in magnetic resonance imaging studies in individuals with anxiety symptoms and in bipolar depression. In bipolar patients, MBCT resulted in increased brain activity in prefrontal regions (i.e., the part of the cortex related to cognitive flexibility and regulation of emotions) during mindfulness practice (Ives-Deliperi, Howells, Stein, Meintjes, & Horn, 2013). In social anxiety, mindfulness resulted in changes in activation in the parietal cortex, an area involved in attentional processing (Goldin and Gross, 2010). Participation in a mindfulness training resulted in decreased amygdala activation during facial processes and increased functional connectivity between the amygdala and prefrontal cortex in patients with GAD (Hölzel et al. 2013). Taken together, mindfulness practice appears to affect brain activity in areas that are related to attentional processing and emotional regulation, which are in turn important for risk of psychopathology.

In addition to attentional bias being studied as an MBCT working mechanism, memory bias has also been implicated as a mechanistic process within MBCT. First, MBCT reduces overgeneral memory in remitted depressed patients (Williams, Teasdale, Segal, & Soulsby, 2000). MBCT also affects negative memory bias. Again in a remitted depressed sample, more positive and less negative recall of verbal information was found in remitted depressed patients after MBCT (Van Vugt, Hitchcock, Shahar, & Britton, 2012). The effect of MBCT on memory bias is explained in terms of diminished ruminative thinking: MBCT may weaken the strength of negative schemata that form the basis of repetitive negative thinking. Repeatedly retrieving emotional information from memory is a process akin to rumination (Nolen-Hoeksema, Wisco, & Lyubomirsky, 2008).

There is some work on cognitive processes as a working mechanism of MBCT in clinical samples other than remitted depressed patients, for example in alcohol-dependent individuals. Higher trait mindfulness skills were associated with less difficulty disengaging attention from alcohol-related stimuli (i.e., less attentional bias) in a sample of recovering alcohol-dependent inpatients (Garland, Boettiger, Gaylord, Chanon, & Howard, 2012). MBCT specifically targeted at alcohol dependence diminished attentional bias toward subliminal alcohol cues (Garland, Gaylord, Boettiger, & Howard, 2010). However, the results in alcohol-dependent individuals are sparse and not as clear-cut as in remitted depressed patients. Taken together, research indicates that MBCT indeed manages to change cognitive processing and this in turn facilitates treatment.

Treatment of Trauma Targeting Cognitive Processes

The very successful cognitive therapy treatment for posttraumatic stress disorder (PTSD) by Ehlers, Clark, Hackmann, McManus, and Fennell (2005) is based on a model that focuses on cognitive process. In this model, "data-driven" processing predominates during a traumatic event while "conceptual" processing is impaired. Data-driven processing involves sensory information whereas conceptual processing of the traumatic event creates a more or less coherent trauma narrative. Information processing and encoding are thought to play an important role in intrusion development, which in turn promotes the development of PTSD. In treatment, the emphasis is on creating a narrative that imbeds the sensory information into the conceptual processing. Several laboratory studies have shown that visuospatial processing of trauma information is an ingredient in the formation of intrusive trauma memories (e.g., Holmes, Brewin, & Hennessy, 2004). Impairing the visual spatial memory reduces intrusions (e.g., James et al., 2015) in the laboratory.

Memory Processes in COMET

Besides MBCT, COMET is another frequently applied psychological treatment that is based on cognitive behavioral principles (see Korrelboom, 2011). COMET was developed to strengthen self-esteem in the context of psychopathology. Low self-esteem is a risk factor for the development, maintenance and recurrence of a broad spectrum of psychiatric problems. As the name suggests, COMET assumes memory processing as the key working mechanism. COMET is a 5 to 12 session intervention that is based on the Competitive Memory Retrieval Account for emotional disorders (Brewin, 2006). All concepts, including the concept of the "self," are stored in long-term memory and all concepts have multiple meanings. A trigger can activate a certain meaning of a concept and only *one* meaning can be activated at a certain time, resulting in competition between meanings. Based on our experiences, we form a hierarchy of these meanings and the strongest most frequently activated meaning is triggered more easily than the weaker meanings. As in many aspects of life, the strongest defeats the weaker. The competition between meanings is biased in psychopathology, with low self-esteem as a frequent symptom. COMET aims to strengthen the competitive value of weaker but functional (or even positive) meanings of the self-concept. This is done in different ways: through repetition, through making the functional meaning more emotional and hence more salient, and lastly through counter-conditioning (i.e., making sure the trigger that used to trigger the negative meaning becomes linked to the functional or positive meaning). To date, COMET has mostly been implemented in the treatment of depression, schizophrenia-spectrum disorders, eating disorders, personality disorders, and obsessive–compulsive disorder (e.g., Ekkers et al., 2011; Van der Gaag, van Oosterhout, Daalman, Sommer, & Korrelboom, 2012, 2009; Korrelboom, Marissen, & van Assendelft, 2011, Korrelboom, De Jong, Huijbrechts, & Daansen, 2009; Schneider, Wittekind, Talhof, Korrelboom, & Moritz, 2015).

COMET is a relatively new treatment option in psychopathology. Hence, there is currently very little published work on (biased) cognitive processes as a working mechanism of COMET. One study in schizophrenia patients found improvement of cognitive interpretations of auditory hallucinations after COMET (Van der Gaag et al., 2012). However, the clear focus retrieval of emotional information from memory, as well as the use of associations between (possibly meaningless) triggers or cues and emotional representations in the treatment assumes that processing of emotional information is of key importance to the effectiveness of COMET. This is a research area that will hopefully attract more attention in the near future.

Cognitive Processes in Metacognitive Therapy

Metacognitive therapy (MCT) (Wells, 2008) is another popular third wave psychological treatment that explicitly targets cognitive processes. MCT was developed as a treatment for generalized anxiety disorders targeting the worry process. More recently, MCT has also been applied in the treatment of anxiety disorders (Normann, Emmerik, & Morina, 2014), schizophrenia (Moritz & Woodward, 2006), as well as personality disorders (Dimaggio & Attinà, 2012; Fiore, Dimaggio, Nicoló, Semerari, & Carcione, 2008), with promising results. MCT took a close look at thoughts and beliefs about the worry process itself (e.g., patients with generalized anxiety disorder think that worry might help to prevent misfortunes in the future). On the other hand, they also have negative metacognitive thoughts, such as "I cannot control my worries" or "Worrying is bad for my health." Both sorts of meta-cognitions, positive as well as negative, maintain the disorder and are targeted and addressed with cognitive restructuring. In the further development of MCT, the component of attention training was added to increase awareness of thoughts and to restore or gain flexible control over attentional processes. Patients' attention is trained through daily exercises, which consist of actively listening and focusing attention in the context of simultaneous sounds presented at different loudness and spatial locations.

Studies on the effectiveness of MCT are increasing rather rapidly; however, studies on the mechanisms underlying the effect of MCT are sparse. In a nonclinical sample of children around the age of 12 years old, Autin and Croizet (2012) found that a brief metacognitive intervention had a positive effect on children's working memory span. More evidence for working memory and attention as working mechanisms of MCT were found in a pilot study in depressed patients (Groves et al., 2015). Compared to CBT, depressed patients showed improvement in working memory performance as well as sustained attention—above and beyond mood effects—after 12 weeks of MCT. A type of bias that we have not touched upon is the "bias against disconfirmatory evidence." This bias can be considered as a form of rigidity, and is used to investigate the (reduced) tendency of schizophrenics to disconfirm their own answers. Schizophrenic patients showed less bias against disconfirmatory evidence after MCT (Buonocore et al., 2015). However, no effects on general nonemotional cognitive processes were found (i.e., working memory, recall, selective attention). All in all, more research is needed, however MCT is probably successful in changing cognitive processes.

Memory Processes in MEST

As explained, overgeneral memory is a key bias in depression (Williams et al., 2007) associated with slower recovery (e.g., Peeters et al., 2002; Raes et al., 2006). Quite recently, the evidence for overgeneral memory in depression and the following assumption that reduction of overgeneral memory may be a therapeutic target has resulted in the development of the MEST (Raes et al., 2009). MEST is a group-based intervention specifically designed to increase memory specificity and hence decrease overgenerality of memory. First evidence suggests that the MEST intervention is indeed successful in increasing memory specificity and decreasing depressive symptoms (Neshat-Doost et al., 2012; Raes et al., 2009). However, MEST needs to be compared to an active control group (e.g., treatment as usual or another affective treatment option) before conclusions about the effectively as a depression treatment can be drawn.

CONCLUSION

Cognitive processes are important in what we "see" and how we interpret it, and what we remember of the world. Thus, biased processing is influencing our view of the world and our reactions to the world, but also how we see ourselves. This is important when considering patients in treatment. What they hear, how they interpret it, and what they remember from therapy will all be influenced by biased information processing. It is important to realize that these are automatic processes and there is very little voluntary control, nevertheless, these biases might hinder treatment success considerably.

Cognitive biases underlie all psychopathology and can be regarded as common factors; however, research shows that different disorders form those biases in specific ways. Anxiety is supposed to prevent danger, thus attention to threat is heightened. When the anxiety becomes dysfunctional, so does the heightened attention. Sadness is supposed to help us to take a break in action and to take time to consider what are the reasons for the misfortune, but in depression this leads to rumination and changed memory, tipping the scales from realism to pessimism.

It is important to target those cognitive processes in therapy: for their importance as causal and maintaining factors as well as for their potential to hinder treatment. It is therefore not surprising that there is evidence that biases are an important working mechanism of psychological treatments. CBT seems to be able to change those biases, but also direct approaches to change those biases result in good treatment results. Most of those direct therapies are rather recent developments, mirroring the new interest in cognitive processing as a potential for change. However, we do lack studies, and there are still many unanswered questions. Some are more fundamental, e.g., do biases interact; if we target one bias will other biases change, too? Some are more practical, e.g., how can we best target and change biases and in which patients is this most effective? Many of the patients seeking help have more than one disorder, could we treat them more efficiently by targeting common underlying processes, like the cognitive processes described here? Because cognitive processing is a focus of research in clinical psychology, neuro-cognition, genetics, and psychiatry we will hopefully get more answers in the coming years.

References

Alloy, L. B., & Abramson, L. Y. (1988). Depressive realism: Four theoretical perspectives. In L. B. Alloy (Ed.), *Cognitive processes in depression* (pp. 223–265). New York, NY: Guilford Press.

Amir, N., Beard, C., Taylor, C. T., Klumpp, H., Elias, J., Burns, M., & Chen, X. (2009). Attention training in individuals with generalized social phobia: A randomized controlled trial. *Journal of Consulting and Clinical Psychology, 77,* 961–973.

Amir, N., & Taylor, C. T. (2012). Combining computerized home-based treatments for generalized anxiety disorder: An attention modification program and cognitive behavioral therapy. *Behavior Therapy, 43,* 546–559.

Anderson, J. R. (1990). *Cognitive psychology and its implications.* New York, NY: WH Freeman/Times Books/Henry Holt & Co.

Anderson, N. D., Lau, M. A., Segal, Z. V., & Bishop, S. R. (2007). Mindfulness-based stress reduction and attentional control. *Clinical Psychology and Psychotherapy, 14,* 449–463.

Autin, F., & Croizet, J. C. (2012). Improving working memory efficiency by reframing metacognitive interpretation of task difficulty. *Journal of Experimental Psychology: General, 141,* 610–618.

Baddeley, A. (1992). Working memory. *Science, 255,* 556–559.

Bar-Haim, Y. (2010). Research review: Attention bias modification (ABM): A novel treatment for anxiety disorders. *Journal of Child Psychology and Psychiatry, 51,* 859–870.

Bar-Haim, Y., Lamy, D., Pergamin, L., Bakermans-Kranenburg, M. J., & Van Ijzendoorn, M. H. (2007). Threat-related attentional bias in anxious and nonanxious individuals: A meta-analytic study. *Psychological Bulletin, 133,* 1–24.

Barkby, H., Dickson, J. M., Roper, L., & Field, M. (2012). To approach or avoid alcohol? Automatic and self-reported motivational tendencies in alcohol dependence. *Alcoholism: Clinical and Experimental Research, 36,* 361–368.

Beard, C., Sawyer, A. T., & Hofmann, S. G. (2012). Efficacy of attention bias modification using threat and appetitive stimuli: A meta-analytic review. *Behavior Therapy, 43,* 724–740.

Becker, E., & Rinck, M. (2004). Sensitivity and response bias in fear of spiders. *Cognition and Emotion, 18,* 961–976.

Bishop, S. J. (2007). Neurocognitive mechanisms of anxiety: An integrative account. *Trends in Cognitive Sciences, 11,* 307–316.

Blair, K., Shaywitz, J., Smith, B. W., Rhodes, R., Geraci, M. R. N., Jones, M., ... Mondillo, K. (2008). Response to emotional expressions in generalized social phobia and generalized anxiety disorder: Evidence for separate disorders. *American Journal of Psychiatry, 165,* 1193–1202.

Blanchette, I., & Richards, A. (2010). The influence of affect on higher level cognition: A review of research on interpretation, judgement, decision making and reasoning. *Cognition and Emotion, 24,* 561–595.

Boettcher, J., Hasselrot, J., Sund, E., Andersson, G., & Carlbring, P. (2014). Combining attention training with internet-based cognitive-behavioural self-help for social anxiety: A randomised controlled trial. *Cognitive Behaviour Therapy, 43,* 34–48.

Bower, G. H. (1981). Mood and memory. *American Psychologist, 36,* 129–148.

Bower, G. H. (1987). Commentary on mood and memory. *Behaviour Research and Therapy, 25,* 443–455.

Bowler, J. O., Mackintosh, B., Dunn, B. D., Mathews, A., Dalgleish, T., & Hoppitt, L. (2012). A comparison of cognitive bias modification for interpretation and computerized cognitive behavior therapy: Effects on anxiety, depression, attentional control, and interpretive bias. *Journal of Consulting and Clinical Psychology, 80,* 1021–1033.

Bradley, B., & Mathews, A. (1983). Negative self-schemata in clinical depression. *British Journal of Clinical Psychology, 22,* 173–181.

Brewin, C. R. (2006). Understanding cognitive behaviour therapy: A retrieval competition account. *Behaviour Research and Therapy, 44*, 765–784.

Brittlebank, A. D., Scott, J., Williams, J. M., & Ferrier, I. N. (1993). Autobiographical memory in depression: State or trait marker? *The British Journal of Psychiatry, 162*, 118–121.

Brosch, T., Pourtois, G., & Sander, D. (2010). The perception and categorisation of emotional stimuli: A review. *Cognition and Emotion, 24*, 377–400.

Buchanan, T. W. (2007). Retrieval of emotional memories. *Psychological Bulletin, 133*, 761–779.

Buonocore, M., Bosia, M., Riccaboni, R., Bechi, M., Spangaro, M., Piantanida, M., ... Cavallaro, R. (2015). Combined neurocognitive and metacognitive rehabilitation in schizophrenia: Effects on bias against disconfirmatory evidence. *European Psychiatry, 30*, 615–621.

Cahill, L., Prins, B., Weber, M., & McGaugh, J. L. (1994). β-Adrenergic activation and memory for emotional events. *Nature, 371*, 702–704.

Calamaras, M. R., Tone, E. B., & Anderson, P. L. (2012). A Pilot Study of attention bias subtypes: Examining their relation to cognitive bias and their change following cognitive behavioral therapy. *Journal of Clinical Psychology, 68*, 745–754.

Chambers, R., Lo, B. C. Y., & Allen, N. B. (2008). The impact of intensive mindfulness training on attentional control, cognitive style, and affect. *Cognitive Therapy and Research, 32*, 303–322.

Cisler, J. M., & Koster, E. H. (2010). Mechanisms of attentional biases towards threat in anxiety disorders: An integrative review. *Clinical Psychology Review, 30*, 203–216.

Clancy, S. A., McNally, R. J., Schacter, D. L., Lenzenweger, M. F., & Pitman, R. K. (2002). Memory distortion in people reporting abduction by aliens. *Journal of Abnormal Psychology, 111*, 455–461.

Clark, D. A., & Beck, A. T. (1999). *Scientific foundations of cognitive theory and therapy of depression*. Oxford, England: John Wiley & Sons.

Clark, D. M. (1986). A cognitive approach to panic. *Behaviour Research and Therapy, 24*, 461–470.

Corwin, D. L., & Olafson, E. (1997). Videotaped discovery of a reportedly unrecallable memory of child sexual abuse: Comparison with a childhood interview videotaped 11 years before. *Child Maltreatment, 2*, 91–112.

Dalgleish, T., & Watts, F. N. (1990). Biases of attention and memory in disorders of anxiety and depression. *Clinical Psychology Review, 10*, 589–604.

De Houwer, J., Crombez, G., Baeyens, F., & Hermans, D. (2001). On the generality of the affective Simon effect. *Cognition and Emotion, 15*, 189–206.

De Raedt, R., Baert, S., Demeyer, I., Goeleven, E., Raes, A., Visser, A., ... Speckens, A. (2012). Changes in attentional processing of emotional information following mindfulness-based cognitive therapy in people with a history of depression: Towards an open attention for all emotional experiences. *Cognitive Therapy and Research, 36*, 612–620.

De Raedt, R., & Koster, E. H. (2010). Understanding vulnerability for depression from a cognitive neuroscience perspective: A reappraisal of attentional factors and a new conceptual framework. *Cognitive, Affective, & Behavioral Neuroscience, 10*, 50–70.

Dimaggio, G., & Attinà, G. (2012). Metacognitive interpersonal therapy for narcissistic personality disorder and associated perfectionism. *Journal of Clinical Psychology, 68*, 922–934.

Docteur, A., Mirabel-Sarron, C., Guelfi, J. D., Rouillon, F., & Gorwood, P. (2013). The role of CBT in explicit memory bias in bipolar I patients. *Journal of Behavior Therapy and Experimental Psychiatry, 44*, 307–311.

Dolcos, F., LaBar, K. S., & Cabeza, R. (2005). Remembering one year later: Role of the amygdala and the medial temporal lobe memory system in retrieving emotional memories. *Proceedings of the National Academy of Sciences of the United States of America, 102*, 2626–2631.

Eberl, C., Wiers, R. W., Pawelczack, S., Rinck, M., Becker, E. S., & Lindenmeyer, J. (2013). Approach bias modification in alcohol dependence: Do clinical effects replicate and for whom does it work best? *Developmental Cognitive Neuroscience, 4*, 38–51.

Edelstein, R. S. (2006). Attachment and emotional memory: Investigating the source and extent of avoidant memory impairments. *Emotion, 6*, 340–345.

Ehlers, A., Clark, D. M., Hackmann, A., McManus, F., & Fennell, M. (2005). Cognitive therapy for post-traumatic stress disorder: Development and evaluation. *Behaviour Research and Therapy, 43*, 413–431.

Ekkers, W., Korrelboom, K., Huijbrechts, I., Smits, N., Cuijpers, P., & van der Gaag, M. (2011). Competitive memory training for treating depression and rumination in depressed older adults: A randomized controlled trial. *Behaviour Research and Therapy, 49*, 588–596.

Ellsworth, P. C., & Scherer, K. R. (2003). Appraisal processes in emotion. In R. J. Davidson, K. R. Scherer, & H. Goldsmith (Eds.), *Handbook of affective sciences* (pp. 572–595). Oxford, England: Oxford University Press.

Eriksen, C. W., & James, J. D., St (1986). Visual attention within and around the field of focal attention: A zoom lens model. *Perception & Psychophysics, 40*, 225–240.

Ernst, L. H., Plichta, M. M., Dresler, T., Zesewitz, A. K., Tupak, S. V., Haeussinger, F. B., ... Ehlis, A.-C. (2014). Prefrontal correlates of approach preferences for alcohol stimuli in alcohol dependence. *Addiction Biology, 19*, 497–508.

Everaert, J., Koster, E. H., & Derakshan, N. (2012). The combined cognitive bias hypothesis in depression. *Clinical Psychology Review, 32*, 413–424.

Eysenck, M. W., Mogg, K., May, J., Richards, A., & Mathews, A. (1991). Bias in interpretation of ambiguous sentences related to threat in anxiety. *Journal of Abnormal Psychology, 100*, 144–150.

Fiore, D., Dimaggio, G., Nicoló, G., Semerari, A., & Carcione, A. (2008). Metacognitive interpersonal therapy in a case of obsessive–compulsive and avoidant personality disorders. *Journal of Clinical Psychology, 64*, 168–180.

Freud, S. (1896). Zur Ätiologie der Hysterie. *Wiener klinische Runddschau, 10*(22), 379–381.

Freud, S. (1924). The passing of the Oedipus complex. *The International Journal of Psychoanalysis, 5*, 419.

Frewen, P. A., Dozois, D. J., Joanisse, M. F., & Neufeld, R. W. (2008). Selective attention to threat versus reward: Meta-analysis and neural-network modeling of the dot-probe task. *Clinical Psychology Review, 28*, 307–337.

Garland, E. L., Boettiger, C. A., Gaylord, S., Chanon, V. W., & Howard, M. O. (2012). Mindfulness is inversely associated with alcohol attentional bias among recovering alcohol-dependent adults. *Cognitive Therapy and Research, 36*, 441–450.

Garland, E. L., Gaylord, S. A., Boettiger, C. A., & Howard, M. O. (2010). Mindfulness training modifies cognitive, affective, and physiological mechanisms implicated in alcohol dependence: Results of a randomized controlled pilot trial. *Journal of Psychoactive Drugs, 42*, 177–192.

Gibb, B. E., McGeary, J. E., & Beevers, C. G. (2015). Attentional biases to emotional stimuli: Key components of the RDoC constructs of sustained threat and loss. *American Journal of Medical Genetics Part B: Neuropsychiatric Genetics, 171*, 65–80.

Gladwin, T. E., Figner, B., Crone, E. A., & Wiers, R. W. (2011). Addiction, adolescence, and the integration of control and motivation. *Developmental Cognitive Neuroscience, 1*, 364–376.

Gleaves, D. H., Smith, S. M., Butler, L. D., & Spiegel, D. (2004). False and recovered memories in the laboratory and clinic: A review of experimental and clinical evidence. *Clinical Psychology: Science and Practice, 11*, 3–28.

Goddard, L., Dritschel, B., & Burton, A. (1996). Role of autobiographical memory in social problem solving and depression. *Journal of Abnormal Psychology, 105*, 609–616.

Goldin, P. R., & Gross, J. J. (2010). Effects of mindfulness-based stress reduction (MBSR) on emotion regulation in social anxiety disorder. *Emotion, 10,* 83–91.

Gotlib, I. H., & Joormann, J. (2010). Cognition and depression: current status and future directions. *Annual Review of Clinical Psychology, 6,* 285–312.

Groves, S. J., Porter, R. J., Jordan, J., Knight, R., Carter, J. D., McIntosh, V. V., ... Joyce, P. R. (2015). Changes in neuropsychological function after treatment with metacognitive therapy or cognitive behavior therapy for depression. *Depression and Anxiety, 32,* 437–444.

Hadwin, J. A., Garner, M., & Perez-Olivas, G. (2006). The development of information processing biases in childhood anxiety: A review and exploration of its origins in parenting. *Clinical Psychology Review, 26,* 876–894.

Hakamata, Y., Lissek, S., Bar-Haim, Y., Britton, J. C., Fox, N. A., & Leibenluft, E. (2010). Attention bias modification treatment: A meta-analysis toward the establishment of novel treatment for anxiety. *Biological Psychiatry, 68,* 982–990.

Hallion, L. S., & Ruscio, A. M. (2011). A meta-analysis of the effect of cognitive bias modification on anxiety and depression. *Psychological Bulletin, 137,* 940–958.

Hamann, S. B., Ely, T. D., Grafton, S. T., & Kilts, C. D. (1999). Amygdala activity related to enhanced memory for pleasant and aversive stimuli. *Nature Neuroscience, 2,* 289–293.

Heinrichs, N., & Hofmann, S. G. (2001). Information processing in social phobia: A critical review. *Clinical Psychology Review, 21,* 751–770.

Hertel, P. (2004). Memory for emotional and nonemotional events in depression. *Memory and Emotion,* 186–216.

Hofmann, S. G., Ellard, K. K., & Siegle, G. J. (2012). Neurobiological correlates of cognitions in fear and anxiety: A cognitive-neurobiological information processing model. *Cognition and Emotion, 26,* 282–299.

Holmes, E. A., Brewin, C. R., & Hennessy, R. G. (2004). Trauma films, information processing, and intrusive memory development. *Journal of Experimental Psychology: General, 133,* 3–22.

Hölzel, B. K., Hoge, E. A., Greve, D. N., Gard, T., Creswell, J. D., Brown, K. W., & Lazar, S. W. (2013). Neural mechanisms of symptom improvements in generalized anxiety disorder following mindfulness training. *NeuroImage: Clinical, 2,* 448–458.

Homack, S., & Riccio, C. A. (2004). A meta-analysis of the sensitivity and specificity of the Stroop Color and Word Test with children. *Archives of Clinical Neuropsychology, 19,* 725–743.

Hunot, V., Moore, T., Caldwell, D. M., Furukawa, T., Davies, P., Jones, H., ... Churchill, R. (2013). Third wave'cognitive and behavioural therapies versus other psychological therapies for depression. *Cochrane Database Syst Rev, 10,* CD008704.

Hyman, I. E., Husband, T. H., & Billings, F. J. (1995). False memories of childhood experiences. *Applied Cognitive Psychology, 9,* 181–197.

Hyman, S. E., Malenka, R. C., & Nestler, E. J. (2006). Neural mechanisms of addiction: The role of reward-related learning and memory. *Annual Review of Neuroscience, 29,* 565–598.

Ives-Deliperi, V. L., Howells, F., Stein, D. J., Meintjes, E. M., & Horn, N. (2013). The effects of mindfulness-based cognitive therapy in patients with bipolar disorder: A controlled functional MRI investigation. *Journal of Affective Disorders, 150,* 1152–1157.

James, E. L., Bonsall, M. B., Hoppitt, L., Tunbridge, E. M., Geddes, J. R., Milton, A. L., & Holmes, E. A. (2015). Computer game play reduces intrusive memories of experimental trauma via reconsolidation-update mechanisms. *Psychological Science, 26,* 1201–1215.

James, W. (1890). *The Principles of Psychology, 1.*

Jersild, A. T. (1927). Mental set and shift. *Archives of Psychology, 89,* 5–82.

Joormann, J., & Gotlib, I. H. (2008). Updating the contents of working memory in depression: Interference from irrelevant negative material. *Journal of Abnormal Psychology, 117,* 182–192.

Kabat-Zinn, J. (1994). *Where ever you go there you are*. New York, NY: Hyperion.

Klein, A. M., Titulear, G., Simons, C., Allart, E., de Gier, E., Bögels, S. M., ... Rinck, M. (2014). Biased interpretation and memory in children with varying levels of spider fear. *Cognition and Emotion, 28*, 182–192.

Klein, S. B., Loftus, J., & Burton, H. A. (1989). Two self-reference effects: The importance of distinguishing between self-descriptiveness judgments and autobiographical retrieval in self-referent encoding. *Journal of Personality and Social Psychology, 56*, 853.

Klumpp, H., Fitzgerald, D. A., Cook, E., Shankman, S. A., Angstadt, M., & Phan, K. L. (2014). Serotonin transporter gene alters insula activity to threat in social anxiety disorder. *Neuroreport, 25*, 926–931.

Korrelboom, K. (2011). *COMET voor negatief zelfbeeld*. Houten: Bohn Stafleu van Loghum.

Korrelboom, K., de Jong, M., Huijbrechts, I., & Daansen, P. (2009). Competitive memory training (COMET) for treating low self-esteem in patients with eating disorders: A randomized clinical trial. *Journal of Consulting and Clinical Psychology, 77*, 974–980.

Korrelboom, K., Marissen, M., & van Assendelft, T. (2011). Competitive memory training (COMET) for low self-esteem in patients with personality disorders: A randomized effectiveness study. *Behavioural and Cognitive Psychotherapy, 39*, 1–19.

LeDoux, J. (1998). *The emotional brain: The mysterious underpinnings of emotional life*. New York, NY: Simon and Schuster.

Loftus, E. F., & Pickrell, J. E. (1995). The formation of false memories. *Psychiatric Annals, 25*, 720–725.

Ma, S. H., & Teasdale, J. D. (2004). Mindfulness-based cognitive therapy for depression: Replication and exploration of differential relapse prevention effects. *Journal of Consulting and Clinical Psychology, 72*, 31–40.

MacLeod, C. M. (2005). The Stroop Task in cognitive research. In A. Wenzel, & D. C. Rubin (Eds.), *Cognitive methods and their application to clinical research* (pp. 17–40). Washington, DC: American Psychological Association.

MacLeod, C., Mathews, A., & Tata, P. (1986). Attentional bias in emotional disorders. *Journal of Abnormal Psychology, 95*, 15–20.

Mathews, A., & MacLeod, C. (2002). Induced processing biases have causal effects on anxiety. *Cognition & Emotion, 16*, 331–354.

Mathews, A., & MacLeod, C. (2005). Cognitive vulnerability to emotional disorders. *Annual Review of Clinical Psychology, 1*, 167–195.

Matt, G. E., Vázquez, C., & Campbell, W. K. (1992). Mood-congruent recall of affectively toned stimuli: A meta-analytic review. *Clinical Psychology Review, 12*, 227–255.

McBride, C., Segal, Z., Kennedy, S., & Gemar, M. (2007). Changes in autobiographical memory specificity following cognitive behavior therapy and pharmacotherapy for major depression. *Psychopathology, 40*, 147–152.

McNally, R. J., & Geraerts, E. (2009). A new solution to the recovered memory debate. *Perspectives on Psychological Science, 4*, 126–134.

Meyersburg, C. A., Bogdan, R., Gallo, D. A., & McNally, R. J. (2009). False memory propensity in people reporting recovered memories of past lives. *Journal of Abnormal Psychology, 118*, 399–404.

Mobini, S., Mackintosh, B., Illingworth, J., Gega, L., Langdon, P., & Hoppitt, L. (2014). Effects of standard and explicit cognitive bias modification and computer-administered cognitive-behaviour therapy on cognitive biases and social anxiety. *Journal of Behavior Therapy and Experimental Psychiatry, 45*, 272–279.

Mogg, K., & Bradley, B. P. (1998). A cognitive-motivational analysis of anxiety. *Behaviour Research and Therapy, 36*, 809–848.

Moritz, S., & Woodward, T. S. (2006). A generalized bias against disconfirmatory evidence in schizophrenia. *Psychiatry Research, 142*, 157–165.

Neshat-Doost, H. T., Dalgleish, T., Yule, W., Kalantari, M., Ahmadi, S. J., Dyregrov, A., & Jobson, L. (2012). Enhancing autobiographical memory specificity through cognitive training: An intervention for depression translated from basic science. *Clinical Psychological Science*, 1, 84−92.

Nolen-Hoeksema, S., Wisco, B. E., & Lyubomirsky, S. (2008). Rethinking rumination. *Perspectives on Psychological Science*, 3, 400−424.

Normann, N., Emmerik, A. A., & Morina, N. (2014). The efficacy of metacognitive therapy for anxiety and depression: A meta-analytic review. *Depression and Anxiety*, 31, 402−411.

Öhman, A. (1992). Fear and anxiety as emotional phenomena: Clinical phenomenology, evolutionary perspectives, and information-processing mechanisms. In M. Lewis, & J. M. Haviland (Eds.), *Handbook of emotions* (pp. 511−536). New York, NY: Guilford.

Öhman, A. (1996). Preferential pre-attentive processing of threat in anxiety: Preparedness and attentional biases. In R. Rapee (Ed.), *Current controversies in the anxiety disorders* (pp. 253−290). New York, NY: Guilford Press.

Pashler, H. (1994). Dual-task interference in simple tasks: Data and theory. *Psychological Bulletin*, 116, 220−244.

Pearson, R. M., O'Mahen, H., Burns, A., Bennert, K., Shepherd, C., Baxter, H., ... Evans, J. (2013). The normalisation of disrupted attentional processing of infant distress in depressed pregnant women following cognitive behavioural therapy. *Journal of Affective Disorders*, 145, 208−213.

Peeters, F., Wessel, I., Merckelbach, H., & Boon-Vermeeren, M. (2002). Autobiographical memory specificity and the course of major depressive disorder. *Comprehensive Psychiatry*, 43, 344−350.

Raes, F., Hermans, D., Williams, J. M. G., Beyers, W., Eelen, P., & Brunfaut, E. (2006). Reduced autobiographical memory specificity and rumination in predicting the course of depression. *Journal of Abnormal Psychology*, 115, 699−704.

Raes, F., Williams, J. M. G., & Hermans, D. (2009). Reducing cognitive vulnerability to depression: A preliminary investigation of memory specificity training (MEST) in inpatients with depressive symptomatology. *Journal of Behavior Therapy and Experimental Psychiatry*, 40, 24−38.

Reinecke, A., Hoyer, J., Rinck, M., & Becker, E. S. (2013). Cognitive-behavioural therapy reduces unwanted thought intrusions in generalized anxiety disorder. *Journal of Behavior Therapy and Experimental Psychiatry*, 44, 1−6.

Reinecke, A., Rinck, M., Becker, E. S., & Hoyer, J. (2013). Cognitive-behavior therapy resolves implicit fear associations in generalized anxiety disorder. *Behaviour Research and Therapy*, 51, 15−23.

Reinecke, A., Soltau, C., Hoyer, J., Becker, E. S., & Rinck, M. (2012). Treatment sensitivity of implicit threat evaluation, avoidance tendency and visual working memory bias in specific phobia. *Journal of Anxiety Disorders*, 26, 321−328.

Reinecke, A., Waldenmaier, L., Cooper, M. J., & Harmer, C. J. (2013). Changes in automatic threat processing precede and predict clinical changes with exposure-based cognitive-behavior therapy for panic disorder. *Biological Psychiatry*, 73, 1064−1070.

Rinck, M., & Becker, E. S. (2007). Approach and avoidance in fear of spiders. *Journal of Behavior Therapy and Experimental Psychiatry*, 38, 105−120.

Roberts-Wolfe, D., Sacchet, M., Hastings, E., Roth, H., & Britton, W. (2012). Mindfulness training alters emotional memory recall compared to active controls: Support for an emotional information processing model of mindfulness. *Frontiers in Human Neuroscience*, 6, 1−13.

Robinson, T. E., & Berridge, K. C. (1993). The neural basis of drug craving: An incentive-sensitization theory of addiction. *Brain Research Reviews*, 18, 247−291.

Robinson, T. E., & Berridge, K. C. (2003). Addiction. *Annual Review of Psychology*, 54, 25−53.

Schacter, D. L. (2008). *Searching for memory: The brain, The mind, and the past.* New York, NT: Basic Books.

Schneider, B. C., Wittekind, C. E., Talhof, A., Korrelboom, K., & Moritz, S. (2015). Competitive memory training (COMET) for OCD: A self-treatment approach to obsessions. *Cognitive Behaviour Therapy, 44,* 142–152.

Schneider, S., & Nündel, B. (2002). Familial transmission of panic disorder: The role of separation anxiety disorder and cognitive factors. *European Neuropsychopharmacology, 12,* 149–150.

Schneider, S., Unnewehr, S., Florin, I., & Margraf, J. (2002). Priming panic interpretations in children of patients with panic disorder. *Journal of Anxiety Disorders, 16,* 605–624.

Segal, Z. V., Williams, J. M. G., & Teasdale, J. D. (2012). *Mindfulness-based cognitive therapy for depression.* New York, NY: Guilford Press.

Sharot, T., & Phelps, E. A. (2004). How arousal modulates memory: Disentangling the effects of attention and retention. *Cognitive, Affective, & Behavioral Neuroscience, 4,* 294–306.

Siegle, G. J., Thompson, W., Carter, C. S., Steinhauer, S. R., & Thase, M. E. (2007). Increased amygdala and decreased dorsolateral prefrontal BOLD responses in unipolar depression: Related and independent features. *Biological Psychiatry, 61,* 198–209.

Solarz, A. K. (1960). Latency of instrumental responses as a function of compatibility with the meaning of eliciting verbal signs. *Journal of Experimental Psychology, 59,* 239–245.

Stacy, A. W., & Wiers, R. W. (2010). Implicit cognition and addiction: A tool for explaining paradoxical behavior. *Annual Review in Clinical Psychology, 6,* 551–575.

Teachman, B. A., Marker, C. D., & Smith-Janik, S. B. (2008). Automatic associations and panic disorder: Trajectories of change over the course of treatment. *Journal of Consulting and Clinical Psychology, 76,* 988–1002.

Teasdale, J. D., Segal, Z., & Williams, J. M. G. (1995). How does cognitive therapy prevent depressive relapse and why should attentional control (mindfulness) training help? *Behaviour Research and Therapy, 33,* 25–39.

Van der Gaag, M., van Oosterhout, B., Daalman, K., Sommer, I. E., & Korrelboom, K. (2012). Initial evaluation of the effects of competitive memory training (COMET) on depression in schizophrenia-spectrum patients with persistent auditory verbal hallucinations: A randomized controlled trial. *British Journal of Clinical Psychology, 51,* 158–171.

Van Vugt, M. K., Hitchcock, P., Shahar, B., & Britton, W. (2012). The effects of mindfulness-based cognitive therapy on affective memory recall dynamics in depression: a mechanistic model of rumination. *Frontiers in Human Neuroscience, 6,* 257.

Verhoeven, J. E., Vrijsen, J. N., van Oostrom, I., Speckens, A. E. M., & Rinck, M. (2014). Attentional control effects of mindfulness-based cognitive therapy in formerly depressed patients. *Journal of Experimental Psychopathology, 5,* 414–424.

Vrijsen, J. N., van Oostrom, I., Arias-Vásquez, A., Franke, B., Becker, E. S., & Speckens, A. (2014). Association between genes, stressful childhood events and processing bias in depression vulnerable individuals. *Genes, Brain and Behavior, 13,* 508–516.

Vrijsen, J. N., Vogel, S., Arias-Vásquez, A., Franke, B., Fernández, G., Becker, E. S., ... Van Oostrom, I. (2015). Depressed patients in remission show an interaction between variance in the mineralocorticoid receptor NR3C2 gene and childhood trauma on negative memory bias. *Psychiatric Genetics, 25,* 99–105.

Watkins, E. (2015). Overgeneral autobiographical memories and their relationship to rumination. In L. A. Watson, & D. Berntsen (Eds.), *Clinical perspectives on autobiographical memory* (pp. 199–220). Cambridge, England: Cambridge University Press.

Wegner, D. M. (1994). Ironic processes of mental control. *Psychological Review, 101,* 34–52.

Wells, A. (2008). *Metacognitive therapy for depression and anxiety.* New York, NY: Guilford Press.

Wells, A. (2011). *Metacognitive therapy for anxiety and depression*. New York, NY: Guilford press.

Wiers, R. W., Eberl, C., Rinck, M., Becker, E. S., & Lindenmeyer, J. (2011). Retraining automatic action tendencies changes alcoholic patients' approach bias for alcohol and improves treatment outcome. *Psychological Science, 22*, 490–497.

Wiers, R. W., Rinck, M., Dictus, M., & Van den Wildenberg, E. (2009). Relatively strong automatic appetitive action-tendencies in male carriers of the OPRM1 G-allele. *Genes, Brain and Behavior, 8*, 101–106.

Williams, J. M. G. (2004). Experimental cognitive psychology and clinical practice: Autobiographical memory as a paradigm case. In J. Yiend (Ed.), *Cognition, emotion and psychopathology* (pp. 251–269). Cambridge, England: Cambridge University Press.

Williams, J. M. G., Barnhofer, T., Crane, C., Herman, D., Raes, F., Watkins, E., & Dalgleish, T. (2007). Autobiographical memory specificity and emotional disorder. *Psychological Bulletin, 133*, 122–148.

Williams, J. M. G., & Dritschel, B. H. (1988). Emotional disturbance and the specificity of autobiographical memory. *Cognition & Emotion, 2*, 221–234.

Williams, J. M. G., Ellis, N. C., Tyers, C., Healy, H., Rose, G., & MacLeod, A. K. (1996). The specificity of autobiographical memory and imageability of the future. *Memory & Cognition, 24*, 116–125.

Williams, J. M. G., Mathews, A., & MacLeod, C. (1996). The emotional Stroop task and psychopathology. *Psychological Bulletin, 120*, 3–24.

Williams, J. M. G., Teasdale, J. D., Segal, Z. V., & Soulsby, J. (2000). Mindfulness-based cognitive therapy reduces overgeneral autobiographical memory in formerly depressed patients. *Journal of Abnormal Psychology, 109*, 150–155.

Williams, J. M. G., Watts, F. N., MacLeod, C., & Mathews, A. (1988). *Cognitive psychology and emotional disorders*. Oxford, England: John Wiley & Sons.

Woud, M. L., & Becker, E. S. (2014). Editorial for the special issue on cognitive bias modification techniques: An introduction to a time traveller's tale. *Cognitive Therapy and Research, 38*, 83–88.

Wrase, J., Grusser, S. M., Klein, S., Diener, C., Hermann, D., Flor, H., ... Heinz, A. (2002). Development of alcohol-associated cues and cue-induced brain activation in alcoholics. *European Psychiatry, 17*, 287–291.

5

Emotion Regulation in Cognitive-Behavioral Therapy: Bridging the Gap Between Treatment Studies and Laboratory Experiments

Andre J. Plate and Amelia Aldao

The Ohio State University, Columbus, OH, United States

INTRODUCTION

Cognitive-behavioral therapy (CBT) is a problem-focused and goal-oriented therapy that emphasizes the reciprocal relationship between thoughts, feelings, and behaviors (Beck, 1979; Beck, Emery, & Greenberg, 1985; Beck, 2011). One of the primary goals of CBT is to teach patients to identify, evaluate, and modify their dysfunctional thoughts and beliefs (i.e., cognitive restructuring) through therapeutic techniques such as the Daily Record of Dysfunctional Thinking (i.e., thought record; Beck, 1979). Additionally, an integral component of CBT is its emphasis on reducing problematic behaviors (e.g., avoidance and social withdrawal) and promoting more functional ones (e.g., through behavioral activation, exposure) (e.g., Barlow et al., 2010; Craske & Barlow, 2006; Gilson, Freeman, Yates, & Freeman, 2009; Hope, Heimberg, & Turk, 2010). Critically, CBT teaches patients skills that not only facilitate symptom reduction, but also lead to long-lasting improvements in mental health and reduce the risk of relapse (Hollon et al., 2005; Hollon, Thase, & Markowitz, 2002). Although CBT was

The Science of Cognitive Behavioral Therapy.
DOI: http://dx.doi.org/10.1016/B978-0-12-803457-6.00005-2

initially developed to treat depression (Beck, 1979), it is now successfully utilized to treat a wide range of additional psychological disorders, including a host of anxiety disorders (e.g., Barlow, 2002; Craske & Barlow, 2006; Hope et al., 2010; Zinbarg, Craske, & Barlow, 2006), eating disorders (Fairburn, Cooper, Shafran, & Terence, 2008), psychotic-spectrum disorders (Tarrier & Taylor, 2008), personality disorders (Linehan, 1993), and attention deficit hyperactivity disorder (Safren, Perlman, Sprich, & Otto, 2005), among many other problems (Hofmann, Asnaani, Vonk, Sawyer, & Fang, 2012).

A key philosophical underpinning of CBT is the bidirectional relationship between research and clinical practice. That is, findings derived from basic psychopathology research influence treatment development and implementation (e.g., Chambless, 1996; McHugh & Barlow, 2010), whereas clinical experiences inspire new areas of research (e.g., Baker, McFall, & Shoham, 2008; Mischel, 2008). Consequently, the empirical literature on CBT can be divided into two major lines of work: (1) randomized controlled trials (RCTs) evaluating treatment efficacy and effectiveness and (2) laboratory-based experiments identifying the mechanisms underlying the effects of specific CBT techniques. On the contrary, many research programs often focus on only one of these methods rather than combining them, which creates a chasm between treatment studies and laboratory-based experimental work. This is a crucial limitation that largely precludes the field of clinical psychology from further expanding our understanding of psychopathology and enhancing cognitive-behavioral treatments.

In this chapter, we argue for the integration of RCTs and laboratory-based experiments in order to improve diagnoses, prevention, and treatment of psychological disorders. To do so, we focus on the concept of emotion regulation, which is the processes by which people modify which emotions they have, when they have them, and how they experience and express them (Gross, 1998, 2015). Contemporary conceptualizations of CBT are increasingly placing an emphasis on the role that emotion dysregulation plays in the development and maintenance of psychopathology (e.g., Aldao et al., 2010; Berking & Wupperman, 2012; Gross & Jazaieri, 2014; Hofmann, Sawyer, Fang, & Asnaani, 2012; Kring & Sloan, 2009; Linehan, 1993; Tracy, Klonsky, & Proudfit, 2014). As such, emotion regulation is now a focal point of newer, emotion-focused versions of CBT (e.g., Barlow et al., 2010; Hayes et al., 1999; Mennin & Fresco, 2013; Roemer & Orsillo, 2009; Watkins et al., 2011). In addition, laboratory-based studies that seek to identify mechanisms underlying the efficacy of CBT have also begun to focus on emotion regulation (e.g., Kircanski, Lieberman, & Craske, 2012; Levitt, Brown, Orsillo, & Barlow, 2004). Overall, as a translational framework for studying psychopathology that spans both applied and basic clinical science (as reviewed by Gross & Jazaieri, 2014; Mennin & Fresco, 2009; Sheppes, Suri, & Gross, 2015).

In this chapter, we first review the current status of RCTs testing the efficacy of emotion regulation-focused interventions for psychological disorders that fall under the cognitive-behavioral umbrella. Then, we discuss laboratory-based experimental studies that attempt to explore the specific emotion regulation processes that parallel those used in clinical practice and seek to enhance emotion regulation skills in people suffering from psychopathology. Lastly, we conclude with guidelines and suggestions for integrating these two research methods in order to bridge the gap between treatment studies and laboratory-based experiments with the goal of bolstering our understanding of emotion regulation in the context of psychopathology and cognitive-behavioral approaches to treatment.

RANDOMIZED CONTROLLED TRIALS THAT EVALUATE THE EFFICACY OF CBT

Given the myriad of RCTs supporting its efficacy, CBT falls within the scope of evidence-based medicine (e.g., Barlow, Gorman, Shear, & Woods, 2000; DeRubeis et al., 2005; Roy-Byrne et al., 2005; Schnurr et al., 2007; see meta-analyses by Butler, Chapman, Forman, & Beck, 2006; Hofmann & Smits, 2008; Stewart & Chambless, 2009). RCTs for CBT are typically used to test its *efficacy*—evaluating treatment outcomes under rigorously controlled conditions characterized by high internal validity (Chambless & Hollon, 1998). Such a step is essential when seeking to determine whether new forms of CBT (or "traditional" CBT delivered to new populations) can result in clinically significant improvements. To evaluate treatment efficacy, RCTs randomize patients to various treatment conditions (e.g., CBT versus antidepressant medication). RCTs typically span approximately 12–20 weeks, and often include follow-up assessments (e.g., 6 months to 1 year) to evaluate the long-term outcomes of the intervention. They tend to have strict exclusion criteria in order to ensure that the treatment is tested in a homogeneous clinical population. In addition, RCTs often entail the delivery of highly structured treatment manuals and great emphasis is placed on adherence to such protocols. Given these characteristics of RCTs, one limitation is that they might have lower external validity. That is, the samples included in RCTs often exclude the most severe patients or those most likely to seek treatment. As such, RCTs may not accurately represent samples of treatment-seeking individuals typically seen in outpatient or community settings (e.g., Stirman, DeRubeis, Crits-Christoph, & Brody, 2003; Westen & Morrison, 2001). In other words, these treatments tested under well-controlled conditions may not always translate to "real-world" clinical settings.

A number of RCTs have sought to test the efficacy of newer, cutting-edge cognitive-behavioral interventions that explicitly incorporate emotion regulation as a primary target in treatment. For example, one of the earliest emotion regulation-focused treatments was Marsha Linehan's dialectical behavior therapy (DBT), which emerged out of an effort to treat chronically suicidal patients diagnosed with borderline personality disorder and views emotion dysregulation as a key form of pathology underlying this condition (Linehan, 1993). As such, patients are taught various DBT skills to improve emotional functioning, such as observing and describing their emotions and their functions, decreasing the frequency of intense, negative emotions, and increasing the ability to cope with distressing emotions in order to reduce emotional suffering (Linehan, 1993, 2014). Overall, DBT is now considered the "gold-standard" treatment for borderline personality disorder and empirical support has mounted for the efficacy of DBT in reducing suicide attempts, non-suicidal self-injury (NSSI), inpatient psychiatric care and hospitalizations, and utilization of crisis services (e.g., emergency department visits)—all costly and potentially life-threatening outcomes (e.g., Linehan et al., 2006, 2015; Linehan, Armstrong, Suarez, Allmon, & Heard, 1991; Verheul et al., 2003; see Linehan, 2014 for a detailed review of the efficacy of DBT and DBT skills training). Research has also found that the use of DBT skills mediates reductions in suicide attempts, NSSI, and depression (Neacsiu, Rizvi, & Linehan, 2010). Moreover, emerging research suggest that the specific emotion regulation DBT skills may mediate differential changes in emotion dysregulation and symptoms of psychopathology, emphasizing the importance of emotion regulation as a key target for intervention and as a mechanism of therapeutic change (Neacsiu, Eberle, Kramer, Wiesmann, & Linehan, 2014).

A focal point of many emotion-focused psychotherapies is the use of acceptance, which in some cases, can be viewed as a regulatory strategy to effectively manage emotions (Aldao & Plate, in press). One such treatment is acceptance and commitment therapy (ACT; Hayes et al., 1999), which proposes that the primary source of psychopathology is psychological inflexibility that is often maintained or exacerbated by experiential avoidance, or attempts to evade unpleasant emotions, thoughts, bodily sensations, and/or behaviors (Hayes, Luoma, Bond, Masuda, & Lillis, 2006; Hayes, Wilson, Gifford, Follette, & Strosahl, 1996). Thus, rather than attempting to change the form, frequency, or intensity of one's emotions (i.e., experiential avoidance), clients are taught to stay in contact with the present moment, allow themselves to experience their emotions, and observe these experiences in a nonjudgmental way (i.e., acceptance). RCTs have demonstrated that acceptance-based treatments such as ACT are efficacious in treating anxiety disorders and depression (e.g., Arch et al., 2012; Bohlmeijer, Fledderus, Rokx, & Pieterse, 2011; Roemer, Orsillo, & Salters-Pedneault, 2008), obsessive—compulsive disorder (OCD; Twohig et al., 2010), psychotic-spectrum disorders (Bach & Hayes, 2002), substance use disorders (Smout et al., 2010), and even managing chronic pain (Wetherell et al., 2011). Significantly, there is evidence that acceptance mediates treatment outcomes in depression and anxiety (Forman, Herbert, Moitra, Yeomans, & Geller, 2007).

Another innovative emotion-focused treatment is the Unified Protocol (UP) for the Transdiagnostic Treatment of Emotional Disorders (Barlow et al., 2010), which was designed to treat disorders in which the experience and regulation of emotion plays a prominent role, such as anxiety, depressive, obsessive-compulsive, and trauma-related disorders (Payne, Ellard, Farchione, Fairholme, & Barlow, 2014). The UP is a modular intervention that seeks to improve specific areas of emotional functioning, such as increasing awareness (i.e., nonjudgmental acceptance) of emotional experiences, enhancing cognitive flexibility (i.e., cognitive appraisal and reappraisal), and identifying and reducing patterns of emotional and behavioral avoidance (Barlow et al., 2010). A RCT examining the efficacy of the UP demonstrated preliminary evidence supporting its utility in reducing symptoms of anxiety and depression, and improving overall emotional functioning (Farchione et al., 2012).

Another intervention that was developed on the basis of basic and translational findings in the field of affective science is emotion regulation therapy (ERT; Mennin & Fresco, 2013), a novel treatment for generalized anxiety disorder (GAD) and co-occurring depression that views treatment of these highly comorbid conditions (Kessler et al., 2005) entirely through the lens of an emotion regulation framework. That is, both GAD and depression are both characterized by heightened intensity and reactivity to emotions, poor understanding of emotions, and the use of maladaptive strategies to manage emotions such as worry and rumination (Mennin, Holaway, Fresco, Moore, & Heimberg, 2007). Specifically, ERT is a mechanism-targeted intervention that seeks to enhance emotion-regulation skills over the course of two phases of treatment. In the first phase, patients are taught to identify their emotional reactions, either stay in contact with them or generate distance from them, and practice nonjudgmental acceptance (see Roemer, Orsillo, & Salters-Pedneault, 2008 for a similar acceptance-based behavioral approach to treating GAD). Additionally, clients develop cognitive change capacities through practicing various forms of cognitive reappraisal. In the second phase of treatment, they conduct experiential and behavioral exposures that allow them to counteract emotional avoidance tendencies (e.g., worry and rumination). A recently published open trial suggests that ERT is effective at reducing symptoms of GAD and depression, improving quality of life, and increasing the habitual use of adaptive emotion regulation strategies such as acceptance and cognitive reappraisal (Mennin & Fresco, 2013; Mennin, Fresco, Ritter, & Heimberg, 2015).

Overall, there are a variety of well-established treatments and newer, emotion-focused psychotherapies that are efficacious in treating those with psychological disorders. Nonetheless, although the majority of the empirical evidence from RCTs suggests that CBT is efficacious for a host of mental health conditions (e.g., Butler, Chapman, Forman, & Beck, 2006; Hofmann & Smits, 2008), it is also the case that this treatment is not equally helpful for all patients. For instance, a meta-analysis of 28 studies that collectively included 1880 adults diagnosed with MDD found that 54% of patients who experienced symptom reduction as a function of CBT ended up relapsing within the next 2 years (Vittengl, Clark, Dunn, & Jarrett, 2007). A similar pattern has been observed in the treatment of GAD with CBT, for which studies suggest that nearly 50% of those treated with CBT fail to return to high end-state functioning (Borkovec & Ruscio, 2001; Borkovec & Whisman, 1996).

One potential reason underlying this discrepancy in treatment outcomes is that much remains to be known about the specific mechanisms by which these treatments work. That is, it is largely unclear to what extent emotion regulation is a central process underlying the efficacy of these interventions. One way of addressing this limitation is by attempting to identify moderators and mediators of treatment outcomes in RCTs (Kraemer, Frank, & Kupfer, 2006; Kraemer, Wilson, Fairburn, & Agras, 2002). Moderators, on one hand, allow researchers to determine *who* does or does not respond to the intervention under *which* circumstances. As such, identifying moderators of treatment has great potential for specifying who might be more likely to respond to CBT versus other treatment modalities (e.g., psychopharmacology, CBT + psychopharmacology, other forms of psychotherapy) and could facilitate a more effective dissemination of mental health resources and enhance personalized medicine (Cuijpers et al., 2012). On the other hand, mediators allow clinical scientists to determine specifically *how* an intervention works (i.e., its mechanisms). As such, identifying mediators of symptom reductions and improvements in mental health can lead to a better understanding of what aspects of treatment might need to be emphasized and which deemphasized in order to achieve optimal treatment outcomes.

In order to elucidate the function that emotion regulation plays as a necessary mechanism to achieve the best outcomes in cognitive-behavioral interventions, researchers are beginning to systematically test whether changes in emotion regulation abilities mediate reductions in symptoms and improvements in psychological functioning and well-being. For instance, a RCT comparing the effectiveness of CBT and ACT for anxiety and depression found that changes in observing and describing one's experiences mediated outcomes for patients who received CBT, whereas acting with awareness and acceptance mediated outcomes for patients receiving ACT (Forman et al., 2007). Another RCT found that increases in cognitive reappraisal self-efficacy (i.e., the belief that one can successfully implement reappraisal when they wish to regulate their emotions) mediated the effects of CBT for social anxiety disorder (Goldin et al., 2012). As mentioned previously, emotion regulation skills have also been found to mediate DBT treatment outcomes for borderline personality disorder (Neacsiu et al., 2014).

Although specifying the role of emotion regulation as a key mediator of treatment efficacy is critical and bolsters our understanding of how cognitive-behavioral treatments work, this is merely a starting point in the field of clinical psychology. Further investigation into the specific mechanisms that contribute to superior treatment outcomes is imperative because it may underscore the role of emotion regulation as an essential process necessary for therapeutic change. In turn, this may provide opportunities to refine and enhance psychological interventions in order to emphasize the components of treatment that are known to be most effective. One robust way for developing and improving cognitive-behavioral treatments is through laboratory-based experimental studies that can help identify emotion regulation processes that might enhance the effects of CBT. In the following section, we provide a detailed review of how laboratory-based experimental work can be utilized to shed light on the specific mechanisms used to treat psychological disorders.

LABORATORY-BASED EXPERIMENTAL STUDIES: A FRAMEWORK FOR IDENTIFYING EMOTION REGULATION MECHANISMS UNDERLYING CBT

In contrast to RCTs, laboratory-based studies present clinical scientists with a context in which they can manipulate variables of interest that offer insight into the nature and function of CBT mechanisms. A primary advantage to this laboratory-based experimental approach is that it permits researchers to isolate the processes that are relevant to therapy elements (e.g., emotion regulation) and test their causal relationships to symptom change. For instance, a number of laboratory-based studies have sought to examine the detrimental impact that safety behaviors (SBs) (i.e., overt actions, thoughts, behaviors, or other strategies commonly used by anxious individuals to reduce their anxiety or escape from it) have on the effectiveness of exposure therapy for anxiety disorders. This is a crucial research question that has paramount implications for clinicians delivering CBT for anxiety disorders. That is, it provides practitioners with clinically useful information about whether or not they should permit their clients to judiciously use SBs during exposure therapy. A recent study explored the link between SBs and social judgments in social anxiety disorder by manipulating the use of these behaviors during a controlled social interaction with a confederate in the laboratory. Participants diagnosed with social anxiety disorder were randomized to a SB *reduction* plus exposure condition (SB + EXP) or an exposure-only (EXP) control condition. Participants in the SB + EXP group made more accurate and less negative judgments about their performance relative to EXP participants. Critically, they also exhibited less judgments about the likelihood of negative outcomes in a subsequent social interaction compared to those in the EXP control condition (Taylor & Alden, 2010). Mediational analyses also found that reductions in the use of SBs mediated changes in negative judgments about themselves and their performance in future social interactions. Although this is just one example, laboratory-based studies such as these afford researchers greater precision in testing their scientific hypotheses by providing them the opportunity to isolate specific mechanisms underlying psychopathology and how they can be treated—in this case the causal role of SBs interfering with the effectiveness of exposure.

Nonetheless, a few limitations of this type of laboratory-based experimental research are worth noting. Specifically, these studies only offer a snapshot of these mechanisms at work and the participant's level of psychological functioning. That is, laboratory-based studies rarely follow participants over time and only provide a glimpse into their thoughts, emotions, and behaviors as they are experienced in a brief session in the laboratory. This precludes clinical scientists from observing how these mechanisms or other important outcome variables (e.g., symptoms, quality of life, and behaviors) may change longitudinally. This is in contrast to RCTs, which typically track patients over 12–20 weeks of treatment and often conduct follow-up assessments in the year or two following treatment termination. However, laboratory-based studies can ameliorate this issue by incorporating follow-up sessions or symptom assessments in the months following a session in the laboratory.

Laboratory-based studies also share a common limitation with RCTs that examine treatment efficacy. For instance, similar to RCTs, laboratory-based studies may not always have high levels of external validity. The results of a laboratory-based study, which can be regarded as an artificial context, may not always generalize to other situations or other people outside of the laboratory setting. However, it should be noted that the external validity of any research study might not be best characterized as dichotomous (i.e., valid or not valid), but rather as falling along a continuum where researchers need to determine *to what extent* their results are valid and translate to the "real world" (Messick, 1989).

Despite these limitations, the overarching benefit to laboratory-based experimental studies is that they can help clinical scientists identify the nuanced processes underlying psychological disorders characterized by emotion dysregulation and how they can be treated. Indeed, there has been an increasing enthusiasm in adopting emotion regulation as a translational framework that can be used to shed led on the specific treatment-relevant mechanisms studied in the laboratory that have direct implications for the implementation of cognitive-behavioral treatments used by practitioners in clinical settings. In the next section, we discuss how the study of emotion regulation processes through laboratory-based experiments advances our knowledge of the mechanisms by which cognitive-behavioral techniques can be enhanced to effectively treat psychological disorders. Specifically, we discuss a few commonly used laboratory-based paradigms—exposure and distress tolerance—that allow clinical scientists to study psychopathology in the context of approach behaviors [e.g., exposure, behavioral approach tests (BATs)] and resisting tendencies to avoid or escape difficult emotional experiences (e.g., distress tolerance, carbon dioxide inhalation challenge). A large body of research has demonstrated that many forms of psychopathology (e.g., anxiety disorders, depression) are characterized by excessive and maladaptive patterns of avoidance (see Hayes et al., 1996 for a review). As such, many empirically supported treatments emphasize behavioral *approach* toward (rather than *avoidance* of) emotions, thoughts, situations, objects, activities, or memories that are perpetuating symptoms of psychopathology (i.e., exposure; e.g., Craske & Barlow, 2006; Foa, Hembree, & Rothbaum, 2007; Foa et al., 2012; Hope et al., 2010; Zinbarg et al., 2006; see also Fairburn et al., 2008 for exposure that has been extended to eating disorders). As such, this approach versus avoidance framework has great potential for helping us deepen our understanding of the role of emotion regulation processes in the treatment of psychological disorders.

EXPOSURE AND BEHAVIORAL APPROACH TESTS

A commonly used laboratory-based method to study the mechanisms underlying the effectiveness of *exposure* are BATs (Öst, Salkovskis, & Hellström, 1991), which typically consist of asking participants to engage in a series of steps that put them in progressively closer contact with a feared stimulus. The main dependent variable consists of the number of steps taken, with higher numbers reflecting greater approach behavior. Other dependent variables often include subjective anxiety ratings [e.g., subjective units of distress scale (SUDS)] and physiological arousal. BATs have been widely used in the study of phobias including those to spiders (e.g., Kircanski, Lieberman, & Craske, 2012; Öst et al., 1991; Öst, Stridh, & Wolf, 1998), blood/injections (e.g., Hellström, Fellenius, & Öst, 1996; Koch, O'Neill, Sawchuk, & Connolly, 2002), and heights or elevators (Biran & Terence, 1981). They have also been used in the study of fear of contamination in the context of OCD (e.g., Milosevic & Radomsky, 2008; Najmi & Amir, 2010; Rachman et al., 2011).

Researchers have recently been taking advantage of the BAT paradigm in order to identify the role of using emotion regulation strategies in the context of exposure. In this vein, a recent study examined the effect of implementing different emotion regulation strategies during a BAT to a live tarantula (Kircanski et al., 2012). Participants with spider phobias were randomized into the following conditions: Affect labeling (i.e., verbalizing their negative emotional response to the spider such as saying "I feel anxious that the disgusting spider will jump on me), reappraisal (i.e., changing their perspective to feel less negative about the spider), distraction (i.e., focus on an object or piece of furniture in the room to redirect attention away from the spider), or exposure alone." The researchers found that, at a 1-week posttest, those participants in the affect labeling condition exhibited attenuated skin conductance response (a physiological index of emotional arousal) compared to those in all other conditions (Cohen's $d = 0.64-0.85$). Moreover, participants completed approximately one step more in the BAT compared to those in the distraction condition (Cohen's $d = 0.59$), although this finding was only marginally significant. Interestingly, both of these results were characterized by a dose—response effect. That is, as participants verbalized more anxiety and fear words during the exposure, the magnitude of the skin conductance reduction became more pronounced and resulted in greater approach behavior. Overall, these findings highlight that an early state of emotion regulation, namely affect labeling, can augment exposure. However, more work remains to be done in order to determine whether using other regulation strategies, such as reappraisal or acceptance, might also be beneficial in the context of BATs.

In this respect, a recent study in our research laboratory (Wilson & Aldao, in preparation) tested the effects of two forms of cognitive reappraisal during BATs to contaminated objects (e.g., rub one's face with a dollar bill) in participants with elevated OCD contamination concerns. We assigned participants to one of three conditions: (1) reappraise the emotion-eliciting stimulus (i.e., the contaminated object), (2) reappraise their emotional response (i.e., anxiety and fear), or (3) a control condition where participants were given no specific emotion regulation instructions. We found that reappraising the contaminated object led to significantly greater approach behaviors across multiple BAT domains in the participant's fear hierarchy compared to the no-instruction condition. Interestingly, there were no significant differences in subjective anxiety (i.e., SUDS ratings) between either of the reappraisal conditions and the no-instruction control condition. Overall, these findings suggest that one form of cognitive reappraisal (i.e., reframing one's thoughts about the contaminated object) may augment the effectiveness of exposure in OCD by increasing approach behaviors, even in the absence of subjective changes in emotions (i.e., anxiety). Additionally, this study demonstrates how the investigation of emotion regulation processes (e.g., cognitive reappraisal) is intricate, complex, and needs to be studied at a nuanced level in laboratory-based experimental studies.

DISTRESS TOLERANCE

Although exposure seeks to increase behavioral approach toward anxiety-provoking situations or objects, another central goal underlying exposure is teaching people the skills needed to cope with and tolerate distressing emotions (e.g., Craske & Barlow, 2006; Foa et al., 2007, 2012). In translating some of these therapeutic techniques to the laboratory, some experimental methods explore how people endure stressors that are already present. That is, they assess *distress tolerance*. A widely studied distress tolerance paradigm is the cold pressor test, which is designed to experimentally induce pain by placing a person's hand or forearm in near-freezing water. Although there is variability in how the cold pressor test is implemented (Birnie, Petter, Boerner, Noel, & Chambers, 2012), distress tolerance is often operationalized as the time it takes for an individual to report that the pain or discomfort is no longer tolerable and/or terminates the procedure by removing her/his hand from the cold water (Burns, Bruehl, & Caceres, 2004). Overall, the cold pressor test has been found to be a reliable and valid assessment of pain tolerance (Edens & Gil, 1995).

Recently, researchers have begun to examine how emotion regulation processes may facilitate distress tolerance abilities in a cold pressor task. For example, one study found that people instructed to use cognitive reappraisal reported feeling greater self-efficacy and control in tolerating distress prior to a cold pressor task (i.e., during an anticipatory anxiety phase) as well as greater self-efficacy after the task was completed (Denson, Creswell, Terides, & Blundell, 2014). Cognitive reappraisal has also been found to be more effective than other emotion regulation strategies (i.e., acceptance and suppression) at reducing negative emotions such as anger during a Mirror-Tracing Persistence Task (Rodman, Daughters, & Lejuez, 2009), which is a widely used paradigm that serves as a behavioral indicator of distress tolerance (Szasz, Szentagotai, & Hofmann, 2011). Research has also supported to utility of acceptance as an emotion regulation strategy to tolerate distress. A recent study demonstrated that teaching participants to accept pain-related negative thoughts, emotions, and physical sensations through a brief mindfulness intervention significantly improved their pain tolerance and reduced their distress during immersion in the freezing water (Liu, Wang, Chang, Chen, & Si, 2013).

Another experimental method frequently used to investigate how people endure, rather than avoid, unpleasant experiences (e.g., emotions, physical symptoms) is through the carbon dioxide inhalation challenge. In this experiment, participants typically inhale a mixture of 21% oxygen, 73.5% nitrogen, and 5.5% carbon dioxide gradually for 15 min through a breathing apparatus. Although this procedure does not pose any serious health risks, participants frequently experience panic-like symptoms or even full-blown panic attacks. As such, this experimental paradigm has been widely studied in the context of panic disorder given that these patients often exhibit interoceptive avoidance, or the avoidance of physical sensations that might trigger panic attacks (e.g., Craske & Barlow, 1990; Sanderson, Rapee, & Barlow, 1989). Similar to the aforementioned studies, the use of emotion regulation strategies has been found to reduce interoceptive avoidance in panic disorder. In a study of 60 patients diagnosed with panic disorder, participants listened to a 10-min audiotape instructing them to either accept or suppress their emotions during an upcoming carbon dioxide inhalation challenge, or a neutral narrative that was used as a control group. The researchers found that those in the acceptance group were significantly less anxious in terms of subjective anxiety compared to those in the suppression and control groups. Significantly, those individuals in the acceptance group also reported greater willingness to participate in a second challenge immediately after the first challenge relative to the suppression or control groups. These results suggest that when participants with panic disorder implemented an adaptive emotion regulation strategy (i.e., acceptance), they were less anxious when enduring panic-like symptoms that they experienced during the challenge and also demonstrated greater approach behaviors as suggested by their greater willingness to participate in a second carbon dioxide inhalation challenge (Levitt et al., 2004). A critical finding is that participants were less likely to exhibit avoidance behaviors—a primary target for intervention in the highly efficacious treatment of panic disorder that can serve as a key mechanism of therapeutic change (Craske & Barlow, 2006).

As the previous studies demonstrate, there is mounting evidence suggesting that utilizing emotion regulation strategies may actually enhance distress tolerance capabilities in such experimental settings. Importantly, distress tolerance is a skill that is an integral component of empirically supported treatments, most notably DBT. In DBT, teaches patients skills at tolerating distress such as "radical acceptance," which involves dealing with, getting through, and accepting events that cause intense emotional distress (which Linehan states is an inevitable part of life) without making them worse (e.g., engaging in problematic behaviors). Linehan refers to some of these distress tolerance skills as "crisis survival strategies" (Linehan, 1993, p. 147–148) given the grave importance for patients with borderline personality disorder to persevere through difficult situations that elicit intense distress and negative affect (e.g., anger, sadness) rather than turning to impulsive, self-destructive behaviors that can have life-threatening consequences (e.g., suicidal behaviors, NSSI, and substance use). Interestingly, a coping strategy that is frequently taught in DBT is to encourage patients who are in distress to hold ice cubes in their hands, splash cold water on their face, or to take an ice-cold shower (Linehan, 1993)—all distress tolerance techniques that are analogous to the cold pressor test.

Overall, the use of paradigms such as BATs, the cold pressor test, or the carbon dioxide inhalation challenge demonstrate the robust opportunities for studying specific emotion regulation processes that enhance our understanding and treatment of psychological disorders. Importantly, investigating the specific emotion regulation mechanisms that are directly relevant to those used in treatment (e.g., exposure and distress tolerance) might help clinical scientists translate experimental research conducted in the laboratory to the therapy room. Doing so is vital if we want to improve the cognitive-behavioral techniques used in clinical practice and reduce the suffering for those suffering from psychopathology by delivering more effective, cutting-edge versions of CBT that emphasize emotion regulation. In the following section, we conclude with a series of recommendations for bridging the gap between treatment studies and laboratory-based experimental studies by integrating these two research methodologies in a more unified and cohesive manner.

TOWARD A BETTER UNDERSTANDING OF EMOTION REGULATION IN CBT: INTEGRATING TREATMENT STUDIES AND LABORATORY-BASED EXPERIMENTS

The utility of coalescing RCTs and experimental studies in a more unified and cohesive manner is potentially limitless, particularly because mental health issues still pose a large burden to our society

(Kazdin & Blase, 2011). First, integrating these approaches would lead to a better understanding of the specific mechanisms (e.g., emotion regulation) by which cognitive-behavioral treatments lead to improvements in mental health and emotional functioning. Thus, clinical scientists are presented with an opportunity to improve emotion-focused interventions by fine-tuning and emphasizing the treatment components that are most important to attain optimal outcomes. Second, a promising opportunity for improving currently available cognitive-behavioral interventions lies in the possibility of whether enhancing emotion regulation skills in laboratory settings translates to increased treatment efficacy.

One promising way of amalgamating these two approaches is to ask patients enrolled in RCTs to participate in laboratory-based paradigms such as those described above. For instance, let us imagine that clinical scientists want to conduct a RCT to systematically test the efficacy of a novel emotion-focused intervention for comorbid GAD and depression. In addition to receiving the treatment they are randomized to over the course of 16–20 weeks, patients could also complete laboratory-based experiments at the beginning, middle, and end of treatment, as well as at follow-up assessments. Adopting this integrated methodology would allow researchers to assess whether the emotion regulation strategies and skills that patients are learning in treatment (e.g., reappraisal, acceptance, and regulatory flexibility) are being used in laboratory settings. Importantly, this approach would improve our knowledge about the specific mechanisms (i.e., emotion regulation) necessary for therapeutic change to obtain the most robust treatment outcome. For instance, patients might benefit from participating in distress tolerance tasks to learn more effective ways of coping with the distressing uncertainty of the future, which is a prevalent worry theme that is frequently targeted using cognitive-behavioral interventions (Zinbarg et al., 2006). They could complete a distress tolerance task such as the cold pressor while being instructed to utilize the emotion regulation strategies they are being taught in treatment (e.g., cognitive reappraisal and acceptance). An alternative, and perhaps even more valuable, approach is for researchers to assess how these patients are spontaneously regulating their emotions (Sheppes et al., 2014), as this would allow researchers to verify whether patients utilize the emotion regulation strategies they are learning in therapy outside of the therapy room. The insight that researchers can gain from combining these two methods has the potential to shed light on mechanisms by which cognitive-behavioral treatments are effective at reducing symptoms of psychopathology and improving overall mental health.

Another primary goal of this integrated approach would be to determine whether improved performance on such experimental tasks in the laboratory would translate to greater abilities to utilize these techniques (e.g., exposure, distress tolerance) in a patient's day-to-day lives, which in turn, could bolster treatment efficacy. For instance, patients could participate in exposure analogs in a laboratory setting such as imaginal exposures where they imagine that their most distressing worries are coming true (e.g., "what if I lose my job and cannot provide for my family financially?") and they are required to cope with this distress by implementing emotion regulation strategies from their repertoire. Additionally, these patients with co-occurring GAD and depression might also benefit from completing BATs in the laboratory that could be used to facilitate the reduction of avoidance (e.g., avoiding worries and the physical symptoms that typically go along with worrying) and increasing a patient's engagement in more functional, adaptive behaviors (e.g., less procrastinating) outside the therapy room. Importantly, many laboratory studies are beginning to show that emotion regulation might actually enhance therapeutic techniques that parallel those used in clinical practice such as exposure analogs for anxiety disorders (Kircanski et al., 2012; Wilson & Aldao, in preparation). Consequently, it remains to be tested whether building emotion regulation abilities in the laboratory has a positive influence on treatment outcomes.

CONCLUDING REMARKS

A remarkable aspect of CBT is that it is continually evolving. In recent years, this growth has focused on incorporating the flourishing field of affective science. RCTs have provided empirical support for the efficacy of emotion-focused interventions and laboratory-based studies have helped identify mechanisms underlying treatment success. However, these two lines of work have largely been disconnected from each other, and this does not bode well for the growth of emotion regulation in CBT. We hope that our suggestions inspire clinical scientists to more regularly bridge the gap between the clinic and the laboratory, and ultimately, to develop more effective emotion regulation-based forms of CBT that have the potential to reduce the suffering and improve the mental health in those with psychological disorders on a larger scale.

References

Aldao, A., Nolen-Hoeksema, S., & Schweizer, S. (2010). Emotion-regulation strategies across psychopathology: A meta-analytic review. *Clinical Psychology Review, 30*(2), 217–237. Available from http://dx.doi.org/10.1016/j.cpr.2009.11.004.

Aldao, A., & Plate, A. J. (in press). Coping and emotion regulation. In S. Hayes & S. Hofmann (Eds.), *Core competencies of behavioral and cognitive therapies*. Oakland, CA: New Harbinger Publications.

Arch, J. J., Eifert, G. H., Davies, C., Plumb, C., Rose, R. D., & Craske, M. G. (2012). Randomized clinical trial of cognitive behavioral therapy (CBT) versus acceptance and commitment therapy (ACT) for mixed anxiety disorders. *Journal of Consulting and Clinical Psychology, 80*(5), 750−765. http://doi.org/10.1037/a0028310.

Bach, P., & Hayes, S. C. (2002). The use of acceptance and commitment therapy to prevent the rehospitalization of psychotic patients: A randomized controlled trial. *Journal of Consulting and Clinical Psychology, 70*(5), 1129−1139. http://doi.org/10.1037/0022-006X.70.5.1129.

Baker, T. B., McFall, R. M., & Shoham, V. (2008). Current status and future prospects of clinical psychology: Toward a scientifically principled approach to mental and behavioral health care. *Psychological Science in the Public Interest, 9*(2), 67−103. http://doi.org/10.1111/j.1539-6053.2009.01036.x.

Barlow, D. H. (2002). *Anxiety and its disorders: The nature and treatment of anxiety and panic* (2nd ed.). New York, NY: Guilford Press.

Barlow, D. H., Farchione, T. J., Fairholme, C. P., Ellard, K. K., Boisseau, C. L., Allen, L. B., & May, J. T. E. (2010). *Unified protocol for transdiagnostic treatment of emotional disorders: Therapist guide.* New York, NY: Oxford University Press.

Barlow, D. H., Gorman, J. M., Shear, M. K., & Woods, S. W. (2000). Cognitive-behavioral therapy, imipramine, or their combination for panic disorder: A randomized controlled trial. *The Journal of the American Medical Association, 283*(19), 2529−2536. http://doi.org/10.1001/jama.283.19.2529.

Beck, A. T. (1979). *Cognitive therapy of depression.* New York, NY: Guilford Press.

Beck, A. T., Emery, G., & Greenberg, R. L. (1985). *Anxiety disorders and phobias: A cognitive perspective.* New York, NY: Basic Books.

Beck, J. S. (2011). *Cognitive behavior therapy: Basics and beyond.* New York, NY: Guilford Press.

Berking, M., & Wupperman, P. (2012). Emotion regulation and mental health: Recent findings, current challenges, and future directions. *Current Opinion in Psychiatry, 25*(2), 128−134.

Biran, M., & Terence, G. (1981). Treatment of phobic disorders using cognitive and exposure methods: A self-efficacy analysis. *Journal of Consulting and Clinical Psychology, 49* (6), 886−899. http://doi.org/10.1037/0022-006X.49.6.886.

Birnie, K. A., Petter, M., Boerner, K. E., Noel, M., & Chambers, C. T. (2012). Contemporary use of the cold pressor task in pediatric pain research: A systematic review of methods. *The Journal of Pain, 13*(9), 817−826. http://doi.org/10.1016/j.jpain.2012.06.005.

Bohlmeijer, E. T., Fledderus, M., Rokx, T. A. J. J., & Pieterse, M. E. (2011). Efficacy of an early intervention based on acceptance and commitment therapy for adults with depressive symptomatology: Evaluation in a randomized controlled trial. *Behaviour Research and Therapy, 49*(1), 62−67. http://doi.org/10.1016/j.brat.2010.10.003.

Borkovec, T. D., & Ruscio, A. M. (2001). Psychotherapy of generalized anxiety disorder. *The Journal of Clinical Psychiatry, 62*, 37−42, discussion 43−5.

Borkovec, T. D., & Whisman, M. A. (1996). Psychosocial treatment for generalized anxiety disorder. In M. R. Mavissakalian, & R. F. Prien (Eds.), *Long-term treatments of anxiety disorders* (pp. 171−199). Arlington, VA: American Psychiatric Association.

Burns, J. W., Bruehl, S., & Caceres, C. (2004). Anger management style, blood pressure reactivity, and acute pain sensitivity: Evidence for "Trait × Situation" models. *Annals of Behavioral Medicine: A Publication of the Society of Behavioral Medicine, 27*(3), 195−204. http://doi.org/10.1207/s15324796abm2703_7.

Butler, A. C., Chapman, J. E., Forman, E. M., & Beck, A. T. (2006). The empirical status of cognitive-behavioral therapy: A review of meta-analyses. *Clinical Psychology Review, 26* (1), 17−31. http://doi.org/10.1016/j.cpr.2005.07.003.

Chambless, D. L. (1996). In defense of dissemination of empirically supported psychological interventions. *Clinical Psychology: Science and Practice, 3*(3), 230−235. http://doi.org/10.1111/j.1468-2850.1996.tb00074.x.

Chambless, D. L., & Hollon, S. D. (1998). Defining empirically supported therapies. *Journal of Consulting and Clinical Psychology, 66*(1), 7−18. http://doi.org/10.1037/0022-006X.66.1.7.

Craske, M. G., & Barlow, D. H. (1990). Nocturnal panic: Response to hyperventilation and carbon dioxide challenges. *Journal of Abnormal Psychology, 99*(3), 302−307. http://doi.org/10.1037/0021-843X.99.3.302.

Craske, M. G., & Barlow, D. H. (2006). *Mastery of your anxiety and panic (therapist guide)* (4th ed.). New York, NY: Oxford University Press.

Cuijpers, P., Reynolds, C. F., Donker, T., Li, J., Andersson, G., & Beekman, A. (2012). Personalized treatment of adult depression: Medication, psychotherapy, or both? A systematic review. *Depression and Anxiety, 29*(10), 855−864. http://doi.org/10.1002/da.21985.

Denson, T. F., Creswell, J. D., Terides, M. D., & Blundell, K. (2014). Cognitive reappraisal increases neuroendocrine reactivity to acute social stress and physical pain. *Psychoneuroendocrinology, 49*, 69−78. http://doi.org/10.1016/j.psyneuen.2014.07.003.

DeRubeis, R. J., Hollon, S. D., Amsterdam, J. D., Shelton, R. C., Young, P. R., Salomon, R. M., Gallop, R.... (2005). Cognitive therapy vs medications in the treatment of moderate to severe depression. *Archives of General Psychiatry 62*(4), 409−416. http://doi.org/10.1001/archpsyc.62.4.409.

Edens, J. L., & Gil, K. M. (1995). Experimental induction of pain: Utility in the study of clinical pain. *Behavior Therapy, 26*(2), 197−216. http://doi.org/10.1016/S0005-7894(05)80102-9.

Fairburn, C. G., Cooper, Z., Shafran, R., & Terence, G. (2008). *Eating disorders: A transdiagnostic protocol . Clinical handbook of psychological disorders: A step-by-step treatment manual* (4th ed.). New York, NY: Guilford Press.

Farchione, T. J., Fairholme, C. P., Ellard, K. K., Boisseau, C. L., Thompson-Hollands, J., Carl, J. R., ... Barlow, D. H. (2012). Unified protocol for transdiagnostic treatment of emotional disorders: A randomized controlled trial. *Behavior Therapy, 43*(3), 666−678. http://doi.org/10.1016/j.beth.2012.01.001.

Foa, E. B., Hembree, E. A., & Rothbaum, B. O. (2007). *Prolonged exposure therapy for PTSD: Emotional processing of traumatic experiences (therapist guide)*. New York, NY: Oxford University Press.

Foa, E. B., Yadin, E., & Lichner, T. K. (2012). *Exposure and response (ritual) prevention for obsessive compulsive disorder: Therapist guide* (2nd ed.). New York, NY: Oxford University Press.

Forman, E. M., Herbert, J. D., Moitra, E., Yeomans, P. D., & Geller, P. A. (2007). A randomized controlled effectiveness trial of acceptance and commitment therapy and cognitive therapy for anxiety and depression. *Behavior Modification, 31*(6), 772−799. http://doi.org/10.1177/0145445507302202.

Gilson, M., Freeman, A., Yates, M. J., & Freeman, S. M. (2009). *Overcoming depression: A cognitive therapy approach (therapist guide)* (2nd ed.). New York, NY: Oxford University Press.

Goldin, P. R., Ziv, M., Jazaieri, H., Werner, K., Kraemer, H., Heimberg, R. G., & Gross, J. J. (2012). Cognitive reappraisal self-efficacy mediates the effects of individual cognitive-behavioral therapy for social anxiety disorder. *Journal of Consulting and Clinical Psychology, 80*(6), 1034−1040. http://doi.org/10.1037/a0028555.

Gross, J. J. (1998). The emerging field of emotion regulation: An integrative review. *Review of General Psychology, 2*(3), 271−299. http://doi.org/10.1037/1089-2680.2.3.271.

Gross, J. J. (2015). Emotion regulation: Current status and future prospects. *Psychological Inquiry, 26*(1), 1−26. http://doi.org/10.1080/1047840X.2014.940781.

Gross, J. J., & Jazaieri, H. (2014). Emotion, emotion regulation, and psychopathology: An affective science perspective. *Clinical Psychological Science, 2*(4), 387−401. http://doi.org/10.1177/2167702614536164.

Hayes, S. C., Luoma, J. B., Bond, F. W., Masuda, A., & Lillis, J. (2006). Acceptance and commitment therapy: Model, processes and outcomes. *Behaviour Research and Therapy*, *44*(1), 1–25. http://doi.org/10.1016/j.brat.2005.06.006.

Hayes, S. C., Strosahl, K. D., & Wilson, K. G. (1999). *Acceptance and commitment therapy: An experiential approach to behavior change* (Vol. xvi). New York, NY: Guilford Press.

Hayes, S. C., Wilson, K. G., Gifford, E. V., Follette, V. M., & Strosahl, K. (1996). Experiential avoidance and behavioral disorders: A functional dimensional approach to diagnosis and treatment. *Journal of Consulting and Clinical Psychology*, *64*(6), 1152–1168. http://doi.org/10.1037/0022-006X.64.6.1152.

Hellström, K., Fellenius, J., & Öst, L.-G. (1996). One versus five sessions of applied tension in the treatment of blood phobia. *Behaviour Research and Therapy*, *34*(2), 101–112 . http://doi.org/10.1016/0005-7967(95)00060-7.

Hofmann, S. G., Asnaani, A., Vonk, I. J. J., Sawyer, A. T., & Fang, A. (2012). The efficacy of cognitive behavioral therapy: A review of meta-analyses. *Cognitive Therapy and Research*, *36*(5), 427–440. http://doi.org/10.1007/s10608-012-9476-1.

Hofmann, S. G., Sawyer, A. T., Fang, A., & Asnaani, A. (2012). Emotion dysregulation model of mood and anxiety disorders. *Depression and Anxiety*, *29*(5), 409–416. http://doi.org/10.1002/da.21888.

Hofmann, S. G., & Smits, J. A. J. (2008). Cognitive-behavioral therapy for adult anxiety disorders: A meta-analysis of randomized placebo-controlled trials. *The Journal of Clinical Psychiatry*, *69*(4), 621–632.

Hollon, S. D., DeRubeis, R. J., Shelton, R. C., Amsterdam, J. D., Salomon, R. M., O'Reardon, J. P., . . . Gallop, R. (2005). Prevention of relapse following cognitive therapy vs medications in moderate to severe depression. *Archives of General Psychiatry*, *62*(4), 417–422. http://doi.org/10.1001/archpsyc.62.4.417.

Hollon, S. D., Thase, M. E., & Markowitz, J. C. (2002). Treatment and prevention of depression. *Psychological Science in the Public Interest*, *3*(2), 39–77. http://doi.org/10.1111/1529-1006.00008.

Hope, D. A., Heimberg, R. G., & Turk, C. L. (2010). *Managing social anxiety: A cognitive-behavioral therapy approach (therapist guide)* (2nd ed.). New York, NY: Oxford University Press.

Kazdin, A. E., & Blase, S. L. (2011). Rebooting psychotherapy research and practice to reduce the burden of mental illness. *Perspectives on Psychological Science*, *6*(1), 21–37. http://doi.org/10.1177/1745691610393527.

Kessler, R. C., Berglund, P., Demler, O., Jin, R., Merikangas, K. R., & Walters, E. E. (2005). Lifetime prevalence and age-of-onset distributions of DSM-IV disorders in the National Comorbidity Survey Replication. *Archives of General Psychiatry*, *62*(6), 593–602.

Kircanski, K., Lieberman, M. D., & Craske, M. G. (2012). Feelings into words: Contributions of language to exposure therapy. *Psychological Science*, *23*(10), 1086–1091. http://doi.org/10.1177/0956797612443830.

Koch, M. D., O'Neill, H. K., Sawchuk, C. N., & Connolly, K. (2002). Domain-specific and generalized disgust sensitivity in blood-injection-injury phobia: The application of behavioral approach/avoidance tasks. *Journal of Anxiety Disorders*, *16*(5), 511–527. http://doi.org/10.1016/S0887-6185(02)00170-6.

Kraemer, H. C., Frank, E., & Kupfer, D. J. (2006). Moderators of treatment outcomes: Clinical, research, and policy importance. *JAMA*, *296*(10), 1286–1289. http://doi.org/10.1001/jama.296.10.1286.

Kraemer, H. C., Wilson, G. T., Fairburn, C. G., & Agras, W. S. (2002). Mediators and moderators of treatment effects in randomized clinical trials. *Archives of General Psychiatry*, *59*(10), 877–883. http://doi.org/10.1001/archpsyc.59.10.877.

Kring, A. M., & Sloan, D. M. (2009). *Emotion regulation and psychopathology: A transdiagnostic approach to etiology and treatment*. New York, NY: Guilford Press.

Levitt, J. T., Brown, T. A., Orsillo, S. M., & Barlow, D. H. (2004). The effects of acceptance versus suppression of emotion on subjective and psychophysiological response to carbon dioxide challenge in patients with panic disorder. *Behavior Therapy, 35*(4), 747−766. http://doi.org/10.1016/S0005-7894(04)80018-2.

Linehan, M. (1993). *Cognitive-behavioral treatment of borderline personality disorder*. New York, NY: Guilford Press.

Linehan, M. M. (2014). *DBT skills training manual* (2nd ed.). New York, NY: The Guilford Press.

Linehan, M. M., Armstrong, H. E., Suarez, A., Allmon, D., & Heard, H. L. (1991). Cognitive-behavioral treatment of chronically parasuicidal borderline patients. *Archives of General Psychiatry, 48*(12), 1060−1064.

Linehan, M. M., Comtois, K. A., Murray, A. M., Brown, M. Z., Gallop, R. J., Heard, H. L., ... Lindenboim, N. (2006). Two-year randomized controlled trial and follow-up of dialectical behavior therapy vs therapy by experts for suicidal behaviors and borderline personality disorder. *Archives of General Psychiatry, 63*(7), 757−766.

Linehan, M. M., Korslund, K. E., Harned, M. S., Gallop, R. J., Lungu, A., Neacsiu, A. D., ... Murray-Gregory, A. M. (2015). Dialectical behavior therapy for high suicide risk in individuals with borderline personality disorder: A randomized clinical trial and component analysis. *JAMA Psychiatry, 72*(5), 475−482. http://doi.org/10.1001/jamapsychiatry.2014.3039.

Liu, X., Wang, S., Chang, S., Chen, W., & Si, M. (2013). Effect of brief mindfulness intervention on tolerance and distress of pain induced by cold-pressor task. *Stress and Health, 29*(3), 199−204. http://doi.org/10.1002/smi.2446.

McHugh, R. K., & Barlow, D. H. (2010). The dissemination and implementation of evidence-based psychological treatments: A review of current efforts. *American Psychologist, 65*(2), 73−84. http://doi.org/10.1037/a0018121.

Mennin, D. S., & Fresco, D. M. (2009). Emotion regulation as an integrative framework for understanding and treating psychopathology. *Emotion Regulation and Psychopathology: A Transdiagnostic Approach to Etiology and Treatment*, 356−379.

Mennin, D. S., & Fresco, D. M. (2013). Emotion regulation therapy. In J. J. Gross (Ed.), *Handbook of emotion regulation* (2nd ed., pp. 469−490). New York, NY: Guilford Press.

Mennin, D. S., Fresco, D. M., Ritter, M., & Heimberg, R. G. (2015). An open trial of emotion regulation therapy for generalized anxiety disorder and co-occurring depression. *Depression and Anxiety, 32*(8), 614−623. http://doi.org/10.1002/da.22377.

Mennin, D. S., Holaway, R. M., Fresco, D. M., Moore, M. T., & Heimberg, R. G. (2007). Delineating components of emotion and its dysregulation in anxiety and mood psychopathology. *Behavior Therapy, 38*(3), 284−302. http://doi.org/10.1016/j.beth.2006.09.001.

Messick, S. (1989). Validity. In R. L. Linn (Ed.), *Educational measurement* (3rd ed., pp. 13−103). New York: Macmillan.

Milosevic, I., & Radomsky, A. S. (2008). Safety behaviour does not necessarily interfere with exposure therapy. *Behaviour Research and Therapy, 46*(10), 1111−1118. http://doi.org/10.1016/j.brat.2008.05.011.

Mischel, W. (2008). Connecting clinical practice to scientific progress. *Psychological Science in the Public Interest, 9*(2), i−ii. http://doi.org/10.1111/j.1539-6053.2009.01035.x.

Najmi, S., & Amir, N. (2010). The effect of attention training on a behavioral test of contamination fears in individuals with subclinical obsessive-compulsive symptoms. *Journal of Abnormal Psychology, 119*(1), 136−142. http://doi.org/10.1037/a0017549.

Neacsiu, A. D., Eberle, J. W., Kramer, R., Wiesmann, T., & Linehan, M. M. (2014). Dialectical behavior therapy skills for transdiagnostic emotion dysregulation: A pilot randomized controlled trial. *Behaviour Research and Therapy, 59*, 40−51. http://doi.org/10.1016/j.brat.2014.05.005.

Neacsiu, A. D., Rizvi, S. L., & Linehan, M. M. (2010). Dialectical behavior therapy skills use as a mediator and outcome of treatment for borderline personality disorder. *Behaviour Research and Therapy*, *48*(9), 832–839. http://doi.org/10.1016/j.brat.2010.05.017.

Öst, L.-G., Salkovskis, P. M., & Hellström, K. (1991). One-session therapist-directed exposure vs. self-exposure in the treatment of spider phobia. *Behavior Therapy*, *22*(3), 407–422. http://doi.org/10.1016/S0005-7894(05)80374-0.

Öst, L. G., Stridh, B. M., & Wolf, M. (1998). A clinical study of spider phobia: Prediction of outcome after self-help and therapist-directed treatments. *Behaviour Research and Therapy*, *36*(1), 17–35. http://doi.org/10.1016/S0005-7967(97)10018-3.

Payne, L. A., Ellard, K. K., Farchione, T. J., Fairholme, C. P., & Barlow, D. H. (2014). *Emotional disorders: A unified transdiagnostic protocol. Clinical handbook of psychological disorders, fifth edition: A step-by-step treatment manual* (5th ed.) New York, NY: Guilford Publications, Inc.

Rachman, S., Shafran, R., Radomsky, A. S., & Zysk, E. (2011). Reducing contamination by exposure plus safety behaviour. *Journal of Behavior Therapy and Experimental Psychiatry*, *42*(3), 397–404. http://doi.org/10.1016/j.jbtep.2011.02.010.

Rodman, S. A., Daughters, S. B., & Lejuez, C. W. (2009). Distress tolerance and rational-emotive behavior therapy: A new role for behavioral analogue tasks. *Journal of Rational-Emotive & Cognitive-Behavior Therapy*, *27*(2), 97–120. http://doi.org/10.1007/s10942-009-0090-4.

Roemer, L., & Orsillo, S. M. (2009). *Mindfulness- and acceptance-based behavioral therapies in practice.* New York, NY: Guilford Press.

Roemer, L., Orsillo, S. M., & Salters-Pedneault, K. (2008). Efficacy of an acceptance-based behavior therapy for generalized anxiety disorder: Evaluation in a randomized controlled trial. *Journal of Consulting and Clinical Psychology*, *76*(6), 1083–1089. http://doi.org/10.1037/a0012720.

Roy-Byrne, P. P., Craske, M. G., Stein, M. B., Sullivan, G., Bystritsky, A., Katon, W., ... Sherbourne, C. D. (2005). A randomized effectiveness trial of cognitive-behavioral therapy and medication for primary care panic disorder. *Archives of General Psychiatry*, *62*(3), 290–298. http://doi.org/10.1001/archpsyc.62.3.290.

Safren, S. A., Perlman, C. A., Sprich, S., & Otto, M. W. (2005). *Mastering your adult ADHD: A cognitive-behavioral treatment program (therapist guide).* New York; NY: Oxford University Press.

Sanderson, W. C., Rapee, R. M., & Barlow, D. H. (1989). The influence of an illusion of control on panic attacks induced via inhalation of 5.5% carbon dioxide-enriched air. *Archives of General Psychiatry*, *46*(2), 157–162. http://doi.org/10.1001/archpsyc.1989.01810020059010.

Schnurr, P. P., Friedman, M. J., Engel, C. C., Foa, E. B., Shea, M. T., Chow, B. K., Bernardy, N.... (2007). Cognitive behavioral therapy for posttraumatic stress disorder in women: A randomized controlled trial. *The Journal of the American Medical Association*, *297*(8), 820–830. http://doi.org/10.1001/jama.297.8.820.

Sheppes, G., Scheibe, S., Suri, G., Radu, P., Blechert, J., & Gross, J. J. (2014). Emotion regulation choice: A conceptual framework and supporting evidence. *Journal of Experimental Psychology: General*, *143*(1), 163–181. http://doi.org/10.1037/a0030831.

Sheppes, G., Suri, G., & Gross, J. J. (2015). Emotion regulation and psychopathology. *Annual Review of Clinical Psychology*, *11*(1), 379–405. http://doi.org/10.1146/annurev-clinpsy-032814-112739.

Smout, M. F., Longo, M., Harrison, S., Minniti, R., Wickes, W., & White, J. M. (2010). Psychosocial treatment for methamphetamine use disorders: A preliminary randomized controlled trial of cognitive behavior therapy and acceptance and commitment therapy. *Substance Abuse*, *31*(2), 98–107. http://doi.org/10.1080/08897071003641578.

Stewart, R. E., Chambless, D. L., & Linehan, M. M. (2009). Cognitive–behavioral therapy for adult anxiety disorders in clinical practice: A meta-analysis of effectiveness studies. *Journal of Consulting and Clinical Psychology, 77*(4), 595–606. https://doi.org/10.1037/a0016032

Stirman, S. W., DeRubeis, R. J., Crits-Christoph, P., & Brody, P. E. (2003). Are samples in randomized controlled trials of psychotherapy representative of community outpatients? A new methodology and initial findings. *Journal of Consulting and Clinical Psychology, 71*(6), 963–972. http://doi.org/10.1037/0022-006X.71.6.963.

Szasz, P. L., Szentagotai, A., & Hofmann, S. G. (2011). The effect of emotion regulation strategies on anger. *Behaviour Research and Therapy, 49*(2), 114–119. http://doi.org/10.1016/j.brat.2010.11.011.

Tarrier, N., & Taylor, R. (2008). *Schizophrenia and other psychotic disorders. Clinical handbook of psychological disorders: A step-by-step treatment manual* (4th ed.) New York, NY: Guilford Press.

Taylor, C. T., & Alden, L. E. (2010). Safety behaviors and judgmental biases in social anxiety disorder. *Behaviour Research and Therapy, 48*(3), 226–237. http://doi.org/10.1016/j.brat.2009.11.005.

Tracy, J. L., Klonsky, E. D., & Proudfit, G. H. (2014). How affective science can inform clinical science: An introduction to the special series on emotions and psychopathology. *Clinical Psychological Science, 2*(4), 371–386. http://doi.org/10.1177/2167702614551692.

Twohig, M. P., Hayes, S. C., Plumb, J. C., Pruitt, L. D., Collins, A. B., Hazlett-Stevens, H., & Woidneck, M. R. (2010). A randomized clinical trial of acceptance and commitment therapy versus progressive relaxation training for obsessive-compulsive disorder. *Journal of Consulting and Clinical Psychology, 78*(5), 705–716. http://doi.org/10.1037/a0020508.

Verheul, R., Van Den Bosch, L. M. C., Koeter, M. W. J., De Ridder, M. A. J., Stijnen, T., & Van Den Brink, W. (2003). Dialectical behaviour therapy for women with borderline personality disorder: 12-month, randomised clinical trial in The Netherlands. *The British Journal of Psychiatry: The Journal of Mental Science, 182*, 135–140.

Vittengl, J. R., Clark, L. A., Dunn, T. W., & Jarrett, R. B. (2007). Reducing relapse and recurrence in unipolar depression: A comparative meta-analysis of cognitive-behavioral therapy's effects. *Journal of Consulting and Clinical Psychology, 75*(3), 475–488. http://doi.org/10.1037/0022-006X.75.3.475.

Watkins, E. R., Mullan, E., Wingrove, J., Rimes, K., Steiner, H., Bathurst, N., . . . Scott, J. (2011). Rumination-focused cognitive-behavioural therapy for residual depression: Phase II randomised controlled trial. *The British Journal of Psychiatry, 199*(4), 317–322. http://doi.org/10.1192/bjp.bp.110.090282.

Westen, D., & Morrison, K. (2001). A multidimensional meta-analysis of treatments for depression, panic, and generalized anxiety disorder: An empirical examination of the status of empirically supported therapies. *Journal of Consulting and Clinical Psychology, 69*(6), 875–899. http://doi.org/10.1037/0022-006X.69.6.875.

Wetherell, J. L., Afari, N., Rutledge, T., Sorrell, J. T., Stoddard, J. A., Petkus, A. J., . . . Hampton Atkinson, J. (2011). A randomized, controlled trial of acceptance and commitment therapy and cognitive-behavioral therapy for chronic pain. *Pain, 152*(9), 2098–2107. http://doi.org/10.1016/j.pain.2011.05.016.

Wilson, A.C. & Aldao, A. (in preparation). Appraising reappraisal: Exploring its role in the context of behavioral exposure for obsessive-compulsive disorder.

Zinbarg, R. E., Craske, M. G., & Barlow, D. H. (2006). *Mastery of your anxiety and worry (therapist guide)* (2nd ed.). New York, NY: Oxford University Press.

EXTENSIONS, INNOVATIONS, AND MODIFICATIONS OF TREATMENT STRATEGIES

6

Combined Treatment With CBT and Psychopharmacology

Josie Lee[1], Bridget A. Hearon[2] and Michael W. Otto[1]

[1]Boston University, Boston, MA, United States [2]Albright College, Reading, PA, United States

Affective disorders are highly prevalent (Kessler et al., 2003, 2005) and are associated with a number of adverse outcomes including increased utilization of healthcare services (Mathers & Loncar, 2006), lower quality of life (Saarni et al., 2007), and high levels of economic costs (Smit et al., 2006). A robust body of literature has demonstrated support for the use of both cognitive-behavioral therapy (CBT) and pharmacologic interventions in the treatment of these disorders. As part of the search for more powerful interventions, clinicians and researchers have investigated combining these treatment modalities to examine potential additive benefits. Given the prominence of the combination treatment literature for anxiety and mood disorders, we more extensively review the literature within these clinical domains, but we also address the successful use of combination treatments observed in other disorders [e.g., schizophrenia and attention-deficit hyperactivity disorder (ADHD)].

MONOTHERAPY: CBT OR PHARMACOTHERAPY

An extensive body of literature has demonstrated strong support for the efficacy of both cognitive behavioral and pharmacologic monotherapy for adults across a range of disorders. Among individuals who receive CBT, randomized controlled trials (RCTs) and meta-analytic reviews have demonstrated its efficacy for the treatment of both mood (Jones & Hayward, 2004; Cuijpers, Andersson, Donker, & van Straten, 2011) and anxiety disorders (Deacon & Abramowitz, 2004; Hofmann & Smits, 2008). Likewise, several classes of pharmacological agents including selective-serotonin reuptake inhibitors (SSRIs), monoamine oxidase inhibitors (MAO-Is), and tricyclic antidepressants have also been shown to reduce mood and anxiety disorder symptom severity reliably, with similar evidence for benzodiazepine treatment of many anxiety disorders (Abramowitz, 1997; Gould, Buckminster, Pollack, Otto, & Yap, 1997; Hidalgo et al., 2001; Pollack, 2005; Rocha et al., 2012).

Although CBT and pharmacological treatments often offer comparable acute outcomes, some reliable differences have emerged over time. Roshanaei-Moghaddam et al. (2011) compared the relative effects of CBT and pharmacotherapy in the treatment of depression and anxiety disorders in a meta-analytic review of 21 studies that included randomized treatment conditions examining both CBT and psychopharmacology. Findings for the anxiety disorders evinced differential effects for each treatment modality depending on the particular disorder at hand. CBT was observed to have the greatest advantage of over pharmacotherapy in panic disorder (medium effect size; $d = 50$). Although nonsignificant, a similar trend was observed for obsessive compulsive disorder (OCD). Favorable outcomes for pharmacotherapy over CBT were observed at the trend level in social anxiety disorder (SAD; $d = 22$). No relative advantage between treatment modalities was found for depression. These results, based on trials examining both CBT and pharmacotherapy in the same trial are consistent with the general conclusion of meta-analyses that have compared the controlled effect sizes when CBT and pharmacotherapy are studied independently for panic disorder (e.g., Gould et al., 1997; Furukawa, Watanabe, & Churchill, 2006) and generalized anxiety disorder (GAD; Mitte, 2005).

These data for acute outcomes have been complemented by trials examining the efficacy of each treatment modality in maintaining treatment gains over the long term. In general, one substantial advantage of CBT is its ability to provide ongoing benefit in the absence of ongoing treatment, whereas relapse is common upon discontinuation of pharmacologic treatment (Keller et al., 2007; Reynolds et al., 2006; Stein, Versiani, Hair, & Kumar, 2002; Walker et al., 2000). Indeed, for the treatment of recurrent major depressive disorder (MDD), long-term maintenance therapy using antidepressant medication is recommended (Anderson, Nutt, & Deakin, 2000), with a trial conducted by Keller et al. (2007) indicating continued medication may be required for 2 years or more to adequately prevent relapse. Evidence does suggest that those patients who are able to achieve remission from their disorder rather than just symptom reduction may be more successful in avoiding relapse after discontinuing pharmacotherapy (Mavissakalian & Perel, 1999). However, those who achieve remission during the acute phase of treatment represent a minority of individuals who initiate pharmacotherapy, and the remaining majority of patients likely need to continue pharmacotherapy in the long term to maintain treatment gains. In contrast, short-term CBT interventions have demonstrated stronger maintenance of treatment gains for both anxiety (Deacon & Abramowitz, 2004; Gould et al., 1997; Otto, Pollack, & Maki, 2000) and depression (Dobson et al., 2008; Evans et al., 1992; Hollon et al., 2005). Indeed, a recent meta-analytic review of nine studies indicates that patients who receive CBT are significantly less likely to relapse than patients who discontinue their pharmacotherapy on the order of an odds ratio (OR) of 2.61. Interestingly, this advantage continued at a trend level (OR = 1.62) even if brief CBT was compared to continued pharmacotherapy (Cuijpers et al., 2013). Also, due to the need for ongoing pharmacotherapy, the two treatment modalities have different cost efficacy estimates. Studies of anxiety disorders (Heuzenroeder et al., 2004; McHugh et al., 2007; Otto, Pollack, & Maki, 2000) and depression (Haby et al., 2004) indicate that CBT offers a significantly better cost benefit ratio than pharmacotherapy.

COMBINATION TREATMENT—THE FOREST BEFORE THE TREES

The characteristics of monotherapy give rise to a number of considerations for the strategy of combination treatment. First, both monotherapies can be applied simultaneously at treatment onset. Second, combination treatment can be applied judiciously, targeting only nonresponders to the other monotherapy. Third, combination treatment can be applied in a maintenance treatment phase, where one treatment is used to aid the discontinuation of the other. In the sections below, we consider each of these strategies. However, prior to proceeding to the evidence from outcome trials, it is important to first consider the nature of beneficial effects in combination treatment.

Concerning the simultaneous combination of treatments, the magnitude of treatment response should logically depend on the degree to which (1) nonresponders to one treatment will receive benefit from the other treatment, so that the overall number of responders in any given trial is larger or (2) that one treatment will aid response to the other treatment, so that there are true additive actions within the treatment of an individual. Despite the large number of combination treatment trials to date, there has been only limited clarification on which of these actions tend to dominate. At least for the anxiety disorders, there is evidence that treatment with antidepressants does not aid core therapeutic learning mechanisms of CBT (Otto et al., 2010a, 2016a). As for benzodiazepines, there is increasing evidence that benzodiazepines, if administered at CBT onset, retard some of the therapeutic benefits of CBT (Otto et al., 2016b; Rothbaum et al., 2014). Accordingly, there is a relative absence of evidence that anxiety or mood pharmacotherapy specifically enhances learning mechanisms of CBT, and instead we are inclined to consider that the benefit offered by combination treatment may reflect the treatment of nonresponders to the other modality of treatment.

Consider that, in the context of a combination treatment trial, there will be (1) a group of patients who can respond to either treatment, (2) a group that responds to neither intervention, (3) a group that responds primarily to CBT, (4) a group that responds primarily to pharmacotherapy, and (5) a group that may need both treatments offered together to respond. Accordingly, a combination treatment would show an advantage over CBT alone to the degree that Groups 3 and 5 are represented, and combination treatment would show an advantage over pharmacotherapy alone to the degree to which Groups 4 and 5 are represented. Also, to the extent to which there is a smaller proportion of Group 1 patients in a treatment trial (perhaps conferred by choosing patients with greater severity or chronicity, or demonstrated nonresponse to previous treatment), it will be easier to detect combination treatment benefits, unless this selection overly increases Group 2 patients. Finally, when one modality of treatment tends to outperform the other, there should be fewer benefits for combination treatment. For example, using findings from Roshanaei-Moghaddam et al.'s (2011) meta-analysis noted above, this should translate to a greater proportion of Group 3 than Group 4 patients for the treatment of panic disorder and perhaps OCD (where CBT outcomes dominate), and a greater proportion of Group 4 than Group 3 patients for SAD.

Unfortunately, there are little data that have successfully identified which patients might belong to these treatment groups. Keller et al. (2000) have provided circumstantial evidence, based on the time course of treatment response to each modality (early for antidepressants and later for CBT), that combination treatment effects may indeed represent the summation of separate responders to CBT and psychopharmacology. Later these researchers conducted retrospective analyses indicating that, for the treatment of depression, those with a history of childhood trauma may be more responsive to CBT and those without this history may have greater relative response to antidepressant treatment (Nemeroff et al., 2003). Yet, we are unaware of a replication of this effect in other trials.

Also, using data from a recent clinical trial comparing CBT, antidepressant medication, and placebo in the treatment of 231 (moderate-to-severe) depressed outpatients, Fournier et al. (2013) examined advantages for either treatment modality in attenuating specific depressive symptom clusters (i.e., mood, cognitive/suicide, anxiety, typical-vegetative, and atypical-vegetative symptoms). Interestingly, active treatments (i.e., antidepressant medication and CBT) did not differ from placebo in the reduction of three out of five symptom clusters, whereas differential treatment effects relative to placebo were observed for cognitive/suicide and atypical-vegetative symptoms. Specifically, by 4 weeks, antidepressant medication led to a greater reduction in cognitive/suicide symptoms relative to placebo and by 8 weeks, both antidepressant and CBT treatments reduced these symptoms relative to placebo. With regard to atypical-vegetative symptoms (i.e., hypersomnia and weight gain/increased appetite), CBT reduced symptoms more than medications throughout the trial (Fournier et al., 2013). Again, these findings have not been replicated, but they are supportive of the notion that modality-specific groups of treatment responsive patients can be identified. Again, it is these (Groups 3 and 4, and perhaps the as-yet-to-be-identified Group 5) patients that should be one important source of advantages of combination treatment over the component monotherapies. As we review the combination treatment evidence for each disorder in the sections below, we will consider further the evidence for and predictors of each of these theoretical groups.

COMBINATION TREATMENT FOR UNIPOLAR DEPRESSION—ACUTE OUTCOMES

A multitude of studies have examined the efficacy of combination strategies for the treatment of depression, with overall findings indicating a significant but relatively modest advantage for the use of combination strategies as compared to pharmacotherapy alone (de Maat, Dekker, Schoevers, & de Jonghe, 2007; Cuijpers et al., 2014), psychotherapy alone (Pampallona, Bollini, Tibaldi, Kupelnick, & Munizza, 2004), and the combination of psychotherapy and placebo (Cuijpers et al., 2014). For example, in a recent meta-analysis of 53 RCTs comparing combined treatment against pharmacotherapy alone and psychotherapy alone, combined treatment was found to have a moderate effect on adult depression compared with pill placebo ($g = 0.46$), and small-to-moderate effects compared against pharmacotherapy alone ($g = 0.38$), psychotherapy alone ($g = 0.34$), and psychotherapy and placebo ($g = 0.23$) (see also, de Maat et al., 2007; Cuijpers et al., 2014).

There is evidence suggesting these overall small-to-medium effects of combination treatment might be moderated by treatment severity or chronicity (Otto, Smits, & Reese, 2005). That is, relative to our model for combination treatment effects, biasing the sample away from the most easy-to-treat patients (Group 1), should lead to a greater magnitude of combination treatment effects. In support of this, Fournier et al. (2010) examined the benefit of antidepressants relative to placebo across a wide range of initial symptom severity in patients diagnosed with depression. Ultimately, they found that the magnitude of benefit of antidepressant medication compared with placebo varied as a function of baseline severity of depressive symptoms, where minimal benefit was observed for patients with mild or moderate symptoms, and substantial benefit was observed for patients with very severe depression. These data suggest that greater effects of adding pharmacotherapy (i.e., antidepressant medication) to CBT will be achieved primarily for those at the highest level of baseline clinical severity.

Consistent with this notion, a randomized clinical trial comparing effects of combined CBT ($n = 227$) with antidepressant medication alone ($n = 225$) found modest enhancement of recovery in a sample of 452 adults outpatients with chronic or recurrent MDD. Patients with severe (nonchronic) depression evinced substantially greater benefit from combined treatment as compared to antidepressant medication alone (Hollon et al., 2014). These findings are consistent with findings from earlier studies that found patients with severe recurrent depression were particularly likely to benefit from combined treatment relative to psychotherapy alone (Thase et al., 1997). Furthermore, Thase and colleagues found that less-severely depressed patients treated with CBT alone achieved comparable results to those who received combined therapy— a finding that has been observed in other studies examining patients with chronic depression (Kocsis et al., 2009). Thus, it may be that combination strategies may confer most benefit to those with severe, refractory, or significantly debilitating clinical disorders (Thase & Howland, 1994), whereas, individuals with chronic, less severe depression may not necessarily benefit from this additive strategy.

Studies that examine combination treatment as a sequential treatment strategy also tend to show additive treatment benefits. For these trials, Group 1 patients have been effectively eliminated. For example, combination treatments may confer greater benefits in treatment-refractory populations (Lynch et al., 2011; Spijker et al., 2013). RCTs have evinced support that CBT as an adjunctive to usual care (which included pharmacotherapy) is more cost-effective and effective in reducing depressive symptoms in treatment-resistant adults (as compared to usual care alone; Wiles et al., 2014). For instance, in the multisite RCT, researchers examined the effectiveness of CBT as an adjunct to usual care (including pharmacotherapy) for primary care (73 UK general practices) patients with treatment-resistant depression as compared with usual care alone (Wiles et al., 2014). The final sample included 469 patients (aged 18–75 years) who were randomly assigned to either: usual care ($n = 235$) or CBT in addition to usual care ($n = 234$). Participants who received CBT achieved near double the response relative to usual care. However, this study only shows that sequential treatment works for patients like these with treatment-resistant depression, not that CBT might be necessary as an alternative to psychopharmacology in all cases. For example, results from the largest trial conducted to date examining the effectiveness of using combination strategies in a medication nonresponsive population (Sequenced Treatment Alternatives to Relieve Depression; STAR*D), indicated that no particular augmentation strategy emerged as superior in achieving remission rates for patients (Warden et al., 2007).

COMBINATION TREATMENT FOR UNIPOLAR DEPRESSION—MAINTENANCE OF TREATMENT GAINS

Despite the relatively mixed findings for the overall use of combination treatment in depression, there is clearer evidence for significant benefits for adding CBT during the acute phase of medication treatment for the purpose of maintaining gains. Specifically, one study found a 15% relapse rate among patients in combination treatment (CBT with antidepressant) as compared to higher rates of 20%, 32%, and 50% in patients with CBT alone, pharmacotherapy alone (maintained), and pharmacotherapy (short-term), respectively (Evans et al., 1992). Moreover, a meta-analytic review of eight studies (442 patients; Guidi, Fava, Fava, & Papakostas, 2011) examined whether the sequential integration of psychotherapy and pharmacotherapy in the prevention of relapse and recurrence in MDD could serve as a viable strategy. Ultimately, findings suggest a relative advantage in preventing relapse/recurrence for the sequential administration of treatments. Patients that were randomized to receive psychotherapy while antidepressants were discontinued were significantly less likely to experience relapse/recurrence compared to controls. Subgroup analyses evinced a trend favoring psychotherapy during continuation of antidepressant drugs compared to antidepressants or treatment as usual (relative risk: 0.84, 95% CI 0.67−1.05). Hence, the sequential administration of psychotherapy after response to acute-phase pharmacotherapy, may serve as a buffer from experiencing relapse and recurrence in MDD.

In summary, combination strategies for the treatment of depression may be beneficial among depressive disorders, although with greatest benefits being observed in specific subgroups (severe, nonchronic) of patients. Moreover, combined treatments show a useful but not unique role in sequential treatment for patients failing to respond to initial pharmacotherapy, and demonstrate a useful role in helping patients responding to pharmacotherapy maintain their gains and discontinue their pharmacotherapy.

Evidence for Bipolar Depression

Given the primacy of pharmacology with mood stabilizers in the management of bipolar disorder, the model for combination treatment for this disorder has been the addition of CBT to ongoing pharmacotherapy. At this writing, the most commonly used mood stabilizers include lithium, Depakote, and Tegretol (carbamazepine) (Davis, Williams, & Cates, 2004; Goodwin, 2003). CBT has then been added to this core frontline treatment with the goals ranging from medication adherence and relapse prevention to treatment of the bipolar depression that represents a core debilitating component of the disorder (Miklowitz et al., 2007).

Typically in patients taking at least a mood stabilizer, and in many cases in patients taking a mood stabilizer in conjunction with other antidepressant or anxiolytic agents, CBT can also be applied as a relapse prevention strategy during a phase of relative euthymia. For instance, recent trials have demonstrated efficacy of adding CBT in enhancing long-term outcome in individuals already on lithium treatment (Fava et al., 2001). In studies of this kind, relatively brief CBT (often in the range of 12 to 18 sessions) has been found to reduce current symptoms as well as the relapse rate over time, particularly for depressive relapse (Lam et al., 2003; Scott, Garland, & Moorhead, 2001; Zaretsky, Lancee, Miller, Harris, & Parikh, 2008). Furthermore, RCTs have demonstrated support for adjunctive psychosocial interventions (e.g., CBT) in aiding mood stabilization, delaying relapses and reducing symptoms and/or symptom severity (Miklowitz, 2008; Szentagotai & David, 2010). In particular, combined treatment can be effective in the long term for patients with refractory bipolar disorder as evinced in a 5-year follow-up study of a combined treatment as compared with a standard pharmacological treatment (Isasi et al., 2014). Specifically, 40 adult patients with a history of severe or severe progression in the disorder despite adequate pharmacological treatment (defined as two or more relapse events in the preceding year), recent suicide attempts, persistent affective symptoms (3 months), or severe difficulties in social—occupational functioning were included. The combined treatment evinced lower depressive and anxiety symptoms at the 6-month, 12-month, and 5-year evaluation time points, indicating that combined therapy is effective for the long-term in patients with refractory bipolar disorder.

Recent applications of CBT to bipolar disorder have also included cost-effective group interventions, with significant benefits to bipolar depression and quality of life, as well as reductions in the frequency and duration of mood episodes (Costa et al., 2012). Also, CBT that is similar to that used for unipolar depression but includes strategies for relapse prevention as well as early detection and intervention for (hypo)mania has been shown to be efficacious (e.g., Miklowitz et al., 2007; Zaretsky et al., 2008). Indeed, findings have shown CBT to be effective in the same cohort of patients taking mood stabilizers for whom antidepressant medication offered no additional efficacy (Miklowitz et al., 2007; Sachs et al., 2007).

Also, mindfulness-based CBT (MBCT), a type of treatment based on mindfulness practices with elements of CBT and originally developed for preventing relapse in remitted patients with recurrent major depressive episodes (Segal, Williams, & Teasdale, 2002; Williams, Teasdale, Segal, & Kabat-Zinn, 2007), has recently been applied to bipolar disorder. This recent application was utilized in part to target the cognitive and role dysfunction that accompanies the disorder. Previous open trials have shown promising outcomes, including reductions in depression, increased well-being and psychosocial functioning, and significant improvements in executive functioning, memory, and the ability to initiate and complete tasks (Williams et al., 2008; Miklowitz et al., 2009; Deckersbach et al, 2012; Stange et al., 2011). However, one randomized trial of MBCT in bipolar disorder did not find significant benefits (as compared to usual care) on depression or hypomania symptoms over 12 months (Perich et al., 2013). Several other psychosocial interventions adjunctive to pharmacological agents have also been developed to treat bipolar disorder; including, interpersonal and social rhythm therapy (IPSRT), and family focused treatment (FFT) (for a review, see Miklowitz, 2008).

ANXIETY-RELATED DISORDERS

The advantages of combination treatment for the anxiety-related disorders are variable, with some evidence indicating smaller combined treatment effects in OCD and SAD, and stronger effects in panic disorder and GAD (Bandelow et al., 2007; Foa, Franklin, & Moser, 2002; Hofmann, Sawyer, Korte, & Smits, 2009), reflecting in part the degree of advantage of CBT over placebo for these disorders (Hofmann & Smits, 2008). Moreover, the degree of acute benefits of combined treatment need to be considered relative to the maintenance of treatment gains. Despite several studies showing increased efficacy for combined treatment strategies during the acute and maintenance phases of treatment, discontinuation of pharmacotherapy has been shown to lead to relapse of symptoms (Barlow et al, 2000; Marks et al.,

1993; for a review, see Otto et al., 2010a). In support of this, a review of 21 randomized trials demonstrated that combined therapy outperformed both antidepressant pharmacotherapy and psychotherapy (e.g., CBT) after the acute phase of treatment. However, during follow-up periods after medication was discontinued, combined therapy remained more efficacious than pharmacotherapy alone yet was not more efficacious than psychotherapy alone (Furukawa, Watanabe, & Churchill, 2007).

Part of the loss of efficacy from medication discontinuation may be explained by context effects. A wealth of animal studies and an increasing number of human studies show that relative safety learned from exposure is learned in relation to both internal and external contexts; when the context changes, some of the learned safety may be lost (for a review, see Otto et al., 2005). That is, the relative safety learned from CBT while taking medications is not necessarily retained when medications are discontinued, thereby conferring a cost to combination treatments that are not faced by CBT alone (Otto et al., 2010a). Engagement in CBT during and after the period of medication discontinuation, thereby bridging the gap between the context of being on and being off medication—helps prevent this relapse and can extend treatment gains (see "CBT for Medication Discontinuation in the Anxiety Disorders" section).

In addition, attributions about treatment effects may also complicate the maintenance of combination treatment for the anxiety disorders. In one of the earliest studies regarding this topic, Başoğlu et al. (1994) examined a subset of individuals with panic disorder with agoraphobia, as part a larger study of the benzodiazepine alprazolam and exposure therapy, alone and in combination. Patients receiving combined treatment who attributed their gains to the medication were more likely to report withdrawal symptoms and more likely to relapse as compared to those who attributed their gains to their own efforts. These findings suggest that stronger attributions to external factors (i.e., medication) are associated with earlier and more severe relapse. Also, it appears that some of the value of combination treatment may be due to expectation (placebo effects) alone. Specifically, a review of three RCTs indicated that patients receiving CBT plus placebo responded better to treatment than those receiving CBT alone at the end of acute treatment (Furukawa, Watanabe, Omori, & Churchill, 2007). Expectations about pill efficacy and attributions about gains in combination treatment may also detract from CBT efficacy over time. For example, Başoğlu et al. (1994) reported that attributions of improvement to a study pill significantly predicted relapse in panic disorder patients treated with exposure in combination with medication. Likewise, Biondi and Picardi (2003) reported that making external, medication attributions about the source of treatment efficacy for panic disorder was associated with a 60% relapse rate, whereas making internal attributions was associated with a 0% relapse rate. Finally, in an experimental paradigm with claustrophobic individuals, that manipulated expectancy about the effects of placebo, Powers et al. (2009) found a relapse rate of 39% among participants who were led to believe that the study pill had a sedating effect, whereas a relapse rate of 0% was observed among participants who were led to believe the pill had a stimulating or no effect.

CBT FOR MEDICATION DISCONTINUATION IN THE ANXIETY DISORDERS

Medication discontinuation for the anxiety disorders is marked by the return of symptoms (Donovan, Glue, Kolluri, & Emir, 2010), much like it is for major depression. In addition, the discontinuation of benzodiazepine medication is associated with anxiety-like withdrawal symptoms similar to those motivating treatment seeking in the first place (Roy-Byrne & Hommer, 1988; Tyrer, Murphy, & Riley, 1990). These symptoms appear to interact with core fears inherent in the disorder, such as the fears of anxiety-related symptoms in panic disorder (Otto, Hong, & Safren, 2002) and posttraumatic stress disorder (Risse et al., 1990). Brief CBT programs have been developed to aid discontinuation success and the maintenance of treatment gains (e.g., Otto et al., 1993, 2010b), with all emphasizing the use of interoceptive exposure (exposure to feared internal sensations) to help patients become resilient to fears of anxiety and withdrawal sensations (for a treatment manual see Otto & Pollack, 2009). These treatments have been met with consistent success, and support the hypothesis that CBT offered during the medication taper and thereafter can help patients discontinue their benzodiazepine medication and maintain or extend their treatment gains (Bruce, Spiegel, & Hegel, 1999; Otto et al., 2010b). Moreover, there is similar evidence for the application of brief CBT to aid antidepressant discontinuation in panic disorder (e.g., Whittal, Otto, & Hong, 2001), as well as CBT for benzodiazepine discontinuation for patients with GAD (Gosselin et al., 2006) and insomnia (Morin, Bélanger, Bastien, & Vallières, 2005).

COMBINATION TREATMENTS FOR OTHER DISORDERS

There are also a number of disorders for which combination treatment represents the standard application for CBT—namely, psychiatric disorders where pharmacotherapy has long been considered the core treatment modality. In recent years, studies have shown that CBT can add significantly to the outcomes provided by medication in disorders such as schizophrenia, and adult ADHD.

Schizophrenia

Recent research has documented an important role for CBT in the management of schizophrenia. Yet, as CBT approaches to schizophrenia have been expanded, there has been some evidence of decreasing effect sizes from the promising initial medium to large effects reported by Gould, Mueser, Bolton, Mays, and Goff (2001). Recent meta-analyses of 34 studies examining CBT for the symptoms of schizophrenia indicate effects in the small-to-medium range for overall and positive symptoms, and very small for negative symptoms (Jauhar et al., 2014). Somewhat larger effect sizes (in the medium range) have been reported when CBT strategies are applied specifically to medication-resistant cases (Burns, Erickson, & Brenner, 2014), perhaps providing a more exact measure of CBT benefit when variability in response to medication is minimized by choosing nonresponsive cases. Regardless of reason, it is promising that CBT can exert beneficial effects to those patients for whom medication offers limited benefits.

Attention-Deficit Hyperactivity Disorder

ADHD is another disorder where medication treatment is the primary intervention. Nonetheless, studies have shown that CBT interventions can add significant benefit. In an initial trial, Safren et al. (2005) showed that adults with ADHD who were stabilized on medication achieved clinically significant gains, including lower severity of ADHD symptoms, as well as lower anxiety and depression with the addition of CBT. Utilizing a similar design, Emilsson et al. (2011) found advantages for CBT compared to usual medication treatment reflecting medium-to-large effect sizes, with evidence of continued treatment gains over follow-up. Use of a more stringent control group continued to support the efficacy of CBT (Safren et al., 2010). Also, there is tentative evidence that these specialized CBT programs for ADHD are effective for individuals off medication, but the trial was too small to delineate the additive effect of medication to CBT alone (Weiss et al., 2012). Other studies investigating adjunctive treatments such as cognitive remediation (as compared to waitlist; Stevenson et al., 2002), metacognitive therapies (Safren et al., 2010; Solanto et al., 2010), and an open-label trial on mindfulness meditation (Zylowska et al., 2008) have contributed to the literature on cognitive and behavioral therapies (more broadly defined) enhance improvements in adults with ADHD.

PREFERENCE, TOLERABILITY, AND AVAILABILITY OF COMBINED TREATMENT

Psychological treatment for anxiety and mood disorders is preferred to pharmacologic treatment, on the order of a threefold preference for psychological therapy when each treatment type is offered individually (McHugh, Whitton, Peckam, Weige, & Otto, 2013). Yet, preference for treatment does appear to be dependent on treatment history. There is some evidence that when patients initiate treatment with pharmacotherapy and are given a subsequent choice of additional pharmacotherapy or CBT, the latter may be selected by only a minority of patients (Wisniewski et al., 2007), in direct opposition to the near 3:1 preference seen across studies in general (McHugh et al., 2013). Hence, initial selection and acculturation to treatment may affect the acceptability of a subsequent switch to an alternative treatment modality. In the STAR*D trial, patients who were better educated and had a family history of a mood disorder were more likely to accept CBT as a second step treatment strategy (Wisniewski et al., 2007).

There is also evidence for greater retention of patients in CBT than pharmacotherapy. For example, in meta-analyses examining treatment discontinuation rates across anxiety disorders treated with CBT and pharmacotherapy either alone or in combination, dropout rates in CBT were lower or equivalent to rates for pharmacotherapy alone (Otto, Smits, & Reese, 2005). Moreover, combined CBT and SSRIs was found to lead to dropout rates comparable to pharmacotherapy alone among panic disorder, while rates of discontinuation in CBT alone were significantly less. Large-scale studies of OCD (Foa et al., 2005) and SAD (Davidson et al., 2004) demonstrated trends toward higher dropout in combined treatment as compared to CBT alone as well. This trend, however, was not observed in a multicenter trial examining panic disorder (Barlow et al., 2000).

Similarly, in a meta-analysis comparing pharmacological and psychological interventions for depression, Cuijpers et al. (2008) found significantly lower dropout rates for psychological interventions as compared to medication. With regard to combination treatment, Cuijpers et al. (2009) examined the addition of psychotherapy as an augmentation of pharmacotherapy for depression and revealed a significantly lower dropout rate for combined treatment than pharmacotherapy alone.

Taken together, studies indicate that for both anxiety and depression, treatment with psychotherapy is preferred at the outset of treatment and appears equally, if not more, tolerable than pharmacotherapy alone and combined strategies. Given such findings, it is possible to conclude that combination strategies offer no discernible advantage to CBT with regard to retention of patients.

Although CBT has proven to be a well-tolerated and efficacious intervention, availability of state-of-the art CBT differs greatly from pharmacotherapy, making the attainment of combination treatment out of reach for many individuals. Although both psychiatric specialists and primary care physicians are available to administer pharmacological interventions, the dissemination of CBT to community settings has proceeded slowly. Indeed, despite evidence that CBT can successfully be disseminated to community settings (Addis et al., 2004; Stuart, Treat, & Wade, 2000), studies of patients with anxiety disorders in primary care and specialty care settings indicate that only about one-tenth to one-third of these patients receive CBT (Goisman, Warshaw, & Keller, 1999; Stein et al., 2004). Despite more recent studies showing some promise for both the implementation and acceptability of computerized CBT Kaltenthaler et al. (2008), limitations with this method exist and pharmacotherapy still remains the more easily obtained form of treatment.

NEW DIRECTIONS

Given the modest findings regarding traditional combination strategies in the treatment of psychiatric disorders, a novel approach in enhancing learning through the use of pharmacotherapy during CBT has recently emerged. In particular, research in the past decade has investigated the use of D-cycloserine (DCS), a N-methyl-D-aspartate (NMDA) partial agonist, as one particular adjunctive method to enhance exposure-based treatments for anxiety disorders (Ressler et al., 2004). Informed by basic animal findings where DCS has reliably augmented extinction learning in animals (Walker, Ressler, Lu, & Davis, 2002; Ledgerwood et al., 2003; Norberg et al., 2012), DCS has now been used in humans undergoing exposure-based CBT (EBT; Bontempo, Panza, & Bloch, 2012). This model of treatment reflects the use of pharmacotherapy not to directly treat a disorder but to enhance the learning processes of CBT; as such, it represents attention to Group 5 patients (those patients who may need an augmented version of CBT to respond). Enhanced extinction learning with DCS has been demonstrated in studies of varying clinical disorders including height phobia, social anxiety, and OCD (e.g., Ressler et al., 2004; Hofmann et al., 2006; Hofmann et al., 2013; Wilhelm et al., 2008). Meta-analytic review supports the overall efficacy of DCS in enhancing treatment for anxiety disorders (Bontempo et al., 2012; Norberg et al., 2012), as compared to

CBT-alone, although ongoing research indicates that effect sizes for this strategy may be decreasing over time, and that important moderators will suggest more judicious use of this strategy (Otto et al., 2016a). Nonetheless, the relative success of DCS has ignited the search for other novel combination treatment strategies that may target the augmentation of CBT effects rather than direct anxiolysis (Hofmann et al., 2011; Nations et al., 2012; Powers et al., 2009; Telch et al., 2014).

SUMMARY AND CONCLUSIONS

Overall, the research literature provides a complex picture on the efficacy of combination treatments. In general, benefits of combination treatment appear to be modest at best for unselected samples of patients and come with issues of medication adherence and discontinuation for the longer term management of patients. Nonetheless, there is a stronger role for combination treatment for selected cohorts of patients, although clear designation of the specific characteristics of this cohort (e.g., severity or chronicity) is still lacking replication. There is also more consistent evidence for the benefits of combination treatment when nonresponders to one modality are crossed over to the other modality of treatment. In addition, there is hope for a new model for combination treatment, where pharmacotherapy is used to enhance the therapeutic learning from CBT, rather than providing direct mood or anxiety reductions. Yet, as with other combination treatment strategies even this new strategy is evolving toward judicious use, with assumptions that important treatment moderators may be at work.

References

Abramowitz, J. S. (1997). Effectiveness of psychological and pharmacological treatments for obsessive-compulsive disorder: A quantitative review. *Journal of Consulting and Clinical Psychology, 65*, 44.

Addis, M. E., Hatgis, C., Krasnow, A. D., Jacob, K., Bourne, L., & Mansfield, A. (2004). Effectiveness of cognitive-behavioral treatment for panic disorder versus treatment as usual in a managed care setting. *Journal of Consulting and Clinical Psychology, 72*, 625.

Anderson, I. M., Nutt, D. J., & Deakin, J. F. W. (2000). Evidence-based guidelines for treating depressive disorders with antidepressants: A revision of the 1993 British Association for Psychopharmacology guidelines. *Journal of Psychopharmacology, 14*, 3–20.

Bandelow, B., Seidler-Brandler, U., Becker, A., Wedekind, D., & Rüther, E. (2007). Meta-analysis of randomized controlled comparisons of psychopharmacological and psychological treatments for anxiety disorders. *The World Journal of Biological Psychiatry, 8*, 175–187.

Barlow, D. H., Gorman, J. M., Shear, M. K., & Woods, S. W. (2000). Cognitive-behavioral therapy, imipramine, or their combination for panic disorder: A randomized controlled trial. *Journal of the American Medical Association, 283*, 2529–2536.

Başoğlu, M., Marks, I. M., Swinson, R. P., Noshirvani, H., O'Sullivan, G., & Kuch, K. (1994). Pre-treatment predictors of treatment outcome in panic disorder and agoraphobia treated with alprazolam and exposure. *Journal of Affective Disorders, 30*, 123–132.

Biondi, M., & Picardi, A. (2003). Increased probability of remaining in remission from panic disorder with agoraphobia after drug treatment in patients who received concurrent cognitive-behavioural therapy: A follow-up study. *Psychotherapy and Psychosomatics, 72*, 34–42.

Bontempo, A., Panza, K. E., & Bloch, M. H. (2012). D-Cycloserine augmentation of behavioral therapy for the treatment of anxiety disorders: A meta-analysis. *Journal of Clinical Psychiatry, 73*, 533–537.

Bruce, T. J., Spiegel, D. A., & Hegel, M. T. (1999). Cognitive-behavioral therapy helps prevent relapse and recurrence of panic disorder following alprazolam discontinuation: A long-term follow-up of the Peoria and Dartmouth studies. *American Journal of Psychiatry, 67*, 151–156.

Burns, A. M., Erickson, D. H., & Brenner, C. A. (2014). Cognitive-behavioral therapy for medication-resistant psychosis: A meta-analytic review. *Psychiatric Services, 65*, 874–880.

Costa, R. T., Cheniaux, E., Rangé, B. P., Versiani, M., & Nardi, A. E. (2012). Group cognitive behavior therapy for bipolar disorder can improve the quality of life. *Brazilian Journal of Medical and Biological Research, 45*, 862–868.

Cuijpers, P., Andersson, G., Donker, T., & van Straten, A. (2011). Psychological treatment of depression: Results of a series of meta-analyses. *Nordic Journal of Psychiatry, 65*, 354–364.

Cuijpers, P., Dekker, J., Hollon, S. D., & Andersson, G. (2009). Adding psychotherapy to pharmacotherapy in the treatment of depressive disorders in adults: A meta-analysis. *Journal of Clinical Psychiatry, 70*, 1–478.

Cuijpers, P., Hollon, S. D., van Straten, A., Bockting, C., Berking, M., & Andersson, G. (2013). Does cognitive behaviour therapy have an enduring effect that is superior to keeping patients on continuation pharmacotherapy? A meta-analysis. *BMJ Open, 3*, e002542.

Cuijpers, P., Turner, E. H., Mohr, D. C., Hofmann, S. G., Andersson, G., Berking, M., & Coyne, J. (2014). Comparison of psychotherapies for adult depression to pill placebo control groups: A meta-analysis. *Psychological Medicine, 44*, 685–695.

Cuijpers, P., van Straten, A., van Oppen, P., & Andersson, G. (2008). Are psychological and pharmacologic interventions equally effective in the treatment of adult depressive disorders? A meta-analysis of comparative studies. *Journal of Clinical Psychiatry, 69*, 1–478.

Davidson, J. R., Foa, E. B., Huppert, J. D., Keefe, F. J., Franklin, M. E., Compton, J. S., ... Gadde, K. M. (2004). Fluoxetine, comprehensive cognitive behavioral therapy, and placebo in generalized social phobia. *Archives of General Psychiatry, 61*, 1005–1013.

Davis, L. L., Williams, R., & Cates, M. (2004). Divalproex sodium in the treatment of adults with bipolar disorder. *Expert Review Neurotherapeutics, 4*(3), 349–362.

Deacon, B. J., & Abramowitz, J. S. (2004). Cognitive and behavioral treatments for anxiety disorders: A review of meta-analytic findings. *Journal of Clinical Psychology, 60*, 429–441.

Deckersbach, T., Hölzel, B. K., Eisner, L. R., Stange, J. P., Peckham, A. D., Dougherty, D. D., ... Nierenberg, A. A. (2012). Mindfulness-based cognitive therapy for nonremitted patients with bipolar disorder. *CNS Neuroscience & Therapeutics, 18*, 133–141.

de Maat, S. M., Dekker, J., Schoevers, R. A., & de Jonghe, F. (2007). Relative efficacy of psychotherapy and combined therapy in the treatment of depression: A meta-analysis. *European Psychiatry, 22*, 1–8.

Dobson, K. S., Hollon, S. D., Dimidjian, S., Schmaling, K. B., Kohlenberg, R. J., Gallop, R. J., ... Jacobson, N. S. (2008). Randomized trial of behavioral activation, cognitive therapy, and antidepressant medication in the prevention of relapse and recurrence in major depression. *Journal of Consulting and Clinical Psychology, 76*, 468.

Donovan, M. R., Glue, P., Kolluri, S., & Emir, B. (2010). Comparative efficacy of antidepressants in preventing relapse in anxiety disorders: A meta-analysis. *Journal of Affective Disorders, 123*, 9−16.

Emilsson, B., Gudjonsson, G., Sigurdsson, J. F., Baldursson, G., Einarsson, E., Olafsdottir, H., & Young, S. (2011). Cognitive behaviour therapy in medication-treated adults with ADHD and persistent symptoms: A randomized controlled trial. *BMC Psychiatry, 11*, 116.

Evans, M. D., Hollon, S. D., DeRubeis, R. J., Piasecki, J. M., Grove, W. M., Garvey, M. J., & Tuason, V. B. (1992). Differential relapse following cognitive therapy and pharmacotherapy for depression. *Archives of General Psychiatry, 49*, 802.

Fava, G. A., Bartolucci, G., Rafanelli, C., & Mangelli, L. (2001). Cognitive-behavioral management of patients with bipolar disorder who relapsed while on lithium prophylaxis. *Journal of Clinical Psychiatry, 62*, 556−559.

Foa, E. B., Franklin, M. E., & Moser, J. (2002). Context in the clinic: How well do cognitive-behavioral therapies and medications work in combination? *Biological Psychiatry, 52*, 987−997.

Foa, E. B., Liebowitz, M. R., Kozak, M. J., Davies, S., Campeas, R., Franklin, M. E., ... Simpson, H. B. (2005). Randomized, placebo-controlled trial of exposure and ritual prevention, clomipramine, and their combination in the treatment of obsessive-compulsive disorder. *American Journal of Psychiatry, 162*, 151−161.

Fournier, J. C., DeRubeis, R. J., Hollon, S. D., Dimidjian, S., Amsterdam, J. D., Shelton, R. C., & Fawcett, J. (2010). Antidepressant drug effects and depression severity: a patient-level meta-analysis. *Journal of the American Medical Association, 303*, 47−53, PubMed Central PMCID: PMC3712503

Fournier, J. C., DeRubeis, R. J., Hollon, S. D., Gallop, R., Shelton, R. C., & Amsterdam, J. D. (2013). Differential change in specific depressive symptoms during antidepressant medication or cognitive therapy. *Behaviour Research and Therapy, 51*, 392−398.

Furukawa, T. A., Watanabe, N., & Churchill, R. (2006). Psychotherapy plus antidepressant for panic disorder with or without agoraphobia: Systematic review. *British Journal of Psychiatry, 188*, 305−312.

Furukawa, T. A., Watanabe, N., Omori, I. M., & Churchill, R. (2007). Can pill placebo augment cognitive-behavior therapy for panic disorder? *BMC Psychiatry, 7*, 73, PubMed Central PMCID: PMC2225396.

Goisman, R. M., Warshaw, M. G., & Keller, M. B. (1999). Psychosocial treatment prescriptions for generalized anxiety disorder, panic disorder, and social phobia, 1991−1996. *American Journal of Psychiatry, 156*, 1819−1821.

Goodwin, F. K. (2003). Rationale for using lithium in combination with other mood stabilizers in the management of bipolar disorder. *Journal of Clinical Psychiatry, 64*(Suppl 5), 18−24.

Gosselin, P., Ladouceur, R., Morin, C. M., Dugas, M. J., & Baillargeon, L. (2006). Benzodiazepine discontinuation among adults with GAD: A randomized trial of cognitive-behavioral therapy. *Journal of Consulting and Clinical Psychology, 74*, 908−919.

Gould, R. A., Buckminster, S., Pollack, M. H., Otto, M. W., & Yap, L. (1997). Cognitive-behavioral and pharmacological treatment for social phobia: A meta-analysis. *Clinical Psychology: Science and Practice, 4*, 291−306.

Gould, R. A., Mueser, K. T., Bolton, E., Mays, V., & Goff, D. (2001). Cognitive therapy for psychosis in schizophrenia: An effect size analysis. *Schizophrenia Research, 48*, 335−342.

Guidi, J., Fava, G. A., Fava, M., & Papakostas, G. I. (2011). Efficacy of the sequential integration of psychotherapy and pharmacotherapy in major depressive disorder: A preliminary meta-analysis. *Psychological Medicine, 41*, 321−331.

Haby, M. M., Tonge, B., Littlefield, L., Carter, R., & Vos, T. (2004). Cost-effectiveness of cognitive behavioural therapy and selective serotonin reuptake inhibitors for major depression in children and adolescents. *Australian and New Zealand Journal of Psychiatry, 38,* 579–591.

Hidalgo, R. B., Barnett, S. D., & Davidson, J. R. (2001). Social anxiety disorder in review: Two decades of progress. *International Journal of Neuropsychopharmacology, 4,* 279–298.

Heuzenroeder, L., Donnelly, M., Haby, M. M., Mihalopoulos, C., Rossell, R., Carter, R., . . . Vos, T. (2004). Cost-effectiveness of psychological and pharmacological interventions for generalized anxiety disorder and panic disorder. *Australian and New Zealand Journal of Psychiatry, 38,* 602–612.

Hofmann, S. G., Meuret, A. E., Smits, J. A., Simon, N. M., Pollack, M. H., Eisenmenger, K., . . . Otto, M. W. (2006). Augmentation of exposure therapy with D-cycloserine for social anxiety disorder. *Archives of General Psychiatry, 63,* 298–304.

Hofmann, S. G., Sawyer, A. T., Korte, K. J., & Smits, J. A. J. (2009). Is it beneficial to add pharmacotherapy to cognitive-behavioral therapy when treating anxiety disorders? A meta-analytic review. *International Journal of Cognitive Therapy, 2,* 160–175.

Hofmann, S. G., & Smits, J. A. J. (2008). Cognitive-behavioral therapy for adult anxiety disorders: A meta-analysis of randomized placebo-controlled trials. *Journal of Clinical Psychiatry, 69,* 621.

Hofmann, S. G., Smits, J. A., Asnaani, A., Gutner, C. A., & Otto, M. W. (2011). Cognitive enhancers for anxiety disorders. *Pharmacology, Biochemistry, and Behavior, 99,* 275–284.

Hofmann, S. G., Smits, J. A. J., Rosenfield, D., Simon, N., Otto, M. W., Meuret, A. E., . . . Pollack, M. H. (2013). D-Cycloserine as an augmentation strategy of cognitive behavioral therapy for social anxiety disorder. *American Journal of Psychiatry, 170,* 751–758.

Hollon, S. D., DeRubeis, R. J., Fawcett, J., Amsterdam, J. D., Shelton, R. C., Zajecka, J., . . . Gallop, R. (2014). Effect of cognitive therapy with antidepressant medications versus antidepressants alone on the rate of recovery in major depressive disorder: A randomized clinical trial. *JAMA Psychiatry, 71,* 1157–1164.

Hollon, S. D., Garber, J., & Shelton, R. C. (2005). Treatment of depression in adolescents with cognitive behavior therapy and medications: A commentary on the TADS project. *Cognitive and Behavioral Practice, 12,* 149–155.

Isasi, A. G., Echeburua, E., Liminana, J. M., & Gonzalez-Pinto, A. (2014). Psychoeducation and cognitive-behavioral therapy for patients with refractory bipolar disorder: A 5-year controlled clinical trial. *European Psychiatry, 29,* 134–141.

Jauhar, S., McKenna, P. J., Radua, J., Fung, E., Salvador, R., & Laws, K. R. (2014). Cognitive-behavioural therapy for the symptoms of schizophrenia: A systematic review and meta-analysis with examination of potential bias. *British Journal of Psychiatry, 204,* 20–29.

Jones, S., & Hayward, P. (2004). *Coping with schizophrenia: A CBT guide for patients, families and caregivers.* Oneworld Publications.

Kaltenthaler, E., Parry, G., Beverley, C., & Ferriter, M. (2008). Computerised cognitive–behavioural therapy for depression: A systematic review. *The British Journal of Psychiatry, 193,* 181–184.

Keller, M. B., McCullough, J. P., Klein, D. N., Arnow, B., Dunner, D. L., Gelenberg, A. J., . . . Zajecka, J. (2000). A comparison of nefazodone, the cognitive behavioral-analysis system of psychotherapy, and their combination for the treatment of chronic depression. *New England Journal of Medicine, 342,* 1462–1470.

Keller, M. B., Yan, B., Musgnung, J., Dunner, D., Ferguson, J., Friedman, E., . . . Nemeroff, C. (2007). Two-year placebo-controlled maintenance study to assess recurrence prevention with venlafaxine XR in patients with recurrent unipolar major depression. *European Psychiatry, 22,* S241.

Kessler, R. C., Berglund, P., Demler, O., Jin, R., Koretz, D., Merikangas, K. R., . . . Wang, P. S. (2003). The epidemiology of major depressive disorder: Results from the National Comorbidity Survey Replication (NCS-R). *JAMA, 289*, 3095–3105.

Kessler, R. C., Berglund, P., Demler, O., Jin, R., Merikangas, K. R., & Walters, E. E. (2005). Lifetime prevalence and age-of-onset distributions of DSM-IV disorders in the National Comorbidity Survey Replication. *Archives of General Psychiatry, 62*, 593–602.

Kocsis, J. H., Leon, A. C., Markowitz, J. C., Manber, R., Arnow, B., Klein, D. N., . . . Thase, M. E. (2009). Patient preference as a moderator of outcome for chronic forms of major depressive disorder treated with nefazodone, cognitive behavioral analysis system of psychotherapy, or their combination. *Journal of Clinical Psychiatry, 70*, 354–361.

Lam, D. H., Watkins, E. R., Hayward, P., Bright, J., Wright, K., Kerr, N., . . . Sham, P. (2003). A randomized controlled study of cognitive therapy for relapse prevention for bipolar affective disorder: Outcome of the first year. *Archives of General Psychiatry, 60*, 145–152.

Ledgerwood, L., Richardson, R., & Cranney, J. (2003). Effects of D-cycloserine on extinction of conditioned freezing. *Behavioral Neuroscience, 117*, 341–349.

Lynch, F. L., Dickerson, J. F., Clarke, G., Vitiello, B., Porta, G., Wagner, K. D., . . . Ryan, N. D. (2011). Incremental cost-effectiveness of combined therapy vs medication only for youth with selective serotonin reuptake inhibitor–resistant depression: Treatment of SSRI-resistant depression in adolescents trial findings. *Archives of General Psychiatry, 68*, 253–262.

Marks, I. M., Swinson, R. P., Başoğlu, M., Kuch, K., Noshirvani, H., O'Sullivan, G., . . . Wickwire, K. (1993). Alprazolam and exposure alone and combined in panic disorder with agoraphobia: A controlled study in London and Toronto. *British Journal of Psychiatry, 162*, 776–787.

Mathers, C. D., & Loncar, D. (2006). Projections of global mortality and burden of disease from 2002 to 2030. *PLoS Medicine, 3*, e442.

Mavissakalian, M. R., & Perel, J. M. (1999). Long-term maintenance and discontinuation of imipramine therapy in panic disorder with agoraphobia. *Archives of General Psychiatry, 56*, 821–827.

McHugh, R. K., Otto, M. W., Barlow, D. H., Gorman, J. M., Shear, M. K., & Woods, S. W. (2007). Cost-efficacy of individual and combined treatments for panic disorder. *Journal of Clinical Psychiatry, 68*, 1–478.

McHugh, R. K., Whitton, S. W., Peckham, A. D., Welge, J. A., & Otto, M. W. (2013). Patient preference for psychological vs pharmacologic treatment of psychiatric disorders: A meta-analytic review. *Journal of Clinical Psychiatry, 74*, 1–478.

Miklowitz, D. J. (2008). Adjunctive psychotherapy for bipolar disorder: State of the evidence. *American Journal of Psychiatry, 165*, 1408–1419.

Miklowitz, D. J., Alatiq, Y., Goodwin, G. M., Geddes, J. R., Fennell, M. J., Dimidjian, S., . . . Williams, J. M. G. (2009). A pilot study of mindfulness-based cognitive therapy for bipolar disorder. *International Journal of Cognitive Therapy, 2*, 373–382.

Miklowitz, D. J., Otto, M. W., Frank, E., Reilly-Harrington, N. A., Wisniewski, S. R., Kogan, J. N., . . . Araga, M. (2007). Psychosocial treatments for bipolar depression: A 1-year randomized trial from the Systematic Treatment Enhancement Program. *Archives of General Psychiatry, 64*, 419–426.

Mitte, K. (2005). Meta-analysis of cognitive-behavioral treatments for generalized anxiety disorder: A comparison with pharmacotherapy. *Psychological Bulletin, 131*, 785.

Morin, C. M., Bélanger, L., Bastien, C., & Vallières, A. (2005). Long-term outcome after discontinuation of benzodiazepines for insomnia: A survival analysis of relapse. *Behavior Research and Therapy, 43*, 1–14.

Nations, K. R., Smits, J. A. J., Tolin, D. F., Rothbaum, B. O., Hofmann, S. G., Tart, C. D., . . . Otto, M. W. (2012). Evaluation of the glycine transporter inhibitor ORG 25935 as augmentation to cognitive-behavioral therapy for panic disorder. *Journal of Clinical Psychiatry, 73,* 647–653.

Nemeroff, C. B., Heim, C. M., Thase, M. E., Klein, D. N., Rush, A. J., Schatzberg, A. F., . . . Keller, M. B. (2003). Differential responses to psychotherapy versus pharmacotherapy in patients with chronic forms of major depression and childhood trauma. *Proceedings of the National Academy of Sciences of the United States of America, 100,* 14293–14296.

Norberg, M. M., Gilliam, C. M., Villavicencio, A., Pearlson, G. D., & Tolin, D. F. (2012). D-Cycloserine for treatment nonresponders with obsessive-compulsive disorder: A case report. *Cognitive Behavioral Practice, 19,* 338–345.

Otto, M. W., Hong, J. J., & Safren, S. A. (2002). Benzodiazepine discontinuation difficulties in panic disorder: Conceptual model and outcome for cognitive-behavior therapy. *Current Pharmaceutical Design, 8,* 75–80.

Otto, M. W., Kredlow, M. A., Smits, J. A. J., Hofmann, S. G., Tolin, D. F., de Kleine, R. A., . . . Pollack, M. H. (2016a). Enhancement of psychosocial treatment with D-cycloserine: Models, moderators, and future directions. *Biological Psychiatry, 80,* 274–283.

Otto, M. W., McHugh, R. K., & Kantak, K. M. (2010a). Combined pharmacotherapy and cognitive-behavioral therapy for anxiety disorders: Medication effects, glucocorticoids, and attenuated treatment outcomes. *Clinical Psychology: Science and Practice, 17,* 91–103.

Otto, M. W., McHugh, R. K., Simon, N. M., Farach, F. J., Worthington, J. J., & Pollack, M. H. (2010b). Efficacy of CBT for benzodiazepine discontinuation in patients with panic disorder: Further evaluation. *Behaviour Research and Therapy, 48,* 720–727.

Otto, M. W., & Pollack, M. H. (2009). *Stopping anxiety medication* (Therapist guide, 2nd ed.). New York: Oxford University Press.

Otto, M. W., Pollack, M. H., Dowd, S. M., Hofmann, S. G., Pearlson, G., Szuhany, K., . . . Tolin, D. F. (2016b). Randomized trial of D-cycloserine enhancement of cognitive-behavioral therapy for panic disorder. *Depression and Anxiety, 33,* 737–745.

Otto, M. W., Pollack, M. H., & Maki, K. M. (2000). Empirically supported treatments for panic disorder: Costs, benefits, and stepped care. *Journal of Consulting and Clinical Psychology, 68,* 556–563.

Otto, M. W., Pollack, M. H., Sachs, G. S., Reiter, S. R., Meltzer-Brody, S., & Rosenbaum, J. F. (1993). Discontinuation of benzodiazepine treatment: Efficacy of cognitive-behavioral therapy for patients with panic disorder. *American Journal of Psychiatry, 150,* 1485–1490.

Otto, M. W., Smits, J. A. J., & Reese, H. E. (2005). Combined psychotherapy and pharmacotherapy for mood and anxiety disorders in adults: Review and analysis. *Clinical Psychology: Science and Practice, 12,* 72–86.

Pampallona, S., Bollini, P., Tibaldi, G., Kupelnick, B., & Munizza, C. (2004). Combined pharmacotherapy and psychological treatment for depression: A systematic review. *Archives of General Psychiatry, 61,* 714–719.

Perich, T., Manicavasagar, V., Mitchell, P. B., Ball, J. R., & Hadzi-Pavlovic, D. (2013). A randomized controlled trial of mindfulness-based cognitive therapy for bipolar disorder. *Acta Psychiatrica Scandinavica, 127,* 333–343.

Pollack, M. H. (2005). The pharmacotherapy of panic disorder. *Journal of Clinical Psychiatry, 66*(Suppl 4), 23–27.

Powers, M. B., Smits, J. A. J., Otto, M. W., Sanders, C., & Emmelkamp, P. M. (2009). Facilitation of fear extinction in phobic participants with a novel cognitive enhancer: A randomized placebo controlled trial of yohimbine augmentation. *Journal of Anxiety Disorders, 23,* 350–356.

Ressler, K. J., Rothbaum, B. O., Tannenbaum, L., Anderson, P., Graap, K., Zimand, E., . . . Davis, M. (2004). Cognitive enhancers as adjuncts to psychotherapy: Use of D-cycloserine in phobic individuals to facilitate extinction of fear. *Archives of General Psychiatry, 61,* 1136–1144.

Reynolds, C. F., III, Dew, M. A., Pollock, B. G., Mulsant, B. H., Frank, E., Miller, M. D., ... Schlernitzauer, M. A. (2006). Maintenance treatment of major depression in old age. *New England Journal of Medicine, 354,* 1130–1138.

Risse, S. C., Whitters, A., & Burke, J. (1990). Severe withdrawal symptoms after discontinuation of alprazolam in eight patients with combat-induced posttraumatic stress disorder. *Journal of Clinical Psychiatry, 51,* 206–209.

Rocha, F. L., Fuzikawa, C., Riera, R., & Hara, C. (2012). Combination of antidepressants in the treatment of major depressive disorder: A systematic review and meta-analysis. *Journal of Clinical Psychopharmacology, 32,* 278–281.

Roshanaei-Moghaddam, B., Pauly, M. C., Atkins, D. C., Baldwin, S. A., Stein, M. B., & Roy-Byrne, P. (2011). Relative effects of CBT and pharmacotherapy in depression versus anxiety: Is medication somewhat better for depression, and CBT somewhat better for anxiety? *Depression and Anxiety, 28,* 560–567.

Rothbaum, B. O., Price, M., Jovanovic, T., Norrholm, S. D., Gerardi, M., Dunlop, B., ... Ressler, K. J. (2014). A randomized, double-blind evaluation of D-cycloserine or alprazolam combined with virtual reality exposure therapy for posttraumatic stress disorder in Iraq and Afghanistan War veterans. *American Journal of Psychiatry, 171,* 640–648, PubMed Central PMCID: PMC4115813.

Roy-Byrne, P. P., & Hommer, D. (1988). Benzodiazepine withdrawal: Overview and implications for the treatment of anxiety. *American Journal of Medicine, 84,* 1041–1052.

Saarni, S. I., Suvisaari, J., Sintonen, H., Pirkola, S., Koskinen, S., Aromaa, A., & Lonnqvist, J. (2007). Impact of psychiatric disorders on health-related quality of life: General population survey. *British Journal of Psychiatry, 190,* 326–332.

Sachs, G. S., Nierenberg, A. A., Calabrese, J. R., Marangell, L. B., Wisniewski, S. R., Gyulai, L., ... Ketter, T. A. (2007). Effectiveness of adjunctive antidepressant treatment for bipolar depression. *New England Journal of Medicine, 356,* 1711–1722.

Safren, S. A., Otto, M. W., Sprich, S., Perlman, C. L., Wilens, T. E., & Biederman, J. (2005). Cognitive behavioral therapy for ADHD in medication-treated adults with continued symptoms. *Behaviour Research and Therapy, 43,* 831–842.

Safren, S. A., Sprich, S., Mimiaga, M. J., Surman, C., Knouse, L., Groves, M., & Otto, M. W. (2010). Cognitive behavioral therapy vs relaxation with educational support for medication-treated adults with ADHD and persistent symptoms: A randomized controlled trial. *JAMA, 304,* 875–880.

Scott, J., Garland, A., & Moorhead, S. (2001). A pilot study of cognitive therapy in bipolar disorders. *Psychological Medicine, 31,* 459–467.

Segal, Z. V., Williams, J. M. G., & Teasdale, J. D. (2002). *Mindfulness-based cognitive therapy for depression.* New York: The Guilford Press.

Smit, F., Cuijpers, P., Oostenbrink, J., Batelaan, N., de Graaf, R., & Beekman, A. (2006). Costs of nine common mental disorders: Implications for curative and preventive psychiatry. *Journal of Mental Health Policy and Economics, 9,* 193–200.

Solanto, M. V., Marks, D. J., Wasserstein, J., Mitchell, K., Abikoff, H., Alvir, J. M. J., & Kofman, M. D. (2010). Efficacy of meta-cognitive therapy for adult ADHD. *American Journal of Psychiatry, 167,* 958–968.

Spijker, J., van Straten, A., Bockting, C. L., Meeuwissen, J. A., & van Balkom, A. J. (2013). Psychotherapy, antidepressants, and their combination for chronic major depressive disorder: A systematic review. *Canadian Journal of Psychiatry: Revue Canadienne de Psychiatrie, 58,* 386–392.

Stange, J. P., Eisner, L. R., Hölzel, B. K., Peckham, A. D., Dougherty, D. D., Rauch, S. L., ... Deckersbach, T. (2011). Mindfulness-based cognitive therapy for bipolar disorder: Effects on cognitive functioning. *Journal of Psychiatric Practice, 17,* 410.

Stein, D. J., Versiani, M., Hair, T., & Kumar, R. (2002). Efficacy of paroxetine for relapse prevention in social anxiety disorder: A 24-week study. *Archives of General Psychiatry, 59,* 1111–1118.

II. EXTENSIONS, INNOVATIONS, AND MODIFICATIONS

Stein, M. B., Sherbourne, C. D., Craske, M. G., Means-Christensen, A., Bystritsky, A., Katon, W., ... Roy-Byrne, P. P. (2004). Quality of care for primary care patients with anxiety disorders. *American Journal of Psychiatry, 161*(12), 2230–2237.

Stevenson, C. S., Whitmont, S., Bornholt, L., Livesey, D., & Stevenson, R. J. (2002). A cognitive remediation programme for adults with attention deficit hyperactivity disorder. *Australian and New Zealand Journal of Psychiatry, 36*, 610–616.

Stuart, G. L., Treat, T. A., & Wade, W. A. (2000). Effectiveness of an empirically based treatment for panic disorder delivered in a service clinic setting: 1-year follow-up. *Journal of Consulting and Clinical Psychology, 68*, 506.

Szentagotai, A., & David, D. (2010). The efficacy of cognitive-behavioral therapy in bipolar disorder: A quantitative meta-analysis. *Journal of Clinical Psychiatry, 71*, 66–72.

Telch, M. J., Bruchey, A. K., Rosenfield, D., Cobb, A. R., Smits, J., Pahl, S., & Gonzalez-Lima, F. (2014). Effects of post-session administration of methylene blue on fear extinction and contextual memory in adults with claustrophobia. *American Journal of Psychiatry, 171*, 1091–1098.

Thase, M. E., Greenhouse, J. B., Frank, E., Reynolds, C. F., Pilkonis, P. A., Hurley, K., ... Kupfer, D. J. (1997). Treatment of major depression with psychotherapy or psychotherapy-pharmacotherapy combinations. *Archives of General Psychiatry, 54*, 1009–1015.

Thase, M. E., & Howland, R. (1994). Refractory depression: relevance of psychosocial factors and therapies. *Psychiatric Annals, 24*, 232–240.

Tyrer, P., Murphy, S., & Riley, P. (1990). The benzodiazepine withdrawal symptom questionnaire. *Journal of Affective Disorders, 19*, 53–61.

Walker, D. L., Ressler, K. J., Lu, K. T., & Davis, M. (2002). Facilitation of conditioned fear extinction by systemic administration or intra-amygdala infusions of D-cycloserine as assessed with fear-potentiated startle in rats. *Journal of Neuroscience, 22*, 2343–2351.

Walker, J. R., Van Ameringen, M. A., Swinson, R., Bowen, R. C., Chokka, P. R., Goldner, E., ... Lane, R. M. (2000). Prevention of relapse in generalized social phobia: Results of a 24-week study in responders to 20 weeks of sertraline treatment. *Journal of Clinical Psychopharmacology, 20*, 636–644.

Warden, D., Rush, A. J., Trivedi, M. H., Fava, M., & Wisniewski, S. R. (2007). The STAR*D Project results: A comprehensive review of findings. *Current Psychiatry Reports, 9*, 449–459.

Weiss, M., Murray, C., Wasdell, M., Greenfield, B., Giles, L., & Hechtman, L. (2012). A randomized controlled trial of CBT therapy for adults with ADHD with and without medication. *BMC Psychiatry, 12*, 30.

Wiles, N., Thomas, L., Abel, A., Barnes, M., Carroll, F., Ridgway, N., ... Owen-Smith, A. (2014). Clinical effectiveness and cost-effectiveness of cognitive behavioural therapy as an adjunct to pharmacotherapy for treatment-resistant depression in primary care: The CoBalT randomised controlled trial. *Health Technology Assessment, 18*, 1–167.

Wilhelm, S., Buhlmann, U., Tolin, D. F., Meunier, S. A., Pearlson, G. D., Reese, H. E., ... Rauch, S. L. (2008). Augmentation of behavior therapy with D-cycloserine for obsessive-compulsive disorder. *American Journal of Psychiatry, 165*, 335–341.

Whittal, M. L., Otto, M. W., & Hong, J. J. (2001). Cognitive-behavior therapy for discontinuation of SSRI treatment of panic disorder: A case series. *Behavior Research and Therapy, 39*, 939–945.

Williams, J. M. G., Alatiq, Y., Crane, C., Barnhofer, T., Fennell, M. J., Duggan, D. S., ... Goodwin, G. M. (2008). Mindfulness-based cognitive therapy (MBCT) in bipolar disorder: Preliminary evaluation of immediate effects on between-episode functioning. *Journal of Affective Disorders, 107*, 275–279.

Williams, M. W., Teasdale, J. D., Segal, Z., & Kabat-Zinn, J. (2007). *The mindful way through depression. Freeing yourself from chronic unhappiness.* New York: Guilford.

Wisniewski, S. R., Fava, M., Trivedi, M. H., Thase, M. E., Warden, D., Niederehe, G., ... Rush, A. J. (2007). Acceptability of second-step treatments to depressed outpatients: A STAR*D report. *American Journal of Psychiatry, 164*, 753–760.

Zaretsky, A., Lancee, W., Miller, C., Harris, A., & Parikh, S. V. (2008). Is cognitive-behavioural therapy more effective than psychoeducation in bipolar disorder? *Canadian Journal of Psychiatry, 53*, 441–448.

Zylowska, L., Ackerman, D. L., Yang, M. H., Futrell, J. L., Horton, N. L., Hale, T. S., ... Smalley, S. L. (2008). Mindfulness meditation training in adults and adolescents with ADHD a feasibility study. *Journal of Attention Disorders, 11*, 737–746.

Further Reading

Prien, R. F., & Potter, W. Z. (1990). NIMH workshop report on treatment of bipolar disorder. *Psychopharmacology Bulletin, 26*, 409–427.

Scott, J. (2006). Psychotherapy for bipolar disorders-efficacy and effectiveness. *Journal of Psychopharmacology, 20*, 46–50.

Acceptance and Commitment Therapy and the Cognitive Behavioral Tradition: Assumptions, Model, Methods, and Outcomes

Fredrick Chin and Steven C. Hayes

University of Nevada, Reno, NV, United States

Acceptance and commitment therapy (ACT, said as one word; Hayes, Strosahl, & Wilson, 2012) is an evidence-based therapeutic approach that combines acceptance and mindfulness methods with commitment and behavior change methods for the purposes of promoting psychological flexibility. Emerging from a functional and contextual wing of behavior analysis, and based on traditional behavioral principles, ideas drawn from evolution science, and an experimental program in human language and higher cognition in the form of relational frame theory (RFT: Hayes, Barnes-Holmes, & Roche, 2001), ACT presents a challenge of categorization as an evidence-based therapy. Theoretically, ACT can be categorized as a form of clinical behavior analysis, but it does not sound classically behavioral in its firm link to a program in cognitive research, its rejection of the bottom up model of application, and its focus on topics such as values, self-acceptance, or spirituality. It can be categorized as a form of humanistic therapy but does not sound classically humanistic in its interest in laboratory research, experimentally established processes, component analyses, or its commitment to outcome evaluation using randomized controlled trials. It can be

The Science of Cognitive Behavioral Therapy.
DOI: http://dx.doi.org/10.1016/B978-0-12-803457-6.00007-6

classified as a form of cognitive behavior therapy (CBT), but it does not sound like classical CBT in its contextualistic philosophical assumptions, its rejection of cognitive causality, and its concern over many traditional cognitive methods.

ACT is best evaluated relative to its own goals, which are to be found in a knowledge development strategy called contextual behavioral science (CBS; Zettle, Hayes, Barnes-Holmes, & Biglan, 2016). A CBS approach emphasizes contextualistic philosophical assumptions, the value of a behavioral approach to language and cognition, a reticulated model of the relationship of basic and applied theory and practice, and the development of procedures that impacts impact clinically relevant processes of change. Because of the unique features of the ACT tradition in these areas, ACT cannot be well understood as a protocol or package, and especially not as a syndrome-focused package. ACT is an approach to creating behavior change, but it is an approach based on a particular set of philosophical assumptions; on basic principles and theory; on an applied model; and on a cross disciplinary knowledge development strategy. In this chapter, we will briefly review these features of ACT, and will examine the state of the evidence on ACT and its underlying model.

PHILOSOPHICAL ASSUMPTIONS: FUNCTIONAL CONTEXTUALISM

CBT in particular and evidence-based theory in general are best viewed as a broad umbrella covering a wide variety of theories, principles, and sets of philosophical assumptions (Dobson & Dozois, 2010). ACT is based on the foundational assumptions of contextualism (Pepper, 1942), which suppose that human behavior can only be understood in reference to the historical and situational context in which it occurs (Hayes, Hayes, & Reese, 1988). The fundamental unit of analysis within contextualism is the act-in-context, in which individual components of behavior are viewed as abstractions that are derived from the whole, purposive act.

The idea of behavior as a whole, purposive act applies just as clearly to the behavior of scientists. Scientific truth, from a contextualistic framework, is a matter of "successful working." Such a pragmatic truth criterion demands that the analytic goals of scientists be defined a priori, otherwise any reinforced operant behavior would have to be "true" (Hayes, 1993). It is this characteristic that establishes the varieties of scientific contextualism: Different forms can emerge in science linked to their different analytic goals.

There can be no evaluation process regarding ultimate analytic goals: Such goals can only be stated and owned. If a goal was evaluated in contextualism, it would require an evaluation relative to the successful accomplishment of still more goals. Stating analytic goals clearly is necessary to prevent just such an infinite regress. Stating analytic goals prior to performing an analysis constrains and determines the nature and breadth of contextual variables that can be usefully included in a given analysis (Hayes, 1993).

The stated goal of functional contextualism (Hayes, 1993) is to predict and influence, with precision, scope, and depth, the actions of whole organisms interacting in and with a context considered historically and situationally. Precision means that only a limited set of analytic constructions can be applied to a given event; scope that these constructions apply to a range of such events; and depth that they are not contradicted by well-developed knowledge in other domains or levels of analysis. Functional contextualism can be distinguished from various forms of descriptive contextualism, such as social constructionism, dramaturgy, narrative psychology, or hermeneutics, which apply the same analytic unit of the act-in-context but do so in order to have a personal appreciation of the participants in that whole act.

Functional contextualism is meant to be a more refined way of speaking about the philosophy of science underlying behavior analysis and traditional radical behaviorism (Hayes et al., 1988). The goal of science generally, from a contextualistic standpoint, is to "develop increasingly organized statements of relations among events that allow an analytic goal to be accomplished based on verifiable experience" (Vilardaga, Hayes, Levin, & Muto, 2009, p. 113). Because it views truth as the accomplishment of a goal, however, functional contextualism truth claims are not settled by making ontological claims: the basis of knowledge is instead intensely epistemological (Barnes-Holmes, 2000; Hayes, Barnes-Holmes, & Wilson, 2012). This does not mean that anything goes. To the contrary, fully accomplishing the goal of prediction-and-influence of behavior requires analyses that begin and end outside of the individual (Hayes & Brownstein, 1986). Thus, functional contextualism rejects mentalism, and views environmental causes as the ultimate focus of psychological science, not because behavior does not influence the environment but because only knowledge that includes variables that the analyst or clinician can directly change can accomplish its purposes.

BASIC PRINCIPLES: BEHAVIORAL PRINCIPLES, RELATIONAL FRAME THEORY, AND EVOLUTION SCIENCE

At the foundational level, ACT is based on behavioral principles as augmented by a specific theory of language and cognition, and as situated under the umbrella of evolution science. Behavioral principles are relied upon to some degree by most of CBT, and because of their ubiquity we will not spend time explicating them here. RFT (Hayes et al., 2001; Torneke, 2010) is much less well known and a brief summary seems in order.

Traditional behavior analysts have difficulty in accounting for human language and cognition and its relationship to nonverbal behavior. In essence, Skinner suggested that human language was merely the use of characteristic behavior—environment relations to acquire socially mediated reinforcers from a verbal community trained to provide them (Skinner, 1957). The account was largely theoretical, rather than empirical and never led to a robust experimental analysis that applied to the full range of concerns contacted in the psychology of human language and cognition.

Even though it is behavioral, RFT takes a very different approach. From an RFT perspective, human language and cognition involves learning to (1) derive mutual relationships among events under the control in part of arbitrary cues and to combine these into networks and (2) to change the functions of related events based on the relations among them and cues that select the relevant functions that are being changed. Most living organisms, with an appropriate training history, are able to respond to relations among the physical properties of two or more stimuli. For example, adult rhesus monkeys can be trained to select the taller of two stimuli. When later presented with a previous "correct" stimulus and a novel, taller stimulus, the monkeys will select the novel stimulus, demonstrating a response system based on relational (taller) rather than absolute stimulus properties (Harmon, Strong, & Pasnak, 1982). However, humans appear to be unique in their capacity to abstract higher order relationships from these relations (Penn, Holyoak, & Povinelli, 2008).

A well-studied example is stimulus equivalence: an individual trained to match spoken words to printed words will, without additional training, produces spoken words when provided printed words (Sidman, 1971). This process, referred to as mutual entailment in RFT terminology, is apparently absent in nonhuman species—even language-trained chimpanzees that are taught to select an object when seeing a characteristic sign will fail to produce the sign when seeing the object (Dugdale & Lowe, 2000). This lack of mutual entailment makes perfect sense when evaluated from an evolutionary context. A primate may naturally learn to seek out brush when it encounters a lion, but it would make little sense for the primate to then derive that it should seek out a lion when it encounters brush. Why, then, should humans behave differently?

Humans are a highly social, cooperative species of primate, possessing the capacity to engage in social referencing and nonverbal theory of mind skills from infancy (e.g., Tomasello, Carpenter, Call, Behne, & Moll, 2005). These skills alone provide a framework from which social mutual entailment skills would develop (Hayes & Sanford, 2014). If a person emits a characteristic sound in the presence of an object, it would be socially cooperative to provide the object in a content in which the speaker seemingly needed it upon hearing the sound. This extension of cooperation would give advantages to social groups that could that advantage of it and genetic adaptation responsive to the selection pressure provided by that group advantage would lead to greater readiness to learn and internalize mutual entailment, which is a defining feature of relational framing.

According to RFT, human language and higher cognition is based on relational framing, which refers to the learned ability to relate stimuli to one another based in part on arbitrary contextual cues, putting these relations into networks that alter behavior. Specific types of relational responses (e.g., same, opposite, more than) are controlled by specific kinds of contextual cues, allowing learned relational responses to become arbitrarily applicable. For example, very young children, when given a choice between a nickel and a dime, will choose the nickel because it is physically larger. As arbitrarily applicable comparative relational framing is acquired, older children will prefer the dime based on the social convention that the dime "is larger than" the nickel.

Relational framing allows for stimulus functions of events in a verbal network to be transformed by other events in network based on the derived relation between them and cues that select the relevant functions (Dymond & Rehfeldt, 2000). For example, Dougher, Hamilton, Fink, and Harrington (2007) taught some participants but not others an arbitrary relationship between three graphic symbols on a computer screen (which we will call here A, B, C) such that $A < B < C$. All participants were then repeatedly shocked in the presence of B and the arousal to the three stimuli was measured by galvanic skin response. B was highly arousing, as would be expected. Participants who were not exposed to the relational training showed little arousal when A or C were presented. Participants with the history of relational training were not aroused when A was presented but became *more* fearful in the presence of stimulus C than they were to stimulus B, despite never having been shocked when exposed to C. Thus, the fearful functions of stimulus B were not just transferred to C (as might be expected if the two were merely "associated"), they were actively *transformed* by the "greater than" relation between B and C.

Such transformation of stimulus functions is necessarily limited by contextual control: if all the functions of a stimulus transferred to another the two would be psychological equivalent. As a practical example, imagine a person is told to picture an apple. Though an apple has several stimulus functions (including the near-universal perceptual functions of taste, smell, texture, and sight), the phrase "picture an" acts as a context that emphasizes the visual stimulus functions of the apple.

Twenty years ago, a fairly comprehensive list of empirical ways to test and disprove RFT was published (Hayes, Gifford, & Ruckstuhl, 1996). Most of the studies then called for have since been conducted, and not a single empirical flaw has yet appeared. No theory is ever fully and finally proven in science, but the data in support of RFT as a relatively adequate empirical account of human language and cognition is large, growing, and highly consistent (for a recent summary of the state of the evidence, see Dymond & Roche, 2013).

As an applied matter RFT can do a number of important things such as increasing perspective taking skills (Weil, Hayes, & Capurro, 2011), assessing motivators for behavior change (Jackson, Williams, & Hayes, 2016), or increasing IQ (Cassidy, Roche, & Hayes, 2011).

In the area of psychotherapy, RFT helps explain how verbal and cognitive processes can lead to dysfunctional behaviors. Due to the effects of transformation of stimulus functions, words and thoughts themselves take on aversive stimulus properties. As a result, at times thoughts and feelings that are connected verbally to painful or distressing events are avoided as if they were equivalent to the event itself, a process known as experiential avoidance (Hayes, Wilson, Gifford, Follette, & Strosahl, 1996). Such processes often inhibit the learning of more adaptive behavior. Though the immediate effects of such experiential avoidance are negatively reinforcing, they come at the expense of an increase in the frequency and intensity of those experiences (Wegner, 1994).

Consider the example of thought suppression. Private events, such as thoughts of death, are targeted verbally for change via the construction of verbal rules design to solve the problem of pain. A person might decide to "think about the beach instead" in order to avoid the sadness or fear that comes from thinking about death. However, now the beach, death, and sadness, are now all in a relational network with one another, and the stimulus functions of the beach may change dramatically through a transformation of stimulus function. Similar to the way "dark" can be evoked by the word "light," the word "beach," actual beaches, or pictures of beaches may all paradoxically evoke thoughts of death or feelings of fear or sadness. By expanding the verbal network in a futile attempt to escape fear or sadness, a previously neutral stimulus has become death-related, and will now evoke aversive thoughts or feelings.

There is no psychological process called "unlearning." If RFT is correct and verbal/cognitive relations are learned, it can be clinically dangerous and unhelpful to expand verbal networks in an attempt to eliminate verbal events. A safer course of action is to change the functions of verbal/cognitive events. This implication of an the RFT account has been most extensively explored in ACT.

APPLIED MODEL: ACT PROCESSES OF CHANGE

Within the families of CBT models, the ACT model is characteristic in suggesting that it is the *context* surrounding verbal/cognitive activity, rather than the *content* of verbal/cognitive activity itself, that is key in producing or in reducing human suffering. The core target of ACT is "psychological flexibility", contacting the present moment as a conscious human being, fully and without needless defense—as it is and not as what it says it is—and persisting with or changing a behavior in the service of chosen behaviors (i.e., increasing psychological flexibility; Hayes et al., 2012, p. 96). The repertoire narrowing and self-amplifying processes of experiential avoidance, thought suppression, or other forms of cognitive entanglement are reduced by attempting to alter the functions of thoughts and feelings via acceptance, mindfulness, flexible attention to the now, and cognitive defusion. Theoretically, the aim is to bring the functions of verbal and cognitive events under more precise and voluntary contextual control, to broaden behavioral repertoires in the direction of chosen values.

According to the ACT model, six core processes produce psychological flexibility: enhancing client acceptance of distressing experiential content, utilizing cognitive defusion techniques to mitigate the deleterious effects of cognitions, increasing client ability to attend to the present moment, enhancing a self-as-context perspective within the client, identifying core values meaningful to the client, and supporting committed, effective action toward reaching those valued ends. These core processes are commonly diagramed as a hexagon (the tongue in cheek name for the diagram is the "hexaflex") (see Fig. 7.1), with the four processes on the left considered to be mindfulness and acceptance processes, whereas the four on the right are taken to be commitment and behavior change processes. Note that flexible attention to the present moment and self-as-context are invoked in both groups of processes. The hexaflex illustrates all processes as connected to one another—in practice, movement in one ACT process almost always results in changes in one or more other processes (Hayes et al., 2012).

Before psychological flexibility processes are directly targeted, steps are taken to increase motivation and to establish an agenda for change. Most clients seeking treatment have struggled with, worked around, and fought through their problems for some time. Often, clients have attempted many different solutions, to little success. Almost

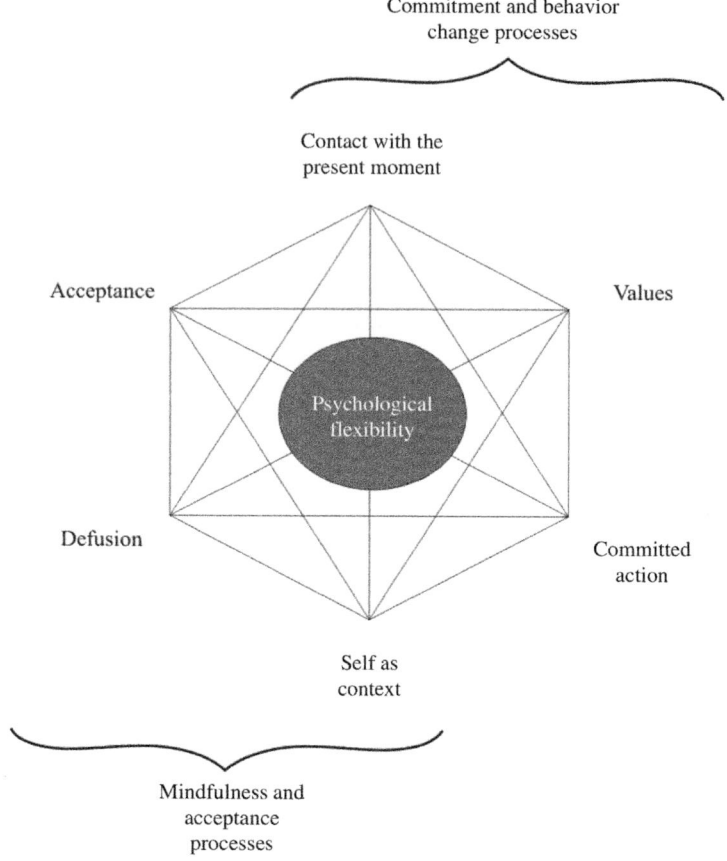

FIGURE 7.1 The ACT "Hexaflex" model. *Source: Copyright Steven C. Hayes. Used by permission.*

universally, clients believe that their failure to reduce their emotional distress is due to an inability to find the "correct" way to fix the problem. However, the ACT model proposes a second alternative: that trying directly to reduce or eliminate distress can itself become a problem. Such a message may initially seem counterintuitive to clients, who live in the context of a culture that promotes the control and elimination of painful memories, feelings, thoughts and sensations. Thus, the first step in ACT is often to aid the client in considering alternative, culturally incongruent methods of dealing with the problem. Typically, clients are asked such questions as:

1. What does a "better" life look like?
2. What strategies have you tried so far?
3. How have those strategies worked?

4. What has been the cost of following those strategies?
5. If they had worked what would you then have hoped for?
6. What does your experience tell you: are these outcomes closer or farther away?

The goal of this line of questioning is to utilize the client's direct experience to highlight the problems with an experiential control strategy and to encourage the client to give up such a strategy, only knowing that the next step is to try something different.

Acceptance. Etymologically, *acceptance* refers to the act of "taking what is offered." In ACT, acceptance refers to the active, voluntary embracing of moment-to-moment experience. Unfortunately, clients sometimes mistake this posture with a passive stance of "grinning and bearing." Such confusion should be clarified as soon as it is recognized, as the latter form of acceptance is not associated with positive health outcomes, regardless of the cultural or ethnic group (Cook & Hayes, 2010; see also Monestès et al., 2016). Rather, the client should be guided to adopt a willful experiencing of feelings as feelings, thoughts as thoughts, sensations as sensations, and so forth. Notably, an exposure paradigm is invoked via acceptance, with an important distinction: in ACT, exposure is not utilized as a vehicle for emotional regulation (Farmer & Chapman, 2008), but rather done in service of building out a heightened awareness of the contingencies, both positive and negative, that act as a context for behavior.

Defusion. From an RFT perspective, the functions of language processes are contextual, rather than mechanical: the specific stimulus properties of words depend on their context (e.g., *picture* an apple). Due to the transformation of stimulus functions, verbal/cognitive events can at times dominate over other sources of behavioral regulation. This process is termed "cognitive fusion." For example, a thought like "I am worthless" can seem to mean that the individual having the thought actually *is* worthless. To remedy this, ACT utilizes *cognitive defusion* techniques, deliberately altering the context of language to alter it automatic functions. An example of a way that ACT therapists might facilitate defusion is the "Leaves on a Stream" metaphor, in which clients are asked to imagine their thoughts as leaves floating by on a stream (e.g., Hayes & Smith, 2005).

Present moment focus exercises are designed to increase flexible attention to internal and external events in the here and now. Empirical research supports the association between rigid, nonpresent attention and psychological dysfunction (e.g., Davis & Nolen-Hoeksema, 2000), as well as a positive relationship between present-moment awareness and psychological well-being (Bowlin & Baer, 2012). Skills-building in this domain allows the client to create a space from which to experience both positive and negative psychological content without it encompassing the entirety of attention and behavior.

Self-as-context. Clients often enter therapy heavily fused with stories of themselves and others, and as a result are less able to react flexibly from moment to moment. This inflexibility is not strictly associated with negative thoughts—clients may be fused to the thought, "I am a caring person," and thus be unwilling to discuss the ways in which they are hurtful to others. Perspective taking allows clients to loosen the attachment to rigid self-stories. The "I" invoked by a sense of perspective is a locus from which experience occurs. In one sense it holds or contains all of experience, and in another sense there is a separation between self-as-awareness and self as the content of psychological events. These qualities of inclusion and distinction arguably foster more flexible behavioral patterns.

These first four flexibility processes are a kind of operational definition of mindfulness. The overlaps with Kabat-Zinn's (1990) well-known definition of mindfulness, "Paying attention in a particular way: on purpose, in the present moment, nonjudgmentally" (p. 4).

Values. Values in ACT are chosen qualities of being and doing. Engaging in values-based actions has advantages in establishing adaptive behavioral repertoires: The reinforcing effects of a quality of action exist in the present moment of behavioral engagement rather than external outcomes that may or may not follow. Values construction exercises are used in ACT to orient the client toward overt behaviors and away from private events. A critical component of the ACT values formulation is the emphasis on *choosing* values, rather than *deciding* upon values. Decisions are based on a verbal problem-solving strategy, whereby an individual weighs the costs and benefits associated with an array of options and selects the most attractive based on relative merits. Conversely, though values choices are often made within a context of reasons for and against, they are not made *for* those reasons. Choice is the natural state of affairs for nonverbal organisms. When defusion skills are applied to reason-giving itself, something approximating choice is afforded. The distinction between decision and choice is crucial in ACT because it aids the client in transitioning from a control-based agenda to a willingness-based agenda by allowing the client to engage in values even if there is a constant flow of reason-giving linked to a problem-solving, control-based agenda.

Committed action. The final component of the psychological flexibility model is *committed action,* the active, behavioral expression of personal values identified by the client and their construction into larger and broader patterns of flexible, effective, values-consistent habits of living. Commitments, from an ACT perspective, are not promises about actions to be made in the future. Rather, a commitment is a moment-to-moment decision to build patterns of meaningful action. Slips in committed action are not construed as therapeutic failures, but as opportunities to take responsibility for the lapse and to recommit to values-based action. A common misunderstanding regarding committed action is to confuse the distinction between values and goals. Clients may believe that the road to happiness and life satisfaction lies in goal attainment. Functionally, this mantra is intrinsically connected to a state of deprivation, as equating goal achievement to happiness constructs a context in which what is important is constantly missing. Concrete goals can be useful as a kind of values-compass, so long as emphasis is placed on living within a process of committed action. The primary outcome of interest is in the act of living: the habits of action embodying chosen qualities.

TRANSDIAGNOSTIC EFFECTIVENESS OF ACT

Because of its philosophical roots in functional contextualism, the scientific strategy propelling ACT is based on a contextual analysis of human behavior, rather than out of a symptomatic diagnostic nosology. In other words, the focus within ACT is not the specific topographical manifestations of human suffering (i.e., symptoms and syndromes), but rather the functional processes in the historical and situational context that are believed to act as a root cause for such suffering. The theorized processes of psychological dysfunction and prosperity are designed to be applicable across a range of psychological disorders, and beyond disorders onto the promotion of human prosperity. This process-focused strategy seeks broadly applicable interventions protocols—with the hope that interventions that act upon processes that liberate a person from pathology and promote prosperity in one domain should often be effective within other domains.

The wide ranging impact of these processes and the methods that target them suggest that this hope turned out to be true. Psychological flexibility processes appear to be key in a broad variety of psychological disorders. For example, many forms of psychopathology appear to emerge or to be exacerbated by experiential avoidance (Hayes et al., 1996). Behaviors that appear formally disparate across diagnoses may, in fact, serve a short-term reinforcing function of allowing the individual to escape from unwanted private events. In a large longitudinal study, Spinhoven, Drost, de Rooij, van Hemert, & Penninx (2014) found that elevated levels of experiential avoidance predict the development of both mood and anxiety disorders. Experiential avoidance also mediated the future development of distress-related disorders (e.g., major depression) given preexisting fear disorders (e.g., panic disorder) and vice versa. Thus, the high rates of comorbidity across psychological disorders may reflect common processes being manifested across topographies.

Fused patterns of thinking interfere with psychological flexibility, and thus context-insensitive fusion should lead to a variety of psychological disorders. The evidence from a traditional CBT framework (Beck, 2011) bears on this claim, where thought-action fusion has long been known to be troublesome (e.g., Shafran, Thordarson, & Rachman, 1996; see also Clark & Wells, 1995). More ACT specific measures of cognitive fusion and defusion are gathering a broader range of supportive data as well, as predictors of pathology and as mediators of change in CBT as well as ACT (e.g., Arch, Wolitzky-Taylor, Eifert, & Craske, 2012; Gillanders et al., 2014).

Component studies appear to support the psychologically active nature of methods designed to target the elements of psychological flexibility. For example, Masuda et al. (2004, 2009) showed that defusion-based word repetition exercises significantly reduced discomfort and believability of negative self-referential thoughts among participants, and such a strategy was more effective than distraction and thought control tasks. Additionally, Healy et al. (2008) found that prefacing a negative statement with the defusion phrase, "I am having the thought that" was effective at reducing discomfort and increasing willingness to engage with the content of the statement among participants. This effect remained consistent regardless of whether participants were told that the defusion technique would increase or decrease the emotional impact of the statement. Similarly, acceptance-based strategies have been shown to be more effective than control-based strategies in decreasing physiological reactivity in response to emotionally provocative film material (Campbell-Sills, Barlow, Brown, & Hofmann, 2006), increasing the duration of time spent in a cold-pressor task (Hayes et al., 1999) and increased ability to engage in exposure to carbon dioxide and reduced anxiety symptoms and anxiety-related cognitions for panic-disordered individuals (Levitt, Brown, Orsillo, & Barlow, 2004).

The outcome literature on ACT provides further evidence in support of the transdiagnostic effectiveness of the model. There are over 170 randomized trials on ACT (https://contextualscience.org/ACT_Randomized_Controlled_Trials). Meta-analyses show that ACT is effective across a panoply of mental health disorders (A-Tjak et al., 2015), substance abuse disorders (Lee, An, Levin, & Twohig, 2015), and chronic disease problems (Graham, Gouick, Krahé, & Gillanders, 2016). ACT has also been applied to a wide range of other issues such as promoting healthier eating (e.g., Forman, Hoffman, Juarascio, Butryn, & Herbert, 2013), reducing racial prejudice (e.g., Lillis & Hayes, 2007), and improving learning (e.g., Brown et al., 2011; Varra, Hayes, Roget, & Fisher, 2008) among many other areas. ACT interventions do not need to be face to face. For example, web-based, phone-based, and smartphone app-based ACT is more effective at aiding individuals in quitting smoking than extent federal and state government interventions of that kind (e.g., Bricker et al., 2014).

Although the details differ, in general meta-analyses show that ACT solidly outperforms wait lists or treatment as usual controls and shows broadly similar effectiveness compared to CBT or other established evidence-based psychological treatments, with small effect sizes in favor of ACT that are sometimes statistically significant (e.g., Lee et al., 2015) and sometimes are not (e.g., A-Tjak et al., 2015) depending on the problem area and the range and number of studies selected.

MEDIATORS AND MODERATORS OF ACT PROCESSES

Within the CBS approach, identification of moderators and mediators associated with a model are crucial (Hayes et al., 2012). Research on moderators identifies contextual, idiographic features that contribute to treatment outcomes, while mediational research provides evidence that theoretically important processes of change are altered by intervention and are functionally important in eliciting positive outcomes.

Because the ACT model is based on the idea that psychological inflexibility, broadly, is responsible for a multitude of dysfunctional behaviors, it would be theorized that complex, multiproblem individuals would benefit more from ACT than traditional CBT. Preliminary data support this hypothesis. For example, among individuals with mixed-anxiety disorders, ACT showed better outcomes than CBT primarily among those who also had comorbid depressive symptoms (Wolitzky-Taylor, Arch, Rosenfield, & Craske, 2012).

Several measures have been developed to assess aspects of the psychological flexibility model. One of the most commonly utilized measures, the Acceptance and Action Questionnaire-II (AAQ-II), evaluates experiential avoidance and psychological inflexibility in a general, broadly contextual sense (Bond et al., 2011). As predicted by the ACT model, higher levels of psychological flexibility are related to greater levels of psychological distress, and decreases in AAQ-II score (i.e., increased psychological flexibility) mediate ACT outcomes across a range of problem areas (see the review in Hayes et al., 2012). Versions of the AAQ have been developed for use among specific problems and populations, and have been effective at providing mediators of ACT interventions for those domains (e.g., Gifford et al., 2004; Lundgren, Dahl, & Hayes, 2008). Similar mediational results have been found for alternative measures of flexibility processes, such as the Multidimensional Experiential Avoidance Questionnaire (MEAQ; Gámez, Chmielewski, Kotov, Ruggero, & Watson, 2011), and the Cognitive Fusion Questionnaire (CFQ; Gillanders et al., 2014), or similar measures (Bach, Gaudiano, Hayes, & Herbert, 2013).

Wings and Waves of CBT

During the years that immediately followed the declaration of the arrival of "third-wave" behavioral and cognitive therapy (Hayes, 2004), it was sometimes argued that ACT was old CBT wine in a new bottle (Hofmann & Asmundson, 2008). Over time, as these similarities and differences have been more thoroughly explored, it appears that a more nuanced perspective has taken hold. At the level of methods, most appear to agree (as do we, largely) with Hofmann, Sawyer, and Fang (2010)'s assertion that "treatment-specific techniques between mindfulness-based treatments, ACT, and CBT are not incompatible" (p. 707). At the level of theory, integration is more difficult. Cognitive reappraisal, for example, makes sense to ACT providers if it is a way of speaking about cognitive flexibility, but not so much if it is a way of speaking about cognitive disputation.

The field itself appears to have been changed by this discussion, however, so the theoretical ideas and methods are blending. Mainstream CBT has begun to incorporate many of the concepts and methods of the acceptance and mindfulness wing of CBT. The field has been going through a transition toward a more process-oriented approach and appears to be drawing these various wings, traditions, or waves closer together.

What is difficult to integrate fully are the philosophical assumptions, and knowledge development strategies that characterize the CBS development community as distinct from traditional CBT. Theoretical differences become more intractable as they bear on philosophical assumptions. For example, many in mainstream CBT are still wanting to say that maladaptive cognitions play a *causal* role in the development of emotional distress, and thus that logically modifying such cognitions must be a crucial component of treatment. This causal relationship is not so much indicative of a theoretical difference as it is reflective of a different philosophy of science. ACT rests upon a different framework, in which all events are contextually interrelated. The purposes brought to science from a functional contextual positive require that "causes" be, at least in principle, be accessible to direct manipulation (Hayes, 2004). In this view, emotions and thoughts relate to overt action only in a historical and situational context, and while these contexts can be causal, the emotions and thoughts themselves are not. This is not an empirical issue and thus these core differences about the causal role of thought appear unlikely to change.

Integration at the level of basic principles or knowledge development strategy is more possible. The CBS approach to balancing the need for basic principles and applied technologies has been to develop a reticulated (web-like) approach, wherein theoretical and practical work are interconnected, and build upon one another. ACT was developed in conjunction with, and intimately draws from a basic, comprehensive analysis of human language and cognition, RFT, that has not yet been seriously entertained or applied by mainstream CBT. There seems to be no reason that it could not be borrowed and applied there, and a new book has built a beginning bridge of that kind (Villatte, Villatte, & Hayes, 2016).

If a process-oriented development strategy continues to strengthen in mainstream CBT it will advance this pattern of integration. This in fact appears to be occurring now that the "packages for syndromes" approach is weakening. When combined with mediation and moderation research, a more process-oriented approach may provide a clear and efficient avenue for the ACT and CBS community, and the rest of the behavioral and cognitive therapy community generally, to work together more vigorously and to focus on the processes and procedures that best reduce problems and foster prosperity in people. This is an exciting possibility given that Paul's (1969) famous clinical question still remains unanswered: "What treatment, by whom, is most effective for this individual with that specific problem, under which set of circumstances, and how does it come about? (p. 44)."

References

Arch, J. J., Woliztky-Taylor, K. B., Eifert, G. H., & Craske, M. G. (2012). Longitudinal treatment mediation of traditional cognitive behavioral therapy and acceptance and commitment therapy for anxiety disorders. *Behavior Research and Therapy, 50*, 469–478.

A-Tjak, J. G. L., Davis, M. L., Morina, N., Powers, M. B., Smits, J. A. J., & Emmelkamp, P. M. G. (2015). A meta-analysis of the efficacy of Acceptance and Commitment Therapy for clinically relevant mental and physical health problems. *Psychotherapy and Psychosomatics, 84*, 30–36.

Bach, P., Gaudiano, B. A., Hayes, S. C., & Herbert, J. D. (2013). Acceptance and Commitment Therapy for psychosis: Intent to treat hospitalization outcome and mediation by believability. *Psychosis, 5*, 166–174.

Barnes-Holmes, D. (2000). Behavioral pragmatism: No place for reality and truth. *The Behavior Analyst, 23*, 191–202.

Beck, J. S. (2011). *Cognitive behavior therapy: Basics and beyond* (2nd ed.). New York: Guilford Press.

Bond, F. W., Hayes, S. C., Baer, R. A., Carpenter, K. C., Guenole, N., Orcutt, H. K., ... Zettle, R. D. (2011). Preliminary psychometric properties of the Acceptance and Action Questionnaire − II: A revised measure of psychological flexibility and acceptance. *Behavior Therapy, 42*, 676–688.

Bowlin, S. L., & Baer, R. A. (2012). Relationships between mindfulness, self-control and psychological functioning. *Personality and Individual Differences, 52*, 411–415.

Bricker, J. B., Mull, K. E., Kientz, J. A., Vilardaga, R., Mercer, L. D., Akiokaa, K. J., & Heffner, J. L. (2014). Randomized, controlled pilot trial of a smartphone app for smoking cessation using Acceptance and Commitment Therapy. *Drug and Alcohol Dependence, 143*, 87–94.

Brown, L. A., Forman, E. M., Herbert, J. D., Hoffman, K. L., Yuen, E. K., & Goetter, E. M. (2011). A randomized controlled trial of acceptance-based behavior therapy and cognitive therapy for test anxiety: A pilot study. *Behavior Modification, 35*, 31–53.

Campbell-Sills, L., Barlow, D. H., Brown, T. A., & Hofmann, S. G. (2006). Effects of suppression and acceptance on emotional responses of individuals with anxiety and mood disorders. *Behavior Research and Therapy, 44*, 1251–1263.

Cassidy, S., Roche, B., & Hayes, S. C. (2011). A relational frame training intervention to raise intelligence quotients: A pilot study. *The Psychological Record, 61*, 173–198.

Clark, D. M., & Wells, A. (1995). A cognitive model of social phobia. In R. G. Heimberg, M. R. Liebowitz, D. A. Hope, & F. R. Schneier (Eds.), *Social phobia: Diagnosis, assessment and treatment* (pp. 69–93). New York: Guilford Press.

Cook, D., & Hayes, S. C. (2010). Acceptance-based coping and the psychological adjustment of Asian and Caucasian Americans. *International Journal of Behavioral Consultation and Therapy, 6*, 186–197.

Davis, R. N., & Nolen-Hoeksema, S. (2000). Cognitive inflexibility among ruminators and nonruminators. *Cognitive Therapy and Research, 24*, 699–711.

Dobson, K. S., & Dozois, D. J. A. (2010). Historical and philosophical bases of the cognitive-behavioral therapies. In K. S. Dobson (Ed.), *Handbook of cognitive-behavioral therapies* (pp. 3–38). New York: Guilford Press.

Dougher, M. J., Hamilton, D. A., Fink, B. C., & Harrington, J. (2007). Transformation of the discriminative and eliciting functions of generalizing relational stimuli. *Journal of the Experimental Analysis of Behavior, 88*(2), 179–197.

Dugdale, N., & Lowe, C. F. (2000). Testing for symmetry in the conditional discriminations of language-trained chimpanzees. *Journal of Experimental Analysis of Behavior, 73*, 5–22.

Dymond, S., & Roche, B. (2013). *Advances in relational frame theory: Research and application.* Oakland, CA: New Harbinger Publications/Context Press.

Dymond, S., & Rehfeldt, R. A. (2000). Understanding complex behavior: The transformation of stimulus functions. *Behavior Analyst, 23*, 239–254.

Farmer, R. E., & Chapman, A. L. (2008). *Behavioral interventions in cognitive behavior therapy: Practical guidance for putting theory into action.* Washington, DC: American Psychological Association.

Forman, E. M., Hoffman, K. L., Juarascio, A. S., Butryn, M. L., & Herbert, J. D. (2013). Comparison of acceptance-based and standard cognitive-based coping strategies for craving sweets in overweight and obese women. *Eating Behaviors, 14*, 64–68.

Gámez, W., Chmielewski, M., Kotov, R., Ruggero, C., & Watson, D. (2011). Development of a measure of experiential avoidance: The Multidimensional Experiential Avoidance Questionnaire. *Psychological Assessment, 23*, 692–713.

Gifford, E. V., Kohlenberg, B. S., Hayes, S. C., Antonuccio, D. O., Piasecki, M. M., Rasmussen-Hall, M. L., & Palm, K. M. (2004). Acceptance theory-based treatment for smoking cessation: An initial trial of Acceptance and Commitment Therapy. *Behavior Therapy, 35*, 689–705.

Gillanders, D. T., Bolderston, H., Bond, F. W., Dempster, M., Flaxman, P. E., Campbell, L., ... Remington, R. (2014). The development and initial validation of the Cognitive Fusion Questionnaire. *Behavior Therapy, 45*, 83–101.

Graham, C. D., Gouick, J., Krahé, C., & Gillanders, D. (2016). A systematic review of the use of Acceptance and Commitment Therapy (ACT) in chronic disease and long-term conditions. *Clinical Psychology Review, 46*, 46–58.

Harmon, K., Strong, R., & Pasnak, R. (1982). Relational responses in tests of transposition with rhesus monkeys. *Learning and Motivation, 13*, 495–504.

Hayes, S. C. (1993). Analytic goals and the varieties of scientific contextualism. In S. C. Hayes, L. J. Hayes, H. W. Reese, & T. R. Sarbin (Eds.), *Varieties of scientific contextualism* (pp. 11–27). Reno, NV: Context Press.

Hayes, S. C. (2004). Acceptance and commitment therapy, relational frame theory, and the third wave of behavioral and cognitive therapies. *Behavior Therapy, 35*, 639−665.

Hayes, S. C., Barnes-Holmes, D., & Roche, B. (Eds.), (2001). *Relational frame theory: A Post-Skinnerian account of human language and cognition.* New York: Plenum Press.

Hayes, S. C., Barnes-Holmes, D., & Wilson, K. G. (2012). Contextual behavioral science: Creating a science more adequate to the challenge of the human condition. *Journal of Contextual Behavioral Science, 1*, 1−16.

Hayes, S. C., Bisset, R., Korn, Z., Zettle, R. D., Rosenfarb, I., Cooper, L., & Grundt, A. (1999). The impact of acceptance versus control rationales on pain tolerance. *Psychological Record, 49*, 33−47.

Hayes, S. C., & Brownstein, A. J. (1986). Mentalism, behavior-behavior relatoins, and a behavior-analytic view of the purposes of science. *The Behavior Analyst, 9*(2), 175−190.

Hayes, S. C., Gifford, E. V., & Ruckstuhl, L. E., Jr. (1996). Relational frame theory and executive function. Chapter. In G. R. Lyon, & N. A. Krasnegor (Eds.), *Attention, memory and executive function* (pp. 279−305). Baltimore: Brookes.

Hayes, S. C., Hayes, L. J., & Reese, H. W. (1988). Finding the philosophical core: A review of Stephen C. Pepper's World Hypotheses. *Journal of Experimental Analysis of Behavior, 50*, 97−111.

Hayes, S. C., & Sanford, B. T. (2014). Cooperation came first: Evolution and human cognition. *Journal of Experimental Analysis of Behavior, 101*, 112−129.

Hayes, S. C., & Smith, S. (2005). *Get out of your mind and into your life: The new acceptance and commitment therapy.* Oakland, CA: New Harbinger.

Hayes, S. C., Strosahl, K. D., & Wilson, K. G. (2012). *Acceptance and commitment therapy: The process and practice of mindful change* (2nd ed.). New York: Guilford Press.

Hayes, S. C., Wilson, K. G., Gifford, E. V., Follette, V. M., & Strosahl, K. D. (1996). Experiential avoidance and behavioral disorders: A functional dimensional approach to diagnosis and treatment. *Journal of Consulting and Clinical Psychology, 64*, 1152−1168.

Healy, H. A., Barnes-Holmes, Y., Barnes-Holmes, D., Keogh, C., Luciano, C., & Wilson, K. G. (2008). An experimental test of a cognitive defusion exercise: Coping with negative and positive self-statements. *Psychological Record, 58*, 623−640.

Hofmann, S. G., & Asmundson, G. J. G. (2008). Acceptance and mindfulness-based therapy: New wave or old hat? *Clinical Psychology Review, 28*, 1−16.

Hofmann, S. G., Sawyer, A. T., & Fang, A. (2010). The empirical status of the "new wave" of CBT. *Psychiatric Clinics of North America, 33*, 701−710.

Jackson, M. L., Williams, W. L., & Hayes, S. C. (2016). Whatever gets your heart pumping: The impact of implicitly selected reinforcer-focused statements on exercise intensity. *Journal of Contextual Behavioral Science, 5*, 48−57.

Kabat-Zinn, J. (1990). *Full catastrophe living: Using the wisdom of your body and mind to face stress, pain and illness.* New York: Delacorte.

Lee, E. B., An, W., Levin, M. E., & Twohig, M. P. (2015). An initial meta-analysis of Acceptance and Commitment Therapy for treating substance use disorders. *Drug and Alcohol Dependence, 155*, 1−7.

Levitt, J. T., Brown, T. A., Orsillo, S. M., & Barlow, D. H. (2004). The effects of acceptance versus suppression of emotion on subjective psychophysiological response to carbon dioxide challenge in patients with panic disorder. *Behavior Therapy, 35*, 747−766.

Lillis, J., & Hayes, S. C. (2007). Applying acceptance, mindfulness, and values to the reduction of prejudice: A pilot study. *Behavior Modification, 31*, 389−411.

Lundgren, T., Dahl, J., & Hayes, S. C. (2008). Evaluation of mediators of change in the treatment of epilepsy with Acceptance and Commitment Therapy. *Journal of Behavior Medicine, 31*, 225−235.

Masuda, A., Hayes, S. C., Sackett, C. F., & Twohig, M. P. (2004). Cognitive defusion and self-relevant negative thoughts: Examining the impact of a ninety year old technique. *Behavior Research and Therapy, 42*, 477−485.

Masuda, A., Hayes, S. C., Twohig, M. P., Drossel, C., Lillis, J., & Washio, Y. (2009). A parametric study of cognitive defusion and the believability and discomfort of negative thoughts. *Behavior Modification, 33*, 250–262.

Monestès, J. L., Karekla, M., Jacobs, N., Michaelides, M., Hooper, N., Kleen, M., ... Hayes, S. C. (2016). Experiential avoidance as a common psychological process in European cultures. *European Journal of Psychological Assessment*. Available from http://dx.doi.org/10.1027/1015-5759/a000327.

Paul, G. L. (1969). Behavior modification research: design and tactics. In C. M. Franks (Ed.), *Behavior therapy: Appraisal and status* (pp. 29–62). New York: McGraw-Hill.

Penn, D. C., Holyoak, K. J., & Povinelli, D. J. (2008). Darwin's mistake: Explaining the discontinuity between human and nonhuman minds. *Behavioral and Brain Sciences, 31*, 109–178.

Pepper, S. C. (1942). *World hypotheses: A study in evidence*. Berkeley, CA: University of California Press.

Shafran, R., Thordarson, D., & Rachman, S. (1996). Thought action fusion in obsessive compulsive disorder. *Journal of Anxiety Disorders, 5*, 379–391.

Sidman, M. (1971). Reading and auditory-visual equivalences. *Journal of Speech and Hearing Research, 39*, 61–68.

Skinner, B. F. (1957). *Verbal behavior*. New York: Crofts-Century-Crofts.

Spinhoven, P., Drost, J., de Rooij, M., van Hemert, A. M., & Penninx, B. W. (2014). A longitudinal study of experiential avoidance in emotional disorders. *Behavior Therapy, 45*(6), 840–850.

Tomasello, M., Carpenter, J., Call, J., Behne, T., & Moll, H. (2005). Understanding and sharing intentions: The origins of cultural cognition. *Behavioral and Brain Sciences, 28*, 675–735.

Torneke, N. (2010). *Learning RFT: An introduction to relational frame theory and its clinical application*. Oakland, CA: New Harbinger Publications/Context Press.

Varra, A. A., Hayes, S. C., Roget, N., & Fisher, G. (2008). A randomized control trial examining the effect of Acceptance and Commitment Training on clinician willingness to use evidence-based pharmacotherapy. *Journal of Consulting and Clinical Psychology, 76*, 449–458.

Vilardaga, R., Hayes, S. C., Levin, M. E., & Muto, T. (2009). Creating a strategy for progress: A contextual behavioral science approach. *The Behavior Analyst, 32*, 105–133.

Villatte, M., Villatte, J. L., & Hayes, S. C. (2016). *Mastering the clinical conversation: Language as intervention*. New York, NY: Guilford Press.

Wegner, D. M. (1994). *White bears and other unwanted thoughts*. New York: Guilford Press.

Weil, T. M., Hayes, S. C., & Capurro, P. (2011). Establishing a deictic relational repertoire in young children. *Psychological Record, 61*, 371–390.

Wolitzky-Taylor, K. B., Arch, J. J., Rosenfield, D., & Craske, M. G. (2012). Moderators and non-specific predictors of treatment outcome for anxiety disorders: A comparison of cognitive behavioral therapy to acceptance and commitment therapy. *Journal of Consulting and Clinical Psychology, 80*, 786–799.

Zettle, R. D., Hayes, S. C., Barnes-Holmes, D., & Biglan, T. (Eds.), (2016). *The Wiley handbook of Contextual Behavioral Science*. Chichester, UK: Wiley/Blackwell.

Further Reading

Gross, J. J., & John, O. P. (2003). Individual differences in two emotion regulation processes: Implications for affect, relationships, and well-being. *Journal of Personality and Social Psychology, 85*, 348–362.

Guidano, V. F., & Liotti, G. (1987). *Cognitive processes and emotional disorders: A structural approach to psychotherapy*. New York: Guilford Press.

Hayes, S. C., Levin, M. E., Plumb-Vilardaga, J., Villatte, J. L., & Pistorello, J. (2013). Acceptance and commitment therapy and contextual behavioral science: Examining the progress of a distinct model of behavioral and cognitive therapy. *Behavior Therapy, 44*, 180−198.

Kessler, R. C., Berglund, P., Demler, O., Jin, R., Merikangas, K. R., & Walters, E. E. (2005). Lifetime prevalence and age-of-onset distributions of DSM-IV disorders in the national comorbidity survey replication. *Archives of General Psychiatry, 62*, 593−602.

Marlatt, G. A. (1985). Relapse prevention: Theoretical rationale and overview of the model. In G. A. Marlatt, & J. R. Gordon (Eds.), *Relapse prevention: Maintenance strategies in the treatment of addictive behaviors* (pp. 3−70). New York: Brunner/Mazel.

Michael, J. (1986). Repertoire-altering effects of remote contingencies. *Analysis of Verbal Behavior, 4*, 10−18.

Parrott, L. J. (1984). Listening and understanding. *The Behavior Analyst, 7*, 29−39.

Rippere, V. (1977). "What's the thing to do when you're feeling depressed?"—A pilot study. *Behvior Research and Therapy, 15*, 185−191.

Skinner, B. F. (1938). *Behavior of organisms.* New York: D. Appleton & Co.

Skinner, B. F. (1971). *Beyond freedom and dignity.* New York: Knopf.

Skinner, B. F. (1974). *About behaviorism.* New York: Knopf.

Wulfert, E., & Hayes, S. C. (1988). The transfer of conditional sequencing through conditional equivalence classes. *Journal of Experimental Analysis of Behavior, 50*, 125−144.

Mindfulness-Based Cognitive Behavioral Treatments

Lizabeth Roemer[1], Natalie Arbid[1], Jennifer H. Martinez[1] and Susan M. Orsillo[2]

[1]University of Massachusetts Boston, Boston, MA, United States [2]Suffolk University, Boston, MA, United States

Mindfulness- (and acceptance-) based strategies have been integrated into a wide range of cognitive behavioral therapies (CBTs) to target the problematic, reactive, fused, entangled relationship individuals have with their internal experiences (thoughts, feelings, sensations, memories), which underlie many clinical presentations (cf. Baer, 2014; Hayes, Follette, & Linehan, 2004; Irving, Farb, & Segal, 2015). This broad class of treatments underneath the CBT umbrella has been called acceptance-based behavioral therapies (ABBTs; e.g., Roemer & Orsillo, 2009), "third wave" behavioral therapies (e.g., Hayes, 2004), or, more recently, contextual CBTs (Hayes, Villatte, Levin, & Hildebrandt, 2011). The term ABBT is used because these treatments all target enhancing acceptance based on the model that nonacceptance of internal experiences (and some external events) contributes to psychological distress and interference. Mindfulness strategies within these treatments are used to cultivate acceptance. This group of therapies includes mindfulness-based treatments, such as mindfulness-based cognitive therapy (MBCT; Segal, Williams, & Teasdale, 2013) and mindfulness-based relapse prevention (MBRP; Bowen, Chawla, & Marlatt, 2011), as well as acceptance and commitment therapy (ACT; Hayes, Strosahl, & Wilson, 2011) and dialectical behavior therapy (DBT; Linehan, 1993, 2015). The latter two approaches are described in other chapters in this volume, so we will not discuss them in-depth here. Some authors have defined

The Science of Cognitive Behavioral Therapy.
DOI: http://dx.doi.org/10.1016/B978-0-12-803457-6.00008-8

mindfulness-based treatments as those that exclude any other treatment elements (e.g., Khoury et al., 2013); however, in fact even these "purer" approaches include strategies commonly used in CBTs, such as monitoring chains of reactions, or pleasant and unpleasant events (Baer, 2014). Instead, we will focus here on all approaches that integrate mindfulness strategies and CBT strategies, with the exception of ACT and DBT. Literature on integrating mindfulness into other therapeutic approaches (e.g., Stewart, 2014) and the impact of therapists' mindfulness practice on the effectiveness of therapy (e.g., Shapiro, Thakur, & de Sousa, 2014) is outside the scope of this chapter.

ACCEPTANCE-BASED BEHAVIORAL MODEL OF CLINICAL PROBLEMS

Our application of mindfulness within the context of CBT is based on an acceptance-based behavioral model of clinical challenges that draws from cognitive behavioral research and theory (cf., Antony & Roemer, 2011; Craske, 2010), ACT (Hayes et al., 2011), and mindfulness-based theory and research (cf., Brown, Cresswell, & Ryan, 2015) and is presented in more detail elsewhere (Roemer & Orsillo, 2009, 2014). In this model, biological and environmental influences shape a learning history that leads to three interrelated processes that elicit and maintain clinical presentations: (1) a problematic relationship with internal experiences (thoughts, emotions, sensations, and memories) that is critical, entangled, and self-defining, (2) rigid, habitual efforts to avoid these internal experiences (i.e., experiential avoidance; Hayes, Wilson, Gifford, Follette, & Strosahl, 1996), which in turn increase reactivity to internal experiences and paradoxically increase distress, and (3) restrictions (behaviorally and/or attentionally) in engaging in meaningful actions (Wilson & Murrell, 2004), which reduce quality of life and increase distress. This model is closely related to the ACT hexaflex model (Hayes et al., 2011).

Extensive research provides evidence that clinical problems are characterized by problematic ways of relating to internal experiences, rather than by the mere occurrence of thoughts, sensations, and/or emotions. For instance, decades of research on anxiety sensitivity (i.e., the fear of behaviors or sensations associated with the experience of anxiety) demonstrate an association between responding to internal sensations as signs of danger and anxiety disorders (cf., Olatunji & Wolitzky-Taylor, 2009). More recently, anxiety sensitivity has also been linked to other clinical presentations such as problematic drinking (DeMartini & Carey, 2011) and chronic pain (Ocañez, McHugh, & Otto, 2010). Further, beyond anxiety, fear of/distress about the full range of one's emotions (Williams, Chambless, & Ahrens, 1997) has been shown to correlate with a broad array of psychological symptoms including depression (Werner-Seidler, Banks, Dunn, & Moulds, 2013), posttraumatic stress (Sippel & Marshall, 2013), borderline personality (Sauer & Baer, 2009), and generalized anxiety (Mennin, Heimberg, Turk, & Fresco, 2005). Similarly, mood-induced reactivity is predictive of relapse among individuals with recurrent major depressive disorders (van Rijsbergen et al., 2013). In fact, emotional reactivity predicts treatment outcome in treatment of emotional disorders above and beyond measures of negative affect (Sauer-Zavala et al., 2012). Negative beliefs about one's thoughts (i.e., meta-cognitions, Wells, 2000), including worry, are associated with both depression (Sarısoy et al., 2014) and generalized anxiety (Wells & Carter, 2001). Further, the extent to which individuals believe their anxious thoughts and worries to be true is related to higher psychological distress and poorer quality of life (Herzberg et al., 2012). Theory and research highlight the way that judgment and criticism of internal experiences can promote reactivity, as well as how interpreting internal experiences as self-defining and permanent contributes to symptoms and quality of life (see Hayes et al., 2011; Roemer & Orsillo, 2009 for reviews).

This heightened reactivity to thoughts, emotions, and sensations, as well as defining these experiences as indicators of truth will naturally lead to efforts to avoid these experiences. Yet experimental studies show that rigid, repeated efforts to put thoughts, feelings, sensations or memories out of our minds (e.g., experiential avoidance; Hayes et al., 1996) are often unsuccessful and can actually increase distressing thoughts, feelings, or sensations (e.g., Gross, 2002; Levitt, Brown, Orsillo, & Barlow, 2004; Najmi & Wegner, 2008). Furthermore, instructed efforts not to think of situations can increase reported anxiety associated with the target situation (Roemer & Borkovec, 1994), suggesting that experiential avoidance increases distress about thoughts and emotions. Experience sampling research using a sample of outpatients diagnosed with a psychotic disorder recently confirmed that attempts to control uncomfortable thoughts subsequently increased both the severity of, and distress over, persecutory delusions (Hartley, Haddock, Vasconcelos e Sa, Emsley, & Barrowclough, 2015). As such, these rigid efforts to avoid can paradoxically contribute to prolonged distress.

Finally, experiential avoidance often takes the form of either engaging in problematic behaviors (such as substance use, restricted eating) or avoiding actions (such as engaging socially, asserting oneself) that are initially negatively reinforced by reduced distress but lead to more prolonged difficulties in living, such as narrowed lives and relationships (e.g., Michelson, Lee, Orsillo, & Roemer, 2011). Other times avoidance is more attentional than behavioral, with people engaging in meaningful actions while preoccupied in rumination or worry so that they are not attentionally or emotionally present in their lives (Roemer & Orsillo, 2014).

Mindfulness-based approaches target each of these processes and, instead, encourage (1) an expansive, decentered relationship with internal experiences, (2) acceptance of and willingness to have internal experiences, and (3) intentional engagement in personally meaningful, valued actions. That is, these approaches help clients learn to see their internal experiences as phenomena that arise (e.g., thoughts are just thoughts, not facts, *decentering*), to allow these experiences when they arise (although this does not preclude emotion regulation efforts as long as clients are not rigidly attempting to remove or avoid distress), and to engage in what matters to them, regardless of the emotions that arise. This final component overlaps with cognitive behavioral strategies of exposure, behavioral activation, opposite action (from DBT, Linehan, 1993), and facilitating action tendencies that are not associated with dysregulated emotions (from the unified protocol; Barlow, Allen, & Choate, 2004).

MINDFULNESS IN PSYCHOLOGICAL INTERVENTIONS

Within Western psychological approaches, mindfulness is commonly defined as "paying attention in particular way, on purpose, in the present moment, and nonjudgmentally" (Kabat-Zinn, 1994, p. 4), or "open or receptive attention to and awareness of ongoing events and experience" (Brown & Ryan, 2004, p. 245). Another, related, often-cited definition is "the awareness that arises through intentionally attending in an open, kind, and discerning way" (Shapiro & Carlson, 2009, p. 15). Shapiro et al. (2014) further describe three components of mindfulness: intention, attention, and attitude (e.g., openhearted, curious, compassionate). Within intention, they include a growing awareness of "unconscious values" and choosing whether to pursue these values (not in terms of striving for outcome, but as a direction for action). Within ACT (current chapter), this attention to clarification of values and choosing actions is an additional element of treatment (as it is in our ABBT approach to treating GAD, in which we draw from ACT; Roemer & Orsillo, 2014); however, Shapiro and colleagues' description highlights how intentionality and chosen action can also flow directly from mindfulness practices. Garland, Farb, Goldin, and Frederickson (2015) similarly argue that mindfulness facilitates the ability to choose to live a meaningful life.

The term mindfulness is used to refer to (1) the state of paying attention, in the present moment, with kindness and care, (2) a dispositional quality of often being aware, in the present moment, with kindness and care, and (3) the practices that cultivate this state and this dispositional quality by making this type of awareness a habit and more easily accessed throughout one's life. Often mindfulness is narrowly associated with meditative practices. However, not all meditative practices cultivate a state of open or receptive attention and awareness (for instance, some practices narrow awareness or attempt to "clear" the mind), and meditative practices are not the only way to cultivate awareness.

Most mindfulness-based treatments do incorporate "formal" practices, sometimes referred to as meditative practices. These involve setting aside a varying amount of time and practicing bringing attention to different aspects of experience (e.g., breath, physical sensations, sounds, thoughts, and emotions). The practice involves bringing attention to the target again and again, noticing when the mind wanders, and once again returning attention to the focus of the practice. This practice helps one to develop the skill of noticing, without judgment, and offers the practitioner an opportunity to observe how busy minds are and how easily attention wanders. This experience helps one to cultivate acceptance and self-compassion, and the recognition that internal experiences are fleeting, rather than enduring and self-defining. Mindfulness-based treatments vary in the centrality and length of formal practices, with MBCT and MBRP [as well as mindfulness-based stress reduction (MBSR; Kabat-Zinn, 1994) the general health promotion program that both were adapted from] including regular lengthy practices, whereas others (e.g., DBT; Linehan, 1993; ABBT; Roemer & Orsillo, 2014) use briefer, more flexible formal practices. Formal practices can also include movement, such as mindful walking, yoga, or martial arts.

Mindfulness-based treatments typically include formal practice in sessions as well as home practice. However, a recent meta-analysis of mindfulness-based treatments (which did not include more integrative approaches, but only those with a central focus on these types of practices) found that duration of home practice did not moderate the effects of these mindfulness-based treatments on clinical outcomes (Khoury et al., 2013). In a review of studies specifically examining the role of home practice in mindfulness-based treatments on outcome, Vettese, Toneatto, Stea, Nguyen, and Wang (2009) reported inconsistent findings, with half the studies showing no associations between formal practice and outcomes. However, the same meta-analysis described above did find that improvements in dispositional mindfulness significantly moderated outcome at both posttreatment and follow-up (Khoury et al., 2013), indicating that developing the skill of mindfulness is an active component of these treatments, even if home formal practice may not be necessary.

Informal practices are also an integral part of mindfulness-based treatments (Baer, 2014; Roemer & Orsillo, 2009; Shapiro et al., 2014). These practices involve practicing being aware, in the moment, on purpose, with kindness and care, while engaging in daily activities. Often people begin with neutral activities, such as washing the dishes, folding laundry, or eating, and then begin practicing mindfulness in more challenging contexts, like job interviews, first dates, or difficult conversations. Informal practices provide an opportunity to apply new skills into daily life, and therefore are an essential part of using mindfulness to address clinical problems. For instance, among clients with generalized anxiety disorder, maintenance of treatment gains was associated with reported frequency of informal, but not formal, mindfulness practice (Morgan, Graham, Hayes-Skelton, Orsillo, & Roemer, 2014). Similarly, among smokers who received mindfulness training, reported informal mindfulness, but not formal practice, moderated the relations between craving and smoking such that among those who practiced informally, cravings were decoupled from smoking (Elwafi, Witkiewitz, Mallik, Thornhill, & Brewer, 2013).

Hayes-Skelton and Wadsworth (2015) and Szabo, Long, Villatte, and Hayes (2015) note that other commonly used CBT strategies may also cultivate mindfulness and should be studied. For instance, a case series illustrated ways that applied relaxation increased reports of mindfulness, even though no explicit references to mindfulness were included (Hayes-Skelton, Usmani, Lee, Roemer, & Orsillo, 2012). Findings from a recent randomized controlled trial also support this hypothesis: increases in reported mindfulness predicted reductions in social anxiety across clients who received a mindfulness and acceptance-based group therapy, as well as those who received traditional cognitive behavioral group therapy for social anxiety with no explicit mindfulness component (Kocovski, Fleming, Hawley, Ho, & Antony, 2015).

CONCEPTUAL CONNECTIONS BETWEEN MINDFULNESS AND CBT

Skillful integration of novel approaches necessitates a coherent conceptual basis for intervention so that clinicians can flexibly use strategies with clear understanding of why they are using a specific strategy, and what they hope it will accomplish, and so that clients can similarly understand the function behind different strategies; in essence, a comprehensive case formulation is needed to guide flexible clinical application (cf., Persons, 1989). Our integration of mindfulness into CBTs (Orsillo, Roemer, Block, & Tull, 2004) was precipitated by the findings that indicated that a critical, judgmental, fused relationship with internal experiences, rigid attempts to experiential avoid, and restrictions in meaningful actions were important clinical targets, as well as the conceptual overlap between proposed functions of mindfulness and those associated with other CBT approaches. Conceptualizing mindfulness as a skill that can be practiced and applied in daily living is consistent with a CBT skills-based approach. Mindfulness-based strategies are an additional tool that can help clients to notice their experience, relate differently to internal experiences, learn to tolerate and regulate distress, and develop a more flexible, adaptive behavioral repertoire to promote life satisfaction. To help guide others in this integration, we review some of the areas of overlap often identified in the literature.

Cultivating Awareness—Monitoring Experiences

At its core, mindfulness practices involve bringing attention to the present moment, to cultivate awareness. Self-monitoring in CBT can be thought of as serving a similar function; clients are asked to observe, in the moment, specific aspects of their experience and note them. This includes several skills highlighted in mindfulness practice—noticing what arises, in the moment, and noticing it with curiosity, as an observer. We find in our clinical practice that when clients are able to notice their experience and write it on a monitoring form, separating out the different aspects of experience, they often have a more curious, observational stance toward these experiences, consistent with other mindfulness practices. Conversely, formal and informal mindfulness practices can facilitate this self-monitoring so that clients are better able to notice responses in the moment.

The process of engaging in self-monitoring and mindfulness practice helps clients to notice patterns as they unfold. This serves several functions in CBT and in mindfulness-based interventions. It provides psychoeducation about the nature of interrelations among thoughts, emotions, and behaviors, as well as triggers, responses, and consequences. Baer (2014) describes how chain analyses in DBT and the process of inquiry after mindfulness practice in MBCT and MBSR help clients to recognize habitual, reactive responses and the process through which they arise. Noticing these patterns may also naturally increase self-compassion and reduce self-criticism because seemingly irrational, intense responses become more understandable. Finally, noticing these patterns facilitates the process of early cue detection (Borkovec & Sharpless, 2004), through which clients are eventually able to engage in new, nonhabitual responses in response to early cues, and strengthen new, more flexible, adaptive patterns of responding. Baer (2003) suggests that this early recognition allows for self-management and behavior change.

These proposed functions for mindfulness and self-monitoring lead to two clinical suggestions. First clinicians should help clients problem-solve how to complete monitoring forms in the moment that their responses are unfolding rather than later; otherwise clients are not learning the important skills of early cue detection and present moment focus that they will need to facilitate behavior change. Also, clinicians often overlook the role of inquiry after formal mindfulness practice. Without guided inquiry, clients often mistakenly think the purpose of formal practice is to clear their minds or feel relaxed. Through skillful inquiry, therapists can help clients use their formal practice to notice their experience as it unfolds, and bring compassion to those observations, so that they begin to relate differently to these experiences.

Expanding Rather Than Narrowing Awareness

Information processing models of clinical problems highlight the way that clinical problems are associated with narrowed awareness (e.g., noticing threatening cues and ignoring safety cues, remembering sad events or failure, rather than successes; Tolin, 2016). Mindfulness practices encourage more expansive awareness, which does not ignore or suppress these aspects of experiences but also allows for other experiences (e.g., noticing a whole audience, instead of only those who are frowning or falling asleep). In fact, research indicates that mindfulness is associated with a broader awareness, with less affective bias, so that both external and internal stimuli (including one's own reactions) are more accurately perceived (Davis & Thompson, 2015). As such, these practices may help to alter these rigid styles of information processing.

If mindfulness is being used to counter rigid, narrow processing of information, clinicians need to intentionally promote this more expansive, flexible attention through practices and inquiry. Clients may begin to use mindfulness practices as another way of narrowing attention (e.g., focusing on the breath as a way to avoid feeling anxious or worrying) or as a rigid style of responding to distress. When this happens, practices that promote broadened awareness and flexibility may be particularly important.

Interacting Differently With Thoughts

Although there are notable differences between mindfulness approaches to thoughts and traditional cognitive restructuring, there are also important commonalities. Both emphasize recognizing that thoughts are just thoughts, rather than enduring facts (e.g., Irving et al., 2015). Mindfulness practices aimed at decentering from thoughts (e.g., imagining putting thoughts on leaves on a stream; Hayes et al., 2011; or picturing thoughts and feelings as clouds passing through the sky; Linehan, 2015; Roemer & Orsillo, 2009) can help promote this awareness. Research also shows that cognitive therapy, including cognitive restructuring, can similarly lead to increased decentering (metacognitive awareness, Teasdale et al., 2002), suggesting that, even though challenging thoughts is not a typical mindfulness-based strategy, it may also lead to a different relationship to thoughts.

Another similarity between mindfulness-based approaches and cognitive restructuring is that both help clients to incorporate new information. In mindfulness-based treatments, the broadening of attention described above can help clients become aware of new information, which may disconfirm rigidly held beliefs, although these beliefs are not replaced by new ones and they may reemerge in the future. Both treatment approaches also highlight that thoughts do not have to control behavior and that new learning can occur when we look at our experience rather than focusing solely on the thoughts that arise or what we believe.

One particular type of thought that mindfulness-based treatments target particularly is self-critical thoughts. Again, these thoughts are not challenged through cognitive restructuring, but the underlying assumption of mindfulness- and ABBTs that thoughts, sensations, and feelings are all natural, human, understandable occurrences (similar to a traditional cognitive-behavioral model of the cycle of internal experiences) directly contradicts commonly arising thoughts that symptoms are a sign of weakness or a flaw in the individual. Cultivating "friendly" or "kind" attention to one's experiences counters the common habit of judging and criticizing these experiences. As a result, mindfulness-based treatments directly target self-critical thoughts and cultivate self-compassion. Compassion-focused treatments (e.g., Germer & Neff, 2013; Gilbert, 2010) and specific mindfulness practices like loving kindness meditation (Hofmann, Grossman, & Hinton, 2011) more explicitly cultivate self-compassion and target self-critical thoughts; these approaches are beyond the scope of this chapter, but they overlap in many ways with mindfulness-based approaches.

This distinction of function rather than form is important to keep in mind in clinical practice. Rather than adhering to certain strategies (e.g., mindfulness practices) and eschewing others (e.g., cognitive restructuring), therapists can focus on how to help clients relate differently to their thoughts rather than treating them as enduring facts. Clinicians should remain sensitive to whether any strategies (including mindfulness practice) are instead being used as a way to change one thought to another or to suppress certain thoughts, as this sends an inconsistent message and may instead strengthen judgment and avoidance of thoughts.

Turning Intentionally Toward Instead of Habitually Away—Exposure

Baer (2003) reviews how Kabat-Zinn, Linehan, and others have described exposure as an underlying mechanism of mindfulness practices, as these practices involve turning toward avoided experiences (e.g., painful sensations, emotions, thoughts), and learning that they are not as threatening as imagined. Bowen, Vieten, Witkiewitz, and Carroll (2015) observe that mindfulness can be thought of as exposure with response prevention in that practitioners are encouraged to notice unpleasant experiences and to refrain from avoidance or suppression strategies. Relatedly, Treanor (2011) suggests that mindfulness may enhance extinction learning by broadening awareness of stimuli and acting as a retrieval cue. A pilot study indicates that a brief version of ACT can be effectively integrated with exposure therapy for panic disorder, leading to increases in mindfulness and decreases in symptoms (Meuret, Twohig, Rosenfield, Hayes, & Craske, 2012).

The continual practice of turning toward internal experiences in mindfulness practice (and self-monitoring) is likely to naturally reduce suppression (i.e., experiential avoidance), which should also result in reduction in symptoms. Supporting this proposed mechanism, reports of suppressing unwanted thoughts partially mediated the effects of a mindfulness meditation intervention on alcohol use at follow-up (Bowen, Witkiewitz, Dillworth, & Marlatt, 2007). Mindfulness has also been associated with increased voluntary exposure in several studies (see Arch & Landy, 2015 for a review).

This proposed function highlights the potential of mindfulness practices facilitating exposure-based strategies in CBT, as well as the importance of including mindfulness practices that involve awareness of thoughts and emotions in clinical practice. The mindfulness exercise "Inviting a difficulty in and working it through the body" (Segal et al., 2013) may be particularly beneficial in facilitating this extinction (or inhibitory) learning aspect of treatment. This model also highlights the importance of noticing when mindfulness is leading to experiences of relaxation or reduced distress for clients. This can be a natural outcome of the practices, because of the reduced struggle with internal experiences. However, clients also benefit from opportunities to practice when they do not experience calm or relaxation, so clinicians can make sure these opportunities arise. By focusing on the function of approaching threatening internal experiences, clinicians can use a range of strategies flexibly and avoid the risk of encouraging suppression (Arch & Craske, 2008).

Learning to Tolerate and Regulate Emotional Distress

One suggestion of how the exposure function of mindfulness-based approaches may be beneficial is through the distress tolerance and emotion regulation abilities that are developed from mindfulness skills. Development of tolerance of fear and anxiety is now seen as one of the central goals of exposure, to facilitate inhibitory learning (Craske et al.,

2008). Many theorists and researchers have explored how challenges in noticing, clarifying, modulating, and recovering from emotional states relate to clinical problems (e.g., Gross, 2015; Hofmann, Sawyer, Fang, and Asnaani, 2012; Mennin & Fresco, 2015). Through the processes described above (noticing emotions as they arise, decentering from these experiences so that they are not experienced as permanent and defining, turning toward these experiences rather than avoiding or suppressing them), clients who practice mindfulness are likely to experience enhanced tolerance of emotions, as well as regulation of these emotional states. Specifically, research suggests that mindfulness may lead to reduced intensity of distress, enhanced emotional recovery, reduced negative self-referential processing, and/or enhanced ability to engage in goal-directed behaviors while distressed (see Roemer, Williston, & Rollins, 2015 for a review). Mediation studies indicate that reduced emotional and cognitive reactivity may be a mechanism of change in MBSR and MBCT (Gu, Strauss, Bond, & Cavanaugh, 2015).

In clinical practice, mindfulness skills may be effectively integrated with other emotion regulation strategies (such as in DBT). When synthesizing these strategies, an acceptance-based model of emotion regulation, in which the focus is on understanding and accepting emotions, feeling able to respond skillfully to them, and being able to choose to act or refrain from actions while distressed (Gratz & Roemer, 2004) will facilitate a coherent conceptualization that clients can follow. Within this frame, strategies that may reduce distress are seen as lessening the struggle or reactivity to emotions (e.g., "muddy," Roemer & Orsillo, 2009; or "dirty," Hayes et al., 2011; emotions), rather than lessening or avoiding natural human responses to experiences. An emphasis on reducing intensity or duration rather than occurrence of emotions is less likely to lead to experiential avoidance and suppression.

Enhancing New Learning, Flexible Behavioral Repertoires, Responsiveness to Context, and Intentional, Autonomous Action

Each of the sections above described a specific type of new learning that mindfulness may facilitate. Mindfulness may also enhance flexible new learning more broadly. A central principle of behavioral approaches to clinical change is to reduce habitual, rigid responding and to promote more flexible behavioral repertoires that are responsive to context, and to intention, so as to allow behaviors that are not immediately reinforced but lead to long-term desirable consequences (Antony & Roemer, 2011). Greater awareness of the present moment can allow individuals to notice opportunities to engage in new, nonhabitual behaviors. Decentering or "decoupling" internal responses from the actions they are associated with facilitates engagement in these new behaviors (Levin, Luoma, & Haeger, 2015). In a review of studies that investigated decoupling across a wide range of clinical presentations, Levin et al. (2015) found evidence that mindfulness and acceptance-based treatments led to greater decoupling, with the strongest evidence to date emerging for decoupling of urges and substance use. Finally, mindfulness may help individuals to connect more fully with what matters to them in the moment so that they are able to make autonomous choices, rather than being affected by immediate circumstances or reactivity (Deci, Ryan, Schultz, & Niemiec, 2015; Hayes et al., 2011; Roemer & Orsillo, 2009; Shapiro et al., 2014).

In our clinical application of mindfulness-based strategies, we incorporate psychoeducation about the function of emotions and the distinction between action tendencies and required actions (Linehan, 1993), so as to facilitate this decoupling, and to enhance clients' ability to choose their actions. We also draw from ACT in helping clients to clarify what matters to them so that they are more able, in the moment, to choose an action that is consistent with how they want to be, rather than one that stems from reactivity or experiential avoidance. Finally, we emphasize informal practice and self-monitoring in part so that clients are able to apply awareness in the context of their lives, helping them to choose meaningful actions and change their habitual behavioral patterns.

EVIDENCE BASE FOR MINDFULNESS-BASED TREATMENTS

Brief Description of Treatments

The first, most widely used mindfulness-based intervention, MBSR, was explicitly designed as an education- rather than therapeutic-oriented, complementary health promotion program to be offered to mixed groups of medical patients (i.e., not diagnosis-specific; Kabat-Zinn, 1996). It consists of eight sessions, typically 2.5—3.5 hours long, as well as an all-day retreat, offered to a class of 15—40 participants. Classes are highly experiential, including formal practices like the body scan, mindfully eating a raisin, mindful yoga, mindful walking, as well as informal mindfulness practices. Participants are expected to practice at least 45 minutes 6 days a week throughout the program. The program also includes inquiry and monitoring of pleasant and unpleasant events (Baer, 2014).

Other programs adapt the MBSR program to specifically target clinical presentations. For instance, MBCT integrates MBSR with CBT for depression in order to reduce relapse in major depressive disorders. Specifically, it incorporates psychoeducation about automatic thoughts and mood, identification of early triggers and warnings, and monitoring pleasure and mastery daily into MBSR (Irving et al., 2015). MBRP integrates MBSR and MBCT with CBT relapse prevention strategies to directly target addiction with strategies such as urge surfing, identifying antecedents of relapse, and cultivating self-efficacy and life balance, in addition to formal and informal mindfulness practices (Witkiewitz et al., 2014). Mindfulness-based eating awareness training (MB-EAT; Kristeller & Wolever, 2014) integrates MBSR with cognitive-behavioral strategies, eating meditations, and nutrition and exercise information to help individuals increase their awareness of triggers and reactivity and to promote wise choices.

A number of interventions have been developed that integrate mindfulness-based strategies, often drawing from MBSR and MBCT, into broader cognitive-behavioral protocols that are administered in groups or individually for a wide range of clinical presentations. For instance, our own ABBT for generalized anxiety disorder (ABBT for GAD; Roemer & Orsillo, 2014) integrates mindfulness-based strategies with interventions drawn from ACT and CBT for GAD in a 14 session (with two tapered sessions for relapse prevention) individual treatment for GAD and comorbid clinical disorders. Similarly, Mindfulness and Acceptance-Based Group Therapy for Social Anxiety Disorders integrates exercises from MBCT into an ACT intervention for social anxiety disorder that includes exposure exercises with an acceptance-based rationale (Kocovski, Fleming, & Rector, 2009).

Meta-Analysis and Selected Randomized Clinical Trial Findings

A recent systematic review and meta-analysis of systematic reviews of MBSR and MBCT in both medical and psychiatric settings revealed significant effects of both MBSR and MBCT on depressive symptoms, anxiety symptoms, stress, and quality of life among individuals with cancer; depressive symptoms, pain burden, and physical health among individuals with chronic pain; depression, anxiety, stress, and hypertension among individuals with cardiovascular disease, reduced risk of depression (compared to treatment as usual) for individuals with major depressive disorder and a history of three or more episodes, reduced anxiety symptoms for individuals with anxiety disorders, reduced anxiety and depressive symptoms in clients with bipolar disorders, and improved clinical functioning among individuals with schizophrenia (Gotink et al., 2015). The authors describe further complexity in their review: MBCT was found to be superior to MBSR among individuals with an anxiety or depressive disorder, and a cognitive behavioral treatment for social anxiety disorder yielded larger effects than MBSR for social anxiety. However, in two more recent trials, MBSR yielded comparable effects to a group CBT for social anxiety (Goldin et al., 2016) and an adapted MBSR (with shortened practices and psychoeducation related to anxiety) yielded comparable effects to a group CBT for clients with mixed anxiety disorders (Arch et al., 2013). In their meta-analysis, Khoury et al. (2013) found that mindfulness-based treatments were more effective than active treatments such as psychoeducation, relaxation, supportive therapy, imagery, and art therapy, but not than cognitive-behavioral therapies. Taken together, these reviews and meta-analyses indicate that MBSR and MBCT both lead to significant decreases in a range of symptoms among medical and clinical samples, although not more than those associated with CBT for specific clinical presentations.

Chiesa and Serretti (2014) conducted a systematic review of studies that examined any intervention that included mindfulness (including ACT and DBT, as well as MBRP) and a comparison condition in the treatment of substance use. They concluded that mindfulness-based interventions can decrease the use of a number of substances, including alcohol, cigarettes, cocaine, opiates, and amphetamines more than wait-list conditions and nonspecific educational support groups, but not CBT, although these findings are not always replicated. An RCT published after this review revealed that both MBRP and relapse prevention (RP, a CBT for addiction) led to reduced alcohol and drug use in comparison to an abstinence-based treatment as usual, with RP showing longer time to first drug use at the 6-month follow-up and MBRP showing significantly fewer days of substance use and less heavy drinking than RP at a 12-month follow-up (Bowen et al., 2014).

Recently, internet-based mindfulness interventions have been developed and tested. A recent meta-analysis indicates that these approaches (broadly defined to include ACT and other integrative programs) show promise: small-to-medium effects on measures of stress, anxiety, depression, and well-being emerged, with preliminary evidence that guided interventions may be more effective (Spijkerman, Pots, & Bohlmeijer, 2016). However, these findings are preliminary and more research is needed to examine the long-term effects of these interventions. In addition, many studies used healthy participants, which may have underestimated effect sizes (due to ceiling and floor effects). Finally, although mindfulness-based treatment research (similar to others) does not sufficiently include individuals from marginalized backgrounds (e.g., racial minorities, low socioeconomic status), a preliminary meta-analysis of studies that included large proportions of clients from nondominant backgrounds revealed small to large effect sizes for mindfulness-based treatments broadly defined (Fuchs, Lee, Roemer, &

Orsillo, 2013), suggesting promise in this area although much more research is needed.

Studies of ABBT for GAD have revealed significant large effects on symptoms of worry, anxiety, and depression, as well as quality of life and number of comorbid disorders that is greater than waitlist and comparable to an empirically based CBT for GAD (see Roemer & Orsillo, 2014 for a review). An internet-based ABBT for GAD has also shown large effect sized reductions in GAD symptoms and moderate effect sized reductions in depressive symptoms, compared to a waitlist condition (Dahlin et al., 2016). Similarly, Mindfulness and Acceptance-Based Group Therapy yielded significantly greater outcomes than waitlist, which were comparable to group CBT, in treating social anxiety disorder (Kocovski, Fleming, Hawley, Huta, & Antony, 2013).

Evidence for Mechanisms of Change

Gu et al. (2015) conducted a systematic review of 20 studies that examined mediators of clinical outcomes in studies of MBSR and MBCT, and meta-analyses when sufficient published studies of a given mediator were identified. They concluded that there was strong and consistent evidence for reduced cognitive and emotional reactivity as a mediator, as well as consistent, moderate evidence for mindfulness and reduced negative repetitive thought, while evidence for self-compassion and psychological flexibility was preliminary and insufficient. However, they note that the majority of studies did not establish temporal precedence or include an active treatment comparison group, indicating that more research is needed to confirm these findings. Penberthy et al. (2015) review the limited research to date on mechanisms of change in MBRP, noting preliminary evidence for awareness, acceptance, and nonjudgment as mediators of levels of craving at posttreatment. Latent difference score analyses (which examine temporal precedence) indicate that changes in self-reported decentering precede changes in anxiety among individuals with GAD who receive both ABBT and applied relaxation (Hayes-Skelton, Roemer, & Orsillo, 2015), whereas changes in mindfulness and social anxiety are bidirectionally related in both mindfulness and acceptance group therapy and cognitive behavior group therapy (Kocovski et al., 2015).

FUTURE DIRECTIONS

Research has established the potential utility of mindfulness-based interventions in targeting a broad range of clinical interventions, with strongest evidence for targeting depressive and anxiety symptoms, while also indicating that these interventions may work through increasing decentering and reducing emotional and cognitive reactivity. However, considerably more research is needed. Studies are needed that better establish the temporal precedence of examined mechanisms, explore how proposed mechanisms relate to one another, distinguish between common and specific mechanisms of change and how best to target each, and identify any moderators of treatment effects that can help us determine who is most likely to benefit from these approaches. We also need a better understanding of the role of formal and informal practice in promoting these mechanisms and meaningful change. These studies, in turn, will help us determine how best to disseminate these approaches, while retaining their core therapeutic features, and how to integrate them with other CBT approaches. This will include exploring efficacy of differing lengths and modalities of treatments.

We need to learn more about cultural adaptations of these approaches so that we can use them skillfully in diverse contexts (Fuchs et al., 2013; see Hinton, Pich, Hofmann, & Otto, 2013 for an example). One interesting area for future study is the potential role that mindfulness may play in buffering the negative psychological impact of discrimination for individuals from marginalized backgrounds. Preliminary correlational research indicates that dispositional mindfulness is associated with a reduced or eliminated relation between experiences of discrimination and symptoms of anxiety and depression (e.g., Brown-Iannuzzi, Adair, Payne, Richman, & Frederickson, 2014; Graham, West, & Roemer, 2013; Lyons, 2016). We need to determine how to effectively use mindfulness strategies to buffer the negative impact of these experiences. Validation of the reality and pain of these experiences will be an important first step, based on our clinical experiences. Mindfulness may, however, help to reduce the internalization of these experiences that likely promotes and prolongs clinical symptoms (e.g., Graham, West, Martinez, & Roemer, 2016).

SUMMARY

Mindfulness- (and acceptance-) based strategies have been integrated with a wide range of CBT strategies to target a range of clinical presentations among both medical and psychological populations. Many of these approaches involve MBSR or adaptations of MBSR and have a central emphasis on length formal mindfulness practices (e.g., 45 minutes) practiced in session and at home, in addition to informal practices that are applied to daily life. Other approaches, such as DBT, use briefer more flexible mindfulness practices as well as numerous other cognitive behavioral strategies. Approaches also vary on whether they are adapted for specific clinical presentations or meant to address well-being more broadly.

Theory and research suggests that these strategies overlap with other CBT strategies in that they enhance awareness (monitoring), broaden attention/information processing, help clients to relate differently to thoughts, encourage approaching distressing material rather than avoiding/suppressing, enhance distress tolerance/emotion regulation (i.e., reduced emotional and cognitive reactivity), and build flexible, adaptive behavioral repertoires. Awareness of these proposed functions of mindfulness and other strategies can help clinicians to flexibly, skillfully apply and integrate them in a coherent, effective way with their clients.

Meta-analyses and systemic reviews document the efficacy of these approaches, although more research is needed on mechanisms of action, with particular attention to both common and specific mechanisms of change and how a range of strategies may promote some of the mechanisms associated with mindfulness. We also need to learn more about how to culturally adapt these approaches so that they are acceptable and responsive to clients from a range of backgrounds. Research in these areas will help us more skillfully apply, integrate, and disseminate these promising interventions.

References

Arch, J. J., Ayers, C. R., Baker, A., Almklov, E., Dean, D. J., & Craske, M. G. (2013). Randomized clinical trial of adapted mindfulness-based stress reduction versus group cognitive behavioral therapy for heterogeneous anxiety disorders. *Behaviour Research and Therapy*, 51, 185–196. Available from http://dx.doi.org/10.1016/j.brat.2013.01.003.

Arch, J. J., & Craske, M. G. (2008). Acceptance and commitment therapy and cognitive behavioral therapy for anxiety disorders: Different treatments, similar mechanisms? *Clinical Psychology: Science and Practice*, 15, 263–279. Available from http://dx.doi.org/ 10.1111/j.1468-2850.2008.00137.x.

Arch, J. J., & Landy, L. N. (2015). Emotional benefits of mindfulness. In K. W. Brown, J. D. Cresswell, & R. M. Ryan (Eds.), *Handbook of mindfulness: Theory, research, and practice*. New York: The Guilford Press.

Antony, M. M., & Roemer, L. (2011). *Behavior therapy*. Washington, DC: American Psychological Association Press.

Baer, R. A. (2003). Mindfulness training as a clinical intervention: A conceptual and empirical review. *Clinical Psychology: Science and Practice*, 10, 125–143. Available from http://dx.doi.org/10.1093/clipsy.bpg015.

Baer, R. (2014). Introduction to the core practices and exercises. In R. Baer (Ed.), *Mindfulness-based treatment approaches: Clinician's guide to evidence base and practice*. New York: Elsevier.

Barlow, D. H., Allen, L. B., & Choate, M. L. (2004). Toward a unifed protocol for emotional disorders. *Behavior Therapy*, 35, 205–230. Available from http://dx.doi.org/10.1080/ 07317100802701228.

Borkovec, T. D., & Sharpless, B. (2004). Generalized anxiety disorder: Bringing cognitive-behavioral therapy into the valued present. In S. C. Hayes, V. M. Follette, & M. M. Linehan (Eds.), *Mindfulness and acceptance: Expanding the cognitive-behavioral tradition* (pp. 209−242). New York: Guilford Press.

Bowen, S., Chawla, N., & Marlatt, G. A. (2011). *Mindfulness-based relapse prevention for addictive behaviors: A clinician's guide.* New York: The Guilford Press.

Bowen, S., Witkiewitz, K., Clifasefi, S. L., Grow, J., Chawla, N., Hsu, S. H., ... Larimer, M. E. (2014). Relative efficacy of mindfulness-based relapse prevention, standard relapse prevention, and treatment as usual for substance use disorders: A randomized clinical trial. *JAMA Psychiatry, 71*, 547−556. Available from http://dx.doi.org/10.1001/jamapsychiatry.2013.4546.

Bowen, S., Witkiewitz, K., Dillworth, T. M., & Marlatt, G. A. (2007). The role of thought suppression in the relationship between mindfulness mediation and alcohol use. *Addictive Behaviors, 32*, 2324−2328. Available from http://dx.doi.org/10.1016/j.addbeh.2007.01.025.

Bowen, S., Vieten, C., Witkiewitz, K., & Carroll, H. (2015). A mindfulness approach to addiction. In K. W. Brown, J. D. Cresswell, & R. M. Ryan (Eds.), *Handbook of mindfulness: Theory, research, and practice.* New York: The Guilford Press.

Brown, K. W., Cresswell, Jd, & Ryan, R. M. (Eds.), (2015). *Handbook of mindfulness: Theory, research, & practice* New York: The Guilford Press.

Brown, K. W., & Ryan, R. M. (2004). Perils and promise in defining and measuring mindfulness: Observations from experience. *Clinical Psychology: Science & Practice, 11*, 242−248. Available from http://dx.doi.org/10.1093/clipsy.bph078.

Brown-Iannuzzi, J. L., Adair, K. C., Payne, B. K., Richman, L. S., & Frederickson, B. L. (2014). Discrimination hurts, but mindfulness may help: Trait mindfulness moderates the relationship between perceived discrimination and depressive symptoms. *Personality and Individual Differences, 56*, 201−205. Available from http://dx.doi.org/10.1016/j.paid.2013.09.015.

Chiesa, A., & Serretti, A. (2014). Are mindfulness-based interventions effective for substance use disorders? A systematic review of the evidence. *Substance Use & Misuse, 49*, 492−512. Available from http://dx.doi.org/10.3109/10826084.2013.770027.

Craske, M. G. (2010). *Cognitive behavioral therapy.* Washington, DC: American Psychological Association Press.

Craske, M. G., Kircanski, K., Zelikowsky, M., Mystkowski, J., Chowdhury, N., & Baker, A. (2008). Optimizing inhibitory learning during exposure therapy. *Behaviour Research and Therapy, 46*, 5−27. Available from http://dx.doi.org/10.1016/j.brat.2007.10.003.

Dahlin, M., Andersson, G., Magnusson, K., Johansson, T., Sjögren, J., Håkansson, A., ... Carlbring, P. (2016). Internet-delivered acceptance-based behaviour therapy for generalized anxiety disorder: A randomized controlled trial. *Behaviour Research and Therapy, 77*, 86−95. Available from http://dx.doi.org/10.1016/j.brat.2015.12.007.

Davis, J. H., & Thompson, E. (2015). Developing attention and decreasing affective bias: Toward a cross-cultural cognitive science of mindfulness. In K. W. Brown, J. D. Cresswell, & R. M. Ryan (Eds.), *Handbook of mindfulness: Theory, research, & practice.* New York: The Guilford Press.

Deci, E. L., Ryan, R. M., Schultz, P. P., & Niemiec, C. P. (2015). Being aware and functioning fully: Mindfulness and interest-taking within self-determination theory. In K. W. Brown, J. D. Creswell, & R. M. Ryan (Eds.), *Handbook of mindfulness: Theory, research, and practice.* New York, NY: Guilford Press.

DeMartini, K. S., & Carey, K. B. (2011). The role of anxiety sensitivity and drinking motives in predicting alcohol use: A critical review. *Clinical Psychology Review, 31*, 169−177. Available from http://dx.doi.org/10.1016/j.cpr.2010.10.001.

Elwafi, H. M., Witkiewitz, K., Mallik, S., Thornhill, T. A., & Brewer, J. A. (2013). Mindfulness training for smoking cessation: Moderation of the relationship between craving and cigarette use. *Drug and Alcohol Dependence*, *130*(0), 222–229. Available from http://dx.doi.org/10.1016/j.drugalcdep.2012.11.015.

Fuchs, C., Lee, J. K., Roemer, L., & Orsillo, S. M. (2013). Using mindfulness- and acceptance-based treatments with clients from nondominant cultural and/or marginalized backgrounds: Client considerations, meta-analysis findings and introduction to the special series. *Cognitive and Behavioral Practice*, *20*, 1–12. Available from http://dx.doi.org/10.1016/j.cbpra.2011.12.004.

Garland, E. L., Farb, N. A., Goldin, P. R., & Frederickson, B. L. (2015). Mindfulness broadens awareness and builds eudaimonic meaning: A process model of mindful positive emotion regulation. *Psychological Inquiry*, *26*, 293–314. Available from http://dx.doi.org/10.1080/1047840X.2015.1064294.

Germer, C. K., & Neff, K. D. (2013). Self-compassion in clinical practice. *Journal of Clinical Psychology*, *69*, 856–867. Available from http://dx.doi.org/10.1002/jclp.22021.

Gilbert, P. (2010). *The compassionate mind: A new approach to life's challenges*. Oakland, CA: New Harbinger.

Goldin, P. R., Morrison, A., Jazaieri, H., Brozovich, F., Heimberg, R. G., & Gross, J. J. (2016). Group CBT versus MBSR for social anxiety disorder: A randomized controlled trial. *Journal of Consulting and Clinical Psychology*, *84*, 427–437. Available from http://dx.doi.org/10.1037/ccp0000092.

Gotink, R. A., Chu, P., Busschbach, J. J. V., Benson, H., Fricchione, G. L., & Myriam Hunink, M. G. M. (2015). Standardised mindfulness-based interventions in healthcare—An overview systematic reviews and meta-analyses of RCTs. *PLoS ONE*, *10*, 1–17. Available from http://dx.doi.org/10.1371/journal.pone.0124344.

Graham, J. R., West, L. M., Martinez, J., & Roemer, L. (2016). The mediating role of internalized racism in the relationship between racist experiences and anxiety symptoms in a Black American sample. *Cultural Diversity and Ethnic Minority Psychology*, *22*, 369–376. Available from http://dx.doi.org/10.1037/cpd0000073.

Graham, J. R., West, L., & Roemer, L. (2013). The experience of racism and anxiety symptoms in an African American Sample: Moderating effects of trait mindfulness. *Mindfulness*, *4*, 332–341. Available from http://dx.doi.org/10.1007/s12671-012-0133-2.

Gratz, K. L., & Roemer, L. (2004). Multidimensional assessment of emotion regulation and dysregulation: Development, factor structure, and initial validation of the difficulties in emotion regulation scale. *Journal of Psychopathology and Behavioral Assessment*, *26*, 41–54. Available from http://dx.doi.org/10.1023/B:JOBA.0000007455.08539.94.

Gross, J. J. (2015). Emotion regulation: Current status and future prospects. *Psychological Inquiry*, *26*, 1–26. Available from http://dx.doi.org/10.1080/1047840X.2014.940781.

Gross, J. (2002). Emotion regulation: Affective, cognitive, and social consequences. *Psychophysiology*, *39*(3), 281–291. https://dx.doi.org/10.1017.S0048577201393198.

Gu, J., Strauss, C., Bond, R., & Cavanaugh, K. (2015). How do mindfulness-based cognitive therapy and mindfulness-based stress reduction improve mental health and wellbeing? A systematic review and meta-analysis of mediation studies. *Clinical Psychology Review*, *37*, 1–12. Available from http://dx.doi.org/10.1016/j.cpr.2015.01.006.

Hartley, S., Haddock, G., Vasconcelos e Sa, D., Emsley, R., & Barrowclough, C. (2015). The influence of thought control on the experience of persecutory delusions and auditory hallucinations in daily life. *Behaviour Research and Therapy*, *65*, 1–4. Available from http://dx.doi.org/10.1016/j.brat.2014.12.002.

Hayes, S. C. (2004). Acceptance and commitment therapy, relational frame theory, and the third wave of behavioral and cognitive therapies. *Behavior Therapy*, *35*, 639–665. Available from http://dx.doi.org/10.1016/S0005-7894(04)80013-3.

Hayes, S. C., Follette, V. M., & Linehan, M. M. (Eds.), (2004). *Mindfulness and acceptance: Expanding the cognitive-behavioral tradition*. New York: Guilford Press.

Hayes, S. C., Strosahl, K. D., & Wilson, K. G. (2011). *Acceptance and commitment therapy. The process and practice of mindful change* (2nd ed). New York: The Guilford Press.

Hayes, S. C., Villatte, M., Levin, M., & Hildebrandt, M. (2011). Open, aware, and active: Contextual approaches as an emerging trend in the behavioral and cognitive therapies. *Annual Review of Clinical Psychology, 7,* 141–168. Available from http://dx.doi.org/ 10.1146/annurev-clinpsy-032210-104449.

Hayes, S. C., Wilson, K. G., Gifford, E. V., Follette, V. M., & Strosahl, K. (1996). Experiential avoidance and behavioral disorders: A functional dimensional approach to diagnosis and treatment. *Journal of Consulting and Clinical Psychology, 64,* 1152–1168.

Hayes-Skelton, S. A., Roemer, L., & Orsillo, S. M. (2015). Decentering as a potential common mechanism across two therapies for generalized anxiety disorder. *Journal of Consulting and Clinical Psychology, 83,* 395–404. Available from http://dx.doi.org/ 10.1037/a0038305.

Hayes-Skelton, S. A., Usmani, A., Lee, J. K., Roemer, L., & Orsillo, S. M. (2012). A fresh look at potential mechanisms of change in applied relaxation for generalized anxiety disorder: A case series. *Cognitive and Behavioral Practice, 19,* 451–462. Available from http://dx.doi.org/10.1016/j.cbpra.2011.12.005.

Hayes-Skelton, S. A., & Wadsworth, L. P. (2015). Mindfulness in the treatment of anxiety. In K. W. Brown, J. D. Cresswell, & R. M. Ryan (Eds.), *Handbook of mindfulness: Theory, research, and practice.* New York: The Guilford Press.

Herzberg, K. N., Sheppard, S. C., Forsyth, J. P., Credé, M., Earleywine, M., & Eifert, G. H. (2012). The believability of anxious feelings and thoughts questionnaire (BAFT): A psychometric evaluation of cognitive fusion in a nonclinical and highly anxious community sample. *Psychological Assessment, 24*(4), 877–891. Available from http://dx.doi. org/10.1037/a0027782.

Hinton, D. E., Pich, V., Hofmann, S. G., & Otto, M. W. (2013). Acceptance and mindfulness techniques as applied to refugee and ethnic minority populations with PTSD: Examples from "Culturally Adapted CBT". *Cognitive and Behavioral Practice, 20,* 33–46. Available from http://dx.doi.org/10.1016/j.cbpra.2011.09.001.

Hofmann, S. G., Grossman, P., & Hinton, D. E. (2011). Loving-kindness and compassion meditation: Potential for psychological interventions. *Clinical Psychology Review, 31,* 1126–1132. Available from http://dx.doi.org/10.1016/j.cpr.2011.07.003.

Hofmann, S. G., Sawyer, A. T., Fang, A., & Asnaani, A. (2012). Emotion dysregulation model of mood and anxiety disorders. *Depression and Anxiety, 29,* 409–416. Available from http://dx.doi.org/10.1002/da.21888.

Irving, J. A., Farb, N. A. S., & Segal, Z. V. (2015). Mindfulness-based cognitive therapy for chronic depression. In K. W. Brown, J. D. Cresswell, & R. M. Ryan (Eds.), *Handbook of mindfulness: Theory, research, and practice.* New York: The Guilford Press.

Kabat-Zinn, J. (1994). *Wherever you go, there you are: Mindfulness meditation in everyday life.* New York: Hyperion.

Kabat-Zinn, J. (1996). Mindfulness meditation: What it is, what it isn't, and it's role in health care and medicine. In Y. Haruki, Y. Ishii, & M. Suzuki (Eds.), *Comparative and psychological study on meditation* (pp. 161–169). Netherlands: Eburon.

Khoury, B., Lecomte, T., Fortin, G., Masse, M., Therien, P., Bouchard, V., . . . Hofmann, S. G. (2013). Mindfulness-based therapy: A comprehensive meta-analysis. *Clinical Psychology Review, 33,* 763–771. Available from http://dx.doi.org/10.1016/j. cpr.2013.05.005.

Kocovski, N. L., Fleming, J. E., Hawley, L. L., Ho, M. H., & Antony, M. M. (2015). Mindfulness and acceptance-based group therapy and traditional cognitive behavioral group therapy for social anxiety disorder: Mechanisms of change. *Behaviour Research and Therapy, 70,* 11–22. Available from http://dx.doi.org/10.1016/j.brat.2015.04.005.

Kocovski, N. L., Fleming, J. E., Hawley, L. L., Huta, V., & Antony, M. M. (2013). Mindfulness and acceptance-based group therapy versus traditional cognitive behavioral group therapy for social anxiety disorder: A randomized controlled trial. *Behaviour Research and Therapy, 51,* 889–898. Available from http://dx.doi.org/10.1016/j.brat.2013.10.007.

Kocovski, N. L., Fleming, J. E., & Rector, N. A. (2009). Mindfulness and acceptance-based group therapy for social anxiety disorder: An open trial. *Cognitive and Behavioral Practice, 16,* 276–289. Available from http://dx.doi.org/10.1016/j.cbpra.2008.12.004.

Kristeller, J. L., & Wolever, R. Q. (2014). Mindfulness-based eating awareness training: Treatment of overeating and obesity. In R. Baer (Ed.), *Mindfulness-based treatment approaches, second edition* (pp. 121–141). MA: Elsevier, Waltham.

Levin, M. D., Luoma, J. B., & Haeger, J. A. (2015). Decoupling as a mechanism of change in mindfulness and acceptance: A literature review. *Behavior Modification, 39,* 870–911. Available from http://dx.doi.org/10.1177/0145445515603707.

Levitt, J. T., Brown, T. A., Orsillo, S. M., & Barlow, D. H. (2004). The effects of acceptance versus suppression of emotion on subjective and psychophysiological response to carbon dioxide challenge in patients with panic disorder. *Behavior Therapy, 35,* 747–766. Available from http://dx.doi.org/10.1016/S0005-7894(04)80018-2.

Linehan, M. M. (1993). *Cognitive-behavioral treatment of borderline personality disorder.* New York: The Guilford Press.

Linehan, M. M. (2015). *DBT skills manual* (2nd ed). New York: The Guilford Press.

Lyons, A. (2016). Mindfulness attenuates the impact of discrimination on the mental health of middle-aged and older gay men. *Psychology of Sexual Orientation and Gender Diversity, 3,* 227–235. Available from http://dx.doi.org/10.1037/sgd0000164.

Mennin, D. S., & Fresco, D. M. (2015). Advancing emotion regulation perspectives on psychopathology: The challenge of distress disorders. *Psychological Inquiry, 26,* 80–92. Available from http://dx.doi.org/10.1080/1047840X.2015.969624.

Mennin, D. S., Heimberg, R. G., Turk, C. L., & Fresco, D. M. (2005). Preliminary evidence for an emotion dysregulation model of generalized anxiety disorder. *Behaviour Research and Therapy, 43*(10), 1281–1310. Available from http://dx.doi.org/10.1016/j.brat.2004.08.008.

Meuret, A. E., Twohig, M. P., Rosenfield, D., Hayes, S. C., & Craske, M. G. (2012). Brief acceptance and commitment therapy and exposure for panic disorder: A pilot study. *Cognitive and Behavioral Practice, 19*(4), 606–618. Available from http://dx.doi.org/10.1016/j.cbpra.2012.05.004.

Michelson, S. E., Lee, J. K., Orsillo, S. M., & Roemer, L. (2011). The role of values-consistent behavior in generalized anxiety disorder. *Depression and Anxiety, 28*(5), 358–366. Available from http://dx.doi.org/10.1002/da.20793.

Morgan, L., Graham, J. R., Hayes-Skelton, S. A., Orsillo, S. M., & Roemer, L. (2014). Relationships between amount of post-intervention of mindfulness practice and follow-up outcome variables in an acceptance-based behavior therapy for generalized anxiety disorder: The importance of informal practice. *Journal of Contextual Behavioral Science, 3,* 173–178. Available from http://dx.doi.org/10.1016/j.jcbs.2014.05.001.

Najmi, S., & Wegner, D. M. (2008). Thought suppression and psychopathology. In A. Elliot (Ed.), *Handbook of approach and avoidance motivation* (pp. 447–459). New York: Psychology Press.

Ocañez, K. L., McHugh, R. K., & Otto, M. W. (2010). A meta-analytic review of the association between anxiety sensitivity and pain. *Depression and Anxiety, 27,* 760–767. Available from http://dx.doi.org/10.1002/da.20681.

Olatunji, B. O., & Wolitzky-Taylor, K. B. (2009). Anxiety sensitivity and the anxiety disorders: A meta-analytic review and synthesis. *Psychological Bulletin, 135,* 974–999. Available from http://dx.doi.org/10.1037/a0017428.

Orsillo, S. M., Roemer, L., Block, J., & Tull, M. T. (2004). Acceptance, mindfulness, and cognitive behavioral therapy: Comparisons, contrasts and application to anxiety. In S. C. Hayes, V. M. Follette, & M. M. Linehan (Eds.), *Mindfulness and acceptance: Expanding the cognitive-behavior tradition*. New York: Guilford Press.

Penberthy, J. K., Konig, A., Gioia, C. J., Rodríguez, V. M., Starr, J. A., Meese, W., ... Natanya, E. (2015). Mindfulness-based relapse prevention: History, mechanisms of action, and effects. *Mindfulness, 6*, 151−158. Available from http://dx.doi.org/10.1007/s12671-013-0239-1.

Persons, J. B. (1989). *Cognitive therapy in practice: A case formulation approach*. New York: W.W. Norton & Company.

Roemer, L., & Borkovec, T. D. (1994). Effects of suppressing thoughts about emotional material. *Journal of Abnormal Psychology, 103*(3), 467−474.

Roemer, L., & Orsillo, S. M. (2009). *Mindfulness and acceptance-based behavioral therapies in practice*. New York: The Guilford Press.

Roemer, L., & Orsillo, S. M. (2014). An acceptance-based behavioral therapy for generalized anxiety disorder. In D. H. Barlow (Ed.), *Clinical handbook of psychological disorders: A step-by-step treatment manual* (5th ed., pp. 206−236). New York: The Guilford Press.

Roemer, L., Williston, S. K., & Rollins, L. G. (2015). Mindfulness and emotion regulation. *Current Opinion in Psychology, 3*, 52−57. Available from http://dx.doi.org/10.1016/j.copsyc.2015.02.006.

Sarısoy, G., Pazvantoğlu, O., Özturan, D. D., Ay, N. D., Yilman, T., Mor, S., & Gümüş, K. (2014). Metacognitive beliefs in unipolar and bipolar depression: A comparative study. *Nordic Journal of Psychiatry, 68*(4), 275−281. Available from http://dx.doi.org/10.3109/08039488.2013.814710.

Sauer, S. E., & Baer, R. A. (2009). Relationships between thought suppression and symptoms of borderline personality disorder. *Journal of Personality Disorders, 23*(1), 48−61. Available from http://dx.doi.org/10.1521/pedi.2009.23.1.48.

Sauer-Zavala, S., Boswell, J. F., Gallagher, M. W., Bentley, K. H., Ametaj, A., & Barlow, D. H. (2012). The role of negative affectivity and negative reactivity to emotions in predicting outcomes in the unified protocol for the transdiagnostic treatment of emotional disorders. *Behaviour Research and Therapy, 50*, 551−557. Available from http://dx.doi.org/10.1016/j.brat.2012.05.005.

Segal, Z. V., Williams, J. M. G., & Teasdale, J. D. (2013). *Mindfulness-based cognitive therapy for depression* (2nd ed). New York: The Guilford Press.

Shapiro, S. L., & Carlson, L. E. (2009). *The art and science of mindfulness: Integrating mindfulness into psychology and the helping professions*. Washington, DC: American Psychological Association.

Shapiro, S., Thakur, S., & de Sousa, S. (2014). Mindfulness for health care professionals and therapists in training. In R. Baer (Ed.), *Mindfulness-based treatment approaches: Clinicians' guide to evidence base and applications*. New York: Elsevier.

Sippel, L. M., & Marshall, A. D. (2013). Posttraumatic stress disorder and fear of emotions: The role of attentional control. *Journal of Traumatic Stress, 26*(3), 397−400. Available from http://dx.doi.org/10.1002/jts.21806.

Spijkerman, M. P. J., Pots, W. T. M., & Bohlmeijer, E. T. (2016). Effectiveness of online mindfulness- based interventions in improving mental health: A review and meta-analysis of randomized controlled trials. *Clinical Psychology Review, 45*, 102−114. Available from http://dx.doi.org/10.1016/j.cpr.2016.03.009.

Stewart, J. M. (Ed.), (2014). *Mindfulness, acceptance, and the psychodynamic evolution: Bringing valued into treatment planning and enhancing psychodynamic work with Buddhist psychology*. New York: Context Press.

Szabo, T. G., Long, D. M., Villatte, M., & Hayes, S. C. (2015). Mindfulness in contextual cognitive-behavioral models. In K. W. Brown, J. D. Cresswell, & R. M. Ryan (Eds.), *Handbook of mindfulness: Theory, research, and practice*. New York: The Guilford Press.

Teasdale, J. D., Moore, R. G., Hayhurst, H., Pope, M., Williams, S., & Segal, Z. V. (2002). Metacognitive awareness and prevention of relapse in depression: Empirical evidence. *Journal of Consulting and Clinical Psychology, 70*, 275−287. Available from http://dx.doi.org/10.1037//0022-006X.70.2.275.

Tolin, D. T. (2016). *Doing CBT: A comprehensive guide to working with behaviors, thoughts, and emotions*. New York: The Guilford Press.

Treanor, M. (2011). The potential impact of mindfulness on exposure and extinction learning in anxiety disorders. *Clinical Psychology Review, 31*, 617−625. Available from http://dx.doi.org/10.1016/j.cpr.2011.02.003.

van Rijsbergen, G. D., Bockting, C. H., Burger, H., Spinhoven, P., Koeter, M. J., Ruhé, H. G., & Schene, A. H. (2013). Mood reactivity rather than cognitive reactivity is predictive of depressive relapse: A randomized study with 5.5-year follow-up. *Journal of Consulting and Clinical Psychology, 81*(3), 508−517. Available from http://dx.doi.org/10.1037/a0032223.

Wells, A. (2000). *Emotional disorders and metacognition: Innovative cognitive therapy*. New York: Wiley.

Wells, A., & Carter, K. (2001). Further tests of a cognitive model of generalized anxiety disorder: Metacognitions and worry in GAD, panic disorder, social phobia, depression, and non-patients. *Behavior Therapy, 32*. Available from http://dx.doi.org/10.1016/S0005-7894(01)80045-9.

Werner-Seidler, A., Banks, R., Dunn, B. D., & Moulds, M. L. (2013). An investigation of the relationship between positive affect regulation and depression. *Behaviour Research and Therapy, 51*(1), 46−56. Available from http://dx.doi.org/10.1016/j.brat.2012.11.001.

Williams, K. E., Chambless, D. L., & Ahrens, A. (1997). Are emotion frightening? An extension of the fear of fear context. *Behaviour Research and Therapy, 35*, 239−248.

Wilson, K. G., & Murrell, A. R. (2004). Values work in acceptance and commitment therapy: Setting a course for behavioral treatment. In S. C. Hayes, V. M. Follette, & M. M. Linehan (Eds.), *Mindfulness and acceptance: Expanding the cognitive-behavioral tradition* (pp. 120−151). New York: Guilford Press.

Witkiewitz, K., Bowen, S., Harrop, E. N., Douglas, H., Enkema, M., & Sedgwick, C. (2014). Mindfulness-based treatment to prevent addictive behavior relapse: Theoretical models and hypothesized mechanisms of change. *Substance Use & Misuse, 49*, 513−524. Available from http://dx.doi.org/10.3109/10826084.2014.891845.

Vettese, L. C., Toneatto, T., Stea, J. N., Nguyen, L., & Wang, J. J. (2009). Do mindfulness meditation participants do their homework? And does it make a difference? A review of the empirical evidence. *Journal of Cognitive Psychotherapy, 23*, 198−225. Available from http://dx.doi.org/10.1891/0889-8391.23.3.198.

9

Global to Local: Adapting CBT for Cross-Cultural Expressions of Psychopathology

Anushka Patel[1] and Devon Hinton[2,3]

[1]The University of Tulsa, Tulsa, OK, United States [2]Arbour Counseling Services, Lowell, MA, United States [3]Massachusetts General Hospital and Harvard Medical School, Boston, MA, United States

GLOBAL TO LOCAL: ADAPTING CBT FOR CROSS-CULTURAL EXPRESSIONS OF PSYCHOPATHOLOGY

In this chapter on culturally sensitive treatments, we first make a case for the need to culturally adapt mental health treatments and review debates concerning when adaptation is warranted; we follow this by reviewing what components scholars believe should be adapted in addition to prominent models of how to adapt treatment. We then present a model of how anxiety disorders are generated across cultural contexts. Based in large part on this model of how anxiety is produced, we discuss how culturally sensitive treatment can be conducted, focusing again on the anxiety disorders.

WHY DO WE NEED CULTURALLY ADAPTED TREATMENTS?

According to the World Health Organization survey conducted in 28 countries, mental illness has a lifetime prevalence of 18%–36% (Kessler et al., 2009). This report concluded that not only are mental disorders common across cultures but they are also "often seriously impairing in many countries" (Kessler et al., 2009, p. 23). Although mental illness is prevalent across cultures, psychological treatments associated with them are often developed in Western countries (Kirmayer, 2007). We will present a case for the importance of using culturally adapted treatments in the United States and across the globe.

Projections of the United States' population by the year 2050 portend a truly diverse cultural mosaic. Hispanics, African Americans, Asian Americans, and Pacific Islanders are predicted to be the fastest growing groups, whereas non-Hispanic whites are predicted to decline in growth, constituting just 63% of the national population by 2050 (Day, 1992). Such rapidly changing demographics may influence how the national burden of disease clusters. For instance, the incidence, prevalence and mortality risk of health conditions differs by ethnic grouping (Chaturvedi, 2003; Laumann & Youm, 1999), presumably due to common risk and resilience factors borne from shared genetic and/or environmental influences. With such rapid growth in ethnic minority populations, healthcare providers must be culturally competent to treat various health conditions with diverse groups. Clinical providers, in particular, must be prepared for this task for two reasons: cultural forces shape the expression and amelioration of mental illness (Kleinman, 1977; Lopez & Guarnaccia, 2000) and treatments developed in Western cultures are being increasingly disseminated globally (Weisman, Duarte, Koneru, & Wasserman, 2006). Therefore, culturally adapting treatments may be necessary to increase their utility.

Attitudes toward mental healthcare and use of services vary widely by ethnicity (Alvidrez, 1999). Ethnic minorities in the USA have historically had less access to and availability of mental health services (U.S. DHHS, 2001). Even when they do use mental health services, the quality of care tends to be lower than those offered to majority cultural groups (U.S. DHHS, 2001). Disparities in *access to care* can be attributed to fear/ mistrust (via service-seekers) and explicit/implicit institutionalized racism (via mental healthcare systems). Disparities in *quality of care* may be attributed to intersections between racial discrimination, socioeconomic status (SES), acculturation levels, and language barriers. For instance, ethnic minority status may overlap with being from a historically marginalized race, having a low SES, and lacking fluency in English. All these factors, in turn, can impact the service experience. As one example, a clinician who fails to understand the extent and nature of a client's symptoms because of language barriers may misdiagnose and/or implement suboptimal treatment that is incommensurate with the client's key complaints (United States Department of Health and Human Services, 2001).

Similar issues are relevant in other countries. There is a global refugee crisis, with over 42 million people estimated to be forcibly displaced from their home countries (United Nations High Commissioner for Refugees, 2005; Norwegian Refugee Council, 2005). A meta-analysis by Porter and Haslam (2005) found that a number of postdisplacement conditions moderated mental health outcomes. For instance, worse outcomes were observed for refugees who live in institutional accommodation, have fewer economic opportunities, are internally displaced within their own country, and repatriate to a previously fled country (Porter & Haslam, 2005). Similarly, refugees who were older, more educated, female, and with a higher predisplacement SES were at higher risk for worse outcomes (Porter & Haslam, 2005). Refugees typically experience a great deal of trauma exposure (e.g., prolonged violence, forced migration, economic, housing, and food insecurity) that predisposes them to having posttraumatic stress disorder (PTSD). A recent review found that refugees resettled in Western countries were 10 times more likely to have PTSD than age-matched populations in the same countries (Fazel, Wheeler, & Danesh, 2005).

In light of (1) ethnic diversification in many countries across the globe, (2) diminished access to and satisfaction with services among ethnic minorities, and (3) global refugee crisis and globalization of treatment dissemination, there is a pressing need to offer culturally appropriate services. In line with the American Psychological Association's call to increase cultural competence in mental healthcare (APA, 2003), we aim to translate the latest research findings into targeted care recommendations for ethnic minorities and refugees. As culturally appropriate treatments for anxiety disorders and PTSD are understudied (Cardemil, 2008; Hinton, Rivera, Hofmann, Barlow, & Otto, 2012), we focus on this set of disorders. Given the extensive evidence-base for CBT in alleviating anxiety (Norton & Barrera, 2012), we focus on CBT adaptation in local and global contexts. We will begin by presenting relevant debates pertaining to cultural adaptation. We will then generate a model of anxiety disorders and PTSD that is sensitive to cultural influences. Finally, we will illustrate how to culturally adapt a treatment for anxiety disorders and PTSD by providing examples of adaptations in various cultural groups.

HOW TO ADAPT: DEVELOP NEW TREATMENTS OR MODIFY WHAT WORKS?

Although the importance of providing high-quality care to ethnic minorities is universally acknowledged, there is some disagreement on exactly how to go about this process. Specifically, there exists a debate between the cultural compatibility and universalist schools of thought (Bernal, Jiménez-Chafey, & Domenech Rodríguez, 2009). Advocates of the cultural compatibility hypothesis believe in developing entirely new treatments for ethnic minorities from a ground-up culturally informed approach. Meanwhile, advocates of the universalist hypothesis contend that mechanisms of change in psychotherapy are universal and should be tested as they currently exist *before* undertaking the arduous task of adaptation (Elliot & Mihalic, 2004). Culturally adapted treatments are situated in the nexus of tension between these competing hypotheses. Bernal et al. (2009, p. 362) define cultural adaptation as the "systematic modification of an evidence-based treatment (EBT) to account for language, culture, and context in a way that is consistent with the client's cultural patterns, meanings and values." In this sense, culturally adapted treatments are a middle ground that can allow the best of both worlds—a kind of "flexibility within fidelity" to EBTs (Kendall & Beidas, 2007).

Let us examine how to apply this logic to making decisions about whether cultural adaptation is warranted. Castro, Barrera, and Steiker (2010) have identified four concrete situations in which cultural adaptation of an EBT is justified. Any (or a combination) of the following conditions must exist to warrant adaptation:

1. *Ineffective clinical engagement.* If a treatment is unable to engage clients from a subcultural group due to (a) awareness of treatment availability, (b) entry/enrollment into treatment, (c) participation in treatment, and (d) retention and completion of treatment (Castro et al., 2010).
2. *Unique risk and resilience factors.* Sometimes culturally specific mechanisms common to an entire ethnic group (or subgroup) influence clinical outcomes in distinct ways from the original group on which the treatment was tested. If this is the case, etiology—or causes—may be different in the given group, and adapting treatment components can be justified (Castro et al., 2010).
3. *Unique symptoms of a common disorder.* When an ethnic group exhibits unique symptoms associated with a common disorder, then adaptation to target these unique symptoms is justified (Castro et al., 2010; Hinton, Pich, Chhean, & Pollack, 2005; Lau, 2006).
4. *Nonsignificant intervention efficacy.* If an EBT is followed with strict fidelity and it demonstrates smaller effect sizes in a specific group than expected, then adapting it may be warranted for a particular cultural group (Castro et al., 2010).

EVIDENCE FOR EFFICACY OF CULTURAL ADAPTATION: WHAT TO ADAPT

Griner and Smith (2006) reviewed 76 studies on culturally adapted mental health interventions for a wide range of disorders. They found a random effects weighted average effect size of $d = 0.45$ for culturally adapted treatments, indicating a moderately strong effect. Interventions targeted to specific ethnic groups produced four times stronger effects than those provided to diverse ethnic groups. Similarly, interventions delivered in client's first languages were twice as effective as those conducted only in English (Griner & Smith, 2006).

In response to how culturally adapted treatments perform against unadapted ones, Benish, Quintana, and Wampold (2011) conducted a direct-comparison meta-analysis with 21 studies. They confirmed that culturally adapted treatment is more effective than unadapted treatment ($d = 0.32$). However, the only significant moderator accounting for this difference was modification of the "illness myth," also known as the explanatory model.

Simply put, the explanatory model is the way in which a person understands his or her illness experience. How psychological distress is experienced, labeled, caused, and cured all form part of this explanation. Although an explanatory model can reflect individual differences, it is heavily influenced by one's sociocultural environment. Therefore, it may be internally consistent within an ethnic group. Benish et al.'s (2011) study highlights the importance of eliciting a group's explanatory model and adapting treatment in accordance with it. In fact, understanding the client's interpretation of symptoms—invariably influenced by the prevailing cultural interpretation—and providing treatment congruent with their explanatory model appears to be the "active ingredient" in culturally adapted treatment.

Although the explanatory model appears to be an important consideration for cultural adaptation, there are other frameworks arguing for adapting a range of dimensions. For instance, the ecological validity framework, posited by Bernal, Bonilla, and Bellido (1995), is a prominent framework for culturally adapting interventions. This framework posits eight dimensions on which to adapt a given intervention:

1. *Language*. As language is the "carrier of culture" (Bernal, Bonilla, & Bellido, 1995, p. 74) and is used to convey emotion and distress, this dimension refers to adapting interventions for language-match.
2. *Persons*. This refers to the relationship between the client and clinician, including culturally sensitive ways to address inter-racial dynamics in a safe space.
3. *Metaphors*. This includes the idioms, proverbs, and sayings prominent in a cultural group to communicate a warmth and understanding of the uniqueness of the client's cultural group.
4. *Content*. This refers to the cultural knowledge that makes cultural groups unique, and adapting a treatment on this dimension entails

using this cultural knowledge to validate a cultural group's uniqueness.

5. *Concepts.* This indicates the constructs used in psychosocial models. Creating an overlap or cultural consonance between psychopathological models and cultural understandings of the same can be beneficial.

6. *Goals.* This refers to the aims of therapy. Discrepancy between clinician's goals and the client's goals can hamper the therapeutic alliance and outcomes. Therefore, using culturally congruent concepts to cement goal agreement is desirable.

7. *Methods.* This refers to evaluating therapeutic techniques for cultural acceptability. If a treatment method is incompatible with the client's cultural group expectations, then it is less likely to be successful.

8. *Context.* This attends to the current environmental factors, such as acculturation stress, and financial stress, to be sensitive to the client's context. Although the ecological validity framework was initially conceptualized for Latin American populations, this framework is applicable to other cultural groups.

Another prominent framework, developed by Hwang (2006), is the Psychotherapy Adaptation and Modification Framework. This model denotes six domains, along with principles and rationales, on which adaptation can occur. The domains are as follows:

1. *Dynamic issues.* Evaluating intersecting identities (i.e., age, gender, sexual orientation, disability status, religion, nationality, etc.) is imperative to avoid rigid application of EBTs to a group. Hwang (2006) notes that "dynamic sizing," or the process of knowing when to generalize to a group versus individualizing to a person, can help make such decisions.

2. *Orientation.* Socializing clients to the aim, format, and expected outcomes of therapy can facilitate their therapeutic engagement. This can involve formulating culturally congruent goals early in the therapeutic process.

3. *Cultural beliefs.* Understanding how cultural knowledge influences treatment is integral. This understanding can be used to bridge between psychotherapy concepts and culturally accepted practices.

4. *Client–therapist relationship.* Training cultural awareness in a clinician can foster stronger alliances with clients. Similarly, understanding the social structures that prevail in a cultural group—levels of hierarchy, individual/collectivist grouping, and attitude toward authority—can inform what kind of relationship clients expect of the therapist.

5. *Cultural differences in expression and communication.* Learning differences in communication styles can benefit therapeutic alliance.

This awareness can also facilitate accuracy in communication more generally, which is crucial for diagnosis and treatment planning.

6. *Cultural issues of salience.* Developing rationales and goals for therapy that are culturally consistent can aid in adherence. Talking about issues such as stigma and demystifying what therapy entails can help assuage inconsistencies between Western therapy norms and culturally sanctioned ideas of healing.

The Ecological Validity framework and the Psychotherapy Adaptation and Modification Framework are the only two models that have been tested in adapting a host of EBTs (Walker, Trupin, & Hansen, 2011). Although both models use different terminology, they share many overlapping features to guide delivery of culturally sensitive care. Broadly speaking, these models delineate the main focus areas and content to adapt. Let us now turn to adaptation that is based on a model of how psychopathology is generated.

A MODEL OF ANXIETY GENERATION ACROSS CULTURAL CONTEXTS

We have demonstrated why culturally sensitive conceptualization of psychopathology is a necessary first step for cultural adaptation of treatment. We will now turn to a model that delineates how to generate a culturally informed model of anxiety. This model is transdiagnostic; it is basic enough that it is widely applicable to generation of anxiety in general and therefore relevant to understanding diverse anxiety-related disorders including PTSD. Further, this conceptualization is superior to disorder-specific ones as transdiagnostic CBT has been known to produce better outcomes than disorder-specific CBT (Norton & Barrera, 2012).

Fig. 9.1 (Hinton & La Roche, 2013) delineates this model of anxiety generation. The model takes into account catastrophic cognitions and the role they play in related symptomatology. Catastrophic cognitions constitute a key producer of anxiety disorders. Catastrophic cognitions about anxiety-related somatic and psychological symptoms can worsen panic disorder and generate panic attacks (Clark, 1986; Hedley et al., 2000). Catastrophic cognitions about PTSD-related symptoms can lead to more chronic symptoms (Clark & Ehlers, 2004; Dunmore, Clark, & Ehlers, 2001; Halligan, Michael, Clark, & Ehlers, 2003). Catastrophic cognitions about the bodily and mental consequences of worry, and about the danger posed by worry-induced somatic and psychological symptoms, may worsen—and even produce—generalized anxiety disorder; this, in turn, may cause worry to escalate to panic (Wells, 2007, p. 20).

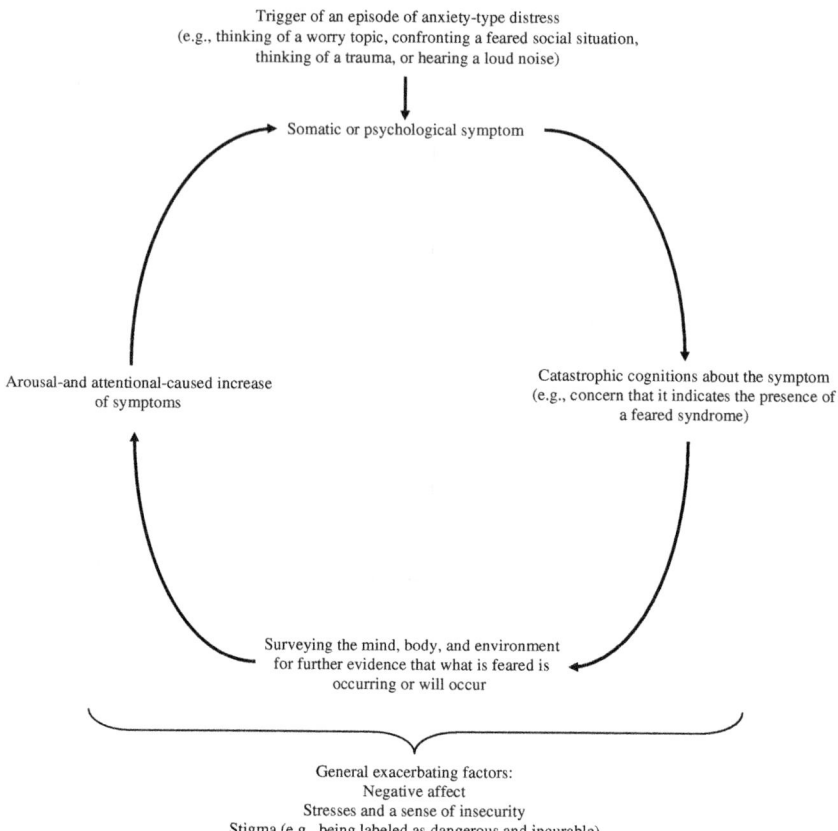

FIGURE 9.1 A culturally informed model of how psychopathology is generated (Hinton & La Roche, 2013).

Lastly, catastrophic cognitions increase anxiety sensitivity, which is a known risk factor for exacerbating *all* anxiety disorders (Hinton, Pich, Safren, Pollack, & McNally, 2005, 2006).

How do these catastrophic cognitions arise? If physiological symptoms of anxiety are interpreted as triggering a feared cultural syndrome, multiple catastrophic cognitions may result: if a Cambodian considers anxiety symptoms such as dizziness to be the start of a *khyâl* attack (in which *khyâl* and blood rush upward in the body to cause bodily disasters), or a Puerto Rican considers shakiness to be the start of an *ataque de nervios* (in which disordered "nerves" result in loss of control, asphyxia, and other disasters), he or she may experience catastrophic cognitions. Once a symptom is attributed to a particular cultural syndrome, fears of having the cultural syndrome will increase that symptom by increasing arousal and narrowing attention on the sensation in question (Fig. 9.1). In this way, someone's expectation of what a somatic symptom can mean for his or her future health can lead to a self-fulfilling prophecy. For instance, a person who considers joint pain to be a key sign of a disorder (e.g., fibromyalgia)—and fears that the disorder is dangerous—will be hypervigilant to those sensations. If he then experiences joint discomfort, he may get very fearful and inadvertently worsen joint pain by increasing muscular tension and amplifying attention on the pain. This example illustrates how syndrome expectations, which are culturally generated, interact with fear biology to produce anxiety symptomatology.

HOW TO CULTURALLY ADAPT TREATMENT?

In this section, we will provide broad domains of adaptation that merit careful attention, with regards to treating anxiety disorders and PTSD with CBT. We will focus specifically on four main sections: (1) how to select appropriate treatment targets, (2) how to engage in effective psychoeducation and treatment engagement, (3) how to teach culturally consistent emotion regulation, and (4) how to conduct culturally sensitive exposure.

Selecting Treatment Targets

Treatment must be targeted very specifically to the needs of the group it is intended for in order to optimize treatment utility. Choosing appropriate treatment targets is crucial, and there are several pieces of information we can use to decide on these.

Elicit explanatory models and link symptoms to local cultural syndromes. In order to effectively treat a client's problems, it is necessary to determine how the client views their problem. Assessing clients' explanatory models for their specific symptoms and learning about prevailing cultural syndromes has a twofold benefit: It gives the clinician a broader context for exactly how symptoms are impairing the client's functioning and can foster alliance and adherence if self-reported concerns are being attended to (Hinton & Lewis-Fernández, 2010a). It is also the single biggest predictor of treatment improvement (Benish et al., 2011).

Hinton and colleagues, who have worked extensively with Cambodian refugees, ask about locally relevant cultural syndromes: they ask if clients experience "weak heart" or "*khyâl* attacks," how they treat these conditions and what fears they have about them (for a review of these syndromes, see Hinton & Lewis-Fernández, 2010b). In this way, they are able to understand whether the cultural syndrome is diagnostically relevant to the individual client, what their explanations for these syndromes are, how they seek help or treat these symptoms and what kinds of catastrophic cognitions may be accompanying them. Hinton and colleagues have developed a measure to systematically examine such questions in a standardized and culturally sensitive manner. The Cambodian Somatic Syndrome Inventory (SSI; Hinton, Kredlow, Bui, Pollack, & Hofmann, 2012; Hinton, Pich, Kredlow, Bui, & Hofmann, 2013) is one such measure. The SSI has the benefit of measuring key symptoms outlined in the DSM-5 in addition to specific Cambodian cultural syndromes.

Target somatic symptoms. There is evidence to show that clients experience and express psychological distress through somatic complaints in several cultural groups (Gureje, Simon, Ustun & Goldberg, 1997; Hinton & Lewis-Fernández, 2011; Hinton & Otto, 2006; Kleinman, 1977). This evidence, in and of itself, merits careful attention for somatic symptoms especially for clients presenting to primary care settings.

Additionally, Fig. 9.1 presents a model for how somatic symptoms interact with prominent knowledge about what these symptoms mean. Extreme somatization can trigger anxiety responses and exacerbate existing psychopathology. Gureje et al. (1997) found higher rates of somatic complaints among South American populations (Gureje et al., 1997). Using this knowledge, it would be useful to assess whether these somatic complaints—and their accompanying catastrophic cognitions—sensitize Latin American populations to fears of having an *ataque de nervios* (a common syndrome among Latin Americans with wide-ranging anxiety presentation, including reported panic attacks). Targeting somatic symptoms is important because if somatic symptoms predispose anxiety sensitivity and catastrophic cognitions, then treating the somatic symptom itself may derail the cycle that leads to panic.

Address sleep-related phenomena. Sleep-related problems may be a precursor to developing anxiety disorders (Alfano, Ginsberg, & Kingery, 2007; Gregory et al., 2005). Further, there is evidence to support that sleep-related phenomena and amount of REM-sleep are influenced by ethnicity among people with depression (Poland et al., 1999; Stepnowsky, Moore, & Dimsdale, 2003). Sleep disturbance is a chief concern reported by trauma-exposed clients (Davis & Wright, 2007). As sleep-related concerns may vary by ethnic group and are common in trauma-exposed individuals, it may be an important clinical target to adapt in treatment.

Common sleep-related pathology include nightmares, sleep paralysis, and nocturnal panic. Nightmares refer to distressing dreams that are frightening enough to wake the individual up. Sleep paralysis occurs upon falling asleep or awakening and is characterized by an inability to move or speak, even though the individual is conscious. Nocturnal panic indicates awaking in a panic and being able to move but unable to recall a nightmare.

Hinton and colleagues have examined all these sleep-related phenomena in several groups. They assess the subjective meaning of nightmares according to the client. In many cultural contexts, nightmares are considered a portal for a deceased relative to visit or a state of physical and/or spiritual vulnerability (Hinton, Rasmussen, Nou, Pollack, & Good, 2009). They specifically ask about sleep paralysis as it is common in some cultural groups, and clients provide extensive cultural elaboration on the subject (Hinton et al., 2005). For example, distressed Cambodian refugees often have sleep paralysis, and they attribute this to the visitation of a malevolent spirit or dangerous physiological problems. African American groups also indicate sleep paralysis and give it a catastrophic interpretation (Hinton, Pich, Chhean, & Pollack, 2005). They also assess for nocturnal panic and its interpretation.

Target Worry and GAD. Regardless of the client's anchoring diagnosis, chronic worry—uncontrollable in nature—is a key clinical target among refugee and minority populations. Clients often attribute PTSD and anxiety symptoms to a cultural syndrome. Such an attribution may trigger anxiety sensitivity, making them more prone to catastrophizing that the symptoms indicate severe physical dysfunction and/or insanity (see Fig. 9.1). If such catastrophic cognition spiral, they can trigger panic attacks (in the immediate moment) and result in generalized worry (in the long term).

Similarly, refugees and ethnic minorities often engage in worry due to current stressors in their environmental context (e.g., food insecurity). This prolonged stress results in difficulty disengaging from worry and sensitivity to arousal. Such "arousal inducibility" (Hinton, Nickerson, & Bryant, 2011) is another mechanism by which catastrophic cognitions relate to trauma recall and worry to create a ruminative hypervigilance to threat.

Therefore, targeting prominent worry themes can help with two major areas: (1) determining if the catastrophic cognitions are inducing panic attacks or trauma recall and (2) building therapeutic alliance by communicating that the client's problems are being understood by the clinician. A host of relaxation techniques to regulate emotion are later described to target these.

Adapting Psychoeducation to Optimize Treatment Engagement

Psychoeducation refers to educating individuals with a mental disorder about what is currently known about their condition and how to best handle it. Effective psycheducation is empowering in that it can provide a validating context for difficulties in an individual's life. Aside from being brief, cost-effective and easily disseminated, psychoeducation can reduce symptoms (Donker, Griffiths, Cuijpers, & Christensen, 2009). As psychoeducation is typically delivered early in treatment, it can also be used to foster therapeutic alliance and adherence to treatment in various ways.

Create positive expectancy and treatment credibility. Positive expectancy results when clients believe that treatment will improve outcomes that matter most to them. Eliciting a client's chief complaint, along with their explanatory models for what caused this can create this positive expectancy (Lewis-Fernández & Diaz, 2002; Sue & Sue, 2007). For instance, Japanese individuals who meet diagnostic criteria for social phobia may consider symptoms such as fearing one's odor is offending others as their chief concern. In such a case, symptoms consistent with *taijin kyofusho* rather than Western-centric diagnoses such as social phobia may be beneficial to target first. Similarly, a Cambodian may view "weak heart," dizziness, sleep paralysis, and nightmares as their key problems. Although such symptoms, and prior trauma exposure, may be consistent with panic attacks and PTSD, the latter is a concept of which they have little familiarity. Therefore, couching treatment benefits in terms that matter most to them can increase positive expectancy.

A parallel idea in creating positive expectancy lies in creating treatment credibility, or the hope that treatment will actually address their problems in a meaningful way. It may be necessary to bridge psychoeducation for social phobia used in ESTs with the chief complaints identified by clients. Hinton and colleagues provide an example of this: going back to the Japanese individual experiencing *taijin kyofusho*, recall that the most feared outcome for the client is a negative social interaction. The clinician can use this knowledge to explain that constant fear of emitting an offending odor leads to worsened social interaction by taking up all attentional resources and inducing negative somatic and psychological symptoms (Hinton & La Roche, 2013). In this manner, the clinician can link a desired clinical outcome to the client's desired social outcome.

Similarly, for the Cambodian with GAD and frequent *khyâl* attacks, the clinician can explain that rumination increases arousal, which in turn caused somatic symptoms, poor sleep, and dizziness (all typical symptoms of a *khyâl* attack), and that muscle relaxation and stretching can decrease the arousal. This strategy bridges the psychoeducation of how the biopsychosocial model generates distress by couching it in terms of a key concern that is relevant to the client: *khyâl* attacks.

Proverbs can serve to prime adaptive cognitive schemas and interpret reality in ways that promote positive affect (Aviera, 1996; Hyman, Ortiz, Añez, Paris, & Davidson, 2006; Otto, 2000). Proverbs and analogies can be used to create positive expectancy about treatment and to promote adherence. For instance, using the analogy of cooking with Cambodian clients can liken the step-wise nature of the treatment process to preparing a certain traditional noodle dish (Hinton & La Roche, 2013). In order to make this specialty, there are several steps that build upon each other (e.g., making a paste, noodles, and sauce). They explain that each part of the therapy is like one step in making this dish, and it is only at the end of therapy that one knows exactly what has been accomplished (Hinton & La Roche, 2013). Such culturally consonant analogies and proverbs can demystify the therapeutic process and communicate respect and knowledge of the client's cultural world.

Proverbs and cultural analogies can likewise be used to convey relevant CBT information and point out how to regulate emotions in a culturally consistent way. For example, in teaching a Latin American client how to extricate him or herself from the negative spiral of focusing too much on one negative thought, one can use the proverb, "No se ahoge en un vaso do agua." This loosely translates to "Do not drown in a glass of water." Such sayings harken back to traditional ways of handling distress and point out the effects of attending too narrowly to one subject. Similarly, the term "rebound" is a powerful sports motivator among African American teenagers: It is a reminder that recovering after a missed "shot" or opportunity is possible.

Present CBT in terms of the local psychology and physiology. Every culture has a set of ideas on how to manage distress. In the Spanish language, there are several tropes describing negative events in terms of images of suffocation or drowning (Hinton, Lewis-Fernández, & Pollack, 2009). Therefore, the expression, *desahogarse*, which means to "undrown yourself," can be used to encourage clients to talk about trauma memories. The underlying assumption being that if trauma is left unspoken, it could be intolerable and analogous to drowning.

Reduce stigma. Informing the client that the disorder in question is treatable and targeting less stigmatizing symptoms of the disorder can help reduce stigma associated with seeking mental healthcare. For example, one can frame the treatment as reducing a somatic symptom such as dizziness or improving vegetative functions such as sleep or appetite. The client may then describe their treatment to family or friends as targeting those culturally acceptable and nonstigmatizing symptoms.

Address key stressors and issues of security. Ethnic minorities and refugees confront multiple practical issues that range from medical problems, financial strain, safety issues, and parenting difficulties in their culture of resettlement. In treating clients from other cultural contexts, it is important to ensure that these problems are being addressed (Ell et al., 2011; Lesser et al., 2008; Miranda, Azocar, Organista, Dwyer, & Areane, 2003).

For example, a woman in an abusive relationship may not make expected treatment gains due to the current stressor in her life. Therefore, problem-solving for this may be a necessary first step before resuming treatment. In some cases, it may be imperative to conduct a hybrid therapy in which these safety and practical issues are discussed to some extent in each session. It is also important to teach how to handle emotional arousal given current levels of stress. There are several ways in which to teach emotion regulation in culturally consistent ways, which are outlined below.

Improving Emotion Regulation

Poor emotion regulation is a common feature in PTSD and the anxiety disorders more generally (Fairholme, Boisseau, Ellard, Ehrenreich, & Barlow, 2010). In this section, we describe key themes to keep in mind when developing emotion regulation strategies for a cultural group and provide examples of how emotion regulation techniques can be culturally adapted for CBT.

Bridge therapeutic techniques from local healing traditions. The first step to introducing healthy coping techniques is to ask about how clients cope with anxiety, anger, and trauma recall. In this way, a clinician understands the client's typical ways of dealing with distress, including their use of culturally specific healing techniques. Following this, various emotion regulation techniques, from locally salient proverbs to adaptive healing rituals, can be used in culturally adapted CBT. For instance, there is a Cambodian proverb to help teach anger restraint: "If you control your anger once, you gain a hundred days of happiness." Ideally, therapeutic metaphors, models of causation (e.g., historical trauma), ideas of cure, and ideas about ontology (e.g., the nature of personhood) consistent with their tradition should be integrated into treatment.

Likewise, the treatment can be couched in terms of the traditional spiritual and religious traditions to the extent that clients are involved in and gain benefit from them (Lewis-Fernández & Diaz, 2002). Meditation in Buddhist societies or yoga in Indic societies are robust sources of local resilience. Meditation and yoga are CBT-consistent in that they regulate cognitive and physiological distress through relaxation techniques that can help regulate emotions. These techniques have demonstrated effective reduction in anxiety in multiple studies; their efficacy has been explained in terms of CBT principles (Hinton, Pich, Hofmann, & Otto, 2013), so it would be consistent to incorporate them into culturally adapted CBT.

Interestingly, although these techniques historically originated in these cultural traditions, it is common that group members have used them minimally. Teaching them in the context of a structured therapy can generate positive results. It is best to select techniques that are culturally appropriate and also map onto CBT principles. Counting beads on the rosary in the Catholic tradition or opening the Bible to read a passage are examples of traditional healing practices that focus attention on a positively charged task. These can be applied to Christians in many cultural groups. Likewise, in Islam, repeatedly saying *dhikr*, the name of Allah, or reading *namaz* from the Quran can offer similar results. These examples can be conceptualized in terms of CBT in that they regulate emotion by narrowing attention through repetition on a positive focus of interest. In American Indian traditions, the Indian steam ritual can also be used therapeutically: it can be conceived of as interoceptive exposure to symptoms of arousal. By creating positive associations to symptoms of arousal (that can potentially lead to negative consequences such as asphyxia), the clinician can create new associations using the CBT technique of interoceptive exposure (Gone, 2009, 2010).

Use meditation to regulate emotions. Much research has demonstrated that meditation can reduce anxiety and regulate emotions (Goyal et al., 2014; Van Dam, Hobkirk, Sheppard, Aviles-Andrews, & Earleywine, 2014). For a Buddhist client, loving kindness meditation is already ingrained in their tradition. Therefore, capitalizing on this technique for treatment is culturally consistent with existent practices. A key Buddhist principle, equanimity (*upekkha*), can be taught by distancing from emotions by treating them as like clouds in the sky. Similarly, using imagery of light and warmth—common motifs in Catholic traditions—during guided imagery and meditative practice for Catholics is culturally consistent.

Increase emotional and cognitive flexibility in a culturally appropriate way. Psychological inflexibility is a key cause of psychopathology (Ehrenreich, Fairholme, Buzzella, Ellard, & Barlow, 2007; Hinton, Hofmann, Pollack, & Otto, 2009). Psychological flexibility is defined as the ability to distance from current mindsets and consider other possible mindsets (Kashdan, 2010). Psychological flexibility creates a new adaptive processing mode that competes with the threat mode (Hinton et al., 2013; Kashdan, 2010; Kok & Fredrickson, 2010) and is a key aspect of emotion regulation.

Psychological flexibility is a crucial skill for refugees and ethnic minorities who are dealing with multiple adaptations that require great flexibility. They must reconcile their own culture and their new one, to learn a new social and geographic location, to learn to switch language registers, to deal with different ideas about proper behavior and social interaction, such as how children should behave. Practicing the labeling and distancing from affect (Ayduk & Kross, 2010; Hinton, 2008) can assist in emotional flexibility. Similarly, progressive muscle relaxation can help reduce physiological arousal. To promote flexibility among

Christian Latino clients, Hinton and colleagues instruct them to note how the flame of a votive candle moves with the breeze—the image in question serves to prime flexibility (Hinton, 2008).

Making Exposure Culturally Appropriate

Exposure is a central part of treating anxiety disorders and is especially relevant for PTSD. Prolonged exposure (Foa & Rothbaum, 1998) takes exposure to trauma memories to be the central part of treatment for PTSD. Similarly, Cognitive processing therapy (Resick & Schnicke, 1996) also uses exposure as a central component by having the client write down the trauma event in detail and repeatedly read it. In this section, we will address the (1) cultural acceptability of exposure as it is currently conceptualized in EBTs and (2) provide culturally adapted methods of exposure.

Problems with exposure in standard EBTs. Even Western populations often find traditional exposure hard to tolerate, and this may worsen during treatment (Cahill, Foa, Hembree, Marshall, & Nacash, 2006; Markowitz, 2010). Given that ethnic minority and refugee populations are often highly distressed (due to contextual stressors outlined above), these techniques may have iatrogenic effects. Lester and colleagues found that traditional exposure was poorly tolerated by these groups, with African Americans dropping out of treatment at approximately twice the rate of Caucasian clients (Lester, Resick, Young-Xu, & Artz, 2010).

Second, the mechanisms of change involved in exposure are being reconceptualized. It was initially theorized that exposure allowed habituation to the "hot thought" and thereby reduced its vividness and distress (Foa & Rothbaum, 1998). However, there is evidence to show that the trauma memory is never erased through treatment (Craske et al., 2008; Hofmann, 2008). The mechanism by which exposure works is through creating new nonthreatening associations to the trauma memory network; these new associations, in turn, decrease the memory's "hotness" (Brewin, Dalgleish, & Joseph, 1996; Craske et al., 2008). Using this framework, it is possible to confer the benefit of new associations to trauma memories *without* exposing a client to high levels of distress (Craske et al., 2008; Hofmann, 2008).

Third, teaching emotion regulation techniques before conducting exposure can reduce arousal during exposure. This is delivered in a phase approach and is used in a new 16-session treatment (Cloitre, Cohen, & Koenen, 2006; Cloitre, Koenen, Cohen, & Han, 2002). Phase treatment is especially important in highly traumatized populations and with clients under great current stress (Markowitz, 2010) such as refugees.

Finally, exposure should be conducted not only for certain event memories but also for somatic sensations linked to traumatic experiences (Hinton, Hofmann, Pitman, Pollack, & Barlow, 2008; Otto & Hinton, 2006; Wald & Taylor, 2007, 2008). Interoceptive exposure is especially indicated for those with prominent somatic complaints, catastrophic cognitions about somatic symptoms, and extensive trauma associations to somatic sensations. For instance, a client whose trauma involved forced labor may have memories of the event (cognitively encoded trauma recall) and remember chronically tense muscles and his back bent over in pain (somatically encoded trauma recall). Interoceptive exposure to such somatic sensations decreases catastrophic cognitions about them reduces their ability to recall trauma events and reduces anxiety sensitivity that may trigger panic symptomatology (Barlow, 2002; Craske et al., 2009; Wald & Taylor, 2007, 2008).

Conduct "exposure" in a culturally acceptable way. In light of the iatrogenic effects of traditional exposure techniques with highly traumatized populations, there is a need to develop culturally sensitive exposure techniques for these cultural groups. Hinton and colleagues have developed the following protocol, using a strategic phase approach, to deliver culturally adapted exposure.

1. *Phase approach.* They use a phase approach, teaching emotion regulation skills, such as applied muscle relaxation, applied stretching, and meditation for the first three sessions before conducting exposure.
2. *Trauma protocol.* To promote acceptability of exposure, they have clients discuss trauma memories at the beginning of several sessions (sessions 5–10). When the client becomes upset, they have him or her perform a trauma protocol. This protocol consists of several emotion regulation techniques, including mindfulness and applied stretching with visualization.
3. *Interoceptive exposure with reassociation.* Hinton and colleagues also conduct interoceptive exposure to sensations such as dizziness while creating positive reassociations to them to compete with sensation-type trauma associations and catastrophic cognitions. An example of this would be to induce dizziness and then prompt the client to recall other times that induced a similar sensation in more positive circumstances (e.g., playing games in childhood or using the image of a lotus in slow repetitive rotation).

Emotion exposure paired with emotion regulation. Emotion regulation deficits are a key treatment issue among persons with emotional disorders (Fairholme et al., 2010; Hofmann, Sawyer, Fang, & Asnaani, 2012; Kring & Sloan, 2010). Other than the emotion of fear, ethnic minorities and refugees with anxiety disorders often have problems with anger, general anxiety, and worry (Hinton et al., 2011; Hinton, Rasmussen, et al., 2009). These emotions often give rise to arousal, trauma recall, and catastrophic cognitions, which start vicious cycles of worsening symptoms. Therefore, an important treatment target is to expose clients to intense emotions in such a way that the client learns to tolerate the affect and react more adaptively to it. This is a central part of Barlow's unified protocol in which he expands his work on interoceptive exposure to include emotional exposure (Ellard, Fairholme, Boisseau, Farchione, & Barlow, 2010; Fairholme et al., 2010; Otto, Powers, & Fischmann, 2005; Wilamowska et al., 2010). Hinton and colleagues have used trauma exposure—which elicits negative emotions—followed by the practice of emotion regulation. The client verbalizes the trauma, creating frontal representations that should decrease automaticity of recall (Brewin et al., 1996; Clark & Ehlers, 2004). The client is then encouraged to practice emotion regulation techniques in response to the trauma recall and other dysphoric states. In this way, the client learns to pair a positive memory state to the trauma memory, so that the sense of agency can start being associated with it instead. The ultimate goal is to reinforce the practice of this pairing so much so that it induces self-image of strength, resilience, and self-respect in relation to the trauma recall.

SUMMARY

In this chapter, we first reviewed debates about the need to adapt treatment and how to do so. We then presented a model of how anxiety-type psychopathology is generated and proceeded to demonstrate how culturally sensitive treatment might be conducted. We selected broad transdiagnostic targets in the generation of psychopathology, with an emphasis on anxiety. There are many challenges to effectively diagnosing and treating disorders in varying cultural contexts. In this chapter, we have provided a model to accomplish this goal. It should be noted that low-and-middle-income countries are resource-poor and lack access to psychological treatment, let alone evidence-based culturally adapted care. Similarly, there are special treatment challenges with refugee populations. Refugees living in currently difficult environments (e.g., war zones) and those in challenging conditions in countries of relocation will require greater attention to contextual stressors in the implementation of culturally sensitive CBT (Arbona et al., 2010; Betancourt et al., 2015).

References

Alfano, C. A., Ginsburg, G. S., & Kingery, J. N. (2007). Sleep-related problems among children and adolescents with anxiety disorders. *Journal of the American Academy of Child & Adolescent Psychiatry, 46,* 224–232.

Alvidrez, J. (1999). Ethnic variations in mental health attitudes and service use among low-income African American, Latina, and European American young women. *Community Mental Health Journal, 35,* 515–530.

American Psychological Association (2003). Guidelines on multicultural education, training, research, practice, and organizational change for psychologists. *American Psychologist, 58,* 377–402.

Arbona, C., Olvera, N., Rodriguez, N., Hagan, J., Linares, A., & Wiesner, M. (2010). Acculturative stress among documented and undocumented Latino immigrants in the United States. *Hispanic Journal of Behavioral Sciences, 32,* 362–384.

Aviera, A. (1996). "Dichos" therapy group: A therapeutic use of Spanish language proverbs with hospitalized Spanish-speaking psychiatric patients. *Cultural Diversity and Mental Health, 2,* 73–87.

Ayduk, O., & Kross, E. (2010). From a distance: Implications of spontaneous self-distancing for adaptive self-reflection. *Journal of Personality and Social Psychology, 98,* 809–829.

Barlow, D. H. (2002). *Anxiety and its disorders: The nature and treatment of anxiety and panic* (2nd ed.). New York, NY: Guilford Press.

Benish, S. G., Quintana, S., & Wampold, B. E. (2011). Culturally adapted psychotherapy and the legitimacy of myth: A direct-comparison meta-analysis. *Journal of Counseling Psychology, 58,* 279.

Bernal, G., Bonilla, J., & Bellido, C. (1995). Ecological validity and cultural sensitivity for outcome research: Issues for the cultural adaptation and development of psychosocial treatments with Hispanics. *Journal of Abnormal Child Psychology, 23,* 67–82.

Bernal, G., Jiménez-Chafey, M. I., & Domenech Rodríguez, M. M. (2009). Cultural adaptation of treatments: A resource for considering culture in evidence-based practice. *Professional Psychology: Research and Practice, 40,* 361.

Betancourt, T. S., Abdi, S., Ito, B. S., Lilienthal, G. M., Agalab, N., & Ellis, H. (2015). We left one war and came to another: Resource loss, acculturative stress, and caregiver-child relationships in Somali refugee families. *Cultural Diversity and Ethnic Minority Psychology, 21,* 114.

Brewin, C., Dalgleish, T., & Joseph, S. (1996). A dual representation theory of posttraumatic stress disorder. *Psychological Review, 103,* 670–686.

Cahill, S. P., Foa, E. B., Hembree, E. A., Marshall, R. D., & Nacash, N. (2006). Dissemination of exposure therapy in the treatment of posttraumatic stress disorder. *Journal of Traumatic Stress, 19,* 597–610.

Cardemil, E. V. (2008). Commentary: Culturally sensitive treatments: Need for an organizing framework. *Culture & Psychology, 14,* 357–367.

Castro, F. G., Barrera, M., Jr, & Steiker, L. K. H. (2010). Issues and challenges in the design of culturally adapted evidence-based interventions. *Annual Review of Clinical Psychology, 6,* 213.

Chaturvedi, N. (2003). Ethnic differences in cardiovascular disease. *Heart, 89,* 681–686.

Clark, D. M. (1986). A cognitive approach to panic. *Behaviour Research and Therapy, 24,* 461–470.

Clark, D. M., & Ehlers, A. (2004). Posttraumatic stress disorder: From cognitive theory to therapy. In R. L. Leahy (Ed.), *Contemporary cognitive therapy* (pp. 141–160). New York, NY: Guilford Press.

Cloitre, M., Cohen, L. R., & Koenen, K. C. (2006). *Treating survivors of childhood abuse: Psychotherapy for the interrupted life.* New York, NY: Guilford Press.

Cloitre, M., Koenen, K. C., Cohen, L. R., & Han, H. (2002). Skills training in affective and interpersonal regulation followed by exposure: A phase-based treatment for PTSD related to childhood abuse. *Journal of Consulting and Clinical Psychology, 70,* 1067–1074.

Craske, M. G., Kircanski, K., Zelikowsky, M., Mystkowski, J., Chowdhury, N., & Baker, A. (2008). Optimizing inhibitory learning during exposure therapy. *Behaviour Research and Therapy, 46*, 5–27.

Craske, M. G., Roy-Byrne, P. P., Stein, M. B., Sullivan, G., Sherbourne, C., & Bystritsky, A. (2009). Treatment for anxiety disorders: Efficacy to effectiveness to implementation. *Behaviour Research and Therapy, 47*, 931–937.

Davis, J. L., & Wright, D. C. (2007). Randomized clinical trial for treatment of chronic nightmares in trauma-exposed adults. *Journal of Traumatic Stress, 20*, 123–133.

Day, J.C. (1992). *Population projections of the United States, by age, sex, race, and Hispanic origin: 1992 to 2050* (No. 1092). US Department of Commerce, Economics and Statistics Administration, Bureau of the Census.

Donker, T., Griffiths, K. M., Cuijpers, P., & Christensen, H. (2009). Psychoeducation for depression, anxiety and psychological distress: A meta-analysis. *BMC Medicine, 7*, 79.

Dunmore, E., Clark, D. M., & Ehlers, A. (2001). A prospective investigation of the role of cognitive factors in persistent posttraumatic stress disorder (PTSD) after physical and sexual assault. *Behaviour Research and Therapy, 39*, 1063–1084.

Ehrenreich, J. T., Fairholme, C. P., Buzzella, B. A., Ellard, K. K., & Barlow, D. H. (2007). The role of emotion in psychological therapy. *Clinical Psychology: Science and Practice, 14*, 422–428.

Ell, K., Xie, B., Kapetanovic, S., Quinn, D. I., Lee, P. J., Wells, A., et al. (2011). One-year follow-up of collaborative depression care for low-income, predominantly Hispanic patients with cancer. *Psychiatric Services, 62*, 162–170.

Ellard, K. K., Fairholme, C. P., Boisseau, C. L., Farchione, T. J., & Barlow, D. H. (2010). Unified protocol for the transdiagnostic treatment of emotional disorders: Protocol development and initial outcome data. *Cognitive and Behavioral Practice, 77*, 88–101.

Elliot, D. S., & Mihalic, S. (2004). Issues in disseminating and replicating effective prevention programs. *Prevention Science, 5*, 47–53.

Fairholme, C. P., Boisseau, C. L., Ellard, K. K., Ehrenreich, J. T., & Barlow, D. H. (2010). Emotions, emotion regulation, and psychological treatment: A unified perspective. In A. M. Kring, & D. M. Sloan (Eds.), *Emotion regulation and psychopathology: A transdiagnostic approach to etiology and treatment* (pp. 283–309). New York, NY: Guilford Press.

Fazel, M., Wheeler, J., & Danesh, J. (2005). Prevalence of serious mental disorder in 7000 refugees resettled in western countries: A systematic review. *The Lancet, 365*, 1309–1314.

Foa, E. B., & Rothbaum, B. O. (1998). *Treating the trauma of rape: Cognitive-behavioral therapy for PTSD*. New York, NY: Guilford Press.

Gone, J. P. (2009). A community-based treatment for Native American historical trauma: Prospects for evidence-based practice. *Journal of Consulting and Clinical Psychology, 77*, 751–761.

Gone, J. P. (2010). Psychotherapy and traditional healing for American Indians: Exploring the prospects for therapeutic integration. *The Counseling Psychologist, 38*, 166–235.

Goyal, M., Singh, S., Sibinga, E. M., Gould, N. F., Rowland-Seymour, A., Sharma, R., & Haythornthwaite, J. A. (2014). Meditation programs for psychological stress and well-being: A systematic review and meta-analysis. *JAMA Internal Medicine, 174*, 357–368.

Gregory, A. M., Caspi, A., Eley, T. C., Moffitt, T. E., O'Connor, T. G., & Poulton, R. (2005). Prospective longitudinal associations between persistent sleep problems in childhood and anxiety and depression disorders in adulthood. *Journal of Abnormal Child Psychology, 33*, 157–163.

Griner, D., & Smith, T. B. (2006). Culturally adapted mental health intervention: A meta-analytic review. *Psychotherapy: Theory, Research, Practice, Training, 43*, 531.

Gureje, O., Simon, G. E., Ustun, T. B., & Goldberg, D. P. (1997). Somatization in cross-cultural perspective: A World Health Organization study in primary care. *American Journal of Psychiatry, 154*, 989–995.

Halligan, S. L., Michael, T., Clark, D. M., & Ehlers, A. (2003). Posttraumatic stress disorder following assault: The role of cognitive processing, trauma memory, and appraisal. *Journal of Consulting and Clinical Psychology, 71*, 410−431.

Hedley, L. M., Hoffart, A., Dammen, T., Ekeberg, Ø., & Friis, S. (2000). The relationship between cognitions and panic attack intensity. *Acta Psychiatrica Scandinavica, 102*(4), 300−302.

Hinton, D. E. (2008). Healing through flexibility primers. In B. Keon (Ed.), *The Oxford handbook of medical ethnomusicology* (pp. 121−163). Oxford, UK: Oxford University Press.

Hinton, D. E., Hofmann, S. G., Pitman, R. K., Pollack, M. H., & Barlow, D. H. (2008). The panic attack−posttraumatic stress disorder model: Applicability to orthostatic panic among Cambodian refugees. *Cognitive Behaviour Therapy, 37*, 101−116.

Hinton, D. E., & La Roche, M. (2013). Culturally appropriate CBT for the anxiety disorders. In G. Simos, & S. G. Hofmann (Eds.), *CBT for anxiety disorders: A practitioner book* (pp. 191−224). Oxford: John Wiley & Sons Ltd.

Hinton, D. E., & Lewis-Fernández, R. (2010a). Idioms of distress among trauma survivors: Subtypes and clinical utility. *Culture, Medicine and Psychiatry, 34*, 209−218.

Hinton, D. E., & Lewis-Fernández, R. (2010b). "Idioms of distress" (culturally salient indicators of distress) and anxiety disorders. In H. B. Simpson, Y. Neria, R. Lewis-Fernández, & F. Schneier (Eds.), *Anxiety disorders: Theory, research, and clinical perspectives* (pp. 127−138). Cambridge: Cambridge University Press.

Hinton, D. E., & Lewis-Fernández, R. (2011). The cross-cultural validity of posttraumatic stress disorder: Implications for DSM-5. *Depression and Anxiety, 28*, 783−801.

Hinton, D. E., & Otto, M. W. (2006). Symptom presentation and symptom meaning among traumatized Cambodian refugees: Relevance to a somatically focused cognitive-behavior therapy. *Cognitive and Behavioral Practice, 13*, 249−260.

Hinton, D. E., Hofmann, S. G., Pollack, M. H., & Otto, M. W. (2009). Mechanisms of efficacy of CBT for Cambodian refugees with PTSD: Improvement in emotion regulation and orthostatic blood pressure response. *CNS Neuroscience and Therapeutics, 15*, 255−263.

Hinton, D. E., Kredlow, M. A., Bui, E., Pollack, M. H., & Hofmann, S. G. (2012). Treatment change of somatic symptoms and cultural syndromes among Cambodian refugees with PTSD. *Depression and Anxiety, 29*, 148−155.

Hinton, D. E., Kredlow, M. A., Pich, V., Bui, E., & Hofmann, S. G. (2013). The relationship of PTSD to key somatic complaints and cultural syndromes among Cambodian refugees attending a psychiatric clinic: The Cambodian Somatic Symptom and Syndrome Inventory (CSSI). *Transcultural Psychiatry, 0*, 1−24.

Hinton, D. E., Lewis-Fernández, R., & Pollack, M. H. (2009). A model of the generation of ataque de nervios: The role of fear of negative affect and fear of arousal symptoms. *CNS Neuroscience and Therapeutics, 15*, 264−275.

Hinton, D. E., Nickerson, A., & Bryant, R. A. (2011). Worry, worry attacks, and PTSD among Cambodian refugees: A path analysis investigation. *Social Science & Medicine, 72*, 1817−1825.

Hinton, D. E., Pich, V., Chhean, D., & Pollack, M. H. (2005). "The ghost pushes you down": Sleep paralysis-type panic attacks in a Khmer refugee population. *Transcultural Psychiatry, 42*, 46−78.

Hinton, D. E., Pich, V., Hofmann, S. G., & Otto, M. W. (2013). Acceptance and mindfulness techniques as applied to refugee and ethnic minority populations with PTSD: Examples from "culturally adapted CBT". *Cognitive and Behavioral Practice, 20*, 33−46.

Hinton, D. E., Pich, V., Safren, S. A., Pollack, M. H., & McNally, R. J. (2005). Anxiety sensitivity in traumatized Cambodian refugees: A discriminant function and factor analytic investigation. *Behaviour Research and Therapy, 43*, 1631−1643.

Hinton, D. E., Pich, V., Safren, S. A., Pollack, M. H., & McNally, R. J. (2006). Anxiety sensitivity among Cambodian refugees with panic disorder: A factor analytic investigation. *Journal of Anxiety Disorders, 20,* 281–295.

Hinton, D. E., Rasmussen, A., Nou, L., Pollack, M. H., & Good, M. J. (2009). Anger, PTSD, and the nuclear family: A study of Cambodian refugees. *Social Science and Medicine, 69,* 1387–1394.

Hinton, D. E., Rivera, E. I., Hafmann, S. G., Barlow, D. H., & Otto, M. W. (2012). Adapting CBT for traumatized refugees and ethnic minority patients: Examples from culturally adapted CBT (CA-CBT). *Transcultural Psychiatry, 49*(2), 340–365.

Hofmann, S. G. (2008). Cognitive processes during fear acquisition and extinction in animals and humans: Implications for exposure therapy of anxiety disorders. *Clinical Psychology Review, 28,* 199–210.

Hofmann, S. G., Sawyer, A. T., Fang, A., & Asnaani, A. (2012). Emotion dysregulation model of mood and anxiety disorders. *Depression and Anxiety, 29,* 409–416.

Hwang, W. (2006). The psychotherapy adaptation and modification framework: Application to Asian Americans. *American Psychologist, 61,* 702–715.

Hyman, R., Ortiz, J., Añez, L., Paris, M., & Davidson, L. (2006). Culture and clinical practice recommendations for working with Puerto Ricans and other Latinos in the United States. *Professional Psychology: Research Practice, 37,* 694–701.

Kashdan, T. B. (2010). Psychological flexibility as a fundamental aspect of health. *Clinical Psychology Review, 30,* 865–878.

Kendall, P. C., & Beidas, R. S. (2007). Smoothing the trail for dissemination of evidence-based practices for youth: Flexibility within fidelity. *Professional Psychology: Research and Practice, 38,* 13–20.

Kessler, R. C., Aguilar-Gaxiola, S., Alonso, J., Chatterji, S., Lee, S., Ormel, J., & Wang, P. S. (2009). The global burden of mental disorders: An update from the WHO World Mental Health (WMH) surveys. *Epidemiologia e Psichiatria Sociale, 18,* 23–33.

Kirmayer, L. J. (2007). Psychotherapy and the cultural concept of the person. *Transcultural Psychiatry, 44,* 232–257.

Kleinman, A. M. (1977). Depression, somatization and the new cross-cultural psychiatry. *Social Science and Medicine, 11*(1), 3–10. Available from http://dx.doi.org/10.1016/0037-7856(77)90138-X.

Kok, B. E., & Fredrickson, B. L. (2010). Upward spirals of the heart: Autonomic flexibility, as indexed by vagal tone, reciprocally and prospectively predicts positive emotions and social connectedness. *Biological Psychology, 85,* 432–436.

Kring, A. M., & Sloan, D. M. (Eds.), (2010). *Emotion regulation and psychopathology: A transdiagnostic approach to etiology and treatment* New York, NY: Guilford Press.

Lau, A. S. (2006). Making a case for selective and directed cultural adaptations of evidence-based treatments: Examples from parent training. *Clinical Psychology Science & Practice, 13,* 295–310.

Laumann, E. O., & Youm, Y. (1999). Racial/ethnic group differences in the prevalence of sexually transmitted diseases in the United States: A network explanation. *Sexually Transmitted Diseases, 26,* 250–261.

Lesser, I., Rosales, A., Zisook, S., Gonzalez, C., Flores, D., Trivedi, M., & Epstein, M. (2008). Depression outcomes of Spanish- and English-speaking Hispanic outpatients in STAR*D. *Psychiatric Services, 59,* 1273–1284.

Lester, K., Resick, P. A., Young-Xu, Y., & Artz, C. (2010). Impact of race on early treatment termination and outcomes in posttraumatic stress disorder treatment. *Journal of Consulting and Clinical Psychology, 78,* 480–489.

Lewis-Fernández, R., & Diaz, N. (2002). The cultural formulation: A method for assessing cultural factors affecting the clinical encounter. *Psychiatric Quarterly, 73,* 271–295.

Lopez, S. R., & Guarnaccia, P. J. (2000). Cultural psychopathology: Uncovering the social world of mental illness. *Annual Review of Psychology, 51*, 571–598.

Markowitz, J. C. (2010). IPT and PTSD. *Depression and Anxiety, 27*, 879–881.

Miranda, J., Azocar, F., Organista, K. C., Dwyer, E., & Areane, P. (2003). Treatment of depression among impoverished primary care patients from ethnic minority groups. *Psychiatric Services, 54*, 219–225.

Norton, P. J., & Barrera, T. L. (2012). Transdiagnostic versus diagnosis-specific CBT for anxiety disorders: A preliminary randomized controlled noninferiority trial. *Depression and Anxiety, 29*, 874–882.

Norwegian Refugee Council (2005). *Internal displacement: Global overview of trends and developments in 2004.* Geneva: Global IDP Project.

Otto, M. W. (2000). Stories and metaphors in therapy. *Cognitive and Behavioral Practice, 7*, 166–172.

Otto, M. W., & Hinton, D. E. (2006). Modifying exposure-based CBT for Cambodian refugees with posttraumatic stress disorder. *Cognitive and Behavioral Practice, 13*, 261–270.

Otto, M. W., Powers, M. B., & Fischmann, D. (2005). Emotional exposure in the treatment of substance use disorders: Conceptual model, evidence, and future directions. *Clinical Psychology Review, 25*, 824–839.

Poland, R. E., Rao, U., Lutchmansingh, P., McCracken, J. T., Lesser, I. M., Edwards, C., & Lin, K. M. (1999). REM sleep in depression is influenced by ethnicity. *Psychiatry Research, 88*, 95–105.

Porter, M., & Haslam, N. (2005). Predisplacement and postdisplacement factors associated with mental health of refugees and internally displaced persons: A meta-analysis. *Journal of the American Association, 294*, 602–612.

Resick, P. A., & Schnicke, M. K. (1996). *Cognitive processing therapy for rape victims: A treatment manual* Vol. 4, Sage: Newbury Park, CA.

Stepnowsky, C. J., Moore, P. J., & Dimsdale, J. E. (2003). Effect of ethnicity on sleep: Complexities for epidemiologic research. *SLEEP, 26*, 329–332.

Sue, D. W., & Sue, D. (2007). *Counseling the culturally diverse: Theory and practice.* Hoboken, NJ: Wiley.

U.S. Department of Health and Human Services (2001). Youth violence: A report of the Surgeon General, Rockville, MD.

United Nations High Commissioner for Refugees (2005). *The 2004 global report.* Geneva: United Nations High Commissioner for Refugees.

Van Dam, N. T., Hobkirk, A. L., Sheppard, S. C., Aviles-Andrews, R., & Earleywine, M. (2014). How does mindfulness reduce anxiety, depression, and stress? An exploratory examination of change processes in wait-list controlled mindfulness meditation training. *Mindfulness, 5*, 574–588.

Wald, J., & Taylor, S. (2007). Efficacy of interoceptive exposure therapy combined with trauma-related exposure therapy for posttraumatic stress disorder: A pilot study. *Journal of Anxiety Disorders, 21*, 1050–1060.

Wald, J., & Taylor, S. (2008). Responses to interoceptive exposure in people with posttraumatic stress disorder (PTSD): A preliminary analysis of induced anxiety reactions and trauma memories and their relationship to anxiety sensitivity and PTSD symptom severity. *Cognitive Behaviour Therapy, 37*, 90–100.

Walker, S. C., Trupin, E. W., & Hansen, J. (2011). *A toolkit for applying the cultural enhancement model to evidence-based practic.* Available from http://www.modelsforchange.net/publications/476.

Weisman, A., Duarte, E., Koneru, V., & Wasserman, S. (2006). The development of culturally informed, family-focused treatment for schizophrenia. *Family Process, 45*, 171–186.

Wells, A. (2007). Cognition about cognition: Metacognitive therapy and change in general-ized anxiety disorder and social phobia. *Cognitive and Behavioral Practice, 14*(1), 18–25.

Wilamowska, Z. A., Thompson-Hollands, J., Fairholme, C. P., Ellard, K. K., Farchione, T. J., & Barlow, D. H. (2010). Conceptual background, development, and preliminary data from the unified protocol for transdiagnostic treatment of emotional disorders. *Depression and Anxiety, 27*, 882–890.

Further Reading

Begeer, S., El Bouk, S., Boussaid, W., Terwogt, M. M., & Koot, H. M. (2009). Underdiagnosis and referral bias of autism in ethnic minorities. *Journal of Autism and Developmental Disorders, 39*, 142–148.

Hinton, D. E., Park, L., Hsia, C., Hofmann, S., & Pollack, M. H. (2009). Anxiety disorder presentations in Asian populations: A review. *CNS Neuroscience and Therapeutics, 15*, 295–303.

Iwamasa, G. Y. (1997). Behavior therapy and a culturally diverse society: Forging an alli-ance. *Behavior Therapy, 28*, 347–358.

Rossello, J., & Bernal, G. (1999). The efficacy of cognitive-behavioral and interpersonal treatments for depression in Puerto Rican adolescents. *Journal of Consulting and Clinical Psychology, 67*, 734.

Weiss, M. G., Doongaji, D. R., Siddhartha, S., Wypij, D., Pathare, S., Bhatawdekar, M., & Fernandes, R. (1992). The Explanatory Model Interview Catalogue (EMIC). Contribution to cross-cultural research methods from a study of leprosy and mental health. *The British Journal of Psychiatry, 160*, 819–830.

10

Cognitive-Behavioral Therapy in Older Adults

Elizabeth C. Conti, Cynthia Kraus-Schuman and Melinda A. Stanley

Baylor College of Medicine, Houston, TX, United States

INTRODUCTION

The number of Americans over age 60 is anticipated to double from 2010 to 2050 (Administration on Aging, 2010), echoing trends in Europe and around the world (Beard, 2014). As the population ages, mental health professionals will increasingly be presented with older adult clients, clients caring for older relatives, and the psychosocial concerns prevalent among older adults. Evidence for the effectiveness of cognitive-behavioral therapy (CBT) with older adults has mounted over the last four decades (Areán & Cook, 2002; Laidlaw & Thompson, 2014). This chapter summarizes the evidence for the use of CBT in older adults, as well as considerations for clinicians when working with this population in research and practice.

GENERAL CONSIDERATIONS FOR WORKING WITH OLDER ADULTS

Common Themes in CBT With Older Adults

Older adults are a highly diverse group, including individuals as young as 50 or 55 years to centenarians. Older adults have lower rates of psychiatric disorders than younger and middle-aged adults (Hasin & Grant, 2015) but may also experience new and worsening mental health

The Science of Cognitive Behavioral Therapy.
DOI: http://dx.doi.org/10.1016/B978-0-12-803457-6.00010-6

problems with age (e.g., Laborde-Lahoz et al., 2015; Zhang et al., 2015). Although many older adults retain good health and independent lifestyles well into their later years, other individuals in this group may experience substantial limits in functioning, live in long-term care, or be at the end of life. Nevertheless, some common themes are encountered when engaging in CBT with older adults.

As people age, they experience normal changes in cognitive and physical abilities, changes in finances or work role, and increased risk of mortality (Bishop, Lu, & Yankner, 2010). Older adults may engage in fewer activities inside and outside the home because of shifts in their work role (e.g., retirement), or because of reduced physical capabilities. Changes in family and community roles, as well as reduced independence, are also common. Older adults are more likely than younger adults to experience the deaths of friends, relatives, and partners. Grief and widowhood are important considerations. Preparatory grief for the end of one's own life may also be present (Periyakoil & Hallenbeck, 2002), as well as the experience of constructing meaningfulness at the end of life. Mental health concerns in later life are frequently comorbid with physical disease (El-Gabalawy, Mackenzie, Pietrzak, & Sareen, 2014). Physical health burden may increase the severity and persistence of mental disorders and is critical for clinicians to consider and integrate into their work (Erlangsen, Stenager, & Conwell, 2015; Mackenzie, El-Gabalawy, Chou, & Sareen, 2014).

Older adults may present to mental health settings with a long history of mental health concerns, dating back to their young or middle adulthood. Persistent psychiatric conditions can result in a cascade of other problems in the individual's life (e.g., relationship problems, lower educational, and vocational attainment, disability; Byers, Covinsky, Neyland, & Yaffe, 2014). Older adults with persistent mental health symptoms are more likely to have sought help and, thus, may have experienced unsuccessful rounds of treatment (Mackenzie et al., 2014). On the other hand, a substantial proportion of psychiatric conditions in older adults are new; that is, they began in late life and may be related to recent adverse events and life changes (e.g., Zhang et al., 2015).

Delivery of CBT to Older Adults

Delivery of CBT to older adults sometimes requires modifications, defined as changes in the delivery of the therapy, such as reducing the amount of content in each individual session or using worksheets with larger print. Modifying the delivery of CBT for a range of hearing, vision, mobility, memory, and other limitations requires clinician creativity and flexibility. Typical changes associated with aging include moderate decrements in short-term memory, processing speed, and executive functioning (Bishop et al., 2010). If these changes interfere with therapy, they might be accommodated with strategies such as a slower pace, written or verbal reminders between sessions, using mnemonic memory devices, simplifying concepts, and minimizing distractions (Dreer, Copeland, & Cheavens, 2011). A mid-week telephone call may be particularly helpful to remind patients of their goals for that week and to encourage homework completion. Other practical strategies include reducing jargon, encouraging the proper use of hearing aids and magnifying devices and conducting therapy in a well-lit room (Areán & Feliciano, 2008). Therapists are encouraged to use focusing and redirection to keep older adult clients on task. Involving caregivers is another key strategy for increasing the effectiveness of CBT with older adults, discussed in the following section on cognitive impairment. Even when cognitive impairment is not present, communicating with other healthcare providers can help maximize treatment for late-life mental health conditions and their interaction with physical diseases.

Not all older adults require modifications, and there may not always be existing empirical evidence to support the use of modifications to CBT (Laidlaw & Thompson, 2014). Older adults can engage successfully in even complex and intense treatments, such as prolonged exposure (PE) therapy for posttraumatic stress disorder (PTSD; Thorp, Stein, Jeste, Patterson, & Wetherell, 2012). Some older adults also are able to learn cognitive restructuring in one session without modifications, although increased depression and anxiety and decreased cognitive flexibility impact the quality of cognitive restructuring (Johnco, Wuthrich, & Rapee, 2015). Clinicians should consider the individual strengths and needs of older adult clients before applying modifications.

Incorporating CBT into medical settings, especially primary care, may help to increase older adults' engagement in mental health care (Laidlaw et al., 2008; Serfaty et al., 2009). Older adults have more frequent medical appointments than younger people and may prefer to see a mental health provider during the same visit and in a place with which they are familiar. Rates of mental health problems among older adults in primary care are high. However, they are not often detected (Calleo et al., 2009; Jameson and Cully, 2011). CBT is also a natural fit with an emphasis on managing chronic conditions by implementing behavioral and lifestyle changes, which are often recommended but not thoroughly discussed during regular medical appointments (Jameson & Cully, 2011). After a referral is offered, a "warm handoff" (face-to-face introduction) between the primary care team and a mental health professional is recommended. Brief, modular CBT (e.g., individual, structured sessions emphasizing cognitive restructuring, relaxation training, and behavioral activation) is best suited to primary care, with initial goal-setting and conceptualization occurring in the first one to two sessions. However, older adults may require more sessions than younger people in primary care to adequately learn and practice CBT material (Serfaty et al., 2009).

Long-term care is another setting that serves predominantly older adults and provides opportunities for CBT and consultation rooted in CBT principles. Rates of mental illness, including serious mental illness, and psychotropic medication use in long-term care are high (Carlson & Snowden, 2014). Facilities in the United States are not required to provide specialized mental health personnel or to demonstrate that their staff is trained in geriatric mental health (Carlson & Snowden, 2014). Psychologists in these settings often take on an "on-call" or consulting role, including assessing and recommending practical CBT strategies to manage depression, behavioral problems associated with dementia, and end-of-life concerns (Zarit & Zarit, 2007). In these settings, mental health professionals typically work closely with the family, nursing and other staff, physicians, and social service providers to understand the causes and consequences of behavior, as well as to implement interventions. Using nurse case managers to track psychotropic medication use and symptoms is recommended to improve mental health care in nursing homes (Carlson & Snowden, 2014).

Although older adults often prefer psychotherapy over medication for psychological problems, they are much more likely to be prescribed medication than to receive regular psychotherapy (Gum, Iser, & Petkus, 2010). One reason may be the lack of accessible and affordable psychotherapy services. To meet the mental health needs of a diverse older-adult population, it is crucial to expand services so that they are available in community settings and through existing aging services organizations (Areán, Raue, Sirey, & Snowden, 2012). Providing services in patients' homes and over the telephone can also increase access for older adults (Areán et al., 2012). One challenge to providing mental health services in nontraditional settings is the lack of insurance reimbursement for travel, telephone services, or staff training (Areán et al., 2012). Trained lay providers, such as community health workers and social workers, can help to address workforce issues (Institute of Medicine [IOM], 2012). However, quality care requires that expert staff spend time training and supervising these clinicians (Areán et al., 2012). Broader models of care, including attention to case management and resource needs, are also critical to the treatment of psychological distress in older adults. These issues are discussed throughout this chapter.

SPECIFIC DISORDERS

CBT for Depression in Late Life

Depression is a substantial and undertreated problem for older adults. Current prevalence estimates for major depressive disorder (MDD) range from 1% to 4%, but the percentage of older adults with clinically significant depressive symptoms is estimated to be 8%−16% in the community, and substantially higher in nursing homes (Blazer, 2003). Considering lifetime prevalence, older adults are equally likely to have experienced subsyndromal depression (13.8%) as they are a major depressive episode (13.7%; Laborde-Lahoz et al., 2015). Subsyndromal depression is a significant risk factor for developing MDD in late life (Laborde-Lahoz et al., 2015) and is associated with increased risk of dementia, physical disease, and reduced quality of life (Lee et al., 2012). CBT shows promise at treating subsyndromal depression and preventing the development of MDD (Lee et al., 2012).

Several meta-analyses and reviews of treatment for late-life depression support the efficacy and effectiveness of CBT (Cuijpers, van Straten, & Smit, 2006; Mackin & Areán, 2005). One meta-analysis calculated a large effect size (i.e., greater than 0.8) for CBT (Pinquart, Duberstein, & Lyness, 2007) but noted that more scientifically rigorous studies with active control groups tended to show smaller effects (e.g., Serfaty et al., 2009). CBT is equivalent to antidepressant medication in older primary care patients (Laidlaw et al., 2008) and produces comparable effects to other psychotherapies for late-life depression (Cuijpers et al., 2006). Among samples of older adults, age was not found to impact CBT treatment outcome (Pinquart et al., 2007). Future research on the effectiveness of CBT in real-world settings is critical to understanding how disadvantaged, frail, or cognitively impaired older adults respond to CBT for depression. The following sections will summarize recommendations for implementing CBT for depression with older adults, models to increase access and reach of CBT for depression, and research related to using CBT for suicide prevention for older patients.

General Recommended Strategies for CBT for Late-Life Depression

Thompson and colleagues completed some of the earliest randomized controlled trials (RCTs) of CBT for depression among older adults (e.g., Thompson & Gallagher, 1984), showing that men and women in their 60s, 70s, and older could benefit from psychotherapy. Their CBT protocol for treating late-life depression includes simple illustrations, vignettes featuring older adults, and a CBT model of depression that includes physiology along with mood, behavior, and thoughts (Thompson, Dick-Siskin, Coon, Gallagher-Thompson, & Powers, 2009;

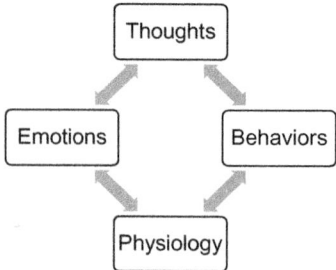

FIGURE 10.1   CBT model of depression including physical health status.

see Fig. 10.1). "Physiology" includes acute or chronic illness and states such as fatigue, hunger, and pain. Including this facet emphasizes that physical health has an impact on behaviors, thoughts, and mood, as well as that depressed mood can impact the experience of pain, fatigue, and medical conditions. Although this model may be useful for clients of all ages, it is indispensable among older adults.

Behavioral activation that is generally incorporated into CBT for depression may be useful on its own for improving mood among older adults, especially if the preferred activities of the older individual have been curtailed or there has been an increase in unpleasant or negative events (e.g., medical procedures or caregiving responsibilities). The California Older Person's Pleasant Event Scale was developed to assess the frequency and pleasantness of 66 activities thought to be pleasurable and available for older people (Rider, Gallagher-Thompson, & Thompson, 2016). Several other pleasant events inventories exist, including one for individuals in nursing homes (Meeks, Shah, & Ramsey, 2009). Clinicians should strive to be creative in identifying and scheduling pleasant events for older adults with functional limitations. As these inventories show, simple activities, such as giving someone a compliment, taking care of plants, writing a card, or even wearing favorite clothes, may contribute to improved mood.

Problem-solving therapy (PST) is a brief cognitive-behavioral treatment focused on taking an optimistic view of solving daily problems, addressing practical concerns, and overcoming social adversity as they are related to depression or chronic illness in late life (Areán et al., 2010). This approach has emerged as a flexible therapy that can be used by older adults with deficits in executive functioning and a range of disabilities. A meta-analysis of PST for depression in older adults concluded that the treatment had a large effect size compared with control conditions across studies (Kirkham, Seitz, & Choi, 2015).

Age, income, and executive dysfunction impact response to depression treatment, and one should consider them when selecting treatments (Areán & Niu, 2014). Despite the evidence base for PST, a recent

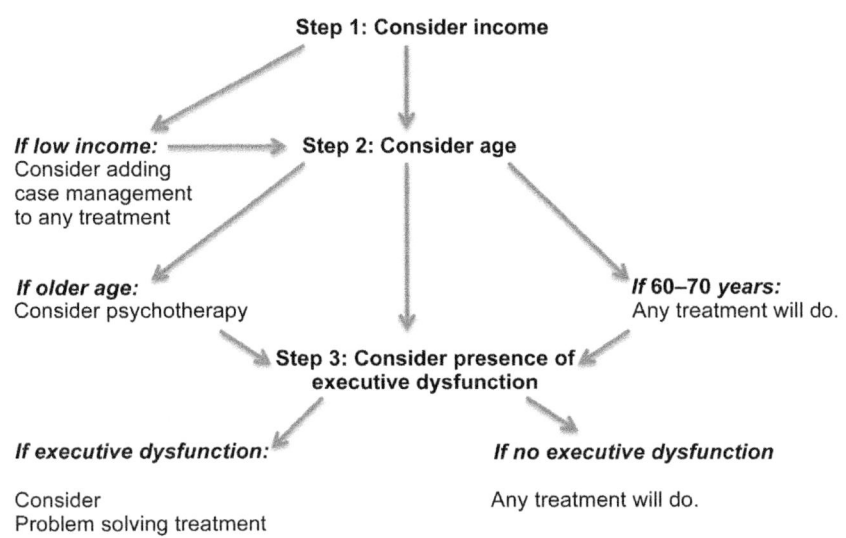

Step 1: Consider income

If low income:
Consider adding
case management
to any treatment

Step 2: Consider age

If older age:
Consider psychotherapy

If 60–70 years:
Any treatment will do.

Step 3: Consider presence of executive dysfunction

If executive dysfunction:

Consider
Problem solving treatment

If no executive dysfunction

Any treatment will do.

FIGURE 10.2   Treatment selection model for depression treatments in late life. "Any treatment will do" refers to medication and a range of psychotherapies. *Source: Reprinted from Clinics in Geriatric Medicine, Vol 30, Patricia A. Areán & Grace Niu, Choosing Treatment for Depression in Older Adults and Evaluating Response, 535–551, Copyright (2014), with permission from Elsevier.*

RCT found that low-income, disabled older adults with MDD receiving case management benefitted just as much as those receiving PST (Alexopoulos et al., 2015). This study points to the importance of addressing basic needs in treating depression among low-income older adults. Fig. 10.2 shows a decision tree developed by Areán and Niu (2014) that provides recommendations based on existing evidence for treatment of late-life depression. Case management is recommended for depressed older adults with low income. Adults over 70 do not respond as well to antidepressant medication, compared to adults in their 60s and younger (Areán & Niu, 2014). Older adults with executive dysfunction also respond poorly to antidepressants but respond well to PST, which directly addresses deficits in decision-making and judgment (Areán & Niu, 2014). Taken together, CBT or other evidence-based psychotherapies (rather than medications) are recommended for adults over 70 and PST, specifically, is recommended for older adults with depression and executive dysfunction (Areán & Niu, 2014).

Novel Models to Address Challenges to Effective Treatment and Access

Although CBT for late-life depression is effective, individuals who cannot or do not access specialty mental health care are unlikely to receive it. Among older adults, these individuals may include those with low income or functional limitations; members of underserved ethnic groups; and men, who are less likely to seek mental health care. To address challenges to delivering effective care, several research groups have initiated novel models of depression treatment for older adults.

Collaborative Depression Care

Two major studies have attempted to address the challenges of identifying and treating the large numbers of depressed older adults in primary care. The PROSPECT (Bruce et al., 2004) and IMPACT (Unützer et al., 2002) studies randomized a heterogeneous group of primary care practices to implement large-scale screening of patients and a stepped, collaborative-care algorithm. Depression care managers provided guidance and facilitated communication between patients and physicians. Interventions consisted of pharmacotherapy and either PST or interpersonal therapy, an intervention that shares characteristics with CBT (i.e., it focuses on current functioning, links mood to behaviors and environment, and uses collaboratively agreed-upon behavioral assignments). In PROSPECT, patients with major depression showed significant decreases in depressive symptoms at 4, 8, and 12 months, compared with patients receiving usual care (Bruce et al., 2004). Patients with minor depression did not show significant improvements. The IMPACT trial found that, although patients in the collaborative-care group had greater reductions in depressive symptoms than patients in the usual care group, most patients did not achieve remission of depression (Unützer et al., 2002). Collaborative care increased the numbers of patients receiving treatment for depression, including psychotherapy, but the prevalence of chronic illness in this population may have dampened the effect of the treatments (Unützer et al., 2002). A depression care model similar to PROSPECT was tested in individuals over 65 who were receiving home health care (Bruce et al., 2015). Like the PROSPECT trial, significant reductions in depressive symptoms were found only in individuals with major depression but not minor depression (Bruce et al., 2015). These studies support the use of depression care managers and collaborative care but demonstrate that the care algorithms may not be helpful for older adults experiencing minor or subsyndromal depression.

Reaching Underserved Older Adults

Older adults with physical limitations and low income face substantial challenges to accessing CBT for depression (Choi, 2009). Research involving community partners has stressed the importance of addressing motivation, inadequate housing and other basic needs, stigma, inadequate insurance, and the quality of available services, among other concerns (Dobransky-Fasiska et al., 2012). Providing home-based care combined with PST is thought to be a promising treatment option for depressed older adults with low income and lower socioeconomic status (Areán et al., 2010). The PEARLS intervention consisted of home-based PST, behavioral activation that included social activities and exercise, and communication between a study psychiatrist and community primary care physicians (Ciechanowski et al., 2004). A group of low-income, disabled, and racially diverse older adults with minor depression or dysthymia receiving PEARLS was more likely to experience reductions in and remission from depressive symptoms than a group receiving usual care.

Other recommendations for increasing access to care include using community health workers and family members to extend the reach of care into the community (Hoeft, Hinton, Liu, & Unützer, 2016). For example, a streamlined, stepped treatment model for depression ("Engage") was designed to facilitate the training of community-based social workers and lay therapists (Alexopoulos et al., 2015). In a preliminary study, the intervention showed similar effects to PST but required one-third of the training time for study clinicians (Alexopoulos et al., 2015).

Including elders of diverse racial and ethnic backgrounds in depression outcomes research is a challenge, but there have been several relevant studies. Integrating mental health into primary care services substantially improved the percentage of African-American elders receiving mental health treatment (Ayalon, Aréan, Linkins, Lynch, & Estes, 2007). However, African-American older adults, compared with White older adults, were less likely to engage in psychotherapy for minor depression, even as part of an algorithm-based, collaborative-care trial (Joo, Morales, de Vries, & Gallo, 2010). Provider bias, internal and external stigma, and cultural beliefs about mental illness and treatment likely impact the participation of minority older adults in psychotherapy for depression (Schraufnagel, Wagner, Miranda, & Roy-Byrne, 2006). In both research and practice, building relationships with gatekeepers and agencies that serve these communities is particularly important to increasing access to and reach of CBT (Bistricky, Mackin, Chu, & Aréan, 2010).

Treatments to Prevent Suicidal Behaviors in Late Life

Suicide risk is of special concern in later life. Older adults make fewer suicide attempts but die by suicide at higher rates than younger adults (Drapeau & McIntosh, 2015). Middle-aged and older White men are at particularly high risk and drive the high rates of suicide deaths seen in these age groups (Drapeau & McIntosh, 2015). Suicide in late life is usually associated with a mood disorder; although, hopelessness, lack of social connection, physical illness, and feeling like a burden are also implicated (Cukrowicz, Cheavens, van Orden, Ragain, & Cook., 2011; De Leo, Draper, Snowdon, & Kõlves, 2013; Erlangsen et al., 2015). Several CBT protocols have been developed to target suicidality in a variety of settings (Bryan, 2015; Wenzel, Brown, & Beck, 2009). Typical elements include safety planning and creation of a "Hope Kit," cognitive therapy targeting suicide-related thoughts, behavioral activation, and relapse prevention. A randomized trial of cognitive therapy showed reductions in suicide attempts, depression, and hopelessness (but not suicidal ideation) in a mixed-age sample (Brown et al., 2005). These therapies have not been systematically tested in older adults. However, treatments for depression previously reviewed have a positive effect on suicidal ideation. In the collaborative-care model tested in PROSPECT (Bruce et al., 2004), suicidal ideation resolved faster and decreased more than with usual care but was not eliminated. A more recent study found that PST, compared with supportive therapy, reduced suicidal ideation among patients 65 and older with MDD (Gustavson et al., 2016).

Dialectical behavior therapy (DBT) is an efficacious treatment for preventing suicidal behavior in young to middle-aged women (e.g., Koons et al., 2001). DBT targets emotion- regulation strategies and directly applies behavioral theory to suicidal and emotional crises. It is similar to CBT in its focus on antecedent and consequences of behavior, understanding links between behavior and mood, and using strategies such as relaxation and mindfulness. In an RCT, modified DBT plus antidepressant medication resulted in a higher proportion of participants over 60 reaching remission of depression than did medication alone (Lynch et al., 2007). DBT may reduce suicide risk in older adults, but it requires further study.

Treating suicidal ideation and risk in older men is a substantial challenge for the field (Lapierre et al., 2011). In response to the gendered phenomenon of late-life suicide, researchers have initiated an RCT of cognitive therapy for suicidality, specifically for older men (Bhar & Brown, 2012). This protocol emphasizes managing medical illness; decreasing loneliness and increasing a sense of purpose; and simple, practical homework (Bhar & Brown, 2012). Results have not yet been published, but components are based on empirically supported techniques and are promising.

CBT for Anxiety Disorders in Late Life

Anxiety disorders occur more frequently than depression in later life, with lifetime prevalence up to 15% (Kessler et al., 2005) and significant negative health outcomes (Wolitzky-Taylor, Castriotta, Lenze, Stanley, & Craske, 2010). Here, we review the evidence for CBT efficacy among older adults with anxiety and discuss recent work designed to develop and test innovative models of care to improve outcomes, reach, and access.

Overview of Traditional Efficacy Trials

Meta-analyses of late-life anxiety efficacy trials demonstrate that the effects of CBT for a range of anxiety disorders [generalized anxiety disorder (GAD), panic disorder (PD), mixed anxiety samples] are large and equivalent to medication effects when analyses control for nonspecific changes (Pinquart & Duberstein, 2007). The effects of CBT across this range of disorders, however, are larger relative to inactive (i.e., wait-list) control conditions than alternative active treatments (Gould, Coulson, & Howard, 2012); and, relaxation therapy alone is comparable to more comprehensive CBT (Thorp et al., 2009).

The majority of late-life treatment research has focused on GAD, given its high prevalence and public health impact (Wolitzky-Taylor et al., 2010). Meta-analytic review of GAD trials also suggests equivalent outcomes for CBT and medication (Gonçalves & Byrne, 2012), although CBT effects are significant across these trials only with comparison to wait-list, minimal contact or treatment as usual control conditions. The effects of CBT for late-life GAD are not significant relative to active treatment comparisons (e.g., supportive therapy), suggesting the need for adaptations to enhance outcomes for this disorder. Outcomes following CBT for late-life PD with or without agoraphobia are even more positive, with moderate-to-large effects for older adults that are comparable to or greater than those for younger adults (Hendriks, Kampman, Keijsers, Hoogduin, & Voshaar, 2014). No RCTs are available for other anxiety disorders in later life, although case studies suggest positive outcomes for specific phobia (Pachana, Woodward, & Byrne, 2007), and obsessive-compulsive disorder (Calamari, Pontarelli, Armstrong, & Salstrom, 2012).

Until recently, treatment of older adults with PTSD had been examined only in case studies, with interventions including imaginal exposure (Knaevelsrud, Böttche, & Kuwert, 2009) and general CBT (Snell & Padin-Rivera, 1997). The utility of these evidence-based treatments for older adults with PTSD has been questioned, given potential age-associated cognitive limitations (Schuitevoerder et al., 2013) and concerns about possible adverse outcomes of intensive exposure. In an RCT of PE with older adult male combat Veterans, significantly greater PTSD symptom reduction was associated with PE, compared to relaxation training (Thorp & Sones, 2013). Veterans also reported reduced symptoms of depression. This research supports the value of PE for older patients, and the Veterans Health Administration efforts to disseminate the treatment, even when traumas targeted during treatment occurred four to five decades prior to study enrollment (Thorp et al., 2012).

Though the literature addressing PTSD treatment in older adults remains nascent, current findings and continuing efforts in addressing treatment efficacy are promising.

Although available evidence supports the efficacy of CBT for late-life anxiety, effects are not consistently as robust in older as in younger adults (Wetherell et al., 2013b), and modifications in treatment content and delivery may be required to meet the unique needs of older people. Most studies to date have focused on homogeneous samples with regard to diagnosis (i.e., GAD or PD) and demographic characteristics (e.g., Caucasian, middle-to-high socioeconomic status, mostly young-old) and trials have largely been conducted in academic clinical settings with expert CBT providers, which do not generalize well to real-world care. These study limitations restrict generalizability and suggest the need for research that focuses on unique presentations of anxiety symptoms among older adults (e.g., hoarding or fear of falling) and innovative models of care to enhance outcomes, reach, and access (IOM, 2012).

Research Addressing Anxiety Symptoms Unique to Older Adults

Research focused on addressing anxiety symptoms unique to older adults includes studies addressing treatment of hoarding and fear of falling.

Hoarding

Hoarding is more common among older than younger adults, and severity increases with age (Ayers et al., 2013a). Hoarding in later life is associated with functional impairment and disability (Ayers et al., 2013a), reduced quality of life (Saxena et al., 2011), and poor executive functioning (Ayers et al., 2013b). A cognitive-behavioral model for the treatment of hoarding among younger adults includes attention to education, motivational interviewing, exposure, cognitive restructuring, and problem solving (Steketee, Frost, Tolin, Rasmussen, & Brown, 2010). This model is efficacious for younger adults but failed to demonstrate positive outcomes among older patients (Ayers, Wetherell, Golshan, & Saxena, 2011). In an initial open trial, only three of 12 older adults who completed the treatment were responders, and gains for these individuals were not maintained at six-month follow-up. Given the increased risk of cognitive deficits among older adults with hoarding (Ayers et al., 2011), as well as their significant behavioral and experiential avoidance (Ayers, Castriotta, Dozier, Espejo, & Porter, 2014a), an adapted treatment protocol was developed to reduce attention to traditional cognitive components of treatment, increase attention to behavioral strategies (i.e., exposure), and add elements of cognitive rehabilitation. A recent open trial of this intervention demonstrated clinically significant improvement for eight of 11 older adults (Ayers et al., 2014b). A follow-up RCT with a larger and more diverse sample is needed.

Fear of Falling

Fear of falling is a common and unique concern for older adults that is associated with reduced functional impairment, physical instability and poor health, and diminished quality of life (Li, Fisher, Harmer, McAuley, & Wilson, 2003). Home-based exercise programs and a variety of assessment strategies (e.g., fall risk and home-safety assessments, cognition, and visual acuity testing) are effective for managing fear of falling (Gillespie et al., 2012); but these treatments typically do not incorporate evidence-based anxiety-reduction procedures. The activity, balance, learning, and exposure (ABLE) intervention is an innovative, eight-session, home-based treatment for fear of falling that includes exposure exercises, cognitive restructuring, review of medications, exercise, and a home safety evaluation (Wetherell et al., 2013a). A physical therapist delivers ABLE. Preliminary data suggest decreased symptoms of fear of falling and reduced avoidance following ABLE relative to a falls education control condition (Wetherell et al., 2013a). Future studies will need to address the integration of ABLE into existing home health care systems.

Innovations to Enhance Outcomes and Access

Innovations to enhance outcomes and access include novel treatment models and delivery options.

Novel Treatment Models

Two treatment models that expand CBT with attention to mindfulness theory and practice, namely, acceptance and commitment therapy (ACT) and mindfulness-based stress reduction (MBSR), may be useful approaches for older adults with worry and anxiety (Lenze et al., 2014; Wetherell et al., 2011). These approaches include components of behavioral models (i.e., breathing retraining in MBSR, behavioral activation in ACT) but focus more explicitly on the need to adapt to life events that are not always modifiable (e.g., declining health, loss of family or friends, functional impairment). Recent open trials of ACT and MBSR suggest benefits for older adults with GAD (Wetherell et al., 2011) and significant worry (Lenze et al., 2014). However, larger clinical trials are needed to examine the effectiveness of these approaches.

Modular interventions that incorporate elements of CBT also may be particularly useful for older adults, given their ability to facilitate person-centered treatment and mirror real-world care. An early version of modular treatment for late-life GAD allowed patients to choose from traditional CBT skills (e.g., relaxation, thought stopping, behavioral activation) and/or alternative approaches (e.g., life review, acceptance and commitment; Wetherell et al., 2009). Initial outcome data suggested feasibility and acceptability of the treatment, although benefits were equivalent to enhanced community treatment. In a more recent and larger primary care trial, modular CBT led to reductions in a range of mental health symptoms relative to usual care for older adults with GAD (Stanley et al., 2014).

In an effort to meet the needs of older adults with significant worry/anxiety in underserved, low-income, mostly minority communities, an innovative model of CBT-based treatment was developed to incorporate attention to religion and/or spirituality and basic unmet needs (e.g., chronic illness, personal-care needs, financial difficulties). Integrating religion and/or spirituality was thought to be particularly valuable for increasing reach among older minority populations (African Americans, Hispanics) that endorse high levels of religious involvement and spirituality (Newport, 2006). Addressing unmet basic needs was expected to broaden the potential limited value of a solely skills-based approach for worry among people in underserved communities. In the Calmer Life intervention, participants may choose to incorporate religion or spirituality into some or all coping skills or may elect to omit religion or spirituality completely (Shrestha et al., 2012). Calmer Life counselors also guide participants in the identification of community resources to address unmet needs and suggest ways to enhance communication about anxiety with healthcare providers. Over 70% of older adults who participated in Calmer Life chose to integrate religion or spirituality (Shrestha et al., 2012, 2014), and preliminary data suggest positive outcomes relative to enhanced community care for participants with GAD or anxiety disorder not otherwise specified (Shrestha et al., 2014). A larger trial is ongoing to address the treatment of clinically significant worry, irrespective of diagnosis (Shrestha et al., 2015).

Novel Delivery Options

To increase access, a variety of innovative delivery models for late-life anxiety treatments are being tested, including delivery by telephone, in nontraditional settings (e.g., primary care, home, community settings), and with nontraditional providers. Telephone-based treatment is used in the modular approaches reviewed earlier, with treatment reflecting a mix of both in person and telephone delivery according to participant preference (Shrestha et al., 2012, 2014; Stanley et al., 2014). Treatment delivered entirely by telephone also is effective relative to nondirective supportive treatment among rural older adults with GAD (Brenes, Danhauer, Lyles, Hogan, & Miller, 2015), with outcomes comparable with in-person delivery.

CBT-based treatments for late-life worry/anxiety also are being delivered in a variety of nontraditional settings, including primary care (Stanley et al., 2014; Wetherell et al., 2009), patients' homes (Cummings et al., 2013), and community settings (social service agencies, churches, residential settings; Shrestha et al., 2012, 2014, 2015). This flexibility in delivery options facilitates person-centered care and extends reach and access (IOM, 2012).

Training nontraditional providers to deliver care may also be key to expanding reach and access (IOM, 2012). Bachelor-level lay providers were trained to deliver care in a recent clinical trial of modular CBT for late-life anxiety (Stanley et al., 2014). Outcomes in this group were equivalent to those when Ph.D.-level providers delivered care. Bachelor-level and Ph.D.-level provider outcomes were both improved relative to usual care, and both groups produced comparable patient expectations and satisfaction (Kraus-Schuman et al., 2015). In more recent work, community providers (community health workers, case managers) are trained to deliver care (Shrestha et al., 2014, 2015).

CBT for Insomnia

Insomnia is common among older adults, especially older women (Foley, Ancoli-Israel, Britz, & Walsh, 2004). Factors contributing to insomnia in late life include less structure in daily schedules, increased napping, and normal age-related changes in sleep patterns. Healthy older adults spend more time in lighter stages of sleep and are more easily awakened (Petrov, Vandder Wal, & Lichstein, 2014). However, previous studies suggest that insomnia may be more closely related to physical disease than chronological age (Foley et al., 2004; Smagula, Stone, Fabio, & Cauley, 2016). Older adults do not need less sleep than younger people; but, their more fragmented sleep puts them at risk for insomnia (Petrov et al., 2014). Though common, insomnia can be a very distressing condition and is associated with depression (Smagula et al., 2016), as well as suicidal ideation and suicide attempts in older adults (Kay et al., 2015; Nadorff, Fiske, Sperry, Petts, & Gregg, 2013).

CBT-I is a manualized, brief treatment including components of stimulus control and sleep hygiene, sleep restriction or compression, cognitive restructuring, and relaxation (Perlis, Jungquist, Smit, & Posner, 2005). The patient carefully tracks his or her sleep, resulting in sleep prescriptions based on current sleep efficiency (i.e., how much of the time in bed the individual is actually sleeping). Age or physical illness does not contraindicate use of the treatment, although clients may be initially more fatigued as they adjust to their new schedules (Perlis et al., 2005).

In several RCTs, CBT-I was efficacious for improving insomnia in older adults. CBT-I was more effective at improving sleep, both objectively and subjectively, and its effects were longer lasting than sleep medication alone (Morin, Colecchi, Stone, Sood, & Brink, 1999; Sivertsen et al., 2006). Insomnia can be effectively treated when it is comorbid or even a symptom of other physical and psychological conditions. In the context of chronic medical conditions in late life, CBT-I was more effective than general stress-management techniques for improving sleep efficiency (Rybarczyk et al., 2005). The effects of CBT-I are durable over long-term follow-up (1 year) and outcomes extend to physical health, for example, reductions in self-reported osteoarthritis pain (Vitiello, Rybarczyk, Von Korff, & Stepanski, 2009). An integrated CBT protocol for late-life insomnia and pain was more effective for comorbid, severe, chronic pain than CBT for chronic pain alone (McCurry et al., 2014). Thus, insomnia can be treated even in the presence of other serious medical conditions, and pain that is comorbid with insomnia may be lessened by CBT-I.

Older adults are frequently prescribed benzodiazepines or hypnotic medications for sleep problems (e.g., zolpidem; Weich et al., 2014), even though these medications are generally contraindicated for geriatric populations because of their sedating effects, risk of falls, and increased risk of cognitive impairment over time (American Geriatrics Society, 2015; Moore, Pariente, & Bégaud, 2015). Older adults using benzodiazepines for sleep can be effectively tapered using CBT-I, with subjective improvements in sleep; although, measurable improvements in sleep might not be seen for several months after the medications are discontinued (Morin et al., 2004). Based on the effectiveness of CBT-I and the risks associated with sleep medications, CBT-I should be a first-line treatment for older adults with insomnia. As with other forms of CBT, access to treatment is limited by the number of trained providers and the availability of services in convenient locations, such as primary care clinics.

CBT for Individuals With Cognitive Impairment

Thirty-five million people are estimated to have dementia worldwide (World Health Organization, 2012). Major neurocognitive disorder (i.e., dementia) is characterized by significant cognitive decline in one or more cognitive domains (complex attention, executive function, learning and memory, language, perceptual-motor, or social cognition), and these cognitive deficits interfere with independence in everyday activities (American Psychiatric Association, 2013). Mild neurocognitive disorder (i.e., mild cognitive impairment MCI) is characterized by modest cognitive decline in one or more cognitive domains without interference with independence in everyday activities (American Psychiatric Association, 2013). Neuropsychiatric symptoms (e.g., depression, aggression, anxiety, delusions, and hallucinations) are common across all types of dementia (Kales, Gitlin, & Lyketsos, 2014). A total of 75% of individuals with dementia had one neuropsychiatric symptom in the past month, 55% had experienced two or more symptoms in the past month, and 44% of individuals experienced three or more symptoms (Lyketsos et al., 2002). The most common neuropsychiatric symptoms in individuals with dementia were apathy (36%), depression (32%), and agitation/aggression (30%). Forty-three percent of individuals with MCI had experienced neuropsychiatric symptoms in the previous month (Lyketsos et al., 2002), with depression (20%), apathy (15%), and irritability (15%) being the most common.

Psychosocial interventions for neuropsychiatric symptoms may be preferable over medication because of preexisting medical conditions, increased vulnerability to adverse drug reactions, and complicated medication regimens often present in this population. In addition, given the mixed evidence-base for psychotropic use for neuropsychiatric symptoms in dementia, a multidisciplinary expert panel recommended use of psychotropic medication only after attempting behavioral and environmental modifications and needed medical interventions (Kales et al., 2014). Exceptions to these recommendations include the presence of major depression with or without suicidal ideation, psychosis causing harm or with significant risk of causing harm, and aggression causing risk to self or others (Kales et al., 2014). Despite their promise and recommendations for their use, nonpharmacological therapies for individuals with dementia are limited and warrant continued development. The following sections will provide a review of CBT for individuals with varying levels of cognitive impairment, including how to address depression, anxiety, pain, and behavioral challenges in these patients.

Modifications of CBT for Individuals With Mild-to-Moderate Cognitive Difficulties

One challenge in implementing CBT for individuals with dementia is that cognitive limitations affect an individual's ability to comprehend, remember, and apply new skills (Kraus et al., 2008). Modifications are needed in the content, structure, and learning strategies of CBT protocols (Kraus et al., 2008). A coach, such as a caregiver or supportive other, can be used when the individual cannot retain information in brief conversations and when he/she needs assistance with practice and skill use outside the therapy session (Charlesworth, Sadek, Schepers, & Spector, 2015; Kraus et al., 2008; Stanley et al., 2013).

Basic elements of CBT can be simplified and abbreviated to make the skills more accessible to individuals with cognitive difficulties. For example, instead of using all the steps of cognitive restructuring, the therapist and/or supportive other can suggest "calming thoughts" as a means to decrease distress (Kraus et al., 2008; Paukert et al., 2013; Stanley et al., 2013). Although the basic session structure (homework review, skill acquisition or review, new homework) can remain the same (Charlesworth et al., 2015; Paukert et al., 2013; Stanley et al., 2013), sessions, generally, will be briefer (30 to 40 minutes) to accommodate limitations in attention and the presence of fatigue. The complexity of skill development needs to match the abilities of the individual and the availability of a coach to practice the skills (Charlesworth et al., 2015). In general, the more cognitively impaired the individual, the more behaviorally focused interventions should be. As with traditional CBT, the therapist needs to assess the patient's and coach's understandings of the skill during session. This assessment could involve having the patient and/or coach describe the skill, observing the patient and coach practice a skill together, or using a concrete homework plan and written homework directions (Kraus et al., 2008). Organization and memory aides, such as a therapy binder for handouts and skill reminder cards to keep in a wallet or posted in a prominent place (i.e., bedside or kitchen table, television screen), can also enhance the individual's use of the skill (Kraus et al., 2008; Paukert et al., 2013; Stanley et al., 2013). Spaced retrieval, a cognitive rehabilitation technique during which the individual remembers material in incrementally longer increments, has also been used in CBT for individuals with cognitive difficulties (Camp, Kloss, & Judge, 1999; Kraus et al., 2008; Paukert et al., 2010; Stanley et al., 2013).

Anxiety and Depression

Anxiety and depressive symptoms are common among individuals with dementia or MCI. Varying estimates of prevalence rates may be related to differences in methodologies, settings (clinical or residential), and severity and type of participants' impairments (physical, cognitive, and/or functional; Neville & Teri, 2011). A review of anxiety disorder prevalence in dementia suggests a range of 5% to 21% for current to 6 month prevalence (Seignorel, Kunik, Snow, Wilson, & Stanley, 2008). Anxiety symptoms are estimated to occur in 10% to 74% of individuals with MCI (Lopez, Becker, & Sweet, 2005). Current depressive symptom prevalence in dementia of the Alzheimer's type is estimated to range from 20% to 30%, with a higher prevalence in individuals with dementia with Lewy Bodies and vascular dementia (Enache, Winblad, & Aarsland, 2011). Estimates of current prevalence for depressive symptoms in individuals with MCI range from 36% (Palmer et al., 2007) to 63% (Solfrizzi et al., 2007). Anxiety and depression in individuals with dementia have been linked to decreased quality of life. Associated difficulties include increased behavioral problems, limitations in activities of daily living (Neville & Teri, 2011; Schultz, Hoth, & Buckwalter, 2004), and risk of nursing-home placement (Gibbons et al., 2002; Lyketsos et al., 1997; Stern et al., 1997).

There is a research base for CBT-based interventions for individuals with dementia and anxiety or depression. Case studies (Kipling, Bailey, & Charlesworth, 1999; Koder, 1998; Kraus et al., 2008) and RCTs (Spector et al., 2015; Stanley et al., 2013) have shown support for CBT-based interventions targeting anxiety in individuals with dementia. The Peaceful Mind program combined home visits and telephone sessions to teach patients with dementia and their coaches (adults who spent at least 8 hours per week with patients) simplified CBT skills (self-monitoring, deep breathing, coping self-statements, behavioral activation, and sleep management; Stanley et al., 2013). After the first 3 months of skills training sessions, patients reported a higher quality of life, clinicians rated patients as less anxious than individuals receiving usual care, and coaches reported less distress related to their loved ones' anxiety. A lack of maintenance of positive effects at 6 months might have been related to participants' needing a longer interval of treatment with providers, possible changes in the patient-coach relationship, or cognitive changes in the patients. Another trial targeted depression in dementia by training patient—carer dyads to use CBT skills (psychoeducation about CBT and anxiety in dementia, self-monitoring, identifying and practicing strategies for feeling safe, identifying and challenging unhelpful cognitions, addressing realistic negative automatic thoughts, calming thoughts, and behavioral experiments) over 10 weekly sessions (Spector et al., 2015). This program also offered optional modules for considering long-standing unhelpful "rules for living" and for addressing interpersonal difficulties between the carer and person with dementia. At 15 weeks and at six months, differences in anxiety between CBT and treatment as usual approached significance. Depression remained significantly different between both groups at 15 weeks and 6 months. Larger studies and further investigation of the effectiveness of CBT for depression in dementia are recommended (Spector et al., 2015).

Pain

Individuals with dementia commonly experience pain (Shega, Hougham, Stocking, Cox-Hayley, & Sachs, 2004; Zwakhalen, Koopmans, Geels, Berger, & Hamers, 2009), regardless of mental health diagnoses or functional status (Breland et al., 2015). Approximately 50% of individuals with dementia regularly experience pain (Corbett et al., 2012). Community-dwelling older adults with dementia had a significantly higher prevalence of bothersome pain (63.5%) than a matched cohort without dementia (54.5%; Hunt et al., 2015). This study also found a higher percentage of activity-limiting pain in individuals with dementia (43.3%) than without dementia (27.2%) (Hunt et al., 2015). Unfortunately, pain is often undertreated in adults with dementia because of patients' difficulties with communication and challenges for providers to interpret altered behavioral patterns (pacing, vocalizations, etc.) that may reflect different forms of distress (e.g., boredom, pain, anxiety; Husebo et al., 2012). Pain may also contribute to aggressive behaviors in adults with dementia in nursing homes (Ahn & Horgas, 2014; Kunik et al., 2010; Norton, Allen, Snow, Hardin, & Bargio, 2010).

Psychosocial interventions for pain help the individual cope, minimize the negative impact on emotional well-being, and may provide distraction from pain (Snow & Jacobs, 2014). Interventions such as relaxation techniques are effective for pain management in older adults (Morone & Greco, 2007); however, research on relaxation and related techniques is lacking with older adults with dementia (Snow & Jacobs, 2014). CBT is the best-documented psychosocial intervention for pain in individuals with mild-to-moderate dementia (Snow & Jacobs, 2014). One treatment for pain in dementia is geriatric multimodal CBT (GMCBT), which is inclusive of a broad range of psychotherapeutic techniques that can be operationalized in cognitive-behavioral terms (Clifford, Cipher, Roper, Snow, & Molinari, 2008). Examples of GMCBT treatment goals include improved pain tolerance, increased involvement in pleasurable activity, behavioral pain management (e.g., ice and heat, distraction), reductions in negative moods (e.g., depression, anxiety, irritability), improved care plan adherence, and decreased frequency of inappropriate behaviors (Clifford et al., 2008). During early sessions, there is discussion of the patient's personal values (e.g., being active in one's faith, being a hard worker), which contributes to the development of motivational themes for family and staff to use in facilitating behavioral change (Cipher, Clifford, & Roper, 2007; Clifford et al., 2008). Sessions are conducted with other healthcare providers present, who then participate in skill implementation. Cognitive restructuring is based on stated values and facilitates patients' reappraisal of their medical conditions, which may be contributing to mood disturbances, problematic behaviors, and interpersonal strain (Cipher et al., 2007; Clifford et al., 2008). Eight sessions of GMCBT resulted in significant reductions in pain and other factors related to pain in nursing-home residents with mild-to-moderate cognitive impairment (Cipher et al., 2007).

Modifications, such as working collaboratively with family members and nursing-home staff, developing structured treatment plans with an interdisciplinary team, and addressing problems relevant and valued by the residents, can contribute to favorable outcomes in pain management for individuals with dementia (Cipher, Clifford, & Roper, 2006). Snow and Jacobs present a Distress First model of integrative clinical assessment and intervention approach (Snow & Jacobs, 2014). Clinicians are encouraged to use the term *distress* rather than *pain*, reflecting the diversity of behaviors that can indicate pain or other discomfort. Through a process of Look-Listen-Guess-Respond-Repeat, clinicians make educated guesses about what is causing distress, alter the environment or other factors, and then reassess to determine if the change was associated with improvement. Within this approach, nonpharmacologic and pharmacologic treatments are considered.

Treating Behavioral and Psychological Symptoms in Moderate-to-Severe Dementia

As dementia progresses in severity, additional challenging and problematic behaviors emerge. These can include agitation, hitting, screaming, pacing, wandering, and decreased inactivity, which may be referred to as behavioral and psychological symptoms of dementia (BPSD; Moniz Cook, De Vugt, Verhey, & James, 2009) or neuropsychiatric symptoms of dementia (Finkel, Silva, Cohen, Miller, & Sartorius, 1997). Individuals with advanced dementia almost universally have at least one BPSD (Kverno, Black, Nolan, & Rabins, 2009; Lyketsos et al., 2011). Because of the multiple factors contributing to BPSD, including environmental and interpersonal elements, CBT conceptualizations can guide the development of interventions for individuals with dementia and for their caregivers.

Conceptual models directing the treatment of challenging behaviors include the Cohen-Mansfield "unmet needs" perspective, the environmental vulnerability paradigm, and the learning/behavior paradigm (Cohen-Mansfield, 2001; McGee & Bratkovich, 2011). The unmet needs paradigm focuses on unmet social (i.e., being lonely), emotional (i.e., sadness, fear), and physical (e.g., pain, hunger) needs as precipitants of the expression of BPSD. In the environmental vulnerability paradigm, as dementia progresses, individuals may need assistance in modifying and/or coping with environmental stimuli, for example, decreasing noise, as a way to decrease BPSD. The learning/behavior paradigm focuses on teaching providers and families to use analyses of antecedents, behaviors, and consequences (ABCs) to understand the origin and maintenance of problematic behaviors. These models are not exclusive, and one can use them collaboratively to understand problematic behaviors and develop interventions (Cohen-Mansfield, 2001).

Numerous psychosocial interventions for BPSD include elements of CBT, such as relaxation; encouraging pleasurable events or behavioral activation; and behavior-focused interventions, including differential reinforcement. A literature review of 83 nonpharmacological intervention studies for BPSD (Cohen-Mansfield, 2001) provided support for a variety of treatments to decrease inappropriate behaviors in patients with advanced dementia, including combination therapies, medical/nursing care interventions, environmental interventions, structured activities, staff training, behavior therapy, and sensory or social contact (real or simulated). However, the majority of studies reviewed had small numbers of participants or were case studies.

Staff Training in Assisted Living Residences (STAR) is a psychosocial intervention training program for direct care staff working with residents with challenging dementia-related behaviors (Teri, Huda, Gibbons, Young, & van Leynseele, 2005). Staff members are trained to examine ABCs of behavioral distress to facilitate altering the sequence of events that begin or maintain problematic behaviors. Training includes basic information about dementia, skills for communicating with dementia residents, pleasant events for residents, improving communication between staff and families, and using the ABC approach to identify and decrease resident distress. Within this training program are staff workshops, individualized sessions with trainer and trainee, and meetings with residence leadership. Following training, residents had significantly reduced levels of behavioral and affective distress compared with control residents. Staff trained with STAR also reported more job satisfaction and less adverse impact and negative reaction to resident problems. The STAR program has been implemented in the Veterans Health Administration (STAR-VA), with positive results; specifically, the frequency and severity of depression, anxiety, and agitation all significantly decreased in Veterans Health Administration Community Living Centers (Karel, Teri, McConnell, Visnic, & Karlin, 2016).

The implementation of nonpharmacological approaches for managing challenging dementia-related behaviors in long-term care settings has been limited because of staff time, staff training needs, and organizational implementation requirements, such as leadership buy-in (Karel et al., 2016). Cohen-Mansfield (2001) recommends continued progress on individualizing interventions, understanding the mechanics of successful interventions (e.g., timing, duration) and addressing issues of implementation and cost.

SUMMARY AND FUTURE DIRECTIONS

Evidence is strong for the use of CBT in late life, especially for depressive symptoms and insomnia. More research is needed on effective therapies for preventing late-life suicidal behavior. Cognitive-behavioral treatments for late-life anxiety are promising, although many older adults with anxiety do not seek treatment (Byers, Aréan, & Yaffe, 2012), and outcomes among older adult samples are not as robust as for younger adults (Wetherell et al., 2013b). The evidence base for interventions for older adults with cognitive impairments is growing. When caregivers or a coach are involved, CBT is effective for a range of problems facing these individuals. Research is currently focused on developing and testing novel care models to address access to care for older adults. Therapy provided in the home, over the telephone, and by nontraditional providers is both patient-centered and practical (Hoeft et al., 2016).

Future studies should continue to involve underserved and ethnic and racial minority older adults in CBT effectiveness and implementation research (Areán et al., 2010). Many trials of CBT in late life have included predominantly women, so recruiting older men for research is also critical (Price, Fiske, & Edelstein, 2015). Because of the frequency of insomnia, depressive symptoms, worry, and concerns about cognitive functioning among older primary care populations, behavioral health care should be routine in medical settings. In long-term care, training staff in behavioral interventions for problem behaviors in dementia can provide a nonmedication option for the prevention and treatment of distressing neuropsychiatric symptoms. CBT, in various forms, is well positioned to continue to be the treatment of choice in settings serving older adults. Future research should focus on issues of access and reach in order to provide effective CBT to older adults, regardless of income, health, or living situation.

References

Administration on Aging. (2010). *Older population by age group: 1900 to 2050 with chart of the 60 + population.* Available from http://www.aoa.gov/AoARoot/Aging_Statistics/future_growth/future_growth.aspx#age.

Ahn, H., & Horgas, A. (2014). Does pain mediate or moderate the effect of cognitive impairment on aggression in nursing home residents with dementia? *Asian Nursing Research, 8*, 105–109.

Alexopoulos, G. S., Raue, P. J., Kiosses, D. N., Seirup, J. K., Banerjee, S., & Areán, P. A. (2015). Comparing engage with PST in late-life major depression: A preliminary report. *The American Journal of Geriatric Psychiatry, 23*, 506–513.

American Geriatrics Society (2015). American Geriatrics Society 2015 updated Beers criteria for potentially inappropriate medication use in older adults. *Journal of the American Geriatric Society, 63*, 2227–2246.

American Psychiatric Association (2013). *Diagnostic and statistical manual of mental disorders* (5th Ed.). Washington, DC: Author.

Aréan, P. A., & Niu, G. (2014). Choosing treatment for depression in older adults and evaluating response. *Clinics in Geriatric Medicine, 30*, 535–551.

Aréan, P. A., & Feliciano, L. (2008). Older adults. In M. A. Whisman (Ed.), *Adapting cognitive therapy for depression: Managing complexing and comorbidity* (pp. 417–438). New York, NY: The Guildford Press.

Aréan, P. A., & Cook, B. L. (2002). Psychotherapy and combined psychotherapy/pharmacotherapy for late life depression. *Biological Psychiatry, 52*, 293–303.

Aréan, P. A., Mackin, S., Vargas-Dwyer, E., Raue, P., Sirey, J. A., Kanellopolos, D., & Alexopoulos, G. S. (2010). Treating depression in disabled, low-income elderly: A conceptual model and recommendations for care. *International Journal of Geriatric Psychiatry, 25*, 765–769.

Aréan, P. A., Raue, P. J., Sirey, J. A., & Snowden, M. (2012). Implementing evidence-based psychotherapies in settings serving older adults: Challenges and solutions. *Psychiatric Services, 63*, 605–607.

Ayalon, L., Areán, P. A., Linkins, K., Lynch, M., & Estes, C. L. (2007). Integration of mental health services into primary care overcomes ethnic disparities in access to mental health services between black and white elderly. *The American Journal of Geriatric Psychiatry, 15*, 906–912.

Ayers, C., Castriotta, N., Dozier, M., Espejo, E., & Porter, B. (2014a). Behavioral and experiential avoidance in patients with hoarding disorder. *Journal of Behavior Therapy and Experimental Psychiatry, 45*, 408–414.

Ayers, C., Ly, P., Howard, I., Mayes, T., Porter, B., & Iqbal, Y. (2013a). Hoarding severity predicts functional disability in late-life hoarding disorder patients. *International Journal of Geriatric Psychiatry, 29*, 741–746.

Ayers, C., Saxena, S., Espejo, E., Twamley, E., Granholm, E., & Wetherell, J. (2014b). Novel treatment for geriatric hoarding disorder: An open trial of cognitive rehabilitation paired with behavior therapy. *American Journal of Geriatric Psychiatry, 22*, 248–252.

Ayers, C., Wetherell, J., Golshan, S., & Saxena, S. (2011). Cognitive-behavioral therapy for geriatric compulsive hoarding. *Behaviour Research and Therapy, 49*, 689–694.

Ayers, C., Wetherell, J., Schiehser, D., Almklov, E., Golshan, S., & Saxena, S. (2013b). Executive functioning in older adults with hoarding disorder. *International Journal of Geriatric Psychiatry, 28*, 1175–1181.

Beard, J. R. (2014). The demography and epidemiology of population aging. In N. A. Pachana, & K. Laidlaw (Eds.), *The Oxford handbook of clinical geropsychology* (pp. 26–39). New York, NY: Oxford University Press.

Bhar, S. S., & Brown, G. K. (2012). Treatment of depression and suicide in older adults. *Cognitive and Behavioral Practice, 19*, 116–125.

Bishop, N. A., Lu, T., & Yankner, B. A. (2010). Neural mechanisms of ageing and cognitive decline. *Nature, 464*, 529–535.

Bistricky, S. L., Mackin, R. S., Chu, J. P., & Areán, P. A. (2010). Recruitment of African Americans and Asian Americans with late-life depression and mild cognitive impairment. *The American Journal of Geriatric Psychiatry, 18*, 734–742.

Blazer, D. G. (2003). Depression in late life: Review and commentary. *Journals of Gerontology Series A, 58*, 249–265.

Breland, J. Y., Barrera, T. L., Snow, A. L., Sansgiry, S., Stanley, M. A., Wilson, N., ... Kunik, M. E. (2015). Correlates of pain intensity in community-dwelling individuals with mild to moderate dementia. *American Journal of Alzheimer's Disease and Other Dementias, 30*, 320–325. Available from http://dx.doi.org/10.1177/1533317515458273317514545827.

Brenes, G., Danhauer, S., Lyles, M., Hogan, P., & Miller, M. (2015). Telephone-delivered cognitive behavioral therapy and telephone-delivered nondirective supportive therapy for rural older adults with generalized anxiety disorder. *JAMA Psychiatry, 72*, 1012–1020.

Brown, G. K., Ten Have, T., Henriques, G. R., Xie, S. X., Hollander, J. E., & Beck, A. T. (2005). Cognitive therapy for the prevention of suicide attempts: A randomized controlled trial. *JAMA, 294*, 563–570.

Bruce, M. L., Raue, P. J., Reilly, C. F., Greenberg, R. L., Meyers, B. S., Banerjee, S., ... Rosas, V. H. (2015). Clinical effectiveness of integrating depression care management into Medicare home health: The depression CAREPATH Randomized Trial. *JAMA Internal Medicine, 175*(1), 55–64.

Bruce, M. L., Ten Have, T. R., Reynolds, C. F., III, Katz, I. I., Schulberg, H. C., Mulsant, B. H., ... Alexopoulos, G. S. (2004). Reducing suicidal ideation and depressive symptoms in depressed older primary care patients: A randomized controlled trial. *Journal of the American Medical Association, 291*, 1081–1091.

Bryan, C. K. (Ed.), (2015). *Cognitive behavioural therapy for preventing suicide attempts: A guide to brief treatments across clinical settings* New York, NY: Routledge.

Byers, A. L., Aréan, P. A., & Yaffe, K. (2012). Low use of mental health services among older Americans with mood and anxiety disorders. *Psychiatric Services, 63,* 66–72.

Byers, A. L., Covinsky, K. E., Neylan, T. C., & Yaffe, K. (2014). Chronicity of posttraumatic stress disorder and risk of disability in older persons. *JAMA Psychiatry, 71,* 540–546.

Calamari, J., Pontarelli, N., Armstrong, K., & Salstrom, S. (2012). Obsessive-compulsive disorder in late life. *Cognitive and Behavioral Practice, 19,* 136–150.

Calleo, J., Stanley, M. A., Greisinger, A., Wehmanen, O., Johnson, M., Novy, D., . . . Kunik, M. (2009). Generalized anxiety disorder in older medical patients: Diagnostic recognition, mental health management and service utilization. *Journal of Clinical Psychology in Medical Settings, 16,* 178–185.

Camp, C. J., Koss, E., & Judge, K. (1999). Cognitive assessment in late-stage dementia. In P. A. Lichtenberg (Ed.), *Handbook of assessment in clinical gerontology* (pp. 442–467). Hoboken, NJ: John Wiley & Sons, Inc.

Carlson, W. L., & Snowden, M. (2014). Community treatment of older adults: Principles and evidence supporting mental health service interventions. *Clinical Geriatric Medicine, 30,* 655–661.

Charlesworth, G., Sadek, S., Schepers, A., & Spector, A. (2015). Cognitive behavior therapy for anxiety in people with dementia: A clinician guideline for a person-centered approach. *Behavior Modification, 39,* 390–412.

Choi, N. G. (2009). The integration of social and psychologic services to improve low-income homebound older adults' access to depression treatment. *Family & Community Health, 32,* S27–S35.

Ciechanowski, P., Wagner, E., Schmaling, K., Schwartz, S., Williams, B., Diehr, P., & LoGerfo, J. (2004). Community-integrated home-based depression treatment in older adults: A randomized controlled trial. *Journal of the American Medical Association, 291,* 1569–1577.

Cipher, D. J., Clifford, P. A., & Roper, K. D. (2006). Behavioral manifestations of pain in the demented elderly. *Journal of the American Medical Directors Association, 7,* 355–365. doi: 10.1016/j.jamda.2005.11.012.

Cipher, D. J., Clifford, P. A., & Roper, K. D. (2007). The effectiveness of geropsychological treatment in improving pain, depression, behavioral disturbances, functional disability, and health care utilization in long-term care. *Clinical Gerontologist, 30,* 23–40.

Clifford, P. A., Cipher, D. J., Roper, K. D., Snow, A. L., & Molinari, V. (2008). Cognitive-behavioral interventions for long-term care residents with physical and cognitive disabilities. In D. Gallagher-Thompson, A. M. Steffen, & L. W. Thompson (Eds.), *Handbook of behavioral and cognitive therapist with older adults* (pp. 76–101). New York: Springer New York.

Cohen-Mansfield, J. (2001). Nonpharmacologic interventions for inappropriate behaviors in dementia: A review, summary, and critique. *The American Journal of Geriatric Psychiatry, 9,* 361–381.

Corbett, A., Husebo, B., Malcangio, M., Staniland, A., Cohen-Mansfield, J., Aarsland, D., & Ballard, C. (2012). Assessment and treatment of pain in people with dementia. *National Review of Neurology, 8,* 264–274. doi: 10.1038/nrneurol.2012.53.

Cuijpers, P., van Straten, A., & Smit, F. (2006). Psychological treatment of late-life depression: A meta-analysis of randomized controlled trials. *International Journal of Geriatric Psychiatry, 21,* 1139–1149.

Cukrowicz, K. C., Cheavens, J. S., Van Orden, K. A., Ragain, R. M., & Cook, R. L. (2011). Perceived burdensomeness and suicide ideation in older adults. *Psychology and Aging, 26,* 331.

Cummings, J.P., Armento, M.E., Kunik, M.E., Cully, J., Wilson, N.L., Amspoker, A.B., . . . Stanley, M.A. (2013, November 21–24). A brief intervention for home-bound veterans with anxiety and/or depressive symptoms. Poster presentation at The Association for Behavioral and Cognitive Therapies, Nashville, Tennessee.

De Leo, D., Draper, B. M., Snowdon, J., & Kõlves, K. (2013). Suicides in older adults: A case-control psychological autopsy study in Australia. *Journal of Psychiatric Research, 47,* 980–988. doi:10.1016/j.jpsychires.2013.02.009.

Dobransky-Fasiska, D., Nowalk, M. P., Cruz, M., McMurray, M. L., Castillo, E., Begley, A. E., . . . Brown, C. (2012). A community–academic partnership develops a more responsive model to providing depression care to disadvantaged adults in the US. *International Journal of Social Psychiatry, 58,* 295–305.

Drapeau, C. W., & McIntosh, J. L. (2015). *U.S.A. suicide 2014: Official final data.* Washington, DC: American Association of Suicidology. Available from http://www.suicidology.org.

Dreer, L. E., Copeland, J. N., & Cheavens, J. S. (2011). Integrating neuropsychological functioning into cognitive behavioral therapy: Implications for older adults. In K. H. Sorocco, & S. Lauderdale (Eds.), *Cognitive behavior therapy with older adults* (pp. 317–366). New York, NY: Springer Publishing Company.

El-Gabalawy, R., Mackenzie, C. S., Pietrzak, R. H., & Sareen, J. (2014). A longitudinal examination of anxiety disorders and physical health conditions in a nationally representative sample of US older adults. *Experimental Gerontology, 60,* 46–56.

Enache, D., Winblad, B., & Aarsland, D. (2011). Depression in dementia: Epidemiology, mechanisms, and treatment. *Current Opinion in Psychiatry, 24,* 461–472.

Erlangsen, A., Stenager, E., & Conwell, Y. (2015). Physical diseases as predictors of suicide in older adults: A nationwide, register-based cohort study. *Social Psychiatry and Psychiatric Epidemiology, 50,* 1427–1439.

Finkel, S. I., Silva, J. C., Cohen, G., Miller, S., & Sartorius, N. (1997). Behavioral and psychological signs and symptoms of dementia: A consensus statement on current knowledge and implications for research and treatment. *International Journal of Geriatric Psychiatry, 12,* 1060–1061.

Foley, D., Ancoli-Israel, S., Britz, P., & Walsh, J. (2004). Sleep disturbances and chronic disease in older adults: Results of the 2003 National Sleep Foundation Sleep in America Survey. *Journal of Psychosomatic Research, 56,* 497–502.

Gibbons, L. E., Teri, L., Logsdon, R., McCurry, S. M., Kukull, W., Bowen, J., . . . Larson, E. (2002). Anxiety symptoms as predictors of nursing home placement in patients with Alzheimer's disease. *Journal of Clinical Geropsychology, 8,* 335–342.

Gillespie, L. D., Robertson, M. C., Gillespie, W. J., Sherirngton, C., Gates, S., Clemson, L. M., & Lamb, S. E. (2012). Interventions for preventing falls in older people in the community. *Cochrane Database Systematic Review, 9,* CD007146.

Gonçalves, D., & Byrne, G. (2012). Interventions for generalized anxiety disorder in older adults: Systematic review and meta-analysis. *Journal of Anxiety Disorders, 26,* 1–11.

Gould, R., Coulson, M., & Howard, R. (2012). Efficacy of cognitive behavioral therapy for anxiety disorders in older people: A meta-analysis and meta-regression of randomized controlled trials. *Journal of the American Geriatrics Society, 60,* 218–229.

Gum, A. M., Iser, L., & Petkus, A. (2010). Behavioral health service utilization and preferences of older adults receiving home-based aging services. *American Journal of Geriatric Psychiatry, 18,* 491–501.

Gustavson, K. A., Alexopoulos, G. S., Niu, G. C., McColloch, C., Meade, T., & Arean, P. A. (2016). Problem-solving therapy reduces suicidal ideation in depressed older adults with executive dysfunction. *American Journal of Geriatric Psychiatry, 24,* 11–17.

Hasin, D. S., & Grant, B. F. (2015). The National Epidemiologic Survey on Alcohol and Related Conditions (NESARC) Waves 1 and 2: Review and summary of findings. *Social Psychiatry and Psychiatric Epidemiology, 50,* 1609−1640.

Hendriks, G., Kampman, M., Keijsers, G., Hoogduin, C., & Voshaar, R. (2014). Cognitive-behavioral therapy for panic disorder with agoraphobia in older people: A comparison with younger patients. *Depression and Anxiety, 31,* 669−677.

Hoeft, T. J., Hinton, L., Liu, J., & Unützer, J. (2016). Directions for effectiveness research to improve health services for late-life depression in the United States. *The American Journal of Geriatric Psychiatry, 24,* 18−30.

Hunt, L. J., Covinsky, K. E., Yaffe, K., Stephens, C. E., Miao, Y., Boscardin, W. J., & Smith, A. K. (2015). Pain in community-dwelling older adults with dementia: Results from the National Health and Aging Trends Study. *Journal of the American Geriatrics Society, 63,* 1503−1511.

Husebo, B. S., Achterberg, W. P., Lobbezoo, F., Kunz, M., Lautenbacher, S., Kappesser, J., ... Strand, L. I. (2012). Pain in patients with dementia: A review of pain assessment and treatment challenges. *Norsk Epidemiologi, 22,* 243−251.

Institute of Medicine (2012). *Mental health and substance use workforce for older adults. In whose hands?* Washington, DC: National Academy Press.

Jameson, J. P., & Cully, J. A. (2011). Cognitive behavioral therapy for older adults in the primary care setting. In K. H. Sorocco, & S. Lauderdale (Eds.), *Cognitive behavior therapy with older adults* (pp. 291−316). New York, NY: Springer Publishing Company.

Johnco, C., Wuthrich, V. M., & Rapee, R. M. (2015). The impact of late-life anxiety and depression on cognitive flexibility and cognitive restricting skill acquisition. *Depression and Anxiety, 32,* 752−762.

Joo, J. H., Morales, K. H., de Vries, H. F., & Gallo, J. J. (2010). Disparity in use of psycho-therapy offered in primary care between older African-American and white adults: Results from a practice-based depression intervention trial. *Journal of the American Geriatrics Society, 58,* 154−160.

Kales, H. C., Gitlin, L. N., & Lyketsos, C. G. (2014). Management of neuropsychiatric symptoms of dementia in clinical settings: Recommendations from a multidisciplinary expert panel. *Journal of American Geriatrics Society, 62,* 762−769.

Karel, M. J., Teri, L., McConnell, E., Visnic, S., & Karlin, B. E. (2016). Effectiveness of expanded implementation of STAR-VA for managing dementia-related behaviors among veterans. *The Gerontologist, 56,* 126−134.

Kay, D. B., Dombrovski, A. Y., Buysse, D. J., Reynolds, C. F., Begley, A., & Szanto, K. (2015). Insomnia is associated with suicide attempt in middle-aged and older adults with depression. *International Psychogeriatrics, 28,* 1−7.

Kessler, R., Berglund, P., Demler, O., Jin, R., Merikangas, K., & Walters, E. (2005). Lifetime prevalence and age-of-onset distributions of DSM-IV disorders in the National Comorbidity Survey Replication. *Archives of General Psychiatry, 62,* 593−602.

Kipling, T., Bailey, M., & Charlesworth, G. (1999). The feasibility of a cognitive behaviour-al therapy group for men with mild/moderate cognitive impairment. *Behavioural and Cognitive Psychotherapy, 27,* 189−193.

Kirkham, J., Seitz, D., & Choi, N. G. (2015). Meta-analysis of problem solving therapy for the treatment of depression in older adults. *The American Journal of Geriatric Psychiatry, 3,* S129−S130.

Knaevelsrud C., Böttche M., & Kuwert P. (2009). Long-term effects of civilian war trauma: Epidemiological, sociological and psychotherapeutic aspects. Presented at the 11th European Conference on Traumatic Stress, June 15−18, 2009, Oslo, Norway.

Koder, D. A. (1998). Treatment of anxiety in the cognitively impaired elderly: Can cognitive-behavior therapy help? *International Psychogeriatrics, 10,* 173−182.

Koons, C. R., Robins, C. J., Tweed, J. L., Lynch, T. R., Gonzalez, A. M., Morse, J. Q., . . . Bastian, L. A. (2001). Efficacy of dialectical behavior therapy in women veterans with borderline personality disorder. *Behavior Therapy, 32,* 371−390.

Kraus, C. A., Seignourel, P., Balasubramanyam, V., Snow, A. L., Wilson, N. L., Kunik, M. E., . . . Stanley, M. A. (2008). Cognitive behavioral treatment for anxiety in patients with dementia: Two case studies. *Journal of Psychiatric Practice, 14,* 186−192.

Kraus-Schuman, C., Wilson, N., Amspoker, A., Wagener, P., Calleo, J., Diefenbach, G., . . . Stanley, M. A. (2015). Enabling lay providers to conduct CBT for older adults: Key steps for expanding treatment capacity. *Translational Behavioral Medicine, 5,* 247−253.

Kunik, M. E., Snow, A. L., Davila, J. A., Steele, A. B., Balasubramanyam, V., Doody, R. S., . . . Morgan, R. O. (2010). Causes of aggressive behavior in patients with dementia. *The Journal of Clinical Psychiatry, 71,* 1145−1152.

Kverno, K. S., Black, B. S., Nolan, M. T., & Rabins, P. V. (2009). Research on treating neuropsychiatric symptoms of advanced dementia with non-pharmacological strategies, 1998−2008: A systematic literature review. *International Psychogeriatrics, 21,* 825−843.

Laborde-Lahoz, P., El-Gabalawy, R., Kinley, J., Kirwin, P. D., Sareen, J., & Pietrzak, R. H. (2015). Subsyndromal depression among older adults in the USA: Prevalence, comorbidity, and risk for new-onset psychiatric disorders in late life. *International Journal of Geriatric Psychiatry, 30,* 67i7−85.

Laidlaw, K., & Thompson, L. W. (2014). Cognitive-behavior therapy with older people. In N. A. Pachana, & K. Laidlaw (Eds.), *The Oxford handbook of clinical geropsychology* (pp. 603−621). New York, NY: Oxford University Press.

Laidlaw, K., Davidson, K., Toner, H., Jackson, G., Clark, S., Law, J.,et al. (2008). A randomised controlled trial of cognitive behaviour therapy vs treatment as usual in the treatment of mild to moderate late life depression. *International Journal of Geriatric Psychiatry 23,* 843−850.

Lapierre, S., Erlangsen, A., Waern, M., De Leo, D., Oyama, H., Scocco, P., . . . International Research Group for Suicide among the Elderly. (2011). A systematic review of elderly suicide prevention programs. *Crisis, 32,* 88−98.

Lee, S. Y., Franchetti, M. K., Imanbayev, A., Gallo, J. J., Spira, A. P., & Lee, H. B. (2012). Non-pharmacological prevention of major depression among community-dwelling older adults: A systematic review of the efficacy of psychotherapy interventions. *Archives of Gerontology and Geriatrics, 55,* 522−529.

Lenze, E., Hickman, S., Hershey, T., Wendleton, L., Ly, K., Dixon, D., . . . Wetherell, J. (2014). Mindfulness-based stress reduction for older adults with worry symptoms and co-occurring cognitive dysfunction. *International Journal of Geriatric Psychiatry, 29,* 991−1000.

Li, F., Fisher, K. J., Harmer, P., McAuley, E., & Wilson, N. L. (2003). Fear of falling in elderly persons: Association with falls, functional ability, and quality of life. *Journals of Gerontology Series B: Psychological Sciences and Social Sciences, 58,* P283−P290.

Lopez, O. L., Becker, I. T., & Sweet, R. A. (2005). Non-cognitive symptoms in mild cognitive impairment subjects. *Neurocase, 11,* 65−71.

Lyketsos, C. G., Carillo, M. C., Ryan, J. M., Khatchaturian, A. S., Trzepac, P., Amatniek, J., . . . Miller, D. S. (2011). Neuropsychiatric symptoms in Alzheimer's disease. *Alzheimer's and Dementia: The Journal of the Alzheimer's Association, 7,* 532−539. Available from http://dx.doi.org/10.1016/j.jalz.2011.05.2410.

Lyketsos, C. G., Lopez, O., Jones, B., Fitzpatrick, A. L., Breitner, J., & DeKosky, S. (2002). Prevalence of neuropsychiatric symptoms in dementia and mild cognitive impairment: Results from the cardiovascular health study. *Journal of the American Medical Association, 288,* 1475−1483.

Lyketsos, C. G., Steele, C., Baker, L., Galik, E., Kopunek, S., Steinberg, M., & Warren, A. (1997). Major and minor depression in Alzheimer's disease: Prevalence and impact. *Journal of Neuropsychiatry and Clinical Neurosciences, 9,* 556—561.

Lynch, T. R., Cheavens, J. S., Cukrowicz, K. C., Thorp, S. R., Bronner, L., & Beyer, J. (2007). Treatment of older adults with co-morbid personality disorder and depression: A dialectical behavior therapy approach. *International Journal of Geriatric Psychiatry, 22,* 131—143. doi: 10.1002/gps.1703.

Mackenzie, C. S., El-Gabalawy, R., Chou, K. L., & Sareen, J. (2014). Prevalence and predictors of persistent versus remitting mood, anxiety, and substance disorders in a national sample of older adults. *The American Journal of Geriatric Psychiatry, 22,* 854—865.

Mackin, R. S., & Aréan, P. A. (2005). Evidence-based psychotherapeutic interventions for geriatric depression. *Psychiatric Clinics of North America, 28,* 805—820.

McCurry, S. M., Shortreed, S. M., Von Korff, M., Balderson, B. H., Baker, L. D., Rybarczyk, B. D., & Vitiello, M. V. (2014). Who benefits from CBT for insomnia in primary care? Important patient selection and trial design lessons from longitudinal results of the Lifestyles trial. *Sleep, 37,* 299—308.

McGee, J. S., & Bratkovich, K. L. (2011). Assessment and cognitive-behaviorally oriented interventions for older adults with dementia. In K. H. Sorocco, & S. Lauderdale (Eds.), *Cognitive behavior therapy with older adults: Innovations across settings* (pp. 219—261). New York, NY: Springer Publishing Company.

Meeks, S., Shah, S. N., & Ramsey, S. K. (2009). The Pleasant Events Schedule—Nursing home version: A useful tool for behavioral interventions in long-term care. *Aging and Mental Health, 13,* 445—455.

Moniz Cook, E., De Vugt, M., Verhey, F., & James, I. (2009). Functional analysis-based interventions for challenging behavior in dementia. *The Cochrane Database of Systematic Reviews, 3,* 1—7.

Moore, N., Pariente, A., & Bégaud, B. (2015). Why are benzodiazepines not yet controlled substances? *JAMA Psychiatry, 72,* 110—111.

Morin, C. M., Bastien, C., Guay, B., Radouco-Thomas, M., Leblanc, J., & Valliéres, A. (2004). Randomized clinical trial of supervised tapering and cognitive behavioral therapy to facilitate benzodiazepine discontinuation in older adults with chronic insomnia. *American Journal of Psychiatry, 161,* 332—342.

Morin, C. M., Colecchi, C., Stone, J., Sood, R., & Brink, D. (1999). Behavioral and pharmacological therapies for late-life insomnia: A randomized controlled trial. *Journal of the American Medical Association, 281,* 991—999.

Morone, N. E., & Greco, C. M. (2007). Mind-body interventions for chronic pain in older adults: A structured review. *Pain Medicine, 8,* 359—375. Available from http://dx.doi.org/10.1111/j.1526-4637.2007.00312.x.

Nadorff, M. R., Fiske, A., Sperry, J. A., Petts, R., & Gregg, J. J. (2013). Insomnia symptoms, nightmares, and suicidal ideation in older adults. *The Journals of Gerontology Series B: Psychological Sciences and Social Sciences, 68,* 145—152.

Neville, C., & Teri, L. (2011). Anxiety, anxiety symptoms, and associations among older people with dementia in assisted-living facilities. *International Journal of Mental Health Nursing, 20*(19), 5—201.

Newport, F. (2006). Religion most important to blacks, women, and older Americans. [online] Gallup.com. Available from: http://www.gallup.com/poll/25585/Religion-Most-Important-Blacks-Women-Older-Americans.aspx [accessed 27 .07. 2015].

Norton, M. J., Allen, R. S., Snow, A. L., Michael Hardin, J., & Burgio, L. D. (2010). Predictors of need-driven behaviors in nursing home residents with dementia and associated certified nursing assistant burden. *Aging & Mental Health, 14,* 303—309.

Pachana, N. A., Woodward, R. M., & Byrne, G. J. (2007). Treatment of specific phobia in older adults. *Clinical Interventions in Aging*, 2, 469–476.

Palmer, K., Berger, A. K., Monastero, R., Winblad, B., Bäckman, L., & Fratiglioni, L. (2007). Predictors of progression from mild cognitive impairment to Alzheimer disease. *Neurology*, 68, 1596–1602.

Paukert, A. L., Calleo, J., Kraus-Schuman, C., Snow, Wilson, N., Petersen, N. J., ... Stanley, M. A. (2010). Peaceful mind: An open trial of cognitive-behavioral therapy for anxiety in persons with dementia. *International Psychogeriatrics*, 22, 1012–1021.

Paukert, A. L., Kraus-Schuman, C., Wilson, N., Snow, A. L., Calleo, J., Kunik, M. E., & Stanley, M. A. (2013). The peaceful mind manual: A protocol for treating anxiety in persons with dementia. *Behavior Modification*, 37, 631–664.

Periyakoil, V. S., & Hallenbeck, J. (2002). Identifying and managing preparatory grief and depression at the end of life. *American Family Physician*, 65, 883–900.

Perlis, M. L., Jungquist, C., Smit, M. T., & Posner, D. (2005). *Cognitive behavioral treatment of insomnia: A session-by-session guide*. New York, NY: Springer.

Petrov, M. E., Vandder Wal, G. S., & Lichstein, K. L. (2014). Late-life insomnia. In N. A. Pachana, & K. Laidlaw (Eds.), *The Oxford handbook of clinical geropsychology* (pp. 527–548). New York, NY: Oxford University Press.

Pinquart, M., & Duberstein, P. (2007). Treatment of anxiety disorders in older adults: A meta-analytic comparison of behavioral and pharmacological interventions. *American Journal of Geriatric Psychiatry*, 15, 639–651.

Pinquart, M., Duberstein, P. R., & Lyness, J. M. (2007). Effects of psychotherapy and other behavioral interventions on clinically depressed older adults: A meta-analysis. *Aging & Mental Health*, 11, 645–657.

Price, E. C., Fiske, A., & Edelstein, B. (2015). Efficacy of psychosocial interventions for men over 55: A critical review. *GeroPsych: The Journal of Gerontopsychology and Geriatric Psychiatry*, 28, 87–96.

Rider, K. L., Thompson, L. W., & Gallagher-Thompson, D. (2016). California Older Persons Pleasant Events Scale: A tool to help older adults increase positive experiences. *Clinical Gerontologist*, 39, 64–83.

Rybarczyk, B., Stepanski, E., Fogg, L., Lopez, M., Barry, P., & Davis, A. (2005). A pacebo-controlled test of cognitive-behavioral therapy for comorbid insomnia in older adults. *Journal of Consulting and Clinical Psychology*, 73, 1164–1174.

Saxena, S., Ayers, C., Maidment, K., Vapnik, T., Wetherell, J., & Bystritsky, A. (2011). Quality of life and functional impairment in compulsive hoarding. *Journal of Psychiatric Research*, 45, 475–480.

Schraufnagel, T. J., Wagner, A. W., Miranda, J., & Roy-Byrne, P. P. (2006). Treating minority patients with depression and anxiety: What does the evidence tell us? *General Hospital Psychiatry*, 28, 27–36.

Schuitevoerder, S., Rosen, J., Twamley, E., Ayers, C., Sones, H., Lohr, J., ... Thorp, S. (2013). A meta-analysis of cognitive functioning in older adults with PTSD. *Journal of Anxiety Disorders*, 27, 550–558.

Schultz, S. K., Hoth, A., & Buckwalter, K. (2004). Anxiety and impaired social function in the elderly. *Annals of Clinical Psychiatry*, 16, 47–51.

Seignourel, P. J., Kunik, M. E., Snow, L., Wilson, N., & Stanley, M. A. (2008). Anxiety in dementia: A critical review. *Clinical Psychology Review*, 1071–1082.

Serfaty, M. A., Haworth, D., Blanchard, M., Buszewicz, M., Murad, S., & King, M. (2009). Clinical effectiveness of individual cognitive behavioral therapy for depressed older people in primary care: A randomized controlled trial. *Archives of General Psychiatry*, 66, 1332–1340.

Shega, J. W., Hougham, G. W., Stocking, C. B., Cox-Hayley, D., & Sachs, G. A. (2004). Pain in community-dwelling persons with dementia: Frequency, intensity, and congruence between patient and caregiver report. *Journal of Pain and Symptom Management, 28*, 585−592.

Shrestha, S., Amspoker, A.B., Armento, M., Evans, G., Kunik, M.E., Stanley, M.A., & Wilson, N. (November, 2014). Calmer Life: Expanding reach of late-life anxiety treatment in underserved, mostly African-American communities. Presentation at the 67th Annual Scientific Meeting of the Gerontological Society of America, November 5−9 2014, Washington, D.C.

Shrestha, S., Armento, M. E. A., Bush, A. L., Huddleston, C., Zeno, D., Jameson, J. P., . . . Stanley, M. A. (2012). Pilot findings from a community-based treatment program for late-life anxiety. *International Journal of Person Centered Medicine, 2*, 400−409.

Shrestha, S., Wilson, N.L., Amspoker, A.B., Calleo, J., Kunik, M.E., Bavineau, J., . . . Stanley, M.A. (2015, November): Calmer Life: A hybrid effectiveness-implementation trial for late-life anxiety. Poster presented at the 68th Annual Scientific Meeting of the Gerontological Society of America Conference, November 18−22, 2015, Orlando, FL.

Sivertsen, B., Omvik, S., Pallesen, S., Bjorvatn, B., Havik, O. E., Kvale, G., . . . Nordhus, I. H. (2006). Cognitive behavioral therapy vs zopiclone for treatment of chronic primary insomnia in older adults: A randomized controlled trial. *Journal of the American Medical Association, 295*, 2851−2858.

Smagula, S. F., Stone, K. L., Fabio, A., & Cauley, J. A. (2016). Risk factors for sleep disturbances in older adults: Evidence from prospective studies. *Sleep Medicine Reviews, 25*, 21−30.

Snell, F. I., & Padin-Rivera, E. (1997). Group treatment for older veterans with posttraumatic stress disorders. *Journal of Psychosocial Nursing Mental Health Services, 35*, 10−16.

Snow, A. L., & Jacobs, M. L. (2014). Pain in persons with dementia and communication impairment. In N. A. Pachana, & K. Laidlaw (Eds.), *The Oxford handbook of clinical geropsychology* (pp. 876−908). New York: Oxford University Press.

Solfrizzi, V., D'Introno, A., Colacicco, A. M., Capurso, C., Del Parigi, A., Caselli, R. J., . . . Panza, F. (2007). Incident occurrence of depressive symptoms among patients with mild cognitive impairment—The Italian longitudinal study on aging. *Dementia and Geriatric Cognitive Disorders, 24*, 55−64.

Spector, A., Charlesworth, G., King, M., Lattimer, M., Sadek, L. M., Rehill, A., . . . Orrell, M. (2015). Cognitive-behavioral therapy for anxiety in dementia: Pilot randomized controlled trial. *The British Journal of Psychiatry* , 509−516. Available from http://dx.doi.org/10.1192/bjp.bp.113.140087.

Stanley, M. A., Calleo, J., Bush, A. L., Wilson, N., Snow, A. L., Kraus-Schuman, C., . . . Kunik, M. E. (2013). The Peaceful Mind program: A pilot test of a cognitive-behavioral therapy-based intervention for anxious patients with dementia. *American Journal of Geriatric Psychiatry, 21*, 696−708.

Stanley, M., Wilson, N., Amspoker, A., Kraus-Schuman, C., Wagener, P., Calleo, J., . . . Kunik, M. (2014). Lay providers can deliver effective cognitive behavior therapy for older adults with generalized anxiety disorder: A randomized trial. *Depression and Anxiety, 31*, 391−401.

Steketee, G., Frost, R., Tolin, D., Rasmussen, J., & Brown, T. (2010). Waitlist-controlled trial of cognitive behavior therapy for hoarding disorder. *Depression and Anxiety, 27*, 476−484.

Stern, Y., Tang, M. X., Albert, M. S., Brandt, J., Jacobs, D. M., Bell, K., & Bylsma, F. (1997). Predicting time to nursing home care and death in individuals with Alzheimer disease. *Journal of the American Medical Association, 277*, 806−812.

Teri, L., Huda, P., Gibbons, L., Young, H., & van Leynseele, J. (2005). STAR: A dementia-specific training program for staff in assisted living residences. *The Gerontologist, 45,* 686–693.

Thompson, L. W., & Gallagher, D. (1984). Efficacy of psychotherapy in the treatment of late-life depression. *Advances in Behavior Research & Therapy, 6,* 127–139. Available from http://dx.doi.org/10.1016/0146-6402(84)90007-9.

Thompson, L. W., Dick-Siskin, L., Coon, D. W., Gallagher-Thompson, D., & Powers, D. V. (2009). *Treating late-life depression: A cognitive-behavioral approach.* Oxford: Oxford University Press.

Thorp, S.R. & Sones, H.M. (2013). Prolonged exposure vs. relaxation for older veterans with PTSD. Paper presented at the 33rd Annual Meeting of the Anxiety Disorders Association of America (ADAA), La Jolla, CA.

Thorp, S.R., Ayers, C.R., Nuevo, R. Stoddard, J.A., Sorrell, J.T. & Wetherell, J.L. (2009). Meta-analysis comparing different behavioural treatments for late-life anxiety. *American Journal of Geriatric Psychiatry, 17,* 105–115.

Thorp, S. R., Stein, M. B., Jeste, D. V., Patterson, T. L., & Wetherell, J. L. (2012). Prolonged exposure therapy for older veterans with posttraumatic stress disorder: A pilot study. *The American Journal of Geriatric Psychiatry, 20,* 276–280.

Unützer, J., Katon, W., Callahan, C. M., Williams, J. W., Jr, Hunkeler, E., Harpole, L., ... Areán, P. A. (2002). Collaborative care management of late-life depression in the primary care setting: A randomized controlled trial. *Journal of the American Medical Association, 288,* 2836–2845.

Vitiello, M. V., Rybarczyk, B., Von Korff, M., & Stepanski, E. J. (2009). Cognitive behavioral therapy for insomnia improves sleep and decreases pain in older adults with co-morbid insomnia and osteoarthritis. *Journal of Clinical Sleep Medicine, 5,* 355–362.

Weich, S., Pearce, H. L., Croft, P., Singh, S., Crome, I., Bashford, J., & Frisher, M. (2014). Effect of anxiolytic and hypnotic drug prescriptions on mortality hazards: Retrospective cohort study. *BMJ (Clinical research ed.), 348,* g1996–g1996.

Wenzel, A., Brown, G. K., & Beck, A. T. (2009). *Cognitive therapy for suicidal patients: Scientific and clinical applications.* Washington, DC: American Psychological Association.

Wetherell, J., Ayers, C., Sorrell, J., Thorp, S., Nuevo, R., Belding, W., ... Patterson, T. L. (2009). Modular psychotherapy for anxiety in older primary care patients. *American Journal of Geriatric Psychiatry, 17,* 483–492.

Wetherell, J., Petkus, A., Thorp, S., Stein, M., Chavira, D., Campbell-Sills, L., & Roy-Byrne, P. (2013b). Age differences in treatment response to a collaborative care intervention for anxiety disorders. *British Journal of Psychiatry, 203,* 65–72.

Wetherell, J. L., Afari, N., Ayers, C., Stoddard, J. A., Ruberg, J., Sorrell, J. T., ... Patterson, T. L. (2011). Acceptance and commitment therapy for generalized anxiety disorder in older adults: A preliminary report. *Behavior Therapy, 42,* 127–134.

Wetherell, J.L., Johnson, K., Chnag, D.G., Ward, S.R., Merz, C.C., Petkus, A.J., and Bower, E.S. (2013a). *Activity, balance, learning and exposure (ABLE): A new intervention for excessive fear of falling.* Poster presented at the annual meeting of the American Association for Geriatric Psychiatry, March 14–17, 2013, Los Angeles, California.

Wolitzky-Taylor, K., Castriotta, N., Lenze, E., Stanley, M. A., & Craske, M. G. (2010). Anxiety disorders in late age: A comprehensive review. *Depression and Anxiety, 27,* 190–211.

World Health Organization (2012). *Dementia: A public health priority.* Geneva, Switzerland: Author.

Zarit, S. H., & Zarit, J. M. (2007). *Mental disorders in older adults* (2nd ed.). New York, NY: Guilford.

Zhang, X., Norton, J., Carrière, I., Ritchie, K., Chaudieu, I., & Ancelin, M. L. (2015). Risk factors for late-onset generalized anxiety disorder: Results from a 12-year prospective cohort (The ESPRIT study). *Translational Psychiatry, 5*, e536.

Zwakhalen, S. M., Koopmans, R. T., Geels, P. J., Berger, M. P., & Hamers, J. P. (2009). The prevalence of pain in nursing home residents with dementia measured using an observational pain scale. *European Journal of Pain, 13*, 89–93.

Further Reading

Laidlaw, K. (2001). An empirical review of cognitive therapy for late life depression: Does research evidence suggest adaptations are necessary for cognitive therapy with older adults? *Clinical Psychology & Psychotherapy, 8*, 1–14.

Ramos, K., Barrera, T. L., & Stanley, M. A. (2014). Incorporating non-mainstream spirituality into CBT for anxiety: A case study. *Spirituality in Clinical Practice, 1*, 269–277.

Wetherell, J. L., Thorp, S. R., Patterson, T. L., Golshan, S., Jeste, D. V., & Gatz, M. (2004). Quality of life in geriatric generalized anxiety disorder: A preliminary investigation. *Journal of Psychiatric Research, 38*, 305–312.

11

Cognitive-Behavioral Therapy for Children and Adolescents

Danielle Cornacchio, Amanda L. Sanchez,
Tommy Chou and Jonathan S. Comer

Florida International University, Miami, FL, United States

Children's mental health problems impose a staggering public health burden. Roughly half of the population suffers from a mental disorder at some point in their lifetime (Kessler et al., 2005), with the majority of these problems onsetting during childhood or adolescence. In fact, somewhere between 13% and 40% of youth meet criteria for a mental disorder within the past 12 months (Costello, Egger, & Angold, 2005; Kessler et al., 2012; Merikangas et al., 2010), and without intervention these conditions do not typically remit over time. These estimates are particularly concerning when considering the tremendous individual, familial, and societal costs associated with children's mental health problems, including family dysfunction, peer problems, academic impairments, physical health problems, and criminality, as well as overall reduced quality of life, poorer worker productivity, and increased health care costs across the lifespan (e.g., Comer et al., 2011; Kessler et al., 2012). Indeed, effective intervention for mental health problems presenting in childhood is critical.

Despite daunting statistics regarding the prevalence, scope, and impact of children's mental health problems, the past few decades have witnessed tremendous advances in the development and evaluation of evidence-based psychological procedures with demonstrated success in treating a considerable share of children's mental health problems. These supported practices have largely drawn on developmentally informed cognitive-behavioral models of intervention and have shown

The Science of Cognitive Behavioral Therapy.
DOI: http://dx.doi.org/10.1016/B978-0-12-803457-6.00011-8

257

compelling efficacy across hundreds of controlled studies evaluating indicated treatment methods for children's mental health problems.

Given this progress, in this chapter we provide an overview of the cognitive-behavioral treatment (CBT) model for mental health problems, followed by a discussion of key developmental considerations and distinguishing attributes of CBT when targeting mental health problems in youth. We then turn our attention to how CBT differentially addresses specific domains of child mental health problems (i.e., anxiety, depression, trauma, attention-deficit/hyperactivity disorder (ADHD), and disruptive behavior problems), and then we review major advances and innovations in recent years that hold great promise for meaningfully expanding the reach and quality of CBT for an even a larger proportion of affected children and adolescents. These innovations include the development of transdiagnostic, modular, and intensive CBT formats for child problems, as well as the promising role of technology for improving the accessibility of CBT for traditionally underserved child populations. We conclude by highlighting areas in need of continued empirical attention and laying out an agenda for future research seeking to optimize the public health impact of CBT procedures for redressing children's mental health problems.

THE CBT MODEL OF PSYCHOLOGICAL TREATMENT

Broadly speaking, CBT refers to a family of treatments that target psychopathology by focusing on problematic associations between thoughts, behaviors, and emotions maintained by behavioral (e.g., reinforcement, avoidance) and/or cognitive (e.g., memory, attribution, attention) processes (Boswell et al., 2011; Hofmann, 2011). CBT can be thought of as the systematic integration of behavioral methods of conditioning and reinforcement that grew out of the earlier work of Pavlov (1927), Mowrer (1939), Skinner (1953), Watson and Raynor (1920), and Wolpe (1952) with a focus on cognitive distortions, attributions, and related mental phenomena popularized in the 1960s and 1970s by Ellis (1962) and Beck (1976). In recent decades, findings from affective science have increasingly informed CBT models, leading to emotion and its dysregulation taking a more central role in modern CBT (e.g., Hofmann, Sawyer, Fang, & Asnaani, 2012; Power & Dalgleish, 2008; Samoilov & Goldfried, 2000).

CBT has long been distinguished from more traditional models of psychotherapy by its present-focused and data-driven approach. CBT therapists efficiently focus on symptom-maintaining factors in the "here and now" rather than search for historical antecedents that may or may not be related to present psychopathology. Moreover, CBT is goal-focused and action-oriented, and for these reasons typically time-limited. CBT therapists collaborate with their clients to identify specific and obtainable goals, and together CBT therapists and their clients routinely monitor progress toward these goals. CBT therapists are typically more directive than more traditional therapists. For example, whereas psychoanalysts might prioritize free association and play therapists might prioritize unstructured play in treatment, CBT therapists take an active role in shaping the structure and content of sessions, creating session agendas, and working to actively build new skills and more adaptive coping repertoires in their clients. Moreover, CBT therapists typically assign out-of-session homework in order to facilitate generalization of treatment to real-world situations. Indeed, research indicates that homework completion outside of treatment is an important and significant predictor of treatment success (Kazantzis, Deane, & Ronan, 2000).

EIGHT KEY COMPONENTS OF CBT PRACTICE ACROSS THE LIFESPAN

Before introducing special considerations and distinguishing characteristics of CBT when working with child populations, it is important to first provide a general overview of the key components found across CBT practices for problems regardless of client age. Broadly speaking, CBT protocols for psychological problems across the lifespan typically entail some combination of eight key components of CBT practice. Although we go into further depth regarding many of these components later in this chapter when we discuss focused CBTs for specific child problems, we first briefly introduce these components here as part of our CBT overview.

The first key CBT component is providing *psychoeducation* to clients about the problems that have brought them into treatment. Clients are provided with information about their mental health conditions so that they can better understand, accept, and destigmatize their problems, recognize that they are not alone in their suffering, and accept taking on an active role in making indicated changes. Second, as noted, CBT is a data-driven approach to treatment, and as such *routine symptom monitoring* is a critical component of CBT care. Mood, thoughts, and behaviors are routinely assessed in CBT at regularly fixed intervals and provide data that in turn continually inform the course of treatment over time—including necessary treatment adjustments and course corrections. In addition to informing the direction of treatment, having clients engage in monitoring of their own moods, thoughts, and behaviors can raise their awareness of maladaptive patterns and maintaining influences and produce therapeutic effects. Third, *somatic management* is often incorporated into CBT to reduce tension in the body and can include diaphragmatic breathing exercises and progressive muscle relaxation.

The fourth CBT component is *contingency management,* which entails the use of interpersonal or tangible rewards to reinforce positive behaviors, and sometimes the incorporation of response costs for undesired behaviors. *Behavioral engagement* is the fifth key CBT component and varies depending on the specific problem being treated. For example, for depression, behavioral engagement often takes the form of activity scheduling and behavioral activation, whereas for anxiety, behavioral engagement might take the form of graduated exposure to the situations and stimuli that the client fears or avoids. For many problems, behavioral engagement will mean rehearsal of key skills newly acquired in treatment, such as social skills, assertiveness, anger management, effective communication, distress tolerance, healthy eating, or self-care.

Sixth, CBT often engages clients in *cognitive restructuring and related thought challenging exercises* in which clients learn to identify and adjust maladaptive thoughts and distortions that maintain psychopathology and negatively affect quality of life. Seventh, *problem-solving* entails helping clients take an active role in defining their problems, identifying possible solutions, evaluating the pros and cons of various solutions, determining which solutions are most likely to result in positive outcomes, enacting selected solutions, and then monitoring the effectiveness of enacted solutions. Finally, *relapse prevention* focuses on consolidating skills learned in treatment, with an emphasis on maintaining gains after treatment terminates, preventing the occurrence of symptom or behavioral lapses going forward, identifying early warning signs that problems may be returning, and developing an action plan for lapse-management strategies.

DISTINGUISHING ATTRIBUTES AND KEY CONSIDERATIONS FOR CBT WHEN WORKING WITH CHILD POPULATIONS

Although the underlying theory, science, principles, and components of CBT remain the same regardless of client age, a number of distinguishing attributes and key considerations are specific to the treatment of children and adolescents, and merit focused consideration. These include considerations of (1) developmental compatibility, (2) therapeutic alliance and the posture of the therapist, and (3) therapy participants and settings.

Developmental Compatibility

Many of the CBT strategies that have shown great success in adult populations rely heavily on methods and tasks that are beyond the developmental capacities of younger children and adolescents, and so simple downward extensions of treatments designed for older individuals to address the clinical needs of youth are misguided (Carpenter, Puliafico, Kurtz, Pincus, & Comer, 2014; Grave & Blissett, 2004; Kingery et al., 2006). Importantly, supported CBT for adults requires a basic understanding of causality and of mental states and requires the individual to engage in representational thought and systematic problem-solving (Weisz & Weiss, 1989). Although common strategies such as the use of pictorial representations have been suggested as ways to increase the "digestibility" of content in light of linguistic challenges (Kingery et al., 2006), deficits in reasoning and other advanced cognitive functions still impinge on children's capacity to engage in content focusing on maladaptive or inaccurate cognition and perception (Grave & Blissett, 2004).

Consider the following clinical misstep from a CBT trainee working with a 5-year old child with social anxiety disorder:

Therapist: *What if you were to have thought "the other kids are not going to laugh at me"? Do you think you would've still felt scared?*
Child: *(Blank stare from child)*
Therapist: *Do you think in the future you could try to think "the other kids aren't going to laugh at me"*
Child: *(Blank stare from child)*

This very brief vignette illustrates a great number of ways that a CBT therapist can fail to take into account a younger child's restricted but expanding cognitive development. We now consider five overlapping domains of developing cognition in youth as they pertain to this brief vignette and how they pertain to successful engagement in various CBT tasks.

Mental Representation

Mental representation refers to the ability to go beyond what is observable and immediately available to the senses (Flavell, Miller, & Miller, 2001). One of the very earliest accomplishments in this area is found in the infant's emerging appreciation for object permanence, in which they develop an awareness that objects and people exist independent of their physical perceptions of them. By the end of the first year of life, if you cover a toy with a blanket in front of the child, the child will likely pick up the blanket to find the toy. Although typically developing children develop a sophisticated appreciation for object permanence by the end of their first year, increasingly sophisticated capacities for mental representation continue to unfold deep into young adulthood. Language development is a critical accomplishment in this arena, as children progressively learn that sounds, words, and then clusters of words can have increasingly nuanced representational meanings. Imagery then entails going beyond simple mental representations and zooming in on the sights, sounds, smells, tastes, and textures of mental constructions of the world. Although there's evidence of basic imagery in infancy, this process becomes more and more refined as children develop—and even into adulthood we are still developing increasing abilities for detail and vividness in our imagery.

With regard to CBT for youth, any in-office cognitive approach directly working with children requires the child to have a basic ability to mentally represent objects, persons, situations, and scenarios. When asking children to consider anything *outside* of the office—whether it is consideration of the home, family life, school, or peer scenarios—the child essentially has to be able to mentally leave the office. For example, in the misguided therapy vignette above, the therapist had the child consider his classroom situation while in the therapy office, but it is not clear how well the child was actually able to mentally represent his classroom or to recreate that specific day while in the therapy office and while in the presence of so much novel perceptual stimuli.

Even after children have acquired a basic ability to mentally represent, and they are able to engage broadly in various forms of cognitive therapy, more sophisticated representational abilities are required for many conventional CBT techniques originally developed for use with adults. For example, imaginal exposures for anxiety have the client imagine in detail certain aspects of feared objects or situations, with the assumption that repeatedly encountering feared material, even in imaginal forms, can extinguish feared associations. If a child is unable to achieve vivid images, he or she may be unable to imagine feared objects or situations in sufficient detail to allow for meaningful deconditioning to actually occur.

It is also critical to consider the child's developing ability to mentally represent the self. When asked to describe themselves, preschoolers will tend to focus on physical characteristics (e.g., that they are boy or girl) and then self-representations progress to actions (e.g., defining themselves as someone who walks to school or who plays baseball). In middle childhood, children begin to define themselves in more psychological terms (e.g., that they are a child who *likes* to play baseball), and then in the context of other children (e.g., that they are someone who plays baseball *better* than other kids). Children's self-representations become more differentiated and nuanced with age (Flavell et al., 2001) and so, for example, an adolescent may be able to understand himself as better than *most* kids at *baseball* but *not* as good as other kids at *math* or *art*. Given that cognitive work with youth suffering from depression often targets children's representations of the self, including self-esteem and self-worth, it is important that care is taken by the therapist to ensure that the encouraged new attitudes are consistent with the child's developing capacity to represent him or herself. For example, if a therapist were working with a young child who is feeling bad about her soccer abilities, it might be ineffective if the therapist were to encourage the child to consider that she is still better at soccer than a lot of kids, that she does not even like playing soccer, and that she is also really great at baseball.

Causal Reasoning

Causal reasoning refers to the ability to recognize the causes of events with the effects they produce. As early as 6 months, infants have already developed at least a rudimentary understanding of cause-and-effect relationships in the physical world, and by 10 months children can appreciate cause-and-effect relationships that cross sensory modalities, such as sight and sound (e.g., learning that when one squeezes a rubber duck, it produces a squeak) (Flavell et al., 2001). As children mature, they develop an improved capacity to comprehend temporal relationships among increasingly distal events and can begin to appreciate complex causal chains. But a more sophisticated understanding of causal relationships among thoughts, feelings, and behavior may not emerge until late adolescence and young adulthood (Flavell et al., 2001). For a young child who has not yet developed an ability to recognize cause-and-effect relationships between the mind and behavior, it might be misguided to attempt to engage the child in cognitive treatment tasks that emphasize the associations between thoughts, feelings, situations, and behavior. For example, when treating a young child with depression, it may be more appropriate to target behavioral activation and increasing positive reinforcement in the child's life, rather than working to convey to the child how thoughts can influence behavior and mood.

Counterfactual Reflection

Counterfactual reflection refers to the ability to consider what we know about the past and present in the context of what could have also been (Flavell et al., 2001). Essentially, it is the emergence of an ability to entertain *alternatives to reality*—to recognize what has happened or what is happening, and to simultaneously conceive of alternatives that could have happened instead. At around the age of four, children's language begins to reflect a rudimentary acknowledgment of realistic counterfactuals, but as late as age 7 children still show great difficulty entertaining multiple possibilities in reasoning tasks that require consideration of counterfactuals (e.g., asking a child "what else could have happened?"). It then takes several more years before children are able to go beyond simply identifying alternatives and to report *why* alternatives are possible.

In the misguided clinical vignette above, when the therapist asked the 5-year-old child to consider how he would have felt if he had thought to himself that "maybe the other kids wouldn't laugh at me," not only was the therapist asking him to consider a causal relationship between thought and behavior, but the therapist was also asking him to imagine an alternative reality in which he thought and behaved differently from how things unfolded in reality.

Consideration of counterfactual reflection abilities is extremely important even as early as the first session, when the therapist considers what to explain to children about what therapy is. Explaining to a child that therapy is an activity that helps kids *change* things about themselves—whether the goal is to become a happier kid, or to be less anxious, or to make any other changes—requires the child to consider how they currently are and to appreciate that there are *alternatives* (e.g., appreciating that "I am sad, but it is a possibility that I could instead be happy"). Given younger children's limited capacity for counterfactual reasoning, when working with very young children it can be most important to simply convey that the therapy is a time for the child to enjoy him or herself and have fun, rather than a confusing time, which could potentially offset the alliance by communicating a notion that is beyond their comprehension (i.e., that the therapist and child are going to work together to try to change some things about the way the child is).

Consideration of Future States and Hypotheticals

The ability to predict future states and hypotheticals refers to the ability to go beyond what *is* happening and to consider what *could* happen. By the age of three, children begin to offer future-oriented language, and soon after there is evidence of future-oriented behavior (e.g., planning, anticipation, and delay of gratification; Flavell et al., 2001). But young children still have great difficulty considering future states in the context of *uncertainty*—they might be able to consider what *will* happen but might have more difficulty considering what *could* happen. For example, a young child might understand that if you throw a ball up, it will come down, but it may be more difficult for the child to anticipate what their mother or father could do next. In the misguided clinical vignette above, when the therapist asked the 5-year old child *"Do you think in the future you could try to think that other kids might not laugh at you?,"* the therapist was asking the child to engage in a sort of "mental time travel" that may have been beyond his abilities.

Among the activities that require an ability to consider future states, let us consider problem-solving and planning, both of which are often key components of CBT protocols for older clients. Of course, in some cases, the child might have a somewhat delayed ability for problem-solving and planning, and this is the very target of treatment (e.g., in organizational skills training for kids with ADHD; Abikoff et al., 2013). But, particularly in earlier childhood, a limited capacity to engage in formal problem-solving and planning is not the treatment target itself; rather, limitations associated with typical development simply present obstacles to engaging children in treatment tasks. Accordingly, with younger children, CBT therapists have to focus less on the Socratic dialogues therapists use when engaging adults in problem-solving and planning and, instead, must rely more heavily on providing concrete practical skills, multiple opportunities for practice, and contingent reinforcement for positive behaviors.

Theory of Mind

Building on all of these cognitive abilities is theory of mind, which refers to the child's ability to develop a basic understanding and appreciation of the mind, an awareness of mental states and processes, and the ability to attribute mental states to others—particularly when these mental states *differ* from the child's *own* mental states (Flavell et al., 2001; Flavell, Green, & Flavell, 1998, 2000). Theory of mind considers the child's ability to recognize that other people's behavior can be attributed to their mental states (e.g., their thoughts, beliefs, desires, intentions, and knowledge) and that by attending to others' mental states the child can make the social world more predictable. These abilities are closely linked to perspective-taking, which involves being able to coordinate multiple points of view.

Children with autism and other pervasive developmental disorders struggle with tasks requiring a theory of mind (e.g., when being asked to predict the behavior of someone who does not have the same information and knowledge about the situation as the child). But, in typically developing children, theory of mind emerges rapidly, with even toddlers talking about actions in terms of mental states (Flavell et al., 1998, 2000). By the age of 4 or 5, children have developed a basic understanding of beliefs, desires, intentions, and visual perspectives; but, for the next several years children still struggle to develop an ability to engage in more sophisticated abstract reasoning tasks that require more than two perspectives at once or that require consideration of the role of mental states in hypothetical scenarios. Well into adolescence, typically developing teens are still developing abilities to coordinate multiple coexisting and seemingly competing perspectives (Devine & Hughes, 2013; Grazzani & Ornaghoi, 2012).

In the misguided clinical vignette above, when the therapist asked the 5-year-old child whether he could have considered in the past or in the future that other children would not laugh at him, the therapist was not only attempting to engage the child in mental time travel that was likely beyond his abilities, but the therapist was also asking the child to attribute others' thoughts and emotions and to link these mental states to their behavior in the context of hypothetical scenarios. According to the developmental literature (Flavell et al., 2001), this complicated task is considerably beyond a 5-year-old child's cognitive capacities. Similarly, in cognitive restructuring tasks, CBT therapists often use Socratic methods to have adults consider *how else* a given situation could be construed or perceived and how *other* people might consider a situation *differently*. These methods would require a child to consider multiple perspectives and their differential relationships to mood. As such, when working with younger children, it is best to stay away from tasks that emphasize the relativism and pluralism of perspectives. Instead, therapists should more concretely teach children optimistic perspectives, rather than engaging them to consider how particular outlooks might be associated more positive or negative mood states. However, research has shown that theory of mind training can result in meaningful improvements in theory of mind related skills when working with children with pervasive developmental delays (Hofmann et al., 2016).

Emotion Understanding and Regulation

Kingery et al. (2006) have considered emotional understanding and emotional regulation in the context of CBT for youth. Emotional understanding refers to identifying and appropriately labeling emotional experiences, whereas emotional regulation refers to managing ones emotions given fluctuating situational contexts and environmental demands. Emotional understanding develops throughout early childhood and shows dramatic growth through middle childhood and adolescence. Similarly, emotion regulation abilities advance in early childhood and into middle childhood and continue to gain sophistication in adolescence. Assessment of a child's emotional understanding and regulation capacity can play a major role in shaping the delivery of CBT.

Youth with deficits in emotional understanding may benefit from exercises working to improve the identification of emotions and their explanatory nature and relationship to thoughts and behaviors (Kingery et al., 2006; Suveg, Kendall, Comer, & Robin, 2006). Whereas younger children may have difficulty fully elaborating and grasping concepts related to emotions, adolescents might more readily adopt and cultivate an understanding of their own and others' thoughts and emotions as well as more complex motivations (Kingery et al.,

2006; Southam-Gerow & Kendall, 2000). Moreover, although activities such as labeling emotions of popular icons or cartoon characters may be the upper limit to which younger children are able to participate, adolescents may be able to take advantage of more detailed discussion and didactic presentation of emotion- and cognition-related content (Southam-Gerow & Kendall, 2000). Understanding these limitations in early and middle childhood can also prove essential when considering whether to shift to more active, practice-based content versus spending time in didactic sessions that may offer little benefit to the child (Kingery et al., 2006; Southam-Gerow & Kendall, 2000).

Therapeutic Alliance and the Posture of the Therapist

Therapeutic alliance is a broad construct that refers to the affective bond between the therapist and client and the agreement and collaboration between the therapist and client on therapy tasks and goals (DiGiuseppe, Linscott, & Jilton, 1996). Therapeutic alliance is a process that evolves across a course of treatment and a positive therapeutic alliance can be thought of as a necessary but not sufficient ingredient for effective treatment response. Indeed, across treatments for child mental health problems, therapeutic alliance has been found to be a predictor of treatment outcome (McLeod, 2011; Shirk, Karver, & Brown, 2011). A favorable therapeutic alliance may be needed to complete challenging therapy tasks, such as the exposure tasks that are critical for improvement. In recent years, research has emerged suggesting that there is a dynamic and reciprocal interplay across the course of CBT between therapeutic alliance and symptom improvement, such that positive therapeutic alliance predicts subsequently improved symptom response in treatment which, in turn, subsequently predicts further growth in therapeutic alliance and so on (e.g., Marker, Comer, Abramova, & Kendall, 2013).

Promoting a positive therapeutic alliance requires special consideration when working with youth populations. Importantly, youth typically do not self-refer to mental health services and many interventions are either advised or mandated by others. Children are often referred by parents, school, agency, court, or other social service provider for treatment of problems that they do not believe they have. It is not uncommon for children to have limited insight into their symptoms and, accordingly, they can be less motivated to collaborate in order to make improvements that others have deemed necessary.

In contrast to CBT for adults, supported CBTs for child problems often incorporate games, artwork, and other activities that children may enjoy. Importantly, in supported CBT the games and artwork are not the active ingredients of treatment. Whereas in play therapy and other traditional forms of psychotherapy play can be seen as cathartic and therapeutic by itself, in supported protocols the play is included to promote positive engagement between the therapist and child (e.g., so the child looks forward to attending sessions and working with the therapist) and/or the CBT content is directly woven into these playful activities. For example, the CBT therapist might play a game of "feelings charades" with a child in order to build awareness in the context of a playful activity of emotions and their expressions.

Parents and other central adults in children's lives are often involved in children's treatment. The involvement of multiple therapy participants introduces further obstacles to therapeutic alliance in CBT for youth. Therapists must carefully attend to all of the treatment participants and their concerns. Children are very sensitive to whether the therapist is on their "side" or their parents' "side," and the therapist who does not carefully balance the needs and interests of both the child and the parents can inadvertently alienate one party or the other.

The optimal posture of the CBT therapist in child therapy merits special attention, as CBT therapists fulfill many different roles to promote treatment gains. Functionally, CBT therapists simultaneously serve as *teachers* giving knowledge and skills to their clients, as *health care providers* delivering expert services for improved functioning, and as *coaches* encouraging youth to challenge themselves with fun and creative activities. Kendall (2012b) specifies three different roles that CBT therapists should fulfill: the "collaborator/consultant," the "diagnostician," and the "educator." The "collaborator/consultant" works with the child to set goals with the notion that the therapist is an expert on the CBT treatment techniques and the child is the expert on him or herself. The expertise of both the therapist and the child are equally needed to meet treatment goals. The "diagnostician" is continually observing, collecting, and combining information about the child and their current difficulties to fully understand the child's symptoms and how best to progress in treatment. The therapist integrates information from multiple sources (e.g., from the child, his or her parents, and teachers) across the backdrop of development, family values and preferences, culture, socioeconomic status, and other family variables to best understand the child's needs and plan treatment appropriately. The "educator" teaches children specific skills and tailors his or her teaching methods to the child's individual needs.

As the effective CBT therapist integrates the roles of collaborator, diagnostician, and educator to guide children throughout the course of treatment, the term "coach" is often used to describe the optimal posture (or attitude) of the therapist. The metaphor of "therapist as coach" connotes a supportive yet exacting and challenging individual who can bring out the best in each child.

Therapy Participants and Settings

Children, particularly young children, are highly dependent on their environments and various adults in their environments (e.g., parents, school personnel). Accordingly, CBT for child problems often incorporates a broader range of participants and settings than encountered in typical CBT for adult problems. We now consider the roles of parents and school personnel in child CBT.

Parental Involvement

Parents and other caregivers are viewed as the primary agents of change in the lives of children and, as noted, young children may not have the cognitive capacity to understand and implement treatment techniques on their own. Consequently, parents often take a lead role in treatment. CBT therapists work with parents to reshape the primary context of their child's development by working to reduce maladaptive patterns of interaction (e.g., parental accommodation and reinforcement of anxious or disruptive behaviors).

Once treatment begins, parents may take different roles, such as consultant, collaborator, or coclient (Kendall, 2012b). Parents act as consultants by providing information for diagnoses, treatment goals, and progress. Parents act as collaborators by participating in the treatment process; they may be taught the skills the therapist uses in session to further implement them at home and guide their child in implementing the skills on their own. Lastly, parents can be participating in treatment as a coclient if the focus of treatment is also the parent's psychopathology (e.g., reducing parental anxiety or depression related to child symptoms). It is critical to establish clear expectations and orient parents to the necessary roles they may need to fulfill from the onset.

The optimal level of parental involvement in treatment varies across treatment protocols and the age of the child. For example, in CBT for older adolescents, parents might participate in as little as one or two parent-only sessions to collaborate on treatment goals. For younger children in CBT, the majority of the treatment may be parent training with or without child involvement.

School Personnel Involvement

Children spend the majority of their waking hours at school interacting with school personnel (e.g., teachers, counselors, paraprofessionals) and the majority of children who seek services initially seek them in schools (Burns et al., 1995). School personnel can be recruited for assessment purposes, as collaborators in the treatment process, or as direct treatment providers. Therapists commonly work with teachers to reinforce positive classroom behaviors (e.g., attending to the teacher, finishing work, participating in class) and decrease negative or avoidant classroom behaviors (e.g., interrupting, aggression, social withdrawal). School personnel employ various techniques in order to aid in behavior change, including developing and monitoring reward charts and daily report cards (DRCs), carrying out exposure tasks in the school setting, and setting up classroom contingencies. Additionally, school personnel may employ more in-depth cognitive and social skills training. In a recent randomized trial by Masia Warner et al. (2016), school counselors implemented a group CBT program for youth with social anxiety with outcomes as favorable as those found for youth randomized to receive CBT from trained clinical psychologists.

Despite the added benefits of working within the school setting to promote and generalize behavior change in children, there are several obstacles to working within school settings. First, teachers and other school personnel are often overburdened with other tasks and adding additional responsibilities related to a child's mental health care may discourage them from participating in assessment and treatment. Moreover, a teacher's primary responsibility is meeting the educational needs of their students. As such, school-based CBT efforts should emphasize how targeting children's mental health will likely improve children's overall learning (e.g., treating a child's ADHD will prevent that child's disruptive symptoms from further disruptive the learning of other children in the classroom, treating a child's anxiety will help him or her demonstrate their full comprehension of classroom material on examinations).

CHILD AND ADOLESCENT CBT COMPONENTS FOR SPECIFIC PROBLEM AREAS

As we noted earlier, CBT protocols target associations between thoughts, behaviors, and emotions that are maintained by behavioral and/or cognitive processes and they typically entail some combination of eight key components of CBT practice: psychoeducation, routine symptom monitoring, somatic management, contingency management, behavioral engagement, cognitive restructuring and related thought challenging, problem-solving, and relapse prevention. That said, clinical trials have demonstrated that the optimal balance of these components, and the specific foci and structure of CBT, varies depending on the specific domain of child problems being targeted in treatment. To illustrate the heterogeneity and flexibility of modern CBT for various child problems, we now briefly present the most well-supported CBT practices for a number of the most common problem areas that bring youth into treatment: anxiety, depression, trauma, and attention-deficit/hyperactivity disorder and disruptive behavior problems. Although we provide an overview of these practices here, more comprehensive details about specific protocols and session-by-session guides can be found elsewhere (e.g., Kendall, 2012a).

CBT for Child Anxiety

Although there are many overlapping and neighboring CBT protocols that target child anxiety, supported CBT protocols typically share the same core components: psychoeducation about child anxiety, relaxation strategies, cognitive restructuring, and exposure tasks.

CBT for child anxiety typically begins with psychoeducation about anxiety and teaches children (and parents if they are involved in treatment) that fear and anxiety are normal human responses to different stimuli in the environment. Children are taught that anxiety is normal and that it is only a problem when it becomes difficult to manage and interferes with everyday activities. Children are taught how their body physiologically responds to fear and that the feelings in their bodies, their maladaptive thoughts, and their behavior can all influence one another. Children are additionally taught that the more they confront and remain in age-appropriate anxiety-provoking situations, the more their ability to cope with anxiety will improve and they will feel more confident to face their fears in the future. Children are also taught relaxation strategies that target physiological responses to anxiety. Children often learn diaphragmatic breathing exercises, progressive muscle relaxation, and are engaged in guided imagery.

CBT for child anxiety typically then proceeds to focus on restructuring maladaptive cognitions. Children are taught to identify their dysfunctional thoughts in specific anxiety-provoking situations (e.g., a boy with social anxiety disorder might learn to recognize that when he is in the classroom he is commonly thinking to himself "if I answer the question wrong, everyone will laugh at me and think I'm dumb"). Anxious youth are then given skills to challenge the validity and accuracy of their thoughts and to reframe those thoughts to be more adaptive and accurate (e.g., for the socially anxious child a more adaptive thought might be "I've answered questions incorrectly before and nobody has laughed; I know the answer to the question and if I mess up, that's okay—everybody makes mistakes sometimes!"). Problem-solving strategies are also emphasized in these earlier stages of CBT treatment for child anxiety.

Treatment then shifts to exposure tasks. Many experts suggest exposures to be the single most important element of effective CBT for child anxiety (Kendall et al., 2005) and, as such, exposure tasks typically dominate at least half of the treatment sessions in well-supported protocols. Exposure tasks have children gradually confront the situations and stimuli that they most fear and avoid. Typically, the child and therapist (and parents when involved in treatment) together create a hierarchy of feared situations (e.g., a child with a specific phobia of dogs may put "seeing a dog on television or online" low on the hierarchy and may put "giving a dog a hug" at the top of the hierarchy). The CBT therapist encourages the child to use the coping strategies acquired in treatment in increasingly anxiety-provoking situations, always rewarding the child's effort with social reinforcement (e.g., labeled praises) and/or tangible reinforcement (e.g., a sticker).

It has been noted that many providers who do not specialize in CBT regrettably shy away from exposure tasks when working with anxious youth, misperceiving that exposure tasks are inappropriate for youth and may interfere with treatment engagement and a positive therapeutic alliance. Importantly, Kendall et al. (2009) randomly assigned anxious youth to receive either psychoeducation/support or psychoeducation/support plus exposure tasks and found that the addition of exposure tasks did not rupture therapeutic alliance. In fact, growth curve modeling showed that therapeutic alliance for anxious youth who participated in exposure tasks actually continued to improve after the introduction of exposure tasks.

Some CBT protocols targeting child anxiety also involve parents directly in treatment, although for anxious youth 8 years and older it is not clear that including parents in treatment sessions actually improves outcomes (Barmish & Kendall, 2005; Breinholst, Esbjørn, Reinholdt-Dunne, & Stallard, 2012). Importantly, however, every supported CBT protocol for anxiety in children ages 7 years and below takes a parent-focused approach (Cartwright-Hatton et al., 2011; Comer et al., 2012). Given the evidence, it seems as though parental involvement in CBT is critical when treating anxiety in young children; for anxious youth in middle childhood or adolescence, parental involvement is not always critical but can be helpful when parents display maladaptive patterns of symptom accommodation and overprotection.

When working with younger anxious children (i.e., ages 7 years and below), CBT typically de-emphasizes cognitive strategies to accommodate the more restricted cognitive capacities of early childhood. CBTs targeting anxiety in early childhood utilize parents as the agents of change. Programs such as the Coaching Approach Behavior and Leading by Modeling Program (Comer et al., 2012; Puliafico, Comer, & Albano, 2013) teach parents how to reduce symptom accommodation, overprotection, and other child anxiety-maintaining behaviors, and directly coach parents to engage their young child in exposure tasks.

CBT for Child Depression

CBT for depressive disorders in children and adolescents incorporates many of the same components of CBT for anxiety and, as with

CBT for anxiety, there are many overlapping and neighboring CBT protocols that target youth depression that have shown empirical support. Many CBT protocols are family-based, incorporating parents, and sometimes other members of the family, into treatment. Including parents in treatment can be particularly helpful when youth depression is triggered by stressful life/family events.

CBT for youth depression typically incorporates some combination of psychoeducation, problem formulation and goal setting, mood monitoring, behavioral activation/activity scheduling, relaxation strategies, social skills building, problem solving, and cognitive restructuring (Reinecke & Ginsburg, 2008). Psychoeducation entails giving structured information to the child or adolescent (and their parent if involved in treatment) about biological, cognitive, and environmental factors that can be associated with depression, how various factors interact to influence symptoms, and what to expect in a course of CBT for youth depression. Within the first few sessions, the CBT therapist engages the child in problem formulation and goal setting—the therapist and child collaboratively generate a list of problems that the youth is currently experiencing that seem linked with depressive symptoms. *Mood monitoring* is another critical early component of CBT for youth depression. Youth are taught to engage in "detective thinking" to identify their emotions and track their feelings, both positive *and* negative. Youth are taught to identify specific thoughts that accompany their feelings.

Behavioral activation and activity scheduling can be an essential component of CBT for youth depression, particularly for more withdrawn depressed youth or youth under stress. Depressed children or adolescents are encouraged to schedule and participate in activities that are pleasurable and social to improve their mood. The youth and therapist generate a list of realistic activities in which the youth can engage every day; it is expected that increasing participation in pleasurable activities will naturally increase environmental reinforcements.

As in CBT for child anxiety, youth in CBT for depression are often taught relaxation strategies such as diaphragmatic breathing and progressive muscle relaxation. Youth are encouraged to use relaxation strategies during times of mood dysregulation and stressful situations. Focusing on relaxation and affect regulation can help direct youth away from maladaptive responses such as rumination and poor thinking patterns. Depressive symptoms commonly have a negative impact on interpersonal relationships and, accordingly, social skills training can be another commonly used CBT component for youth depression. Social skills building for depressed youth teaches children and adolescents how to more appropriately interact with others via role plays and guided practice. For example, youth practice appropriate body language and conversation skills and are taught to reduce excessive reassurance-seeking in conversation.

Problem-solving components of CBT for youth depression provides children and adolescents with strategies to resolve specific difficulties or dilemmas in their interpersonal lives via role-plays and in-session practice. The RIBEYE acronym is frequently used to facilitate recall of problem-solving strategies: Relax, Identify the problem, Brainstorm possible solutions, Evaluate their strengths and weaknesses, say Yes to one (or two), and Encourage oneself for success (Reinecke & Ginsburg, 2008).

Finally, cognitive components of CBT for youth depression often target negative views the child or adolescent holds of themselves, others/the world, and their future. Cognitive restructuring aims to reframe maladaptive perspectives into more positive and adaptive thinking. Youth are encouraged to identify automatic thoughts and cognitive distortions (e.g., catastrophizing, jumping to conclusions) and challenge the validity of distorted thoughts. Subsequently, youth are encouraged to generate counter-thoughts to more adaptively interpret and think about stressful situations.

CBT for Child Trauma

CBT for youth who have experienced trauma, or trauma-focused CBT (TF-CBT; Cohen, Mannarino, & Deblinger, 2012; Cohen, Mannarino, Perel, & Staron, 2007; Scheeringa, Weems, Cohen, Amaya-Jackson, & Guthrie, 2011), emphasizes making meaning of traumatic experiences and coping with the reminders of and stressors related to traumatic experiences. Family involvement can be particularly important in TF-CBT, especially when family members are also deeply impacted by the traumas their children have experienced. Parents are taught skills, such as active listening, and strategies to make the child feel safe in their environment. TF-CBT emphasizes a strong therapeutic relationship with the assumption that these youth and families may have a hard time discussing their traumatic experiences and must feel they are in a safe and accepting environment in order to make use of treatment.

Psychoeducation in TF-CBT focuses on normalizing responses to trauma as well as information on the trauma itself; for example, families might be provided with information on the prevalence and impact of a specific trauma endured. Psychoeducation about trauma and youth reactions can also help begin to make the child feel more comfortable discussing the traumatic experience and being in treatment. TF-CBT therapists also incorporate relaxation strategies, such as diaphragmatic breathing, progressive muscle relaxation, and guided imagery to help youth calm their bodies during stressful times or when recalling or remembering traumatic events. Youth often experience a confusing array of emotions in response to trauma. Accordingly, affective expression is a key component of TF-CBT that helps youth identify emotions and connect situations to certain emotions those situations might evoke. In addition, youth are encouraged to use specific coping strategies to help manage their emotions (e.g., listening to music, going on a walk).

As treatment shifts to focus on the specific traumatic experiences, developing a *trauma narrative* becomes a central component of TF-CBT. Youth are asked to generate a narrative discussing the specific occurrences of the trauma and any relevant feelings or thoughts experienced during the trauma. Youth are encouraged to gradually and repeatedly expose themselves to their traumatic memories until they become increasingly desensitized to those memories, and the memories become less challenging to tolerate. Exposure is also used to target avoidant behaviors related to their traumatic experience. Youth are encouraged to practice going to certain places or doing specific things that they have come to avoid due to painful reminders of their traumatic experience. As in CBT for other child problems, cognitive restructuring in TF-CBT helps youth identify and adjust maladaptive thinking patterns. Youth are encouraged to identify faulty and inaccurate thoughts related to their trauma and memories of the trauma and replace them with more positive and valid thoughts.

CBT for Disruptive Behavior Problems and Attention-Deficit/Hyperactivity Disorder

Most supported CBT protocols for disruptive behavior problems in children and ADHD place a predominant focus on the behavioral aspects of treatment and work to change the environments serving to maintain problem behaviors. For example, many target parenting behavior and family interaction patterns, effective commands and adaptive discipline techniques, and/or contingency management in the classroom (Eyberg, Nelson, & Boggs, 2008; Pelham & Fabiano, 2008). Changing the child's environment is emphasized over changing the child's cognitions because children with disruptive behavior problems and ADHD often have poor insight into their symptoms and how they may be impairing their interpersonal and academic lives. Their attention problems may also interfere with their ability to directly engage in cognitive therapy.

CBTs that work to disrupt coercive cycles of negative reinforcement in family interactions that promote oppositional and aggressive behaviors are collectively referred to as "behavioral parent training" or "parent management training." These programs focus on giving parents the skills they need to better manage their child's behavior. Most protocols place importance on having parents give positive attention, such as praise, to their child for appropriate behaviors in order to build a positive relationship with their child. Prior to treatment, many children with ADHD and disruptive behavior problems are receiving extensive attention from the adults and peers in their lives for negative behaviors and positive behaviors are going unnoticed. Behavioral parent training teaches parents to use differential attention to child behaviors, such that they are giving positive attention (e.g., labeled praise) to positive behaviors and ignoring instances of minor misbehavior. Behavioral parent training for child disruptive behavior problems also gives parents disciplinary strategies and guides parents in how to give children effective direct commands and follow through with praise for compliance or a consistent time out procedure for noncompliance.

A DRC may be used in school settings to track child behavior and reinforce appropriate behavior through a point system. The DRC also serves as a way for parents and teachers to regularly communicate with one another about the child's behavior. A small number of specific areas are selected for improvement (e.g., child gets aggressive) and three to eight related target behaviors are identified (e.g., plays without fighting at recess). Target behaviors are evaluated at regular intervals throughout the day and a home-based reward system is set such that parents provide daily and weekly rewards as appropriate for the child meeting specified target goals in school.

CBTs for older children and adolescents with disruptive behavior problems or ADHD typically engage children more directly and incorporate more cognitive components. One well-supported program for disruptive children between 3rd and 7th grade is the Coping Power program (Lochman, Wells, & Lenhart, 2008), which targets aggression and can be implemented in a group or individual format. In addition to providing parent training groups, Coping Power provides child group sessions (typically offered in the school setting) that teach youth skills in anger management, social problem-solving, and resisting peer-pressure. For adolescents with ADHD, there is growing support for the Supporting Teens' Autonomy Daily Program (STAND; Sibley et al., 2013), which focuses on academics, organization, and time management, and encourages parents and adolescents to work together to fix problematic behaviors, monitor progress, and reinforce good behavior and skill usage. STAND also encourages parents and teachers to communicate to monitor the adolescent's academic work and behavior.

RECENT ADVANCES AND INNOVATIONS

Despite the enormous success of CBT practices for treating child and adolescent problems in specialty care settings and research laboratories, our current mental health service delivery models fail to reach adequate numbers of affected youth. With hundreds of controlled evaluations having now demonstrated overwhelming support for the efficacy of CBT for a broad range children's mental health problems (Kendall, 2012a; Weisz, Weiss, Han, Granger, & Morton, 1995), the next great challenge is to develop innovative solutions for meaningfully broadening the reach of quality CBT for youth in need. Indeed, systematic barriers prevent large numbers of children from receiving timely care and gaps persist between CBT provided in specialty care settings and various services provided in the settings where the majority of youth actually receive mental health care (Comer & Barlow, 2014; Sandler, Ostrom, Bitner, Ayers, & Wolchik, 2005; Weisz, Sandler, Durlak, & Anton, 2005).

For most affected youth, problems persist in the availability, accessibility, and acceptability of quality CBT. Regarding CBT availability, there are inadequate numbers of CBT-trained therapists providing care in frontline practice settings. Professional workforce shortages in mental health care abound, with a considerable proportion of U.S. counties lacking any child psychologist, psychiatrist, or social worker (Comer, 2015). Problems in CBT availability for youth are particularly problematic in remote regions, with over three-quarters of federally designated Mental Health Professional Shortage Areas situated in rural areas (Bird, Dempsey, & Hartley, 2001; Comer, Elkins, Chan, & Jones, 2014; National Advisory Committee on Rural Health, 2002). Long wait lists at poorly funded clinics considerably slow the speed of service delivery. Comer and Barlow (2014) have suggested that collectively these factors may help to explain, in part, recent national trends showing that psychotherapies such as CBT have assumed a decreasingly prominent role in outpatient care (Olfson & Marcus, 2010). Poor quality of care in frontline practice settings presents a further obstacle to CBT availability for many children and adolescents, as those receiving mental health care are not necessarily receiving supported services such as CBT. Treatments receiving the strongest support, such as CBT, are rarely disseminated effectively on a broad level.

We now turn our attention to four recent advances in the field that are working to transform the availability of quality CBT for affected children and adolescents. These innovations include transdiagnostic, modular, and intensive CBT formats, as well as the promising role of technology for improving the accessibility of CBT for traditionally underserved child populations.

Transdiagnostic CBT

The development of traditional CBT manuals over the past two decades has yielded a proliferation of "single-disorder protocols" that provide guided intervention for single mental health diagnoses and their clinical correlates. It has been noted that many of these single-disorder protocols have only minor and somewhat trivial variations from one another. Although the development of these manuals was intended, in part, to support CBT training, single-disorder protocols have grown so numerous that it has now become unnecessarily burdensome and near impossible for practicing clinicians to become familiar with, let alone to develop adequate proficiency in, every supported CBT manual. Moreover, it has not been clear how best to choose among or prioritize these single-disorder protocols for training. This state of affairs has regrettably hampered efforts at widespread dissemination and uptake of CBT (Barlow, Sauer-Zavala, Carl, Bullis, & Ellard, 2014).

In contrast to single-disorder protocols, transdiagnostic CBTs for youth focus on similarities and overlying features across child disorders, particularly those from neighboring classes of diagnoses and showing high levels of comorbidity. Although the early roots of behavioral and cognitive therapies, as well as client-centered and psychoanalytic approaches, were intrinsically transdiagnostic (see Comer, Elkins et al., 2014), it is now in light of major advances in knowledge in the affective neuroscience, underlying etiology, and latent structure of disorders (see Barlow, 2004; Wilamowska et al., 2010) that research groups have been able to develop unifying CBT protocols that can be flexibly applied across a range of diagnoses sharing common components and etiological mechanisms. For example, transdiagnostic CBT protocols simultaneously targeting the range of anxiety and unipolar mood disorders in youth are beginning to show strong promise (see Chu, 2012; Ehrenreich, Goldstein, Wright, & Barlow, 2009; Weersing, Rozenman, Maher-Bridge, & Campo, 2012). A downward extension of the unified protocol (UP) for transdiagnostic treatment of emotional disorders (Barlow et al., 2010) is an emotion-focused CBT for application to all internalizing child disorders that was developed by distilling and incorporating the common principles among existing child CBTs—namely restructuring maladaptive cognitions, changing maladaptive action tendencies, preventing emotional avoidance, and engaging emotion exposure procedures (Ehrenreich-May et al., 2008). In addition, the UP for youth places great emphasis on the adaptive, functional nature of emotions, building the child's awareness of physical sensations, cognitions, and behaviors and their relationships with emotional experiences and ability to identify and adjust maladaptive reactions to these experiences.

Transdiagnostic CBT approaches for treating child mental health problems have begun to show promising empirical support in a growing set of clinical evaluations (Bilek & Ehrenreich-May, 2012; Ewing, Monsen, Thompson, Cartwright-Hatton, & Field, 2015). In the event of continued evidence of success for transdiagnostic CBTs, among the many advantages includes a more parsimonious application of CBT and a dramatic reduction in the number of CBT protocols in which we would expect providers to be well versed. These multidisorder interventions consolidate traditional CBT components across diagnostic boundaries for flexible implementation, allowing for more resource-efficient dissemination and implementation with the added advantage of simultaneously addressing comorbid problems. Transdiagnostic CBTs may indeed have the potential to make dissemination efforts less burdensome, thus elevating the public health significance of the availability of supported CBTs (McHugh & Barlow, 2010).

Modular CBT

Another increasingly popular approach to combatting the single-disorder manual proliferation barrier to broad dissemination of children's CBT has been modular approaches to CBT delivery. Whereas traditional CBT protocols apply treatment components in a bound and linear format, it has become apparent that not every child will benefit comparably from each and every treatment component in an indicated CBT (Chorpita, Daleiden, & Weisz, 2005). And, of course, CBT providers encounter a broad range of sometimes unrelated, comorbid problems across internalizing and externalizing dimensions. Thus, many children may benefit from various treatment elements found across a range of single-diagnosis CBT protocols. For the heterogeneous cases that populate practice settings, employing a linear sequence of single-diagnosis CBT manuals may not be optimal from either a dissemination or treatment efficiency standpoint. Modular treatments address such problems through strategic treatment redesign—procedures from supported CBTs for specific identified problems are structured as free-standing modules and decision flowcharts based on individual client characteristics guide module selection and individualized treatment component sequencing (Chiu et al., 2013; Chorpita & Weisz, 2005; Weisz et al., 2012).

Modular approaches to child CBT delivery are already showing success in controlled evaluations, with modular CBT and dynamic treatment regimens (i.e., treatments that systematically adapt to children's shifting symptom presentations) distinguishing themselves from usual care in practice settings (Weisz et al., 2012). For example, the MATCH (modular approach to therapy for children) program produced steeper improvement trajectories in a broad clinical child sample than usual care and standard linear single-disorder CBT protocols. Following treatment, MATCH was also linked with significantly fewer children meeting criteria for their presenting diagnosis than usual care, whereas outcomes of standard single-disorder CBTs did not differ from usual care outcomes (Weisz et al., 2012). Importantly, therapists trained in standard linear single-disorder CBTs held more negative views of treatment manuals than did therapists trained in supported modular programs that incorporate potentially shifting treatment needs and tailor treatment sequences to individual child presentations (Borntrager, Chorpita, Higa-McMillan, & Weisz, 2009).

Intensive CBT

Given regional shortages in the availability of quality CBT (see Comer, Elkins et al., 2014; Elkins, McHugh, Santucci, & Barlow, 2011), it has become increasingly common for CBT specialty providers to offer intensive treatment formats in their practices. This typically requires that families travel for brief (e.g., 1–3 week) periods of all-day sessions of CBT not offered in their local community. Intensive treatments can deliver an entire course of a CBT in a shorter period of time through longer individual sessions (Comer, Elkins et al., 2014; Ehrenreich & Santucci, 2009) and, as such, can be preferable over traditional weekly CBT with respect to the necessary time commitment, travel requirements, and reduction of stigma. Intensive treatments may be conducted during times convenient for the family, such as summer or holiday breaks, during which times children have fewer academic demands. Group intensive CBT formats, in particular, have grown in popularity for children as they can help children feel less isolated by their condition in the context of peers experiencing similar symptoms. Peer interaction may also provide unique opportunities for modeling and practice. Summer "camp-based" intensive group CBTs, in particular, have risen in popularity (e.g., Carpenter et al., 2014; Santucci & Ehrenreich-May, 2013). To date, clinical trials evaluating intensive CBTs have shown positive support in the treatment of child anxiety disorders (e.g., Gallo, Cooper-Vince, Hardaway, Pincus, & Comer, 2014; Hardway, Pincus, Gallo, & Comer, 2015; Ollendick et al., 2009), OCD (e.g., Storch et al., 2007), ADHD (e.g., Sibley, Smith, Evans, Pelham, & Gnagy, 2012), and selective mutism (Carpenter et al., 2014).

Technology and CBT

Recent advances in technology and the rapid uptake of both advanced consumer products and Internet use have yielded a potentially transformative opportunity to reconsider the means by which supported clinic-based CBTs are provided. Given the far-reaching functionality of personal and home-based technologies for transmitting and collecting rich information across a variety of formats, current research efforts have worked to leverage technology in a variety of ways to develop innovative means by which to expand the accessibility to quality CBT (see Comer, 2015; Myers & Comer, 2016). In fact, according to Web of Science, there were 145 scientific publications between 2000 and 2014 that addressed "child telemental health" (and/or "child behavioral telehealth," "child telepsychology," or "child telepsychiatry") and roughly half of these publications were printed in just the past 5 years (Comer & Myers, 2016).

Various platforms have been leveraged to expand the scope and reach of CBT—including PCs, smartphones, and tablets—and technology-based programs range from those that are fully self-administered to those incorporating minimal therapist involvement to those entailing full therapist involvement. Stand-alone (no therapist involvement) computer-based programs and software create platforms through which CBT concepts can be more widely disseminated and self-implemented (Kendall, Khanna, Edson, Cummings, & Harris, 2011; Khanna & Kendall, 2008). Increasing research is finding that client continued use and adherence to self-administered technology-based CBTs can be problematic in the absence of some degree of involvement and check-ins from a professional or paraprofessional (Mohr, Cuijpers, & Lehman, 2011). What the nature of that involvement optimally entails is still unclear, but research is pointing to the importance of "supportive accountability" that has clients' sustained participation in and adherence to technology-based programs is improved when clients feel accountable to a coach who is seen as trustworthy, benevolent, and having expertise (Mohr et al., 2011). Such findings have led to increased incorporation of minimal therapist involvement formats of technology-based services, in which a supportive coach may briefly check in on a semi-regular basis (e.g., weekly or bi-weekly phone calls or emails) to discuss the content of the program, assess adherence to assignments, and answer any questions the child or family may have. Moreover, smartphones and mobile apps have been increasingly used as adjunctive components to clinic-based CBT, collecting ecologically valid data about children's and adolescents' symptoms and impairments *in situ* and affording asynchronous communication between therapists and clients (Pramana, Pramanto, Kendall, & Silk, 2014; Whiteside, 2016).

The use of videoconferencing to deliver real-time CBT has been one of the fastest growing trends in CBT practice and research (Comer, 2015; Crum & Comer, 2016). For mental health care, a discipline that relies primarily on verbal communication and visual observation, videoconferencing methods can offer strategic opportunities to overcome geographical barriers to quality CBT by extending the availability of CBT providers.

Children dwelling in rural or impoverished regions—areas typically beset by insufficient availability of CBT care—can participate in real-time interactive CBT conducted by experts, regardless of geographic proximity to a CBT clinic. A growing body of empirical work supports the preliminary efficacy, feasibility, tolerability, sustainability, and efficacy of applying videoconferencing methods to remotely deliver CBT to children and families in need (Comer et al., 2015; Comer, Furr et al., 2014; Crum & Comer, 2016; Nelson, Barnard, & Cain, 2003).

FUTURE DIRECTIONS AND CONCLUDING THOUGHTS

Children's mental health problems are highly prevalent and impose enormous burdens at the individual, family, and societal level. Fortunately, the past few decades have witnessed tremendous advances in the development and evaluation of CBT procedures with demonstrated success in treating a considerable share of children's mental health problems. Simple downward extensions of treatments designed for older individuals to address the clinical needs of youth are misguided. Developmentally informed models of care that account for the cognitive abilities of youth and that incorporate special considerations inherent in working with child populations are increasingly showing great success. In recent years, advances in transdiagnostic and modularized CBT for youth have been working to improve the efficiency, acceptability, and uptake of CBT for children and adolescents. Researchers and providers are also increasingly leveraging new technologies to meaningfully expand the scope and reach of CBT for youth.

Given these extraordinary advances in developing developmentally sensitive CBT procedures for youth, the challenge ahead will now be to improve training models and dissemination procedures in order to maximize the quality and availability of CBT for the majority of youth in need. Considerable attention and large financial commitments of over several billion dollars have focused in recent years on innovative solutions to the problems of CBT availability and quality (McHugh & Barlow, 2010). Formal evaluations of large-scale dissemination and implementation programs are ongoing, but early efforts do reveal some consistent findings—quality dissemination efforts are expensive and hard to sustain. The larger, more successful programs that have incorporated didactics and extended competency training and consultation have cost hundreds of millions of dollars each and many still have not actualized the large and lasting impacts aspired to at initiative outset (Comer & Barlow, 2014). Regrettably, the present availability of quality CBT for youth is largely concentrated in major academic hubs and metropolitan regions. Accordingly, future research that supports cost-efficient models for promoting effective and sustainable CBT training on a broad scale is critical to optimize the public health impact of the past several decades of successful research on CBT for children's mental health problems.

References

Abikoff, H., Gallagher, R., Wells, K. C., Murray, D. W., Huang, L., Lu, F., & Petkova, E. (2013). Remediating organizational functioning in children with ADHD: Immediate and long-term effects from a randomized controlled trial. *Journal of Consulting and Clinical Psychology, 81,* 113–128.

Barlow, D. H. (2004). Psychological treatments. *American Psychologist, 59,* 869–878.

Barlow, D. H., Farchione, T. J., Fairholme, C. P., Ellard, K. K., Boisseau, C. L., Allen, L. B., & Ehrenreich-May, J. T. (2010). *Unified protocol for transdiagnostic treatment of emotional disorders: Therapist guide.* New York, NY: Oxford University Press.

Barlow, D. H., Sauer-Zavala, S., Carl, J. R., Bullis, J. R., & Ellard, K. K. (2014). The nature, diagnosis, and treatment of neuroticism: Back to the future. *Clinical Psychological Science, 2,* 344–365. Available from http://dx.doi.org/10.1177/2167702613505532.

Barmish, A. J., & Kendall, P. C. (2005). Should parents be co-clients in cognitive-behavioral therapy for anxious youth? *Journal of Clinical Child and Adolescent Psychology, 34,* 569–581.

Beck, A. T. (1976). *Cognitive therapy and the emotional disorders.* New York: New American Library.

Bilek, E., & Ehrenreich-May, J. (2012). An open trial investigation of a transdiagnostic treatment for children with anxiety and depressive symptoms. *Behavior Therapy, 43,* 887–897.

Bird, D. C., Dempsey, P., & Hartley, D. (2001). *Addressing mental health workforce needs in underserved rural areas: Accomplishments and challenges.* Portland, ME: Maine Rural Health Research Center.

Borntrager, C. F., Chorpita, B. F., Higa-McMillan, C., & Weisz, J. R. (2009). Provider attitudes toward evidence-based practices: Are the concerns with the evidence or with the manuals? *Psychiatric Services, 60,* 677–681. doi: 10.1176/appi.ps.60.5.677.

Boswell, J. F., Sharpless, B. A., Greenberg, L. S., Heatherington, L., Huppert, J. D., Barber, J. P., . . . Castonguay, L. G. (2011). Schools of psychotherapy and the beginning of a scientific approach. In D. H. Barlow (Ed.), *The Oxford handbook of clinical psychology.* New York: Oxford University Press.

Breinholst, S., Esbjørn, B. H., Reinholdt-Dunne, M. L., & Stallard, P. (2012). CBT for the treatment of child anxiety disorders: A review of why parental involvement has not enhanced outcomes. *Journal of Anxiety Disorders, 26,* 416–424.

Burns, B. J., Costello, E. J., Angold, A., Tweed, D., Stangl, D., Farmer, E. M. Z., & Erkanli, A. (1995). Children's mental health service use across service sectors. *Health Affairs, 14,* 147–159.

Carpenter, A. L., Puliafico, A. C., Kurtz, S. M. S., Pincus, D. B., & Comer, J. S. (2014). Extending parent–child interaction therapy for early childhood internalizing problems: New advances for an overlooked population. *Clinical Child and Family Psychology Review, 17,* 340–356.

Cartwright-Hatton, S., McNally, D., Field, A. P., Rust, S., Laskey, B., Dixon, C., . . . Woodham, A. (2011). A new parenting-based group intervention for young anxious children: Results of a randomized controlled trial. *Journal of the American Academy of*

Child and Adolescent Psychiatry, 50, 242−251. Available from http://dx.doi.org/10.1016/j.jaac.2010.12.015.

Chiu, A. W., Langer, D. A., McLeod, B. D., Har, K., Drahota, A., Galla, B. M., ... Wood, J. J. (2013). Effectiveness of modular CBT for child anxiety in elementary schools. *School Psychology Quarterly, 28*, 141−153. Available from http://dx.doi.org/10.1037/spq0000017.

Chorpita, B. F., Daleiden, E. L., & Weisz, J. R. (2005). Modularity in the design and application of therapeutic interventions. *Applied and Preventive Psychology, 11*, 141−156.

Chorpita, B. F., & Weisz, J. R. (2005). *Modular approach to therapy for children with anxiety, depression, or conduct problems*. Honolulu, HI: University of Hawaii at Manoa.

Chu, B. (2012). Translating transdiagnostic approaches to children and adolescents. *Cognitive and Behavioral Practice, 19*, 1−4.

Cohen, J. A., Mannarino, A. P., & Deblinger, E. (Eds.) (2012). *Trauma-focused CBT for children and adolescents: Treatment applications*. New York, NY: Guilford Press.

Cohen, J. A., Mannarino, A. P., Perel, J. M., & Staron, V. (2007). A pilot randomized controlled trial of combined trauma-focused CBT and sertraline for childhood PTSD symptoms. *Journal of the American Academy of Child & Adolescent Psychiatry, 46*, 811−819.

Comer, J. S. (2015). Introduction to the special section: Applying new technologies to extend the scope and accessibility of mental health care. *Cognitive and Behavioral Practice, 22*, 253−257.

Comer, J. S., & Barlow, D. H. (2014). The occasional case against broad dissemination and implementation: Retaining a role for specialty care in the delivery of psychological treatments. *American Psychologist, 69*, 1−18.

Comer, J. S., Blanco, C., Grant, B., Hasin, D., Liu, S. M., Turner, J. B., & Olfson, M. (2011). Health-related quality of life across the anxiety disorders: Results from the National Epidemiologic Survey on Alcohol and Related Conditions. *Journal of Clinical Psychiatry, 72*, 43−50.

Comer, J. S., Elkins, R. M., Chan, P. T., & Jones, D. J. (2014). New methods of service delivery for children's mental health care. In C. A. Alfano, & D. Beidel (Eds.), *Comprehensive evidence-based interventions for school-aged children and adolescents*. New York: Wiley.

Comer, J. S., Furr, J. M., Cooper-Vince, C., Kerns, C. E., Chan, P. T., Edson, A. L., ... Freeman, J. B. (2014). Internet-delivered, family-based treatment for early-onset OCD: A preliminary case series. *Journal of Clinical Child and Adolescent Psychology, 43(1)*, 74−87. Available from http://dx.doi.org/10.1080/15374416.2013.855127.

Comer, J. S., Furr, J. M., Cooper-Vince, C., Madigan, R. J., Chow, C., Chan, P. T., ... Eyberg, S. M. (2015). Rationale and considerations for the Internet-based delivery of parent−child interaction therapy. *Cognitive and Behavioral Practice, 22*, 302−316.

Comer, J. S., & Myers, K. M. (2016). Future directions in the use of telemental health to improve the accessibility and quality of children's mental health services. *Journal of Child and Adolescent Psychopharmacology, 26*, 296−300.

Comer, J. S., Puliafico, A. C., Aschenbrand, S. G., McKnight, K., Robin, J. A., Goldfine, M. E., & Albano, A. M. (2012). A pilot feasibility evaluation of the CALM program for anxiety disorders in early childhood. *Journal of Anxiety Disorders, 26*, 40−49. Available from http://dx.doi.org/10.1016/j.janxdis.2011.08.011.

Costello, E. J., Egger, H., & Angold, A. (2005). 10-year research update review: The epidemiology of child and adolescent psychiatric disorders, I: Methods and public health burden. *Journal of the American Academy of Child and Adolescent Psychiatry, 44*, 972−986.

Crum, K. I., & Comer, J. S. (2016). Using synchronous videoconferencing to deliver family-based mental health care. *Journal of Child and Adolescent Psychopharmacology, 26*, 229−234.

Devine, R. T., & Hughes, C. (2013). Silent films and strange stories: Theory of mind, gender, and social experiences in middle childhood. *Child Development, 84*, 989−1003.

DiGiuseppe, R., Linscott, J., & Jilton, R. (1996). Developing the therapeutic alliance in child-adolescent psychotherapy. *Applied and Preventive Psychology, 5*, 85–100.

Ehrenreich, J. T., Goldstein, C. R., Wright, L. R., & Barlow, D. H. (2009). Development of a unified protocol for the treatment of emotional disorders in youth. *Child and Family Behavior Therapy, 31*, 20–37. doi: 10.1080/07317100802701228.

Ehrenreich, J. T., & Santucci, L. C. (2009). Special series: Intensive cognitive-behavioral treatments for child and adolescent anxiety disorders. *Cognitive and Behavioral Practice, 16*, 290–293. doi: 10.1016/j.cbpra.2009.04.001.

Ehrenreich-May, J., Buzzella, B.A., Trosper, S.E., Bennett, S.M., Wright, L.A. & Barlow, D. H. (2008). *Unified protocol for the treatment of emotional disorders in youth*. Unpublished treatment manual, University of Miami and Boston University.

Elkins, R. M., McHugh, R. K., Santucci, L. C., & Barlow, D. H. (2011). Improving the transportability of CBT for internalizing disorders in children. *Clinical Child and Family Psychology Review, 14*, 161–173. Available from http://dx.doi.org/10.1007/s10567-011-0085-4.

Ellis, A. (1962). *Reason and emotion in psychotherapy*. New York: Lyle Stuart.

Ewing, D. L., Monsen, J. J., Thompson, E. J., Cartwright-Hatton, S., & Field, A. (2015). A meta-analysis of transdiagnostic cognitive behavioural therapy in the treatment of child and young person anxiety disorders. *Behavioural and Cognitive Psychotherapy, 43*, 562–577. Available from http://dx.doi.org/10.1017/S1352465813001094.

Eyberg, S. M., Nelson, M. M., & Boggs, S. R. (2008). Evidence-based psychosocial treatments for children and adolescents with disruptive behavior. *Journal of Clinical Child and Adolescent Psychology, 37*, 215–237.

Flavell, J. H., Green, F. L., & Flavell, E. R. (1998). The mind has a mind of its own: Developing knowledge about mental uncontrollability. *Cognitive Development, 13*, 127–138.

Flavell, J. H., Green, F. L., & Flavell, E. R. (2000). Development of children's awareness of their own thoughts. *Journal of Cognition and Development, 1*, 97–112.

Flavell, J. H., Miller, P. H., & Miller, S. A. (2001). *Cognitive development* (4th Ed.). New York, NY: Prentice Hall.

Gallo, K. P., Cooper-Vince, C. E., Hardway, C., Pincus, D. B., & Comer, J. S. (2014). Trajectories of change across outcomes in intensive treatment for adolescent panic disorder and agoraphobia. *Journal of Clinical Child and Adolescent Psychology, 43*, 742–750.

Grave, J., & Blissett, J. (2004). Is cognitive behavior therapy developmentally appropriate for young children? A critical review of the evidence. *Clinical Psychology Review, 24*, 399–420. Available from http://dx.doi.org/10.1016/j.cpr.2004.03.002.

Grazzani, I., & Ornaghoi, V. (2012). How do use and comprehension of mental-state language relate to theory of mind in middle childhood? *Cognitive Development, 27*, 99–111.

Hardway, C. L., Pincus, D. B., Gallo, K. P., & Comer, J. S. (2015). Parental involvement in intensive treatment for adolescent panic disorder and its impact on depression. *Journal of Child and Family Studies, 24*, 3306–3317.

Hofmann, S. G. (2011). *An introduction to modern CBT: Psychological solutions to mental health problems*. New York: Wiley-Blackwell.

Hofmann, S. G., Doan, S. N., Sprung, M., Wilson, A., Ebesutani, C., Andrews, L. A., … Harris, P. L. (2016). Training children's theory-of-mind: A meta-analysis of controlled studies. *Cognition, 150*, 200–212.

Hofmann, S. G., Sawyer, A. T., Fang, A., & Asnaani, A. (2012). Emotion dysregulation model of mood and anxiety disorders. *Depression and Anxiety, 29*, 409–416.

Kazantzis, N., Deane, F. P., & Ronan, K. R. (2000). Homework assignments in cognitive and behavioral therapy: A meta-analysis. *Clinical Psychology: Science and Practice, 7*, 189–202.

Kendall, P. C. (2012a). *Child and adolescent therapy: Cognitive-behavioral procedures* (4th Ed.). New York: Guilford Press.

Kendall, P. C., Comer, J. S., Marker, C. D., Creed, T. A., Puliafico, A. C., Hughes, A. A., . . . Hudson, J. L. (2009). In-session exposure tasks and therapeutic alliance across the treatment of childhood anxiety disorders. *Journal of Consulting and Clinical Psychology, 77,* 517−525. Available from http://dx.doi.org/10.1097/CHI.0b013e31817eed2f.

Kendall, P. C., Khanna, M. S., Edson, A., Cummings, C., & Harris, M. S. (2011). Computers and psychosocial treatment for child anxiety: Recent advances and ongoing efforts. *Depression and Anxiety, 28,* 58−66.

Kendall, P. C. (2012b). Guiding theory for therapy with children and adolescents. In P. C. Kendall (Ed.), *Child and adolescent therapy: Cognitive-behavioral procedures* (4th Ed.). New York: Guilford Press.

Kendall, P. C., Robin, J. A., Bertzos, K., Suveg, C., Flannery-Schroeder, E., & Gosch, E. (2005). Considering CBT with anxious youth? Think exposures. *Cognitive and Behavioral Practice, 12,* 136−148.

Kessler, R. C., Avenevoli, S., Costello, E. J., Georgiades, K., Green, J. G., Gruber, M. J., . . . Merikangas, K. R. (2012). Prevalence, persistence, and sociodemographic correlates of DSM-IV disorders in the National Comorbidity Survey Replication Adolescent Supplement. *Archives of General Psychiatry, 69,* 372−380.

Kessler, R. C., Berglund, P., Demler, O., Jin, R., Merikangas, K. R., & Walters, E. E. (2005). Lifetime prevalence and age-of-onset distributions of DSM-IV disorders in the National Comorbidity Survey Replication. *Archives of General Psychiatry, 62,* 593−602.

Khanna, M. S., & Kendall, P. C. (2008). Computer-assisted CBT for child anxiety: The coping cat CD-ROM. *Cognitive and Behavioral Practice, 15,* 159−165. Available from http://dx.doi.org/10.1016/j.cbpra.2008.02.002.

Kingery, J. N., Roblek, T. L., Suveg, C., Grover, R. L., Sherrill, J. T., & Bergman, R. L. (2006). They're not just little adults: Developmental considerations for implementing cognitive-behavioral therapy with anxious youth. *Journal of Cognitive Psychotherapy, 20,* 263−273. Available from http://dx.doi.org/10.1891/jcop.20.3.263.

Lochman, J. E., Wells, K. C., & Lenhart, L. A. (2008). *Coping power program.* New York, NY: Oxford University Press.

Marker, C. D., Comer, J. S., Abramova, V., & Kendall, P. C. (2013). The reciprocal relationship between alliance and symptom improvement across the treatment of childhood anxiety. *Journal of Clinical Child and Adolescent Psychology, 42,* 22−33.

Masia Warner, C., Colognori, D., Brice, C., Herzig, K., Mufson, L., Lynch, C., . . . Ryan, J. (2016). Can school counselors deliver cognitive-behavioral treatment for social anxiety effectively? A randomized controlled trial. *Journal of Child Psychology and Psychiatry,* 1229−1238.

McHugh, R. K., & Barlow, D. H. (2010). The dissemination and implementation of evidence-based psychological treatments: A review of current efforts. *American Psychologist, 65,* 73−84.

McLeod, B. D. (2011). Relationship of the alliance with outcomes in youth psychotherapy: A meta-analysis. *Clinical Psychology Review, 31,* 603−616.

Merikangas, K. R., He, J. P., Brody, D., Fisher, P. W., Bourdon, K., & Koretz, D. S. (2010). Prevalence and treatment of mental disorders among US children in the 2001−2004 NHANES. *Pediatrics, 125,* 75−81.

Mohr, D. C., Cuijpers, P., & Lehman, K. (2011). Supportive accountability: A model for providing human support to enhance adherence to eHealth interventions. *Journal of Medical Internet Research, 13*(1), e30.

Mowrer, O. H. (1939). A stimulus-response analysis of anxiety and its role as a reinforcing agent. *Psychology Review, 46,* 553−565.

Myers, K., & Comer, J. S. (2016). The case for telemental health for improving the accessibility and quality of children's mental health services. *Journal of Child and Adolescent Psychopharmacology, 26,* 186−191.

National Advisory Committee on Rural Health. (2002). A targeted look at the rural health care safety net: A report to the secretary, U.S. Department of Health and Human Services. Washington, DC: National Advisory Committee on Rural Health.

Nelson, E., Barnard, M., & Cain, S. (2003). Treating childhood depression over videoconferencing. *Telemedicine Journal and e-Health*, 9, 49–55. Available from http://dx.doi.org/10.1089/153056203763317648.

Olfson, M., & Marcus, S. C. (2010). National trends in outpatient psychotherapy. *American Journal of Psychiatry*, 167, 1456–1463. doi:10.1176/appi.ajp.2010.10040570.

Ollendick, T. H., Öst, L. G., Rueterskiöld, L., Costa, N., Cederlund, R., Sirbu, C., . . . Jarrett, M. A. (2009). One-session treatment of specific phobia in youth: A randomized clinical trial in the United States and Sweden. *Journal of Consulting and Clinical Psychology*, 77, 54–57. doi: 10.1037/a0015158.

Pavlov, I. P. (1927). *Conditioned reflexes*. London: Oxford University Press.

Pelham, W. E., & Fabiano, G. A. (2008). Evidence-based psychosocial treatments for attention-deficit/hyperactivity disorder. *Journal of Clinical Child & Adolescent Psychology*, 37, 184–214.

Power, M. J., & Dalgleish, T. (2008). *Cognition and emotion: From order to disorder* (2nd Ed.). New York: Psychology Press.

Pramana, G., Parmanto, B., Kendall, P. C., & Silk, J. S. (2014). The SmartCAT: An m-health platform for ecological momentary intervention in child anxiety treatment. *Telemedicine and e-Health*, 20, 419–427. Available from http://dx.doi.org/10.1089/tmj.2013.0214.

Puliafico, A. C., Comer, J. S., & Albano, A. M. (2013). Coaching approach behavior and leading by modeling: Rationale, principles, and a session-by-session description of the CALM Program for early childhood anxiety. *Cognitive and Behavioral Practice*, 20, 517–528.

Reinecke, M. A., & Ginsburg, G. S. (2008). Cognitive-behavioral treatment of depression during childhood and adolescence. In J. R. Z. Abela, & B. L. Hankin (Eds.), *Handbook of depression in children and adolescents* (pp. 179–206). New York: Guilford.

Samoilov, A., & Goldfried, M. R. (2000). Role of emotion in cognitive-behavior therapy. *Clinical Psychology: Science and Practice*, 7, 373–385.

Sandler, I. N., Ostrom, A., Bitner, M. J., Ayers, T. S., & Wolchik, S. (2005). Developing effective prevention services for the real world: A prevention service development model. *American Journal of Community Psychology*, 35, 127–142.

Santucci, L. C., & Ehrenreich-May, J. (2013). A randomized controlled trial of the Child Anxiety Multi-day Program (CAMP) for separation anxiety disorder. *Child Psychiatry and Human Development*, 44, 439–451.

Scheeringa, M. S., Weems, C. F., Cohen, J. A., Amaya-Jackson, L., & Guthrie, D. (2011). Trauma-focused cognitive-behavioral therapy for posttraumatic stress disorder in three-through six year-old children: a randomized clinical trial. *Journal of Child Psychology and Psychiatry*, 52, 853–860.

Shirk, S. R., Karver, M. S., & Brown, R. (2011). The alliance in child and adolescent psychotherapy. *Psychotherapy*, 48, 17–24.

Sibley, M. H., Pelham, W. E., Jr, Derefinko, K. J., Kuriyan, A. B., Sanchez, F., & Graziano, P. A. (2013). A pilot trial of supporting teens' academic needs daily (STAND): A parent-adolescent collaborative intervention for ADHD. *Journal of Psychopathology and Behavioral Assessment*, 35(4), 436–449.

Sibley, M. H., Smith, B. H., Evans, S. W., Pelham, W. E., & Gnagy, E. M. (2012). Treatment response to an intensive summer treatment program for adolescents with ADHD. *Journal of Attention Disorders*, 16, 443–448. doi: 10.1177/1087054711433424

Skinner, B. F. (1953). *Science and human behavior*. New York: Macmillan.

Southam-Gerow, M., & Kendall, P. C. (2000). Cognitive-behaviour therapy with youth: Advances, challenges, and future directions. *Clinical Psychology and Psychotherapy*, 7, 343–366. Available from http://dx.doi.org.ezproxy.fiu.edu/10.1002/1099-0879(200011)7:5.

Storch, E. A., Geffken, G. R., Merlo, L. J., Mann, G., Duke, D., Munson, M., . . . Goodman, W. K. (2007). Family-based cognitive-behavioral therapy for pediatric obsessive-compulsive disorder: Comparison of intensive and weekly approaches. *Journal of the American Academy of Child and Adolescent Psychiatry, 26,* 469–478. doi: 10.1097/chi.0b013e31803062e7.

Suveg, C., Kendall, P. C., Comer, J. S., & Robin, J. A. (2006). Emotion-focused cognitive-behavioral therapy for anxious youth: A multiple-baseline evaluation. *Journal of Contemporary Psychotherapy, 36,* 77–85.

Watson, J. B., & Raynor, R. (1920). Conditioned emotional reactions. *Journal of Experimental Psychology, 3,* 1–14.

Weersing, V. R., Rozenman, M. S., Maher-Bridge, M., & Campo, J. V. (2012). Anxiety, depression, and somatic distress: Developing a transdiagnostic internalizing toolbox for pediatric practice. *Cognitive and Behavioral Practice, 19,* 68–82. Available from http://dx.doi.org/10.1016/j.cbpra.2011.06.002.

Weisz, J. R., Chorpita, B. F., Palinkas, L. A., Schoenwald, S. K., Miranda, J., Bearman, S. K., . . . Gibbons, R. D. (2012). Testing standard and modular designs for psychotherapy with youth depression, anxiety, and conduct problems: A randomized effectiveness trial. *Archives of General Psychiatry, 69,* 274–282. doi: 10.1001/archgenpsychiatry.2011.147

Weisz, J. R., Sandler, I. N., Durlak, J. A., & Anton, B. S. (2005). Promoting and protecting youth mental health through evidence-based prevention and treatment. *American Psychologist, 60,* 628–648. Available from http://dx.doi.org/10.1037/0003-066X.60.6.628.

Weisz, J. R., & Weiss, B. (1989). Cognitive mediators of the outcome of psychotherapy with children. *Advances in Clinical Child Psychology, 12,* 27–51.

Weisz, J. R., Weiss, B., Han, S., Granger, D. A., & Morton, T. (1995). Effects of psychotherapy with children and adolescents revisited: A meta-analysis of treatment outcome studies. *Psychological Bulletin, 117,* 450–468.

Whiteside, S. P. H. (2016). Mobile device-based applications for childhood anxiety disorders. *Journal of Child and Adolescent Psychopharmacology, 26,* 246–251.

Wilamowska, Z. A., Thompson-Hollands, J., Fairholme, C. P., Ellard, K. K., Farchione, T. J., & Barlow, D. H. (2010). Conceptual background, development, and preliminary data from the unified protocol for transdiagnostic treatment of emotional disorders. *Depression and Anxiety, 27,* 882–890. doi: 10.1002/da.20735.

Wolpe, J. (1952). Experimental neuroses as learned behavior. *British Journal of Psychology, 43,* 243–268.

SECTION III

PROBLEM-FOCUSED APPROACHES

12

Behavioral Activation Treatments for Depression

Leanne Quigley and Keith S. Dobson

University of Calgary, Calgary, AB, Canada

Major depressive disorder (MDD) is defined as a period of decline in mood and functioning, during which an individual experiences persistent low mood and/or decreased interest in formerly enjoyed activities for a minimum of 2 weeks, as well as at least four additional depressive symptoms, which may include a significant change in appetite or weight, insomnia or hypersomnia, psychomotor agitation or slowing, low energy, feelings of worthlessness or excessive guilt, impaired thinking, concentration, or decision-making, and suicidal ideation or behavior (American Psychiatric Association, 2013). Evidence suggests that the annual prevalence rate of MDD is 5%−7%, and that approximately 13%−18% of individuals will meet criteria for MDD in their lifetimes (Hasin, Goodwin, Stinson, & Grant, 2005; Kessler et al., 2003; Williams et al., 2007). The high prevalence of MDD is paralleled by its high burden. The majority of individuals with MDD report significant role impairment (Kessler et al., 2003; Williams et al., 2007), and depression is the fourth-leading cause of disability worldwide (Üstün, Ayuso-Mateos, Chatterji, Mathers, & Murray, 2004). The estimated annual cost of depression in the United States was $210 billion dollars in 2010, comprised of 45%−47% treatment costs, 5% costs related to suicide, and 48%−50% costs related to reduced productivity and absenteeism in the workplace (Greenberg, Fournier, Sisitsky, Pike, & Kessler, 2015).

Despite the tremendous costs of depression, treatment among individuals with MDD remains low. Greenberg et al. (2015) reported that about 50% of individuals with MDD received treatment between 2005 and 2010. Furthermore, only about one in five individuals with MDD

The Science of Cognitive Behavioral Therapy.
DOI: http://dx.doi.org/10.1016/B978-0-12-803457-6.00012-X

receive treatment considered adequate according to duration and intensity guidelines (Kessler et al., 2003). The high prevalence and burden of depression combined with the rising costs of health care has led to pressure to determine cost-effective methods of treating depression. Cost-effective interventions are likely to be those that are brief in duration, simple to deliver, and show rates of efficacy that are comparable with other established treatments for depression.

One seemingly parsimonious and cost-effective intervention for depression is behavioral activation. Behavioral activation has a long history, beginning with early behavioral models of depression (Ferster, 1973; Lewinsohn, 1974). Over the past 20 years, there has been a renewed interest in behavioral activation approaches, evident in the development of two protocols, namely behavioral activation (BA)[1] developed by Jacobson, Martell, and colleagues (Martell, Addis, & Jacobson, 2001), and brief behavioral activation treatment for depression (BATD) developed by Lejuez, Hopko, and Hopko (2001). This chapter reviews the history of behavioral models of depression, key principles of contemporary behavioral activation therapies, and the outcomes associated with these treatments. Extant issues and directions for the future are discussed at the end of the chapter.

HISTORICAL AND THEORETICAL FOUNDATIONS

The conceptual foundations of behavioral activation can be traced to the work of early researchers who first developed behavioral models of depression. Ferster (1973) noted that depressed individuals engaged in increased avoidance and escape behaviors and displayed fewer behaviors that resulted in positive reinforcement. He emphasized the importance of the function rather than the overt form of behavior in terms of understanding depression. Lewinsohn (e.g., Lewinsohn & Graf, 1973; Lewinsohn, 1974) also articulated a behavioral theory of depression in which depression results from a decline in or consistently low rates of response-contingent positive reinforcement. As a function of a lack of or reduction in adequate environmental reinforcers and/or the individual's inability to obtain those reinforcers, the individual receives low positive reinforcement for his or her behavior. Healthy behavior is consequently extinguished through the lack of reinforcement, and the individual's behavior becomes increasingly restricted and passive, which reduces future opportunities for positive reinforcement. Further, low

---

[1]For clarity, the term "behavioral activation" will be used to describe behavioral activation approaches as a whole whereas the acronym "BA" will be used to refer to the specific protocol of Martell, Addis and Jacobson (2001).

positive reinforcement is proposed to have a direct negative effect on mood. Based on this theory, Lewinsohn developed a treatment protocol to increase access to response-contingent positive reinforcement through participation in pleasant events and social skills training (Lewinsohn, Biglan, & Zeiss, 1976).

Despite early attention to the behavioral mechanisms of depression, and related research support, behavioral treatments were soon integrated with or subsumed within cognitive treatments for depression. In a direct comparison of cognitive therapy and behavioral therapy for depression, Shaw (1977) found an advantage for cognitive therapy, which contributed to the rise of cognitive approaches. Lewinsohn incorporated cognitive techniques into his treatment protocol over time (Lewinsohn, Muñoz, Youngren, & Zeiss, 1978). After the introduction of cognitive therapy for depression (Beck, Rush, Shaw, & Emery, 1979), cognitive and cognitive behavioral approaches became the most widely used and studied evidence-based interventions for depression (Butler, Chapman, Forman, & Beck, 2006; Dobson, 1989). Cognitive therapy did incorporate some behavioral strategies, but primarily with the aim to facilitate cognitive change by providing the client with opportunities to test and challenge negative beliefs (Jacobson, Martell, & Dimidjian, 2001).

Interest in a purely behavioral treatment for depression was renewed with the publication of a component analysis of cognitive therapy conducted by Jacobson et al. (1996). This study compared the behavioral activation component of cognitive therapy to the full cognitive therapy protocol and found that behavioral activation alone was as efficacious as cognitive therapy for reducing depression. Furthermore, at a 2-year follow-up, behavioral activation alone remained equivalent to cognitive therapy for the prevention of relapse to depression (Gortner, Gollan, Dobson, & Jacobson, 1998). These findings challenged the notion that cognitive interventions were necessary for optimal depression treatment (Jacobson et al., 1996). Jacobson et al. argued that, given equivalent outcomes, behavioral activation may be preferred over cognitive therapy for depression treatment because of its potential for wider dissemination. The relative parsimony of behavioral activation may allow it to be easily delivered by therapists with less training and/or experience, as well as transported into cost-effective delivery formats including self-help.

These seminal findings led to the development of two contemporary models of behavioral activation. Jacobson, Martell, and colleagues expanded their behavioral activation treatment into a stand-alone intervention for depression, termed BA (Martell et al., 2001). Also recognizing the potential of a parsimonious, easily accessible, and purely behavioral treatment for depression, Lejuez et al. (2001) developed BATD in an independent research endeavor (see also Lejuez, Hopko, Acierno, Daughters, & Pagoto, 2011). The following section describes these two major contemporary models of behavioral activation for depression.

CONTEMPORARY BEHAVIORAL ACTIVATION APPROACHES

Behavioral Activation (BA)

Consistent with the earlier behavioral theories of depression (e.g., Lewinsohn, 1974), BA views depression as primarily a consequence of reduced or low levels of positive reinforcement (Martell et al., 2001; Martell, Dimidjian, & Herman-Dunn, 2010). Low positive reinforcement directly depresses mood and also extinguishes healthy behaviors, leading to a pattern of avoidance, passive coping, and disruption of regular behavioral routines. BA addresses the depressed client's reduced engagement in healthy behaviors through the scheduling of activities that increase opportunities for positive reinforcement.

The BA model emphasizes a contextual understanding of depression (Jacobson et al., 2001). Efforts are directed to understand the conditions in which an individual's depression developed and the environmental factors that maintain and/or worsen the condition. BA assumes that the causes for depression lie in life circumstances rather than in intrapersonal factors or deficits. Thus, therapy focuses on the client's ongoing life events and responses to those events. BA views depressive behavior as primarily avoidance behavior that is an attempt to cope with aversive emotions and life circumstances. BA also attends closely to the function of behavior (Jacobson et al., 2001; Martell et al., 2001, 2010). Behaviors are determined to be adaptive or maladaptive based on their effects on mood and future behavior. A functional analysis of behavior is, therefore, essential to BA and is explicitly taught to the client as a component of therapy.

In addition to the focus from earlier models on the role of low positive reinforcement, the BA model highlights the role of negative reinforcement of avoidance behavior in depression (Martell et al., 2001, 2010). To provide relief from the negative emotion that results from an environment with low rates of positive reinforcement, the depressed individual avoids activities, situations, and responsibilities. Although avoidance provides temporary relief, it ultimately sustains depression by preventing future opportunities for positive reinforcement and contributing to secondary problems that arise from avoiding responsibilities. As avoidance is negatively reinforced through a temporary reduction in negative affect, the depressed individual becomes increasingly fixed in a pattern of restricted, inactive, and passive behavior. BA explicitly addresses avoidance by teaching the client to recognize avoidance patterns and employ alternative coping strategies.

BA draws on acceptance-based approaches (Hayes, Strosahl, & Wilson, 1999), as it encourages the client to act despite low motivation, negative emotions, and desires to avoid (Martell et al., 2001, 2010). The BA therapist acknowledges lack of motivation and energy as common features of depression but coaches the client to work from the "outside-in" instead of the "inside-out," with the rationale that increases in energy, motivation, and positive mood follow rather than precede increases in activation when depressed.

Activity Monitoring

Core processes in BA are activity monitoring and scheduling (Martell et al., 2001, 2010). Activity monitoring entails having the client record his or her daily activities, ideally as soon as possible after actually engaging in them. Although activity monitoring charts are provided in the BA manual (Martell et al., 2001) and clinician's guide (Martell et al., 2010), the exact form of activity monitoring is not essential, and there is considerable flexibility in how the client completes the activity monitoring. Activity monitoring can be done hour-by-hour, in blocks of time (e.g., 3–4 h blocks throughout the day), or by time-sample procedures, whereby the client monitors his or her activities at predetermined times throughout the week (e.g., Monday between 8 and 10 a.m., Wednesday between 12 and 2 p.m., Friday between 8 and 10 p.m., and Sunday between 2 and 4 p.m.). It is important for the client to sample at different times of the day, and on both weekdays and weekends, to allow for a better understanding of the variety in behavior and its contextual influences. The client also monitors and records the nature and intensity of emotions at the time of the activity. The level of mastery/accomplishment and pleasure feelings obtained from the activities may also be recorded, as these ratings can identify activities that are adaptive for the client. Activity monitoring serves several purposes in BA, including providing a baseline assessment of activity level, assessing links between activities and mood, evaluating the client's range of emotions, determining the breadth of the client's behavioral repertoire, identifying avoidance behaviors, and evaluating progress toward treatment and life goals (Martell et al., 2001).

Functional Analysis of Behavior

A key purpose of activity monitoring is to help the client recognize associations between behavior and mood (Martell et al., 2001). The therapist and client review the activity chart from the previous week in detail and discuss observed links between activities and mood. The client is taught an "ABC" analysis, in which "A" stands for the antecedent, "B" stands for the behavior, and "C" stands for the consequences of the behavior. Antecedents may be any internal or external experience that gives rise to the client's behavior. The behavior often seen in depression is avoidance or withdrawal from activity, which tends to lead to increased feelings of depression, hopelessness, and lethargy as consequences.

An acronym used in BA to help the client recognize avoidance is "TRAP," which stands for "Trigger," "Response," and "Avoidance-Pattern" (Martell et al., 2001). The client is taught that certain environmental or internal triggers typically lead to a negative emotional response. In an attempt to avoid aversive emotional states, the client engages in avoidance, which may provide temporary relief but ultimately maintains the response. To counteract TRAPs, the client is taught a second acronym, "TRAC," which stands for "Trigger," "Response," and "Alternative Coping," and learns to respond to the triggers and responses with more active and approach-oriented ways of coping. Thus, the client learns how to "get out of the trap and get back on trac[k]" (Martell et al., 2001, p. 102). A third acronym is used in BA to provide a brief reminder of the entire BA model. This acronym is "ACTION," which encourages the client to "Assess" behavior, "Choose" to avoid or activate, "Try" out the chosen behavior, "Integrate" new behaviors into a routine, "Observe" the outcome, and "Never" give up.

Activity Scheduling

Once the therapist and client determine the client's activity level and develop an understanding of the associations between the client's activities and mood, the next task is activity scheduling and structuring (Martell et al., 2001, 2010). Activity scheduling aims to increase behaviors associated with positive emotions and decrease behaviors that function to maintain depression. The client commits to completing an activity at a specific time during the following week, rather than allowing activity completion to be dependent on emotional or motivational state. The therapist and client can also plan for the frequency, duration, and/or intensity of the planned activity. Structuring the activity involves structuring the finer details of the scheduled activity, such as defining the activity in clear behavioral terms, deciding whether other people will be involved, and determining how success will be measured. The client continues to engage in activity monitoring, recording the completion of scheduled activities and associated emotions on an activity chart. Through monitoring of scheduled activities, the client can observe the changes in mood that accompany activation.

Other Therapeutic Techniques

The BA therapist employs diverse techniques to help the client increase the likelihood of activity completion (Martell et al., 2001, 2010). Challenging tasks can be broken down into smaller, more manageable steps through the use of graded task assignments. Verbal or mental rehearsal of assigned tasks may also be used in session to help the client mentally prepare to complete the task and troubleshoot potential problems. The client may be asked to think about how environmental contingencies may be altered to increase the likelihood of successful completion of activities. For instance, a client who has exercise as a goal can facilitate the completion of this activity by packing running shoes and activewear in a gym bag the day before. In addition to a personal commitment to complete a task at a particular time and place, the client may also make a social commitment to the task by telling someone else about it. Role playing, therapist modeling, and skills training may be used when the client avoids situations due to a lack of skill or comfort level in performing a behavior.

Ruminative thinking is viewed as a form of avoidance in BA, as rumination prevents full engagement in the environment or in an activity and interferes with effective problem solving (Martell et al., 2001, 2010). Once the therapist has assessed the frequency and function of rumination, several interventions may be used to counter ruminative thinking, including attending to present experience, evaluating the consequences of rumination, problem solving, refocusing, and distraction (Martell et al., 2010).

Structure of Therapy

BA typically lasts 20–24 sessions (Martell et al., 2001). Treatment begins with an assessment of the client's depression to provide an initial conceptualization of the context in which the depression developed and its maintaining factors. Initial sessions include an explanation of the BA model and treatment rationale, and introduction of activity monitoring. The client monitors daily activities and moods and the therapist and client begin to determine the activity-mood connections. Once the client has learned the functional analysis of their behavior and recognizes the triggers to avoidance behavior, treatment shifts to activity scheduling and generating alternative coping strategies for triggers. In order to schedule activities that are likely to result in positive reinforcement, the therapist and client brainstorm activities that the client previously enjoyed or desired to try. Barriers to activation are addressed throughout therapy through the various techniques described above. Finally, as the client's depression improves, the focus of therapy moves to maintenance of gains and relapse prevention. Throughout therapy, the style of the BA therapist is collaborative and directive (Martell et al., 2010). The therapist maintains the session structure and the focus on activation. In interactions with the client, the therapist is warm, genuine, and nonjudgmental. The therapist validates the client's experiences and reinforces the client's adaptive behavior and activation attempts.

Behavioral Activation Treatment for Depression (BATD)

BATD was developed by Lejuez and colleagues as a succinct, session-by-session protocol for the treatment of depression. BATD was developed on the basis of Matching Law (Hernstein, 1961, 1970 as cited in Lejuez et al., 2001) and proposes that the frequency of depressed behavior relative to the frequency of nondepressed behavior is proportional to the value of reinforcement provided for depressed behavior relative to the value of reinforcement provided for nondepressed behavior (McDowell, 1982 as cited in Lejuez et al., 2001). BATD is designed to increase contact with positive reinforcement for nondepressed or healthy behavior, in order to increase the likelihood of future healthy behavior and simultaneously decrease the likelihood of future depressed behavior. Like BA, BATD is also influenced by acceptance-based approaches (Hayes et al., 1999). This influence is most apparent in the focus in BATD on life values, as described below.

BATD is a briefer, simpler, and more structured therapy than BA. The manual is provided to the client to use in conjunction with therapy (Lejuez et al., 2001, 2011). Throughout BATD, the client is guided to adopt a contextual perspective and identify factors that may precipitate depressed behavior. Unlike BA, however, the client is not explicitly taught to conduct a functional analysis of his or her behavior. In addition, fewer specific techniques are included in BATD than in BA. These differences between the two treatment approaches result in the relative brevity and simplicity of BATD in comparison to BA.

No studies have directly compared BA and BATD; so, it is unknown whether they yield comparable efficacy in the treatment of depression. If they do have comparable efficacy, and following the argument of parsimony, BATD may be easier for therapists to deliver and for clients to employ (Hopko, Lejuez, Ruggiero, & Eifert, 2003c). In contrast, the more comprehensive treatment approach and wider range of techniques offered by BA may produce better outcomes for more complex and challenging cases, including depression with comorbid diagnoses, although again, this suggestion requires empirical evaluation (Hopko et al., 2003c).

Activity Monitoring

Like BA, the core of BATD is activity monitoring and scheduling (Lejuez et al., 2001, 2011). The BATD manual includes a daily monitoring form for the client to record hourly activities throughout the week. The client is told that activity monitoring measures current activity levels, demonstrates patterns between depressed behaviors and mood, and provides ideas about when and what type of healthy activities may be added throughout the week. In addition to recording activities, the client rates the activity on its level of enjoyment and importance on 0 to 10 rating scales. The client also provides an overall mood rating for each day with a single rating from 0 (most negative mood) to 10 (most positive mood). These forms are reviewed by the therapist and client in subsequent sessions. The client is encouraged to notice the types of activities in which he or she engages throughout the week and how those activities relate to positive or negative feelings.

Life Areas, Values, and Activities

A unique element of BATD is its focus on life values (Lejuez et al., 2001, 2011). The client identifies values in a number of life areas, including relationships, education/career, recreation/interest, mind/body/spirituality, and daily responsibilities. The BATD manual includes a life areas, values, and activities inventory that the client uses to plan activities consistent with his or her values in these areas (Lejuez et al., 2001).

Activity Selection and Ranking

Once the client has identified activities relevant to his or her values in each of the life areas, 15 activities are selected initially (Lejuez et al., 2001, 2011). The client ranks the 15 activities according to their perceived difficulty level, from 1 (easiest to accomplish) to 15 (hardest to accomplish). The client is advised to begin with scheduling one to three of the lowest ranked activities for the following week. As in BA, activities are scheduled for specific days and times throughout the week. The therapist and client discuss potential barriers to completing the activities and brainstorm solutions to those barriers. Throughout the week, the client indicates on the monitoring form whether scheduled activities were completed and rates those activities on their level of enjoyment and importance.

Contracts

Contracts are used in BATD to help the client obtain social support for activity completion, and to address reinforcement of depressive behavior by other people in the client's life (Lejuez et al., 2001, 2011). The BATD model proposes that depressive behavior may be positively reinforced when family or friends pay more attention to depressive behavior than healthy behavior. Depressive behavior may also be negatively reinforced by others, such as when family members take over the depressed individual's avoided tasks and responsibilities. The client uses a form to identify activities that may be easier to complete with the help of others. The client identifies up to three people who could help with the activity and clearly describes how each person could help. The client is instructed to then tell each identified person about the to-be-completed activity and how the person may assist with its completion. BATD emphasizes the importance of seeking support without becoming dependent on others. In the original BATD manual, contracts were used to target the negative behavior of others that maintain the client's depression, such as attending to or enabling depressive behavior. The emphasis of contracts in the revised manual was changed to positive behaviors that others may do to assist and support the depressed client in completing activities, with the notion that increasing positive behaviors will produce a simultaneous decrease in negative behaviors (Lejuez et al., 2011).

Structure of Therapy

BATD provides a 10-session protocol, including five sessions in which the main concepts are presented and five sessions for concept review and planning for ending treatment and after (Lejuez et al., 2011). The first five sessions include the treatment rationale, monitoring of daily activities, discussion and identification of life values, and activity planning/scheduling. Each weekly session incorporates homework assignments to be completed through the week that relate to the topics discussed in that session. Sessions six through nine involve review of the previously learned concepts, and session 10 includes a discussion about preparing for the end of treatment. All of the required forms to conduct BATD are available either in the manual or online as supplemental material to the manual (Lejuez et al., 2001, 2011).

CORE PRINCIPLES AND TECHNIQUES

The following section reviews the core principles and techniques of contemporary behavioral activation approaches. It is argued that the differences between BA and BATD are small relative to the similarities the therapies share, on account of their foundations in traditional behavioral theory and treatment of depression.

Principles

Core principles shared by BA and BATD include an exclusive focus on behavior, adoption of a functional analytic framework, and emphasis on basic behavioral change mechanisms.

Focus on Behavior

Contemporary behavioral activation approaches focus exclusively on behavior as a target for therapeutic change. Behavioral activation views depression as being maintained by decreased engagement in behaviors that elicit positive reinforcement and increased engagement in depressive (i.e., passive, avoidant) behaviors (Lejuez et al., 2001, 2011; Martell et al., 2001, 2010). Behavioral activation approaches aim to counteract these behavioral mechanisms by activating the client. The goals of therapy are to increase behaviors associated with positive emotions and positive reinforcement and to decrease behaviors associated (at least in the long term) with negative emotions and negative reinforcement.

Cognitive influences on depression are not denied in behavioral activation (Lejuez et al., 2001; Martell et al., 2001). Behavioral activation views behavior as the more direct and efficient target for change but assumes that maladaptive cognitions also improve following activation. Indeed, the original component analysis study found that behavioral activation produced comparable reductions in dysfunctional thinking to cognitive therapy (Jacobson et al., 1996). Moreover, changes in attributional style early in treatment predicted improvement in depression in the behavioral activation condition. Thus, engagement in positively reinforced activities may also promote cognitive change by providing opportunities to challenge negative beliefs (Beck et al., 1979). However, there is not yet enough evidence to conclude whether or not cognitive change is a mediator of symptom change in behavioral activation, or whether behavioral activation reliably results in reductions in depressive cognition.

BA differs from cognitive therapy in its conceptualization of rumination and in the strategies used to counteract ruminative thinking. BA attends to the function of rumination as avoidance behavior, as opposed to the content of thoughts. As a strategy to reduce ruminative thinking, BA teaches the client to attend to present sensory experiences. As rumination is thought to prevent an individual from being fully engaged with the environment, attention to present experience counteracts disengagement and brings the individual fully into contact with the environmental surroundings. Attention to experience in BA is similar to mindfulness in other treatments (e.g., Linehan, 1993; Segal, Williams, & Teasdale, 2002) and provides a strategy to reduce rumination without examining, or challenging the validity of, thought content.

Functional Analysis

An important principle of BA and BATD is that behavior is understood according to its function rather than its form. BA teaches the client to conduct a functional analysis of behavior, through the use of the ABC analysis and the acronyms TRAP and TRAC. In contrast, a formal functional analysis is not taught in BATD, although activity monitoring and scheduling are consistent with a functional analytic framework (Lejuez et al., 2011). Daily monitoring forms help the client to learn about the emotional consequences of behaviors. Further, activity selection within BATD is strongly connected to the client's values, to allow the client to identify the reinforcers that serve to maintain depressive behavior, as well as alternative reinforcers that could encourage healthy behavior (Lejuez et al., 2011). The client selects activities consistent with values across multiple life domains, which increase the likelihood that the client will obtain positive reinforcement from completed activities. In subsequent sessions the therapist and client review activation assignments in a manner that is consistent with a functional analysis (Lejuez et al., 2011). If activities were not successfully completed, then the therapist and client determine barriers and develop a plan to overcome those barriers. Activation assignments may be modified on the basis of a new functional analysis. Thus, a functional analysis is embedded within BATD in several ways but is secondary to the primary focus on activation.

Basic Behavioral Change Mechanisms

Behavioral activation treatment can be understood according to basic behavioral change mechanisms, including extinction, fading, and shaping (Hopko et al., 2003c). Both BA and BATD employ a functional analytic perspective to identify positive and negative reinforcers of depressive behavior. The client learns about how avoidance provides temporary relief from aversive situations and emotions but ultimately worsens depression. Once the client understands the consequences of avoidance, avoidance is replaced with healthy approach behaviors that elicit environmental reward. As the value of reinforcement for healthy behavior increases relative to the value of reinforcement for depressive behavior, the depressive behavior is extinguished (Hopko et al., 2003c).

The principle of fading is used in behavioral activation to promote generalization of learned healthy behavior (Hopko et al., 2003c). In the early phases of treatment, there is increased structure, and skills are formally taught in sessions and practiced in homework assignments. As the client demonstrates mastery over concepts, skills, and behaviors, the structured focus on those learned behaviors is faded out to establish these behaviors in the client's daily routine and to focus on other skills and behaviors not yet mastered (Hopko et al., 2003c). Healthy behaviors eventually become maintained by natural reinforcement in the environment, rather than through structured scheduling of activities. If the client has difficulty with a particular assignment or activation in general, then the therapist may increase structure and formal instruction.

Behavioral activation draws on the principle of shaping when the client is working toward a long-term goal that may first require the successive completion of smaller tasks (Hopko et al., 2003c). For instance, a client who has a long-term goal of returning to school in preparation for a new career may first schedule assignments to research the career online, call a friend in a similar field to discuss employment prospects, and seek information on different training programs. The client is more likely to complete and be reinforced for simpler tasks initially and can then move progressively towards the completion of more challenging long-term goals. Hopko et al. (2003c) suggest that the client should initially focus on building fundamental behavior in behavioral activation, in order to obtain immediate reinforcement and interrupt depressive behavior cycles. However, at later phases of treatment, behavioral activation may target long-term goals, and shaping principles may be employed to facilitate goal attainment.

Techniques

The primary categories of techniques employed in contemporary behavioral activation approaches include activity monitoring, goal and value assessment, activity scheduling, skills training, contingency management, and targeting avoidance (Kanter et al., 2010; Lejuez et al., 2001, 2011; Martell et al., 2001, 2010).

Activity Monitoring

The main purposes of activity monitoring in behavioral activation are to provide baseline information about activities and moods and to identify relationships between activities and moods. The therapist and client can employ activity monitoring to determine the type and amount of activity in which the client is currently engaged, and to identify targets for behavior change. Progress throughout treatment can be monitored by comparing the client's current activity level to the baseline data. Identification of the links between activities and moods throughout therapy allows for an ongoing functional analysis of activities. As the function of different activities is determined, assignments can be refined to increase activities that enhance the client's mood and decrease activities that are associated with negative mood. The documented relationship between activities and moods can also strengthen the treatment rationale for the client and build further motivation for behavior change.

Assessment of Goals and Values

Both BA and BATD suggest that assignments should be guided by the client's goals and values. BATD, in particular, uses a values assessment adapted from acceptance and commitment therapy (ACT; Hayes et al., 1999). BA does not include a formal values assessment but does note that activity scheduling should be consistent with the client's goals. BA encourages the client to act in accordance with goals rather than current mood state, akin to the concept of committed action in ACT (Hayes et al., 1999).

A focus on values can increase the client's motivation to engage in activities (Martell et al., 2001). A client who is focused on values will be more likely to choose to engage in activities consistent with those values, despite urges to avoid and escape. The motivating function of values can be particularly important when activation assignments are unpleasant in the short term or not expected to be immediately positively reinforcing (Kanter et al., 2010). Ensuring that activities are consistent with values also increases the likelihood that those activities will be positively reinforced for the client (Lejuez et al., 2001, 2011). Activities that are naturally reinforced are more likely to be incorporated regularly into the client's routine. Even if an activity is not particularly reinforcing, knowledge that one's behavior is in accordance with values is likely to be reinforcing in itself (Kanter et al., 2010).

Activity Scheduling

The main purpose of activity scheduling is to increase positively reinforced behaviors. Both Lejuez et al. (2001, 2011) and Martell et al. (2001) emphasize specificity in scheduling. An activity scheduling form is used to schedule the selected activities for specific days and times throughout the week. This encourages the client to consider when the activity may realistically be accomplished and requires the client to plan out other aspects of his or her schedule in order to facilitate completion of the activity. Activity scheduling should also be consistent with graded task assignment (Lejuez et al., 2011; Martell et al., 2001). The therapist encourages the client to choose easier activities initially that have a higher likelihood of successful completion. Early success provides positive reinforcement and may increase motivation to continue with treatment and to engage in progressively more challenging assignments (Martell et al., 2001). More difficult activities can be broken down into simple component parts to facilitate client progress and success (Lejuez et al., 2011; Martell et al., 2001).

Contingency Management

Contingency management involves changing environmental consequences in order to reinforce adaptive behavior and reduce maladaptive behavior. Behavioral activation approaches emphasize assigning activities that are naturally reinforced on the basis of being important or enjoyable to the client (Lejuez et al., 2011; Martell et al., 2001, 2010). Martell et al. (2001) suggest that natural contingencies, such as the relief that is experienced with the completion of an avoided task, will be more effective reinforcers of behavior than arbitrary rewards. However, some desirable behaviors may not be immediately reinforced by the environment. In such cases, the client may self-reinforce by administering an arbitrary reward after the successful completion of an activity. Occasional self-rewards may encourage the client to attempt new behaviors that would otherwise not be reinforced by the environment, as long as the focus in therapy remains on bringing the client into contact with natural reinforcers (Martell et al., 2001). Similarly, although the original BATD manual included self-rewards for the completion of activity assignments (Lejuez et al., 2001), the revised manual removed this component and instead emphasizes activities that are naturally rewarding (Lejuez et al., 2011).

Contingency management also includes the modification of situational factors to increase the likelihood of completing activities (Martell et al., 2001). Martell and colleagues suggest that the client should brainstorm factors that may facilitate activity completion during activity scheduling. Another strategy that is used in behavioral activation is telling a friend or family member about the activity (Lejuez et al., 2001; Martell et al., 2001). A social commitment to completing the task may be a powerful motivator for some clients. BATD incorporates social commitment and support through the use of contracts with family and friends. Social contracts also help to manage contingencies by addressing situations in which others may inadvertently punish the client's healthy behavior and negatively reinforce unhealthy behavior (Lejuez et al., 2011). Social contracts that specify how family and friends can support the client's healthy behavior are likely to discourage unsupportive responses.

Skills Training

Skills training is suggested for clients who may have a limited behavioral repertoire due to skills deficits. Skills deficits may contribute to the maintenance of depression or interfere with activation assignments. Skills training in the context of behavioral activation for depression would typically target deficits in self-management, social skills, problem solving, and/or emotion regulation (Martell et al., 2001). The therapist may employ various strategies to teach skills relevant to the area of deficit, including direct instruction, modeling, role playing with feedback, reinforcement, and homework assignments.

Given its brevity, the BATD protocol does not include a specific skills training component but assumes that increased activation and engagement in new behaviors will provide the client with the opportunities to develop skills in the real world (Hopko et al., 2003c). However, BATD can be supplemented with more formal skills training if needed. Kanter, Busch, and Rusch (2009) point out that skills training may often be incorporated into activation assignments in behavioral activation. For instance, if a client wishes to apply for a job but is unsure of how to update his resume, the therapist may suggest attendance at a resume writing workshop at a community agency or library. This assignment would bring the client closer to his larger goal of applying for a job and also teach an important skill at the same time. Thus, although BATD may not address skills training specifically, it is likely that skills training occurs in behavioral activation approaches through the completion of activity assignments (Kanter et al., 2010).

Targeting Avoidance

Behavioral activation is incompatible with passive and avoidant behavior. BA includes a more explicit focus on avoidance than other activation approaches (Martell et al., 2001). The conceptual model of BA assigns a prominent role for the negative reinforcement of avoidance in the cycle of depression. In addition to the expanded conceptual model that provides a rationale for the client to work on reducing avoidance, BA includes techniques that directly target avoidant behavior. Through the TRAP and TRAC acronyms, the client is taught to recognize patterns of avoidance and to instead engage in active coping behavior. As discussed, rumination is also viewed as a form of avoidance in BA and is addressed through the strategies of attending to present experience, evaluating the consequences of rumination, problem solving, refocusing, and distraction (Martell et al., 2001).

EMPIRICAL BASIS OF BEHAVIORAL ACTIVATION FOR DEPRESSION

Evidence Specific to BA and BATD

Both BA and BATD have received support for their efficacy in clinical trials. Following the initial component analysis study (Gortner et al., 1998; Jacobson et al., 1996), the expanded version of BA was tested in comparison to cognitive therapy and antidepressant medication (paroxetine) in a placebo-controlled randomized trial (Dimidjian et al., 2006). Among severely depressed participants, BA performed equivalently to antidepressant medication, and both were superior to cognitive therapy. Furthermore, BA had a lower rate of attrition than antidepressant medication. A 2-year follow-up of treatment responders from this trial demonstrated the enduring effects of BA, leading the researchers to conclude that BA was at least as efficacious as continued pharmacotherapy for the prevention of relapse to depression (Dobson et al., 2008).

BATD was evaluated in a small randomized trial conducted in an inpatient psychiatric hospital (Hopko, Lejuez, LePage, Hopko, & McNeil, 2003b). Inpatients received 20-min sessions of either BATD or supportive psychotherapy three times per week for a maximum of 2 weeks or until discharge if earlier than 2 weeks. BATD produced a significantly greater decrease in depressive symptoms than supportive psychotherapy. BATD was also tested with depressed cancer patients (Hopko et al., 2008; Hopko, Bell, Armento, Hunt, & Lejuez, 2005). In the largest of these trials, BATD produced equivalent outcomes to problem solving therapy for women diagnosed with breast cancer and depression (Hopko et al., 2011). Both interventions produced significant decreases in depression and anxiety symptoms, and significant increases in environmental reward, quality of life, social support, and medical outcomes. Treatment gains for both BATD and problem solving therapy were maintained at a 12-month follow-up.

Preliminary findings support the accessibility and cost-effectiveness of BATD. A modified BATD protocol demonstrated efficacy in a randomized trial involving older adult inpatients in a geriatric psychiatry facility, including those with mild-to-moderate cognitive impairment (Snarski et al., 2011). Contracts and daily monitoring forms were omitted due to practical considerations associated with the inpatient setting and the potential burden on participants. Participants who received BATD demonstrated significantly greater reductions in depressive symptoms than participants who received treatment as usual. Moreover, cognitive status was unrelated to change in depressive symptoms, which suggests that the simplicity of BATD may make it accessible to depressed patients with age-related cognitive decline.

Studies also provide support for modified, brief BATD formats. Gawrysiak, Nicholas and Hopko (2009) compared a single 90-min session of BATD to a no-treatment control in university students with moderate symptoms of depression. The single-session modified BATD protocol involved scheduling many activities at once rather than a gradual approach to activation and omitted the contracts element. BATD resulted in significantly greater reductions in depressive symptoms and greater increases in environmental reward after 2 weeks, relative to the control condition. No significant differences were observed between the groups at posttreatment on anxiety symptoms or reported social support. Another randomized controlled trial supported the efficacy of a four-session BATD protocol (McIndoo, File, Preddy, Clark, & Hopko, 2016). University students meeting the diagnostic criteria for MDD and/or reporting elevated depressive symptoms were randomized to BATD, mindfulness-based therapy (MBT), or wait-list control. BATD and MBT produced significantly greater decreases in depression symptoms, perceived stress, and rumination than the control condition, whereas no group differences were observed on pre−post treatment change in anxiety symptoms. Treatment outcomes were maintained at a 1-month follow-up. Although the original format of BATD is already brief at 10 sessions, these studies suggest that BATD may be effectively modified into shorter, more cost-effective formats. The efficacy of briefer protocols may not extend to all outcomes, such as anxiety and social support, however. Thus, shortened BATD protocols may be most appropriate for individuals with mild-to-moderate depressive symptoms without comorbid diagnoses.

Evidence from Meta-Analyses

Three independent meta-analyses have evaluated the efficacy of behavioral activation treatments for depression (Cuijpers, Van Straten, & Warmerdam, 2007; Ekers, Richards, & Gilbody, 2008; Mazzucchelli, Kane, & Rees, 2009). All observed medium (defined as 0.50–0.80) to large (defined as >0.80) mean effect sizes (Hedges' g) ranging from -0.70 to -0.87 for the reduction of symptoms in favor of behavioral activation, compared to control conditions. Behavioral activation also produced better outcomes than noncognitive psychotherapies, including brief psychotherapies and supportive therapy (Ekers et al., 2008; Mazzucchelli et al., 2009). No significant differences were found in comparisons of behavioral activation and cognitive and cognitive behavioral therapies in clinical outcomes or drop-out rates (Ekers et al., 2008). Further, Cuijpers et al. (2007) found no added benefit to treatments that combined cognitive therapy and behavioral activation relative to either behavioral activation or cognitive therapy alone. Outcomes were largely maintained at follow-up, although most studies have examined only short-term results. Mazzucchelli et al. (2009) evaluated the evidence for behavioral activation for depression in relation to the criteria for empirically validated treatments outlined by the APA Division 12 Task Force on Promotion and Dissemination of Psychological Procedures (Chambless et al., 1998; Task Force on Promotion & Dissemination of Psychological Procedures, 1995). They concluded that behavioral activation approaches as a group meet the criteria for a well-established treatment.

Ekers et al. (2014) recently published an update to previous meta-analyses. Moderators of treatment outcome for behavioral activation were explored, including therapist training, delivery mode, multi-morbidity, number of therapy sessions, and severity of depression. Subgroup analyses indicated a significant association between the effect of behavioral activation versus control conditions and two factors: control type and baseline depression severity. Smaller, yet still significant effect sizes in favor of behavioral activation were observed for comparisons with a placebo control ($g = -0.34$) versus wait-list ($g = -0.87$) or usual care ($g = -0.78$) controls, and for studies involving participants with mild-to-moderate ($g = -0.41$) versus moderate-to-severe ($g = -0.82$) baseline depression severity. Behavioral activation was also compared to antidepressant medication in four studies. These comparisons produced a medium-sized mean effect ($g = -0.42$) in favor of behavioral activation.

Evidence for Novel Delivery Formats

A proposed advantage of behavioral activation is that its parsimony relative to other evidence-based therapies for depression may make it particularly suited for wide dissemination (Dimidjian, Barrera, Martell, Muñoz, & Lewinsohn, 2011; Mazzucchelli et al., 2009). Researchers have begun to investigate computer- and internet-based delivery as one method to increase the reach of behavioral activation treatments. A small open trial of a computerized behavioral activation program with moderate to severely depressed individuals found positive results (Spates, Kalata, Ozeki, Stanton, & Peters, 2012). The program was adapted from the BA manual (Martell et al., 2001) and delivered over 10 weeks. Significant decreases in depressive symptoms were observed at posttreatment and maintained through a 6-month follow-up. Activation as measured by the Behavioral Activation for Depression Scale (Kanter, Rusch, Busch, & Sedivy, 2009) significantly increased over treatment.

Ly et al. (2014) conducted the first randomized trial of an 8-week smartphone-based behavioral activation program, based on both the BA (Martell et al., 2001) and BATD (Lejuez et al., 2001) treatment manuals. Study therapists could access data recorded by participants regarding completed activities and provided encouraging messages and weekly personalized feedback. The comparison was an 8-week smartphone-based mindfulness intervention that consisted of psychoeducation and mindfulness exercises and involved similar communication from therapists via e-mail. This study revealed significant decreases in depressive symptoms from pretreatment to posttreatment and from pretreatment to 6-month follow-up among participants with MDD, with no significant difference between the two interventions.

Other potentially cost-effective and/or accessible delivery formats for behavioral activation have received preliminary support in open trials. Porter, Spates, and Smitham (2004) demonstrated positive results for behavioral activation group therapy in community settings. Depressed participants received behavioral activation group therapy either immediately or after a 4—6 week wait period. The therapy protocol was based on the BA manual (Martell et al., 2001) and delivered over 10 95-min weekly sessions. There was no significant change in depressive symptoms from pretreatment to the end of the 4—6 week wait period, but participants who received group behavioral activation demonstrated a significant reduction in symptoms from pretreatment to posttreatment, which was maintained at a 3-month follow-up. A small, uncontrolled pilot study of behavioral activation delivered via videoconferencing also showed positive results for the reduction of depression in older adults (Lazzari, Egan, & Rees, 2011). Treatment gains were achieved with five videoconference sessions and maintained at a 1-month follow-up. These preliminary findings regarding group and videoconference delivery suggest that behavioral activation may be effectively transported into more cost-effective and accessible formats.

The simplicity of behavioral activation relative to other evidence-based therapies may allow it to be effectively delivered by professionals with less training, thus making it more cost-efficient than other therapies (Ekers, Richards, McMillan, Bland, & Gilbody, 2011). Meta-analyses of behavioral activation have not found an association between the training level of therapists and outcome (Cuijpers et al., 2007; Ekers et al., 2008, 2014; Mazzucchelli et al., 2009), supporting the notion that behavioral activation may be effectively delivered by therapists with varying levels of experience. Ekers et al. (2011) evaluated whether behavioral activation could be effectively delivered by nonspecialist mental health workers in primary care. Depressed participants were randomized to a 12-session behavioral activation treatment based on BA and BATD, or treatment as usual. The therapists were mental health nurses who received 5 days of training in behavioral activation. Results demonstrated a significant advantage of behavioral activation compared to treatment as usual for the reduction of depressive symptoms. Although these data suggest that behavioral activation may be effectively delivered by nonspecialist professionals, no study has directly tested therapist training or experience as a moderator of behavioral activation efficacy.

Evidence Related to the Psychopathology and Treatment Model

There have been relatively few attempts to validate the model of psychopathology underlying behavioral activation or its proposed mechanisms (Manos, Kanter, & Busch, 2010). The basic psychopathology model of behavioral activation proposes that decreases in positive reinforcement for healthy behavior and increases in positive and negative reinforcement for depressive behavior lead to (1) more negative mood; (2) reduced healthy behavior and increased depressive behavior; and (3) greater depressive symptoms (Manos et al., 2010). Thus, the behavioral activation model specifies casual associations between reinforcement, mood, behavior, and depression; yet, most of these associations have not been adequately tested. A number of conceptual and measurement issues contribute to the lack of empirical evidence for the behavioral activation psychopathology model (cf. Manos et al., 2010). In particular, positive reinforcement is inherently challenging to measure because it is defined as a process that occurs when a rewarding stimulus introduced after a behavior increases the future likelihood of that behavior. Most measures of reinforcement have, therefore, used pleasant events/behaviors or mood changes following events/behaviors as proxies for the reinforcement process. Unfortunately, this strategy confounds reinforcement with behaviors or mood, which precludes valid testing of these associations. The reader is referred to Manos et al. (2010) for an in-depth discussion of issues related to the assessment of the behavioral activation model.

Several studies have demonstrated that a decreased frequency of pleasant events is associated with depressed mood (e.g., Lewinsohn & Graf, 1973; Lewinsohn & Libet, 1972). However, this association appears to be strongest when pleasant events and mood are measured on the same day, and no clear support has been found for the hypothesized temporal relationship whereby reduced pleasant events or reward predict depressed mood over time (Lewinsohn & Libet, 1972; Rehm, 1978). Similarly, daily diary studies have found an association between mood state and activity, such that more positive mood is associated with greater overall activity level and with engagement in activities of high self-rated reward value (Hopko, Armento, Cantu, Chambers, & Lejuez, 2003a). Thus, there is good evidence that mood is correlated with engagement in reinforcing events and activities. A casual or directional association has yet to be demonstrated, although it would be reasonable to expect bidirectional effects.

Studies also provide support for the relationship between positive reinforcement and depression. Depressed individuals report fewer pleasant activities and lower rates of pleasure obtained from those activities compared to nondepressed individuals (Lewinsohn & Graf, 1973; MacPhillamy & Lewinsohn, 1974). The daily diary study by Hopko et al. (2003a) showed that mildly depressed participants engaged in significantly more behaviors self-rated as minimally pleasurable and significantly fewer behaviors self-rated as extremely pleasurable than nondepressed participants over the course of a week. Engagement in minimally rewarding behaviors also predicted change in depressive symptoms over the week, such that more time spent in minimally rewarding activities was associated with greater depressive symptomatology. Studies have also demonstrated relationships between depressive symptoms and measures of environmental reward (Armento & Hopko, 2007; Carvalho et al., 2011). Overall, there is consistent evidence for a relationship between depression and positive reinforcement as measured by various proxies, but the crucial causal or directional relationship, whereby depression results from a decrease in positive reinforcement, has yet to be established.

Corresponding with the emphasis on avoidance in BA (Martell et al., 2001), there has been a resurgence of research on the relationship between avoidance and depression. Several studies have documented significant associations between depressive symptoms and both cognitive and behavioral forms of avoidance (Cribb, Moulds, & Carter, 2006; Moulds, Kandris, Starr, & Wong, 2007; Ottenbreit & Dobson, 2004; Ottenbreit, Dobson, & Quigley, 2014a). Clinically depressed individuals also report greater levels of avoidance than nondepressed individuals (Ottenbreit, Dobson, & Quigley, 2014b). Thus, there is support for a correlation between avoidance and depression, but little evidence so far for the causal relationship between avoidance and depression as hypothesized in the behavioral activation model. Extending this basic correlational finding, Carvalho and Hopko (2011) found that self-reported environmental reward significantly mediated the relationship between avoidance and depression. This finding is consistent with the notion that avoidance precludes individuals from obtaining positive reinforcement from the environment, which then contributes to depression. However, these results are limited by the cross-sectional nature of the data. Longitudinal data that show that avoidance predicts change in reinforcement which, in turn, predicts change in depression, is needed to support the hypothesized relationships among variables.

A key component of the treatment model of behavioral activation is that increases in positive reinforcement and decreases in avoidance lead to reductions in depression. Early studies showed that intervention led to increased pleasant events and improvement in depressive symptoms (Lewinsohn, Youngren, & Grosscup, 1979), but these studies could not test the mediational hypothesis that increased pleasant events accounted for the symptom improvement. Contemporary behavioral activation research has also demonstrated increases in proxies for positive reinforcement, including pleasant events and self-reported environmental reward, following treatment (Gawrysiak et al., 2009; Hopko et al., 2011; Jacobson et al., 1996). Moreover, Gawrysiak et al. found a strong correlation between increases in environmental reward and decreases in depressive symptoms over the course of therapy. The Jacobson et al. (1996) component analysis study attempted to establish a temporal relationship between mechanisms of change and outcome. Contrary to expectations, however, early increases in pleasant events predicted later improvement in depression in the cognitive therapy intervention but not in the behavioral activation intervention. Together, the limited research on the mechanism model of behavioral activation suggests that intervention does lead to increases in positive reinforcement and reductions in depression. However, no studies have provided evidence for the causal, or even directional, hypothesis that increased positive reinforcement leads to symptom improvement.

SUMMARY AND FUTURE DIRECTIONS

Behavioral activation is an evidence-based, time-limited, and structured psychotherapy for depression that aims to increase behaviors that bring the client into contact with environmental reinforcers and decrease behaviors that preclude contact with positive reinforcement, including inactivity and avoidance. Behavioral activation is based upon a behavioral theory of depression, which proposes that low response-contingent positive reinforcement leads to negative mood, inactivity, and depression (Lewinsohn, 1974). Current behavioral activation models expand upon past theories to suggest that negative and positive reinforcement of depressive behavior also perpetuate the cycle of depression (Lejuez et al., 2001; Martell et al., 2001). Two contemporary behavioral activation protocols exist, namely BA by Martell et al. (2001, 2010) and BATD by Lejuez et al. (2001, 2011). At the core of BA and BATD are activity monitoring and scheduling, through which the client increases engagement in active and approach-oriented behaviors and decreases engagement in inactive and avoidant behaviors. There is considerable evidence that behavioral activation is an efficacious treatment for depression (Cuijpers et al., 2007; Ekers et al., 2008, 2014; Mazzucchelli et al., 2009). Behavioral activation is at least as efficacious as other well-established treatments for depression, including cognitive and cognitive behavioral therapies and antidepressant medication, and may be superior to some other treatment approaches including supportive therapy and psychodynamic therapy.

Several important questions regarding behavioral activation remain for future research. One important question concerns the purported advantages of behavioral activation relative to more complex therapies for depression. Following the finding that behavioral activation produced equivalent outcomes to cognitive therapy, researchers argued that behavioral activation may be preferred to cognitive therapy because it is a more parsimonious treatment (Dimidjian et al., 2006, 2011; Jacobson et al., 1996). In particular, it has been suggested that behavioral activation may be easier for clients to learn, simpler for therapists to deliver, and more amenable to cost-effective delivery methods, including group therapy, computerized therapy, and delivery by therapists with less training. Although there is some evidence for these suggestions, such as the demonstrated efficacy of behavioral activation in a sample of depressed older adults with cognitive impairments (Snarski et al., 2011) and the efficacy of very brief (i.e., 1 to 4 sessions) behavioral activation protocols for the reduction of depression (Gawrysiak et al., 2009; McIndoo et al., 2016), the majority of the purported advantages of behavioral activation over other therapies have not been demonstrated empirically.

Another important question concerns which components of behavioral activation are crucial to treatment outcome. Although behavioral activation is parsimonious relative to other depression treatments, dismantling studies have the potential to increase the efficiency of behavioral activation by reducing it to its essential components. BA and BATD include activity monitoring and scheduling as the primary therapeutic strategies, but both approaches utilize additional strategies, and BA more so than BATD. No studies have directly compared BA and BATD, and, thus, it is unknown whether the increased complexity of BA produces superior outcomes to BATD. BATD also involves strategies beyond activity monitoring and scheduling, including an assessment of life areas and values and contracts with family members and friends, yet it is unclear whether these strategies offer incremental benefit.

The mechanism model of behavioral activation proposes that increasing activation and reducing avoidance through treatment allows the client to obtain greater positive reinforcement from the environment which, in turn, ameliorates depression. Although behavioral activation is associated with increases in pleasant activities and environmental reward and decreases in depressive symptoms (Gawrysiak et al., 2009; Hopko et al., 2011; Jacobson et al., 1996; Lewinsohn et al., 1979), no research has yet adequately tested the causal relationship between increased positive reinforcement and reduced depression; thus, the model lacks strong support. Treatment outcome research employing measurement of variables over time and appropriate statistical tests of mediation is required to determine whether positive reinforcement, or alternative mechanisms, account for symptom improvement in behavioral activation.

In sum, behavioral activation is a brief psychotherapy for depression with comparable efficacy to other established treatments. Behavioral activation holds particular promise as an intervention that may be well-suited for a broad range of populations and wide dissemination via cost-effective delivery methods, given its apparent simplicity relative to other therapies. Future research on the cost-effectiveness, active treatment components, and change mechanisms of behavioral activation is needed to further support its use as a first-line treatment for depression.

References

American Psychiatric Association. (2013). *Diagnostic and statistical manual of mental disorders* (5th ed.). Washington, DC: Author.

Armento, M. E. A., & Hopko, D. R. (2007). The environmental reward observation scale (EROS): Development, validity, and reliability. *Behavior Therapy, 38,* 107–119.

Beck, A. T., Rush, A. J., Shaw, B. F., & Emery, G. (1979). *Cognitive therapy of depression.* New York: Guilford.

Butler, A. C., Chapman, J. E., Forman, E. M., & Beck, A. T. (2006). The empirical status of cognitive-behavioral therapy: A review of meta-analyses. *Clinical Psychology Review, 26,* 17–31.

Carvalho, J. P., Gawrysiak, M. J., Hellmuth, J. C., McNulty, J. K., Magidson, J. F., Lejuez, C. W., & Hopko, D. R. (2011). The reward probability index: Design and validation of a scale measuring access to environmental reward. *Behavior Therapy, 42,* 249–262.

Carvalho, J. P., & Hopko, D. R. (2011). Behavioral theory of depression: Reinforcement as a mediating variable between avoidance and depression. *Journal of Behavior Therapy and Experimental Psychiatry, 42,* 154–162.

Chambless, D. L., Baker, M. J., Baucom, D. H., Beutler, L. E., Calhoun, K. S., Crits-Christoph, P., ... Woody, S. R. (1998). Update on empirically validated therapies, II. *The Clinical Psychologist, 51*, 3−16.

Cribb, G., Moulds, M. L., & Carter, S. (2006). Rumination and experiential avoidance in depression. *Behaviour Change, 23*, 165−176.

Cuijpers, P., Van Straten, A., & Warmerdam, L. (2007). Behavioral activation treatments of depression: A meta-analysis. *Clinical Psychology Review, 27*, 318−326.

Dimidjian, S., Barrera, M., Jr, Martell, C., Muñoz, R. F., & Lewinsohn, P. M. (2011). The origins and current status of behavioral activation treatments for depression. *Annual Review of Clinical Psychology, 7*, 1−38.

Dimidjian, S., Hollon, S. D., Dobson, K. S., Schmaling, K. B., Kohlenberg, R. J., Addis, M. E., ... Jacobson, N. S. (2006). Randomized trial of behavioral activation, cognitive therapy, and antidepressant medication in the acute treatment of adults with major depression. *Journal of Consulting and Clinical Psychology, 74*, 658−670.

Dobson, K. S. (1989). A meta-analysis of the efficacy of cognitive therapy for depression. *Journal of Consulting and Clinical Psychology, 57*, 414−419.

Dobson, K. S., Hollon, S. D., Dimidjian, S., Schmaling, K. B., Kohlenberg, R. J., Gallop, R., ... Jacobson, N. S. (2008). Randomized trial of behavioral activation, cognitive therapy, and antidepressant medication in the prevention of relapse and recurrence in major depression. *Journal of Consulting and Clinical Psychology, 76*, 468−477.

Ekers, D., Richards, D., & Gilbody, S. (2008). A meta-analysis of randomized trials of behavioural treatment of depression. *Psychological Medicine, 38*, 611−623.

Ekers, D., Richards, D., McMillan, D., Bland, J. M., & Gilbody, S. (2011). Behavioural activation delivered by the non-specialist: Phase II randomised controlled trial. *The British Journal of Psychiatry, 198*, 66−72.

Ekers, D., Webster, L., Van Straten, A., Cuijpers, P., Richards, D., & Gilbody, S. (2014). Behavioural activation for depression; an update of meta-analysis of effectiveness and sub group analysis. *PLoS ONE, 9*, e100100.

Ferster, C. B. (1973). A functional analysis of depression. *American Psychologist, 28*, 857−870.

Gawrysiak, M., Nicholas, C., & Hopko, D. R. (2009). Behavioral activation for moderately depressed university students: Randomized controlled trial. *Journal of Counseling Psychology, 56*, 468−475.

Gortner, E. T., Gollan, J. K., Dobson, K. S., & Jacobson, N. S. (1998). Cognitive−behavioral treatment for depression: Relapse prevention. *Journal of Consulting and Clinical Psychology, 66*, 377−384.

Greenberg, P. E., Fournier, A. A., Sisitsky, T., Pike, C. T., & Kessler, R. C. (2015). The economic burden of adults with major depressive disorder in the United States (2005 and 2010). *The Journal of Clinical Psychiatry, 76*, 155−162.

Hasin, D. S., Goodwin, R. D., Stinson, F. S., & Grant, B. F. (2005). Epidemiology of major depressive disorder: Results from the National Epidemiologic Survey on Alcoholism and Related Conditions. *Archives of General Psychiatry, 62*, 1097−1106.

Hayes, S. C., Strosahl, K. D., & Wilson, K. G. (1999). *Acceptance and commitment therapy: An experiential approach to behavior change.* New York: Guilford Press.

Hernstein, R. J. (1961). Relative and absolute strength of a response as a function of frequency of reinforcement. *Journal of the Experimental Analysis of Behavior, 4*, 267−272.

Hernstein, R. J. (1970). On the law of effect. *Journal of the Experimental Analysis of Behavior, 13*, 243−266.

Hopko, D. R., Armento, M. E., Cantu, M. S., Chambers, L. L., & Lejuez, C. W. (2003a). The use of daily diaries to assess the relations among mood state, overt behavior, and reward value of activities. *Behaviour Research and Therapy, 41*, 1137−1148.

Hopko, D. R., Lejuez, C., LePage, J., Hopko, S., & McNeil, D. (2003b). A brief behavioral activation treatment for depression: A randomized pilot trial within an inpatient psychiatric hospital. *Behavior Modification, 27*, 458–469.

Hopko, D. R., Armento, M. E., Robertson, S., Ryba, M. M., Carvalho, J. P., Colman, L. K., ... Lejuez, C. W. (2011). Brief behavioral activation and problem-solving therapy for depressed breast cancer patients: Randomized trial. *Journal of Consulting and Clinical Psychology, 79*, 834–849.

Hopko, D. R., Bell, J., Armento, M. E. A., Robertson, S. M. C., Mullane, C., Wolf, N. J., & Lejuez, C. W. (2008). Cognitive–behavior therapy for depressed cancer patients in a medical care setting. *Behavior Therapy, 39*, 126–136.

Hopko, D. R., Bell, J. L., Armento, M. E. A., Hunt, M. K., & Lejuez, C. W. (2005). Behavior therapy for depressed cancer patients in primary care. *Psychotherapy: Theory, Research, Practice, Training, 42*, 236–243.

Hopko, D. R., Lejuez, C. W., Ruggiero, K. J., & Eifert, G. H. (2003c). Contemporary behavioral activation treatments for depression: Procedures, principles, and progress. *Clinical Psychology Review, 23*, 699–717.

Jacobson, N. S., Dobson, K. S., Truax, P. A., Addis, M. E., Koerner, K., Gollan, J. K., ... Prince, S. E. (1996). A component analysis of cognitive behavioral treatment for depression. *Journal of Consulting and Clinical Psychology, 64*, 295–304.

Jacobson, N. S., Martell, C. R., & Dimidjian, S. (2001). Behavioral activation treatment for depression: Returning to contextual roots. *Clinical Psychology: Science and Practice, 8*, 255–270.

Kanter, J. W., Busch, A. M., & Rusch, L. C. (2009). *Behavioral activation: Distinctive features*. London: Routledge Press.

Kanter, J. W., Manos, R. C., Bowe, W. M., Baruch, D. E., Busch, A. M., & Rusch, L. C. (2010). What is behavioral activation?: A review of the empirical literature. *Clinical Psychology Review, 30*, 608–620.

Kanter, J. W., Rusch, L. C., Busch, A. M., & Sedivy, S. K. (2009). Validation of the Behavioral Activation for Depression Scale (BADS) in a community sample with elevated depressive symptoms. *Journal of Psychopathology and Behavioral Assessment, 31*, 36–42.

Kessler, R. C., Berglund, P., Demler, O., Jin, R., Koretz, D., Merikangas, K. R., ... Wang, P. S. (2003). The epidemiology of major depressive disorder: results from the National Comorbidity Survey Replication (NCS-R). *The Journal of the American Medical Association, 289*, 3095–3105.

Lazzari, C., Egan, S. J., & Rees, C. S. (2011). Behavioral activation treatment for depression in older adults delivered via videoconferencing: A pilot study. *Cognitive and Behavioral Practice, 18*, 555–565.

Lejuez, C. W., Hopko, D. R., Acierno, R., Daughters, S. B., & Pagoto, S. L. (2011). Ten year revision of the brief behavioral activation treatment for depression: Revised treatment manual. *Behavior Modification, 35*, 111–161.

Lejuez, C. W., Hopko, D. R., & Hopko, S. D. (2001). A brief behavioral activation treatment for depression: Treatment manual. *Behavior Modification, 25*, 255–286.

Lewinsohn, P. M. (1974). A behavioral approach to depression. In R. M. Friedman, & M. M. Katz (Eds.), *The psychology of depression: Contemporary theory and research*. New York: Wiley.

Lewinsohn, P. M., Biglan, A., & Zeiss, A. M. (1976). Behavioral treatment for depression. In P. O. Davidson (Ed.), *Behavioral management of anxiety, depression and pain* (pp. 91–146). New York: Brunner/Mazel.

Lewinsohn, P. M., & Graf, M. (1973). Pleasant activities and depression. *Journal of Consulting and Clinical Psychology, 41*, 261–268.

Lewinsohn, P. M., & Libet, J. (1972). Pleasant events, activity schedules, and depressions. *Journal of Abnormal Psychology, 79*, 291–295.

Lewinsohn, P. M., Muñoz, R. F., Youngren, M. A., & Zeiss, A. M. (1978). *Control your depression*. Englewood Cliffs, NJ: Prentice-Hall.

Lewinsohn, P. M., Youngren, M. A., & Grosscup, S. J. (1979). Reinforcement and depression. In R. A. Depue (Ed.), *The psychobiology of the depressive disorders: Implications for the effects of stress* (pp. 291–316). New York: Academic Press.

Linehan, M. (1993). *Cognitive-behavioral treatment of borderline personality disorder*. New York: Guilford Press.

Ly, K. H., Trüschel, A., Jarl, L., Magnusson, S., Windahl, T., Johansson, R., . . . Andersson, G. (2014). Behavioural activation versus mindfulness-based guided self-help treatment administered through a smartphone application: a randomised controlled trial. *BMJ Open, 4*, e003440.

MacPhillamy, D. J., & Lewinsohn, P. M. (1974). Depression as a function of levels of desired and obtained pleasure. *Journal of Abnormal Psychology, 83*, 651–657.

Manos, R. C., Kanter, J. W., & Busch, A. M. (2010). A critical review of assessment strategies to measure the behavioral activation model of depression. *Clinical Psychology Review, 30*, 547–561.

Martell, C. R., Addis, M. E., & Jacobson, N. S. (2001). *Depression in context: Strategies for guided action*. New York: W.W. Norton.

Martell, C. R., Dimidjian, S., & Herman-Dunn, R. (2010). *Behavioral activation for depression: A clinician's guide*. New York: Guilford Press.

Mazzucchelli, T., Kane, R., & Rees, C. (2009). Behavioral activation treatments for depression in adults: A meta-analysis and review. *Clinical Psychology: Science and Practice, 16*, 383–411.

McDowell, J. J. (1982). The importance of Hernstein's mathematical statement of the law and effect for behavior therapy. *American Psychologist, 37*, 771–779.

McIndoo, C. C., File, A. A., Preddy, T., Clark, C. G., & Hopko, D. R. (2016). Mindfulness-based therapy and behavioral activation: A randomized controlled trial with depressed college students. *Behaviour Research and Therapy, 77*, 118–128.

Moulds, M. L., Kandris, E., Starr, S., & Wong, A. (2007). The relationship between rumination, avoidance and depression in a non-clinical sample. *Behaviour Research and Therapy, 45*, 251–261.

Ottenbreit, N. D., & Dobson, K. S. (2004). Avoidance and depression: The construction of the Cognitive-Behavioral Avoidance Scale. *Behaviour Research and Therapy, 42*, 292–313.

Ottenbreit, N. D., Dobson, K. S., & Quigley, L. (2014a). A psychometric evaluation of the cognitive-behavioral avoidance scale in women with major depressive disorder. *Journal of Psychopathology and Behavioral Assessment, 36*, 591–599.

Ottenbreit, N. D., Dobson, K. S., & Quigley, L. (2014b). An examination of avoidance in major depression in comparison to social anxiety disorder. *Behaviour Research and Therapy, 56*, 82–90.

Porter, J. F., Spates, C. R., & Smitham, S. (2004). Behavioral activation group therapy in public mental health settings: A pilot investigation. *Professional Psychology: Research and Practice, 35*, 297–301.

Rehm, L. P. (1978). Mood, pleasant events, and unpleasant events: Two pilot studies. *Journal of Consulting and Clinical Psychology, 46*, 854–859.

Segal, Z. V., Williams, J. M. G., & Teasdale, J. D. (2002). *Mindfulness-based cognitive therapy for depression: A new approach to relapse prevention*. New York: Guilford Press.

Shaw, B. F. (1977). Comparison of cognitive therapy and behavior therapy in the treatment of depression. *Journal of Consulting and Clinical Psychology, 45*, 543–551.

Snarski, M., Scogin, F., DiNapoli, E., Presnell, A., McAlpine, J., & Marcinak, J. (2011). The effects of behavioral activation therapy with inpatient geriatric psychiatry patients. *Behavior Therapy, 42*, 100–108.

Spates, C. R., Kalata, A. H., Ozeki, S., Stanton, C. E., & Peters, S. (2012). Initial open trial of a computerized behavioral activation treatment for depression. *Behavior Modification, 37*, 259–297.

Task Force on Promotion and Dissemination of Psychological Procedures. (1995). Training in and dissemination of empirically validated psychological treatments. *The Clinical Psychologist, 48*, 3–23.

Üstün, T. B., Ayuso-Mateos, J. L., Chatterji, S., Mathers, C., & Murray, C. J. (2004). Global burden of depressive disorders in the year 2000. *The British Journal of Psychiatry, 184*, 386–392.

Williams, D. R., Gonzalez, H. M., Neighbors, H., Nesse, R., Abelson, J. M., Sweetman, J., & Jackson, J. S. (2007). Prevalence and distribution of major depressive disorder in African Americans, Caribbean blacks, and non-Hispanic whites: Results from the National Survey of American Life. *Archives of General Psychiatry, 64*, 305–315.

13

Posttraumatic Stress Disorder

Richard A. Bryant
University of New South Wales, Sydney, NSW, Australia

DIAGNOSTIC DEFINITIONS

Posttraumatic stress disorder (PTSD) is currently defined in the American Psychiatric Association's Diagnostic Statistical Manual for Mental Disorders (DSM). The fifth edition of the DSM (DSM-5; American Psychiatric Association, 2013) maintained the inclusion of a stressor criterion that requires that one must have been exposed to threatened or actual harm to oneself or others (Cluster A). Notably, the stressor criterion was altered in terms of a subjective stressor element such that the previous requirement that the person needed to respond to the trauma with fear, horror, or helplessness was removed. This was done because the subjective element of the stressor criterion does not markedly alter PTSD prevalence, and it also potentially excludes some people who do not respond to the trauma with these reactions at the time (e.g., soldiers, survivors of mild traumatic brain injury) (Friedman, Resick, Bryant, & Brewin, 2011).

In addition, there are four other major clusters of symptoms. First, one needs to have at least of the following: reexperiencing symptoms, including intrusive memories, flashbacks, nightmares, and distress to reminders of the trauma (Cluster B). Second, one is required to have at least one of: active avoidance of internal reminders of the trauma (e.g., thoughts and memories) or external reminders (e.g., situations and conversations) (Cluster C). Third, a new cluster termed "Alterations in Mood and Cognition" requires at least three of the following: exaggerated negative thoughts about oneself or the world, excessive blame, pervasive negative emotions, diminished interest, feeling detached or estranged from others, psychogenic amnesia. The fourth cluster

The Science of Cognitive Behavioral Therapy.
DOI: http://dx.doi.org/10.1016/B978-0-12-803457-6.00013-1

involves arousal symptoms, which requires at least three of exaggerated startle response, reckless behavior, insomnia, aggressive behavior, and sleeping and concentration difficulties (Cluster D). DSM-IV required that the symptoms be present for more than 1 month after the trauma because DSM did not want to pathologize people who may be experiencing a transient stress response.

The DSM-5 definition led to some sharp criticisms, with much concern over the decision to include a broad array of emotional reactions as distinct from the traditional focus on fear and anxiety (Hoge et al., 2016). This shift was done in DSM-5 because of concerns that many traumatized populations experience nonfear-based emotions that can be impairing (e.g., guilt, shame, and anger), such as the military, emergency responders, and victims of crime (Friedman et al., 2011). One concern expressed was that the expansion of the criteria may impact on the prevalence of the disorder; although concordance in identifying PTSD using DSM-IV and DSM-5 definitions is not ideal in some studies (Hoge, Riviere, Wilk, Herrell, & Weathers, 2014), other studies showed more promising concordance (Kilpatrick et al., 2013; O'Donnell et al., 2014).

Another issue raised in relation to DSM-5 was the heterogeneity of how PTSD may be manifested. When we consider other disorders in DSM-5, it is worth noting that there are 227 permutations of how major depression can be displayed, 23,442 for panic disorder, 1 of specific phobia, and 1 of social phobia. In contrast, in DSM-IV, there were 84,645 possible presentations of PTSD; however, the increase in number of symptoms and addition of a cluster in DSM-5 resulted in there being 636,120 possible ways that PTSD can now manifest itself (Galatzer-Levy & Bryant, 2013). This huge increase in possible permutations of how PTSD can be expressed has important research implications, where much energy is currently expended on biological or cognitive markers of the disorder. This task is made much more difficult because the phenotype is very variable in DSM-5.

Alternatively, the World Health Organization's International Classification of Diseases (ICD) offers a much simpler description of PTSD. As a result of the WHO's mission to meet the health needs of low- and middle-income countries, where there are often few mental health specialists. Accordingly, the ICD aims to provide a simple description of each disorder to facilitate diagnoses in poorly resourced settings. A consequence of this is that the proposed ICD-11 definition of PTSD is simpler than the detailed description that we see in DSM-5. The proposed ICD-11 description requires reexperiencing of the traumatic event, avoidance of reminders, and a perception of heightened current threat (reflected by various forms of arousal) (Maercker et al., 2013). There is some evidence that prevalence rates of PTSD between DSM-5 and ICD-11 definitions do not differ markedly; however, worryingly the concordance between the two systems is not strong (O'Donnell et al., 2014).

ACUTE STRESS DISORDER

Although strictly not part of the formal PTSD diagnosis, the acute stress disorder (ASD) diagnosis is a form of PTSD that DSM-IV introduced in 1994 and revised in DSM-5. In DSM-IV, ASD was introduced to diagnose acute stress reactions that occur in the initial month after trauma because this promoted access to health care and also to identify trauma survivors who are at high risk for developing subsequent PTSD (Bryant, 2016). The ASD diagnosis was initially defined with an emphasis on dissociative symptoms (including depersonalization, derealization, and reduced awareness of surroundings), which was argued by some commentators to be important because it can predict subsequent PTSD (Koopman, Classen, Cardena, & Spiegel, 1995) (Koopman et al., 1995). There are numerous longitudinal studies indicating an association between dissociation in the acute phase and subsequent levels of PTSD (Murray, Ehlers, & Mayou, 2002). A series of longitudinal studies were conducted that assessed the relationship between ASD and later PTSD. One review of 22 studies concluded that overall the ASD diagnosis is sensitive in predicting PTSD; that is, the majority of individuals with a diagnosis of ASD do subsequently develop PTSD (Bryant, 2011); however, most people who did develop PTSD did not meet initially display ASD. These studies suggested that although trauma survivors with ASD are at heightened risk for developing PTSD, the ASD diagnosis is overly narrow in identifying people at risk. Accordingly, in DSM-5, the ASD diagnosis was not intended to be predictive of subsequent PTSD but instead was meant to describe people with elevated distress in the initial month who may benefit from mental health assistance. Specifically, the DSM-5 requires at least 9 of 14 potential acute stress reactions be present in the initial month after trauma to make a diagnosis of ASD (Bryant, Friedman, Spiegel, Ursano, & Strain, 2011).

COMPLEX PTSD

A new variant of PTSD has been proposed for ICD-11 termed Complex PTSD (Maercker et al., 2013). This diagnosis is proposed to describe PTSD symptoms that are complicated by three experiencing three additional features: (1) disturbances in self-identity, (2) emotional dysregulation, and (3) significant difficulties in interpersonal relations. Emotion dysregulation may involve emotional reactivity, violent outbursts, reckless or self-destructive behavior, or a tendency toward experiencing prolonged dissociative states. Self-identity disturbance is characterized by negative self-concept, including persistent beliefs about oneself as diminished, defeated, or worthless. Interpersonal disturbances are defined as persistent difficulties in sustaining relationships, which may involve difficulties in feeling close to others, avoidance of relationships, or intense relationships that cannot be maintained. It is suggested that this presentation is most commonly seen in survivors of prolonged and severe trauma, such as childhood abuse or torture (Cloitre et al., 2009).

This proposal has attracted considerable debate. Some commentators propose that the diagnosis is not necessary because the expanded definition of PTSD in DSM-5 allows the features described in Complex PTSD to be accommodated in the main PTSD diagnosis (Resick et al., 2012). Proponents of the diagnosis adopt a different position by demonstrating that this subset of PTSD patients do have this distinctive set of symptoms (Cloitre, Garvert, Brewin, Bryant, & Maercker, 2013), and their profile is different from borderline personality disorder (Cloitre, Garvert, Weiss, Carlson, & Bryant, 2014). It has been argued that phase-based treatments are specifically useful for these patients because it teaches emotion regulation skills, which can then promote better response to exposure-based psychotherapies (Cloitre et al., 2010).

PREVALENCE OF PTSD

Most people exposed to traumatic events are resilient and do not develop a psychological disorder. Indeed, epidemiological studies report lifetime prevalence rates of PTSD of between 13% and 20.4% for women and between 6.2% and 8.2% for men (Breslau, Davis, Andreski, & Peterson, 1991; Kessler, Sonnega, Hughes, & Nelson, 1995). The patterns of women being twice as likely to develop PTSD than men are reflected in many countries across the globe (Olff, Langeland, Draijer, & Gersons, 2007). It is important to note, however, that the likelihood of PTSD developing is highly dependent on a range of factors, including the type of traumatic event. In general, interpersonal violence leads to higher rates of PTSD, and this is particularly the case for sexual violence (Forbes et al., 2012; Forbes et al., 2014). Accordingly, it is observed that prevalence rates for PTSD are higher in survivors of sexual assault than in survivors of natural disasters (Creamer, Burgess, & McFarlane, 2001; Kessler et al., 1995). Reflecting this pattern is meta-analytic evidence that people who are exposed to the most severe interpersonal trauma, including tortured refugees, display the highest rates of PTSD (Steel et al., 2009).

THE COURSE OF PTSD

Much has been learnt about the course of PTSD in recent years, as a result of the many longitudinal studies that have been conducted. One of the major premises of many conceptualizations of PTSD is that although many people exposed to trauma will experience PTSD symptoms in the initial days and weeks after the event, most of these reactions will subside in the following months. This pattern has been observed in decreasing prevalence of PTSD symptoms across different trauma contexts, including assaults, terrorist attacks, and disasters (Galea et al., 2003; Riggs, Rothbaum, & Foa, 1995; Rothbaum, Foa, Riggs, Murdock, & Walsh, 1992; van Griensven et al., 2006).

In recent years, scholars have becoming increasingly aware that PTSD reactions are dynamic over time and do not follow a linear path (Bryant, O'Donnell, Creamer, McFarlane, & Silove, 2013). Researchers have used latent growth mixture modeling to map the trajectories of PTSD over time, which identifies classes of individual variation over time and thereby profiles distinct posttrauma trajectories. This approach has led to remarkable convergence across studies, insofar as they have reliably demonstrated (1) resilient class with consistently shows few PTSD symptoms, (2) a recovery class with initial distress then gradual remission, (3) a delayed reaction class with initial low symptom levels but increased symptoms over time, and (4) a chronic distress class with consistently high PTSD levels (Bonanno et al., 2008; Bryant et al., 2015; deRoon-Cassini, Mancini, Rusch, & Bonanno, 2010; Norris, Tracy, & Galea, 2009).

It is worth noting that the delay reaction class that shows worsening symptoms over time is similar to the DSM conceptualization of delayed-onset PTSD, which has traditionally been recognized in DSM when the onset of PTSD occurs at least 6 months after the traumatic event. Increasingly, this manifestation of PTSD has been shown in military populations, especially after deployment when personnel have returned to their home (Andrews, Brewin, Philpott, & Stewart, 2007). In accordance with studies that have mapped the stress symptoms over time, DSM-5 stipulated that Delayed-onset PTSD may involve presentations in which subsyndromal symptoms were apparent in the acute period after trauma but subsequently worsened over time until syndromal levels of PTSD were met.

IMPAIRMENT

Individuals with PTSD experience marked impairments in occupational (Bolton et al., 2004; Hoge et al., 2008), family and marital (Rona et al., 2009; Sayers, Farrow, Ross, & Oslin, 2009), and social (O'Connell, Kasprow, & Rosenheck, 2008; Schnurr, Hayes, Lunney, McFall, & Uddo, 2006) domains. There is also considerable evidence that trauma survivors who do present with the subsyndromal levels of PTSD also display marked levels of impairment (Stein, Walker, Hazen, & Forde, 1997), even when lifetime PTSD and comorbid depression are controlled (Zlotnick, Franklin, & Zimmerman, 2002). There is also evidence that once PTSD symptoms remit, there can be lingering effects of the disorder on the individual's capacity to function (Bryant et al., 2016).

MODELS OF PTSD

One of the most influential models of PTSD involves fear conditioning (Milad, Rauch, Pitman, & Quirk, 2006). This perspective posits that when a traumatic event (an unconditioned stimulus) occurs, the trauma-exposed person responds with intense fear (an unconditioned response). The trauma-related fear triggers strong learning of associations between the fear and the events surrounding the trauma. As reminders of the trauma occur (the conditioned stimuli), people then respond with fear reactions, such reexperiencing symptoms and distress (the conditioned response). For example, the survivor of a road accident may learn that the smell of petrol, the sound of an engine, or the sight of traffic is a signal of future threat, and hence these previously benign events acquire threatening qualities. Fear conditioning models propose that increased activation off stress hormones (including norepinephrine and epinephrine) results in overconsolidation of trauma memories (Rauch, Shin, & Phelps, 2006). It is also argued that most people are able to recover from a traumatic experience because extinction learning occurs in the following weeks and months, in which repeated exposure to trauma reminders or memories results in new learning that these reminders no longer signal threat.

These models have support from much research that people with chronic PTSD display elevated psychophysiological responses, including heart rate, skin conductance and facial electromyogram (EMG), relative to trauma survivors without PTSD in response to trauma reminders (Pitman, Orr, Forgue, de Jong, & Claiborn, 1987). People who develop PTSD also display higher resting heart rates in the immediate period after trauma, reflecting possible elevated conditioning (Bryant, Creamer, O'Donnell, Silove, & McFarlane, 2008a; Shalev et al., 1998). Other indicators of elevated arousal in the very acute phase after trauma include lower GABA levels (Vaiva et al., 2006) and high rates of panic attacks (Bryant & Panasetis, 2001). Consistent with the notion that PTSD reflects impaired extinction learning, there are multiple studies in military or emergency service personnel that have shown that impaired extinction learning (measured on experimental tasks) prior to commencement of active duty predicts subsequent PTSD levels after personnel have been exposed to traumatic events (Guthrie & Bryant, 2006; Lommen, Engelhard, Sijbrandij, van den Hout, & Hermans, 2013; Orr et al., 2012).

One of the advantages of the parallels between fear conditioning pattern in animals and humans is that the field has been able to make rapid advances in understanding the neural circuitry implicated in PTSD. Neural models typically propose that conditioning occurs in the basolateral nucleus of the amygdala, whereas extinction learning is achieved by regulatory input from the ventral medial prefrontal cortex (Rauch et al., 2006). Supporting this proposition is good evidence that the ventral medial prefrontal cortex is often insufficiently recruited when one is processing fearful emotions in PTSD individuals (Shin & Liberzon, 2010). As the primary form of psychotherapy for PTSD is based on extinction learning, it is perhaps unsurprising that the same neural networks implicated in extinction learning are also involved in predicting successful response to this form of therapy in both functional (Bryant, Felmingham, Kemp, et al., 2008b) and structural (Bryant, Felmingham, Whitford et al., 2008c) imaging studies.

In contrast to biological models, cognitive theorists emphasize the pivotal roles of (a) maladaptive appraisals of the trauma and its aftermath, and (b) disturbances in autobiographical memory (Ehlers & Clark, 2000). Specifically, it is argued that as a result of the elevated arousal at the time of trauma, memories are not embedded in a normal narrative within one's autobiographical memory because memories are perceptually encoded, and this results in fragmented and disorganized memories. Supporting this proposal is evidence that trauma memories are often fragmented (Foa, Molnar, & Cashman, 1995; Harvey & Bryant, 1999), and that development of PTSD is associated with perceptual processing of traumatic information (Ehring, Kleim, & Ehlers, 2011; Sundermann, Hauschildt, & Ehlers, 2013).

Cognitive models also emphasize the role of excessively negative appraisals of the traumatic event, how one is responding to it, and how one perceives the future. Many studies indicate that maladaptive appraisals of the traumatic experience are associated with both ASD (Smith & Bryant, 2000; Warda & Bryant, 1998) and PTSD (Dunmore, Clark, & Ehlers, 1997; Ehring, Ehlers, & Glucksman, 2006), and also such appraisals shortly after trauma exposure are highly predictive of subsequent PTSD (Dunmore, Clark, & Ehlers, 2001; Ehlers, Mayou, & Bryant, 1998).

RISK FOR PTSD

Many of the risk factors for PTSD development are common to risk for other psychiatric disorders. These include prior psychological disturbance, family history of psychological disorders, abusive childhood, low socioeconomic status, and female gender (Brewin, Andrews, & Valentine, 2000). As noted above, it is well documented that PTSD is more likely when the trauma is prolonged, is characterized by exposure to grotesque or extremely distressing events, or involves interpersonal violence (Brewin et al., 2000). The posttrauma environment is also important, with much evidence that low social support and ongoing stressors contributing to risk for PTSD development (Brewin et al., 2000; Bryant et al., 2013).

On the contrary, a large proportion of data from which we infer risk for PTSD come from studies of populations after they have been exposed to trauma, and of course this introduces significant confounds to this information. There is also evidence that has prospectively collected data from people before they have been exposed to traumatic events, and subsequently followed people after exposure. Considerable evidence of this type has been collected in military samples, which has been shown that precombat school problems and lower arithmetic aptitude (Pitman, Orr, Lowenhagen, & Macklin, 1991) and lower intelligence scores (Macklin et al., 1998) predict PTSD. Using the MMPI, certain personality indices assessed prior to deployment (including Hypochondriasis, Psychopathic Deviate, Paranoia, and Femininity) are predictive of PTSD (Schnurr, Friedman, & Rosenberg, 1993). There is also evidence that the tendency to engage in catastrophic thinking before trauma exposure predicts subsequent PTSD in fire-fighters (Bryant & Guthrie, 2005, 2007).

As with other anxiety disorders, twin studies indicate that monozygotic twins are more likely to develop PTSD than dizygotic twins (True et al., 1993). Consistent with much of the psychiatric genomic domain, the search for genotypic bases of PTSD has yielded no robust outcomes (Koenen, Duncan, Liberzon, & Ressler, 2013). Similar candidate genes that have been studied in disorders that are often comorbid with PTSD (such as depression) have been studied considerably in the context of PTSD. Exemplifying this trend is the focus on the functional polymorphism in the promoter region of the serotonin transporter gene (SLC6A4); the short allele (5-HTTLPR S) of this polymorphism reduces serotonergic expression and uptake by nearly 50% (Lesch et al., 1996). There is a greater incidence of 5-HTTLPR S in patients with PTSD (Lee et al., 2005), and the 5-HTTLPR S increases the risk of PTSD when coupled with low social support (Kilpatrick et al., 2007) and also predicts poor response to exposure-based psychotherapy (Bryant et al., 2010). However, gene candidate findings are notorious for not being replicated across studies, and it is safe to conclude that it is most improbable that a PTSD "gene" will be identified.

Beyond the focus on specific genetic candidates, twin studies have been extremely useful in determining the role of characterological factors that can pose risk for PTSD. One important study compared monozygotic co-twins who either did or did not serve in Vietnam according to their PTSD status following their deployment. This study found that Vietnam veterans with PTSD had smaller hippocampi than Vietnam veterans who did not have PTSD (Gilbertson et al., 2002); this was not surprising because numerous studies had previously shown this (Sala et al., 2004; Shucard et al., 2012; Yehuda et al., 2007). The interesting finding of this twin study was the co-twins of those with PTSD (but who had not served in Vietnam) had hippocampi that were just as small. This suggests that small hippocampal volume may constitute a vulnerability factor for PTSD among people exposed to trauma. The study also noted slower habituating skin conductance startle responses in veterans with PTSD and their noncombat-exposed co-twins, compared to veterans without PTSD and their noncombat exposed co-twins (Orr et al., 2003), suggesting that slower habituation may be a pretrauma vulnerability factor for PTSD.

TREATING PTSD

The preferred treatment for PTSD, as recommended by most treatment guidelines around the world (Institute of Medicine, 2008; National Institute of Clinical Excellence, 2005), is trauma-focused psychotherapy. This form of therapy has been shown to be effective with many populations, including traumatic injury and assault, sexual assault, combat, terrorist attacks, refugees, and child sexual abuse (Bryant, Moulds et al., 2008d; Duffy, Gillespie, & Clark, 2007; Foa, Rothbaum, Riggs, & Murdock, 1991; McDonagh et al., 2005; Neuner, Schauer, Klaschik, Karunakara, & Elbert, 2004; Schnurr et al., 2003). Despite the convergent finding of the efficacy of this approach, only two-thirds of PTSD patients adequately respond to this treatment (Bradley, Greene, Russ, Dutra, & Westen, 2005).

The most traditional variant of trauma-focused psychotherapy is trauma-focused cognitive behavior therapy, which comprises psychoeducation about the trauma responses, anxiety management (including breathing retraining or relaxation training), prolonged exposure, and cognitive restructuring. The core component of this treatment involves exposure therapy, which can assume both imaginal and in vivo forms. Imaginal exposure (often termed "Prolonged Exposure") typically asks the patient to vividly imagine their traumatic experience for prolonged periods (45—60 minutes); although evidence suggests that briefer exposures are as efficacious (Nacasch et al., 2015). The goal of this technique is to teach the patient that the distress they experience in response to recalling their trauma, along with all the associated stimuli, can be mastered. In this sense, the goal is to achieve extinction learning because the person learns that the memories are no longer threatening. Imaginal exposure can be supplemented with in vivo exposure, which operates on the same principle but guides the patient through a graded exposure to feared stimuli until the patient learns that they can remain in proximity to each situation with minimal distress (Foa, 2011).

Although prolonged exposure protocols involve supplementing the exercise with discussion about the experience, more cognitively oriented interventions place additional emphasis on specifically targeting the maladaptive reappraisals that may be maintaining the patient's symptoms. Therapies such as Cognitive Therapy (Ehlers et al., 2014) or Cognitive Processing Therapy (Resick et al., 2008) teach the patient to identify and correct appraisals that worsen their condition, and although exposure is often provided in the context of these treatments, correction of cognitive distortions is often regarded as more important.

Other variants of trauma-focused cognitive behavior therapies exist. Eye movement desensitization and reprocessing (EMDR) claims that it is a distinctive form of treatment because unlike other therapies, it involves the patient directing their attention to a trauma memory while also visually tracking the therapist's finger as it is moved across their visual field; the patient then is instructed restructure core elements of the trauma memory with the view of reconsolidating it as a more adaptive memory (Shapiro, 1995). This process is repeated, which is intended to integrate this new information by virtue of the saccadic eye movements promoting relevant neural processes that foster memory adaptation. Although EMDR has been shown to be effective in treating PTSD across numerous controlled trials (Nijdam, Gersons, Reitsma, de Jongh, & Olff, 2012), there is a lack of strong evidence that the eye movements themselves contribute to treatment gains (Australian Centre for Posttraumatic Mental Health, 2007). This pattern has led to the summary that "what is new about EMDR is not effective, and what is effective is not new" (McNally, 1999).

The diagnosis of ASD prompted attempts to identify people who were at high risk for PTSD development and to prevent PTSD by offering them early intervention in the acute period after trauma exposure. These approaches used trauma-focused cognitive behavior therapy in a shortened format (usually 5–6 sessions). Numerous trials demonstrated that have shown that relative to supportive counseling, these interventions were effective in preventing chronic PTSD in most patients who were enrolled in the trials (Bryant, Harvey, Dang, Sackville, & Basten, 1998; Bryant, Mastrodomenico, et al., 2008e; Bryant, Moulds, Guthrie, & Nixon, 2003, 2005; Shalev et al., 2012). Other studies did not employ the ASD criteria, but nonetheless provided cognitive behavior therapy in the period following trauma. These studies led to mixed results with some studies showing long-term benefits in terms of reduced PTSD levels (Bisson, Shepherd, Joy, Probert, & Newcombe, 2004), but another only showed initial gains that were not long-lasting (Sijbrandij et al., 2007). Nonetheless, meta-analytic studies of early interventions have reported the relative risk for a PTSD diagnosis was (0.36; 95% CI 0.17−0.78), supporting the evidence for the utility of brief CBT for ASD (Kornør et al., 2008), which was independently supported by a separate meta-analysis (Roberts, Kitchiner, Kenardy, & Bisson, 2009).

SUMMARY

Despite the advances in our knowledge about PTSD in recent years, there are many challenges ahead as the field attempts to deal with the mental health problems of large numbers of trauma-exposed people around the world. In the wake of war, interpersonal violence, the refugee crisis, natural disasters, and other humanitarian crises, many millions of people experience PTSD and do not currently receive mental health interventions approximating the evidence-based strategies reviewed in this chapter (Saxena, Thornicroft, Knapp, & Whiteford, 2007). There is an urgent need to develop strategies that can be shown to reduce PTSD in ways that can be scaled up for dissemination to large numbers of people in regions that are not serviced by mental health specialists. At the same time, there is a need to improve the success rate of trauma-focused psychotherapies; despite this therapy being well proven for over 20 years, only two-thirds of patients still respond to treatment adequately. Although a range of attempts have been made to augment the effects of trauma-focused cognitive behavior therapy, using both pharmacological (de Kleine, Hendriks, Kusters, Broekman, & van Minnen, 2012; Litz et al., 2012) and psychological (Bryant et al., 2013) strategies, these attempts have not led to reliable improvements. Accordingly, much research attention continues to focus on basic mechanisms underpinning adaptation to trauma with the view of developing novel and effective means to enhance treatment.

References

American Psychiatric Association (2013). *Diagnostic and statistical manual for mental disorders* (5th ed.). Washington, DC: American Psychiatric Association.

Andrews, B., Brewin, C. R., Philpott, R., & Stewart, L. (2007). Delayed-onset posttraumatic stress disorder: A systematic review of the evidence. *American Journal of Psychiatry, 164*(9), 1319−1326.

Australian Centre for Posttraumatic Mental Health. (2007). Australian guidelines for the treatment of adults with acute stress disorder and posttraumatic stress disorder. Melbourne, VIC: ACPMH.

Bisson, J. I., Shepherd, J. P., Joy, D., Probert, R., & Newcombe, R. G. (2004). Early cognitive-behavioural therapy for post-traumatic stress symptoms after physical injury. Randomised controlled trial. *British Journal of Psychiatry, 184*, 63–69.

Bolton, D., Hill, J., O'Ryan, D., Udwin, O., Boyle, S., & Yule, W. (2004). Long-term effects of psychological trauma on psychosocial functioning. *Journal of Child Psychology Psychiatry, 45*(5), 1007–1014.

Bonanno, G. A., Ho, S. M., Chan, J. C., Kwong, R. S., Cheung, C. K., Wong, C. P., & Wong, V. C. (2008). Psychological resilience and dysfunction among hospitalized survivors of the SARS epidemic in Hong Kong: A latent class approach. *Health Psychology, 27*(5), 659–667. Available from http://dx.doi.org/10.1037/0278-6133.27.5.659.

Bradley, R., Greene, J., Russ, E., Dutra, L., & Westen, D. (2005). A multidimensional meta-analysis of psychotherapy for PTSD. *American Journal of Psychiatry, 162*(2), 214–227.

Breslau, N., Davis, G., Andreski, P., & Peterson, E. (1991). Traumatic events and posttraumatic stress disorder in an urban population of young adults. *Archives of General Psychiatry, 48*, 216–222.

Brewin, C. R., Andrews, B., & Valentine, J. D. (2000). Meta-analysis of risk factors for posttraumatic stress disorder in trauma-exposed adults. *Journal of Consulting and Clinical Psychology, 68*(5), 748–766.

Bryant, R. A. (2011). Acute stress disorder as a predictor of posttraumatic stress disorder: A systematic review. *Journal of Clinical Psychiatry, 72*, 233–239.

Bryant, R. A. (2016). *Acute stress disorder: What it is and how to treat it.* New York: Guilford.

Bryant, R. A., Creamer, M., O'Donnell, M., Silove, D., & McFarlane, A. C. (2008a). A multi-site study of initial respiration rate and heart rate as predictors of posttraumatic stress disorder. *Journal of Clinical Psychiatry, 69*(11), 1694–1701.

Bryant, R. A., Felmingham, K., Kemp, A., Das, P., Hughes, G., Peduto, A., & Williams, L. (2008b). Amygdala and ventral anterior cingulate activation predicts treatment response to cognitive behaviour therapy for post-traumatic stress disorder. *Psychological Medicine, 38*(4), 555–561.

Bryant, R. A., Felmingham, K., Whitford, T. J., Kemp, A., Hughes, G., Peduto, A., & Williams, L. M. (2008c). Rostral anterior cingulate volume predicts treatment response to cognitive-behavioural therapy for posttraumatic stress disorder. *Journal of Psychiatry and Neuroscience, 33*(2), 142–146.

Bryant, R. A., Felmingham, K. L., Falconer, E. M., Pe Benito, L., Dobson-Stone, C., Pierce, K. D., & Schofield, P. R. (2010). Preliminary evidence of the short allele of the serotonin transporter gene predicting poor response to cognitive behavior therapy in posttraumatic stress disorder. *Biological Psychiatry, 67*(12), 1217–1219.

Bryant, R. A., Friedman, M. J., Spiegel, D., Ursano, R., & Strain, J. (2011). A review of acute stress disorder in DSM-5. *Depression and Anxiety, 28*(9), 802–817.

Bryant, R. A., & Guthrie, R. M. (2005). Maladaptive appraisals as a risk factor for posttraumatic stress: A study of trainee firefighters. *Psychological Science, 16*(10), 749–752.

Bryant, R. A., & Guthrie, R. M. (2007). Maladaptive self-appraisals before trauma exposure predict posttraumatic stress disorder. *Journal of Consulting and Clinical Psychology, 75*(5), 812–815.

Bryant, R. A., Harvey, A. G., Dang, S. T., Sackville, T., & Basten, C. (1998). Treatment of acute stress disorder: A comparison of cognitive-behavioural therapy and supportive counselling. *Journal of Consulting and Clinical Psychology, 66*(5), 862–866.

Bryant, R. A., Mastrodomenico, J., Felmingham, K. L., Hopwood, S., Kenny, L., Kandris, E., & Creamer, M. (2008e). Treatment of acute stress disorder: A randomized controlled trial. *Archives of General Psychiatry, 65*(6), 659–667.

Bryant, R. A., Mastrodomenico, J., Hopwood, S., Kenny, L., Cahill, C., Kandris, K., & Taylor, K. (2013). Augmenting cognitive behavior therapy for PTSD with emotion tolerance training: A randomized controlled trial. *Psychological Medicine, 43*, 2153–2160.

Bryant, R. A., McFarlane, A. C., Silove, D., O'Donnell, M. L., Forbes, D., & Creamer, M. (2016). The lingering impact of resolved PTSD on subsequent functioning. *Clinical Psychological Science, 4*, 493–498.

Bryant, R. A., Moulds, M., Guthrie, R., & Nixon, R. D. (2003). Treating acute stress disorder following mild traumatic brain injury. *American Journal of Psychiatry, 160*(3), 585–587.

Bryant, R. A., Moulds, M. L., Guthrie, R. M., Dang, S. T., Mastrodomenico, J., Nixon, R. D., & Creamer, M. (2008d). A randomized controlled trial of exposure therapy and cognitive restructuring for posttraumatic stress disorder. *Journal of Consulting and Clinical Psychology, 76*(4), 695–703.

Bryant, R. A., Moulds, M. L., Guthrie, R. M., & Nixon, R. D. V. (2005). The additive benefit of hypnosis and cognitive-behavioral therapy in treating acute stress disorder. *Journal of Consulting and Clinical Psychology, 73*(2), 334–340.

Bryant, R. A., Nickerson, A., Creamer, M., O'Donnell, M., Forbes, D., Galatzer-Levy, I., & Silove, D. (2015). Trajectory of post-traumatic stress following traumatic injury: 6-Year follow-up. *British Journal of Psychiatry, 206*(5), 417–423.

Bryant, R. A., O'Donnell, M., Creamer, M., McFarlane, A. C., & Silove, D. (2013). A multi-site analysis of the fluctuating course of posttraumatic stress disorder. *JAMA: Psychiatry, 70*, 839–846.

Bryant, R. A., & Panasetis, P. (2001). Panic symptoms during trauma and acute stress disorder. *Behaviour Research and Therapy, 39*(8), 961–966.

Cloitre, M., Chase Stovall-McClough, K., Nooner, K., Zorbas, P., Cherry, S., Jackson, C. L., & Petkova, E. (2010). Treatment for PTSD related to childhood abuse: A randomized controlled trial. *American Journal of Psychiatry, 167*, 915–924.

Cloitre, M., Garvert, D. W., Brewin, C. R., Bryant, R. A., & Maercker, A. (2013). Evidence for proposed ICD-11 PTSD and complex PTSD: A latent profile analysis. *European Journal of Psychotraumatology, 4*, p.20706.

Cloitre, M., Garvert, D. W., Weiss, B., Carlson, E. B., & Bryant, R. A. (2014). Distinguishing PTSD, Complex PTSD, and Borderline Personality Disorder: A latent class analysis. *European Journal of Psychotraumatology, 5*, p. 25097.

Cloitre, M., Stolbach, B. C., Herman, J. L., van der Kolk, B., Pynoos, R., Wang, J., & Petkova, E. (2009). A developmental approach to complex PTSD: Childhood and adult cumulative trauma as predictors of symptom complexity. *Journal of Traumatic Stress, 22*(5), 399–408.

Creamer, M., Burgess, P., & McFarlane, A. C. (2001). Post-traumatic stress disorder: Findings from the Australian National Survey of Mental Health and Well-being. *Psychological Medicine, 31*(7), 1237–1247.

de Kleine, R. A., Hendriks, G. J., Kusters, W. J., Broekman, T. G., & van Minnen, A. (2012). A randomized placebo-controlled trial of D-cycloserine to enhance exposure therapy for posttraumatic stress disorder. *Biological Psychiatry, 71*(11), 962–968.

de Roon-Cassini, T. A., Mancini, A. D., Rusch, M. D., & Bonanno, G. A. (2010). Psychopathology and resilience following traumatic injury: A latent growth mixture model analysis. *Rehabilitation Psychology, 55*(1), 1–11.

Duffy, M., Gillespie, K., & Clark, D. M. (2007). Post-traumatic stress disorder in the context of terrorism and other civil conflict in Northern Ireland: Randomised controlled trial. *British Medical Journal, 334*(7604), 1147.

Dunmore, E., Clark, D. M., & Ehlers, A. (1997). Cognitive factors in persistent versus recovered post-traumatic stress disorder after physical or sexual assault: A pilot study. *Behavioural and Cognitive Psychotherapy, 25*(2), 147–159.

Dunmore, E., Clark, D. M., & Ehlers, A. (2001). A prospective investigation of the role of cognitive factors in persistent Posttraumatic Stress Disorder (PTSD) after physical or sexual assault. *Behaviour Research and Therapy, 39*(9), 1063–1084.

Ehlers, A., & Clark, D. M. (2000). A cognitive model of posttraumatic stress disorder. *Behaviour Research and Therapy, 38*(4), 319–345.

Ehlers, A., Hackmann, A., Grey, N., Wild, J., Liness, S., Albert, I., & Clark, D. M. (2014). A randomized controlled trial of 7-day intensive and standard weekly cognitive therapy for PTSD and emotion-focused supportive therapy. *American Journal of Psychiatry, 171*(3), 294–304.

Ehlers, A., Mayou, R. A., & Bryant, B. (1998). Psychological predictors of chronic posttraumatic stress disorder after motor vehicle accidents. *Journal of Abnormal Psychology, 107*(3), 508–519.

Ehring, T., Ehlers, A., & Glucksman, E. (2006). Contribution of cognitive factors to the prediction of post-traumatic stress disorder, phobia and depression after motor vehicle accidents. *Behaviour Research and Therapy, 44*(12), 1699–1716.

Ehring, T., Kleim, B., & Ehlers, A. (2011). Combining clinical studies and analogue experiments to investigate cognitive mechanisms in posttraumatic stress disorder. *International Journal of Cognitive Therapy, 4*(2), 165–177.

Foa, E. B. (2011). Prolonged exposure therapy: Past, present, and future. *Depress Anxiety, 28*(12), 1043–1047.

Foa, E. B., Molnar, C., & Cashman, L. (1995). Change in rape narratives during exposure therapy for posttraumatic stress disorder. *Journal of Traumamatic Stress, 8*(4), 675–690.

Foa, E. B., Rothbaum, B. O., Riggs, D. S., & Murdock, T. B. (1991). Treatment of posttraumatic stress disorder in rape victims: A comparison between cognitive-behavioral procedures and counseling. *Journal of Consulting and Clinical Psychology, 59*(5), 715–723.

Forbes, D., Fletcher, S., Parslow, R., Phelps, A., O'Donnell, M., Bryant, R. A., & Creamer, M. (2012). Trauma at the hands of another: Longitudinal study of differences in the posttraumatic stress disorder symptom profile following interpersonal compared with noninterpersonal trauma. *Journal of Clinical Psychiatry, 73*(3), 372–376.

Forbes, D., Lockwood, E., Phelps, A., Wade, D., Creamer, M., Bryant, R. A., & O'Donnell, M. (2014). Trauma at the hands of another: Distinguishing PTSD patterns following intimate and nonintimate interpersonal and noninterpersonal trauma in a nationally representative sample. *Journal of Clinical Psychiatry, 75*(2), 147–153.

Friedman, M. J., Resick, P. A., Bryant, R. A., & Brewin, C. R. (2011). Considering PTSD for DSM-5. *Depression and Anxiety, 28*(9), 750–769.

Galatzer-Levy, I., & Bryant, R. A. (2013). 636,120 ways to have posttraumatic stress disorder: The relative merits of categorical and dimensional approaches to posttraumatic stress. *Perspectives in Psychological Science, 8*, 651–662.

Galea, S., Vlahov, D., Resnick, H., Ahern, J., Susser, E., Gold, J., & Kilpatrick, D. (2003). Trends of probable post-traumatic stress disorder in New York City after the September 11 terrorist attacks. *American Journal of Epidemiology, 158*(6), 514–524.

Gilbertson, M. W., Shenton, M. E., Ciszewski, A., Kasai, K., Lasko, N. B., Orr, S. P., & Pitman, R. K. (2002). Smaller hippocampal volume predicts pathologic vulnerability to psychological trauma. *Nature Neuroscience, 5*(11), 1242–1247.

Guthrie, R. M., & Bryant, R. A. (2006). Extinction learning before trauma and subsequent posttraumatic stress. *Psychosomatic Medicine, 68*(2), 307–311.

Harvey, A. G., & Bryant, R. A. (1999). A qualitative investigation of the organization of traumatic memories. *British Journal of Clinical Psychology, 38*(4), 401–405.

Hoge, C. W., McGurk, D., Thomas, J. L., Cox, A. L., Engel, C. C., & Castro, C. A. (2008). Mild traumatic brain injury in U.S. soldiers returning from Iraq. *New England Journal of Medicine, 358*(5), 453–463.

Hoge, C. W., Riviere, L. A., Wilk, J. E., Herrell, R. K., & Weathers, F. W. (2014). The prevalence of post-traumatic stress disorder (PTSD) in US combat soldiers: A head-to-head comparison of DSM-5 versus DSM-IV-TR symptom criteria with the PTSD checklist. *Lancet Psychiatry, 1*(4), 269–277.

Hoge, C. W., Yehuda, R., Castro, C. A., McFarlane, A. C., Vermetten, E., Jetly, R., & Rothbaum, B. O. (2016). Unintended consequences of changing the definition of post-traumatic stress disorder in DSM-5: Critique and call for action. *JAMA Psychiatry, 73*(7), 750−752.

Institute of Medicine (2008). *Treatment of posttraumatic stress disorder: An assessment of the evidence.* Washington, DC: Institute of Medicine.

Kessler, R. C., Sonnega, A., Hughes, M., & Nelson, C. B. (1995). Posttraumatic stress disorder in the national comorbidity survey. *Archives of General Psychiatry, 52*, 1048−1060.

Kilpatrick, D. G., Koenen, K. C., Ruggiero, K. J., Acierno, R., Galea, S., Resnick, H. S., & Gelernter, J. (2007). The serotonin transporter genotype and social support and moderation of posttraumatic stress disorder and depression in hurricane-exposed adults. *American Journal of Psychiatry, 164*(11), 1693−1699.

Kilpatrick, D. G., Resnick, H. S., Milanak, M. E., Miller, M. W., Keyes, K. M., & Friedman, M. J. (2013). National estimates of exposure to traumatic events and PTSD prevalence using DSM-IV and DSM-5 criteria. *Journal of Traumatic Stress, 26*(5), 537−547.

Koenen, K. C., Duncan, L. E., Liberzon, I., & Ressler, K. J. (2013). From candidate genes to genome-wide association: The challenges and promise of posttraumatic stress disorder genetic studies. *Biological Psychiatry, 74*(9), 634−636.

Koopman, C., Classen, C., Cardena, E., & Spiegel, D. (1995). When disaster strikes, acute stress disorder may follow. *Journal of Traumatic Stress, 8*(1), 29−46.

Kornør, H., Winje, D., Ekeberg, Ø., Weisaeth, L., Kirkehei, I., Johansen, K., & Steiro, A. (2008). Early trauma-focused cognitive-behavioural therapy to prevent chronic post-traumatic stress disorder and related symptoms: A systematic review and meta-analysis. *BMC Psychiatry, 8*, 81.

Lee, H. J., Lee, M. S., Kang, R. H., Kim, H., Yim, S. D., Kee, B. S., & Paik, I. H. (2005). Influence of the serotonin transporter promoter gene polymorphism on susceptibility to posttraumatic stress disorder. *Depression and Anxiety, 21*(3), 135−139.

Lesch, K. P., Bengel, D., Heils, A., Sabol, S. Z., Greenberg, B. D., Petri, S., & Murphy, D. L. (1996). Association of anxiety-related traits with a polymorphism in the serotonin transporter gene regulatory region. *Science, 274*, 1527−1531.

Litz, B. T., Salters-Pedneault, K., Steenkamp, M. M., Hermos, J. A., Bryant, R. A., Otto, M. W., & Hofmann, S. G. (2012). A randomized placebo-controlled trial of D-cycloserine and exposure therapy for posttraumatic stress disorder. *Journal of Psychiatric Research, 46*(9), 1184−1190.

Lommen, M. J., Engelhard, I. M., Sijbrandij, M., van den Hout, M. A., & Hermans, D. (2013). Pre-trauma individual differences in extinction learning predict posttraumatic stress. *Behaviour Research and Therapy, 51*(2), 63−67.

Macklin, M. L., Metzger, L. J., Litz, B. T., McNally, R. J., Lasko, N. B., Orr, S. P., & Pitman, R. K. (1998). Lower precombat intelligence is a risk factor for posttraumatic stress disorder. *Journal of Consulting and Clinical Psychology, 66*(2), 323−326.

Maercker, A., Brewin, C. R., Bryant, R. A., Cloitre, M., van Ommeren, M., Jones, L. M., & Reed, G. M. (2013). Diagnosis and classification of disorders specifically associated with stress: Proposals for ICD-11. *World Psychiatry, 12*(3), 198−206.

McDonagh, A., Friedman, M., McHugo, G., Ford, J., Sengupta, A., Mueser, K., & Descamps, M. (2005). Randomized trial of cognitive-behavioral therapy for chronic posttraumatic stress disorder in adult female survivors of childhood sexual abuse. *Journal of Consulting and Clinical Psychology, 73*(3), 515−524.

McNally, R. J. (1999). Research on eye movement desensitization and reprocessing (EMDR) as a treatment for PTSD. *Research Quarterly of the National Center for PTSD, 10*(1), 1−7.

Milad, M. R., Rauch, S. L., Pitman, R. K., & Quirk, G. J. (2006). Fear extinction in rats: Implications for human brain imaging and anxiety disorders. *Biological Psychology, 73*(1), 61−71.

III. PROBLEM-FOCUSED APPROACHES

Murray, J., Ehlers, A., & Mayou, R. A. (2002). Dissociation and post-traumatic stress disorder: Two prospective studies of road traffic accident survivors. *British Journal of Psychiatry, 180*, 363–368.

Nacasch, N., Huppert, J. D., Su, Y. J., Kivity, Y., Dinshtein, Y., Yeh, R., & Foa, E. B. (2015). Are 60-minute prolonged exposure sessions with 20-minute imaginal exposure to traumatic memories sufficient to successfully treat PTSD? A randomized noninferiority clinical trial. *Behavior Therapy, 46*(3), 328–341.

National Institute of Clinical Excellence (2005). *The management of PTSD in adults and children in primary and secondary care.* NICE: Wiltshire.

Neuner, F., Schauer, M., Klaschik, C., Karunakara, U., & Elbert, T. (2004). A comparison of narrative exposure therapy, supportive counseling, and psychoeducation for treating posttraumatic stress disorder in an African refugee settlement. *Journal of Consulting Clinical Psychology, 72*(4), 579–587.

Nijdam, M. J., Gersons, B. P., Reitsma, J. B., de Jongh, A., & Olff, M. (2012). Brief eclectic psychotherapy v. eye movement desensitisation and reprocessing therapy for post-traumatic stress disorder: Randomised controlled trial. *British Journal of Psychiatry, 200*(3), 224–231.

Norris, F. H., Tracy, M., & Galea, S. (2009). Looking for resilience: Understanding the longitudinal trajectories of responses to stress. *Social Science and Medicine, 68*(12), 2190–2198.

O'Connell, M. J., Kasprow, W., & Rosenheck, R. A. (2008). Rates and risk factors for homelessness after successful housing in a sample of formerly homeless veterans. *Psychiatric Services, 59*(3), 268–275.

O'Donnell, M. L., Alkemade, N., Nickerson, A., Creamer, M., McFarlane, A. C., Silove, D., & Forbes, D. (2014). Impact of the diagnostic changes to post-traumatic stress disorder for DSM-5 and the proposed changes to ICD-11. *British Journal of Psychiatry, 205*(3), 230–235.

Olff, M., Langeland, W., Draijer, N., & Gersons, B. P. R. (2007). Gender differences in posttraumatic stress disorder. *Psychological Bulletin, 133*(2), 183–204.

Orr, S. P., Lasko, N. B., Macklin, M. L., Pineles, S. L., Chang, Y., & Pitman, R. K. (2012). Predicting post-trauma stress symptoms from pre-trauma psychophysiologic reactivity, personality traits and measures of psychopathology. *Biology of Mood and Anxiety Disorders, 2*(1), 8.

Orr, S. P., Metzger, L. J., Lasko, N. B., Macklin, M. L., Hu, F. B., Shalev, A. Y., & Yehuda, R. (2003). Physiologic responses to sudden, loud tones in monozygotic twins discordant for combat exposure: Association with posttraumatic stress disorder. *Archives of General Psychiatry, 60*(3), 283–288.

Pitman, R. K., Orr, S. P., Forgue, D. F., de Jong, J. T., & Claiborn, J. (1987). Psychophysiologic assessment of posttraumatic stress disorder imagery in Vietnam combat veterans. *Archives of General Psychiatry, 44*(11), 970–975.

Pitman, R. K., Orr, S. P., Lowenhagen, M. J., Macklin, M. L., et al. (1991). Pre-Vietnam contents of posttraumatic stress disorder veterans' service medical and personnel records. *Comprehensive Psychiatry, 32*(5), 416–422.

Rauch, S. L., Shin, L. M., & Phelps, E. A. (2006). Neurocircuitry models of posttraumatic stress disorder and extinction: Human neuroimaging research — Past, present, and future. *Biological Psychiatry, 60*(4), 376–382.

Resick, P. A., Bovin, M. J., Calloway, A. L., Dick, A. M., King, M. W., Mitchell, K. S., & Wolf, E. J. (2012). A critical evaluation of the complex PTSD literature: Implications for DSM-5. *Journal of Traumatic Stress, 25*(3), 241–251.

Resick, P. A., Galovski, T. E., O'Brien Uhlmansiek, M., Scher, C. D., Clum, G. A., & Young-Xu, Y. (2008). A randomized clinical trial to dismantle components of cognitive processing therapy for posttraumatic stress disorder in female victims of interpersonal violence. *Journal of Consulting and Clinical Psychology, 76*(2), 243–258.

Riggs, D. S., Rothbaum, B. O., & Foa, E. B. (1995). A prospective examination of symptoms of posttraumatic stress disorder in victims of nonsexual assault. *Journal of Interpersonal Violence, 10*(2), 201–214.

Roberts, N. P., Kitchiner, N. J., Kenardy, J., & Bisson, J. I. (2009). Systematic review and meta-analysis of multiple-session early interventions following traumatic events. *American Journal of Psychiatry, 166*(3), 293–301.

Rona, R. J., Jones, M., Iversen, A., Hull, L., Greenberg, N., Fear, N. T., & Wessely, S. (2009). The impact of posttraumatic stress disorder on impairment in the UK military at the time of the Iraq war. *Journal of Psychiatric Research, 43*(6), 649–655.

Rothbaum, B. O., Foa, E. B., Riggs, D. S., Murdock, T., & Walsh, W. (1992). A prospective examination of post-traumatic stress disorder in rape victims. *Journal of Traumatic Stress, 5*(3), 455–475.

Sala, M., Perez, J., Soloff, P., di Nemi, S. U., Caverzasi, E., Soares, J. C., & Brambilla, P. (2004). Stress and hippocampal abnormalities in psychiatric disorders. *European Neuropsychopharmacology, 14*(5), 393–405.

Saxena, S., Thornicroft, G., Knapp, M., & Whiteford, H. (2007). Resources for mental health: Scarcity, inequity, and inefficiency. *Lancet, 370*(9590), 878–889.

Sayers, S. L., Farrow, V. A., Ross, J., & Oslin, D. W. (2009). Family problems among recently returned military veterans referred for a mental health evaluation. *Journal of Clinical Psychiatry, 70*(2), 163–170.

Schnurr, P. P., Friedman, M. J., Foy, D. W., Shea, M. T., Hsieh, F. Y., Lavori, P. W., & Bernardy, N. C. (2003). Randomized trial of trauma-focused group therapy for post-traumatic stress disorder: Results from a Department of Veterans Affairs cooperative study. *Archives of General Psychiatry, 60*(5), 481–489.

Schnurr, P. P., Friedman, M. J., & Rosenberg, S. D. (1993). Preliminary MMPI scores as predictors of combat-related PTSD symptoms. *American Journal of Psychiatry, 150*(3), 479–483.

Schnurr, P. P., Hayes, A. F., Lunney, C. A., McFall, M., & Uddo, M. (2006). Longitudinal analysis of the relationship between symptoms and quality of life in veterans treated for posttraumatic stress disorder. *Journal of Consulting and Clinical Psychology, 74*(4), 707–713.

Shalev, A. Y., Ankri, Y., Israeli-Shalev, Y., Peleg, T., Adessky, R., & Freedman, S. (2012). Prevention of posttraumatic stress disorder by early treatment: Results from the Jerusalem trauma outreach and prevention study. *Archives of General Psychiatry, 69*(2), 166–176.

Shalev, A. Y., Sahar, T., Freedman, S., Peri, T., Glick, N., Brandes, D., & Pitman, R. K. (1998). A prospective study of heart rate response following trauma and the subsequent development of posttraumatic stress disorder. *Archives of General Psychiatry, 55*(6), 553–559.

Shapiro, F. (1995). *Eye movement desensitization and reprocessing: Basic principles, protocols, and procedures*. New York: Guilford.

Shin, L. M., & Liberzon, I. (2010). The neurocircuitry of fear, stress, and anxiety disorders. *Neuropsychopharmacology, 35*(1), 169–191.

Shucard, J. L., Cox, J., Shucard, D. W., Fetter, H., Chung, C., Ramasamy, D., & Violanti, J. (2012). Symptoms of posttraumatic stress disorder and exposure to traumatic stressors are related to brain structural volumes and behavioral measures of affective stimulus processing in police officers. *Psychiatry Research, 204*(1), 25–31.

Sijbrandij, M., Olff, M., Reitsma, J. B., Carlier, I. V. E., de Vries, M. H., & Gersons, B. P. R. (2007). Treatment of acute posttraumatic stress disorder with brief cognitive behavioral therapy: A randomized controlled trial. *American Journal of Psychiatry, 164*(1), 82–90.

Smith, K., & Bryant, R. A. (2000). The generality of cognitive bias in acute stress disorder. *Behaviour Research and Therapy, 38*(7), 709–715.

III. PROBLEM-FOCUSED APPROACHES

Steel, Z., Chey, T., Silove, D., Marnane, C., Bryant, R. A., & van Ommeren, M. (2009). Association of torture and other potentially traumatic events with mental health outcomes among populations exposed to mass conflict and displacement: A systematic review and meta-analysis. *JAMA, 302*(5), 537–549.

Stein, M. B., Walker, J. R., Hazen, A. L., & Forde, D. R. (1997). Full and partial posttraumatic stress disorder: Findings from a community survey. *American Journal of Psychiatry, 154*(8), 1114–1119.

Sundermann, O., Hauschildt, M., & Ehlers, A. (2013). Perceptual processing during trauma, priming and the development of intrusive memories. *Journal of Behavior Therapy and Experimental Psychiatry, 44*(2), 213–220.

True, W. R., Rice, J., Eisen, S. A., Heath, A. C., Goldberg, J., Lyons, M. G., & Nowak, J. (1993). A twin study of genetic and environmental contributions to liability for posttraumatic stress symptoms. *Archives of General Psychiatry, 50*, 257–264.

Vaiva, G., Boss, V., Ducrocq, F., Fontaine, M., Devos, P., Brunet, A., & Thomas, P. (2006). Relationship between posttrauma GABA plasma levels and PTSD at 1-year follow-up. *American Journal of Psychiatry, 163*(8), 1446–1448.

van Griensven, F., Chakkraband, M. L. S., Thienkrua, W., Pengjuntr, W., Cardozo, B. L., Tantipiwatanaskul, P., & Tappero, J. W. (2006). Mental health problems among adults in tsunami-affected areas in southern Thailand. *Journal of the American Medical Association, 296*(5), 537–548.

Warda, G., & Bryant, R. A. (1998). Cognitive bias in acute stress disorder. *Behaviour Research and Therapy, 36*(12), 1177–1183.

Yehuda, R., Golier, J. A., Tischler, L., Harvey, P. D., Newmark, R., Yang, R. K., & Buchsbaum, M. S. (2007). Hippocampal volume in aging combat veterans with and without post-traumatic stress disorder: Relation to risk and resilience factors. *Journal of Psychiatric Research, 41*(5), 435–445.

Zlotnick, C., Franklin, C. L., & Zimmerman, M. (2002). Does "subthreshold" posttraumatic stress disorder have any clinical relevance? *Comprehensive Psychiatry, 43*(6), 413–419.

Further Reading

Gadermann, A. M., Alonso, J., Vilagut, G., Zaslavsky, A. M., & Kessler, R. C. (2012). Comorbidity and disease burden in the National Comorbidity Survey Replication (NCS-R). *Depression and Anxiety, 29*(9), 797 –806.

14

Eating Disorders: Transdiagnostic Theory and Treatment

Zafra Cooper[1,2] and Riccardo D. Grave[3]

[1]University of Oxford, Oxford, United Kingdom [2]Yale University Medical School, New Haven, CT, United States [3]Villa Garda Hospital, Garda, Italy

INTRODUCTION

The eating disorders, anorexia nervosa, bulimia nervosa, binge eating disorder, and their variants are serious disorders that are accompanied by significant impairment in physical and psychological functioning as well as in quality of life. They typically begin in adolescence and may run a chronic course; once established they are difficult to treat. They are less common among men than women and represent a significant source of morbidity among adolescent girls and young women in particular. Both anorexia nervosa and bulimia nervosa are associated with increased mortality, and binge eating disorder is associated with an increased risk of obesity. Despite the existence of evidence supported specialist interventions for eating disorders, there is a well-documented unmet need for treatment. Eating disorders are often undetected and even when they come to attention they may not receive appropriate treatment.

CLASSIFICATION AND DIAGNOSIS

Current Scheme for Classification and Diagnosis

The Diagnostic and Statistical Manual of Mental Disorders, 5th edition (DSM-5) scheme for classifying and diagnosing eating disorders

The Science of Cognitive Behavioral Therapy.
DOI: http://dx.doi.org/10.1016/B978-0-12-803457-6.00014-3

recognizes three specific disorders, anorexia nervosa, bulimia nervosa, and binge eating disorder. In addition, there are two residual categories "other specified feeding or eating disorder" and "unspecified feeding or eating disorder" (American Psychiatric Association, 2013). Although there are differences between the clinical presentations of these disorders in terms of their exact symptom patterns and weight status, they share a distinctive core psychopathology that is essentially cognitive in nature. This psychopathology, the overevaluation of shape, and weight and their control, refers to patients' tendency to judge their self-worth largely or even exclusively in terms of weight and shape and their ability to control them. It is shared across anorexia nervosa and bulimia nervosa and occurs in the majority of those with binge eating disorder and the other eating disorders identified in the DSM-5. This core psychopathology is essentially the same in females and males, adults and adolescents. It occurs uniquely in the eating disorders and is rarely seen in the general population.

The Transdiagnostic Perspective

As was the case with earlier versions of the diagnostic criteria, the DSM-5 regards anorexia nervosa, bulimia nervosa and binge eating disorder as distinct clinical states and, as such, suggests that each requires its own form of treatment.

One major concern about the clinical utility of DSM-IV, the predecessor of DSM-5 was the existence of the large residual category of clinically significant eating disorders "not otherwise specified." The majority of eating disorders were thus being classified within a heterogeneous category with little clinical utility. A further concern was that both the observation of the overlapping clinical features of the various disorders and knowledge of their temporal course did little to provide evidence to support the notion that they were sufficiently distinct to constitute separate diagnostic categories. Changes made in DSM-5 were, in most part, designed to reduce the large residual category. Early indications suggest that the inclusion of binge eating disorder as a specific diagnosis and the broadening of the criteria for anorexia nervosa and bulimia nervosa have succeeded in, at most, halving the residual category (Machado, Gonçalves, & Hoek, 2013; Mancuso et al., 2015), although it has been questioned whether the further objections relating to the shared clinical features of the eating disorders and their temporal instability (Ekeroth, Clinton, Norring, & Birgegård, 2013; Smink, van Hoeken, & Hoek, 2013) have been met. Although future research will contribute to assessing the clinical utility of the DSM-5 categories, it is worth also considering an alternative perspective.

In contrast to the DSM, the transdiagnostic perspective focuses on the common features of the eating disorders. Two major considerations support such a perspective. The eating disorders share a distinctive core psychopathology not seen in other psychiatric disorders. This is the overevaluation of shape and weight and their control and according to the cognitive behavioral model it is this distinguishing feature that is of central importance in maintaining the eating disorders (see below). Second studies of the course of the various eating disorders have suggested that, over time, patients moved between the various DSM-IV categories. Research to date suggests that approximately half of those who initially received a diagnosis of anorexia nervosa subsequently met diagnostic criteria for bulimia nervosa and a substantial minority of those with the residual "not otherwise specified disorders" had met criteria for anorexia nervosa and bulimia nervosa in the past. A recent review of studies of the course and outcome of anorexia nervosa and bulimia nervosa showed that no significant differences exist whether DSM-IV or DSM-5 definitions are used, while noting that much less is known about the course and outcome of binge eating disorder (Smink et al., 2013). If this temporal movement between the eating disorders continues to be the norm, it does call into question the claim that these various forms of disorder are indeed separate and distinct states.

The transdiagnostic perspective proposes that the various DSM eating disorders may be maintained by shared processes. The implications of this view are that it would be possible to understand the persistence of these disorders within a unified transdiagnostic theory. Were this to be correct, a treatment developed on the basis of this theory and capable of addressing these maintaining processes should be successful with the full range of eating disorders.

THE TRANSDIAGNOSTIC COGNITIVE BEHAVIORAL THEORY

The cognitive behavioral approach to the understanding and treatment bulimia nervosa was first developed in the early 1980s (Fairburn, Cooper, & Cooper, 1986). Since these early beginnings, the treatment has been theory based and concerned with the processes that maintain the disorder rather than with an account of its development. Subsequently the cognitive behavioral account of the maintenance of bulimia nervosa was enhanced and extended in two major respects: It was extended to cover all eating disorders and to embrace four additional maintaining processes that, in certain patients, interact with the core eating disorder maintaining mechanisms and constitute obstacles to change (Cooper & Fairburn, 2011; Fairburn, Cooper, & Shafran, 2003).

Core Maintaining Processes

According to the cognitive behavioral view, it is the distinctive scheme of self-evaluation shared by patients with eating disorders that is of central importance in maintaining these disorders. Other clinical features can be understood as stemming directly from this "core psychopathology," including the extreme weight-control behavior (e.g., strict dieting, self-induced vomiting, laxative and diuretic misuse, and driven exercising), the various forms of body weight and shape checking and avoidance, and the preoccupation with thoughts about eating, weight, and shape. The one prominent feature that is not obviously a direct expression of the core psychopathology is binge eating, which occurs in many patients with eating disorders whatever their DSM diagnosis. The cognitive behavioral theory proposes that binge eating is largely maintained by attempts to adhere to extreme dietary rules. Patients' tendency to react in a negative and extreme (often, dichotomous) fashion to the almost inevitable breaking of these rules results in even minor dietary slips being interpreted as evidence of poor self-control and personal weakness. The response to this perceived lack of self-control is a temporary abandonment of efforts to restrict eating, and thus these attempts are repeatedly interrupted by episodes of binge eating. This binge eating maintains the core psychopathology by intensifying patients' concerns about their ability to control their eating, shape, and weight and encourages further dietary restraint, thereby increasing the risk of further binge eating. Three further processes also contribute to and maintain binge eating. First, life difficulties and associated mood changes increase the likelihood that patients will break their dietary rules. Second, since binge eating temporarily ameliorates such mood states and distracts patients from thinking about their difficulties, it can become a way of coping with these difficulties. Third, if the binge eating is followed by compensatory vomiting or laxative misuse, this also maintains binge eating because patients' mistaken belief in the effectiveness of such "purging" in preventing energy absorption removes a major deterrent to binge eating.

For those patients who would receive a DSM diagnosis of anorexia nervosa, binge eating may be mainly subjective in nature, or not present at all. Most important is that undereating predominates and patients become underweight. Extremely low weight has certain secondary physiological and psychological consequences that themselves perpetuate undereating. For example, delayed gastric emptying results in a sense of fullness, even after eating modest amounts of food, and the secondary social withdrawal that often occurs magnifies patients' isolation from the influence of others. The core processes involved in the maintenance of eating disorders are shown in the shaded sections of

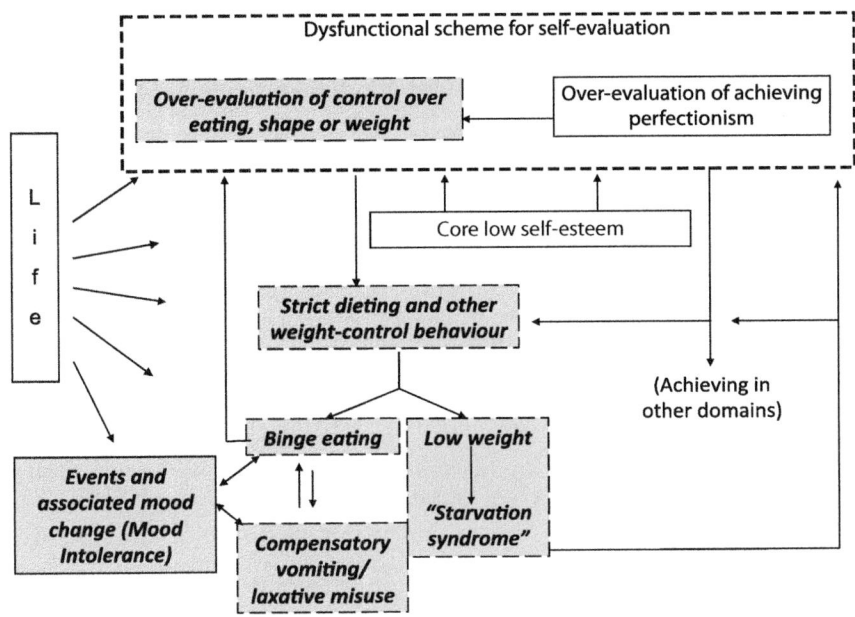

FIGURE 14.1 **The enhanced transdiagnostic cognitive behavioral theory.** "Life" is an abbreviation for interpersonal difficulties. "Mood intolerance" has been assimilated into the core theory. Source: *Adapted from Fairburn, C.G., Cooper, Z., & Shafran, R. (2003). Cognitive behaviour therapy for eating disorders: A "transdiagnostic" theory and treatment. Behaviour Research and Therapy, 41(5), 509—528. http://dx.doi.org/10.1016/S0005-7967(02)00088-8.*

the "transdiagnostic" representation (or "formulation") in Fig. 14.1. [Please note that "Mood intolerance" (shaded box with solid line) is now included in the core theory and treatment as "events and associated mood change" although it was originally one of the additional maintaining processes described below.]

Additional Maintaining Processes

As noted, the enhanced transdiagnostic theory includes four additional maintaining processes that in some patients interact with the core eating disorder maintaining mechanisms. When this occurs they constitute further obstacles to change. These maintaining mechanisms concern: the influence of extreme perfectionism ("clinical perfectionism"); the difficulty coping with intense mood states ("mood intolerance"); the impact of unconditional and pervasive low self-esteem ("core low self-esteem"), and marked interpersonal problems ("interpersonal difficulties"). Fig. 14.1 shows the four hypothesized additional mechanisms together with the core maintaining processes including "Mood intolerance," subsequently incorporated in the core theory and treatment as "events and associated mood change" (see Fig. 14.1).

Clinical Perfectionism

This is seen as an example of a dysfunctional system for self-evaluation much like the "core psychopathology" of eating disorders. In essence, clinical perfectionism refers to the overevaluation of the striving for, and achievement of, personally demanding standards, despite adverse consequences. When present, these demanding standards are applied to eating, weight, and shape and their control thereby intensifying aspects of the eating disorder.

Mood Intolerance

This is defined as either an inability to tolerate intense mood states or a particular sensitivity to such states. In those with mood intolerance, binge eating, vomiting, and driven exercising are further maintained by their role as means of modulating or controlling such moods. Mood intolerance is now included in the core theory and treatment as "events and associated mood change" (see Fig. 14.1).

Core Low Self-Esteem

This creates hopelessness about the capacity to change, thereby undermining patients' compliance with treatment and results in patients pursuing achievement in valued domains, in this case control over eating, shape, and weight, with particular determination.

Interpersonal Difficulties

These difficulties are seen as contributing further to the maintenance of disorder. Examples include family tensions intensifying resistance to eating, especially in younger patients; certain interpersonal environments (both occupational and familial) magnifying concerns about controlling eating, shape, and weight; adverse interpersonal events commonly precipitating episodes of binge eating and long-term interpersonal difficulties undermining self-esteem and leading patients to strive even harder to achieve valued goals such as success at controlling eating, shape, and weight. There is also evidence that disturbed interpersonal functioning predicts a poor response to treatment.

The transdiagnostic cognitive behavioral theory represents the range of processes that maintain any eating disorder whatever its exact form or DSM diagnosis. In some eating disorder presentations, only a limited number of these processes will be active (e.g., in binge eating disorder), whereas for others many more will be active (e.g., in anorexia nervosa with binge eating, purging and accompanying perfectionism).

The theory highlights the processes that need to be tackled in treatment, thereby providing a guide to its individualization.

RESEARCH EVIDENCE FOR THE TRANSDIAGNOSTIC THEORY

There are several sources of direct support for the transdiagnostic theory. Considerable research evidence supports the cognitive view of the maintenance of eating disorders including descriptive, comparative, and experimental studies of the clinical characteristics of these patients (Grilo, 2013; Shafran, Lee, Cooper, Palmer, & Fairburn, 2007; Shafran, Lee, Payne, & Fairburn, 2007; Watson, Raykos, Street, Fursland, & Nathan, 2011). For patients with bulimia nervosa, the relationship between the overevaluation of weight and shape and changes in dietary restraint and binge eating over time have been demonstrated (Fairburn, Stice, et al., 2003); binge eating has been shown to be related to self-reported calorie restriction (Zunker et al., 2011); associations between increased weight concerns and increased restraint and vomiting frequency (Spangler, Baldwin, & Agras, 2004) have been reported; and a reduction in dietary restraint during treatment has been shown to mediate a subsequent reduction in binge eating (Wilson, Fairburn, Agras, Walsh, & Kraemer, 2002). In a more transdiagnostic sample (patients with both bulimia nervosa and anorexia nervosa), a reciprocal relationship has been demonstrated between overevaluation of weight and shape and moderate to extreme dietary restraint and exercising (Tabri et al., 2015).

Cross-sectional evaluations of the transdiagnostic model using structural equation modeling have been completed in treatment seeking patient samples and in community samples. The original cognitive behavioral theory was compared with the enhanced version (including the additional maintaining mechanisms) in patients with bulimia nervosa and atypical forms of the disorder with support being found for both models and the enhanced model accounting for a greater portion of the variance (Lampard, Byrne, McLean, & Fursland, 2011). However, the relationship between dietary restraint and binge eating was not supported. Two further evaluations have been undertaken in transdiagnostic samples, one consisting of referrals for intensive treatment to a tertiary center (Lampard, Tasca, Balfour, & Bissada, 2013; Tasca et al., 2011) and the other comparing the original and enhanced model in referrals to a number of specialist eating disorder centers across one particular country (Dakanalis et al., 2015). In both samples, there was broad support for the theory, although there were some differences between diagnostic groups in the degree of support for some of the relationships tested by the models, and restraint was only indirectly associated with binge eating. Community studies of male students, and women in the community have also provided support for the theory (Dakanalis, Timko, Clerici, Zanetti, & Riva, 2014; Hoiles, Egan, & Kane, 2012).

THE TRANSDIAGNOSTIC TREATMENT

Enhanced cognitive behavior therapy (CBT-E) is a transdiagnostic treatment for eating disorder psychopathology rather than for a particular eating disorder diagnosis. It is derived from the transdiagnostic theory outlined above, which highlights the maintaining processes that need to be addressed in treatment. It is a treatment for patients with an eating disorder of clinical severity and was originally designed as an individual treatment for adult outpatients irrespective of gender with a body mass index (BMI)[1] between 15.0 and 40.0. It has subsequently been adapted for use with younger patients and for more intensive use in outpatient, day patient and inpatient settings (including patients with a BMI below 15.0). Management of patients with a BMI over 40.0 has been addressed elsewhere (de Zwaan, 2010).

CBT-E was designed to be a complete treatment and was not intended to be combined with, or coexist with, other forms of therapy. It is a form of CBT and like many forms of empirically supported CBT it is a time-limited treatment concerned with processes that maintain the patient's psychopathology. It resembles other forms of CBT in style, in that it regards the establishment of a collaborative relationship between the therapist and patient as of paramount importance. However, although it uses a variety of generic cognitive behavioral strategies and procedures (e.g., the use of a formulation, self-monitoring, exploratory questioning, and strategies for addressing cognitive biases), CBT-E differs from other forms of CBT in not using conventional thought records or explicit "Socratic questioning" and in making very limited use of formal behavioral experiments.

Treatment is guided by a personalized formulation of the patient's difficulties, constructed at the beginning of treatment and revised as necessary as treatment progresses. It uses a number of well-specified strategies and procedures designed to target and disrupt the mechanisms maintaining the patient's disorder. This generally involves

---

[1]Body mass index (BMI) is a widely used method of assessing weight adjusted for height. It applies irrespective of gender to those between the ages of 18 and 60. It is calculated by weight in kilograms divided by height in meters squared (wt/ht^2). The healthy range is 18.5−25.0.

encouraging patients to make changes in the way they behave and then helping them to understand and reflect on the effects and implications of these changes. In this way, they learn to decenter from their eating problems and eventually to identify their eating disorder mindset and learn to control and manipulate it.

There are two versions of CBT-E, a "focused" version that exclusively addresses the core processes maintaining the eating disorder psychopathology and a "broad" version that also addresses one or more of the three additional hypothesized maintaining processes (mood intolerance has been incorporated into the focused version of the treatment). Both versions are transdiagnostic in scope with the first stage of treatment being identical and treatment diverging thereafter if there is a clinical need (see below).

In the following discussion, the two versions of CBT-E and its various modifications are discussed in outline only. Full clinical guides are provided elsewhere.

The Core Treatment

The core form of CBT-E is the focused version. It provides the basis for all other variants of the treatment. It is the version of CBT-E that is suitable to treat the vast majority of those with eating disorders provided that they can be safely managed as outpatients. For those patients who are not significantly underweight, generally a BMI equal to or above 18.5, treatment consists of 20 individual sessions over 20 weeks. The focused treatment is described in detail in the complete treatment guide (Fairburn, Cooper, Shafran, Bohn, Hawker, et al., 2008).

The 20-week treatment has four well-defined stages described in outline in Table 14.1.

CBT-E for Underweight Patients

The core treatment does not require major modifications to treat patients who are significantly underweight. As suggested earlier the core psychopathology of patients who are low in weight is very similar to that seen in the majority of patients who are not underweight.

However, it does need to take account of three problems in this group; the first and perhaps most important being the underweight that defines the group. Patients need to regain weight and to accommodate this treatment has to be extended (generally up to 40 weeks) with twice weekly sessions until the patient is consistently gaining weight. The other two problems: limited motivation to change and undereating (dietary restriction) are particularly acute in this group, although they may also occur in those who are not underweight.

TABLE 14.1   The Core Elements of the 20-Week Version of CBT-E

Stage 1

The aims are to engage the patient in treatment and change. Appointments are twice weekly for 4 weeks and involve the following:

- Jointly creating a formulation of the processes maintaining the eating disorder
- Establishing real time monitoring of eating and other relevant thoughts and behavior
- Educating about: body weight regulation and fluctuations; the physical complications of self-induced vomiting and laxative misuse as a means of weight control; the ineffectiveness of purging as a means of weight control and the adverse effects of dieting
- Introducing and establishing weekly in session weighing and becoming practiced in interpreting and coping with weight fluctuations
- Introducing and adhering to a pattern of regular eating with planned meals and snacks
- Involving significant others to facilitate treatment if appropriate

Stage 2

This is a transitional stage, generally involving two appointments, a week apart with the following elements:

- Collaborative reviewing of progress and compliance with treatment
- Identifying barriers to change, both general (e.g., work pressures) and features of the eating disorder itself (e.g., the presence of dietary restraint, not yet addressed)
- Modifying the initial formulation as needed in order to plan Stage 3
- Deciding to continue with the focused version of CBT-E rather than the broad version

Stage 3

The aim is to address the key mechanisms that are maintaining the patient's eating disorder. There are eight weekly appointments addressing:

- Overevaluation of shape and weight as follows: providing education about overevaluation and its consequences; developing previously marginalized domains of self-evaluation; reducing unhelpful body checking and avoidance; relabeling unhelpful thoughts or feelings such as "feeling fat;" exploring the origins of the overevaluation and learning to identify and control the eating disorder mindset
- Dietary restraint as follows: changing inflexible dietary rules into flexible guidelines and introducing previously avoided food
- Event and mood related changes in eating as follows: developing proactive problem solving skills to tackle such triggering events and developing skills to accept and modulate intense moods

Stage 4

The aims are to ensure that progress made in treatment is maintained and that the risk of relapse is minimized. There are three appointments, each 2 weeks apart covering the following:

- Addressing concerns about ending treatment
- Devising a short-term plan to continue to implement changes made in treatment (e.g., reducing body checking, introducing further avoided foods, eating more flexibly, maintaining involvement in new activities) until the post-treatment review session
- Phasing out treatment procedures, in particular self-monitoring and in-session weighing
- Education about realistic expectations and identifying and addressing setbacks
- Devising a long-term plan to cope with setbacks and minimize their occurrence

Posttreatment Review Session

There is a single appointment to review progress and, if necessary, revise the long-term maintenance plan around 20 weeks after treatment has finished

Attention to patients' general health and issues of safety is always of importance in treating eating disorders, but it is especially so in those whose physical health is compromised as it invariably is in patients who are underweight. Therapists need to be aware of such physical complications and be able to manage them or have access to those who can advise on medical management.

The treatment for underweight patients does not neatly map onto the four stages of the 20-week core treatment. The treatment guide also provides fuller details of the treatment for underweight patients (Fairburn, Cooper, Shafran, Bohn, Hawker, et al., 2008).

Briefly, treatment for these patients involves three major steps:

- *Step one.* The aim is to engage patients and help them arrive at the decision to regain weight as well as address the eating disorder psychopathology. This stage lasts up to 8 weeks and involves all of the elements of Stage 1 of the core treatment with the following modifications: provision of personalized education about the effects of being underweight before creating the formulation; emphasis on the role of low weight in maintaining the disorder and a focus on helping the patient make the decision to change and regain weight. If a decision to regain weight is not made, treatment does not proceed to step two and alternative treatment is considered.
- *Step two.* The focus is on achieving weight regain at the same time as addressing the key maintaining mechanisms as in Stage 3 of the core treatment. The goal is to help patients reach a body weight that can be maintained without dietary restriction, is not associated with the symptoms of being underweight, and permits a social life. For the majority of patients, these goals can be achieved with a BMI between 19.0 and 20.0. Once the patient is consistently gaining weight sessions are weekly.
- *Step three.* The aim is to help patients maintain their weight. This phase usually lasts for 8 weeks with appointments toward the end of treatment at intervals of 2 to 3 weeks. Ensuring that progress is maintained and that the risk of relapse is minimized are accomplished as in Stage 4 of the core treatment.

The Broad Version of CBT-E

The focused version of CBT-E is the default version suitable for the vast majority of patients. The decision to use the broad version of CBT-E is made in Stage 2 when the patient and therapist review the progress made during Stage 1. By this time, the therapist has generally gained an understanding of the likely barriers to change. In line with clinical experience and the currently available research evidence (see below), it is only recommended that the broad version of CBT-E be used if, at the Stage 2 review, clinical perfectionism, low self-esteem or interpersonal difficulties are marked, and appear to be maintaining the disorder and obstructing change.

Once the decision has been made to include one of broad modules, Stage 3 of treatment involves addressing both the eating disorder psychopathology and the selected external feature, essentially halving the time allocated to addressing the eating disorder psychopathology at this stage in treatment.

The contents of the three additional modules are described in outline only; greater detail and suggested further reading are available in the treatment guide (Fairburn, Cooper, Shafran, Bohn, & Hawker, 2008).

Clinical Perfectionism

Clinical perfectionism may be evident from early on in treatment. For example, there may be multiple, particularly rigid rules governing eating making it difficult to establish regular eating. The strategy for addressing clinical perfectionism mirrors that used to address the overevaluation of shape and weight, and the two are addressed in concert as part of tackling an overall scheme for self-evaluation. Addressing clinical perfectionism involves the following: providing education about overevaluation of achieving and achievement and its consequences; developing previously marginalized domains and/or new domains of self-evaluation; reducing unhelpful performance checking and avoidance of crucial tests of performance; exploring the origins of the overevaluation of achieving and achievement; and learning to manipulate the perfectionist mindset.

Low Self-Esteem

Low self-esteem is common in patients with eating disorders and may not necessarily obstruct treatment of the disorder; in many patients, it improves with successful treatment. Core low self-esteem is usually evident from the outset as patients tend to be excessively self-critical and tend to discount their achievements and positive qualities.

Core low self-esteem can be addressed in two ways: directly using the cognitive behavioral techniques of this module or indirectly by enhancing interpersonal functioning using the module designed to do this (see below). If time allows, as it may do in the longer form of the treatment, both of these potentially complementary modules may be used.

The strategy for addressing low self-esteem directly involves the following: providing personalized education about the processes maintaining low self-esteem; identifying and addressing the cognitive biases that maintain the low self-esteem (e.g., discounting positive qualities, selective attention to negative information, and different standards for judging themselves); exploring the origins of the low self-esteem using a historical review and helping patients to arrive at a more balanced view of their self-worth and acting in accordance with it.

Interpersonal Difficulties

Many patients with eating disorders have interpersonal difficulties. Generally these lessen with improvements in the eating disorder. If such problems are isolated, they may be addressed with problem solving and work on mood intolerance, but if they are recurrent and interfering with treatment, they may need to be become an additional focus of treatment.

Unlike the other additional modules, interpersonal difficulties are not addressed using CBT but with interpersonal psychotherapy (IPT) (Weissman, Markowitz, & Klerman, 2000). IPT is an empirically supported psychological treatment designed to improve interpersonal functioning that was originally devised for the treatment of clinical depression but was subsequently shown to be an evidence supported treatment for bulimia nervosa (Agras, Walsh, Fairburn, Wilson, & Kraemer, 2000; Fairburn, Jones, Hope, O'Connor, & Peveler, 1993).

IPT and CBT-E are two different psychological treatments with major procedural differences especially in terms of therapist style. In IPT, the therapist is active in encouraging patients to think about interpersonal problems but not directive as in CBT-E and therefore does not suggest solutions or particular courses of action. Because of these differences the two treatments are not integrated; rather there is a brief IPT session embedded within the CBT-E session. The module involves the following: describing the rationale for addressing interpersonal problems; identifying and agreeing one or more interpersonal problems as the focus of treatment; charactering the problems within the four overarching problem areas (grief, role transitions, interpersonal disputes, and interpersonal deficits); using generic and problem specific IPT strategies to address these and ensuring that interpersonal changes are maintained.

CBT-E for Younger Patients

A number of considerations support the view that CBT-E might be particularly suitable for younger patients: The clinical features are very similar to those seen in adults; evidence supporting the use of CBT for other disorders in young people suggests that treatment of this style is likely to be suitable; the treatment is designed to enhance patients' sense of control, an area of concern for many young patients; and CBT-E has well specified ways of enhancing motivation, an issue of particular relevance for adolescent patients. The transdiagnostic nature of the treatment is also an advantage as the limited research to date on the treatment of adolescents has focused on anorexia nervosa and, as with adults, the majority of young patients have other eating disorders, especially those likely to fall within the residual diagnostic categories (Flament et al., 2015; Le Grange, Swanson, Crow, & Merikangas, 2012).

CBT-E for adolescents is very similar in most respects to the treatment for adults. The content of treatment is essentially the same with much the same reliance on individual treatment with a single therapist. Treatment does tend to be shorter, as change often occurs more quickly (e.g., with underweight patients 30 sessions may well be sufficient rather than the 40 more typical for adult patients). More detailed clinical information is available from two sources (Cooper & Stewart, 2008; Dalle Grave, Calugi, Doll, & Fairburn, 2013).

One major modification concerns parental involvement. Given the patients' age range and circumstances, parental involvement is almost invariably necessary. Parental involvement usually comprises a single assessment session with the parents alone within the first 2 weeks of treatment and then, through treatment, a series of brief (15–20 min) joint sessions with the patient and parent that take place immediately after an individual session, the exact number of which varies with the particular nature of the patient's difficulties. The aim of joint sessions with parents and patients is to inform parents about the nature of the eating problem and the treatment being provided; provide a rationale for treatment interventions and an update on progress, and, most importantly, encourage parents to facilitate the young person's efforts to change by supporting the one-to-one treatment as individually appropriate and with the consent and co-operation of the young person.

CBT-E in Intensive Settings

The rationale for extending CBT-E to intensive treatment settings is based on the premise that some patients' lack of progress in treatment may not be due to the inappropriateness of the treatment itself but the need for it to be provided in a more intense form. Two forms of intensive CBT-E have been developed, one being inpatient and day patient-based and the other being a more intensive form of outpatient treatment.

Inpatient CBT-E is designed to ensure a unified, rather than eclectic, approach to the patient's treatment. The program, described in detail elsewhere (Dalle Grave, Bohn, Hawker, & Fairburn, 2008; Dalle Grave, 2013), includes all the main strategies and procedures of CBT-E. Three main features distinguish it from the outpatient version of the treatment. First, a multidisciplinary team of physicians, psychologists, dieticians, and nurses, all fully trained in CBT-E, deliver the treatment. Second, assistance with eating is provided in situ during the first weeks of treatment. Third, although treatment is largely individual, some elements are administered in a group format.

Inpatient CBT-E also includes a number of additional elements designed to reduce the high rate of relapse that typically follows discharge from hospital. Patients are free to leave the hospital as they wish and so they continue to be exposed to the environmental stimuli that tend to provoke their eating disorder psychopathology while at the same time having access to staff support. During the weeks immediately preceding discharge, a concerted effort is made to identify likely environmental triggers of setbacks, which are addressed during individual CBT-E sessions. Also, significant others are helped to create a positive, stress-free environment in readiness for the patient's return home. Perhaps the most important relapse-prevention measure is that inpatient treatment is always followed by stepped-down outpatient CBT-E-based treatment and so a therapist is still available to support and monitor the patient through a potentially difficult transitional phase.

Intensive outpatient CBT-E is designed for patients who may need greater input than outpatient CBT-E can provide, but whose condition is not sufficiently severe to warrant hospitalization. This form of treatment uses all of the procedures and strategies of outpatient CBT-E but also includes several features developed specifically for this group (Dalle Grave et al., 2008; Dalle Grave, 2012, 2013). Intensive treatment lasts for a maximum of 12 weeks but may be shorter if patients successfully make progress in the areas where they were struggling in outpatient CBT-E (examples include lack of progress in weight regain, reducing binge eating, introducing regular meals). It includes the following procedures, on weekdays: supervised daily meals; individual CBT-E twice weekly; sessions with a CBT-E trained dietitian to plan and review weekend meals; and regular reviews with a CBT-E trained physician. The clinical team responsible for such patients meets weekly to monitor each patient's progress. Toward the end of intensive treatment, patients who have responded well are gradually encouraged to eat meals outside the unit, thereby allowing the treatment to evolve into conventional outpatient CBT-E.

RESEARCH EVIDENCE FOR THE TRANSDIAGNOSTIC TREATMENT

CBT-E has been shown to have a wide clinical range. The first controlled trial of CBT-E in a transdiagnostic sample (BMI > 17.5 and < 40.0) compared the broad and focused forms of the treatment with a delayed treatment group in a large two center study (Fairburn et al., 2009). Although the patients in the delayed treatment exhibited little change, those receiving the two active treatments experienced substantial and equivalent change. With those patients for whom at least two of the four original additional mechanisms were judged to be a clinical problem at the beginning of Stage 2 of treatment, the broad form of treatment was superior to the focused form. For the remaining patients, the focused form was superior to the broad form. In another comparison of the focused and broad versions of CBT-E, no differences were found in a sample of adults receiving inpatient treatment for anorexia nervosa (Dalle Grave, Calugi, Conti, Doll, & Fairburn, 2013). The broad and focused versions of the treatment were compared in a relatively small disorder specific sample of patients with bulimia nervosa and threshold or subthreshold borderline personality disorder. Results favored the focused form of treatment and the severity of patients' affective and interpersonal symptoms moderated treatment outcome with those with less severe symptoms benefitting more from the focused treatment, whereas those with more severe symptoms from the broad version (Thompson-Brenner et al., 2016).

The relative efficacy of CBT-E has been investigated in three disorder-specific adult outpatient samples and one further transdiagnostic sample (BMI > 17.5 < 40.0). It has been compared, in focused form, with psychoanalytic psychotherapy (Poulsen et al., 2014) and integrative-affective therapy (ICAT) in adult patients with bulimia nervosa (Wonderlich et al., 2014) with focal psychodynamic treatment in adult patients with anorexia (Zipfel et al., 2014) and with IPT in the transdiagnostic sample (Fairburn et al., 2015). Although CBT-E was superior to psychoanalytic psychotherapy in bulimia nervosa and to IPT in the transdiagnostic sample, no difference was found between CBT-E and ICAT for bulimia nervosa or CBT-E and focal psychodynamic treatment for anorexia nervosa. It should be noted that in the latter study, CBT-E differed in some respects from the previously evaluated treatment described in the treatment guide and a percentage of patients were hospitalized during treatment. A recent further comparison with Maudsley Anorexia Nervosa Treatment for Adults and Specialist Supportive Clinical Management in adult patients with anorexia nervosa is as yet unpublished although results are promising (Byrne et al., 2015).

In addition CBT-E has been investigated as a treatment for anorexia nervosa in a case series consisting of two outpatient samples of adults (Fairburn et al., 2013). It has been investigated in outpatient adolescent samples who are low in weight and those who are not (Dalle Grave, Calugi, Doll, et al., 2013; Dalle Grave, Calugi, Sartirana, & Fairburn, 2015) and in an inpatient sample of adolescents (Dalle Grave, Calugi, El Ghoch, Conti, & Fairburn, 2014). Although CBT-E has shown promise in these various groups, results need to be confirmed in controlled studies. In particular a comparison between CBT-E and family based treatment, the treatment with the most empirical support for adolescents with anorexia nervosa, is warranted.

Of particular interest for clinicians are three large transdiagnostic studies reporting response rates to CBT-E, or slightly modified versions of the treatment, in routine clinical settings. All three uncontrolled studies reported outcome for completers similar to that reported in the previous research trials although treatment completion rates were lower (Byrne, Fursland, Allen, & Watson, 2011; Knott, Woodward, Hoefkens, & Limbert, 2015; Turner, Marshall, Stopa, & Waller, 2015).

CONCLUSION AND FUTURE DIRECTIONS

The transdiagnostic theory of the maintenance of eating disorders and the treatment based on it resulted from extending and enhancing the original cognitive theory of bulimia nervosa. There is evidence supporting the theory and accumulating evidence for the transdiagnostic range of the treatment and for its use in a variety of treatment settings. Support for the treatment comes not only from research trials but also from routine clinical settings.

Despite its successes, CBT-E does not help everyone. There is an urgent need to identify predictors and moderators of treatment response in order to understand for whom, and under what conditions, the treatment is likely to be helpful. There is also a need to improve the treatment further in order to extend the range of patients who might be helped by the approach. A better understanding of how the treatment works is likely to contribute to this goal. Greater understanding of the mechanisms of change would provide the basis for further enhancing the active components of treatment and omitting redundant ones. It might also suggest ways to simplify treatment, generally, or in particular cases.

Another urgent challenge concerns the dissemination and implementation of CBT-E. Despite empirical support, few patients with eating disorders are receiving it. In part this is due to individuals not seeking treatment or eating problems not being correctly detected in primary care. However, even when treatment is sought and offered, many do not receive empirically supported interventions. The barriers to wider dissemination and implementation include clinician attitudes toward such treatment and the lack of sufficient numbers of suitably trained therapists. There is therefore a need to develop and evaluate methods that are suitable for training large numbers of therapists; one that also address therapists' concerns about the use of such treatment. Only with widely available evidence based training are more patients likely to benefit from treatments like CBT-E.

Acknowledgment

ZC is grateful to the Wellcome Trust for its support over many years: ZC was supported by a strategic award (094585).

References

Agras, W. S., Walsh, B. T., Fairburn, C. G., Wilson, G. T., & Kraemer, H. C. (2000). A Multicenter comparison of cognitive-behavioral therapy and interpersonal psychotherapy for bulimia nervosa. *Archives of General Psychiatry, 57*(5), 459−466.

American Psychiatric Association (2013). *Diagnostic and statistical manual of mental disorders* (5th ed.). Washington, DC: American Psychiatric Publishing.

Byrne, S. M., Fursland, A., Allen, K. L., & Watson, H. (2011). The effectiveness of enhanced cognitive behavioural therapy for eating disorders: An open trial. *Behaviour Research and Therapy, 49*(4), 219−226. Available from http://dx.doi.org/10.1016/j.brat.2011.01.006.

Byrne, S. M., Wade, T. D., Hay, P. J., Touyz, S., Fairburn, C. G., Treasure, J., . . . Crosby, R. D. (2015). Principal outcomes of the SWAN Study: A Randomized Controlled Trial of three psychological treatments for anorexia nervosa in adults. Paper presented at XXI Annual Meeting Eating Disorder Research Society. Taormina Sicily.

Cooper, Z., & Fairburn, C. G. (2011). The evolution of "enhanced" cognitive behavior therapy for eating disorders: Learning from treatment nonresponse. *Cognitive and Behavioral Practice, 18*(3), 394−402.

Cooper, Z., & Stewart, A. (2008). CBT-E and the younger patient. In C. G. Fairburn (Ed.), *Cognitive behavior therapy and eating disorders* (pp. 221−231). New York: The Guilford Press.

Dakanalis, A., Carrà, G., Calogero, R., Zanetti, M. A., Gaudio, S., Caccialanza, R., . . . Clerici, M. (2015). Testing the cognitive-behavioural maintenance models across DSM-5 bulimic-type eating disorder diagnostic groups: A multi-centre study. *European Archives of Psychiatry and Clinical Neuroscience, 265*(8), 663−676. Available from http://dx.doi.org/10.1007/s00406-014-0560-2.

Dakanalis, A., Timko, C. A., Clerici, M., Zanetti, M. A., & Riva, G. (2014). Comprehensive examination of the trans-diagnostic cognitive behavioral model of eating disorders in males. *Eating Behaviors, 15*(1), 63−67. Available from http://dx.doi.org/10.1016/j.eatbeh.2013.10.003.

Dalle Grave, R. (2012). *Intensive cognitive behavior therapy for eating disorders*. New York: Nova Science.

Dalle Grave, R. (2013). *Multistep cognitive behavioral therapy: Theory, practice and clinical cases*. New York: Jason Aronson.

Dalle Grave, R., Bohn, K., Hawker, D. M., & Fairburn, C. G. (2008). Inpatient, day patient and two forms of outpatient CBT-E. In C. G. Fairburn (Ed.), *Cognitive behavior therapy and eating disorders* (pp. 231–245). New York: The Guilford Press.

Dalle Grave, R., Calugi, S., Conti, M., Doll, H. A., & Fairburn, C. G. (2013). Inpatient cognitive behaviour therapy for anorexia nervosa: A randomized controlled trial. *Psychotherapy and Psychosomatics, 82*(6), 390–398. Available from http://dx.doi.org/10.1159/000350058.

Dalle Grave, R., Calugi, S., Doll, H. A., & Fairburn, C. G. (2013). Enhanced cognitive behaviour therapy for adolescents with anorexia nervosa: An alternative to family therapy? *Behaviour Research and Therapy, 51*(1), R9–R12. Available from http://dx.doi.org/10.1016/j.brat.2012.09.008.

Dalle Grave, R., Calugi, S., El Ghoch, M., Conti, M., & Fairburn, C. G. (2014). Inpatient cognitive behavior therapy for adolescents with anorexia nervosa: Immediate and longer-term effects. *Frontiers in Psychiatry, 5*(FEB), 1–7. Available from http://dx.doi.org/10.3389/fpsyt.2014.00014.

Dalle Grave, R., Calugi, S., Sartirana, M., & Fairburn, C. G. (2015). Transdiagnostic cognitive behaviour therapy for adolescents with an eating disorder who are not underweight. *Behaviour Research and Therapy, 73*, 79–82. Available from http://dx.doi.org/10.1016/j.brat.2015.07.014.

de Zwaan, M. (2010). Obesity treatment for binge-eating disorder in the obese. In C. M. Grilo, & J. E. Mitchell (Eds.), *The treatment of eating disorders* (pp. 428–436). New York: The Guilford Press.

Ekeroth, K., Clinton, D., Norring, C., & Birgegård, A. (2013). Clinical characteristics and distinctiveness of DSM-5 eating disorder diagnoses: Findings from a large naturalistic clinical database. *Journal of Eating Disorders, 1*(1), 31. Available from http://dx.doi.org/10.1186/2050-2974-1-31.

Fairburn, C. G., Cooper, Z., & Cooper, P. J. (1986). The clinical features and maintenance of bulimia nervosa. In K. D. Brownell, & J. P. Foreyt (Eds.), *Physiology, psychology and treatment of the eating disorders* (pp. 389–404). New York: Basic Books.

Fairburn, C. G., Cooper, Z., & Shafran, R. (2003). Cognitive behaviour therapy for eating disorders: a "transdiagnostic" theory and treatment. *Behaviour Research and Therapy, 41*(5), 509–528. Available from http://dx.doi.org/10.1016/S0005-7967(02)00088-8.

Fairburn, C. G., Cooper, Z., Doll, H. A., O'Connor, M. E., Bohn, K., Hawker, D. M., & Palmer, R. L. (2009). Transdiagnostic cognitive-behavioral therapy for patients with eating disorders: A two-site trial with 60-week follow-up. *American Journal of Psychiatry, 166*(3), 311–319. Available from http://dx.doi.org/10.1176/appi.ajp.2008.08040608.

Fairburn, C. G., Cooper, Z., Doll, H. A., O'Connor, M. E., Palmer, R. L., & Dalle Grave, R. (2013). Enhanced cognitive behaviour therapy for adults with anorexia nervosa: A UK-Italy study. *Behaviour Research and Therapy, 51*(1), R2–R8. Available from http://dx.doi.org/10.1016/j.brat.2012.09.010.

Fairburn, C. G., Cooper, Z., Shafran, R., Bohn, K., & Hawker, D. M. (2008). Clinical perfectionism, core low self-esteem and interpersonal problems. In C. G. Fairburn (Ed.), *Cognitive behavior therapy and eating disorders* (pp. 197–221). New York: The Guilford Press.

Fairburn, C. G., Cooper, Z., Shafran, R., Bohn, K., Hawker, D. M., Murphy, R., & Straebler, S. (2008). Enhanced cognitive behavior therapy for eating disorders: The core protocol. In C. G. Fairburn (Ed.), *Cognitive behavior therapy and eating disorders* (pp. 47–193). New York: The Guilford Press.

Fairburn, C. G., Bailey-Straebler, S., Basden, S., Doll, H. A., Jones, R., Murphy, R., & Cooper, Z. (2015). A transdiagnostic comparison of enhanced cognitive behaviour therapy (CBT-E) and interpersonal psychotherapy in the treatment of eating disorders. *Behaviour Research and Therapy, 70*, 64–71. Available from http://dx.doi.org/10.1016/j.brat.2015.04.010.

Fairburn, C. G., Jones, R., Hope, R. A., O'Connor, M., & Peveler, R. C. (1993). Psychotherapy and bulimia nervosa longer-term effects of interpersonal psychotherapy, behaviour therapy and cognitive behaviour therapy. *Archives of General Psychiatry*, *50*, 419−428.

Fairburn, C. G., Stice, E., Cooper, Z., Doll, H. A., Norman, P. A., & O'Connor, M. E. (2003). Understanding persistence in bulimia nervosa: A 5-year naturalistic study. *Journal of Consulting and Clinical Psychology*, *71*(1), 103−109, doi:10.1037/0022-006X.71.1.103.

Flament, M. F., Buchholz, A., Henderson, K., Obeid, N., Maras, D., Schubert, N., … Goldfield, G. (2015). Comparative distribution and validity of DSM-IV and DSM-5 diagnoses of eating disorders in adolescents from the community. *European Eating Disorders Review*, *23*(2), 163−169. Available from http://dx.doi.org/10.1002/erv.2339.

Grilo, C. M. (2013). Why no cognitive body image feature such as overvaluation of shape/weight in the binge eating disorder diagnosis? *International Journal of Eating Disorders*, *46*(3), 208−211. Available from http://dx.doi.org/10.1002/eat.22082.

Hoiles, K. J., Egan, S. J., & Kane, R. T. (2012). The validity of the transdiagnostic cognitive behavioural model of eating disorders in predicting dietary restraint. *Eating Behaviors*, *13*(2), 123−126. Available from http://dx.doi.org/10.1016/j.eatbeh.2011.11.007.

Knott, S., Woodward, D., Hoefkens, A., & Limbert, C. (2015). Cognitive behaviour therapy for bulimia nervosa and eating disorders not otherwise specified: Translation from randomized controlled trial to a clinical setting. *Behavioural and Cognitive Psychotherapy*, *43* (06), 641−654. Available from http://dx.doi.org/10.1017/S1352465814000393.

Lampard, A. M., Byrne, S. M., McLean, N., & Fursland, A. (2011). An evaluation of the enhanced cognitive-behavioural model of bulimia nervosa. *Behaviour Research and Therapy*, *49*(9), 529−535. Available from http://dx.doi.org/10.1016/j.brat.2011.06.002.

Lampard, A. M., Tasca, G. A., Balfour, L., & Bissada, H. (2013). An evaluation of the transdiagnostic cognitive-behavioural model of eating disorders. *European Eating Disorders Review*, *21*(2), 99−107. Available from http://dx.doi.org/10.1002/erv.2214.

Le Grange, D., Swanson, S. A., Crow, S. J., & Merikangas, K. R. (2012). Eating disorder not otherwise specified presentation in the US population. *International Journal of Eating Disorders*, *45*(5), 711−718. Available from http://dx.doi.org/10.1002/eat.22006.

Machado, P. P. P., Gonçalves, S., & Hoek, H. W. (2013). DSM-5 reduces the proportion of EDNOS cases: Evidence from community samples. *International Journal of Eating Disorders*, *46*(1), 60−65. Available from http://dx.doi.org/10.1002/eat.22040.

Mancuso, S. G., Newton, J. R., Bosanac, P., Rossell, S. L., Nesci, J. B., & Castle, D. J. (2015). Classification of eating disorders: Comparison of relative prevalence rates using DSM-IV and DSM-5 criteria. *The British Journal of Psychiatry*, *206*(6), 519−520. Available from http://dx.doi.org/10.1192/bjp.bp.113.143461.doi:.

Poulsen, S., Lunn, S., Daniel, S. I. F., Folke, S., Mathiesen, B. B., Katznelson, H., & Fairburn, C. G. (2014). A randomized controlled trial of psychoanalytic psychotherapy or cognitive-behavioral therapy for bulimia nervosa. *The American Journal of Psychiatry*, *171*(1), 109−116. Available from http://dx.doi.org/10.1176/appi.ajp.2013.12121511.

Shafran, R., Lee, M., Cooper, Z., Palmer, R. L., & Fairburn, C. G. (2007). Attentional bias in eating disorders. *The International Journal of Eating Disorders*, *40*, 369−380. Available from http://dx.doi.org/10.1002/eat.

Shafran, R., Lee, M., Payne, E., & Fairburn, C. G. (2007). An experimental analysis of body checking. *Behaviour Research and Therapy*, *45*(1), 113−121. Available from http://dx.doi.org/10.1016/j.brat.2006.01.015.

Smink, F. R. E., van Hoeken, D., & Hoek, H. W. (2013). Epidemiology, course, and outcome of eating disorders. *Current Opinion in Psychiatry*, *26*(6), 543−548. Available from http://dx.doi.org/10.1097/YCO.0b013e328365a24f.

Spangler, D. L., Baldwin, S. A., & Agras, W. S. (2004). An examination of the mechanisms of action in cognitive behavioral therapy for bulimia nervosa. *Behavior Therapy, 35*(3), 537–560. Available from http://dx.doi.org/10.1016/S0005-7894(04)80031-5.

Tabri, N., Murray, H. B., Thomas, J. J., Franko, D. L., Herzog, D. B., & Eddy, K. T. (2015). Overvaluation of body shape/weight and engagement in non-compensatory weight-control behaviors in eating disorders: Is there a reciprocal relationship? *Psychological Medicine, 45*(14), 2951–2958. Available from http://dx.doi.org/10.1017/S0033291715000896.

Tasca, G. A., Presniak, M. D., Demidenko, N., Balfour, L., Krysanski, V., Trinneer, A., & Bissada, H. (2011). Testing a maintenance model for eating disorders in a sample seeking treatment at a tertiary care center: A structural equation modeling approach. *Comprehensive Psychiatry, 52*(6), 678–687. Available from http://dx.doi.org/10.1016/j.comppsych.2010.12.010.

Thompson-Brenner, H., Shingleton, R. M., Thompson, D. R., Satir, D. A., Richards, L. K., Pratt, E. M., & Barlow, D. H. (2016). Focused vs. broad enhanced cognitive behavioral therapy for bulimia nervosa with comorbid borderline personality: A randomized controlled trial. *International Journal of Eating Disorders, 49*(1), 36–49. Available from http://dx.doi.org/10.1002/eat.22468.

Turner, H., Marshall, E., Stopa, L., & Waller, G. (2015). Cognitive-behavioural therapy for outpatients with eating disorders: Effectiveness for a transdiagnostic group in a routine clinical setting. *Behaviour Research and Therapy, 68*, 70–75. Available from http://dx.doi.org/10.1016/j.brat.2015.03.001.

Watson, H. J., Raykos, B. C., Street, H., Fursland, A., & Nathan, P. R. (2011). Mediators between perfectionism and eating disorder psychopathology: Shape and weight overvaluation and conditional goal-setting. *International Journal of Eating Disorders, 44*(2), 142–149. Available from http://dx.doi.org/10.1002/eat.20788.

Weissman, M., Markowitz, J. C., & Klerman, G. L. (2000). *Comprehensive guide to interpersonal psychotherapy*. New York: Basic Books.

Wilson, G. T., Fairburn, C. C., Agras, W. S., Walsh, B. T., & Kraemer, H. (2002). Cognitive-behavioral therapy for bulimia nervosa: Time course and mechanisms of change. *Journal of Consulting and Clinical Psychology, 70*(2), 267–274. Available from http://dx.doi.org/10.1037/0022-006X.70.2.267.

Wonderlich, S. A., Peterson, C. B., Crosby, R. D., Smith, T. L., Klein, M. H., Mitchell, J. E., & Crow, S. J. (2014). A randomized controlled comparison of integrative cognitive-affective therapy (ICAT) and enhanced cognitive-behavioral therapy (CBT-E) for bulimia nervosa. *Psychological Medicine, 44*(3), 543–553. Available from http://dx.doi.org/10.1017/S0033291713001098.

Zipfel, S., Wild, B., Groß, G., Friederich, H., Teufel, M., Schellberg, D., . . . de Zwaan, M. (2014). Articles focal psychodynamic therapy, cognitive behaviour therapy, and optimised treatment as usual in outpatients with anorexia nervosa (ANTOP study): Randomised controlled trial. *Lancet, 383*(9912), 127–137. Available from http://dx.doi.org/10.1016/S0140-6736(13)61746-8.

Zunker, C., Peterson, C. B., Crosby, R. D., Cao, L., Engel, S. G., Mitchell, J. E., & Wonderlich, S. A. (2011). Ecological momentary assessment of bulimia nervosa: Does dietary restriction predict binge eating? *Behaviour Research and Therapy, 49*(10), 714–717. Available from http://dx.doi.org/10.1016/j.brat.2011.06.006.

Transdiagnostic Treatment for Anxiety Disorders

Laren R. Conklin[1] *and Hannah Boettcher*[2]

[1]Chalmers P. Wylie VA Ambulatory Care Center, Columbus, OH, United States [2]Boston University, Boston, MA, United States

BACKGROUND

Anxiety disorders are the most common class of psychological disorders; approximately a third of individuals will develop one or more anxiety disorders at some point in their lives (Kessler, Petukhova, Sampson, Zaslavsky, & Wittchen, 2012). Anxiety disorders are often comorbid with each other and other psychological conditions, and the presence of an anxiety disorder is associated with significant impairment in social and work functioning as well as increased utilization of nonpsychiatric medical services (Greenberg et al., 1999; Mojtabai et al., 2015; Olatunji, Cisler, & Tolin, 2007). Following classification changes in the most recent version of the Diagnostic and Statistical Manual of Mental Disorders (DSM-5; American Psychiatric Association, 2013), in which separate designations are made for obsessive-compulsive and trauma-related disorders, the anxiety disorders category currently includes disorders such as panic disorder, agoraphobia, social anxiety disorder, generalized anxiety disorder (GAD), and specific phobias.

The efficacy of treatments for anxiety, particularly those that are behavioral or cognitive-behavioral in nature, has been well established over the years (e.g., Hofmann & Smits, 2008). With the growth of treatment, outcome research has come a similar increase in manualized treatment protocols, developed to delineate which treatment components and strategies merit inclusion in an evidence-based treatment package. This has led to a proliferation of protocols for the treatment of

The Science of Cognitive Behavioral Therapy.
DOI: http://dx.doi.org/10.1016/B978-0-12-803457-6.00015-5

anxiety disorders, most designed to treat a specific primary anxiety disorder (e.g., GAD or panic disorder). These different treatments often overlap considerably, containing very similar components (e.g., psychoeducation, cognitive restructuring, exposure exercises), though a number also contain disorder-specific elements (e.g., interoceptive exposure for panic disorder, Craske, Antony, & Barlow, 2006; progressive muscle relaxation for GAD, Zinbarg, Craske, & Barlow, 2006).

DISADVANTAGES OF A DIAGNOSIS-SPECIFIC APPROACH

This process of developing disorder-specific manualized protocols based on treatment outcome research has been in many ways justified and advantageous; it is reasonable given the constraints of a strong research design and has led to definable treatments with known efficacy. Nevertheless, it has not been without negative consequences. The largely diagnosis-specific nature of treatment development for anxiety disorders means that clinicians who want to adhere to evidence-based practices have to take time to learn and, optimally, receive training in administering each protocol. For a clinician who decides to specialize in treating DSM-5 adult anxiety disorders, and nothing else, this would entail learning at least four separate protocols—more if one also treats disorders that formerly fell under the umbrella of anxiety disorders in the DSM-IV, such as obsessive–compulsive disorder (OCD) and post-traumatic stress disorder (PTSD). The time-related and financial costs of learning individual protocols are among the largest barriers that clinicians report that keep them from achieving competency in the delivery of new evidence-based treatments (Stewart, Chambless, & Baron, 2012).

Another disadvantage of currently available evidence-based protocols is the existence of many similar protocols for treating the same principal diagnosis. For example, over 15 published manuals can be found for the treatment of panic disorder specifically (Wilamowska et al., 2010). Thus, it becomes necessary to sort through and choose among numerous protocols, with the differences in protocols often determined by author preference and not driven by research findings. As a consequence, it has become increasingly difficult for the practicing empirically oriented clinician to select appropriate treatments from the plethora of options, a difficulty compounded by the time, effort, and financial resources needed to learn and deliver the treatment with fidelity once it has been selected.

Although single-diagnosis protocols (SDPs) have been prevalent in anxiety disorder treatment, another challenge for clinicians focused on delivering evidence-based psychotherapies has been deciding what treatment to select when a patient presents with more than one anxiety disorder. Epidemiological and classification research indicate that there are high levels of comorbidity among different anxiety disorders as well as related conditions (e.g., mood disorders). For instance, in a sample of 1127 patients who presented for treatment at a leading cognitive-behavioral clinic, comorbidity was the rule rather than the exception (Brown et al., 2001). For individuals who presented with a current diagnosis of GAD, 83% were also experiencing at least one other cooccurring anxiety/mood disorder. Relatedly, percentages of comorbidity were 59% for individuals with a diagnosis of panic disorder, 70% for individuals with a diagnosis of specific phobia, and 75% for those with social anxiety disorder (Brown et al., 2001). Thus, it is more likely than not that a clinician will need to decide how best to proceed when a patient presents with two (or more) comorbid conditions or when the patient is experiencing other specified anxiety diagnoses or subthreshold symptoms that do not sufficiently match an established SDP. Until recently, options for an evidence-based clinician included choosing an evidence-based protocol for one diagnosis and trying to "fit in" the nontargeted anxiety disorder in using examples or supplementary treatment components, completing multiple SDPs in succession, or forgoing a protocol-based approach entirely, stringing together evidence-based components to treat other specified anxiety diagnoses, subthreshold symptoms, or more than one disorder simultaneously.

COMMONALITIES AMONG ANXIETY DISORDERS

The notable levels of comorbidity among anxiety and related disorders and the complications their presence can bring have led to efforts to identify factors that contribute to the cooccurrence of these disorders as well as to determine how best to treat individuals who are struggling with more than one anxiety disorder. One factor that contributes to comorbidity in anxiety disorders is that, as a class, anxiety disorders have overlapping symptom criteria, such as the experience of frequent anxiety and worry. The specific content of the worry depends on the disorder (e.g., worry about experiencing a panic attack in panic disorder, worry about negative evaluation in social anxiety disorder, or worry about multiple domains as in GAD); however, the distinctions can sometimes be challenging to discern and people often present with more than one domain of anxiety or fearfulness. Researchers have theorized that these distinctions reflect surface-level variations of an underlying "general neurotic syndrome" (Andrews, 1996; Tyrer, Seivewright, Ferguson, & Tyrer, 1992). More recently, there has been a focus on the role that neuroticism/negative affectivity, a core dimension of temperament, plays in the development of anxiety disorders.

Neuroticism is the predisposition to experience negative emotions more frequently and strongly, coupled with a sense of uncontrollability in response to stress (Barlow, Sauer-Zavala, Carl, Bullis, & Ellard, 2014). Neuroticism is strongly heritable, often relatively stable over time, and is considered to be relevant to the etiology of emotional disorders broadly, including anxiety disorders, depressive disorders, trauma- and stressor-related disorders, and obsessive–compulsive spectrum disorders (e.g., Bienvenu et al., 2004; Breslau & Schultz, 2013; Brown, 2007; Fullana et al., 2004; Zinbarg et al., 2016). Low extraversion/positive affectivity, another core dimension of temperament, is also heritable to some extent; although, it seems to be related to a smaller subset of disorders, such as social anxiety disorder, agoraphobia, and depressive disorders (Clark, Watson & Mineka, 1994; Jylhä & Isometsä, 2006; Rosellini, Lawrence, Meyer, & Brown, 2010). A study by Brown, Chorpita, and Barlow (1998) found that almost all the covariance among latent variables related to DSM-IV depression, social phobia, GAD, OCD, and panic disorder/agoraphobia was explained by the higher order dimensions of negative and positive affectivity. These findings are consistent with the idea that the tendency to experience negative emotions is a vulnerability factor for the development of anxiety and other emotional disorders, with the experience of positive emotions conferring important, but more specific, vulnerability to several of these disorders.

With respect to neuroticism, researchers have identified biological and psychological features shared by individuals that are high in neuroticism as well as across multiple anxiety and related disorders. Similarities in neurological functioning, for example, have been found in individuals who have a tendency to experience negative emotions strongly and frequently. Affective neuroscientists have observed individuals that are high in neuroticism display overactivation of the amygdala, an area implicated in anxiety and fear responses (Everaerd, Klumpers, van Wingen, Tendolkar, & Fernández, 2015). This pattern, coupled with lower cortical inhibition, is also found in those diagnosed with GAD (Etkin, Prater, Hoeft, Menon, & Schatzberg, 2010; Monk, et al., 2008), specific phobia (Straube, Mentzel, & Miltner, 2006), and social anxiety disorder (Lorberbaum et al., 2004; Phan, Fitzgerald, Nathan, & Tancer, 2006; Tillfors, Furmark, Marteinsdottir, & Fredrikson, 2002), as well as individuals with depression (Holmes et al., 2012).

Psychological manifestations of neuroticism that are also experienced among those with anxiety disorders include a heightened sense of unpredictability and uncontrollability about the world and the perception that one is ill-equipped to successfully cope with stressors

(Barlow, 2000, 2002). Individuals higher in neuroticism tend to view events as more stressful, believe they are less capable of handling stressful events, and can get more emotionally reactive the more they perceive events to be undesirable or question their ability to cope (Gunthert, Cohen, & Armeli, 1999). Lower perceptions of control have moderate to strong associations with neuroticism, trait anxiety, and the severity of multiple disorders, including GAD, OCD, social anxiety disorder, panic disorder, and PTSD (Darvill, & Johnson, 1991; Gallagher, Bentley, & Barlow, 2014).

THE TRANSDIAGNOSTIC ALTERNATIVE

Evidence of high comorbidity and shared biological and psychological elements related to the development of neuroticism and, accordingly, anxiety disorders suggests that consideration of these elements is essential to identifying effective treatments. There is already some evidence from single-diagnosis treatments that focusing on treating one disorder can result in some improvements in comorbid conditions (Borkovec, Abel, & Newman, 1995; Brown, Antony, & Barlow, 1995; Tsao, Lewin, & Craske, 1998; Tsao, Mystkowski, Zucker, & Craske, 2002). As one example, in a study conducted using CBT for principal panic disorder (Tsao et al., 2002) rates of comorbidity from pre- to posttreatment fell from around 61% to 37%, with the severity of comorbid GAD, depression, and specific phobia improving significantly and remaining stable for six months. It is possible this effect is due to the inclusion of components that are shared across treatments for anxiety and other emotional disorders (e.g., psychoeducation, exposures, cognitive restructuring) and that these components are treating core mechanisms that are maintaining distress and impairment shared among multiple disorders. In support of this, some research has identified that neuroticism, a generally stable construct, can decrease when patients engage in psychological treatments for anxiety and mood disorders (Brown, 2007). It is possible that the durability of these effects could be even greater when treating shared mechanisms and vulnerabilities more directly and helping patients see how skills learned in treatment apply to a wider range of anxieties, fears, or difficult emotions.

The purpose of the remainder of this chapter is to discuss examples of just such an approach. In the sections that follow, we will describe two unified transdiagnostic treatments for anxiety disorders, the Unified Protocol for the Transdiagnostic Treatment of Emotional Disorders (UP) and Transdiagnostic Group Cognitive-Behavioral Therapy (TGCBT). We will include a description of the targets of treatment, the structure of the protocols, and the supporting evidence for their efficacy. Additionally, we will endeavor to describe the major similarities and differences in the treatments.

UNIFIED PROTOCOL FOR THE TRANSDIAGNOSTIC TREATMENT OF EMOTIONAL DISORDERS

Barlow and colleagues (2011a,b) developed the UP to target psychopathology across anxiety, depressive, and related disorders for which responses to negative emotion are of central importance. Decades of research and clinical evidence pointed to underlying common vulnerabilities and maintaining mechanisms across these disorders, as described at the beginning of this chapter. Evidence in support of these processes included high rates of comorbidity, similarities among the treatments found to be most effective for varied emotional disorders, and improvement in the symptoms of comorbid disorders during the treatment for a principal emotional disorder diagnosis. Barlow and colleagues focused on neuroticism/negative affectivity given the supporting evidence that the tendency to experience frequent and intense negative affect—anxiety, fear, depression, or anger—appears to be a central, biologically based vulnerability to developing anxiety and related emotional disorders. Importantly, emotional disorders are developed and maintained when this propensity to experience negative emotions is accompanied by the tendency to have strong aversive reactions to these emotions (e.g., anxiety sensitivity) and to engage in avoidant coping efforts (e.g., situational avoidance, thought suppression, compulsions, withdrawal). For example, a patient with panic disorder may avoid situations in which she has had panic attacks or limit caffeine intake due to fear of anxiety-provoking physical sensations. A patient with social anxiety disorder may avoid eye contact, whereas a depressed patient might stay home or sleep excessively to dampen feelings of low mood. A patient with intrusive thoughts might respond by distracting himself from these thoughts or repeatedly reassure himself that they are untrue, whereas a patient with chronic worry might dampen anxiety by overpreparing for everyday situations.

The UP was developed to target these vulnerabilities and maintaining processes of distress and impairment—negative affectivity, emotion aversion, and maladaptive avoidant coping behaviors—by teaching more effective ways of responding to negative emotion. Specifically, as an alternative to the aversive reactions seen in emotional disorders, the UP promotes an attitude of acceptance toward uncomfortable emotion and a willingness to experience these emotions without avoidance. This is accomplished through the use of evidence-based cognitive-behavioral treatment elements, such as mindfulness, cognitive challenging, and exposure activities.

The UP is delivered in individual sessions of approximately 50 min in length, typically over the course of 12–16 weekly sessions. Importantly, it was designed to be of flexible length, with more or less time devoted to each area of instruction and skills practice based on individual patients' needs. The UP consists of eight modules, including five modules considered "core modules," reflecting specific interventions targeting the core components of emotional disorders, as well as three additional models designed to facilitate the effectiveness of treatment, including motivational enhancement, psychoeducation, and relapse prevention. Barlow and colleagues (2011a, 2011b) developed a patient workbook and therapist guide to facilitate the delivery of the UP (currently under revision).

Description of Treatment

The first session of the UP has several purposes. First, the therapist reviews the patient's presenting problems and diagnoses that have been obtained from an initial assessment. Then, the therapist provides information about the treatment, including a simplified description of why it was developed. The therapist describes common features of emotional disorders, including a propensity for strong negative emotions, aversive reactions to these emotions, and avoidant coping. The therapist also shares the rationale for targeting these common vulnerabilities and mechanisms as well as the rationale for learning a new, different way of coping; specifically, cultivating willingness to approach and remain in contact with uncomfortable emotions, as well as choosing adaptive behavioral responses that are consistent with long-term goals. This discussion is an opportunity for functional assessment of the patient's difficulties (e.g., inquiring about efforts to avoid emotion-provoking situations), which can be used to tailor treatment later.

The second session is typically synonymous with Module 1 of the UP, which focuses on enhancing motivation for treatment. Drawing upon principles of motivational interviewing (Miller & Rollnick, 2012), as well as research highlighting the value of motivation enhancement in the treatment of anxiety (Westra & Dozois, 2006), patients are encouraged to articulate the pros and cons of changing and the pros and cons of staying the same. Therapists can then help the patient weigh the pros and cons to help determine whether the pros outweigh the cons enough to commit to treatment at this time, as well as discuss ways to manage the challenges associated with engaging in treatment. For instance, if a patient is concerned that treatment will take a lot of time, reasonable expectations can be set and the patient can plan to remind themselves of the benefits of treatment during weeks that are busier for them. This discussion may be revisited later in treatment, particularly if the patient is experiencing an increase in ambivalence. Patients also set goals for treatment during the second part of this session, focusing on defining each goal and identifying concrete steps to these goals.

One to two sessions are devoted to Module 2, Understanding Emotions. In this session, the therapist provides psychoeducation on the adaptive nature of emotions and presents in detail the three-component model of emotion—thoughts, physical feelings, and behaviors (or behavioral urges). The therapist briefly introduces the concept of emotion-driven behaviors (EDBs), or the action tendencies associated with strong emotions, which will become an integral focus of later sessions. Module 2 also presents the ARC worksheet [Antecedents (emotional), Response, Consequences]. The focus of the ARC is on helping patients identify triggers of emotions and consequences of their emotions. With respect to identifying triggers, although many patients are able to identify one main trigger that led to their emotions (e.g., their significant other not completing an errand as promised), much fewer patients are able to identify additional triggers or factors that led them to be more vulnerable to experiencing stronger emotional reactions, such as having had a hard day at work, being tired or hungry, or being irritated about something else that is unrelated to their significant other. Identifying the various triggers helps patients start to place their emotional reactions more fully in context and can inform more helpful responses in the future. A second major focus of the ARC is identifying the short- and long-term consequences of emotional responses. This section of the ARC is an opportunity to highlight how responding to strong emotions by avoiding or escaping them can have short-term, seemingly beneficial, consequences (e.g., relief from anxiety) but often has negative long-term consequences (i.e., maintenance of negative affect and reinforcement of avoidance). During this module, patients begin regular monitoring of their emotional experiences and interactions among the three components, in an effort to increase insight about one's own response patterns and identify areas to be targeted in treatment.

The third module, Emotion Awareness Training, is the first module considered a "core" module and typically begins in the fifth session. Over the course of one to two sessions, patients learn to observe their emotional experiences in a mindful way; that is, they learn to observe emotions in a manner that is both present-focused and nonjudgmental. This allows for a distinction to be made between primary emotions (e.g., anxiety about public speaking) and secondary reactions to these emotions (e.g., embarrassment or shame about being nervous), the latter of which often amount to the emotion aversion that is a target of the UP. Furthermore, taking a mindful perspective facilitates the selection of behavioral responses that are consistent with one's long-term goals and needs, rather than engaging in responses that are not present-focused (e.g., worry, rumination) or that are based in strong judgments of one's experience (e.g., escaping an anxiety-provoking situation due to thinking it is intolerable). To facilitate the use of this perspective, the UP uses a guided meditation mindfulness exercise (adapted from Segal, Williams, & Teasdale, 2001) and briefer daily mindfulness exercises to help patients "anchor in the present." In addition, the therapist helps the patient gain the ability to be mindful when experiencing strong emotions by practicing mood induction mindfulness exercises. As part of this exercise, patients listen to evocative music or recall an emotional memory while practicing present-focused and nonjudgmental awareness. Mindfulness is presented as a perspective that facilitates the overarching goal of approaching and tolerating uncomfortable emotions, and this skill is drawn upon when engaging in exposure exercises later in treatment.

The fourth module and second core module is Cognitive Reappraisal, which is similarly delivered over one to two sessions. Here, patients learn about the automatic nature of appraisals (i.e., evaluative thoughts, such as interpretations and predictions) and how these appraisals contribute to negative emotional states. The therapist introduces two major cognitive biases, probability overestimation of negative outcomes and catastrophizing (which includes both thinking the worst and believing one has insufficient capacity to cope with negative outcomes). Using a series of questions designed to challenge these biases, patients practice generating alternative appraisals that are more flexible, realistic, and helpful. Thus, this module is in many ways the cognitive therapy often practiced in single-diagnosis interventions. However, consistent with the emphasis in the UP on the adaptive nature of emotions, Barlow and colleagues place particular emphasis on cognitive *flexibility*, so that patients can notice and be nonjudgmental of their initial appraisals and flexibly generate and weigh alternative appraisals. It does not focus on the correction of thoughts that are inaccurate or "dysfunctional."

Emotion Driven Behaviors and Emotion Avoidance comprise the fifth module and third core module, usually delivered over two sessions. The therapist and patient identify behaviors that are preventing full exposure to and tolerance of strong emotions. Patients first keep track of emotion avoidance, which are strategies a person uses to avoid coming in contact with strong emotions in the first place. These strategies can include overt situational avoidance (i.e., avoiding the situation entirely) and more subtle forms of emotion avoidance, including cognitive avoidance (e.g., distraction), subtle behavioral avoidance (e.g., avoiding eye contact once in a social situation), and safety signals (e.g., carrying a bottle of antianxiety medication with them at all times or entering certain situations only when with a trusted friend or partner). Patients also identify their own EDBs, like overeating when feeling sad, and assess how helpful or unhelpful these behaviors are, with particular attention to EDBs that serve the function of escaping strong emotions and those that have less optimal longer term consequences. The therapist introduces the rationale for practicing "alternative action;" that is, choosing a behavior that allows the patient to approach or remain in contact with strong emotion and is consistent with their goals (e.g., volunteering to lead a group meeting rather than withdrawing when feeling anxious in a professional setting). These practices will serve as the foundation of situational exposures practiced later.

The sixth module and fourth core module, Awareness and Tolerance of Physical Sensations, is focused on interoceptive exposure and typically takes one session to administer. Although interoceptive exposure has traditionally been applied primarily in the treatment of panic, Barlow and colleagues believe this intervention is promising for all emotional disorders, given the physical component inherent in strong emotions and the elevated anxiety sensitivity across these disorders (Boettcher, Brake, & Barlow, 2016). Through repeated practice of interoceptive exposure, patients become more aware of the role played by physical sensations in intensifying strong emotions and contributing to desires to engage in emotion avoidance or maladaptive EDBs. They also learn that these sensations are safe, can be tolerated, and will decrease on their own without the use of avoidance or escape.

The seventh module, Emotion Exposures, is the final core module and, for most patients, is the module to which the most sessions are devoted (typically four to six sessions). Patients learn the rationale for emotion exposures, which emphasizes the goal of using the skills they have learned up to that point to gradually and repeatedly face emotion-provoking situations. This allows patients to see that experiencing negative emotions can be tolerated and that a person can respond to emotion-provoking situations in adaptive ways whether or not they feel anxious, unhappy, or other emotions. Unlike other exposure therapies, the primary goal of emotion exposure is not necessarily to see a reduction of anxiety or fear, although the intensity of emotions does often decrease significantly as patients learn they can tolerate their emotions, cope with the situation, and gain helpful information about the outcomes of situations they face. Situations that provoke anxiety or fear are most commonly chosen for individuals with primary anxiety disorders, but emotion exposures can also include situations that prompt any other emotion patients find aversive and avoid, such as sadness or embarrassment. In the first session of Module 7, a hierarchy is created with situations that the patient finds distressing and/or avoids. Then, the emotion exposures are conducted within and outside of session repeatedly, with attention to learning about the tolerability of strong emotions. Exposures may be in vivo or imaginal and can incorporate additional interoceptive exposures if deemed to be beneficial.

The final session of the UP protocol is reserved for the eighth module, Relapse Prevention. In this session, the patient and therapist collaboratively review treatment skills and develop a practice plan for ongoing application of skills. Patients are informed to expect fluctuations in their symptoms and encouraged to respond to these fluctuations using strategies learned in treatment.

Evidence

A mounting body of evidence points to the effectiveness of the UP in treating anxiety and related disorders. To date, the UP has been used for the treatment of panic disorder, social anxiety disorder, OCD, GAD, PTSD, other-specified anxiety disorders, major depressive disorder, dysthymic disorder (now persistent depressive disorder), bipolar depression, borderline personality disorder, hypochondriasis (now illness anxiety disorder), and comorbid alcohol use disorders (Boswell, Anderson, & Barlow, 2014; Ciraulo et al., 2013; Ellard et al., 2010; Ellard, Deckersbach, Sylvia, Nierenberg, & Barlow, 2012; Farchione et al., 2012; Lopez et al., 2015; Sauer-Zavala, Bentley, & Wilner, 2016). The majority of research has assessed the efficacy of the UP with principal anxiety disorders, with case study or smaller sample size explorations suggesting preliminary evidence for other diagnostic categories.

An early version of the UP was evaluated in two open trials in adults with heterogeneous anxiety and depressive disorders, primarily GAD, OCD, social anxiety disorder, and panic disorder (Ellard et al., 2010). In the first trial of 18 patients, approximately half of patients achieved responder status on their principal diagnosis, defined as an improvement of 30% or more on at least two types of assessment measures (functional impairment, diagnosis-specific symptom severity, and clinician-rated overall severity). In addition, 71% patients reached responder status on their comorbid diagnoses. Barlow and colleagues subsequently modified the protocol to approximate the version used today and described in this chapter. Modifications included adding information about the adaptive nature of emotions and antecedents and consequences of emotional responses, moving emotion awareness training earlier in treatment and adding new mindfulness exercises, increasing emphasis on cognitive flexibility, and expanding the interoceptive exposure module. In the second open trial that followed (also reported in Ellard et al., 2010), 73% of the 15 participants achieved responder status by the end of treatment, and improvement continued such that 85% met responder criteria during the 6-month follow-up period. Furthermore, 64% of participants achieved responder status on their comorbid diagnoses at posttreatment, and 80% achieved responder status on their comorbid diagnoses at 6-month follow-up.

Following these open trials, Farchione et al. (2012) conducted a randomized controlled trial that compared the UP to a waitlist control condition in a sample of 37 adults with heterogeneous anxiety disorders, primarily OCD, GAD, social anxiety disorder, and panic disorder. Participants receiving the UP experienced significant reductions in self- and clinician-rated symptom measures, significant improvement in positive and negative affect, and reduced functional impairment over the course of treatment. Using comparable criteria to that used in the previous open trials, 59% of UP participants achieved responder status at posttreatment, whereas this was true of 0% of waitlist participants. These gains were maintained and continued to improve throughout the 6-month follow-up period. Furthermore, at posttreatment, 50% of UP participants had achieved subclinical status on all of their comorbid diagnoses, compared to 17% of waitlist participants, although the difference was not statistically significant. Similarly, although also not significant, 86% of clinically depressed participants achieved subclinical status on their depressive disorder at posttreatment in the UP group, compared to 40% in the waitlist group. Of additional note, subsequent research using participants from this trial found that, in addition to symptom improvements, individuals who completed the UP also saw improvements in quality of life, intolerance of uncertainty, anxiety sensitivity, neuroticism, and extraversion (Boswell, Farchione, Sauer-Zavala, Murray, Fortune, & Barlow, 2013; Boswell, Thompson-Hollands, Farchione, & Barlow, 2013; Carl, Gallagher, Sauer-Zavala, Bentley, & Barlow, 2014; Gallagher et al., 2013).

After establishing how the UP compares to waitlist, a common early study in treatment outcome research, the next step was to compare the efficacy of the UP to established single-diagnosis treatments for principal anxiety disorders. Barlow and colleagues recently concluded a large ($N = 233$) noninferiority randomized controlled trial comparing the UP against SDPs in the treatment of adults with principal diagnoses of social anxiety disorder, GAD, panic disorder, and OCD (Barlow et al., manuscript submitted for publication). The UP produced equivalent outcomes compared to the SDPs, with some outcomes favoring the UP, and both active treatments were superior to a waitlist control. The UP and SDPs were both associated with significant improvement on clinical severity ratings for principal diagnoses, self-reported symptoms of principal diagnoses, general symptoms of anxiety and depression, and functional impairment. Participants in both conditions were significantly more likely to be below clinical threshold for their principal diagnosis at posttreatment compared to the waitlist condition; 62% of participants treated with UP achieved subclinical status on their principal diagnosis by the end of treatment, and 68% had achieved subclinical status at the 6-month follow-up. Both the UP and SDPs significantly reduced symptoms of comorbid disorders, with no differences between the treatments in this capacity, with one exception: compared to SDPs, the UP led to more lasting reduction of comorbid panic disorder symptoms. Though speculative, this is possibly attributable to the administration of interoceptive exposure exercises to all patients treated with the UP, an element that was not included in the SDPs for social anxiety disorder, GAD, and OCD. There were no significant differences in credibility between the UP and SDPs, and the UP was associated with a significantly higher treatment completion rate (84% compared to 70% in the SDP condition).

The UP has also been adapted for administration in a group format, which was tested in 11 participants with emotional disorders (primarily social anxiety disorder; Bullis et al., 2015). The treatment had a strong effect on reducing symptoms of anxiety, functional impairment, and experiential avoidance, as well as moderate reductions in depressive symptoms and improvements in quality of life, though additional research in larger samples is warranted.

TRANSDIAGNOSTIC GROUP COGNITIVE-BEHAVIORAL THERAPY

Another noteworthy psychotherapy is TGCBT, which was developed by Norton and colleagues (Norton, 2008, 2012b; Norton & Hope, 2008). TGCBT has also proven effective in the treatment of anxiety disorders. Similar to the UP, Norton's intervention grew out of research pointing to a common syndrome underlying anxiety disorders, including high rates of comorbidity, overlap among likely etiological and maintenance mechanisms, responsivity to highly similar interventions across these disorders, and reductions in nontargeted comorbid anxiety symptoms during treatment for a principal anxiety disorder. Norton's conceptualization of a transdiagnostic model for anxiety disorder focuses on the temperamental trait of negative affectivity, particularly heightened sensitivity to negative emotions and a low sense of control over these emotions (Norton & Hope, 2008). Consequently, Norton's group developed a treatment designed to target negative affectivity, which is flexibly applicable across a range of anxiety disorders. The group format provides a cost- and time-efficient means of delivering the treatment, as well as opportunities for drawing upon various members' experiences to exemplify treatment concepts across diagnoses. TGCBT groups are composed of 6–8 adults with heterogeneous anxiety disorders and led by two therapists. The treatment entails 12 two-hour sessions delivered weekly, and homework practice is assigned between each session.

Description of Treatment

TGCBT conceptualizes symptoms in diagnosis-nonspecific terms (e.g., "having an irrational fear of X"; Norton & Hope, 2008). TGCBT consists of two phases. The first phase, spanning the majority of treatment (Sessions 1 through 9), draws upon traditional cognitive-behavioral treatment elements (e.g., psychoeducation, cognitive restructuring, exposure) to extinguish anxiety and fear about each patient's feared and avoided situations. The second phase, spanning the final three sessions, transitions to a focus on targeting general neurotic tendencies in an effort to prevent remission or the acquisition of additional symptoms.

The first session of TGCBT focuses on psychoeducation, as well as providing an opportunity for members to get to know each other. Group leaders provide didactic instruction in the nature of anxiety and cognitive-behavioral therapy. Group leaders differentiate between normal and problematic levels of anxiety in terms of functional impairment and discuss factors that make some individuals prone to anxiety (i.e., biological predisposition and learning experiences). To a greater extent than in the UP, there is an emphasis here on identifying when anxiety is a problem, defined as a misperception and exaggeration of threat (Norton, 2012b). Patients learn about the three components of anxiety and monitor these for homework (i.e., physical sensations, thoughts, and behaviors—the same elements included in the three-component model of emotion in the UP). The leaders explain the purpose of a fear and avoidance hierarchy, and each member begins to develop his or her own hierarchy in this session. In the second session, psychoeducation continues. Much like the psychoeducation provided in the UP, TGCBT highlights the adaptive nature of emotions. The approach differs in that Norton and colleagues focus on fear and anxiety as opposed to all emotional experiences, and they explore the adaptive or benign nature of each component of anxiety individually rather than the adaptive nature of emotions as a whole. This is followed by an introduction to cognitive restructuring, introduced by describing the ways in which perceptions of threat underlie experiences of anxiety. Patients are introduced to the concept of automatic thoughts as those that are more negative, inaccurate, or irrational relative to the situation, after which members monitor automatic thoughts as homework. Here, the focus is on changing irrational or negative thoughts, as in traditional cognitive therapy, as opposed to increasing cognitive flexibility generally, as in the UP. The third session of TGCBT involves additional instruction about cognitive biases, including overestimating the likelihood of negative outcomes and catastrophizing these outcomes (i.e., the same "thinking traps" found in the UP) as well as accurate but generally unhelpful thoughts or "maladaptive thinking." Patients practice using disputing questions to challenge automatic thoughts and generate alternative thoughts, called "rational responses" (again, the focus is on correction of thinking errors). The fourth session of TGCBT introduces the rationale for exposure (e.g., achieving habituation and expectancy disconfirmation), describes types of exposures and the strategy for conducting effective exposure (e.g., elimination of safety behaviors). The next six sessions involve exposure exercises progressing from least to most anxiety-provoking across sessions. These exposures are conducted comparably to those in the UP, with a few differences. Whereas the UP conceptualizes exposure as an opportunity to build tolerance to any uncomfortable emotion, TGCBT maintains a focus on fear and anxiety. TGCBT also places greater emphasis on setting behavioral goals for the exposure. Another difference is that TGCBT highlights the importance of distress reduction over the course of an exposure to a greater extent than the UP. In TGCBT, exposures are continued until distress reduces significantly or plateaus, and patients are reassured that their distress will decrease with repeated exposure. Examples of exposures include role-played social interactions, imaginal exposures targeting worries about feared events, and interoceptive exposure. Some exposures, such as those targeting symptoms of social anxiety, are designed to involve multiple group members. Members plan and perform additional exposures on their own between sessions.

Session 10 begins Phase 2 of TGCBT, in which the focus broadens to core negative beliefs and general neurotic traits, or what Norton and colleagues term the "general anxious style," rather than focusing on specific areas of anxiety. These sessions target negative core beliefs (e.g., "I am a failure") that would otherwise be vulnerability factors for relapse or reacquisition of fear. Sessions 10 and 11 focus on identifying core beliefs, noticing themes across these beliefs, generating evidence that is inconsistent with these beliefs, and challenging the meaning of events that contribute to strong negative emotion. Here, patients take the opportunity to challenge automatic thoughts that lead to a variety of negative emotional states, including anger or depression in addition to anxiety. Because these sessions encourage patients to reflect upon negative thinking styles that extend beyond their principal anxiety disorder (or "fear of X"), these sessions are, in a sense, the most *trans-diagnostic* of TGCBT, and the most resonant with Barlow and colleagues' approach of targeting neurotic traits generally without allegiance to principal diagnosis (or principal object of distress). The final session of TGCBT focuses on relapse prevention and planning continued application of skills to manage lapses.

Evidence

Norton (2008, 2012a), Norton and Barrera (2012), and Norton and Hope (2005) have found this intervention to reduce symptoms of anxiety disorders across both open and randomized controlled trials. A preliminary investigation compared outcomes of nine adults with heterogeneous anxiety disorders who received TGCBT against 10 individuals in a waitlist control group (Norton & Hope, 2005). This study found that the patients receiving TGCBT experienced a significant decrease in clinician-rated severity of their principal anxiety disorder and average clinician-rated severity of all comorbid diagnoses, improvements that were not seen in the waitlist group. The treatment group also uniquely experienced a significant decrease in self-reported fear of personally relevant stimuli. Two-thirds of treatment participants achieved subclinical status on their principal anxiety disorder, whereas none of the waitlist participants did. Nevertheless, other self-reported measures of anxiety symptoms showed no difference between the treatment and control groups. Similarly, the authors' hypothesis that the treatment group would experience an overall decrease in negative affectivity, an important mechanism on which the treatment was based, was not confirmed. Thus, although findings from this study were generally promising, these unexpected results and the small sample size both indicated a need for further research.

A subsequent open trial examined improvements in 52 anxiety disorder patients receiving TGCBT (Norton, 2008). This trial found a significant decrease in state anxiety over the course of treatment. The only diagnostic categories large enough to allow for between-group comparison were principal panic disorder and principal social anxiety disorder, and there was no difference in improvement found between these groups, adding to the preliminary support for the transdiagnostic utility of this treatment.

In a more rigorous examination of TGCBT, Norton and Barrera (2012) compared TGCBT against single-diagnosis group CBT protocols in the treatment of principal social anxiety, GAD, and panic disorder. In the 46 participants randomized to these two conditions, both transdiagnostic and diagnosis-specific treatments led to significant and equivalent improvement, suggesting that a transdiagnostic group intervention can be as effective as more specific interventions. These findings paralleled those of Barlow et al.'s (2016) comparison between the UP and single-diagnosis treatments for anxiety. An additional randomized controlled trial compared TGCBT against a group relaxation training program of the same length (Norton, 2012a). In this study, participants with heterogeneous anxiety disorders (primarily panic disorder, social anxiety disorder, and GAD) were randomly assigned at a 2:1 ratio to receive TGCBT ($N = 65$) or relaxation training ($N = 21$). The study found equivalent reductions on self-report measures of state anxiety and disorder-specific symptoms, as well as clinician-rated severity, and no differences in improvement across diagnostic categories for principal or comorbid diagnoses, supporting the transdiagnostic nature of response to treatment. Furthermore, retention was superior in the TGCBT group (70% completing treatment vs 43%).

Norton also analyzed data across trials of TGCBT and concluded that TGCBT has a greater effect on symptoms of comorbid (i.e., non-principal) anxiety disorders than diagnosis-specific CBT interventions (Norton et al., 2013). Relatedly, some patients experience reductions in symptoms of comorbid depressive disorders over the course of TGCBT (Norton, Hayes, & Hope, 2004; Talkovsky, Green, Osegueda, & Norton, 2016); this is similar to the improvements seen in comorbid diagnoses, including depressive disorders, among those patients treated with the UP (Barlow et al., in preparation). Recent work suggests that TGCBT also improves self-reported quality of life and intolerance of uncertainty (Talkovsky & Norton, 2016; Talkovsky, Paulus, Kuang, & Norton, under review, in Norton & Paulus, 2016). Importantly, reductions in anxiety symptoms over the course of TGCBT appear to be mediated by reductions in negative affectivity (Talkovsky & Norton, 2014). This provides further evidence for the role of this transdiagnostic mechanism in creating and maintaining symptoms across emotional disorders.

CONCLUSIONS

Over the past several decades, the focus on defining anxiety disorders as separate psychopathologies and treating them individually has played an important role in the development of effective treatments. For the subset of individuals who present with one isolated diagnosis, these evidence-based single-diagnosis treatment protocols are still a feasible and excellent option for providers who have the time and inclination to develop good adherence to multiple protocols. Nevertheless, both research evidence and practical considerations increasingly support a broader perspective focusing on shared features and treatment targets that are present across the range of anxiety disorders. Given evidence that anxiety and related disorders often occur in combination, along with the shared vulnerabilities and mechanisms relevant to the development and maintenance of these disorders, it is important to consider the use of unified transdiagnostic treatments like the ones discussed in this chapter. Although the developers of these treatments continue to collect evidence for their efficacy and effectiveness, initial studies of both treatments indicate that they are efficacious, including in comparison to established SDPs. Meta-analytic comparisons across studies examining transdiagnostic and single-diagnosis CBT treatments for anxiety suggest similar comparability in efficacy (Pearl & Norton, 2016). Transdiagnostic treatments have the benefit of reducing therapist burden in acquiring and using evidence-based protocols, and the broader focus can help patients understand how to respond to a variety of emotional problems, whether they present as comorbid diagnoses or subthreshold symptoms that are interfering or distressing. Ongoing research in transdiagnostic treatments for anxiety promises continued improvement in our understanding of and capacity to treat this class of disorders. As part of the development of transdiagnostic treatments hinge on efforts to enhance effectiveness, feasibility, and parsimony, future research will likely examine the efficacy of transdiagnostic treatment for additional diagnoses that fall within the spectrum of emotional disorders, continue to identify ways of making treatments briefer and more efficient, and examine methods of dissemination of transdiagnostic treatments to practicing clinicians in the community.

References

American Psychiatric Association. (2013). *Diagnostic and statistical manual of mental disorders, fifth edition (DSM-5)*. Arlington, Virginia, USA: American Psychiatric Association.

Andrews, G. (1996). Comorbidity and the general neurotic syndrome. *The British Journal of Psychiatry, 168*(Suppl 30), 76–84.

Barlow, D. H. (2000). Unraveling the mysteries of anxiety and its disorders from the perspective of emotion theory. *American Psychologist, 55*, 1247–1263.

Barlow, D. H. (2002). *Anxiety and its disorders: The nature and treatment of anxiety and panic* (2nd ed.). New York: Guilford Press.

Barlow, D. H., Ellard, K. K., Fairholme, C. P., Farchione, T. J., Boisseau, C. L., Allen, L. B., & Ehrenreich-May, J. (2011a). *The unified protocol for transdiagnostic treatment of emotional disorders: Client workbook*. New York: Oxford University Press.

Barlow, D.H., Farchione, T.J., Bullis, J.R., Gallagher, M.W., Latin, H., Sauer-Zavala, S., ... Cassiello-Robbins, C. A randomized equivalence evaluation of the unified protocol for transdiagnostic treatment of emotional disorders compared to diagnosis-specific CBT for anxiety disorders, 2016, manuscript submitted for publication.

Barlow, D. H., Farchione, T. J., Fairholme, C. P., Ellard, K. K., Boisseau, C. L., Allen, L. B., & Ehrenreich-May, J. (2011b). *The unified protocol for transdiagnostic treatment of emotional disorders: Therapist guide*. New York: Oxford University Press.

Barlow, D. H., Sauer-Zavala, S., Carl, J. R., Bullis, J. R., & Ellard, K. K. (2014). The nature, diagnosis, and treatment of neuroticism: Back to the future. *Clinical Psychological Science, 2*(3), 344–365.

Bienvenu, O. J., Samuels, J. F., Costa, P. T., Reti, I. M., Eaton, W. W., & Nestadt, G. (2004). Anxiety and depressive disorders and the five-factor model of personality: A higher- and lower-order personality trait investigation in a community sample. *Depression and Anxiety, 20*(2), 92–97.

Boettcher, H., Brake, C. A., & Barlow, D. (2016). Origins and outlook of interoceptive exposure. *Journal of Behavior Therapy and Experimental Psychiatry, 53*, 41–51.

Borkovec, T. D., Abel, J. L., & Newman, H. (1995). Effects of psychotherapy on comorbid conditions in generalized anxiety disorder. *Journal of Consulting and Clinical Psychology, 63*(3), 479–483.

Boswell, J. F., Anderson, L. M., & Barlow, D. H. (2014). An idiographic analysis of change processes in the unified transdiagnostic treatment of depression. *Journal of Consulting and Clinical Psychology, 82*, 1060–1071.

Boswell, J. F., Farchione, T. J., Sauer-Zavala, S., Murray, H. W., Fortune, M. R., & Barlow, D. H. (2013). Anxiety sensitivity and interoceptive exposure: A transdiagnostic construct and change strategy. *Behavior Therapy, 44*, 417–431.

Boswell, J. F., Thompson-Hollands, J., Farchione, T. J., & Barlow, D. H. (2013). Intolerance of uncertainty: A common factor in the treatment of emotional disorders. *Journal of Clinical Psychology, 69*, 630–645.

Breslau, N., & Schultz, L. (2013). Neuroticism and post-traumatic stress disorder: A prospective investigation. *Psychological Medicine, 43*, 1697–1702.

Brown, T. A. (2007). Temporal course and structural relationships among dimensions of temperament and DSM-IV anxiety and mood disorder constructs. *Journal of Abnormal Psychology, 116*, 313–328.

Brown, T. A., Antony, M. M., & Barlow, D. H. (1995). Diagnostic comorbidity in panic disorder: Effect on treatment outcome and course of comorbid diagnoses following treatment. *Journal of Consulting and Clinical Psychology, 63*(3), 408–418.

Brown, T. A., Campbell, L. A., Lehman, C. L., Grisham, J. R., & Mancill, R. B. (2001). Current and lifetime comorbidity of the DSM-IV anxiety and mood disorders in a large clinical sample. *Journal of Abnormal Psychology, 110*(4), 585–599.

Brown, T. A., Chorpita, B. F., & Barlow, D. H. (1998). Structural relationships among dimensions of the DSM-IV anxiety and mood disorders and dimensions of negative affect, positive affect, and autonomic arousal. *Journal of Abnormal Psychology, 107*(2), 179–192.

Bullis, J. R., Sauer-Zavala, S., Bentley, K. H., Thompson-Hollands, J., Carl, J. R., & Barlow, D. H. (2015). The unified protocol for transdiagnostic treatment of emotional disorders preliminary exploration of effectiveness for group delivery. *Behavior Modification, 39*(2), 295–321.

Carl, J. R., Gallagher, M. W., Sauer-Zavala, S. E., Bentley, K. H., & Barlow, D. H. (2014). A preliminary investigation of the effects of the unified protocol on temperament. *Comprehensive Psychiatry, 55*, 1426–1434.

Ciraulo, D. A., Barlow, D. H., Gulliver, S. B., Farchione, T., Morissette, S. B., Kamholz, B. W., . . . Knapp, C. M. (2013). The effects of venlafaxine and cognitive behavioral therapy alone and combined in the treatment of co-morbid alcohol use-anxiety disorders. *Behaviour Research and Therapy, 51*, 729–735.

Clark, L. A., Watson, D., & Mineka, S. (1994). Temperament, personality, and the mood and anxiety disorders. *Journal of Abnormal Psychology, 103*(1), 103.

Craske, M. G., Antony, M. M., & Barlow, D. H. (2006). *Mastering your fears and phobias (2nd ed.): Therapist guide*. New York, NY, US: Oxford University Press.

Darvill, T. J., & Johnson, R. C. (1991). Optimism and perceived control of life events as related to personality. *Personality and Individual Differences, 12*(9), 951–954.

Ellard, K. K., Deckersbach, T., Sylvia, L. G., Nierenberg, A. A., & Barlow, D. H. (2012). Transdiagnostic treatment of bipolar disorder and comorbid anxiety with the unified protocol: A clinical replication series. *Behavior Modification, 36*, 482–508.

Ellard, K. K., Fairholme, C. P., Boisseau, C. L., Farchione, T. J., & Barlow, D. H. (2010). Unified protocol for the transdiagnostic treatment of emotional disorders: Protocol development and initial outcome data. *Cognitive and Behavioral Practice, 17*(1), 88−101.

Etkin, A., Prater, K. E., Hoeft, F., Menon, V., & Schatzberg, A. F. (2010). Failure of anterior cingulate activation and connectivity with the amygdala during implicit regulation of emotional processing in generalized anxiety disorder. *The American Journal of Psychiatry, 167*(5), 545−554.

Everaerd, D., Klumpers, F., van Wingen, G., Tendolkar, I., & Fernández, G. (2015). Association between neuroticism and amygdala responsivity emerges under stressful conditions. *Neuroimage, 112*, 218−224.

Farchione, T. J., Fairholme, C. P., Ellard, K. K., Boisseau, C. L., Thompson-Hollands, J., Carl, J. R., ... Barlow, D. H. (2012). Unified protocol for transdiagnostic treatment of emotional disorders: A randomized controlled trial. *Behavior Therapy, 43*(3), 666−678.

Fullana, M. À., Mataix-Cols, D., Trujillo, J. L., Caseras, X., Serrano, F., Alonso, P., ... Torrubia, R. (2004). Personality characteristics in obsessive-compulsive disorder and individuals with subclinical obsessive-compulsive problems. *British Journal of Clinical Psychology, 43*(4), 387−398.

Gallagher, M. W., Bentley, K. H., & Barlow, D. H. (2014). Perceived control and vulnerability to anxiety disorders: A meta-analytic review. *Cognitive Therapy and Research, 38*(6), 571−584.

Gallagher, M. W., Sauer-Zavala, S. E., Boswell, J. F., Carl, J. R., Bullis, J., Farchione, T. J., & Barlow, D. H. (2013). The impact of the unified protocol for emotional disorders on quality of life. *International Journal of Cognitive Therapy, 6*, 57−72.

Greenberg, P. E., Sisitsky, T., Kessler, R. C., Finkelstein, S. N., Berndt, E. R., Davidson, J. T., ... Fyer, A. J. (1999). The economic burden of anxiety disorders in the 1990s. *Journal of Clinical Psychiatry, 60*(7), 427−435.

Gunthert, K. C., Cohen, L. H., & Armeli, S. (1999). The role of neuroticism in daily stress and coping. *Journal of Personality and Social Psychology, 77*(5), 1087−1100.

Hofmann, S. G., & Smits, J. A. (2008). Cognitive-behavioral therapy for adult anxiety disorders: a meta-analysis of randomized placebo-controlled trials. *The Journal of Clinical Psychiatry, 69*(4), 621.

Holmes, A. J., Lee, P. H., Hollinshead, M. O., Bakst, L., Roffman, J. L., Smoller, J. W., & Buckner, R. I. (2012). Individual differences in amygdala-medial prefrontal anatomy link negative affect, impaired social functioning, and polygenetic depression link. *Journal of Neuroscience, 32*, 18087−18100.

Jylhä, P., & Isometsä, E. (2006). The relationship of neuroticism and extraversion to symptoms of anxiety and depression in the general population. *Depression and Anxiety, 23*(5), 281−289.

Kessler, R. C., Petukhova, M., Sampson, N. A., Zaslavsky, A. M., & Wittchen, H. (2012). Twelve-month and lifetime prevalence and lifetime morbid risk of anxiety and mood disorders in the United States. *International Journal of Methods in Psychiatric Research, 21*(3), 169−184.

Lopez, M. E., Stoddard, J. A., Noorollah, A., Zerbi, G., Payne, L. A., Hitchcock, C. A., ... Ray, D. B. (2015). Examining the efficacy of the unified protocol for transdiagnostic treatment of emotional disorders in the treatment of individuals with borderline personality disorder. *Cognitive and Behavioral Practice, 22*, 522−533.

Lorberbaum, J. P., Kose, S., Johnson, M. R., Arana, G. W., Sullivan, L. K., Hamner, M. B., ... George, M. S. (2004). Neural correlates of speech anticipatory anxiety in generalized social phobia. *NeuroReport, 15*, 2701−2705.

Miller, W. R., & Rollnick, S. (2012). *Motivational interviewing: Helping people change*. New York: Guilford Press.

Mojtabai, R., Stuart, E. A., Susukida, R., Eaton, W. W., Sampson, N., & Kessler, R. C. (2015). Long-term effects of mental disorders on employment in the National

Comorbidity Survey ten-year follow-up. *Society of Psychiatry and Psychiatric Epidemiology, 50*(11), 1657–1668.

Monk, C. S., Telzer, E. H., Mogg, K., Bradley, B. P., Mai, X., Louro, H. C., . . . Pine, D. S. (2008). Amygdala and ventrolateral prefrontal cortex activation to masked angry faces in children and adolescents with generalized anxiety disorder. *Archives of General Psychiatry, 65*(5), 568–576.

Norton, P. J. (2008). An open trial of a transdiagnostic cognitive-behavioral group therapy for anxiety disorder. *Behavior Therapy, 39*(3), 242–250.

Norton, P. J. (2012a). A randomized clinical trial of transdiagnostic cognitive-behavioral treatments for anxiety disorder by comparison to relaxation training. *Behavior Therapy, 43*(3), 506–517.

Norton, P. J. (2012b). *Group cognitive-behavioral therapy of anxiety: A transdiagnostic treatment manual.* New York: Guilford Press.

Norton, P. J., & Barrera, T. L. (2012). Transdiagnostic versus diagnosis-specific CBT for anxiety disorders: A preliminary randomized controlled noninferiority trial. *Depression and Anxiety, 29*(10), 874–882.

Norton, P. J., Barrera, T. L., Mathew, A. R., Chamberlain, L. D., Szafranski, D. D., Reddy, R., & Smith, A. H. (2013). Effect of transdiagnostic CBT for anxiety disorders on comorbid diagnoses. *Depression and Anxiety, 30*(2), 168–173.

Norton, P. J., Hayes, S. A., & Hope, D. A. (2004). Effects of a transdiagnostic group treatment for anxiety on secondary depression. *Depression and Anxiety, 20*, 198–202.

Norton, P. J., & Hope, D. A. (2005). Preliminary evaluation of a broad-spectrum cognitive-behavioral group therapy for anxiety. *Journal of Behavior Therapy and Experimental Psychiatry, 36*, 79–97.

Norton, P. J., & Hope, D. A. (2008). The "anxiety treatment protocol": A group case study demonstration of a transdiagnostic group cognitive-behavioral therapy for anxiety disorders. *Clinical Case Studies, 7*, 538–554.

Norton, P. J., & Paulus, D. J. (2016). Toward a unified treatment for emotional disorders: Update on the science and practice. *Behavior Therapy, 47*, 854–868.

Olatunji, B. O., Cisler, J. M., & Tolin, D. F. (2007). Quality of life in the anxiety disorders: A meta-analytic review. *Clinical Psychology Review, 27*, 572–581.

Pearl, S. B., & Norton, P. J. (2016). Transdiagnostic versus diagnosis specific cognitive behavioural therapies for anxiety: A meta-analysis*Journal of Anxiety Disorders,* Advance online publication. Available from http://dx.doi.org/10.1016/j.janxdis.2016.07.004.

Phan, K. L., Fitzgerald, D. A., Nathan, P. J., & Tancer, M. E. (2006). Association between amygdala hyperactivity to harsh faces and severity of social anxiety in generalized social phobia. *Biological Psychiatry, 59*, 424–429.

Rosellini, A. J., Lawrence, A. E., Meyer, J. F., & Brown, T. A. (2010). The effects of extraverted temperament on agoraphobia in panic disorder. *Journal of Abnormal Psychology, 119*, 420–426.

Sauer-Zavala, S., Bentley, K. H., & Wilner, J. G. (2016). Transdiagnostic treatment of borderline personality disorder and comorbid disorders: A clinical replication series. *Journal of Personality Disorders, 30*, 35–51.

Segal, Z. V., Williams, J. M. G., & Teasdale, J. D. (2001). *Mindfulness-based cognitive therapy for depression.* New York: Guilford Press.

Stewart, R. E., Chambless, D. L., & Baron, J. (2012). Theoretical and practical barriers to practitioners' willingness to seek training in empirically supported treatments. *Journal of Clinical Psychology, 68*(1), 8–23.

Straube, T., Mentzel, H. J., & Miltner, W. H. (2006). Neural mechanisms of automatic and direct processing of phobogenic stimuli in specific phobia. *Biological Psychiatry, 59*, 162–170.

Talkovsky, A. M., Green, K. L., Osegueda, A., & Norton, P. J. (2016). Secondary depression in transdiagnostic group cognitive behavioral therapy among individuals diagnosed with anxiety disorders*Journal of Anxiety Disorders*, Advance online publication. Available from http://dx.doi.org/10.1016/j.janxdis.2016.09.008.

Talkovsky, A. M., & Norton, P. J. (2014). Mediators of transdiagnostic group cognitive behavior therapy. *Journal of Anxiety Disorders, 28*(8), 919–924.

Talkovsky, A. M., & Norton, P. J. (2016). Intolerance of uncertainty and transdiagnostic group cognitive behavioral therapy for anxiety. *Journal of Anxiety Disorders, 41*, 108–114.

Talkovsky, A.M., Paulus, D.J., Kuang, F., & Norton, P.J. (under review). Quality of life outcomes following Transdiagnostic Group Cognitive-Behavioral Therapy for Anxiety.

Tillfors, M., Furmark, T., Marteinsdottir, I., & Fredrikson, M. (2002). Cerebral blood flow during anticipation of public speaking in social phobia: A PET study. *Biological Psychiatry, 52*, 1113–1119.

Tsao, J. I., Lewin, M. R., & Craske, M. G. (1998). The effects of cognitive-behavior therapy for panic disorder on comorbid conditions. *Journal of Anxiety Disorders, 12*(4), 357–371.

Tsao, J. I., Mystkowski, J. L., Zucker, B. G., & Craske, M. G. (2002). Effects of cognitive-behavioral therapy for panic disorder on comorbid conditions: Replication and extension. *Behavior Therapy, 33*(4), 493–509.

Tyrer, P., Seivewright, N., Ferguson, B., & Tyrer, J. (1992). The general neurotic syndrome: A coaxial diagnosis of anxiety, depression and personality disorder. *Acta Psychiatrica Scandinavica, 85*(3), 201–206.

Westra, H. A., & Dozois, D. J. (2006). Preparing clients for cognitive behavioral therapy: A randomized pilot study of motivational interviewing for anxiety. *Cognitive Therapy and Research, 30*(4), 481–498.

Wilamowska, Z. A., Thompson-Hollands, J., Fairholme, C. P., Ellard, K. K., Farchione, T. J., & Barlow, D. H. (2010). Conceptual background, development, and preliminary data from the unified protocol for transdiagnostic treatment of emotional disorders. *Depression and Anxiety, 27*(10), 882–890.

Zinbarg, R. E., Craske, M. G., & Barlow, D. H. (2006). *Mastery of your anxiety and worry (2nd ed.): Therapist guide*. New York, NY, US: Oxford University Press.

Zinbarg, R. E., Mineka, S., Bobova, L., Craske, M. G., Vrshek-Schallhorn, S., Griffith, J. W., ... Anand, D. (2016). Testing a hierarchical model of neuroticism and its cognitive facets: Latent structure and prospective prediction of first onsets of anxiety and unipolar mood disorders during 3 years in late adolescence. *Clinical Psychological Science, 4*, 805–824.

Cognitive Behavioral Therapy for Sleep Disorders

Caitlin E. Gasperetti, Michael R. Dolsen and
Allison G. Harvey

University of California, Berkeley, CA, United States

INTRODUCTION

We spend approximately one-third of our lives sleeping. Although the study of human sleep is a relatively young science and many fascinating mysteries remain to be solved, there have been great advances in knowledge on the function of sleep as well as the nature and treatment of sleep disorders. This chapter will focus on insomnia, one of the most common sleep disorders. Insomnia is a chronic difficulty that involves problems getting to sleep, maintaining sleep, or waking in the morning not feeling restored. It is a prevalent and increasingly common problem, with 19.2% of adults reporting difficulty sleeping (Ford, Cunningham, Giles, & Croft, 2015). The consequences of sleep deprivation are severe and include decreased quality of life, work absenteeism and work-related problems, decreased productivity, increased rates of accidents, and increased use of medical services (Roth, 2007). Not surprisingly, given the prevalence and associated impairments, the cost to society is enormous. The 6-month cost burden of direct (medical bills) and indirect (missed work, disability) costs is estimated to be an added $1235 per adult suffering from insomnia (Ozminkowski, Wang, & Walsh, 2007). This chapter will give an overview of insomnia as a sleep disorder, take into consideration the effects of age and comorbid medical and psychiatric disorders, and explore psychological and pharmacological treatments most commonly used for sleep disorders.

The Science of Cognitive Behavioral Therapy.
DOI: http://dx.doi.org/10.1016/B978-0-12-803457-6.00016-7

SLEEP BASICS

Human sleep can be divided into two types: nonrapid eye movement (NREM) and rapid eye movement (REM) sleep. NREM sleep can be divided further into the initial transition between wakefulness and sleep (Stage 1), Stage 2, and Stage 3 or slow-wave sleep (SWS), which is the deepest stage of sleep (Iber, Ancoli-Israel, Chesson Jr., & Quan, 2007; Schulz, 2008). During the night, adults experience 70–120 min sleep cycles in which they transition between NREM and REM sleep, with longer SWS episodes during the beginning of the night and longer REM and Stage 2 episodes later in the night (Carskadon & Dement, 2011). NREM sleep is thought to be important for conservation of energy and restoration. It is this phase of sleep that is associated with rapid cell division in some tissues as well as with increased protein synthesis (Shneerson, 2000). The functions of REM sleep include the processing of declarative memories (Walker, 2009), the unlearning of irrelevant information (Crick & Mitchison, 1983), emotional processing and emotion regulation (Walker, 2009), and the consolidation of memories (Walker & Stickgold, 2006). Additionally, sleep deprivation is associated with changes in the immune and neuroendocrine systems, increased inflammation, and cardiovascular disease (Faraut, Boudjeltia, Vanhamme, & Kerkhofs, 2012). Given the important functions of sleep, sleep disturbance and its treatment have major public health implications.

DEFINITION OF INSOMNIA

There are two main classification systems for sleep disorders, including the third edition of the International Classification of Sleep Disorders (American Academy of Sleep Medicine, 2014) and the fifth edition of the Diagnostic and Statistical Manual of Mental Disorders or DSM-5 (American Psychiatric Association, 2013). We will focus on the DSM-5 criteria in this chapter. Within the DSM-5, diagnostic criteria for insomnia are defined by a subjective complaint of trouble falling asleep, staying asleep, or early morning awakening along with dissatisfaction with the quantity or quality of sleep. Additionally, these difficulties must be associated with clinically significant distress or daytime impairment and must not be better accounted for by another medical or psychiatric condition (American Psychiatric Association, 2013). Insomnia often cooccurs with other disorders. Around 75% of people with insomnia have a cooccurring medical problem and around 40% have a cooccurring psychiatric condition (Roth, 2007). Comorbidity is an important consideration when designing treatment for insomnia and will be discussed later in this chapter.

Insomnia is a common disorder. Approximately one-third of the general population reports symptoms of insomnia, and 6% of the general adult population meets diagnostic criteria for a formal diagnosis of insomnia (Roth, 2007). Due to the increasing prevalence of insomnia in the general population, the need for appropriate assessment and treatment is rising.

ASSESSMENT OF INSOMNIA

Subjective Assessment of Insomnia

As evident from the DSM-5 criteria, insomnia is defined subjectively. As such, three types of self-reported sleep data are collected from patients during an assessment for insomnia.

First, a sleep history is taken by a clinician using the DSM-5 diagnostic criteria. Information gathered includes the duration, frequency, and severity of nighttime sleep disturbance including estimates of sleep onset latency (the amount of time it takes to fall asleep), number of awakenings after sleep onset, total amount of time awake after sleep onset, total sleep time, and an estimate of sleep quality. Information about the onset, duration, and type of symptoms (i.e., sleep onset, sleep maintenance, early morning awaking problem, or combinations of these) is collected. A description of the consequences and distress due to insomnia symptoms, including daytime impairment, is also collected. It is important to also obtain information about medications (prescription and over the counter) and screen for the presence of comorbid psychiatric disorders and medical problems (including other sleep disorders). All these pieces of information are used to determine the presence of insomnia and provide a diagnosis.

Second, one or more validated questionnaires can be used to index the presence and severity of sleep disturbance [e.g., Pittsburgh sleep quality index (PSQI); Buysse, Reynolds, Monk, Berman, & Kupfer, 1989], insomnia [e.g., insomnia severity index (ISI); Bastien, Vallières, & Morin, 2001], and daytime sleepiness [e.g., Stanford Sleepiness Scale; Hoddes, Zarcone, Smythe, Phillips, & Dement, 1973]. The two most commonly used and recommended questionnaires in a research setting are the PSQI, which consists of 19 self-rating questions and 4 open-ended questions assessing sleep quality and disturbance over the past month, and the ISI, consisting of 7 self-rating questions assessing insomnia symptoms, impairment in functioning, and concerns related to sleep over the past two weeks. Both measures can be used by clinicians in order to validate assessment screenings and treatment outcomes (Buysse, Ancoli-Israel, Edinger, Lichstein, & Morin, 2006).

Third, the patient might be asked to complete a sleep diary each morning as soon as possible after waking for 2 weeks to provide prospective estimates of sleep. Carney et al. (2012) provide recommendations for sleep diaries to use with insomnia patients. A sleep diary provides information including night-to-night variability of sleep difficulty and sleep—wake patterns and can be used to determine the presence of circadian rhythm problems (Carney et al., 2012). Since the patient is providing information about sleep immediately upon awakening and over the course of several nights, sleep diaries are often a more representative picture of sleep than a one-time questionnaire or one night of polysomnography (PSG; discussed below) (Buysse et al., 2006).

Objective Assessment of Insomnia

The gold standard objective measure of sleep is PSG. PSG involves placing surface electrodes on the scalp and face to measure electrical brain activity (electroencephalogram or EEG), eye movement (electrooculogram or EOG), and muscle tone (electromyogram or EMG). NREM Stage 2, SWS, and REM sleep are all characterized by different patterns of brain activity, and REM sleep is associated with REMs and muscle atonia. The data obtained are used to classify each epoch of data by sleep stage and in terms of sleep cycles (NREM and REM). PSG also provides useful information about sleep onset, sleep onset latency, wake after sleep onset, sleep offset, total sleep time, and sleep efficiency or the amount of time in bed spent sleeping. Disadvantages associated with PSG include its expense, discomfort for participants, and that it is labor-intensive. PSG can be helpful for identifying sleep disorders, including sleep apnea and periodic limb movement disorder, but is not commonly used to assess insomnia (Chesson et al., 2000; Morin et al., 2015).

Actigraphy is another means of providing an objective estimate of sleep and is often used when PSG is not feasible. Unlike PSG, which measures stages of sleep, actigraphy distinguishes between periods of wakefulness and sleep. The actigraphs, which are small, wrist-worn devices containing a sensor that measures movement and sometimes light exposure, sample physical motion and translate it into epochs of specified time duration. Actigraphy provides information about sleep onset, sleep onset latency, wake after sleep onset, sleep offset, total sleep time, and sleep efficiency (Buysse et al., 2006). PSG and actigraphy measures of sleep have been strongly correlated in normal sleepers and a strong correlation between actigraphy and PSG for all sleep measures except sleep onset latency was found in patients with insomnia

(Lichstein et al., 2006). Actigraphy was also found to have an accuracy of 82%, with accuracy defined as the proportion of PSG wake and sleep epochs correctly identified by actigraphy, in normal sleepers (Blood, Sack, Percy, & Pen, 1997). As with PSG, actigraphy is not required for the assessment of insomnia (Buysse et al., 2006); but it is a cost-effective and minimally intrusive measure that is helpful in providing an overview of the sleep—wake cycle.

BRIEF OVERVIEW OF OTHER SLEEP DISORDERS

Although a full description of other sleep disorders and their treatment is beyond the scope of this chapter, a very brief description of each of several other major sleep disorders is provided here. The presence of one of these disorders is among the exclusionary criteria for an insomnia disorder (American Psychiatric Association, 2013). As such, their presence should be assessed in all insomnia cases and is included in the assessment of sleep history. Each of these disorders can have serious consequences for the health and daytime functioning of the sufferer.

Sleep Apnea

Sleep apnea involves the temporary closure of the upper airway during sleep associated with disruption to sleep. Nighttime symptoms can include snoring, pauses in breathing during sleep, shortness of breath during sleep, choking during sleep, headaches upon waking, difficulty getting breath, or breathlessness upon waking. The adverse outcomes include daytime sleepiness and cardiovascular problems. Sleep apnea is more common in men (Peppard et al., 2013).

Restless Legs Syndrome

The symptoms of restless legs syndrome are a sensation or urge to move the limbs (usually legs) and a feeling of restlessness because of sensations in the limbs (usually legs). The sensations start or get worse when resting, relaxing, or first going to bed. A clear circadian pattern must also be present. Restless legs syndrome is more common in women and older adults (Innes, Selfe, & Agarwal, 2011).

Periodic Limb Movement Disorder

The central feature of periodic limb movement disorder is repetitive episodes of stereotyped limb movements (usually the legs) during sleep. The movements are associated with a partial or full awakening. Periodic limb movement disorder is more common in women (Ohayon & Roth, 2002).

Circadian Rhythm Disorders

Circadian rhythm disorders affect the timing of when a person is asleep and awake. Typically, the 24-h circadian rhythm aligns with the timing of the external environment. However, when these two rhythms become misaligned, different patterns of sleep emerge. Two circadian rhythm disorders are advanced sleep phase and delayed sleep phase. Advanced sleep phase involves falling asleep early in the evening and waking up early in the morning. Delayed sleep phase involves not being able to fall asleep until the early hours in the morning and sleeping well into the next day (Reid & Zee, 2009).

Narcolepsy

This is a disorder characterized by excessive sleepiness. Episodes of short uncontrollable naps during the day are typical. Often the nap is associated with cataplexy (loss of muscle tone triggered by strong emotion), sleep paralysis, or hypnogogic hallucinations.

HISTORY OF TREATING INSOMNIA

Treatment for insomnia dates back to the 1920s with Jacobson's progressive muscle relaxation treatment. The primary rationale for this treatment, and for many others that followed, was that heightened arousal disturbed sleep (Jacobson, 1925). During the rise of behaviorism in the 1960s and 1970s, sleep disturbance was attributed to conditioning, where the bedroom environment and heightened arousal became associated with sleeplessness, leading to a learned sleep disturbance (Bootzin, 1979). In the 1980s, biofeedback, which requires patients to learn to monitor their electromyography or sensory-motor rhythm levels, became a popular treatment for insomnia and was shown to be efficacious (Chesson et al., 1999; Morgenthaler et al., 2006). However, the growing popularity of cognitive behavioral therapy (CBT) as well as the time-consuming nature of biofeedback have rendered biofeedback significantly less popular. Currently, cognitive behavioral approaches are the preferred treatment for insomnia (Morin et al., 2015).

COGNITIVE BEHAVIORAL MODELS OF INSOMNIA

Cognitive behavioral approaches for treating insomnia are influenced by two different treatment models. The first model is the "three-factor" or "three-P model" (Spielman, Caruso, & Glovinsky, 1987). The three-factor model is a diathesis-stress model that proposes that insomnia occurs as the result of predisposing factors (e.g., traits), which provide vulnerability for the disorder, and precipitating factors (e.g., life stressors), that trigger the initial onset of the disorder. Insomnia becomes chronic due to perpetuating factors (e.g., poor coping strategies). CBT targets these perpetuating factors. The second model expands on the three-factor model and identifies hyperarousal (cognitive, affective, behavioral, or physiological) as a key precipitating factor for insomnia (Morin, 1993). Stimulus conditioning can then exacerbate this arousal. For example, a person may associate temporal (e.g., bedtime routines) and environmental (e.g., bedroom) stimuli with fear of being unable to sleep. Worry and rumination may result and additional perpetuating factors including daytime fatigue, worry and emotional distress about sleep loss, and maladaptive habits (e.g., excessive time in bed) may ensue. Thus, while hyperarousal may serve as a trigger, a multitude of factors perpetuate the negative cycle. The consequences of sleeplessness may also serve as a trigger for the cycle. This expanded three-factor model provides a helpful theoretical basis for assessing and treating insomnia.

OVERVIEW OF TREATMENT FOR INSOMNIA

Most of the research to date has focused on CBT-I and pharmacologic interventions, each of which is described below.

Cognitive Behavioral Therapy for Insomnia

The primary goal of CBT-I is to address the cognitive and behavioral maintaining mechanisms involved in perpetuating sleep disturbance. A second important goal is to teach coping techniques that patients can use in instances of sleep difficulty once therapy has ended. CBT-I is currently considered the treatment of choice for insomnia (Morgenthaler et al., 2006). It is a multi-component treatment that typically comprises one or more of the following: stimulus control, sleep restriction, sleep education, paradoxical intention, relaxation therapy, and cognitive therapy.

Stimulus Control

Stimulus control requires patients to set a regular sleep schedule with a consistent bedtime and wake time, take no daytime naps, only go to bed when sleep is imminent and leave bed if they are not falling asleep, and eliminate distracting and stimulating activities that are sleep-incompatible (such as upsetting or stimulating conversations, television, and smartphones) from the bedroom (Bootzin, Epstein, & Wood, 1991). When an individual is conditioned to no longer associate their bed with sleep, insomnia arises and stimulus control is designed to alter that association.

Sleep Restriction

Sleep restriction therapy limits time in bed to maximize the sleep drive and strengthen the association between the bed and sleeping (Spielman, Saskin, & Thorpy, 1987). Patients begin by estimating the amount of time they actually spend sleeping and are asked to restrict their time spent in bed so that it is equivalent. For instance, an individual who spends 1 h falling asleep, 1 h awake throughout the night, and 6 h sleeping would reduce their time in bed from 8 to 6 h. This restriction strengthens the homeostatic sleep drive through mild sleep deprivation (Morin, 2011). Time in bed is increased once sleep efficiency is greater than 85%—90% for adults or greater than 80% in older adults. Sleep efficiency is defined as total sleep time divided by time in bed multiplied by 100. Following this restriction, sleep gradually becomes more efficient, at which point time spent in bed is gradually increased to reach an optimal sleep efficiency.

Sleep Education

Patients are provided with information about sleep, factors that can interfere with sleep (e.g., lifestyle, environment), as well as ways to promote better sleep. Some guidelines and areas of education include limiting stimulants and alcohol before bedtime, exercising regularly, allowing for a period of 30—60 min before bed to relax, creating a comfortable sleep environment that is quiet and dark, and maintaining a regular sleep schedule (Morin, 2011). Additional information might also be provided about normal sleep and individual differences in sleep patterns across the lifespan. Although sleep education is a common component of CBT-I, there is no empirical support for it being used as a stand-alone intervention (Morin et al., 2006).

Paradoxical Intention

In paradoxical intention, patients are instructed to stay awake for as long as possible. When patients are focused on staying awake rather than actively trying to fall asleep, there is often a reduction in performance anxiety and sleep effort. The patient is no longer actively involved in trying to get to sleep and instead becomes a passive observer, which more easily facilitates sleep onset. The aim is to reduce excessive monitoring of sleep and worries about insomnia and its consequences (Morin et al., 2006).

Relaxation Therapy

Patients are taught to implement a variety of exercises while in the therapy session and are then encouraged to practice these exercises as much as they can between sessions; but the emphasis is on practice during the day (as opposed to using them only at night in an effort to get to sleep). Relaxation techniques either focus on reducing arousal (e.g., progressive muscle relaxation) or focusing attention (e.g., imagery training and meditation) (Morin, 2011). The type of relaxation technique used often depends on the type of arousal, and it is important for patients to understand the context under which to employ these different techniques. For example, an inability to relax physically (e.g., feelings of restlessness) would benefit more from progressive muscle relaxation that focuses on reducing physical arousal, whereas an inability to relax mentally (e.g., racing thoughts) would benefit more from imagery training that focuses on reducing cognitive arousal (Sharma & Andrade, 2012). One type of relaxation, mindfulness, has also been used as an independent treatment for insomnia and will be discussed in more detail later in this chapter.

Cognitive Therapy

In this version of cognitive therapy (CT-I), the goals are to reverse a broad range of cognitive maintaining mechanisms including unhelpful believes about sleep, worry related to sleep, attentional bias and monitoring for sleep related threat, and misperceptions about sleep. Cognitive therapy was first described by Beck, Rush, Shaw, and Emery (1979). The CT-I component of CBT-I was originally administered over the course of one session. The one session version involves providing education with the aim of altering faulty beliefs about sleep requirements, the biological clock, and the effects of sleep loss on sleep—wake functions. More recently, a broader form of CT-I has been delivered across multiple sessions and interwoven with the behavior therapy components (Harvey et al., 2014).

Evidence for CBT-I Components

A number of randomized controlled trials (RCTs) have compared one or more components of CBT-I to each other and/or to a placebo.

The Standards of Practice Committee of the American Academy of Sleep Medicine found CBT-I to be highly effective and to have sustainable gains over long-term follow-up in adult and older adult samples (Morgenthaler et al., 2006; Morin et al., 2006). This review used the American Psychological Association criteria for well-supported empirically based treatments (Chambless & Hollon, 1998) and concluded that these criteria are met by stimulus control, paradoxical intention, relaxation therapy, sleep restriction approaches, and the administration of multiple components in the form of CBT-I. In addition, several components were concluded to have not yet been tested sufficiently to draw a conclusion, including cognitive therapy, sleep education, and imagery training, which is one component of relaxation therapy. However, since that time a RCT comparing CBT-I to CT-I and behavioral therapy (BT-I) found that while BT-I facilitated faster, short-term benefits and CT-I produced slower but more sustained improvement, CBT-I was the best option for both short and long-term treatment outcomes (Harvey et al., 2014). However, it is worth keeping in mind that all three treatments were found to be effective for the treatment of insomnia and one major limitation of the study was that CBT-I sessions were longer than both CT-I and BT-I.

CBT-I Implementation

Four to ten weekly sessions of CBT-I are typically needed to administer the components chosen from those described above. CBT-I can be implemented as individual therapy, group therapy, or self-help interventions (see Bastien, Morin, Ouellet, Blais, & Bouchard, 2004; Jernelöv et al., 2012).

Pharmacologic Interventions

There are several different types of medications specifically designed to treat sleep disturbance as well as those used off-label. Two commonly used classes of medication are benzodiazepines and nonbenzodiazepines. These two different classes of medication both modulate the gamma-aminobutyric acid type A receptors to enhance inhibitory effects in the brain, including relaxation and sleep enhancement, and are most helpful for sleep onset dysregulation (Morin et al., 2015). All nonbenzodiazepines and some benzodiazepines are approved for use during sleep onset, and some nonbenzodiazepines are also approved for help with sleep maintenance (Morin et al., 2015). Some other FDA approved medications for sleep dysregulation include doxepin, a selective histamine H1 receptor agonist approved for sleep maintenance; ramelteon, a melatonin receptor agonist approved for sleep onset; melatonin, an over-the-counter medication widely used for insomnia symptoms and delayed sleep-phase syndrome; and suvorexant, an antagonist of orexin receptors approved for sleep onset and sleep maintenance (Morin et al., 2015). Benzodiazepines and nonbenzodiazepines have been shown to have a small risk of abuse for certain populations, whereas doxepin, ramelteon, melatonin, and suvorexant do not (Morin et al., 2015). Some antidepressants (amitriptyline, doxepin, trazodone, and mirtazapine), antipsychotics (olanzapine, quetiapine, and risperidone), antihypertensives (prazosin), and anticonvulsants (gabapentin and pregabalin) are used off-label for the treatment of sleep dysregulation. To date, although these drugs show minimal abuse potential, there is little to no data available from RCTs about the efficacy and risk-benefit for treating insomnia using these medications (Morin et al., 2015). Pharmacologic interventions also carry the added risk of tolerance, dependence, and daytime effects; moreover, rebound insomnia is a common problem associated with the discontinuation of these medications, even after only a few days (Morin et al., 2015).

Combined Psychological and Pharmacologic Interventions

It is becoming more common for psychological and pharmacologic treatments to be used together. A recent review found that CBT-I was not only as effective as sleep medications at treating insomnia but also produced more durable results compared to medications (Hood, Rogojanski, & Moss, 2014). Sivertsen et al. conducted a RCT comparing CBT-I, zopiclone (a nonbenzodiazepine hypnotic), and a placebo, finding that the CBT-I group improved over the zopiclone group on measures of total wake time, sleep efficiency, and SWS at 6-week and 6-month follow-ups. Zopiclone was found to be no better than a placebo on most outcomes (Sivertsen et al., 2006). Combined therapy has been shown to produce a higher rate of remission compared to those who received just CBT-I, and results were maintained for 24 months; however, when medication was discontinued after an initial period and just CBT-I was maintained, there was greater improvement compared to those who continued with the medication (Morin et al., 2009). Although it appears that the combination of CBT-I and medication provide enhanced treatment initially, the discontinuation of medications and continuation of therapy appears to be the best option for long-term maintenance.

COMORBIDITY

Comorbidity Between Insomnia and Other Psychiatric Disorders

The cooccurrence between sleep disturbance and psychiatric disorders is considerable and has been reported in 50%–80% of cases

(Harvey, 2001; Ohayon, 2002). The evidence is clear that when insomnia is comorbid with another disorder, there is a bidirectional influence between sleep disturbance and psychiatric illness such that sleep difficulties may lead to a decline in general health and daytime functioning, which can then worsen the sleep problems (Buysse, 2005; Harvey, 2008a; National Institutes of Health, 2005; Smith, Huang, & Manber, 2005).

Sleep disturbance is considered to be the "hallmark" of posttraumatic stress disorder (PTSD; Ross, Ball, Sullivan, & Caroff, 1989). Nearly 70% of patients with PTSD report experiencing insomnia (Ohayon, 2002). Although there is evidence that sleep disturbance can result from sleep-related anxiety connected to the trauma (Inman, Silver, & Doghramji, 1990; Lamarche & De Koninck, 2007), insomnia may also serve as a vulnerability for the development of PTSD. For example, longitudinal evidence from veterans with PTSD suggests that past insomnia is significantly related to future PTSD symptoms whereas symptoms of PTSD do not predict future insomnia (Wright et al., 2011). Additionally, insomnia is a common residual symptom for nearly half of patients successfully treated for PTSD (Belleville, Guay, & Marchand, 2011; Galovski, Monson, Bruce, & Resick, 2009; Zayfert & DeViva, 2004).

Insomnia is one of the most commonly reported symptoms of depression and 60% of patients with depression also have insomnia (Ohayon, 2002; Weissman et al., 1996). Although insomnia is frequently considered a symptom of depression and is included as such in the DSM-5 (American Psychiatric Association, 2013), there is evidence that insomnia can lead to the onset of depression (Buysse et al., 2008; Ford & Kamerow, 1989). Insomnia is also a risk factor for depression across the age span and appears related to increased risk for suicide (Liu et al., 2007; Perlis et al., 2006). Despite a large body of research indicating that insomnia is a risk factor for depression, the relationship between insomnia and depression is clearly bidirectional with both disorders contributing to the maintenance of the other (Staner, 2010).

Sleep disturbance is a core feature of bipolar disorder (Harvey, 2008b) and is often an early indicator of a manic episode (Jackson, Cavanagh, & Scott, 2003). Reduced need for sleep as well as insomnia are often characteristic of mania (Harvey, Talbot, & Gershon, 2009; Holtmann et al., 2007), and both insomnia and hypersomnia can be present during depressive episodes (American Psychiatric Association, 2013). Sleep disturbance appears to contribute to a worsening of symptoms in bipolar disorder, which concurs with findings from affective neuroscience suggesting that emotional memory processing is negatively impacted by sleep deprivation (Walker & van der Helm, 2009; Yoo, Gujar, Hu, Jolesz, & Walker, 2007).

Treatment of Comorbid Insomnia

In the past, it had often been assumed that insomnia that is comorbid with another psychiatric or medical disorder could not be successfully treated if the comorbid condition was not first addressed. Although it is true that cases of comorbid insomnia present additional challenges, Morin et al. (2006) as well as Smith et al. (2005) have concluded that the improvement in sleep following CBT-I treatment has great potential to facilitate improvement in psychological and medical symptoms of the comorbid psychiatric or medical disorders.

There is evidence that CBT-I can be effectively implemented in the context of medical disorders. A RCT comparing CBT-I to an active control condition (in this case, stress management) in a sample of older adults suffering from a range of chronic illnesses (such as osteoarthritis and pulmonary disease) found that CBT-I was associated with a significant improvement in 8 out of 10 sleep measures compared to the control condition (Rybarczyk, Lopez, Schelble, & Stepanski, 2005). Additionally, improvements were also observed in physical health indices such as pain. Other studies confirm that CBT-I can have a positive impact on both insomnia and pain (Pigeon et al., 2012; Smith et al., 2015; Vitiello, Rybarczyk, Von Korff, & Stepanski, 2009). Research has also examined the impact of CBT-I on insomnia comorbid with cancer. In addition to reduced insomnia symptoms, patients with cancer also experience improved quality of life, general health, and mood as a result of CBT-I (Espie et al., 2008; Quesnel, Savard, Simard, Ivers, & Morin, 2003; Savard, Simard, Ivers, & Morin, 2005).

There is also strong evidence for the use of CBT-I in psychiatric disorders. CBT-I has been successfully utilized to reduce sleep disturbance, including insomnia, in PTSD (Germain et al., 2012; Swanson, Favorite, Arnedt, & Horin, 2009; Ulmer, Edinger, & Calhoun, 2011). Both depression and insomnia have been shown to improve with CBT-I combined with selective serotonin reuptake inhibitors, and effectiveness does not appear to depend on depression severity (Manber et al., 2008, 2011). CBT-I has also been successfully and safely implemented in treating insomnia and overall functioning in bipolar disorder (Harvey et al., 2015; Kaplan & Harvey, 2013), despite concerns regarding the use of sleep restriction (see Smith et al., 2005). In both depression and bipolar disorder, adding CBT-I improved mood symptoms relative to a control group who did not receive CBT-I (Harvey et al., 2015; Manber et al., 2008).

Insomnia is often a symptom, cause, and maintaining factor for many psychiatric and medical conditions; so, it is important to incorporate treatment for sleep disturbance because the presence of insomnia can interfere with successful treatment of the cooccurring psychiatric or medical disorder. Existing evidence indicates that CBT-I can effectively reduce symptoms of both insomnia and the comorbid disorder. Notably, Smith et al. (2005) concluded that treatment effects are generally moderate to large for CBT-I administered to medical and psychiatric illnesses and are comparable to treatment effects in insomnia.

EMERGING TREATMENTS

Although outcomes are very good for CBT-I, there remains room for improvement. Effect sizes for CBT-I, while moderate, are much lower than those for CBT for other psychiatric disorders, with a significant proportion of patients not responding to treatment or responding but not moving into the good sleeper range (Harvey & Tang, 2003). As a result, newer treatments that incorporate elements of CBT-I with other types of effective treatments have been emerging.

Mindfulness-Based Therapy for Insomnia

Mindfulness-based stress reduction (MSBR) is a behavioral program involving mindfulness meditations, education on mental and physical stress response, and group support over the course of 8 weeks of treatment (Kabat-Zinn, 1990). Mindfulness-based therapy for insomnia (MBT-I) utilizes the principles of MSBR while specifically tailoring the treatment for individuals with insomnia by incorporating meditation with sleep education and behavioral components, including sleep restriction and stimulus control, to help patients manage daytime sleepiness and nighttime wakefulness (Ong & Sholtes, 2010). A pilot study of 30 patients with insomnia found that all but two patients were below the cutoff for clinically significant insomnia after a 6-week version of MBT-I and half experienced a significant reduction in total wake time (Ong, Shapiro, & Manber, 2008). A recent RCT comparing MBSR and MBT-I to a self-monitoring control condition found that patients who completed 8 weeks of MBSR or MBT-I had a significant decrease in sleep-arousal, as measured by the PSAS, and insomnia severity, as measured by the ISI, compared to the control condition (Ong et al., 2014). The MBT-I condition also showed a significantly greater reduction on the ISI compared to the MBSR condition from baseline to a 6-month follow-up (Ong et al., 2014). These results are most promising for the use of a tailored mindfulness-based treatment program for insomnia patients.

Transdiagnostic Intervention for Sleep and Circadian Dysfunction

Prior treatment studies have been disorder-focused, treating specific sleep problems (e.g., insomnia) in a specific diagnostic group (e.g., depression). However, real life sleep and circadian problems are not so neatly categorized, particularly in severe mental illness where features of insomnia overlap with hypersomnia, delayed sleep phase, and irregular sleep–wake schedules. Transdiagnostic Intervention for Sleep and Circadian Dysfunction (TranS-C) was developed to address the need for a transdiagnostic sleep treatment (Harvey, 2015). TranS-C adopts a modular approach to improving the broad range of sleep problems many patients experience and incorporates components from several existing treatment modalities. TranS-C includes (1) stimulus control, sleep restriction, and cognitive therapy components from CBT-I to increase homeostatic sleep pressure, (2) timed light exposure, regular sleep schedule, and progressive bedtime shifts taken from treatments for delayed sleep phase and chronotherapy, and (3) consistent social rhythms including regular sleep–wake times across weekdays and weekends taken from Interpersonal and Social Rhythms Therapy to stabilize the sleep and circadian systems (Harvey, 2015). It comprises "cross-cutting" modules that are introduced in the first session, including functional analysis, goal setting, motivational interviewing, and sleep education and are typically featured in every session thereafter; "core modules" that apply to the vast majority of clients, such as behavioral components, daytime impairment, unhelpful beliefs, relapse prevention; and "optional modules" that are used less commonly and only if indicated by the case formulation (e.g., bedtime worry) (Harvey, 2015). Two large scale trials of TranS-C, one for youth and one for adults, are currently underway.

SLEEP ACROSS DEVELOPMENT

In this chapter, there has been discussion about the efficacy and effectiveness of CBT-I for the treatment of insomnia and sleep disturbance in adults. However, sleep disturbance is not limited to adulthood. When assessing for sleep disturbance and designing treatment for children and adolescents, it is necessary to consider the recommendations for sleep duration by age. The National Sleep Foundation recommends 10–13 h for preschool (3–5 years), 9–11 h for school age (6–13 years), 8–10 h for adolescents (14–17), and 7–9 h for adults (18 years and older) (Hirshkowitz et al., 2015). These varying recommendations for sleep duration impact how sleep disturbance is conceptualized in children and adolescents compared to adults.

Sleep architecture also changes across the course of development. Newborn infants experience sleep cycles comprising equal parts "active" and "quiet" sleep that are akin to REM and NREM sleep in adults (Harvey & McGlinchey, 2015). As the child grows, the amount of active sleep decreases. By age 2, active sleep accounts for only about a quarter of the sleep a child gets and the child's sleep is dominated by SWS (Harvey & McGlinchey, 2015). The 90-min cycles found in adult sleep first emerge around the second half of the first decade of life. During this time, the amount of SWS and REM sleep decrease, with SWS accounting for only 40% of total sleep by age 11 (Harvey & McGlinchey, 2015; Hoban, 2004). The sleep cycle is mostly stabilized and resembles adult sleep by adolescence (Carskadon & Dement, 2011), with the amount of REM sleep remaining constant throughout the lifespan and the total amount of SWS continuing to decrease (Harvey & McGlinchey, 2015).

Many teenagers are getting fewer than 8 hours of sleep despite a higher recommendation (National Sleep Foundation, 2006), and the adolescent years are also characterized by a delay in the circadian phase with adolescents experiencing a delay in sleep onset of 1–3 h during this period (Hagenauer, Perryman, Lee, & Carskadon, 2009). Another compounding factor in adolescent sleep disturbance is the presence of technology and the increased use of social media around bedtime. Increased exposure to light sources around bedtime and increased stimulation from social media result in a desire to stay awake and not "miss out" on the social interactions happening online (Gradisar et al., 2013). In addition to developmental and social influences, a number of caregiver factors can also contribute to a child's ability to sleep, including caregiver psychiatric disorders (such as depression), work schedule, and difficulty setting bedtime limits for the child (Harvey & McGlinchey, 2015).

CBT-I has been used in adolescents; but, studies on its effectiveness have been limited. A recent RCT comparing CBT-I delivered in either a group setting or online to a waitlist condition found that adolescents with insomnia in both CBT-I conditions improved over the waitlist condition on measures of sleep efficiency, sleep onset latency, wake after sleep onset, and total sleep time and these gains were all maintained at follow-up (de Bruin, Bögels, Oort, & Meijer, 2015). Another pilot study of adolescents with comorbid insomnia and depression compared CBT for depression combined with either sleep hygiene or CBT-I. Participants in CBT-I condition showed improved sleep, including increased total sleep time and decreased insomnia severity, and decreased depression relative to the sleep hygiene condition (Clarke et al., 2015). These findings are promising and demonstrate the effectiveness of CBT-I as a treatment for insomnia in adolescents.

CONCLUSION

This chapter has focused primarily on insomnia, the most common sleep disorder, and has reviewed the diagnosis and assessment as well as the current treatments available, including CBT-I, pharmacologic interventions, and newer therapies such as MBT-I and Trans-C. Additional information related to other common sleep disorders, comorbidity with psychiatric and medical conditions, and sleep across development has also been included because the onset and treatment of sleep disorders is often influenced by other environmental, biological, or social factors. Sleep is a central part of the human experience, but there is still much that we do not know. Although many questions remain about the nature and function of sleep and sleep disorders, it continues to be an exciting area for future research and treatment development.

References

American Academy of Sleep Medicine. (2014). *The international classification of sleep disorders: Diagnostic and coding manual-3rd edition (ICSD-3)* (3rd ed.). Darien, IL.

American Psychiatric Association. (2013). *Diagnostic and statistical manual of mental disorders, fifth edition. Diagnostic and statistical manual of mental disorders* (5th Ed.). Washington DC: American Psychiatric Publishing, Inc.

Bastien, C. H., Morin, C. M., Ouellet, M.-C., Blais, F. C., & Bouchard, S. (2004). Cognitive-behavioral therapy for insomnia: Comparison of individual therapy, group therapy, and telephone consultations. *Journal of Consulting and Clinical Psychology*, 72(4), 653–659. Available from http://dx.doi.org/10.1037/0022-006X.72.4.653.

Bastien, C. H., Vallières, A., & Morin, C. M. (2001). Validation of the insomnia severity index as an outcome measure for insomnia research. *Sleep Medicine*, 2(4), 297–307. Available from http://dx.doi.org/10.1016/S1389-9457(00)00065-4.

Beck, A.T., Rush, A.J., Shaw, B.F., & Emery, G. (1979). *Cognitive therapy of depression*. New York: Guilford.

Belleville, G., Guay, S., & Marchand, A. (2011). Persistence of sleep disturbances following cognitive-behavior therapy for posttraumatic stress disorder. *Journal of Psychosomatic Research*, 70(4), 318–327. Available from http://dx.doi.org/10.1016/j.jpsychores.2010.09.022.

Blood, M. L., Sack, R. L., Percy, D. C., & Pen, J. C. (1997). A comparison of sleep detection by wrist actigraphy, behavioral response, and polysomnography. *Sleep*, 20(6), 388–395.

Bootzin, R. R. (1979). Effects of self-control procedures for insomnia. *American Journal of Clinical Biofeedback*, 2(2), 70–77.

Bootzin, R. R., Epstein, D. R., & Wood, J. M. (1991). Stimulus control instructions. In P. Hauri (Ed.), *Case studies in insomnia SE—2* (pp. 19–28). Springer US. Available from http://dx.doi.org/10.1007/978-1-4757-9586-8_2.

Buysse, D. J. (2005). Insomnia state of the science: An evolutionary, evidence-based assessment. *Sleep, 28*(9), 1045–1046.

Buysse, D. J., Ancoli-Israel, S., Edinger, J. D., Lichstein, K. L., & Morin, C. M. (2006). Recommendations for a standard research assessment of insomnia. *Sleep, 29*(9), 1155–1173.

Buysse, D. J., Angst, J., Gamma, A., Ajdacic, V., Eich, D., & Rössler, W. (2008). Prevalence, course, and comorbidity of insomnia and depression in young adults. *Sleep, 31*(4), 473–480.

Buysse, D. J., Reynolds, C. F., Monk, T. H., Berman, S. R., & Kupfer, D. J. (1989). The Pittsburgh sleep quality index: A new instrument for psychiatric practice and research. *Psychiatry Research, 28*(2), 193–213. Available from http://dx.doi.org/10.1016/0165-1781(89)90047-4.

Carney, C. E., Buysse, D. J., Ancoli-Israel, S., Edinger, J. D., Krystal, A. D., Lichstein, K. L., & Morin, C. M. (2012). The consensus sleep diary: Standardizing prospective sleep self-monitoring. *Sleep, 35*(2), 287–302. Available from http://dx.doi.org/10.5665/sleep.1642.

Carskadon, M. A., & Dement, W. C. (2011). Normal human sleep: An overview. In M. H. Kryger, T. Roth, & W. C. Dement (Eds.), *Principles and practice of sleep medicine* (5th ed., pp. 16–26). St Louis: Elsevier.

Chambless, D. L., & Hollon, S. D. (1998). Defining empirically supported therapies. *Journal of Consulting and Clinical Psychology, 66*(1), 7–18. Available from http://dx.doi.org/10.1037/0022-006X.66.1.7.

Chesson, A. L., Anderson, W. M., Littner, M., Davila, D., Hartse, K., Johnson, S., & Rafecas, J. (1999). Practice parameters for the nonpharmacologic treatment of chronic insomnia. An American Academy of Sleep Medicine report. Standards of Practice Committee of the American Academy of Sleep Medicine. *Sleep, 22*, 1128–1133.

Chesson, A. L., Jr., Hartse, K., Anderson, W. M., Davila, D., Johnson, S., Littner, M., & Rafecas, J. (2000). Practice parameters for the evaluation of chronic insomnia. An American Academy of Sleep Medicine report. Standards of Practice Committee of the American Academy of Sleep Medicine. *Sleep, 23*(2), 237–241.

Clarke, G., McGlinchey, E. L., Hein, K., Gullion, C. M., Dickerson, J. F., Leo, M. C., & Harvey, A. G. (2015). Cognitive-behavioral treatment of insomnia and depression in adolescents: A pilot randomized trial. *Behaviour Research and Therapy, 69*, 111–118. Available from http://dx.doi.org/10.1016/j.brat.2015.04.009.

Crick, F., & Mitchison, G. (1983). The function of dream sleep. *Nature, 304*(5922), 111–114. Available from http://dx.doi.org/10.1038/304111a0.

de Bruin, E. J., Bögels, S. M., Oort, F. J., & Meijer, A. M. (2015). Efficacy of cognitive behavioral therapy for insomnia in adolescents: A randomized controlled trial with internet therapy, group therapy and a waiting list condition. *Sleep, 38*(12), 1913–1926.

Espie, C. A., Fleming, L., Cassidy, J., Samuel, L., Taylor, L. M., White, C. A., & Paul, J. (2008). Randomized controlled clinical effectiveness trial of cognitive behavior therapy compared with treatment as usual for persistent insomnia in patients with cancer. *Journal of Clinical Oncology: Official Journal of the American Society of Clinical Oncology, 26*(28), 4651–4658. Available from http://dx.doi.org/10.1200/JCO.2007.13.9006.

Faraut, B., Boudjeltia, K. Z., Vanhamme, L., & Kerkhofs, M. (2012). Immune, inflammatory and cardiovascular consequences of sleep restriction and recovery. *Sleep Medicine Reviews, 16*(2), 137–149. Available from http://dx.doi.org/10.1016/j.smrv.2011.05.001.

Ford, D. E., & Kamerow, D. B. (1989). Epidemiologic study of sleep disturbances and psychiatric disorders. An opportunity for prevention? *JAMA: The Journal of the American Medical Association, 262*(11), 1479–1484. Available from http://dx.doi.org/10.1001/jama.1989.03430110069030.

Ford, E. S., Cunningham, T. J., Giles, W. H., & Croft, J. B. (2015). Trends in insomnia and excessive daytime sleepiness among U.S. adults from 2002 to 2012. *Sleep Medicine, 16* (3), 372–378. Available from http://dx.doi.org/10.1016/j.sleep.2014.12.008.

Galovski, T. E., Monson, C., Bruce, S. E., & Resick, P. A. (2009). Does cognitive-behavioral therapy for PTSD improve perceived health and sleep impairment? *Journal of Traumatic Stress, 22*(3), 197–204. Available from http://dx.doi.org/10.1002/jts.

Germain, A., Richardson, R., Moul, D. E., Mammen, O., Haas, G., Forman, S. D., & Nofzinger, E. A. (2012). Placebo-controlled comparison of prazosin and cognitive-behavioral treatments for sleep disturbances in US Military Veterans. *Journal of Psychosomatic Research, 72*(2), 89–96. Available from http://dx.doi.org/10.1016/j.jpsychores.2011.11.010.

Gradisar, M., Wolfson, A. R., Harvey, A. G., Hale, L., Rosenberg, R., & Czeisler, C. A. (2013). The sleep and technology use of Americans: Findings from the National Sleep Foundation's 2011 Sleep in America Poll. *Journal of Clinical Sleep, 9*(12), 1291–1299. Available from http://dx.doi.org/10.5664/jcsm.3272.

Hagenauer, M. H. H., Perryman, J. I. I., Lee, T. M. M., & Carskadon, M. A. (2009). Adolescent changes in the homeostatic and circadian regulation of sleep. *Developmental Neuroscience, 31*(4), 276–284. Available from http://dx.doi.org/10.1159/000216538.

Harvey, A. G. (2001). Insomnia: Symptom or diagnosis? *Clinical Psychology Review, 21*(7), 1037–1059. Available from http://dx.doi.org/10.1016/S0272-7358(00)00083-0.

Harvey, A. G. (2008a). Insomnia, psychiatric disorders, and the transdiagnostic perspective. *Current Directions in Psychological Science, 17*(5), 299–303. Available from http://dx.doi.org/10.1111/j.1467-8721.2008.00594.x.

Harvey, A. G. (2008b). Sleep and circadian rhythms in bipolar disorder: Seeking synchrony, harmony, and regulation. *American Journal of Psychiatry, 165*(7), 820–829. Available from http://dx.doi.org/10.1176/appi.ajp.2008.08010098.

Harvey, A. G. (2015). A transdiagnostic intervention for youth sleep and circadian problems. *Cognitive and Behavioral Practice.* Available from http://dx.doi.org/10.1016/j.cbpra.2015.06.001.

Harvey, A. G., Bélanger, L., Talbot, L. S., Eidelman, P., Beaulieu-Bonneau, S., Fortier-Brochu, E., & Morin, C. M. (2014). Comparative efficacy of behavior therapy, cognitive therapy, and cognitive behavior therapy for chronic insomnia: A randomized controlled trial. *Journal of Consulting and Clinical Psychology, 82*(4), 670–683. Available from http://dx.doi.org/10.1037/a0036606.

Harvey, A. G., & McGlinchey, E. L. (2015). *Sleep interventions: A developmental perspective.* Rutter's Child and Adolescent Psychiatry (6th Ed.). Wiley-Blackwell.

Harvey, A. G., Soehner, A. M., Kaplan, K. A., Hein, K., Lee, J., Kanady, J., & Buysse, D. J. (2015). Treating insomnia improves mood state, sleep, and functioning in bipolar disorder: A pilot randomized controlled trial. *Journal of Consulting and Clinical Psychology, 83* (3), 564–577. Available from http://dx.doi.org/10.1037/a0038655.

Harvey, A. G., Talbot, L. S., & Gershon, A. (2009). Sleep disturbance in bipolar disorder across the lifespan. *Clinical Psychology: Science and Practice, 16*(2), 256–277. Available from http://dx.doi.org/10.1111/j.1468-2850.2009.01164.x.

Harvey, A. G., & Tang, N. K. Y. (2003). Cognitive behaviour therapy for primary insomnia: Can we rest yet? *Sleep Medicine Reviews, 7*(3), 237–262. Available from http://dx.doi.org/10.1053/smrv.2002.0266.

Hirshkowitz, M., Whiton, K., Albert, S. M., Alessi, C., Bruni, O., DonCarlos, L., & Ware, J. C. (2015). National Sleep Foundation's updated sleep duration recommendations: Final report. *Sleep Health, 1*(4), 233–243. Available from http://dx.doi.org/10.1016/j.sleh.2015.10.004.

Hoban, T. F. (2004). Sleep and its disorders in children. *Seminars in Neurology, 24*(3), 327–340. Available from http://dx.doi.org/10.1055/s-2004-835062.

Hoddes, E., Zarcone, V., Smythe, H., Phillips, R., & Dement, W. C. (1973). Quantification of sleepiness: A new approach. *Psychophysiology*, *10*(4), 431–436. Available from http://dx.doi.org/10.1111/j.1469-8986.1973.tb00801.x.

Holtmann, M., Bölte, S., Goth, K., Döpfner, M., Plück, J., Huss, M., & Poustka, F. (2007). Prevalence of the Child Behavior Checklist-pediatric bipolar disorder phenotype in a German general population sample. *Bipolar Disorders*, *9*(8), 895–900. Available from http://dx.doi.org/10.1111/j.1399-5618.2007.00463.x.

Hood, H. K., Rogojanski, J., & Moss, T. G. (2014). Cognitive-behavioral therapy for chronic insomnia. *Current Treatment Options in Neurology*, *16*(12), 321. Available from http://dx.doi.org/10.1007/s11940-014-0321-6.

Iber, C., Ancoli-Israel, S., Chesson, A. L., Jr., & Quan, S. F. (2007). *The AASM manual for the scoring of sleep and associated events: Rules terminology and technical specifications* (1st ed.). Westchester, IL: American Academy of Sleep Medicine.

Inman, D. J., Silver, S. M., & Doghramji, K. (1990). Sleep disturbance in post-traumatic stress disorder: A comparison with non-PTSD insomnia. *Journal of Traumatic Stress*, *3* (3), 429–437. Available from http://dx.doi.org/10.1007/BF00974782.

Innes, K. E., Selfe, T. K., & Agarwal, P. (2011). Prevalence of restless legs syndrome in North American and Western European populations: A systematic review. *Sleep Medicine*, *12*(7), 623–634. Available from http://dx.doi.org/10.1016/j.sleep.2010.12.018.

Jackson, A., Cavanagh, J., & Scott, J. (2003). A systematic review of manic and depressive prodromes. *Journal of Affective Disorders*, *74*(3), 209–217. Available from http://dx.doi.org/10.1016/S0165-0327(02)00266-5.

Jacobson, E. (1925). Progressive relaxation. *American Journal of Psychology*, *36*(1), 73–87. Available from http://dx.doi.org/10.2307/1413507.

Jernelöv, S., Lekander, M., Blom, K., Rydh, S., Ljótsson, B., & Axelsson, J. (2012). Efficacy of a behavioral self-help treatment with or without therapist guidance for co-morbid and primary insomnia—A randomized controlled trial. BMC Psychiatry, *12*, 5.

Kabat-Zinn, J. (1990). *Full catastrophe living: Using the wisdom of your body and mind to face stress, pain, and illness*. New York: Delacorte. Available from http://dx.doi.org/10.1037/032287.

Kaplan, K. A., & Harvey, A. G. (2013). Behavioral treatment of insomnia in bipolar disorder. *The American Journal of Psychiatry*, *170*(7), 716–720. Available from http://dx.doi.org/10.1176/appi.ajp.2013.12050708.

Lamarche, L. J., & De Koninck, J. (2007). Sleep disturbance in adults with posttraumatic stress disorder: A review. *The Journal of Clinical Psychiatry*, *68*(August), 1257–1270. Available from http://dx.doi.org/10.4088/JCP.v68n0813.

Lichstein, K. L., Stone, K. C., Donaldson, J., Nau, S. D., Soeffing, J. P., Murray, D., & Aguillard, R. N. (2006). Actigraphy validation with insomnia. *Sleep*, *29*(2), 232–239.

Liu, X., Buysse, D. J., Gentzler, A. L., Kiss, E., Mayer, L., Kapornai, K., & Kovacs, M. (2007). Insomnia and hypersomnia associated with depressive phenomenology and comorbidity in childhood depression. *Sleep*, *30*, 83–90.

Manber, R., Bernert, R. A., Suh, S., Nowakowski, S., Siebern, A. T., & Ong, J. C. (2011). CBT for insomnia in patients with high and low depressive symptom severity: Adherence and clinical outcomes. *Journal of Clinical Sleep Medicine: JCSM: Official Publication of the American Academy of Sleep Medicine*, *7*(6), 645–652. Available from http://dx.doi.org/10.5664/jcsm.1472.

Manber, R., Edinger, J. D., Gress, J. L., San Pedro-Salcedo, M. G., Kuo, T. F., & Kalista, T. (2008). Cognitive behavioral therapy for insomnia enhances depression outcome in patients with comorbid major depressive disorder and insomnia. *Sleep*, *31*(4), 489–495.

Morgenthaler, T., Kramer, M., Alessi, C., Friedman, L., Boehlecke, B., Brown, T., & Swick, T. (2006). Practice parameters for the psychological and behavioral treatment of insomnia: An update. An American academy of sleep medicine report. *Sleep*, *29*(11), 1415–1419.

Morin, C. M. (1993). *Insomnia: Psychological assessment and management.* New York: Guilford Press.

Morin, C. M. (2011). Psychological and behavioral treatment for insomnia I: Approaches and efficacy. In M. Kryger, T. Roth, & W. C. Dement (Eds.), *Principles and practice of sleep medicine* (5th ed., pp. 866–883). St Louis: Elsevier.

Morin, C. M., Bootzin, R. R., Buysse, D. J., Edinger, J. D., Espie, C. A., & Lichstein, K. L. (2006). Psychological and behavioral treatment of insomnia: Update of the recent evidence (1998–2004). *Sleep, 29*(11), 1398–1414.

Morin, C. M., Drake, C. L., Harvey, A. G., Krystal, A. D., Manber, R., Riemann, D., & Spiegelhalder, K. (2015). Insomnia disorder. *Nature Reviews Disease Primers*, 15026. Available from http://dx.doi.org/10.1038/nrdp.2015.26.

Morin, C. M., Vallières, A., Guay, B., Ivers, H., Savard, J., Mérette, C., & Baillargeon, L. (2009). Cognitive behavioral therapy, singly and combined with medication, for persistent insomnia. *The Journal of the American Medical Association, 301*(19), 2005. Available from http://dx.doi.org/10.1001/jama.2009.682.

National Institutes of Health. (2005). National Institutes of Health State of the Science Conference statement on Manifestations and Management of Chronic Insomnia in Adults. *Sleep, 28*(9), 1049.

National Sleep Foundation. (2006). *Summary of findings: 2006 Sleep in America poll.* Washington DC.

Ohayon, M. M. (2002). Epidemiology of insomnia: What we know and what we still need to learn. *Sleep Medicine Reviews, 6*(2), 97–111. Available from http://dx.doi.org/10.1053/smrv.2002.0186.

Ohayon, M. M., & Roth, T. (2002). Prevalence of restless legs syndrome and periodic limb movement disorder in the general population. *Journal of Psychosomatic Research, 53*(1), 547–554. Available from http://dx.doi.org/10.1016/S0022-3999(02)00443-9.

Ong, J. C., Manber, R., Segal, Z. V., Xia, Y., Shapiro, S. L., & Wyatt, J. K. (2014). A randomized controlled trial of mindfulness meditation for chronic insomnia. *Sleep, 37*(9), 1553–1563. Available from http://dx.doi.org/10.5665/sleep.4010.

Ong, J. C., Shapiro, S. L., & Manber, R. (2008). Combining mindfulness meditation with cognitive-behavior therapy for insomnia: A treatment-development study. *Behavior Therapy, 39*(2), 171–182. Available from http://dx.doi.org/10.1016/j.beth.2007.07.002.

Ong, J. C., & Sholtes, D. (2010). A mindfulness-based approach to the treatment of insomnia. *Journal of Clinical Psychology, 66*(11), 1175–1184. Available from http://dx.doi.org/10.1002/jclp.20736.

Ozminkowski, R. J., Wang, S., & Walsh, J. K. (2007). The direct and indirect costs of untreated insomnia in adults in the United States. *Sleep, 30*(3), 263–273.

Peppard, P. E., Young, T., Barnet, J. H., Palta, M., Hagen, E. W., & Hla, K. M. (2013). Increased prevalence of sleep-disordered breathing in adults. *American Journal of Epidemiology, 177*(9), 1006–1014. Available from http://dx.doi.org/10.1093/aje/kws342.

Perlis, M. L., Smith, L. J., Lyness, J. M., Matteson-Rusby, S., Pigeon, W. R., Jungquist, C. R., & Tu, X. (2006). Insomnia as a risk factor for onset of depression in the elderly. *Behavioral Sleep Medicine, 4*(2), 104–113. Available from http://dx.doi.org/10.1207/s15402010bsm0402_3.

Pigeon, W. R., Moynihan, J., Matteson-Rusby, S., Jungquist, C. R., Xia, Y., Tu, X., & Perlis, M. L. (2012). Comparative effectiveness of CBT interventions for co-morbid chronic pain & insomnia: A pilot study. *Behaviour Research and Therapy, 50*(11), 685–689. Available from http://dx.doi.org/10.1016/j.brat.2012.07.005.

Quesnel, C., Savard, J., Simard, S., Ivers, H., & Morin, C. M. (2003). Efficacy of cognitive-behavioral therapy for insomnia in women treated for nonmetastic breast cancer. *Journal of Consulting and Clinical Psychology, 71*(1), 189. Available from http://dx.doi.org/10.1037/0022-006X.71.1.189.

Reid, K. J., & Zee, P. C. (2009). Circadian rhythm disorders. *Seminars in Neurology*. Available from http://dx.doi.org/10.1055/s-0029-1237120.

Ross, R. J., Ball, Wa, Sullivan, K. A., & Caroff, S. N. (1989). Sleep disturbance as the hallmark of posttraumatic stress disorder. *The American Journal of Psychiatry*, 146(6), 697−707.

Roth, T. (2007). Insomnia: Definition, prevalence, etiology, and consequences. *Journal of Clinical Sleep Medicine*, 3(5 SUPPL.), 3−6.

Rybarczyk, B. D., Lopez, M., Schelble, K., & Stepanski, E. J. (2005). Home-based video CBT for comorbid geriatric insomnia: A pilot study using secondary data analyses. *Behavioral Sleep Medicine*, 3(3), 158−175. Available from http://dx.doi.org/10.1207/s15402010bsm0303_4.

Savard, J., Simard, S., Ivers, H., & Morin, C. M. (2005). Randomized study on the efficacy of cognitive-behavioral therapy for insomnia secondary to breast cancer, part I: Sleep and psychological effects. *Journal of Clinical Oncology*, 23(25), 6083−6096. Available from http://dx.doi.org/10.1200/JCO.2005.09.548.

Schulz, H. (2008). Rethinking sleep analysis. *Journal of Clinical Sleep Medicine*, 4(2), 99−103.

Sharma, M. P., & Andrade, C. (2012). Behavioral interventions for insomnia: Theory and practice. *Indian Journal of Psychiatry*, 54(4), 359−366. Available from http://dx.doi.org/10.4103/0019-5545.104825.

Shneerson, J. M. (2000). *Handbook of sleep medicine*. Malden, MA: Wiley-Blackwell.

Sivertsen, B., Omvik, S., Pallesen, S., Bjorvatn, B., Havik, O. E., Kvale, G., & Nordhus, I. H. (2006). Cognitive behavioral therapy vs zopiclone for treatment of chronic primary insomnia in older adults: A randomized controlled trial. *Journal of the American Medical Association*, 295(24), 2851−2858. Available from http://dx.doi.org/10.1001/jama.295.24.2851.

Smith, M. T., Finan, P. H., Buenaver, L. F., Robinson, M., Haque, U., Quain, A., & Haythornthwaite, J. A. (2015). Cognitive-behavioral therapy for insomnia in knee osteoarthritis: A randomized, double-blind, active placebo-controlled clinical trial. *Arthritis & Rheumatology*, 67(5), 1221−1233. Available from http://dx.doi.org/10.1002/art.39048.

Smith, M. T., Huang, M. I., & Manber, R. (2005). Cognitive behavior therapy for chronic insomnia occurring within the context of medical and psychiatric disorders. *Clinical Psychology Review*, 25(5), 559−592. Available from http://dx.doi.org/10.1016/j.cpr.2005.04.004.

Spielman, A. J., Caruso, L. S., & Glovinsky, P. B. (1987). A behavioral perspective on insomnia treatment. *The Psychiatric Clinics of North America*, 10, 541−553.

Spielman, A. J., Saskin, P., & Thorpy, M. J. (1987). Treatment of chronic insomnia by restriction of time in bed. *Sleep*, 10(1), 45−56.

Staner, L. (2010). Comorbidity of insomnia and depression. *Sleep Medicine Reviews*, 14(1), 35−46. Available from http://dx.doi.org/10.1016/j.smrv.2009.09.003.

Swanson, L. M., Favorite, T. K., Arnedt, J. T., & Horin, E. (2009). A combined group treatment for nightmares and insomnia in combat veterans: A pilot study. *Journal of Traumatic Stress*, 22(6), 639−642. Available from http://dx.doi.org/10.1002/jts.

Ulmer, C. S., Edinger, J. D., & Calhoun, P. S. (2011). A multi-component cognitive-behavioral intervention for sleep disturbance in veterans with PTSD: A pilot study. *Journal of Clinical Sleep Medicine*, 7(1), 57−68.

Vitiello, M. V., Rybarczyk, B. D., Von Korff, M., & Stepanski, E. J. (2009). Cognitive behavioral therapy for insomnia improves sleep and decreases pain in older adults with comorbid insomnia and osteoarthritis. *Journal of Clinical Sleep Medicine*, 5(4), 355−362. Available from http://dx.doi.org/10.1111/j.1479-8425.2011.00521.x.

Walker, M. P. (2009). The role of sleep in cognition and emotion. *Annals of the New York Academy of Sciences*, 1156(1), 168−197. Available from http://dx.doi.org/10.1111/j.1749-6632.2009.04416.x.

Walker, M. P., & Stickgold, R. (2006). Sleep, memory, and plasticity. *Annual Review of Psychology*, *57*, 139–166. Available from http://dx.doi.org/10.1146/annurev.psych.56.091103.070307.

Walker, M. P., & van der Helm, E. (2009). Overnight therapy? The role of sleep in emotional brain processing. *Psychological Bulletin, 135*(5), 731–748. Available from http://dx.doi.org/10.1037/a0016570.

Weissman, M. M., Bland, R. C., Canino, G. J., Faravelli, C., Greenwald, S., Hwu, H.-G., & Yeh, E.-K. (1996). Cross-national epidemiology of major depression and bipolar disorder. *JAMA: The Journal of the American Medical Association, 276*(4), 293–299. Available from http://dx.doi.org/10.1001/jama.1996.03540040037030.

Wright, K. M., Britt, T. W., Bliese, P. D., Adler, A. B., Picchioni, D., & Moore, D. (2011). Insomnia as predictor versus outcome of PTSD and depression among Iraq combat veterans. *Journal of Clinical Psychology, 67*(12), 1240–1258. Available from http://dx.doi.org/10.1002/jclp.20845.

Yoo, S.-S. S., Gujar, N., Hu, P., Jolesz, F. A., & Walker, M. P. (2007). The human emotional brain without sleep—A prefrontal amygdala disconnect. *Current Biology, 17*(20), R877–R878. Available from http://dx.doi.org/10.1016/j.cub.2007.08.007.

Zayfert, C., & DeViva, J. C. (2004). Residual insomnia following cognitive behavioral therapy for PTSD. *Journal of Traumatic Stress, 17*(1), 69–73. Available from http://dx.doi.org/10.1023/B:JOTS.0000014679.31799.e7.

Further Reading

Savard, J., Ivers, H., Savard, M. H., & Morin, C. M. (2015). Cancer treatments and their side effects are associated with aggravation of insomnia: Results of a longitudinal study. *Cancer, 121*(10), 1703–1711. Available from http://dx.doi.org/10.1002/cncr.29244.

Cognitive Behavioral Therapy for Somatoform Disorders and Pain

Maria Kleinstäuber and Winfried Rief

Philipps-University, Marburg, Germany

A CASE EXAMPLE: DEBORAH AND HER MULTIPLE SOMATIC SYMPTOMS

Deborah is a 24-year-old student. She reports in her first session with a clinical psychologist multiple, fluctuating physical symptoms that have persisted over the last 2 years. Deborah predominantly experiences breathlessness. It feels like a "resistance" in her throat or as if her "larynx is too tight," and is accompanied by a sensation of pressure in her left chest. Moreover she reports that the breathing and chest complaints are accompanied by nausea and vomiting. Her symptoms partly appear spontaneously and partly after physical exercise and persist between 30 min and several hours. She experienced them for the first time 2 years ago, after she had excessively drunken alcohol. Two months later, symptoms appeared again. During several appointments with medical specialists (e.g., orthopedist, cardiologist, or neurologist), Deborah received contradictory information about options to treat her symptoms. None of the specialists could identify a medical explanation and none of the prescribed interventions (e.g., taking a beta-blocker or physical therapy) was successful. During her appointment with the clinical psychologist, Deborah additionally complains about symptoms such as frequent yawning without being tired, muscle weakness, frequent burping, and a feeling of pressure in the right half of her head.

The Science of Cognitive Behavioral Therapy.
DOI: http://dx.doi.org/10.1016/B978-0-12-803457-6.00017-9

Deborah describes herself as a very active and achievement-oriented student. However, these physical symptoms let her feel weak and less resilient. She avoids more and more physical activity, even everyday life activities such as walking stairs or going by bike to the university. She also reduces her social activities. Deborah says at the end of this appointment that she felt very comfortable and taken seriously. However, she would be still skeptical about how a psychologist could help her. Moreover, she does not know why her GP referred her to a psychologist. She has somatic symptoms but no mental problems!

A JUNGLE OF DIAGNOSTIC TERMS: DEFINING AND CLASSIFYING SOMATOFORM DISORDERS

A key feature of somatoform disorders is the presence of so-called medically unexplained physical symptoms (MUPS). MUPS are somatic symptoms that cannot or have not been sufficiently explained by organic causes after a thorough physical examination (Sharpe, Mayou, & Bass, 1995). According to the criteria of the fourth revision of the Diagnostic and Statistical Manual of Mental Disorders (DSM-IV; American Psychiatric Association, 2000), diagnostic entities including MUPS as their main indication are as follows:

- somatization disorder,
- undifferentiated somatoform disorder, and
- pain disorder.

Somatization disorder comprises at least eight MUPS in different parts of the body with a chronic manifestation (started before the age of 30 and persisted over several years). One or more MUPS being present over the last 6 months or longer are necessary to diagnose an *undifferentiated somatoform disorder*. When pain in one or several parts of the body is the only symptom, the diagnosis of a *pain disorder* should be considered. According to DSM-IV, patients with a *hypochondriasis* can also present with somatic symptoms; however, the belief and fear of having a serious illness are predominant. Other diagnostic entities of somatoform disorders such as *body dysmorphic disorder* (preoccupation with perceived defects or flaws in physical appearance that are not or hardly observable), or *conversion disorder* (MUPS of motor or sensory function have to be associated with distressing events) will be confined in this chapter.

In the actual, fifth revision of the DSM (DSM-5; American Psychiatric Association, 2013), the concept of somatoform disorders has been totally revised. Somatization disorder, undifferentiated somatoform disorder, pain disorder, and partly hypochondriasis are now subsumed under the *somatic symptom disorder* (SSD). This new diagnostic category requires at least one somatic distressing and disabling symptom. In contrast to DSM-IV in DSM-5 medically unexplained as well as *medically explained* symptoms are accepted. Moreover, the SSD criteria require at least one of three psychological features: abnormal persistent thoughts, high levels of anxiety in response to symptom(s), or behaviors associated with excessive time and energy devoted to symptom(s). The specifier "with predominant pain" (DSM-5; American Psychiatric Association, 2013, p. 311) replaces the former pain disorder of DSM-IV. Patients revealing the belief of having or acquiring a serious illness but reporting no somatic or only very mild somatic symptoms are categorized within the *illness anxiety disorder*.

Besides these diagnostic entities in DSM-IV and -5, several other concepts of MUPS have been established. For example in research literature concepts of multiple chronic MUPS such as the somatic symptom index-4/6 (SSI-4/6; ≥4/6 MUPS for men/women; Escobar, Rubio-Stipec, Canino, & Karno, 1989), multisomatoform disorder (≥3 MUPS over the last month; Kroenke et al., 1997), or bodily distress syndrome (BDS; single-organ type: ≥3 MUPS in 1 of 4 symptom categories: gastrointestinal, cardiopulmonary, musculoskeletal, or general symptoms; multiorgan type: ≥4 MUPS from any symptom groups; Fink & Schröder, 2010; Fink, Toft, Hansen, Ornbol, & Olesen, 2007) became popular. Another example are so-called *functional somatic syndromes* such as *irritable bowel syndrome* (functional gastrointestinal disorder characterized by chronic abdominal pain, discomfort, bloating, and alterations of bowel habits; Thompson et al., 1999), *chronic fatigue syndrome, neurasthenia,* or *systemic exertion intolerance disease* (characterized by long-term fatigue worsening after any type of physical or cognitive-emotional exertion; McCarthy, 2015), and *fibromyalgia* (chronic widespread pain accompanied by heightened and painful response to pressure and additional symptoms such as tiredness, sleep disturbance, or joint stiffness; Wolfe et al., 2011). However, several researchers (Fink et al., 2007; Wessely, Nimnuan, & Sharpe, 1999) in this area claim substantial diagnostic overlap and recommend summarizing them in one diagnostic category—the *BDS* or *disorder* (see description above)—which will replace the diagnostic entity of somatoform disorders in the future 11th revision of the European classification manual of diseases by the World Health Organization, the International Classification of Diseases (http://apps.who.int/classifications/icd11/browse/f/en).

In summary, patients whose symptoms fit criteria of diagnostic entities in DSM-IV (somatization disorder, undifferentiated somatoform disorders, pain disorder, hypochondriasis) or equivalent entities in DSM-5 (SSD, illness anxiety disorder), of abridged concepts of MUPS in research literature, or of specific functional syndromes can be treated with the cognitive behavioral therapy (CBT)-approaches described in this chapter. Deborah, in the case example at the beginning of this chapter, received the diagnosis of an undifferentiated somatoform disorder. In the following paragraph, empirical findings on important psychological variables that play an important role in the etiology of somatoform disorders will be illuminated.

TARGETS OF CBT FOR SOMATOFORM DISORDERS AND PAIN: EMPIRICAL EVIDENCE FOR ETIOLOGICAL MECHANISMS AND PSYCHOLOGICAL CORRELATES OF SOMATOFORM SYMPTOMS

Patients with somatoform disorders are characterized by a variety of psychological features that contribute to the development and maintenance of their symptomatology. For example, Brosschot (2002) assumes that somatizing patients undergo processes of cognitive-emotional sensitization. These sensitization processes increase the likelihood of activating cognitive networks associated with topics such as illness or pain and result in different kinds of cognitive biases. One example is an *attention bias* toward somatic stimuli in somatizing patients that can be demonstrated with specific experimental designs. For example, Lupke and Ehlert (1998) identified Stroop task interference effects in regard to health-threatening stimuli in somatoform patients. Pearce and Morley (1989) found similar effects in chronic pain patients in regard to pain-related stimuli. Moreover, it was demonstrated that focusing attention on bodily changes can lead to an increased report of physical symptoms or a decreased pain threshold whereas distraction has reverse effects (De Wied & Verbaten, 2001; Lautenbacher, Pauli, Zaudig, & Birbaumer, 1998). This vicious cycle of attention bias and symptom-intensifying effects of attention focusing is addressed by the concept of *somatosensory amplification* by Barsky and Wyshak (1990). The authors assume that individuals with an increased risk of developing somatoform disorders bear a high vigilance toward bodily changes and tend to experience quickly negative cognitions and emotions in regard to the physical symptoms. They focus their attention more intensively on bodily complaints, which are amplified in turn. In the case example at the beginning of this chapter, Deborah focuses her attention strongly on her body. Even after slight physical exercise, she observes her body thoroughly and often experiences breathlessness. The more she pays attention to this somatic symptom the worse it becomes. Then she withdraws to a quiet place and continues observing her symptoms.

Besides cognitive biases, somatizing patients obtain specific dysfunctional cognitions and cognitive styles such as symptom-related *catastrophizing thoughts* (Barsky et al., 2001; Smeets, De Jong, & Mayer, 2000), and misjudgments of the risk of having a severe somatic disorder (Barsky et al., 2001; Marcus & Church, 2003). In experimental studies, it could be demonstrated that catastrophizing beliefs are associated with a stronger focus of attention on bodily changes and an increased perception of pain (Crombez, Eccleston, Baeyens, & Eelen, 1998). Moreover, a catastrophizing cognitive style is a strong predictor of increased health-care utilization (Severeijns, Vlaeyen, Van den Hout, & Picavet, 2004), distress (Lackner & Quigley, 2005), and pain behavior (Sullivan, Adams, & Sullivan, 2004). Another kind of frequent dysfunctional cognitions in somatizing patients are *illness worries* (Taillefer, Kirmayer, Robbins, & Lasry, 2002; Watt & Stewart, 2000). They have been demonstrated to be a significant predictor of negative interpretations in regard to the own personal physical health status (Hadjistavropoulos, Coons, & Asmundson, 2004). In samples of healthy individuals, it has been demonstrated that modern health worries (e.g., regarding health-threatening influences of pesticides used in farming) are a predictor of health complaints after an exposure to health-threatening stimuli (Petrie et al., 2005). There is the myth that patients with somatoform disorders obtain somatic illness perceptions in general. However, this could not be exactly confirmed in previous research. In the contrary, survey studies showed that many somatizing patients rather have multiple instead of simple explanations for their symptoms (e.g., Rief, Nanke, Emmerich, Bender, & Zech, 2004). Interestingly, comorbid mental disorders (e.g., depression) seemed to be associated with psychological attributions (e.g., stress) whereas in patients with somatoform disorders without psychiatric comorbidity rather somatic symptom attributions were found (Rief et al., 2004). Somatic illness perceptions were rather associated with a bad physical health status, a chronic manifestation of symptoms, and an increased health care utilization (Rief et al., 2004). Finally also *cognitions related to the body image* play a significant etiological role. The body image describes a mental representation of one's appearance, emotions, and thoughts about one's body and its functions and capacities (Cash & Pruzinsky, 2002). Riebel, Egloff, and Witthöft (2013) examined somatoform patients in an experimental study and could demonstrate that they linked illness-related words with themselves more frequently than healthy controls did. Moreover, the authors showed that their self-concept was focused on bodily weakness and was correlated with the number and severity of physical symptoms. A longitudinal study (Klaus et al., 2015) demonstrated that a self-concept of bodily weakness predicts the diagnosis of a somatoform disorder 1 year later. Deborah, in the case example above, also obtains catastrophizig cognitions about her breathlessness and her perceptions of a "resistance in her throat." She often thinks about suffering from a severe cardiovascular disease or larynx cancer. Deborah is able to reassure herself that there is no medical evidence, and she can accept alternative explanations of her symptoms (e.g., bad physical shape, persistingly high workload at university). However, when her symptoms get worse, she cannot control her worries. Deborah has never been very sporty. She now regrets that she has never exercised more frequently. Her body image has never been very positive. Now it even deteriorates. She feels weak and vulnerable. She loses trust in the functions of her body and experiences somatic symptoms as dominating.

Another important psychological variable that seems to play an important role in the etiology of somatoform complaints is *negative affectivity*. Findings of experimental research emphasize that negative affect influences the perception and report of physical symptoms, and attention focusing on the body (Bogaerts et al., 2005; Bogaerts, Janssens, De Peuter, Van Diest, & Van den Bergh, 2010; Brown, Danquah, Miles, Holmes, & Poliakoff, 2010; Constantinou, Bogaerts, Van Diest, & Van den Bergh, 2013). Furthermore, negative affectivity was demonstrated to be a strong predictor of symptom intensity and stability (Bailer, Witthöft, Bayerl, & Rist, 2007). Although Deborah, in the case example above, had originally been an optimistic, energetic, and achievement-oriented person, persisting and disabling somatic symptoms had a strong negative impact on her mood. Moreover, she suffered from the social withdrawal. Being often at home alone and ruminating about her symptoms frustrated her, which, in turn, had a negative impact on her health status and amplified her physical symptoms.

Finally, a substantial subgroup of somatizing patients demonstrates *illness behaviors* (Weiss, Rief, Martin, Rauh, & Kleinstäuber, 2016) such as extensive *health care utilization* and *reassurance behaviors* (e.g., need for physicians' confirmation that somatic symptoms are not caused by severe medical illness), *avoidance behaviors* (e.g., avoiding physical exercise), and *body scanning* (e.g., checking the stool for blood associated with the worry to have intestinal cancer). Health care utilization (or "doctor shopping") can result in negative consequences for the doctor—patient relationship (Murray, Toussaint, Althaus, & Löwe, 2016). A systematic review about challenges in the somatizing patient—GP relationship showed, for example, that practitioners frequently experience caring for patients with MUPS as burden, distressing, frustrating, and difficult (Murray et al., 2016). Somatoform patients in turn fear social stigma of being "mentally disordered" and do not feel taken seriously (Murray et al., 2016). Moreover Rief, Heitmüller, Reisberg, and Rüddel (2006) demonstrated in an experimental study that reassurances given by doctors to their patients in a medical consultation can even have negative effects since patients with MUPS seem to recall the likelihood for medical causes of their symptoms incorrectly. Research on fear of movements and reinjury especially in chronic pain patients—so-called fear-avoidance—showed that avoiding physical exercising is associated with physical deconditioning (Vlaeyen et al., 1999) which in turn can amplify physical complaints. Klaus et al. (2015) demonstrated in a longitudinal study that body checking was a strong predictor of somatoform disorders in a 4-year follow-up. In Deborah's case (see above), several forms of illness behaviors are described. She avoids any kind of physical exercise and activity in her everyday life which deteriorates her physical health status and let her feel weak. Moreover, she consults frequently different medical specialists in order to get an explanation for her symptoms. However, the doctors' attempts to reassure her usually reduce her anxiety only for a short while. Deborah is rather confused about contradictory information she receives from clinicians.

The role of psychological variables and their interactions in the etiology of somatoform disorders are depicted in the cognitive perceptional model of somatoform disorders by Kirmayer and Taillefer (1997) (see Fig. 17.1). This model plays an essential role for the psychoeducation as part of CBT for somatoform disorders and pain and constitutes a rationale for essential therapeutic tools for establishing a trustful therapeutic relationship and compliance, exploring and extending illness beliefs of the patients and psychoeducation, stress management training and biofeedback, attention refocusing, cognitive restructuring of dysfunctional, symptom-related cognitions, and reducing illness behaviors.

CBT FOR SOMATOFORM DISORDERS AND PAIN: BASIC THERAPEUTIC TOOLS

In the following paragraphs, most important tools that are typically part of evidence based CBT programs for somatoform disorders and pain are described (Van Dessel et al., 2014).

Establishing Working Alliance and Therapy Compliance

Many patients with MUPS have a long history of being diagnosed and treated by various medical specialists (Burton, McGorm, Richardson, Weller, & Sharpe, 2012). During these medical appointments, potential psychosocial causes of somatic complaints are usually not or not sufficiently discussed with patients (Ring, Dowrick, Humphris, & Salmon, 2004). In consequence, many patients with MUPS have difficulties in understanding why psychological interventions could be helpful for them. Moreover patients' expectations in regard to psychologists and psychological interventions can be extremely biased.

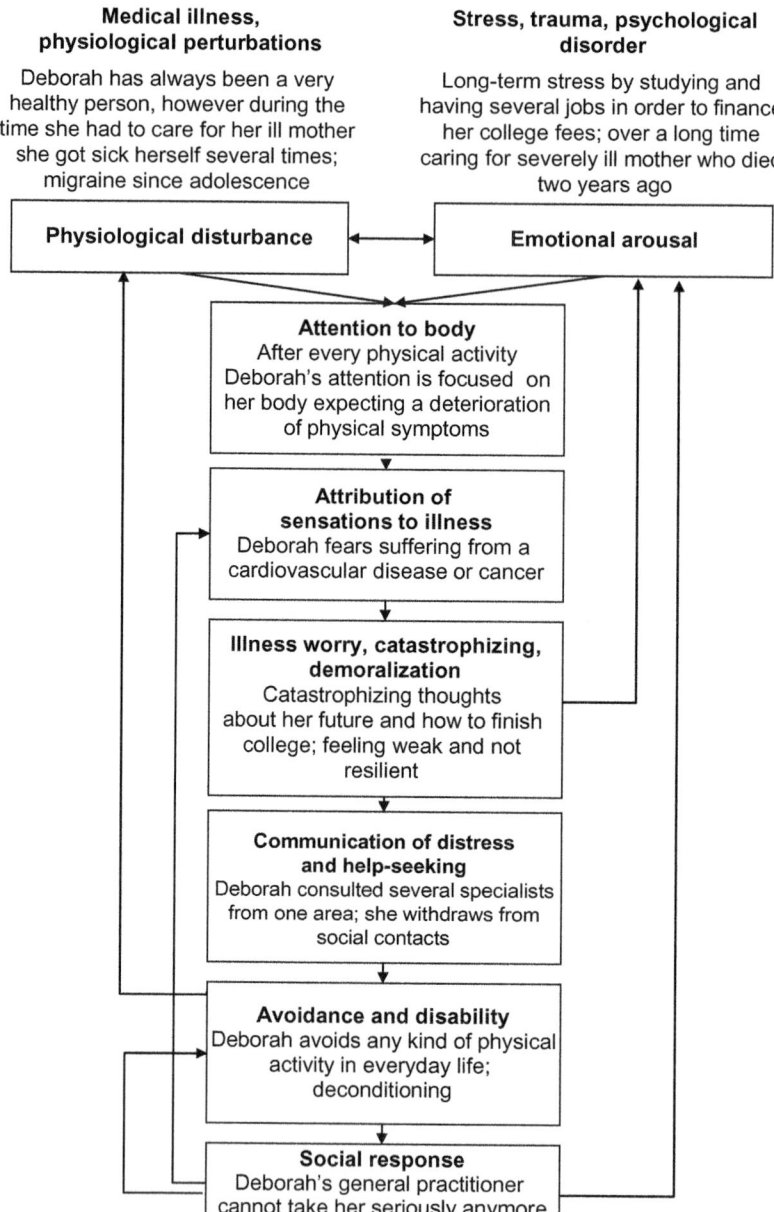

FIGURE 17.1 Cognitive perceptional model of somatoform disorders by Kirmayer and Taillefer (1997) adapted to the case example of Deborah.

Examples of such biased expectations are unrealistic hopes (e.g., "You and this therapy are my last hope."), cognitions that bring a lot of pressure on the therapist and degrades other patients' previous clinicians (e.g., "You are the only one who can help me … all previous doctors I saw couldn't help me anyway."), resigning thoughts (e.g., "It's hopeless, nothing helps."), or rejecting cognitions (e.g., "I don't know how a psychologist can help me. I feel sick, but not crazy.").

These dysfunctional expectations emphasize that it is very important to establish realistic, specifically worded, and operationalized goals that do not only focus on somatic symptoms but also on other areas of problems in the patients' life (e.g. "I want to start cycling again, two times a week for one hour." or "I want to establish a good work-life balance by creating a plan of daily activities and breaks." in contrast to "First my somatic symptoms have to remit completely before I can start doing sports again."). Developing realistic expectations and validating and extending patients' illness beliefs are important steps for establishing a trustful working alliance between patient and therapist. Especially the initial phase but also the whole therapeutic process requires special communication skills (see Royal College General Practitioners, 2011), e.g., validating the symptom-related distress and shifting patients' focus from physical symptoms to the disability in everyday life and limitations of quality of life.

Psychoeducation: Extending Somatic Illness Beliefs by Psychosocial Factors

As already mentioned above, patients with MUPS can have very complex explanations for their somatic symptoms, including psychosocial factors (Martin et al., 2007). Patients' illness beliefs are *explored* thoroughly and *validated* which does not mean to *convince* patients of biopsychosocial explanations. Patients should be slowly encouraged to *extend* their illness beliefs by demonstrating that besides somatic also psychosocial factors play an etiological role. Psychoeducation about the reciprocal relationships between body and mind (e.g., between negative emotions, peripheral arousal, and somatic changes) and using a symptom diary in order to observe associations between external stressors (e.g., conflicts with the partner) and the perception of physical changes are helpful strategies. Dependent on how receptive patients are toward psychosocial besides medical symptom attributions, a cognitive behavioral model of somatoform disorders (see Fig. 17.1) is discussed at this point.

Stress Management and Biofeedback

Stress management training for somatoform patients usually starts with psychoeducation about the relationships between stressors, the activation of the sympathetic nervous system, and physical symptoms. Moreover, patients learn about human relaxation response and activating the parasympathetic nervous system. Patients are provided with strategies to increase their resilience and stress-resistance and improve their relaxation skills. Stress management is a good starting tool of the CBT for somatoform patients since it addresses somatic factors of MUPS. Progressive muscle relaxation is usually recommended to patients to be used as relaxation technique. However, there are a lot of alternatives and patient and therapist have to find out what is the method which fits best patient's abilities and needs. Biofeedback (BFB) is a perfect method to complement relaxation training (e.g., Katsamanis et al., 2011). BFB feedbacks psychophysiological variables (e.g., muscle tone or heart rate). It helps demonstrating the influence of mental processes on bodily reactions and helps patients developing biopsychosocial symptom attributions. Moreover, BFB helps patients experiencing control of bodily reactions.

Refocusing Attention

According to the concept of somatosensory amplification (Barsky & Wyshak, 1990) focusing attention on bodily processes can have amplifying effects on somatic sensations. Brief exercises help patients to experience and understand these relationships. For example, therapists conduct an "alienated" body scan in which patients are guided to shift their attention between different body regions. Typically patients describe perceptions of bodily changes they have not been aware of before the exercise started. This body scan helps demonstrating that bodily processes become conscious as soon as attention is shifted to them. Moreover, exercises demonstrating effects of distraction on somatic sensations are an important therapeutic tool. For example, patients are exposed to a brief, painful, but nonthreatening stimulus (e.g., keeping hands in ice-cold water or keeping arms stretched) under pain-focusing versus distracting instructions. Finally, the therapist and the patient establish individual distraction strategies (e.g., activity-oriented strategies such as positive or attention-consuming activities, physical exercise or exercises where patients shift attention on specific senses such as listening consciously to different sounds in the environment). It is important to emphasize that distraction techniques do not target shifting attention away from bodily symptoms continuously. They are rather used to create short moments in patients' everyday life where individuals with MUPS experience a sense of control over their body. Moreover, patients learn to flexibly shifting attention between somatic symptoms and other stimuli.

Cognitive Restructuring of Dysfunctional, Symptom-Related Cognitions

Contents of dysfunctional symptom-related thoughts in patients with somatoform disorders can vary enormously. Besides catastrophizing thoughts and biased illness attributions (e.g., "The pain in my chest is a sign of a severe cardiovascular disease."), there are a lot of other dysfunctional cognitions. Examples are thoughts about loss of control ("The nausea appears spontaneously and I have no control."), self-blaming thoughts ("I should have gone to the physician when symptoms appeared for the first time. Maybe a medical cause would have been found."), thoughts related to illness behaviors (see next paragraph; e.g. "Due to the spontaneously starting diarrhea I can use only trains which have a restroom."), or biased thoughts regarding the own body or body image (e.g., "I feel weak; my body does not work anymore as it should do.").

Moreover, somatoform patients obtain typical cognitive styles such self-fulfilling prophecies (e.g., "I know that my nausea will start again as soon as I will go the party tonight."). In a first step, these dysfunctional cognitions have to be identified. Then the therapist starts questioning and modifying these thoughts by using methods of cognitive restructuring and Socratic questioning or dialog (e.g., Beck, 2011). In the following (see Table 17.1), some cognitive strategies are presented that can be applied to a dysfunctional thought that typically appears in somatoform patients for example with cardiovascular symptoms or chest pain.

Cognitive strategies are complemented with behavioral experiments where somatic symptoms are prompted intentionally. Such behavioral experiments are especially helpful when patients bear specific symptom attributions and fears of consequences of specific symptoms (e.g., pain in the chest could be a sign of a heart attack). Table 17.2 summarizes examples of such behavioral experiments for different kinds of somatic symptoms. They are usually structured in a standardized way: They start with clarifying and collecting typical dysfunctional cognitions and expectations appearing in situations where somatic symptoms become more severe. In the next step, patients' physical symptoms are triggered (see symptom-triggering exercises in Table 17.2), and patients are instructed to observe if their symptom-related expectations get fulfilled. Finally, patients are asked to contrast their previous dysfunctional

TABLE 17.1 Example of Cognitive Restructuring Techniques Applied on a Typical Dysfunctional Cognition in Somatoform Patients

Cognition: "In fact I trust doctors saying that I have no severe illness. However in this moment when breathlessness and the pressure in my left chest become more severe I'm afraid that it could be a heart attack."

Examples of cognitive restructuring techniques:
1. The therapist clarifies the patient's need associated with this thought (*"What do you need and wish in this moment when your symptoms become more severe?"*). Usually patients express a need of 100% safety and reassurance that they do not have a severe illness.
2. Patient and therapist explore consequences (positive/negative, short- and long term) of this need and this thought (negative consequences are, for example, establishing avoiding behaviors, withdrawal and focusing attention on somatic symptoms, symptom amplification, disability, and limitations in everyday life activities).
3. Patient and therapist find out healthy individuals' risk of having a heart attack. The patient should realize that everybody has a very small risk of suffering a severe illness. As homework, the patient is instructed to ask friends how they think about and cope with this risk.
4. Patient is asked to find out information about signs of a real heart attack. The patient's symptoms and signs of a heart attack are contrasted.

TABLE 17.2 Exercises for Triggering Physical Symptoms

Physical Symptoms	How to Trigger Them
Palpitations, breathlessness	• Walking upstairs quickly and several times • Physical activity, such as running or skipping a rope • Drinking a lot of coffee
Sense of pressure in the chest	• Hyperventilation • Wrap the chest with a scarf tightly • Lying on the ground and placing a heavy object (e.g., a heavy book) on the chest
Gastrointestinal symptoms	• Eating bloating- or diarrhea-triggering food • Taking a herbal laxative • Eating quickly a big amount of food over a short period of time after having been hungry
Pressure in the throat/larynx	• Swallowing repeatedly and holding the hand on the larynx in the same time • Having scarf wrapped around the throat and swallowing repeatedly
Formications in limbs	• Placing a constriction around the upper arm • Keeping arms and hands/legs lifted for a longer while • Lying/sitting on one arm/hand for a longer while
Dizziness	• Lying down and getting up quickly • Sitting on an office chair which is turned many times and quickly • Hyperventilation

thoughts with their new experiences and to phrase more helpful and more functional thoughts.

Reducing Illness Behaviors

Illness behaviors in somatoform patients can be various (Weiss et al., 2016). Typical kinds of illness behaviors are avoidance behaviors, body scanning, extensive healthcare utilization ("doctor shopping"), or other kinds of reassurance behaviors (e.g., excessive search for health-/illness-related information online, so-called "cyberchondriasis"; Muse, McManus, Leung, Meghreblian, & Williams, 2012). Cognitive behavioral techniques mainly aim at reducing these behaviors. In the following for each mentioned kind of illness behavior, basic cognitive behavioral strategies are described.

Avoidance behaviors can be caused by various dysfunctional cognitions. For example, patients avoid activities when they are afraid of being embarrassed (e.g., when a patient often feels dizzy he or she maybe avoids public places where he or she could be judged by others to be drunken) or when they expect a specific activity amplifying symptoms or causing reinjury. Thus, these cognitions are explored and clarified in a first step. Cognitive strategies mentioned above can be applied to restructure these dysfunctional thoughts. Patient and therapist should derive consequences of avoidance behaviors (positive versus negative, short- vs long term). Negative short- and long-term consequences such as deconditioning, lowered quality of life, or worse values in medical screenings should be emphasized and used to foster patients' motivation for change. Finally, the therapist supports patients increasing their levels of physical activity or approaching avoided situations and activities. Instead of avoiding activities, some somatoform patients tend to endurance behaviors and overstep their limits (Hasenbring & Verbunt, 2010). Typical cognitions in such patients are for example "My symptoms will not dominate my life. I continue functioning as I did before I had these symptoms." In this case, patients are supported in finding a healthy balance of physical activities, relaxation, and euthymic strategies, for example, with mindfulness-based exercises.

Body scanning behaviors can be very subtle and have to be thoroughly understood before they can be changed. In the context of a paradox intervention patients are asked for increasing their typical body scanning behavior over a limited period of time (e.g., a week) and completing a diary about their observations. Deborah for example was asked to swallow intensively and repeatedly over 10 min every day. This strategy helps patients understanding the relationship how body scanning amplifies physical perceptions. Finally, the therapist provides strategies for reducing or relinquishing body scanning behaviors. Deborah for example decided to have a fixed period of 5 min every day at 8 p.m. where she planned to check her larynx. Over the day every time she experienced a drive to touch her throat, she tried to distract herself and to postpone her "larynx check" to 8 p.m. At 8 p.m. usually her need to check her throat was low. This strategy helped her getting defused from her drive to scan her body.

Reducing extensive *health care utilizing behaviors* precedes exploring individual motives and needs standing behind this illness behavior. Besides the need for safety (see Table 17.1), also other needs can play a causal role (e.g., need to feel taken seriously or need for care). Moreover, patient and therapist explore consequences of "doctor shopping." Patients should especially become aware of the negative long-term consequences of their behavior. Deborah, for example, realized that she connected lots of hope but also disappointment and frustration with every doctoral appointment. She realized that her illness behaviors make her more and more dependent on physicians' reassurance. Moreover, she realized that her doctor-shopping behavior could pressurize clinicians who in turn will not take her seriously anymore. The therapist encourages the patient to choose one instead of several physicians with whom time- but not symptom-related appointments should be made. This helps breaking up the vicious cycle of the strong anxiety-reducing effect of reassurance.

Specific Issues in CBT for Pain

According to the model of fear avoidance cognitions and behaviors by Vlaeyen, Kolesnijders, Boeren, and Vaneek (1995), patients suffering from chronic pain have an increased risk to develop catastrophizing thoughts and fear of movement. Accordingly patients fear that movements and physical exercise could intensify pain and could lead to reinjury. Disability in everyday life, deconditioning, and depressive mood can be a consequence. Besides the cognitive behavioral strategies mentioned above, patients are treated with exposure therapy with reaction prevention which is similar to exposure for agoraphobia (e.g., Koch, Gloster, & Waller, 2007). The rationale and mechanisms of exposure are explained to patients. Then a hierarchy of feared movements is created. The next step is that patients are gradually exposed to fear-inducing movements (e.g., lifting heavy bags out of the trunk) until the a priori defined level of anxiety is reached and the patient habituated anxiety successfully (Vlaeyen, De Jong, Geilen, Heuts, & Van Breukelen, 2001). These classical concepts of exposure can be complemented by approaches of inhibitory learning. According to this approach, not only habituation is necessary for therapeutic progress in exposure-based interventions but strategies that foster new learning connections in the brain are also important. Examples are dysfunctional expectations regarding the frequency and intensity of bodily symptoms appearing as consequence of movements (Craske, Treanor, Conway, Zbozinek, & Vervliet, 2014).

Specific Issues in CBT for Hypochondriasis or Illness Anxiety Disorder

All strategies for the treatment of somatoform patients mentioned above also play an important role in CBT for patients diagnosed with hypochondriasis. However, they are complemented with exposure-based strategies since in hypochondriasis the symptom "anxiety" is the preliminary therapeutic target but not the somatic symptom. Patients with hypochondriasis usually avoid different places (e.g., hospitals, medical practices, grave yards, apartments of sick friends), situations, activities (e.g., physical exercise, media reports, talking with friends about illnesses, reading list of side effects of medications, medical check-ups) or other things (e.g., "harmful" food). Thus, on the one hand, classical concepts of in vivo exposure (Salkovskis & Warwick, 1986; Warwick, 1989) similar to agoraphobia are applied. On the other hand, in sensu exposure is an impactful intervention in hypochondriasis patients. Similar to evidence-based treatment concept of generalized anxiety disorder (Borkovec, Ray, & Stober, 1998), patients are asked to imagine their most fear-inducing worries (e.g., the imagination of the situation in which a doctor confirms the diagnosis of a severe disorder) and to write a script about this imagination. Patients are guided to end their worries in a worst case-scenario. Then the therapist reads out the script aloud while the patient imagines the content of the worst case scenario. This procedure is repeated until the patient imagines the content of the worst case scenario. Here again this traditional exposure-based approaches can be complemented by modern concepts of inhibitory learning (Craske et al., 2014) mentioned above.

Specific Issues in the Treatment of Patients With Underlying Somatic Disorders

The strategies described above can also be applied to patients with an underlying somatic condition however some specific aspects have to be considered. For somatically ill people, CBT techniques are rather applied in the context of illness management. It has to be considered that there is a real threat by the illness that should not be minimalized. The therapist talks openly about the illness, its consequences, and risks in a sense of illness management and acceptance. Moreover, it should be considered that besides anxiety often other emotions (e.g., grief, anger) play an important role. Although discussing alternative explanations and causes of the somatic symptoms is not a topic in treating patients with underlying medical conditions, of course, specific attentional, cognitive, and behavioral processes that can deteriorate the patient's health status and course of somatic illness can be addressed.

Modern Developments of CBT for Somatoform Disorders and Pain

In the context of "third wave" CBT, the role of emotions in therapeutic work is more emphasized. There are also new developments in the treatment of somatoform disorder applying concepts of mindfulness- and acceptance-based interventions. Fjorback et al. (2013) and Van Ravesteijn, Lucassen, Bor, Van Weel, and Speckens (2013) developed a mindfulness group therapy for patients with MUPS. The intervention is a combination of traditional CBT and mindfulness-based strategies (e.g., different forms of meditation, yoga exercises, body scans). Patients learn to be mindful toward their body, emotions, and mental and mind states and shall move toward acceptance of their symptoms and self-compassion. Eilenberg, Fink, Jensen, Rief, and Frostholm (2015) developed an acceptance and commitment therapy (ACT) for patients with health anxiety. In this treatment, patients learn to commit to alternative behaviors than controlling and avoidance behaviors with applying typical ACT-concepts such as creative hopelessness, defusion strategies, values, and committed actions combined with mindfulness exercises. Especially for patients with chronic pain several ACT and mindfulness-based stress reduction programs do exist (Veehof, Oskam, Schreurs, & Bohlmeijer, 2011). Finally, a cognitive behavioral treatment enriched with emotion regulation training will be evaluated in a study by Kleinstäuber, Gottschalk, Berking, Rau, and Rief (2016). This approach focuses on negative emotions associated with somatic symptoms as well as deficits in emotion regulation in patients with MUPS. Cognitive behavioral strategies are complemented with different forms of emotion regulation techniques.

EMPIRICAL EVIDENCE FOR COGNITIVE BEHAVIORAL THERAPY FOR SOMATOFORM DISORDERS AND PAIN

According to the current state of research, cognitive behavioral treatments are the only psychological interventions for somatoform disorders and pain that have been sufficiently examined in order to allow tentative conclusions about efficacy (Kleinstäuber, Witthöft, & Hiller, 2011; Van Dessel et al., 2014). A recent Cochrane review (Van Dessel et al., 2014) included four randomized controlled trials (RCT) encountering CBT with a waiting list control or a usual medical care control group. A significant, moderate effect regarding severity of somatic symptoms at posttreatment, $g = 0.58$; 95%-CI: 0.38, 0.77, and 1-year follow-up was identified. Regarding secondary outcomes such as quality of life and depressive symptoms only small to even very small, nonsignificant effects were identified.

Regarding *exposure-based therapies* for chronic pain only three randomized controlled trials exist. They demonstrate a significant benefit favoring exposure therapy in contrast to waiting list control group in regard to functioning in everyday life (Linton et al., 2008), perceived severity of pain, depression, and cognitive or emotional variables such as kinesiophobia, fear avoidance cognitions, or catastrophizing thoughts (Woods & Asmundson, 2008). In a third study (Leeuw et al., 2008), exposure-based therapy was even more effective than an active control group with graded physical activity at posttreatment and 6 months after the end of therapy. However, results have to be interpreted cautiously since dropout rates are high, e.g., 58% in the study by Woods and Asmundson (2008).

Third-wave CBTs for somatoform disorders have been only examined in single RCTs. Two RCTs examined the efficacy of *mindfulness therapy* for MUPS. They found significant differences in contrast to an enhanced usual care group regarding the rate of patients experiencing marked improvement at posttreatment in regard to physical health (Fjorback et al., 2013) and social functioning and vitality (Van Ravesteijn et al., 2013). In a RCT on *ACT for hypochondriasis*, a large significant between-group effect size ($d = 0.89$) on health anxiety was identified posttreatment and at the 10-month follow-up (Eilenberg et al., 2015). Dropout rates were low (8%). Research on the efficacy of ACT for treating chronic pain syndromes is much more advanced. A systematic review and meta-analysis (Veehof et al., 2011) obtained small effects for pain depression, physical wellbeing, quality of life ($0.25 \leq g \leq 0.43$), and a moderate effect for anxiety ($g = 0.55$). Veehof et al. (2011) suggest ACT to be not superior however a good alternative to CBT.

SUMMARY

In summary it has been demonstrated that cognitive behavioral interventions target on many factors that have been empirically evidenced to be involved in the etiology and maintenance of somatoform disorders. Moreover, CBT is the only psychological therapy for patients with multiple MUPS that has sufficiently been examined regarding its efficacy. However, the effects of CBT are only moderate or small which raises the question why the efficacy is low in comparison to other mental disorder, e.g., anxiety disorders and depression. A potential explanation could be a methodological problem. Almost all existing studies assess the efficacy of CBT for somatoform disorders with the primary outcome "severity of somatic symptoms" or "general health status." These outcomes are however not the primary target of CBT, but rather symptom-related disability in everyday life. Besides this methodological problem, probably therapeutic tools have to be optimized in order to increase efficacy. Future research will show if additional interventions of third wave CBT can result in better effects. However, it is not only the content of therapy that has to be improved but also the way how medical and psychological care for patients with somatoform disorders is structured. Many somatoform patients receive less helpful and unnecessary medical diagnostic and treatment procedures before they meet a psychologist. National health care systems would have to be restructured in order to facilitate interdisciplinary collaborations. A stepped-care approach for example could encourage physicians and psychologists communicating and coordinating a common treatment plan for patients. In a first step, a medical examination of patients would be conducted by a general practitioner and, if necessary, by medical specialists. If medical causes of physical symptoms cannot be identified clinicians should start early explaining relationships between somatic symptoms and psychosocial factors to patients. In the following step, psychotherapeutic interventions could be conducted in a group setting. If these interventions are not sufficient, individually tailored single therapies are recommended.

References

American Psychiatric Association. (2000). *Diagnostic and statistical manual for mental disorders. Fourth edition, text revision.* Washington, DC: American Psychiatric Press.
American Psychiatric Association. (2013). *Diagnostic and statistical manual of mental disorders. Fifth edition. DSM-5.* Washington, DC: APA.
Bailer, J., Witthöft, M., Bayerl, C., & Rist, F. (2007). Syndrome stability and psychological predictors of symptom severity in idiopathic environmental intolerance and somatoform disorders. *Psychological Medicine, 37,* 271–281. Available from http://dx.doi.org/10.1017/S0033291706009354.
Barsky, A. J., Ahern, D. K., Bailey, E. D., Saintfort, R., Liu, E. B., & Peekna, H. M. (2001). Hypochondriacal patients' appraisal of health and physical risks. *American Journal of Psychiatry, 158,* 783–787. Available from http://dx.doi.org/10.1176/appi.ajp.158.5.783.
Barsky, A. J., & Wyshak, G. (1990). Hypochondriasis and somatosensory amplification. *British Journal of Psychiatry, 157,* 404–409. Available from http://dx.doi.org/10.1192/bjp.157.3.404.

Beck, J. S. (2011). *Cognitive behavior therapy: Basics and beyond* (2nd ed.). New York: Guilford Press.

Bogaerts, K., Janssens, T., De Peuter, S., Van Diest, I., & Van den Bergh, O. (2010). Negative affective pictures can elicit physical symptoms in high habitual symptom reporters. *Psychology & Health, 25*, 685–698. Available from http://dx.doi.org/10.1080/08870440902814639.

Bogaerts, K., Notebaert, K., Van Diest, I., Devriese, S., De Peuter, S., & Van den Bergh, O. (2005). Accuracy of respiratory symptom perception in different affective contexts. *Journal of Psychosomatic Research, 58*, 537–543. Available from http://dx.doi.org/10.1016/j.jpsychores.2004.12.005.

Borkovec, T. D., Ray, W. J., & Stober, J. (1998). Worry: A cognitive phenomenon intimately linked to affective, physiological, and interpersonal behavioral processes. *Cognitive Therapy and Research, 22*, 561–576. Available from http://dx.doi.org/10.1023/A:1018790003416.

Brosschot, J. F. (2002). Cognitive-emotional sensitization and somatic health complaints. *Scandinavian Journal of Psychology, 43*, 113–121. Available from http://dx.doi.org/10.1111/1467-9450.00276.

Brown, R. J., Danquah, A. N., Miles, E., Holmes, E., & Poliakoff, E. (2010). Attention to the body in nonclinical somatoform dissociation depends on emotional state. *Journal of Psychosomatic Research, 69*, 249–257. Available from http://dx.doi.org/10.1016/j.jpsychores.2010.04.010.

Burton, C., McGorm, K., Richardson, G., Weller, D., & Sharpe, M. (2012). Healthcare costs incurred by patients repeatedly referred to secondary medical care with medically unexplained symptoms: A cost of illness study. *Journal of Psychosomatic Research, 72*, 242–247. Available from http://dx.doi.org/10.1016/j.jpsychores.2011.12.009.

Cash, T. F., & Pruzinsky, T. (2002). *Body image. A handbook of theory, research, and clinical practice.* New York: Guilford Press.

Constantinou, E., Bogaerts, K., Van Diest, I., & Van den Bergh, O. (2013). Inducing symptoms in high symptom reporters via emotional pictures: The interactive effects of valence and arousal. *Journal of Psychosomatic Research, 74*, 191–196. Available from http://dx.doi.org/10.1016/j.jpsychores.2012.12.015.

Craske, M. G., Treanor, M., Conway, C. C., Zbozinek, T., & Vervliet, B. (2014). Maximizing exposure therapy: An inhibitory learning approach. *Behaviour Research and Therapy, 58*, 10–23. Available from http://dx.doi.org/10.1016/j.brat.2014.04.006.

Crombez, G., Eccleston, C., Baeyens, F., & Eelen, P. (1998). When somatic information threatens, catastrophic thinking enhances attentional interference. *Pain, 75*, 187–198. Available from http://dx.doi.org/10.1016/S0304-3959(97)00219-4.

De Wied, M., & Verbaten, M. N. (2001). Affective pictures processing, attention, and pain tolerance. *Pain, 90*, 163–172. Available from http://dx.doi.org/10.1016/S0304-3959(0000400-0).

Eilenberg, T., Fink, P., Jensen, J. S., Rief, W., & Frostholm, L. (2015). Acceptance and commitment group therapy (ACT-G) for health anxiety: A randomized controlled trial. *Psychological Medicine.* Available from http://dx.doi.org/10.1017/S0033291715001579.

Escobar, J. I., Rubio-Stipec, M., Canino, G., & Karno, M. (1989). Somatic symptom index (SSI): A new and abridged somatization construct. Prevalence and epidemiological correlates in two large community samples. *Journal of Nervous and Mental Disease, 177*, 140–146. Available from http://dx.doi.org/10.1097/00005053-198903000-00003.

Fink, P., & Schröder, A. (2010). One single diagnosis, bodily distress syndrome, succeeded to capture 10 diagnostic categories of functional somatic syndromes and somatoform disorders. *Journal of Psychosomatic Research, 68*, 415–426. Available from http://dx.doi.org/10.1016/j.jpsychores.2010.02.004.

Fink, P., Toft, T., Hansen, M. S., Ornbol, E., & Olesen, F. (2007). Symptoms and syndromes of bodily distress: An exploratory study of 978 internal medical, neurological, and primary care patients. *Psychosomatic Medicine, 69,* 30–39. Available from http://dx.doi.org/69/1/3010.1097/PSY.0b013e31802e46eb.

Fjorback, L. O., Arendt, M., Ornbøl, E., Walach, H., Rehfeld, E., & Schröder, A. (2013). Mindfulness therapy for somatization disorder and functional somatic syndromes—Randomized trial with one-year follow-up. *Journal of Psychosomatic Research, 74,* 31–40. Available from http://dx.doi.org/10.1016/j.jpsychores.2012.09.006.

Hadjistavropoulos, H. D., Coons, M. J., & Asmundson, G. J. G. (2004). Factor structure and psychometric properties of the Pain Anxiety Symptoms Scale-20 in a community physiotherapy clinic sample. *European Journal of Pain, 8,* 511–516. Available from http://dx.doi.org/10.1016/j.ejpain.2003.11.018.

Hasenbring, M. I., & Verbunt, J. A. (2010). Fear-avoidance and endurance-related responses to pain: New models of behavior and their consequences for clinical practice. *Clinical Journal of Pain, 26,* 747–753. Available from http://dx.doi.org/10.1097/Ajp.0b013e3181e104f2.

Katsamanis, M., Lehrer, P. M., Escobar, J. I., Gara, M. A., Kotay, A., & Liu, R. (2011). Psychophysiologic treatment for patients with medically unexplained symptoms: A randomized controlled trial. *Psychosomatics, 52,* 218–229.

Kirmayer, L. J., & Taillefer, S. (1997). Somatoform disorders. In S. M. Turner, & M. Hersen (Eds.), *Adult psychopathology and diagnosis* (pp. 333–383). New York: Wiley.

Klaus, K., Rief, W., Brahler, E., Martin, A., Glaesmer, H., & Mewes, R. (2015). Validating psychological classification criteria in the context of somatoform disorders: A one- and four-year follow-up. *Journal of Abnormal Psychology, 124,* 1092–1101. Available from http://dx.doi.org/10.1037/abn0000085.

Kleinstäuber, M., Gottschalk, J., Berking, M., Rau, J., & Rief, W. (2016). Enriching cognitive behavior therapy with emotion regulation training for patients with multiple medically unexplained symptoms (ENCERT): Design and implementation of a multicenter, randomized, active-controlled trial. *Contemporary Clinical Trials, 47,* 54–63. Available from http://dx.doi.org/10.1016/j.cct.2015.12.003.

Kleinstäuber, M., Witthöft, M., & Hiller, W. (2011). Efficacy of short-term psychotherapy for multiple medically unexplained physical symptoms: A meta-analysis. *Clinical Psychology Review, 31,* 146–160. Available from http://dx.doi.org/10.1016/j.cpr.2010.09.001.

Koch, E. I., Gloster, A. T., & Waller, S. A. (2007). Exposure treatments for panic disorder with and without agoraphobia. In D. C. S. Richard, & D. Lauterbach (Eds.), *Handbook of exposure therapies* (pp. 221–246). San Diego, CA: Elsevier.

Kroenke, K., Spitzer, R. L., deGruy, F. V., 3rd, Hahn, S. R., Linzer, M., Williams, J. B., Brody, D., & Davies, M. (1997). Multisomatoform disorder: An alternative to undifferentiated somatoform disorder for the somatizing patient in primary care. *Archives of General Psychiatry, 54,* 352–358. Available from http://dx.doi.org/10.1001/archpsyc.1997.01830160080011.

Lackner, J. M., & Quigley, B. M. (2005). Pain catastrophizing mediates the relationship between worry and pain suffering in patients with irritable bowel syndrome. *Behaviour Research and Therapy, 43,* 943–957. Available from http://dx.doi.org/10.1016/j.brat.2004.06.018.

Lautenbacher, S., Pauli, P., Zaudig, M., & Birbaumer, N. (1998). Attentional control of pain perception: The role of hypochondriasis. *Journal of Psychosomatic Research, 44,* 251–259. Available from http://dx.doi.org/10.1016/S0022-3999(97)00214-6.

Leeuw, M., Goossens, M. E. J. B., Van Breukelen, G. J. P., de Jong, J. R., Heuts, P. H. T. G., Smeets, R. J. E. M., Koke, A. J. A., & Vlaeyen, J. W. S. (2008). Exposure in vivo versus operant graded activity in chronic low back pain patients: Results of a randomized controlled trial. *Pain, 138,* 192–207. Available from http://dx.doi.org/10.1016/j.pain.2007.12.009.

Linton, S. J., Boersma, K., Jansson, M., Overmeer, T., Lindblom, K., & Vlaeyen, J. W. S. (2008). A randomized controlled trial of exposure in vivo for patients with spinal pain reporting fear of work-related activities. *European Journal of Pain, 12,* 722–730. Available from http://dx.doi.org/10.1016/j.ejpain.2007.11.001.

Lupke, U., & Ehlert, U. (1998). Attentional bias towards cues prejudicial to health in patients with somatoform disorders [Selektive Aufmerksamkeitslenkung auf gesundheitsbedrohliche Reize bei Patienten mit einer somatoformen Störung]. *Zeitschrift für Klinische Psychologie, Forschung und Praxis, 27,* 163–171.

Marcus, D. K., & Church, S. E. (2003). Are dysfunctional beliefs about illness unique to hypochondriasis? *Journal of Psychosomatic Research, 54,* 543–547. Available from http://dx.doi.org/10.1016/S0022-3999(02)00526-3.

Martin, A., Korn, H. J., Cebulla, M., Saly, M., Fichter, M. M., & Hiller, W. (2007). Causal attributions about bodily sensations in somatoform disorders. *Zeitschrift Fur Psychiatrie Psychologie Und Psychotherapie, 55,* 31–41. Available from http://dx.doi.org/10.1024/1661-4747.55.1.31.

McCarthy, M. (2015). US panel proposes new name and diagnostic criteria for chronic fatigue syndrome. *British Medical Journal, 350,* h775. Available from http://dx.doi.org/ARTNh93210.1136/bmj.h932.

Murray, A. M., Toussaint, A., Althaus, A., & Löwe, B. (2016). The challenge of diagnosing non-specific, functional, and somatoform disorders: A systematic review of barriers to diagnosis in primary care. *Journal of Psychosomatic Research, 80,* 1–10. Available from http://dx.doi.org/10.1016/j.jpsychores.2015.11.002.

Muse, K., McManus, F., Leung, C., Meghreblian, B., & Williams, M. G. (2012). Cyberchondriasis: Fact or fiction? A preliminary examination of the relationship between health anxiety and searching for health information on the Internet. *Journal of Anxiety Disorders, 26,* 189–196. Available from http://dx.doi.org/10.1016/j.janxdis.2011.11.005.

Pearce, J., & Morley, S. (1989). An experimental investigation of the construct-validity of the McGill Pain Questionnaire. *Pain, 39,* 115–121. Available from http://dx.doi.org/10.1016/0304-3959(89)90182-6.

Petrie, K. J., Broadbent, E. A., Kley, N., Moss-Morris, R., Horne, R., & Rief, W. (2005). Worries about modernity predict symptom complaints after environmental pesticide spraying. *Psychosomatic Medicine, 67,* 778–782. Available from http://dx.doi.org/10.1097/01.psy.0000181277.48575.a4.

Riebel, K., Egloff, B., & Witthöft, M. (2013). The implicit health-related self-concept in somatoform disorders. *Journal of Behavior Therapy and Experimental Psychiatry, 44,* 335–342. Available from http://dx.doi.org/10.1016/j.jbtep.2013.02.001.

Rief, W., Heitmüller, A. M., Reisberg, K., & Rüddel, H. (2006). Why reassurance fails in patients with unexplained symptoms—An experimental investigation of remembered probabilities. *PLoS Medicine, 3,* 1266–1272. Available from http://dx.doi.org/10.1371/journal.pmed.0030269.

Rief, W., Nanke, A., Emmerich, J., Bender, A., & Zech, T. (2004). Causal illness attributions in somatoform disorders: Associations with comorbidity and illness behavior. *Journal of Psychosomatic Research, 57,* 367–371. Available from http://dx.doi.org/S002239990400047910.1016/j.jpsychores.2004.02.015.

Ring, A., Dowrick, C., Humphris, G., & Salmon, P. (2004). Do patients with unexplained physical symptoms pressurise general practitioners for somatic treatment? A qualitative study. *British Medical Journal, 328,* 1057–1060. Available from http://dx.doi.org/10.1136/bmj.38057.622639.EE.

Royal College General Practitioners. (2011). Guidance for health professionals on medically unexplained symptoms (MUS). Available from http://www.rcpsych.ac.uk/pdf/CHECKED%20MUS%20Guidance_A4_4pp_6.pdf. Accessed 09.04.14.

Salkovskis, P. M., & Warwick, H. M. (1986). Morbid preoccupations, health anxiety and reassurance: A cognitive-behavioural approach to hypochondriasis. *Behaviour Research and Therapy, 24*, 597–602. Available from http://dx.doi.org/0005-7967(86)90041-0.

Severeijns, R., Vlaeyen, J. W. S., Van den Hout, M. A., & Picavet, H. S. J. (2004). Pain catastrophizing is associated with health indices in musculoskeletal pain: A cross-sectional study in the Dutch community. *Health Psychology, 23*, 49–57. Available from http://dx.doi.org/10.1037/0278-6133.23.1.49.

Sharpe, M., Mayou, R., & Bass, C. (1995). Concepts, theories and terminology. In R. Mayou, C. Bass, & M. Sharpe (Eds.), *Treatment of functional somatic symptoms* (pp. 3–16). Oxford, UK: Oxford University Press.

Smeets, G., De Jong, P. J., & Mayer, B. (2000). If you suffer from a headache, then you have a brain tumour: Domain-specific reasoning "bias" and hypochondriasis. *Behaviour Research and Therapy, 38*, 763–776. Available from http://dx.doi.org/10.1016/S0005-7967(99)00094-7.

Sullivan, M. J. L., Adams, H., & Sullivan, M. E. (2004). Communicative dimensions of pain catastrophizing: Social cueing effects on pain behaviour and coping. *Pain, 107*, 220–226. Available from http://dx.doi.org/10.1016/j.pain.2003.11.003.

Taillefer, S. S., Kirmayer, L. J., Robbins, J. M., & Lasry, J. C. (2002). Psychological correlates of functional status in chronic fatigue syndrome. *Journal of Psychosomatic Research, 53*, 1097–1106. Available from http://dx.doi.org/10.1016/S0022-3999(02)00566-4.

Thompson, W. G., Longstreth, G. F., Drossman, D. A., Heaton, K. W., Irvine, E. J., & Muller-Lissner, S. A. (1999). Functional bowel disorders and functional abdominal pain. *Gut, 45*, 43–47.

Van Dessel, N., Den Boeft, M., Van der Wouden, J. C., Kleinstäuber, M., Leone, S. S., Terluin, B., Numans, M. E., Van der Horst, H. E., & Van Marwijk, H. (2014). Non-pharmacological interventions for somatoform disorders and medically unexplained physical symptoms (MUPS) in adults. *Cochrane Database of Systematic Reviews, Issue 11*. Art. No.: CD011142. Available from http://dx.doi.org/10.1002/14651858.CD011142.pub2.

Van Ravesteijn, H., Lucassen, P., Bor, H., Van Weel, C., & Speckens, A. (2013). Mindfulness-based cognitive therapy for patients with medically unexplained symptoms: A randomized controlled trial. *Psychotherapy and Psychosomatics, 82*, 299–310. Available from http://dx.doi.org/10.1159/000348588.

Veehof, M. M., Oskam, M. J., Schreurs, K. M. G., & Bohlmeijer, E. T. (2011). Acceptance-based interventions for the treatment of chronic pain: A systematic review and meta-analysis. *Pain, 152*, 533–542. Available from http://dx.doi.org/10.1016/j.pain.2010.11.002.

Vlaeyen, J. W. S., De Jong, J., Geilen, M., Heuts, P. H. T. G., & Van Breukelen, G. (2001). Graded exposure in vivo in the treatment of pain-related fear: A replicated single-case experimental design in four patients with chronic low back pain. *Behaviour Research and Therapy, 39*, 151–166. Available from http://dx.doi.org/10.1016/S0005-7967(99)00174-6.

Vlaeyen, J. W. S., Kolesnijders, A. M. J., Boeren, R. G. B., & Vaneek, H. (1995). Fear of movement (re)injury in chronic low-back-pain and its relation to behavioral performance. *Pain, 62*, 363–372. Available from http://dx.doi.org/10.1016/0304-3959(94)00279-N.

Vlaeyen, J. W. S., Seelen, H. A. M., Peters, M., de Jong, P., Aretz, E., Beisiegel, E., & Weber, W. E. J. (1999). Fear of movement/(re)injury and muscular reactivity in chronic low back pain patients: An experimental investigation. *Pain, 82,* 297–304. Available from http://dx.doi.org/10.1016/S0304-3959(99)00054-8.

Warwick, H. M. C. (1989). A cognitive-behavioural approach to hypochondriasis and health anxiety. *Journal of Psychosomatic Research, 33,* 705–710. Available from http://dx.doi.org/10.1016/0022-3999(89)90086-X.

Watt, M. C., & Stewart, S. H. (2000). Anxiety sensitivity mediates the relationships between childhood learning experiences and elevated hypochondriacal concerns in young adulthood. *Journal of Psychosomatic Research, 49,* 107–118. Available from http://dx.doi.org/10.1016/S0022-3999(00)00097-0.

Weiss, F. D., Rief, W., Martin, A., Rauh, E., & Kleinstäuber, M. (2016). The heterogeneity of illness behaviors in patients with medically unexplained physical symptoms. *International Journal of Behavioral Medicine, 23,* 319–326. Available from http://dx.doi.org/10.1007/s12529-015-9533-8.

Wessely, S., Nimnuan, C., & Sharpe, M. (1999). Functional somatic syndromes: One or many? *Lancet, 354,* 936–939. Available from http://dx.doi.org/10.1016/S0140-6736(98)08320-2.

Wolfe, F., Clauw, D. J., Fitzcharles, M. A., Goldenberg, D. L., Hauser, W., Katz, R. S., Mease, P., Russell, A. S., Russell, I. J., & Winfield, J. B. (2011). Fibromyalgia criteria and Severity Scales for Clinical and Epidemiological Studies: A modification of the ACR preliminary diagnostic criteria for fibromyalgia. *Journal of Rheumatology, 38,* 1113–1122. Available from http://dx.doi.org/10.3899/jrheum.100594.

Woods, M. P., & Asmundson, G. J. G. (2008). Evaluating the efficacy of graded in vivo exposure for the treatment of fear in patients with chronic back pain: A randomized controlled clinical trial. *Pain, 136,* 271–280. Available from http://dx.doi.org/10.1016/j.pain.2007.06.037.

Dialectical Behavior Therapy: Overview, Characteristics, and Future Directions

Anita Lungu[1] and Marsha M. Linehan[2]
[1]Lyra Health, Burlingame, CA, United States [2]University of Washington, Seattle, WA, United States

HISTORY OF DIALECTICAL BEHAVIOR THERAPY

Dialectical behavior therapy (DBT) was developed starting in the 1980s as part of a process to effectively treat individuals at high risk for suicide and with complex clinical presentations. Specifically, the focus of treatment was to help individuals who were often chronically suicidal and went in and out of psychiatric hospitals to build lives they experienced as worth living. The treatment development process involved clinical trial and error coupled with detailed observation of clinical work and incorporation of feedback in an iterative process. Early stages of treatment development and research were supported by grant funding that made necessary the selection of a diagnostic category. Borderline personality disorder (BPD) was selected given the high overlap this clinical group had with suicidal behaviors (Leichsenring, Leibing, Kruse, New, & Leweke, 2011).

Initial attempts to develop the treatment focused on a theoretical foundation comprised of behaviorism (Skinner, 1974), social learning theory (Staats & Staats, 1963; Staats, 1975), social psychology (Mischel, 1973), and the cognitive behavioral therapy principles of the time (Goldfried & Davison, 1976; Wilson & O'Leary, 1980). One assumption of the treatment, from the beginning, was that the lives of chronically

429

suicidal individuals were often unbearable as they were. The treatment thus started with a heavy focus on change in order to "fix" the deep and many real problems in the lives of suicidal individuals. Although change was needed to turn those lives around, it was also experienced as invalidating of the individual and unbearable. When asked to change, individuals often became emotionally dysregulated, experiencing the request as a threat to their own identity and worth. The result was often emotional shut-down or dysregulated behaviors like verbally attacking the therapist, attempting to self-harm, or storming out of the room. Research later provided evidence to support that perceived invalidation can lead to increased arousal and an inability to process new invalidation (Swann, Stein-Seroussi, & Giesler, 1992).

As a sole focus on change blatantly back-fired in therapy, the immediate alternative was to heavily focus on complete acceptance of the individual client's emotions, cognitions, and behaviors. However, communicating to clients that they are fully accepted as they are and that no change is needed was perceived as equally invalidating of the suffering of the individual. In other words, if the therapist communicated complete acceptance and did not propose ways, the client could change, this was interpreted as if the therapist was not understanding the depth of suffering and emotional pain in the client and was offering no help. Given the failure of strategies focused solely on change or solely on acceptance, the treatment emerged with the solution of balance between the two; both clients and therapists had to accept client's lives in the moment and simultaneously learn and implement strategies for change so that the client's lives could improve for the future.

At the time DBT was developed, change strategies had significant research support. However, not the same could be said of acceptance strategies. Linehan sought techniques to teach both therapists and their clients to accept reality as it was even as they worked toward change. Client centered therapy contributed significantly to finding ways to accept clients; however, in a sense, it used acceptance to eventually implement change. Linehan was interested also in developing and incorporating strategies for pure acceptance, without an ulterior goal. Linehan's personal experience led to the discovery of contemplative prayer practices and Zen as a trans-confessional practice for increasing awareness and acceptance of the present moment. Early attempts to incorporate Zen into therapy included asking clients to practice meditation. Such attempts were unsuccessful as clients reported being unable to practice and sometimes even got emotionally dysregulated from the practice. Linehan undertook the task of transforming Zen and contemplative prayer practice into behaviors that individuals at high risk for suicide and with complex clinical problems could engage in. Mindfulness, as a term, was adopted from the work of Langer (1989) and of Hahn (1976). Similarly, contemplative prayer practices were transformed into "reality acceptance skills" inspired by the work of May (1987).

Dialectics appeared as a framework that could hold the apparent tensions between opposing perspectives and techniques such as "change" and "acceptance" skills. After adopting dialectics as an underlying philosophical foundation, the entire treatment, including its manual (Linehan, 1993a, 1993b), was modeled to fit that philosophy. At its core, DBT remains true to behavioral principles that place experience above all else as means to know and interact to reality. This emphasis on experience permeates not just the initial development of the treatment but also its evolution over time. DBT is, thus, a treatment heavily based on evidence from clinical experience and research. Close observation of clients and of the therapy process is integrated within the theoretical treatment framework; questions based on theory and clinical experience are asked and answered though research, and the results are incorporated into the treatment administered. This continuous resolution of tensions between clinical experience, theory, and research led to an evolution process for DBT that is similar to the theoretical integration model for psychotherapy (Arkowitz, 1989, 1992; Norcross & Goldfried, 2005; Prochaska & Diclemente, 2005; Ryle, 2005). Research findings have influenced the clinical population targeted by the treatment in terms of age group and clinical problems experienced, the content of the skills included, the order in which clinical problems are addressed, as well as ways in which the treatment is delivered.

DBT THEORY

Three frameworks contribute to DBT theory: dialectics, social behavioral theory, and Zen practice. These are discussed below.

Dialectical Philosophy

As mentioned before, dialectics emerged as a theoretical framework that could hold together DBT's focus on techniques for both acceptance and change. The dialectics philosophy as it relates to DBT has been elaborated elsewhere (Linehan & Schmidt, 1995); so, we include only some major ideas here. Dialectics as a philosophy extends back thousands of years even though the names of Hegel and Marx have been more recently associated with it. Within the context of DBT, dialectics are influential both as a method of persuasion and change and as a worldview (Basseches, 1984; Kaminstein, 1987). At a high level psychotherapy, both in individual and group settings, DBT can be conceptualized as a persuasive process led by the therapist via a dialog with the client; the therapist is attempting to persuade the client to change his/her worldview and behaviors (at least to some extent) in the service of reaching mutually agreed on therapy goals. In this context, dialectics serves as a method of persuasion or argumentation in which the therapist identifies and voices the contradictions (antithesis) in the client's position (thesis) and helps the client arrive at a new stance that can reconcile opposing views (synthesis). Change through a persuasive process not only happens in individual or group sessions with clients but also in DBT team meetings where therapists work on each other as a group to improve the quality of the clinical process and adherence to the treatment. DBT clinicians strive to be dialectical in resolving tensions within the team to see theses and antitheses as they pertain to case conceptualizations and treatment planning and to arrive at syntheses that would qualitatively improve individual and team treatments. DBT clinicians are thus agents of dialectical persuasion for one another.

Several principles speak to dialectics as a worldview. First, the world is seen as being systemic, complex, and interconnected, made of "parts" that together create a "whole." The "parts" cannot be understood in isolation but only when one considers how they relate to one another. Second, the parts of the system are in continuous interaction with one another generating constant change. Change is thus seen as the only constant in the system, something to be fully embraced and accepted.

Such a worldview impacts DBT treatment in multiple ways. First, DBT clients cannot be understood in isolation from their environment, which influences our understanding of the etiology of disorder and also of its maintenance. Second, the biosocial theory of BPD or emotion dysregulation emphasizes the transaction between a child with heightened biological emotion sensitivity and an invalidating environment in the development of disorder. Similarly, the transaction between an individual with heightened sensitivity to invalidation and low skills for regulating emotion and an invalidating environment can maintain disorder. Third, considering the complexity of systems, disorder, or dysregulation is seen as being caused by multiple, not singular factors. This assumption holds at the level of disorder generally but also at the level of a single dysregulated emotion or behavior. Fourth, case conceptualizations in DBT include multiple factors that contributed to the etiology of dysregulation in a particular individual and also multiple factors that are maintaining such dysregulation. Fifth, Linehan's model of emotion (Neacsiu, Bohus, & Linehan, 2015) comprises an array of different factors that all can contribute to a particular dysregulated emotion from distal and proximal vulnerability factors (such as lack of sleep, poor nutrition, chronic pain, or substance use) to cognitive interpretations of the facts.

The most fundamental dialectic tension in DBT is that between acceptance and change. It permeates the treatment in different settings. In individual therapy, the process of each session and the case conceptualization globally needs to be balanced in terms of therapy time and focus allocated to acceptance and change. In group therapy, tension emerges often between accepting clients as they are and pushing for change in their behavior, such that their behavior does not interfere with the therapeutic process for other clients in the group or for the group overall. In DBT teams of clinicians work to accept each others' personal limits while at the same time challenging those limits temporarily when a particular client or group of clients need more clinical effort. Clients themselves need to accept themselves and their limitations while focusing on change.

Close observation of the clinical process with adults and adolescent individuals (and their families) high in emotion dysregulation (many meeting criteria for BPD) has led to the identification of several dialectical dilemmas or tensions that often characterize this clinical group. The dialectical dilemmas are described as oscillations between two opposite poles of behaviors. Not all patterns of such behaviors are present in each individual with high emotion dysregulation and therapists (working individually or as team members) need to do their own assessment to see the extent to which these dilemmas are relevant for each patient (see Linehan & Schmidt, 1995 for a more in-depth discussion of dialectical dilemmas).

Foundation in Social Behavioral Theory

Staat's social behavioral model of personality represented the foundation for the behavioral model of DBT (Staats & Staats, 1963; Staats, 1975). Following this model, three behavior response systems are fundamental for understanding human behavior and function: the overt behavioral response system, the cognitive response system, and the physiological/affective response system. Function takes place within one of these systems or across a combination of these systems. From this perspective, emotions are understood as responses of the entire organism that include all three response systems. To fully comprehend and potentially target for regulation of a particular emotion, one needs to understand the affect, cognitions, and behaviors that occur as part of that emotion. Furthermore, the three response systems are seen as interdependent, such that change in one response system is likely to impact the other response systems. As a consequence of this perspective on emotional functioning, behavioral analysis in DBT includes assessment along variables within individuals but also in their environment. Chain analysis, a DBT behavioral assessment technique, consists of a thorough step-by-step questioning on all environmental variables/triggers, cognitive reactions, and physiological responses connected to a particular target behavior (either functional or dysfunctional). Once a chain is completed and the clinician has a thorough understanding of all components impacting the behavior under analysis the chain can be "resolved"; that is, the client and therapist focus on all "links" of the chain (environmental, cognitive, behavioral, affective) that can be changed, such that the target behavior can be avoided in the future. At a high level, DBT distilled the DBT skills based on social psychology and on observations of what therapists of various effective treatments told clients to do.

An important consequence of this behavioral model is that all dysregulated behaviors (including suicidal and nonsuicidal behaviors) and cognitions that represent therapy targets can be linked to emotion dysregulation and environmental components. DBT as a treatment for emotion dysregulation leverages change on the emotional system by impacting the behavioral, cognitive, and environmental components.

Linehan developed the biosocial model of emotion dysregulation (Crowell, Beauchaine, & Linehan, 2009) to explain developmental factors that contribute to emotion dysregulation. The model comprises two factors that interact with one another: an individual who is biologically vulnerable to have heightened emotional responses (either due to heredity, epigenetics, or due to neural insults), and an invalidating social environment that does not teach the child how to understand, accept, tolerate, and manage emotions (particularly distressing or negative emotions). Emotion dysregulation, and sometimes associated behavioral and cognitive dysregulation, emerges as a result of repeated transactions between emotionally vulnerable individuals and invalidating social environments. Suicidal and nonsuicidal self-injury (NSSI) behaviors are understood, from this perspective as dysfunctional (but often very effective) ways of regulating intolerable suffering in the absence of other more functional emotion regulation (ER) skills.

Foundation in Zen Practice and Contemplative Prayer

As mentioned, the strong influence of Zen practice in DBT stems from Linehan's search for a technology of acceptance that would not have an ulterior goal of change. Although cognitive and behavioral therapies of the 1980s were highly efficacious in teaching change oriented techniques, it was not their strength to teach acceptance techniques. The incorporation of mindfulness into psychotherapy was not yet underway despite some beginning efforts. For example, Alan Marlatt, a colleague of Linehan's at the University of Washington, published the first randomized trial on meditation in 1986 (Murphy, Pagano, & Marlatt, 1986) but did not find it effective for alcohol use, and Jon Kabat-Zinn was teaching meditation and yoga to people with medical disorders (Kabat-Zinn, 1982; Kabat-Zinn, Lipworth, & Burney, 1985). Linehan thus started her own quest for discovering who were the best teachers of acceptance, which resulted in her focusing on Zen practice and contemplative prayer teachings. Zen practice was chosen also because it fit well with a behavioral worldview and techniques that were already at the core of DBT. Both behavioral therapy and Zen: (1) don't have a construct or a focus on individual self; indeed, both would be easier to follow if discourse consisted entirely of verbs; (2) view the world as complex, connected, and interdependent; the ultimate experience for Zen is that of nonself and unity with all things and behavioral therapy recognizes the futility of understanding behavior outside of environment and context; and (3) share practice prescriptions and proscriptions; Zen focuses on experience as paramount in understanding reality and functioning effectively in it—"The first truth . . . is that life is suffering. Avoidance of suffering leads to worse suffering" (Aitken, 1982, p. 49)—whereas behavioral therapy places exposure and experience at the center of overcoming anxiety and fear-related problems.

Once Zen was identified as foundational for DBT's technology of acceptance, the next challenge for Linehan was to find ways to convey Zen teachings and practices to individuals with high emotion dysregulation. Initial attempts at teaching such a clinical group traditional meditation techniques failed. What followed was Linehan's translation of Zen teachings and practices into behavioral skills. The main question to be answered was "What do people do when they practice Zen?," recognizing that while meditation was one way of practicing Zen, it was not the only one. DBT has two different foci in answering this question. First, the DBT skill of "Wise Mind" was derived from the Zen teaching that each individual has an inherent capacity for wisdom. The idea was not that the therapist embarks on a process to teach a client how to be wise, but that the client already had that capacity within and the role of the therapist was to help him/her remove the barriers and develop the habit of accessing that wisdom. "Wise Mind" practices also matched well with behavioral therapy in teaching clients how to rehearse and, thus, have more accessible a context of wise choices and behaviors. Second, DBT deconstructed mindfulness meditation into small pieces that therapists could teach and clients could learn and practice. The focus was radical acceptance of reality as it is in this moment with no judgment and participating in reality with full awareness. Such awareness leads to the skill of describing just what is observed rather than what is interpreted. A common mindfulness description of the thought process can be "The thought has arisen in my mind that you are disappointed." The term mindfulness itself was already used in psychology (Langer, 1989) and was also popularized by Thich Nhat Hanh in *The Miracle of Mindfulness* (Hahn, 1976).

Another set of skills was derived from Christian contemplative practices and developed to teach individuals how to radically accept living the lives they had even when those were not the lives they wanted. The DBT skill of radical acceptance came both from Zen (letting go of attachment) and from that of Christianity ("Thy will be done") and willingness has roots in May's work (May, 1987).

IMPLICATIONS FOR CONCEPTUALIZING EMOTION DYSREGULATION AS TRANS-DIAGNOSTIC MECHANISM OF DISORDER

DBT has the most research supporting its efficacy in treating BPD, a disorder of characterized by pervasive emotion dysregulation (Lynch, Trost, Salsman, & Linehan, 2007). The term pervasive was used to capture how, for individuals meeting criteria for BPD, the emotion dysregulation profoundly impacted all areas of their lives and, considering emotions as full system responses (Linehan, Bohus, & Lynch, 2007), also translated into cognitive dysregulation and behavioral dysregulation (e.g., NSSI, suicide attempts). For individuals with BPD, DBT has been found efficacious in reducing hospitalizations as well as suicidal and self-harm behaviors (Koons et al., 2006; Linehan, Heard, & Armstrong, 1993; McMain et al., 2009; Turner, 2000) and in improving indicators of ER, such as depression, hopelessness, anxiety, and anger (Koons et al., 2006), impulsivity (Verheul et al., 2003), and direct indices of emotion dysregulation (Neacsiu, Rizvi, & Linehan, 2008). DBT has also been adapted to other populations and found effective with depression (Lynch, Cheavens, et al., 2007), eating disorders (Safer, Telch, & Chen, 2009), trichotillomania (Keuthen et al., 2010), substance abuse (Dimeff, Rizvi, Brown, & Linehan, 2000; Linehan et al., 1999; van den Bosch, Verheul, Schippers, & Van den Brink, 2002), ADHD (Fleming, McMahon, Moran, Peterson, & Dreessen, 2014; Hirvikoski et al., 2011), incarcerated adults (Shelton, Sampl, Kesten, Zhang, & Trestman, 2009), and stalking offenders (Rosenfeld et al., 2007). Neacsiu and Linehan have proposed a model that highlights the potential for DBT to treat emotion dysregulation trans-diagnostically (Neacsiu et al., 2015).

The vast majority of psychological disorders reference some disturbance in emotional processes (Kring & Sloan, 2009). For mood disorders, *major depressive disorder* and *bipolar disorder* have been conceptualized as disorders of ER, the former being characterized by failure to upregulate positive emotion and the latter by failure to downregulate positive emotion. Level of depression is positively correlated to increased sadness, guilt, shame, and irritability, whereas level of mania is positively correlated to elevated pride and euphoria (Kring & Bachorowski, 1999). Depression symptoms have also been found to have a strong association with maladaptive ER strategies such as rumination, avoidance, problem solving, and suppression (Aldao, Nolen-Hoeksema, & Schweizer, 2010).

Difficulties regulating emotions are also increasingly recognized in the theoretical understanding and treatment development research for *eating disorders* (Brockmeyer et al., 2014). When problems stem from food restriction, eating can function as an ER strategy in response to stress (Koole, 2009).

The emotions that are difficult to regulate in *anxiety disorders* are fear and anxiety (Kring & Werner, 2004). Failures to effectively regulate emotion have been identified in *generalized anxiety disorder* (Mennin, Heimberg, Turk, & Fresco, 2005) (e.g., heightened emotional intensity, rigid use of ER strategies), *posttraumatic stress disorder* (Litz, 1992; Litz, Orsillo, Kaloupek, & Weathers, 2000), *obsessive compulsive disorder* (e.g., overestimation of threat, intolerance of uncertainty, dysfunctional appraisal and control of thoughts, difficulty coping with anxiety as well as with other intense emotions; McKay et al., 2004), *social phobia* (Goldin, Manber, Hakimi, Canli, & Gross, 2009), and *specific phobia* (Carlsson et al., 2004; Hermann et al., 2009).

Evidence also exists that emphasizes the role of ER in *substance use disorders* (Kober, 2015). Disorders characterized by impulsivity such as *trichotillomania, pathological gambling* can also be linked to difficulties in ER as impulsive action often has the function to avoid an undesirable emotion through a change in mood (Shusterman, Feld, Baer, & Keuthen, 2009; Williams, Grisham, Erskine, & Cassedy, 2012). Evidence has also accumulated to view emotion dysregulation playing an important role in body dysmorphic disorder, where the problematic emotions are fear and disgust. Difficulties in regulating emotions may also underlie problems that don't match a specific diagnosis but can be quite impairing such as problems with anger, aggression (Cohn, Jakupcak, Seibert, Heidebrandt, & Zeichnerm, 2010), marital difficulties (Bloch & Levernson, 2014), complicated grief (Ogrodniczuk, Piper, & Joyce, 2005), and difficulties in care giving (Coon, Thompson, Steffen, Sorocco, & Gallagher-Thompson, 2003).

Given the success of DBT in decreasing emotion dysregulation and the research highlighting emotion dysregulation as trans-diagnostic mechanism of disorder Neacsiu and Linehan proposed DBT as a trans-diagnostic treatment for emotion dysregulation (Neacsiu, Eberle, & Linehan, 2014). In other words, given DBT's success in decreasing emotion dysregulation in BPD, one of the most challenging clinical groups, there is reason to hypothesize that DBT would be successful in decreasing emotion dysregulation in other clinical groups as well. Indeed a one time intervention teaching three DBT ER skills to young drinkers was efficacious in improving indices of ER, depression, and anxiety (Whiteside, 2009). A 4-month DBT skills training targeting ER across mood and anxiety disorders was efficacious in improving skills use, emotion dysregulation, anxiety, depression, and general distress compared to a supportive therapy group; most gains occurred in the first 2 months of therapy (Neacsiu, Eberle, Kramer, Weismann, & Linehan, 2014). A 6-week intervention investigated the specificity of the ER skills in improving indices of emotion dysregulation. Compared to the interpersonal effectiveness (IE) skills module and to an activity group teaching the ER skills was superior on laboratory measures of ER (Bedics, Dixon-Gordon, & Fruzzetti, 2012). These results suggest high potential for DBT skills interventions to impact ER and other general distress.

DBT AS A MODULAR TREATMENT

Modularity is a strategy used across different domains (in computer science, architecture, etc.) for solving complex problems. Modularity can be used in divide-and-conquer design approaches when a complex problem is broken down in smaller subproblems to be solved more or less in isolation and the results to be then incorporated into the full solution for the original problem. The modules can communicate with one another; but clear logical boundaries need to be defined to separate each module in terms of its goals, techniques, and how to communicate with other modules if difficulties are encountered. A psychological treatment can use modularity as an approach to treat clients with particularly challenging clinical presentations if clinical subproblems can be defined and each can be addressed relatively separately from the rest (although exchange of information between modules may be encouraged). When modularity can involve potentially opposing goals for resolving distinct subproblems, clear guidance needs to be provided for how to reach a synthesis and common ground.

DBT is conceptually modular at multiple levels. First, as illustrated in Fig. 18.1, it clearly articulates the functions of treatment, namely to (1) enhance individual's capability by increasing skillful behavior, (2) improve and maintain client's motivation to change and engagement, (3) ensure generalization of change occurring through treatment,

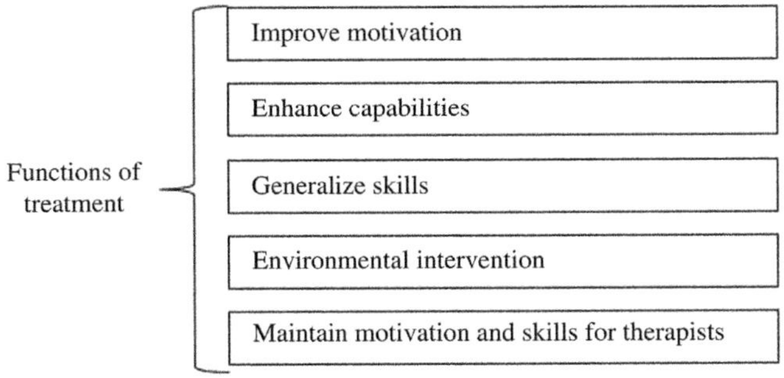

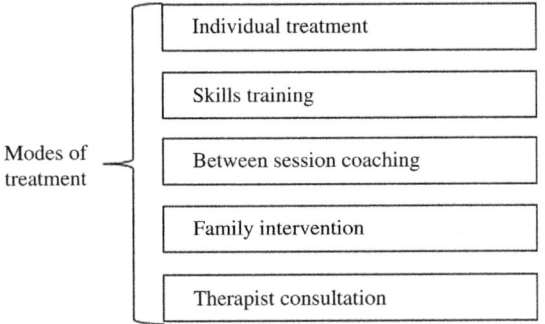

FIGURE 18.1 Modularity of DBT Treatment Functions.

FIGURE 18.2 Modularity of DBT Treatment Modes.

(4) enhance motivation of therapists for treatment delivery, and (5) assist the individual in adjusting his or her environment to supports therapy targets and progress.

Second, DBT delivers treatment using different treatment modes (individual therapy, group skills training, out-of-session coaching, and therapist team consultation). Each of these therapy modes has different treatment goals and employs different techniques (see Fig. 18.2). There is also clarity in how the different modes of treatment communicate and collaborate. Modularity is also present in the structure of the skills training itself, where each session follows a similar structure (mindfulness practice, homework review, teaching of new skill and in session practice, homework assignment). Skilled phone coaching can also follow a predetermined structure of assessing risk and emotion dysregulation and practicing in the moment regulation, assessing situation and willingness to use skills, helping client pick and commit to use appropriate skills, reassessing level of risk, and saying goodbye.

Third, related to the main dialectic in DBT, strategies are grouped into acceptance strategies, change strategies, and dialectical strategies.

Considering how strategies are implemented, they are also grouped into core strategies (problem solving and validation), communication strategies (irreverent and reciprocal styles), and environmental management strategies (consultation to the client that teaches clients to manage their own environments and environmental intervention when the therapist intervenes on behalf of the client). The core strategies problem solving and validation are further deconstructed into smaller parts. Problem solving incorporates five sets of basic behavioral procedures, including (1) behavioral assessment, (2) contingency management, (3) skills training, (4) exposure-based procedures, and (5) cognitive modification. Validation can also be delivered at six different levels, each providing a stronger sense of validation that the previous step (see Fig. 18.3).

Fourth, the structure of a skills training session is also modular, and skills trainers go through a succession of different session sections. DBT skills training sessions start with a brief welcome and conversation while participants join the group, then a brief mindfulness practice followed by feedback on the experience, then homework review and

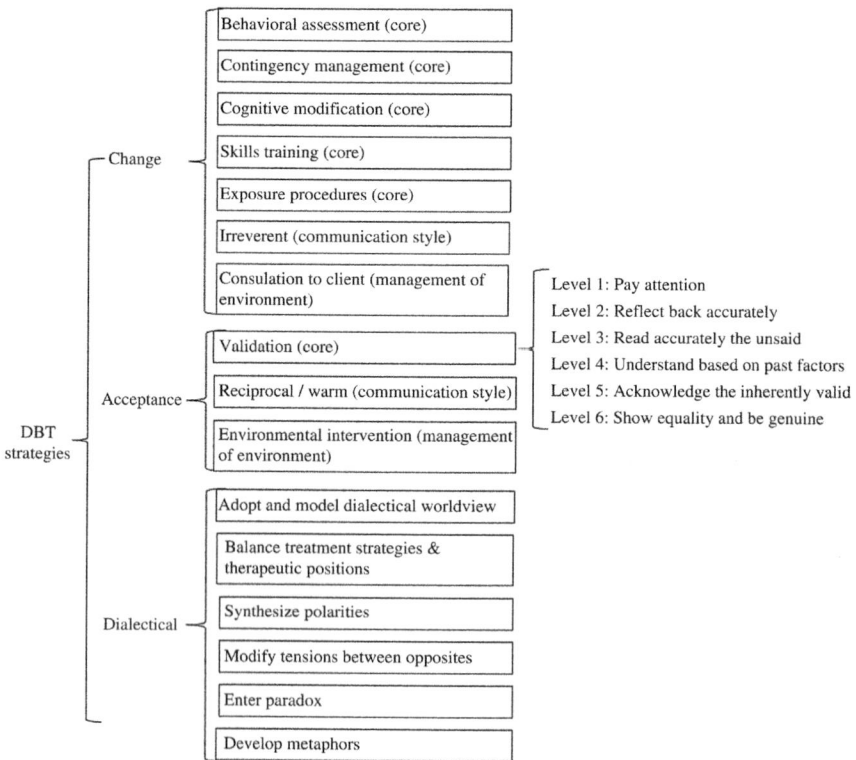

FIGURE 18.3 Modularity of DBT Treatment Strategies.

troubleshooting if homework was not completed, then usually a brief break, followed by teaching of new skills and in session practice, then new homework assignment for the following week and closing with an activity like sharing an observation statement or similar (see Fig. 18.4). The content of the skills training is modular in that skills are organized into different modules (mindfulness, emotion dysregulation, IE, and distress tolerance). Each module is subdivided into sections; for example, the ER module has the following sections: Understanding and Naming Emotions, Changing Emotions, Reducing Vulnerability to Emotions, and Managing Really Difficult Emotions. Each section, in turn, is comprised of a set of individual skills; for example, the Changing Emotions section includes the skills Check the Facts, Opposite Action, and Problem Solving (see Fig. 18.5). Even at the level of an individual skill, complexity is broken down into smaller components that can more easily be taught and practiced. For example, the Problem-Solving skill is broken down into multiple parts of identifying the problem, checking the facts that the problem identified truly is the one causing distress, brainstorming lots of solutions, comparing solutions in terms of their pros and cons, picking a solution to try, putting it into practice, and evaluating whether it effectively solved the problem and if not determining another solution to try (see Fig. 18.5).

Fifth, as mentioned before, DBT was designed to target individuals with complex, multidiagnostic clinical presentations. It was not feasible

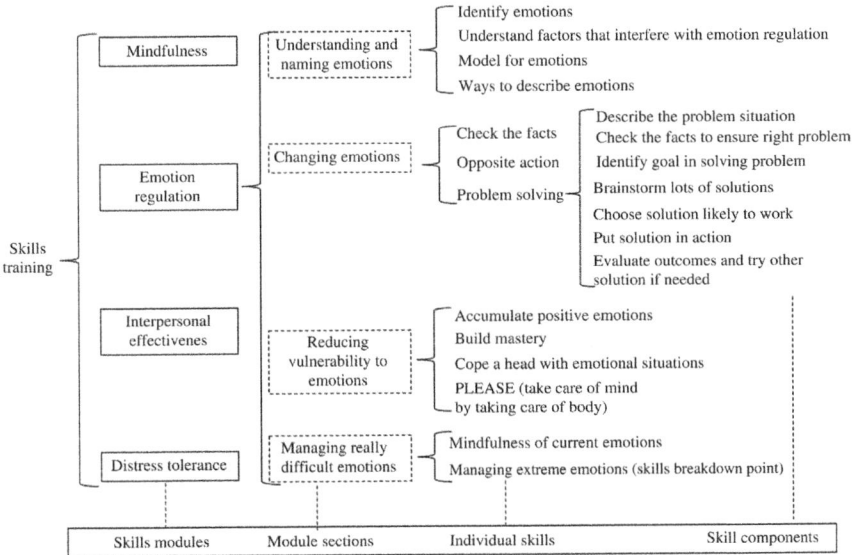

FIGURE 18.4   Modularity of DBT Skills Training.

FIGURE 18.5   DBT Skills Training Session Structure.

and desirable for DBT to develop treatment approaches for the multi-tude of clinical problems that high risk clients presented with. DBT developed to provide what was missing in other treatments to effica-ciously address high risk complex clinical presentations. As such, DBT provides the framework to incorporate other evidence-based treatments (EBTs) to treat particular self-contained clinical problems, such as anxi-ety disorders. Protocols have been developed to safely transition ancil-lary treatments in and out of DBT. One example is the incorporation of prolonged exposure treatment for BPD and individuals at high risk for suicide (Bohus et al., 2013; Harned & Linehan, 2008; Harned, Korslund, Foa, & Linehan, 2012). The transition protocol specifies when it is safe for individuals meeting diagnostic criteria for PTSD to start prolonged exposure, how to reevaluate safety for the duration of treatment, and when to potentially interrupt the exposure treatment in order to strengthen coping skills.

DBT AND THE ALGORITHMIC CHARACTERISTIC OF BEHAVIORAL ASSESSMENT TASKS

Accurate and valid behavioral assessment is a core component of DBT. Treatment interventions are likely to be ineffective if the problem to be solved has not been correctly identified. Over time, DBT has developed behavioral assessment techniques that logically follow a particular structure and workflow that can be represented by an algorithm. At a high level, an algorithm can be defined as a process or sequence of steps to be followed in problem-solving operations. Algorithms are often used in computer science and math, but the term is meaningful in any domain that incorporates problem solving in some manner. In the realm of DBT and behavioral treatments in general, an algorithm can be used to ensure that assessment is uncovering all pieces of information needed to define the problem to be solved. Skilled therapists follow their own unwritten algorithms to conduct comprehensive assessments. High quality assessment is fundamental to DBT given its tendency to not assume an understanding of the problem before exploring the facts. DBT uses behavioral assessments in many forms. Chain analyses and missing links analyses are representative examples that can be transformed in an algorithmic format. Chain analyses represent assessments of the sequence of steps that resulted in a person engaging in a particular behavior that represents a target to be decreased or increased in treatment. For example, a therapist or a client might conduct a chain analyses to understand the steps leading to self-harm behavior or to a particularly effective behavior that represents a change. Once all the links in the chain are revealed for an ineffective behavior, the therapist and client can work together to figure out how to best change a link so that a similar sequence of initial events results in a different outcome. Similarly, for effective behaviors that are uncommon and are targeted to be increased, important links are identified to find ways to solidify/reinforce them. Missing links analysis is conducted to identify the missing behavior that resulted in an expected behavior not taking place. For example, the missing links analysis can be used to identify what led to the client not doing the homework as agreed upon. Fig. 18.6 describes such a missing links analysis for identifying why homework did not happen and the problem-solving steps needed to address the barrier.

Fig. 18.6 illustrates the different points where homework practice can be compromised and how to match a solution to the specific problem. The algorithm goes through assessing if the client knew they had an assignment, if they were willing to do it when they heard it, if they thought about it in between sessions, as well as if they started to do it. There may be no point in working on a client's willingness to do the homework if the primary problem was that they were not aware they had an assignment in the first place.

DBT skills training is structured such that skills practice homework is assigned at the end of each session. As shown in Fig. 18.5 for the Problem-Solving skill in the ER module, some of the DBT skills comprise several steps. The progression through these steps can be described in an

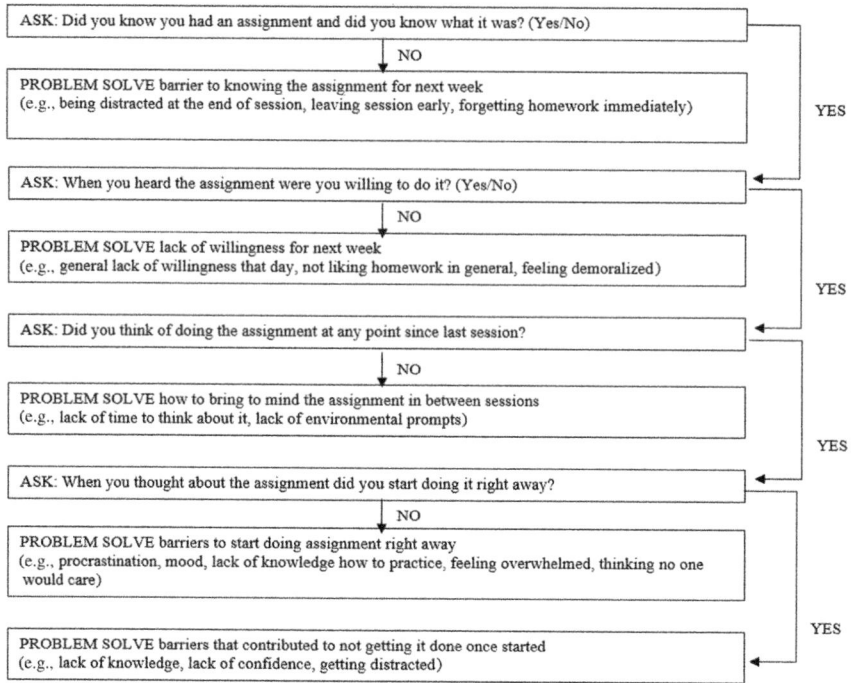

FIGURE 18.6   Missing Links Analysis Homework Review.

algorithmic way. Fig. 18.7 describes such an algorithmic version of the Check the Facts skill in the ER module. The first step of checking the facts is to ask if one wants to change a particular emotion, if not the algorithm stops. If there is a desire to regulate/change emotion, one starts by identifying what emotion one wants to change and the prompting event. Then one identifies interpretations, thoughts, and assumptions made about the facts/prompting event. Checking the facts means looking at the interpretations/thoughts and assumptions and challenging them in light of the facts. One should then think of other interpretations that might also fit the facts and to change interpretations so that they are in line with the facts. After doing this step one checks if the initial emotion has gone down sufficiently or in other words if it was regulated successfully. If not, one asks if there is an assumption of a threat and of a catastrophe and suggestions are made for how to challenge the likelihood of the threat and how to imagine coping well with the catastrophe.

Our point in presenting the algorithmic representation of skills, such as Checking the Facts, was not to suggest that therapists should necessarily follow such a representation when teaching their clients. Our goal was solely to point out that such a logical flow is present in the

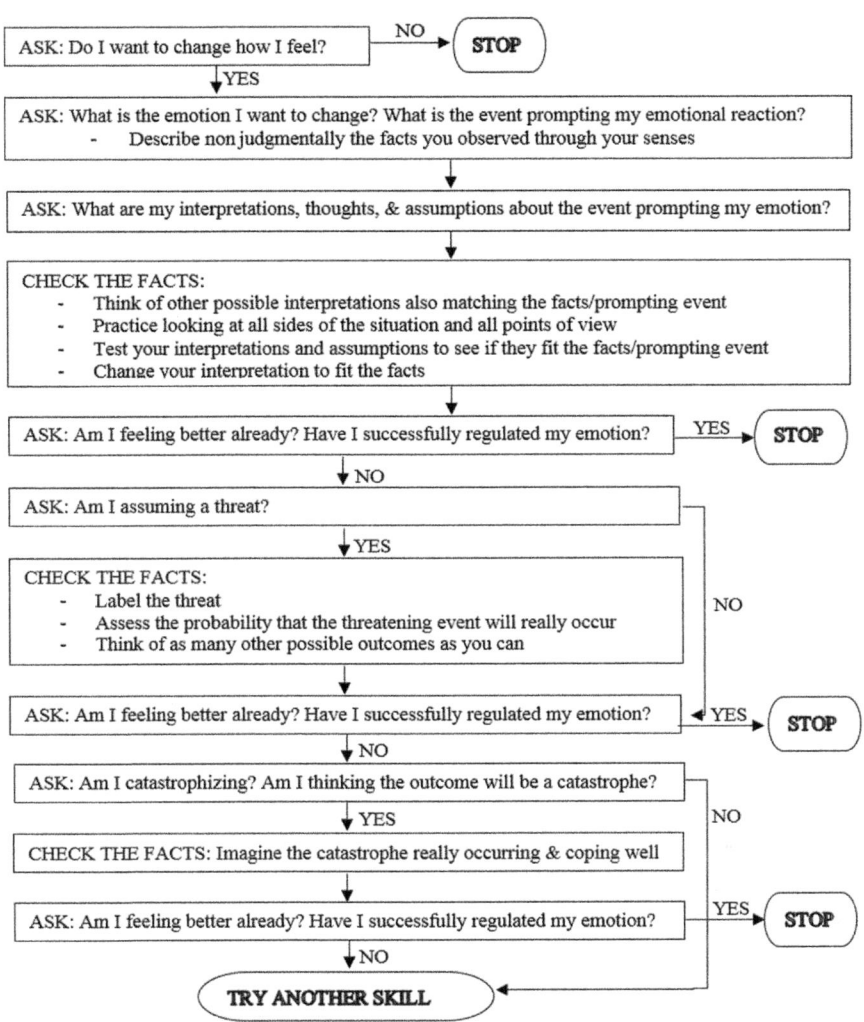

FIGURE 18.7   Checking the Facts DBT Skill in Algorithmic Form.

structure of the skills. Although therapists need not follow the algorithmic representation of the skill, such a representation clarifies how the steps succeed one another and when the skill stops. Reviewing accurate use of that skill in a homework practice needs to ensure that most if not all those steps were correctly applied to a specific situation. Fig. 18.8 shows the homework review for the Check the Facts skill also in an algorithmic form. The flow checks completion of the separate steps of the skill and also helps the client practice the skill on the spot if a particular step was missed during a particular practice.

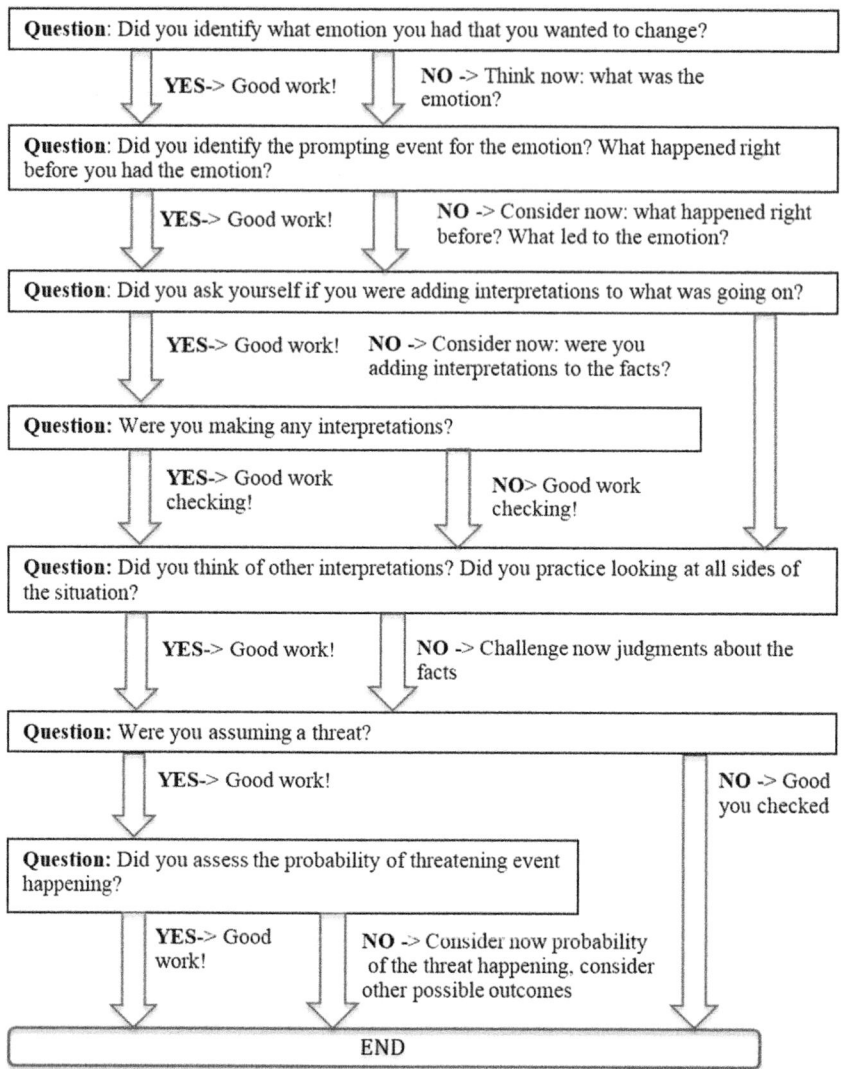

FIGURE 18.8   Check the Facts Homework Review in Algorithmic Form.

BRIEF OVERVIEW OF RESEARCH ON DBT RCTs

Many RCTs of DBT have targeted individuals meeting criteria for BPD and who were at high risk for suicide (Linehan et al., 2006, 2015; Linehan, Armstrong, Suarez, Allmon, & Heard, 1991; McMain et al., 2009; Pistorello, Fruzzetti, MacLane, Gallop, & Iverson, 2012). Compared to treatment as usual (TAU), DBT was superior in decreasing suicide attempts (Linehan et al., 1991). Similar results on the advantage of DBT in impacting suicide attempts were identified for comparison with community treatment by nonbehavioral experts (Linehan et al., 2006) and with psychodynamic treatment conducted by trainees supervised by experts (Pistorello et al., 2012). Specifically, compared to experts in the community DBT decreased suicide attempts by 50% and hospitalizations due to suicidality by 73%. DBT held no advantage when it was compared to psychiatric management plus emotion-focused psychotherapy and suicide management expertise (McMain et al., 2009). These results build strong evidence for DBT as an efficacious treatment for individuals at high risk for suicide.

NSSI is another important behavioral target in DBT. Evidence has emerged linking NSSI as a risk factor for later suicide attempts or suicide (Whitlock et al., 2013). The majority of RCTs found and advantage for DBT in decreasing NSSI compared to control conditions (Bohus et al., 2004; Koons et al., 2001; Linehan et al., 1991) (Pistorello et al., 2012; Turner, 2000; van den Bosch et al., 2002). A minority of studies found DBT to be efficacious in decreasing NSSI but not significantly more so than the control condition (Carter, Willcox, Lewin, Conrad, & Bendit, 2010; Feigenbaum et al., 2012; Linehan et al., 2006).

Suicide ideation is a construct linked to later suicide attempts and suicides (Brent et al., 1993; Gili-Planas, Roca-Bennasar, Ferrer-Perez, & Bernardo-Arroyo, 2001). All RCTs to date have shown DBT to significantly decrease suicide ideation. Some RCTs show an advantage of DBT compared to TAU (Koons et al., 2001)—the control condition was TAU, whereas other have found no significant advantage (Linehan et al., 1991, 2006)—the control conditions were TAU and community treatment by experts (CTBE), respectively.

Another important consideration is the impact of DBT on treatment cost. The majority of studies have found DBT to significantly reduce, compared to the control treatment, visits to the emergency department and number of inpatient hospitalizations for suicidality as well as number of days spent in the hospital once admitted (Koons et al., 2001; Linehan et al., 1991, 2006)—the control conditions were TAU, and CTBE. Some studies though found no advantage to the control condition (Carter et al., 2010; Feigenbaum et al., 2012; Mcmain et al., 2009).

One study also evaluated the impact of DBT on constructs thought to be changed only by insight oriented psychotherapies. DBT had an advantage over the control condition on individuals' development of a positive introject (comprising self-affirmation and self-love).

As mentioned, DBT initially targeted individuals at high risk for suicide but then expanded to BPD. Evidence has accumulated supporting the efficacy of DBT for individuals meeting criteria for BPD and substance dependence (Linehan et al., 1999; 2002). DBT has also been found efficacious in positively impacting disorders commonly cooccurring with BPD, such as depression and anxiety. Some studies have found DBT to have an advantage over control condition in decreasing depression and anxiety in individuals with BPD (Bohus et al., 2004; Koons et al., 2001; Koons, Betts, Chapman, O'Rourke, & Robins, 2004; Pistorello et al., 2012; Soler et al., 2005), whereas other studies found no advantage for either treatment (Linehan et al., 1991; 2006; McMain et al., 2009). Similar remission from depression and anxiety were found at the end of treatment for both DBT and the control condition (CTBE), with higher remission from substance dependence in DBT (Harned et al., 2008). In several studies, no differences were found between DBT and the control condition in decreasing anger, impulsivity, and irritability though both treatments were efficacious (Bohus et al., 2004; Clarkin, Levy, Lenzenweger, & Kernberg, 2007; Feigenbaum et al., 2012; Linehan et al., 1999).

Evidence has emerged to support the fundamental contribution of the skills training component of DBT to its efficacy. DBT has been found at an advantage in increasing skillful behavior compared to the control conditions of standard group therapy (Soler et al., 2009), TAU or waitlist (Evershed et al., 2003; Harley, Sprich, Safren, Jacobo, & Fava, 2008). Furthermore, increase in reported use of skillful behavior has been found to fully mediate the impact of the treatment on suicide attempts, anger control, and depression. DBT skills training appears to be a mechanism of change for DBT treatment. A recent component analysis of DBT that compared comprehensive DBT (S-DBT) with DBT skills training plus case management (DBT-S) and with DBT individual therapy plus activities group (DBT-I) found that the treatments that included DBT skills resulted in greater improvements in the frequency of NSSI acts (Linehan et al., 2015). All three treatment options had similar impact on frequency and severity of suicide attempts, suicide ideation, use of crises serviced due to suicidality, and reasons for living.

Considering the high efficacy of skills training and the appeal in terms of decreased treatment cost, research has significantly increased over the last years evaluating DBT skills-only treatment. DBT skills-only treatment has been found to be efficacious for BPD (Soler et al., 2009), treatment resistant depression (Harley et al., 2008), binge eating disorder (Hill, Craighead, & Safer, 2011; Safer, Robinson, & Jo, 2010; Safer, Telch, & Agras, 2001), incarcerated women with childhood abuse (Bradley & Follingstad, 2003), attention deficit hyperactivity disorder (Fleming et al., 2014; Hirvikoski et al., 2011), bipolar disorder (Van Dijk, Jeffrey, & Katz, 2013), and trans-diagnostically across mood and anxiety disorders (Lungu, Wilks, Zieve, & Linehan, 2015; Neacsiu et al., 2014).

THE TREATMENT DISSEMINATION CHALLENGE

Once research emerged to support DBT as an efficacious treatment for suicidality and BPD, efforts were directed toward the dissemination of the treatment in the community. A training institute was created to lead this mission and standardize training in DBT for clinicians. Despite the increasing number of DBT teams and clinicians across the United States and worldwide, the reality of the field remains that many individuals in need of DBT treatment still do not have access to it. Individuals with acute need for immediate treatment can be placed on waitlists for several months even in DBT's birthplace, Seattle, WA, where many clinicians have been trained in the treatment over the years as part of training events or research studies.

DBT faces a similar challenge to other EBTs of disseminating treatments efficacious in research to the vast number of individuals in need. Over the last several decades research has generated efficacious psychological treatments for a wide range of mental disorders. A review of meta-analyses for cognitive behavioral therapy (CBT) found large effect sizes for unipolar depression, generalized anxiety disorder, panic disorder with or without agoraphobia, social phobia, posttraumatic stress disorder, and childhood depressive and anxiety disorders (Butler, Chapman, Forman, & Beck, 2006). CBT effect sizes for bulimia nervosa and schizophrenia were in the large range. Moderate effect sizes were found for marital distress, anger, childhood somatic disorder, and chronic pain. CBT was even found effective, with small-to-medium effect sizes for reducing psychotic symptoms and distress (Wykes, Steel, Everitt, & Tarrier, 2008).

Barriers to wide-scale dissemination of treatment include: (1) low availability due to dearth of practitioners trained in EBTs; (2) the resource intensive process of performing effectiveness studies when transitioning an EBT from the research lab to clinical practice; (3) the high cost of face-to-face therapy; (4) the logistics involved in getting people in regular face-to-face appointments with professionals; and (5) mental health stigma that keeps people away from professional help (Lyons, Hopley, & Horrocks, 2009; Turner, Beidel, Spaulding, & Brown, 1995; Wright et al., 2009).

The Potential for Computerized Psychotherapy as an Avenue for DBT Treatment Dissemination

In response to these difficulties to disseminate EBTs on a large scale, computerized psychotherapy (CP) has emerged and gained momentum over the last few decades. CP holds great promise to address at least some of the barriers to disseminating efficacious EBTs on a large scale. Treatment delivered entirely through software does not require training, does not tire, remains at fidelity, can be easily replicated, and can be easily updated. Computerized treatments can also be made available to individuals in need, regardless of geographic location, provided computers and potentially an internet connection are available. Cost savings compared to face-to-face psychotherapy can be significant (National Institute for Health & Care Excellence, 2002; Stuhlmiller & Tolchard, 2009). Performing an activity on a computer compared to receiving therapy in a practitioner's office is also more private. People also found it easier to tell computers sensitive information, such as suicide risk or a past criminal record, than telling to a human (Classen & Larkin, 2005; Greist et al., 1973).

Research has found strong evidence to support the efficacy of CPs across a wide variety of problems. Multiple meta-analyses (Andersson & Cuijpers, 2009; Andrews, Cuijpers, Craske, McEvoy, & Titov, 2010; Barak, Hen, & Boniel-Nissim, 2008; Reger & Gahm, 2009; Richards & Richardson, 2012; Spek et al., 2007) have found large-to-medium effect sizes for CPs, primarily for mood and anxiety disorders, but also for other problems targeted by psychotherapy (e.g., body image problems, insomnia). Considering that the demand for DBT treatment far exceeds the available resources to deliver the treatment in a face-to-face modality, developing a CP version of DBT could significantly improve its dissemination.

DBT's High Potential for Computerization and Initial Results

DBT, particularly the DBT skills training component, has several characteristics that make it a good candidate for computerization. The modularity and algorithmic features of the treatment fall into this category. From a technology perspective, the modularity of the treatment implies that different components/modules can be implemented via different technologies. These characteristics are also advantageous for a model of care that complements face-to-face psychotherapy with CP components. All treatment components or techniques that can be described or adapted in an algorithmic form can, with relative ease, be implemented in a computerized workflow.

Prior research has focused only on the generalization of DBT skills through a computerized skills coach (Rizvi, Dimeff, Skutch, Carroll, & Linehan, 2011). More recently, research has created a computerized version of a subset of DBT skills from the ER, Mindfulness, and Distress Tolerance modules called iDBT-ER to highlight the self learning of the DBT skills and the primary focus on ER (Lungu et al., 2015). The iDBT study had two phases. In Phase 1 ($N = 7$), we developed and tested feasibility for the 8-week computerized DBT skills training for high emotion dysregulation and mood and/or anxiety disorders. Participants did the computerized intervention in a research laboratory and provided qualitative and quantitative feedback. Phase 1 qualitative feedback was incorporated to improve the intervention for Phase 2 ($N = 34$), which consisted of an open trial evaluation. Participants went through the intervention online in their own environment. Phase 1 participants found the intervention acceptable and reported reductions in emotion dysregulation, anxiety, and depression and increases in mindfulness and use of skills. Compared to pretreatment, at the end of treatment and at 2-month follow-up, Phase 2 participants reported reductions in emotion dysregulation, depression, and general distress, and increases in mindfulness and use of skillful behavior. Drop-out (defined as not accessing the intervention for 3 weeks or more) rates were 28% for Phase 1 and 17.6% for Phase 2. Large effect sizes were found for all outcomes except for anxiety, where a medium size effect was found. Results were compared to findings from a historical control study that recruited a similar clinical population and taught DBT skills in a face-to-face format. Our findings suggest that DBT skills training can be feasible and efficacious when delivered in a computerized modality, with high engagement and low-drop-out rates.

FUTURE DIRECTIONS FOR RESEARCH

Although the conceptual and theoretical tenets that were fundamental in the initial creation of DBT remain unchanged, the precise form of the treatment and its mode of delivery and dissemination are changing and will continue to change. At its core, DBT is treatment anchored in behavioral science, meaning that the treatment uses its flexibility to adapt to and incorporate new scientific findings. At the same time, change needs to be vetted by science before it can be incorporated into the treatment. DBT is also sensitive to remaining unresolved big challenges to the field that get in the way to delivering efficacious treatment to all individuals in need. As such, developing and trying new avenues for large scale dissemination of DBT emerges as a crucial research target. We briefly explored promising initial results supporting high potential for computerization of DBT as such an avenue for dissemination. Research in progress builds on this initial work and proposes to adapt and evaluate another computerized DBT skills training intervention for individuals at risk for suicide and who use binge drinking as a mechanism to regulate emotion (Wilks, Lungu, Mizimori, Mann, & Linehan, 2016). In current adaptations of DBT skills to a computerized format an array of treatment components (such as the missing links analysis described above) were described in an algorithmic format that was amenable to be computerized. It is likely that such algorithms can be developed for many treatment components, facilitating adaptation of DBT as a CP and increasing fidelity to DBT for such interventions. Adapting DBT to a computerized, online environment also highlights the importance of understanding mechanisms of change in treatment as well as the need for a better understanding of the treatment components that most contribute to change. Once such treatment mechanisms and components are better understood, research can develop and evaluate ways in which they can be implemented or substituted in a computerized environment.

As briefly reviewed above, research has increased tremendously in evaluating various formats of DBT skills training interventions for a wide array of clinical groups. Given the cost-effectiveness and efficacy of DBT skills training such efforts are encouraging, also from the perspective of treatment dissemination priorities. At the same time, it is important for the community to increase its rigor in conducting such research, particularly in defining clearly what the treatments comprise in terms of specific skills taught and presence or absence of treatment modes (such as the presence of a DBT consult team or coaching).

A movement toward trans-diagnostic treatments represents one avenue to expand DBT to a wider clinical group (Barlow, Allen, & Choate, 2004; McHugh, Murray, & Barlow, 2009). From early in its development, DBT has emphasized emotion dysregulation as a critical treatment target for individuals with high suicidality and BPD. As reviewed, emotion dysregulation has been recognized as a mechanism of disorder across diagnoses and DBT, through its sound research evidence, is in a good position to target this characteristic in a trans-diagnostic approach.

References

Aitken, R. (1982). *Taking the path of zen.* San Francisco, CA: North Point Press.

Aldao, A., Nolen-Hoeksema, S., & Schweizer, S. (2010). Emotion-regulation strategies across psychopathology: A meta-analytic review. *Clinical Psychology Review, 30*(2), 217–237.

Andersson, G., & Cuijpers, P. (2009). Internet-based and other computerized psychological treatments for adult depression: A meta-analysis. *Cognitive Behavior Therapy, 38*(4), 196–205.

Andrews, G., Cuijpers, P., Craske, M. G., McEvoy, P., & Titov, N. (2010). Computer therapy for the anxiety and depressive disorders is effective, acceptable and practical health care: A meta-analysis. *PLoS ONE, 5*(10): e13196. Available from http://dx.doi.org/10.1371/journal.pone.0013196.

Arkowitz, H. (1989). The role of theory in psychotherapy integration. *Journal of Integrative and Eclectic Psychotherapy, 8*, 8–16.

Arkowitz, H. (1992). Integrative theories of therapy. In D. Freedheim (Ed.), *The history of psychotherapy: A century of change.* Washington D.C: American Psychologic.

Barak, A., Hen, L., & Boniel-Nissim, N. (2008). A comprehensive review and a meta-analysis of the effectiveness of internet-based psychotherapeutic. *Journal of Technology in Human Services, 26*(2−4), 109−160.

Barlow, D. H., Allen, L. B., & Choate, M. L. (2004). Toward a unified treatment for emotional disorders. *Behavior Therapy, 35*(2), 205−230.

Basseches, M. (1984). *Dialectical thinking and adult development.* Norwood, NJ: Ablex Publishing Cor.

Bedics, J.D., Dixon-Gordon, K., & Fruzzetti, A.E. (2012). *An evaluation of the mechanisms of change in dialectical behavior therapy.* Paper presented at the Annual Meeting of the Society for Psychotherapy Research, Virginia Beach, VA.

Bloch, L., & Levernson, R. W. (2014). Emotion regulation predicts marital satisfaction: More than a wives' tale. *Emotion, 14*(1), 130−144.

Bohus, M., Dyer, A. S., Priebe, K., Kruger, A., Kleindienst, N., Schmahl, C., & Steil, R. (2013). Dialectical behaviour therapy for post-traumatic stress disorder after childhood sexual abuse in patients with and without borderline personality disorder: A randomised controlled trial. *Psychotherapy and Psychosomatics, 82*(4), 221−233.

Bohus, M., Haaf, B., Simms, T., Limberger, M. F., Schmahl, C., Unckel, C., & Linehan, M. M. (2004). Effectiveness of inpatient dialectical behavioral therapy for borderline personality disorder: A controlled trial. *Behaviour Research and Therapy, 42*(5), 487−499.

Bradley, R. G., & Follingstad, D. R. (2003). Group therapy for incarcerated women who experienced interpersonal violence: A pilot study. *Journal of Traumatic Stress, 16*(4), 337−340.

Brent, D. A., Johnson, B., Bartle, S., Bridge, J., Rather, C., Matta, J., & Constantine, D. (1993). Personality disorder, tendency to impulsive violence, and suicidal behavior in adolescents. *Journal of the American Academy of Child and Adolescent Psychiatry, 32*(1), 69−75.

Brockmeyer, T., Skunde, M., Bresslein, E., Rudofsky, G., Herzog, W., & Friederich, H. C. (2014). Difficulties in emotion regulation across the spectrum of eating disorders. *Comprehensive Psychiatry, 55*(3), 565−571.

Butler, A. C., Chapman, J. E., Forman, E. M., & Beck, A. T. (2006). The empirical status of cognitive-behavioral therapy: A review of meta-analyses. *Clinical Psychology Review, 26* (1), 17−31.

Carlsson, K., Petersson, K. M., Lundqvist, D., Karlsson, A., Ingvar, M., & Ohman, A. (2004). Fear and the amygdala: Manipulation of awareness generates differential cerebral responses to phobic and fear-relevant (but nonfeared) stimuli. *Emotion, 4*(4), 340−353.

Carter, G. L., Willcox, C. H., Lewin, T. J., Conrad, A. M., & Bendit, N. (2010). Hunter DBT project: Randomized controlled trial of dialectical behaviour therapy in women with borderline personality disorder. *Australian and New Zealand Journal of Psychiatry, 44*(2), 162−173.

Clarkin, J. F., Levy, K. N., Lenzenweger, M. F., & Kernberg, O. F. (2007). Evaluating three treatments for borderline personality disorder: A multiwave study. *American Journal of Psychiatry, 164*(6), 922−928.

Classen, C. A., & Larkin, G. L. (2005). Ocult suicidality in an emergency department population. *British Journal of Psychiatry, 186*, 352−353.

Cohn, A. M., Jakupcak, M., Seibert, L. A., Heidebrandt, T. B., & Zeichnerm, A. (2010). The role of emotion dysregulation in the association between men's restrictive emotionality and use of physical aggression. *Psychology of Men & Masculinity, 11*, 53−64.

Coon, D. W., Thompson, L., Steffen, A., Sorocco, K., & Gallagher-Thompson, D. (2003). Anger and depression management: Psychoeducational skill training interventions for women caregivers of a relative with dementia. *Gerontologist, 43*, 678−689.

Crowell, S. E., Beauchaine, T. P., & Linehan, M. M. (2009). A biosocial developmental model of borderline personality: Elaborating and extending Linehan's theory. *Psychological Bulletin, 135*(3), 495–510.

Dimeff, L., Rizvi, S. L., Brown, M., & Linehan, M. M. (2000). Dialectical behavior therapy for substance abuse: A pilot application to methamphetamine-dependent women with borderline personality disorder. *Cognitive and Behavioral Practice, 7,* 457–468.

Evershed, S., Tennant, A., Boomer, D., Rees, A., Barkham, M., & Watson, A. (2003). Practice-based outcomes of dialectical behaviour therapy (DBT) targeting anger and violence, with male forensic patients: A pragmatic and non-contemporaneous comparison. *Criminal Behaviour and Mental Health, 13*(3), 198–213.

Feigenbaum, J. D., Fonagy, P., Pilling, S., Jones, A., Wildgoose, A., & Bebbington, P. E. (2012). A real-world study of the effectiveness of DBT in the UK National Health Service. *British Journal of Clinical Psychology, 51*(2), 121–141.

Fleming, A. P., McMahon, R. J., Moran, L. R., Peterson, A. P., & Dreessen, A. (2014). Pilot randomized controlled trial of dialectical behavior therapy group skills training for ADHD among college students. *Journal of Attention Disorders, 19*(3), 260–271.

Gili-Planas, M., Roca-Bennasar, M., Ferrer-Perez, V., & Bernardo-Arroyo, M. (2001). Suicidal ideation, psychiatric disorder, and medical illness in a community epidemiological study. *Suicide and Life Threatening Behavior, 31*(2), 207–213.

Goldfried, M. R., & Davison, G. C. (1976). *Clinical behavior therapy.* New York, NY: Holt, Rinehart & Win.

Goldin, P. R., Manber, T., Hakimi, S., Canli, T., & Gross, J. J. (2009). Neural bases of social anxiety disorder: Emotional reactivity and cognitive regulation during social and physical threat. *Archives of General Psychiatry, 66,* 170–180.

Greist, J. H., Gustafson, D. H., Stauss, F. F., Rowse, G. L., Laughren, T. P., & Chiles, J. A. (1973). A computer interview for suicide-risk prediction. *American Journal of Psychiatry, 130*(12), 1327–1332.

Hahn, T. N. (1976). *The miracle of mindfulness: A manual of meditation.* Boston, MA: Beacon Press.

Harley, R., Sprich, S., Safren, S., Jacobo, M., & Fava, M. (2008). Adaptation of dialectical behavior therapy skills training group for treatment-resistant depression. *Journal of Nervous and Mental Disease, 196*(2), 136–143.

Harned, M. S., Chapman, A. L., Dexter-Mazza, E. T., Murray, A., Comtois, K. A., & Linehan, M. M. (2008). Treating co-occurring Axis I disorders in recurrently suicidal women with borderline personality disorder: A 2-year randomized trial of dialectical behavior therapy versus community treatment by experts. *Journal of Consulting and Clinical Psychology, 76*(6), 1068–1075 , PMID: 19045974

Harned, M. S., Korslund, K. E., Foa, E. B., & Linehan, M. M. (2012). Treating PTSD in suicidal and self-injuring women with borderline personality disorder: Development and preliminary evaluation of a Dialectical Behavior Therapy Prolonged Exposure Protocol. *Behaviour Research and Therapy, 50*(6), 381–386.

Harned, M. S., & Linehan, M. M. (2008). Integrating Dialectical Behavior Therapy and Prolonged Exposure to treat co-occurring borderline personality disorder and PTSD: Two case studies. *Cognitive and Behavioral Practice, 15*(3), 263–276. Available from http://dx.doi.org/210.1016/j.cbpra.2007.1008.1006.

Hermann, A., Schafer, A., Walter, B., Stark, B., Vaitl, D., & Schienle, A. (2009). Emotion regulation in spider phobia: Role of the medial prefrontal cortex. *Social Cognitive & Affective Neuroscience, 4*(3), 257–267.

Hill, D. M., Craighead, L. W., & Safer, D. L. (2011). Appetite-focused dialectical behavior therapy for the treatment of binge eating with purging: A preliminary trial. *International Journal of Eating Disorders, 44,* 249–261.

Hirvikoski, T., Waaler, E., Alfredsson, J., Philgren, C., Holmstrom, A., Johnson, A., & Nordstrom, A. (2011). Reduced ADHD symptoms in adults with ADHD after structured skills training group: Results from a randomized controlled trial. *Behavior Research and Therapy, 49*, 175–185.

Kabat-Zinn, J. (1982). An outpatient program in behavioral medicine for chronic pain patients based on the practice of mindfulness meditation: Theoretical considerations and preliminary results. *General Hospital Psychiatry, 4*(1), 33–47.

Kabat-Zinn, J., Lipworth, L., & Burney, R. (1985). The clinical use of mindfulness meditation for the self-regulation of chronic pain. *Journal of Behavioral Medicine, 8*(2), 163–190.

Kaminstein, D. S. (1987). Toward a dialectical metatheory for psychotherapy. *Journal of Contemporary Psychotherapy, 17*(2), 87–101.

Keuthen, N. J., Rothbaum, B. O., Welch, S. S., Taylor, C., Falkenstein, H. M., Heekin, M., & Jenike, M. A. (2010). Pilot trial of dialectical-behavior therapy-enhanced habit reversal for trichotillomania. *Depression and Anxiety, 27*(10), 953–959.

Kober, H. (2015). Emotion regulation in substance use disorders. In J. Gross (Ed.), *Handbook of emotion regulation* (2nd ed., pp. 428–447). New York, NY: Guilford Press.

Koole, S. (2009). The psychology of emotion regulation. An integrative review. *Cognition & Emotion, 23*, 4–41.

Koons, C. R., Betts, B., Chapman, A. L., O'Rourke, B., & Robins, C. J. (2004). Dialectical behavior therapy for vocational rehabilitation. *Journal of Personality Disorders, 18*(73), 79.

Koons, C. R., Chapman, A. L., Betts, B. B., O'Rourke, B., Morse, N., & Robins, C. J. (2006). Dialectical behavior therapy adapted for the vocational rehabilitation of significantly disabled mentally ill adults. *Cognitive and Behavioral Practice, 13*(2), 146–156.

Koons, C. R., Robins, C. J., Tweed, J. L., Lynch, T. R., Gonzalez, A. M., Morse, J. Q., & Bastian, L. A. (2001). Efficacy of dialectical behavior therapy in women veterans with borderline personality disorder. *Behavior Therapy, 32*, 371–390.

Kring, A. M., & Bachorowski, J. A. (1999). Emotions and psychopathology. *Cognition and Emotion, 13*(5), 575–599.

Kring, A. M., & Sloan, D. M. (2009). *Emotion regulation and psychopathology: A transdiagnostic approach to etiology and treatment.* New York, NY: Guilford Press.

Kring, A. M., & Werner, A. H. (2004). Emotion regulation and psychopathology. In P. Philippot, & R. S. Feldman (Eds.), *The regulation of emotion* (pp. 359–385). Mahwah, NJ: Lawrence Erlbaum Associates, Inc.

Langer, E. J. (1989). *Mindfulness.* Cambridge, MA: Merloyd Lawrence Books.

Leichsenring, F., Leibing, E., Kruse, J., New, A. S., & Leweke, F. (2011). Borderline personality disorder. *Lancet, 377*(9759), 74–84.

Linehan, M., Korslund, K., Harned, M., Gallop, R., Lungu, A., Neacsiu, A. D., & Murray-Gregory, A. (2015). Dialectical Behavior Therapy for high suicide risk in borderline personality disorder: A component analysis. *JAMA Psychiatry, 72*(5), 475–482.

Linehan, M. M. (1993a). *Cognitive-behavioral treatment of borderline personality disorder.* New York, NY: Guilford Press.

Linehan, M. M. (1993b). *Skills training manual for treating borderline personality disorder.* New York, NY: Guilford Press.

Linehan, M. M., Armstrong, H. E., Suarez, A., Allmon, D., & Heard, H. L. (1991). Cognitive-behavioral treatment of chronically parasuicidal borderline patients. *Archives of General Psychiatry, 48*, 1060–1064.

Linehan, M. M., Bohus, M., & Lynch, T. (2007). Dialectical behavior therapy for pervasive emotion dysregulation: Theoretical and practical underpinnings. In J. Gross (Ed.), *Handbook of emotion regulation.* New York, NY: Guilford.

Linehan, M. M., Comtois, K. A., Murray, A. M., Brown, M. Z., Gallop, R. J., Heard, H. L., & Lindenboim, N. (2006). Two-year randomized controlled trial and follow-up of dialectical behavior therapy vs therapy by experts for suicidal behaviors and borderline personality disorder. *Archives of General Psychiatry, 63*(7), 757–766.

Linehan, M. M., Heard, H. L., & Armstrong, H. E. (1993). Standard dialectical behavior therapy compared to psychotherapy in the community for chronically parasuicidal borderline patients.

Linehan, M. M., & Schmidt, H., III (1995). The dialectics of effective treatment of borderline personality disorder. In W. O. O'Donohue, & L. Krasner (Eds.), *Theories in behavior therapy: Exploring behavior change* (pp. 553–584). Washington D.C: American Psychological Association.

Linehan, M. M., Schmidt, H., III, Dimeff, L. A., Craft, J. C., Kanter, J., & Comtois, K. A. (1999). Dialectical behavior therapy for patients with borderline personality disorder and drug-dependence. *The American Journal on Addictions, 8*(4), 279–292.

Litz, B. T. (1992). Emotional numbing in combat-related post-traumatic stress disorder: A critical review and reformulation. *Clinical Psychology Review, 12*(4), 417–432.

Litz, B. T., Orsillo, S. M., Kaloupek, D., & Weathers, F. W. (2000). Emotional processing in posttraumatic stress disorder. *Journal of Abnormal Psychology, 109*(1), 26–39.

Lungu, A., Wilks, C.R., Zieve, G., & Linehan, M. (2015). *iDBT: A computerized dialectical behavior therapy skills training for emotion dysregulation.* Paper presented at the Annual Convention of Association for Behavioral and Cognitive Therapy (ABCT), Chicago, IL.

Lynch, T. R., Cheavens, J. S., Cukrowicz, K. C., Thorp, S. R., Bronner, L., & Beyer, J. (2007). Treatment of older adults with co-morbid personality disorder and depression: A dialectical behavior therapy approach. *International Journal of Geriatric Psychiatry, 22*(2), 131–143.

Lynch, T. R., Trost, W. T., Salsman, N., & Linehan, M. M. (2007). Dialectical behavior therapy for borderline personality disorder. *Annual Review of Clinical Psychology, 3*, 181–205.

Lyons, C., Hopley, P., & Horrocks, J. (2009). A decade of stigma and discrimination in mental health: Plus ca change, plus c'est la meme chose (the more things change, the more they stay the same). *Journal of Psychiatric and Mental Health Nursing, 16*, 501–507.

May, G. G. (1987). *Will and spirit: A contemplative psychology.* San Francisco, CA: Harper & Row.

McHugh, K. R., Murray, K., & Barlow, D. H. (2009). Balancing fidelity and adaptation in the dissemination of empirically supported treatments: The promise of transdiagnostic interventions. *Behaviour Research and Therapy, 47*, 946–953.

McKay, D., Abramowitz, J. S., Calamari, J. E., Kyrios, M., Radomsky, A., & Sookman, D. (2004). A critical evaluation of obsessive-compulsive disorder subtypes: Symptoms versus mechanisms. *Clinical Psychology Review, 24*, 283–313.

McMain, S. F., Links, P. S., Gnam, W. H., Guimond, T., Cardish, R. J., Korman, L., & Streiner, D. L. (2009). A randomized trial of dialectical behavior therapy versus general psychiatric management for borderline personality disorder. *American Journal of Psychiatry, 166*(12), 1365–1374.

Mennin, D. S., Heimberg, R. G., Turk, C. L., & Fresco, D. M. (2005). Preliminary evidence for an emotion dysregulation model of generalized anxiety disorder. *Behaviour Research and Therapy, 43*(10), 1281–1310.

Mischel, W. (1973). Toward a cognitive social learning reconceptualization of personality. *Psychological Review, 80*(4), 252–283.

Murphy, T. J., Pagano, R. R., & Marlatt, G. A. (1986). Lifestyle modification with heavy alcohol drinkers: Effects of aerobic exercise and meditation. *Addictive Behaviors, 11*(2), 175–186.

National Institute for Health and Care Excellence, N (2002). *Guidance on the use of computerised cognitive behavioural therapy for anxiety and depression* (Vol. 51). London: NICE.

Neacsiu, A. D., Bohus, M., & Linehan, M. M. (2015). Dialectical behavior therapy: An intervention for emotion dysregulation. In J. J. Gross (Ed.), *Handbook of emotion regulation* (2nd ed.). New York, NY: Guilford Press.

Neacsiu, A. D., Eberle, J. E., Kramer, R., Weismann, T., & Linehan, M. M. (2014). A treatment mechanism for emotion dysregulation across mood and anxiety disorders: A pilot randomized controlled trial. *Behaviour Research and Therapy, 59*, 40−51.

Neacsiu, A.D., Rizvi, S., & Linehan, M.M. (2008). Skills training as mechanism of change in dialectical behavior therapy. *Symposium presented at the 116th annual convention of the Americal Psychological Association.*

Norcross, J. C., & Goldfried, M. R. (2005). *Handbook of psychotherapy integration* (2nd ed.). New York, NY: Oxford.

Ogrodniczuk, J., Piper, W. E., & Joyce, A. S. (2005). The negative effect of alexithymia on the outcome of group therapy for complicated grief: What role might the therapist play? *Comprehensive Psychiatry, 46*, 206−213.

Pistorello, J., Fruzzetti, A. E., MacLane, C., Gallop, R., & Iverson, K. M. (2012). Dialectical behavior therapy (DBT) applied to college students: A randomized clinical trial. *Journal of Consulting and Clinical Psychology, 80*(6), 982−994.

Prochaska, J. O., & Diclemente, C. C. (2005). The transtheoretical approach. In J. C. Norcross, & M. R. Goldfried (Eds.), *Handbook of psychotherapy integration* (pp. 147−171). New York, NY: Oxford.

Reger, M. A., & Gahm, G. A. (2009). A meta-analysis of the effects of internet- and computer-based cognitive-behavioral treatments for anxiety. *Journal of Clinical Psychology, 65*(1), 53−75.

Richards, D., & Richardson, T. (2012). Computer-based psychological treatments for depression: A systematic review and meta-analysis. *Clinical Psychology Review, 32*, 329−342.

Rizvi, S., Dimeff, L., Skutch, J. M., Carroll, D., & Linehan, M. M. (2011). A pilot study of the DBT Coach: An interactive mobile phone application for individuals with borderline personality disorder and substance use disorder. *Behavior Therapy, 42*, 589−600.

Rosenfeld, B., Galietta, M., Ivanoff, A., Garcia-Mansilla, A., Martinez, R., Fava, J., & Green, D. (2007). Dialectical behavior therapy for the treatment of stalking offenders. *The International Journal of Forensic Mental Health, 6*(2), 95−103.

Ryle, A. (2005). Cognitive analytic therapy. In J. C. Norcross, & M. R. Goldfried (Eds.), *Handbook of psychotherapy integration* (pp. 196−217). New York, NY: Oxford.

Safer, D. J., Telch, C. F., & Chen, E. Y. (2009). *Dialectical behavior therapy for binge eating and bulimia* (Vol. 1). New York, NY: Guilford Press.

Safer, D. L., Robinson, A. H., & Jo, B. (2010). Outcome from a randomized controlled trial of group therapy for binge eating disorder: Comparing dialectical behavior therapy adapted for binge eating to an active comparison group therapy. *Behavior Therapy, 41* (1), 106−120.

Safer, D. L., Telch, C. F., & Agras, W. S. (2001). Dialectical behavior therapy for bulimia nervosa. *American Journal of Psychiatry, 158*(4), 632−634.

Shelton, D., Sampl, S., Kesten, K. L., Zhang, W. L., & Trestman, R. L. (2009). Treatment of impulsive aggression in correctional settings. *Behavioral Sciences & the Law, 27*(5), 787−800.

Shusterman, A., Feld, L., Baer, L., & Keuthen, N. J. (2009). Affective regulation in trichotillomania: Evidence from a large-scale internet survey. *Behaviour Research and Therapy, 47*, 637−644.

Skinner, B. F. (1974). *About behaviorism.* Westminster, MD: Alfred Knoft, Inc.

Soler, J., Pascual, J. C., Campins, J., Barrachina, J., Puigdemont, D., Alvarez, E., & Perez, V. (2005). Double-blind, placebo-controlled study of dialectical behavior therapy plus olanzapine for borderline personality disorder. *The American Journal of Psychiatry, 162* (6), 1221−1224.

III. PROBLEM-FOCUSED APPROACHES

Soler, J., Pascual, J. C., Tiana, T., Cebria, A., Barrachina, J., Campins, M. J., & Perez, V. (2009). Dialectical behaviour therapy skills training compared to standard group therapy in borderline personality disorder: A 3-month randomised controlled clinical trial. *Behaviour Research and Therapy*, 47(5), 353–358.

Spek, V., Cuijpers, P., Nyklicek, I., Riper, H., Keyzer, J., & Pop, V. (2007). Internet-based cognitive behaviour therapy for symptoms of depression and anxiety: A meta-analysis. *Psychological Medicine*, 37(3), 319–328.

Staats, A. W. (1975). *Social behaviorism*. Homewood, IL: Dorsey Press.

Staats, A. W., & Staats, C. K. (1963). *Complex human behavior*. New York, NY: Holt, Rinehart & Win.

Stuhlmiller, C., & Tolchard, B. (2009). Computer-assisted CBT for depression & anxiety: Increasing accessibility to evidence-based mental health treatment. *Journal of Psychosocial Nursing and Mental Health Services*, 47, 32–39.

Swann, W. B., Jr., Stein-Seroussi, A., & Giesler, R. B. (1992). Why people self-verify. *Journal of Personality and Social Psychology*, 62(3), 392–401.

Turner, R. M. (2000). Naturalistic evaluation of dialectical behavioral therapy-oriented treatment for borderline personality disorder. *Cognitive and Behavioral Practice*, 7(4), 413–419.

Turner, S. M., Beidel, D., Spaulding, S., & Brown, J. (1995). The practice of behavior therapy: A national survey of cost and methods. *Behavior Therapist*, 18, 1–4.

van den Bosch, L. M. C., Verheul, R., Schippers, G. M., & Van den Brink, W. (2002). Dialectical Behavior Therapy of borderline patients with and without substance use problems. Implementation and long-term effects. *Addictive Behaviors*, 27, 911–923.

Van Dijk, S., Jeffrey, J., & Katz, M. R. (2013). A randomized, controlled, pilot study of dialectical behavior therapy skills in a psychoeducational group for individuals with bipolar disorder. *Journal of Affective Disorders*, 145(3), 386–393.

Verheul, R., van den Bosch, L. M. C., Koeter, M. W. J., de Ridder, M. A. J., Stijnen, T., & van den, B. W. (2003). Dialectical behaviour therapy for women with borderline personality disorder: 12-month, randomised clinical trial in The Netherlands. *British Journal of Psychiatry*, 182, 135–140.

Whiteside, U. (2009). *A brief motivational intervention incorporating DBT skills for depressed and anxious young drinkers. (PhD)*. Seattle, WA: University of Washington.

Whitlock, J., Muehlenkamp, J. J., Eckenrode, J., Purington, A., Baral Abrams, G., Barreira, P., & Kress, V. (2013). Nonsuicidal self-injury as a gateway to suicide in young adults. *Journal of Adolescent Health*, 52(4), 486–492.

Wilks, C., Lungu, A., Mizimori, B., Mann, A., & Linehan, M. (2016). *Dialectical behavior therapy skills training for suicidal and heavy episodic drinkers: Development and evaluation*. Paper presented at the International Society for Research on Internet Interventions (ISRII), Seattle.

Williams, A. D., Grisham, J. R., Erskine, A., & Cassedy, E. (2012). Deficits in emotion regulation associated with pathological gambling. *British Journal of Clinical Psychology*, 51(2), 223–238.

Wilson, G. T., & O'Leary, K. D. (1980). *Principles of behavior therapy*. Englewood Cliffs, NJ: Prentice Hall.

Wright, K. M., Cabrera, O. A., Bliese, P. D., Adler, A. B., Hoge, C. W., & Castro, C. A. (2009). Stigma and barriers to care in soldiers postcombat. *Psychological Services*, 6(108), 116.

Wykes, T., Steel, C., Everitt, B., & Tarrier, N. (2008). Cognitive behaviour therapy for schizophrenia: effect sizes, clinical models, and methodological rigor. *Schizophrenia Bulletin*, 34, 523–537.

Further Reading

Addis, M. E. (2002). Methods for disseminating research products and increasing evidence-based practice: Promises, obstacles and future directions. *Psychology Science and Practice, 9*, 367–378.

Andrews, G., Henderson, S., & Hall, W. (2001). Prevalence, comorbidity, disability and service utilisation. Overview of the Australian National Mental Health Survey. *Journal of Psychiatry, 178*, 145–153.

Barlow, D. H., Levitt, J. T., & Bufka, L. F. (1999). The dissemination of empirically supported treatments: A view of the future. *Behaviour Research and Therapy, 37*(Suppl. 1), S147–S162.

Bedics, J. D., Atkins, D. C., Comtois, K. A., & Linehan, M. M. (2012). Treatment differences in the therapeutic relationship and introject during a 2-year randomized controlled trial of dialectical behavioral therapy versus non-behavioral psychotherapy experts for borderline personality disorder. *Journal of Consulting and Clinical Psychology.*

Lepine, J. P. (2002). The epidemiology of anxiety disorders: Prevalence and societal costs. *Clinical Psychiatry, 63*(Suppl. 14), 4–8.

COMPUTER-ASSISTED APPLICATIONS

Cognitive Bias Modification

Jennie M. Kuckertz and Nader Amir

San Diego State University/University of California San Diego,
San Diego, CA, United States

INTRODUCTION

Over 30 years of research suggests that individuals with anxiety and depressive disorders display information-processing biases in favor of disorder-related stimuli when compared to neutral stimuli (Bar-Haim, Lamy, Pergamin, Bakermans-Kranenburg, & van IJzendoorn, 2007; Kuckertz & Amir, 2014; Mathews & MacLeod, 2005; Mathews, 2012; Van Bockstaele et al., 2014). Most commonly, cognitive biases in emotional disorders are described as involving either attention or interpretation. For example, this body of research suggests that individuals with anxiety tend to selectively attend to threat stimuli and tend to interpret ambiguous stimuli as threatening.

Although cognitive bias research was initially descriptive in nature, MacLeod and colleagues attempted to apply the same techniques used to assess attention bias to the manipulation of attention bias (MacLeod, Rutherford, Campbell, Ebsworthy, & Holker, 2002). Since that time, the number of studies examining cognitive bias modification (CBM) has rapidly increased. Borne out of the anxiety disorder literature, the CBM technique has spread to other forms of emotional and behavioral disorders, including depression (e.g., Blackwell & Holmes, 2010; Williams, Blackwell, Mackenzie, Holmes, & Andrews, 2013), substance use disorders (e.g., Schoenmakers et al., 2010; Wiers et al., 2015), and eating disorders (e.g., Kemps, Tiggemann, & Hollitt, 2014; Yiend, Parnes, Shepherd, Roche, & Cooper, 2014). In the past 2 years alone, there have been at least six meta-analyses on attention and interpretation bias modification (IBM) programs (Cristea, Kok, & Cuijpers, 2015; Cristea, Mogoașe, David, & Cuijpers, 2015;

The Science of Cognitive Behavioral Therapy.
DOI: http://dx.doi.org/10.1016/B978-0-12-803457-6.00019-2

Heeren, Mogoaşe, Philippot, & McNally, 2015; Linetzky, Pergamin-Hight, Pine, & Bar-Haim, 2015; Menne-Lothmann et al., 2014; Mogoaşe, David, & Koster, 2014). Thus, we reflect on the overall findings of these reviews, including inconsistencies in observed effect sizes across meta-analyses, and highlight issues and controversies in the field for future research. For example, several CBM reviews have examined age as predictor of CBM success (Hakamata et al., 2010; Lau & Pile, 2015; Mogoaşe et al., 2014). Here we attempt to summarize the results of such meta-analytic studies and comment on these findings within a developmental framework.

We discuss two major classes of CBM: attention bias modification (ABM) and IBM. Although memory biases have been reviewed in the context of anxiety and depression (Mathews & MacLeod, 2005), evidence for such biases is generally more ambiguous, and thus relatively fewer efforts have been made toward memory bias modification. Working memory and executive function training has also garnered research interest (e.g., Bomyea & Amir, 2011; Wanmaker, Geraerts, & Franken, 2015); however, their place in the context of CBM is less clear, and outside the scope of the current chapter. Finally, we do not review approach avoidance training here, as this is a relatively new field of CBM research and hence merits a different level of review. For these reasons, we focus our discussion on ABM and IBM.

ATTENTION BIAS MODIFICATION

Description

Individuals with anxiety disorders are characterized by an automatic tendency to attend toward threat while ignoring neutral stimuli (for reviews, see Bar-Haim et al., 2007; Cisler & Koster, 2010). Attempts to correct this bias have largely focused on the area of visual attention rather than other sensory modalities (i.e., auditory) and have used three primary paradigms to manipulate visual attention: probe detection task (MacLeod, Mathews, & Tata, 1986), spatial cueing task (Posner, 1980), and visual search task (e.g., Gilboa-Schechtman, Foa, & Amir, 1999; Rinck, Becker, Kellermann, & Roth, 2003). We note that each of these tasks was originally utilized for assessment of attentional bias but have been adapted as training tasks. For explanatory purposes, we present prominent examples of studies that have used each of these tasks and then discuss ABM findings.

Probe Detection Paradigm (Dot Probe)

The probe detection task is by far the most commonly used paradigm in ABM research (Linetzky et al., 2015). Amir, Beard, Taylor, et al., 2009 utilized a probe detection task to manipulate visual attentional bias in individuals with social anxiety disorder. Participants viewed paired pictures of neutral and angry faces presented vertically for 500 ms on a computer screen. The pictures then disappeared, and a letter probe ("E" or "F") appeared in the location of one of the pictures. Participants had to click the left mouse button if the letter was an E, and the right mouse button if the letter was an F. In the control condition, the probe replaced each face type 50% of the time, whereas in the active training condition, the probe replaced the neutral face 100% of the time, thereby training participants to automatically attend toward the neutral/away from the angry face. This task is argued to reflect attentional bias in the context of competition between stimuli (Cisler & Koster, 2010; MacLeod et al., 1986), similar to real-life situations. However, this task is suboptimal for determining mechanisms of threat bias because it fails to differentiate between fast vigilance for threat versus difficulty disengaging attention from threat once attention has been captured (for review of similar arguments, see Kuckertz & Amir, 2014).

Spatial Cueing Task

The spatial cueing task arguably provides more mechanistic specificity regarding whether attention bias is driven by (1) vigilance for threat or (2) difficulty disengaging from threat (Amir, Elias, Klumpp, & Przeworski, 2003; Yiend & Mathews, 2001). Bar-Haim, Morag, and Glickman (2011) used a spatial cueing task to train high-anxious children to disengage attention from threat. In this study, children saw both neutral and angry faces presented individually on either the left or right side of the screen. The faces then disappeared, and a symbol appeared either in the same (valid trial—reflects attentional vigilance for stimuli) or the opposite (invalid trial—reflects disengagement from stimuli) screen location as the previously presented face. Children had to press a button indicating whether the symbol appeared on the left or right screen location. In the control condition, there was no difference in contingency of valid versus invalid trials for angry versus neutral faces. In the active training condition, angry faces were always invalid trials, thus training children to disengage their attention from threat faces. This task appears infrequently as a training measure for attentional bias.

Visual Search Task

The visual search task is arguably the most ecologically valid tool for training attention (Gilboa-Schechtman et al., 1999); yet, like the spatial cueing task, it has been used infrequently as an ABM tool. This task has primarily been used to speed vigilance for attending to positive stimuli (Dandeneau, Baldwin, Baccus, Sakellaropoulo, & Pruessner, 2007; De Voogd, Wiers, Prins, & Salemink, 2014; Waters, Pittaway, Mogg, Bradley,

& Pine, 2013). For example, Waters et al. (2013) presented clinically anxious children with a 3 × 3 matrix of faces and instructed children in the active training group identify a single happy face amongst a matrix of angry faces. The authors instructed children in the control group to identify a picture of a bird amongst a matrix of flower pictures.

Findings

Clinical Efficacy

Initial investigations of the clinical efficacy of ABM focused on anxiety disorders, suggesting clinically significant symptom reduction in both adult (Amir, Beard, Burns, & Bomyea, 2009; Amir, Beard, Taylor, et al., 2009; Schmidt, Richey, Buckner, & Timpano, 2009) and youth (Eldar et al., 2012; Riemann, Kuckertz, Rozenman, Weersing, & Amir, 2013) populations. Such early findings led to great enthusiasm regarding the potential for ABM to be used as a clinical intervention not only for anxiety, but for other emotional and behavioral disorders as well. For example, Boutelle, Kuckertz, Carlson, and Amir (2014) trained obese children to attend to nonfood cues in the presence of food stimuli; Schoenmakers et al. (2010) trained adults diagnosed with alcohol dependence away from alcohol pictures and toward neutral pictures; and McHugh et al. (2010) attempted to train cigarette smokers to attend to nonsmoking cues. In a meta-analysis examining the differential effects of ABM for training away from threat stimuli (e.g., away from angry faces in anxiety) versus away from appetitive stimuli (i.e., away from alcohol-related cues in alcohol dependence), Beard et al. (2012) reported a medium-sized effect of training for threat studies and a nonsignificant effect of training for appetitive studies on posttreatment measures. Summarizing across eight meta-analyses, ABM appears to exert a small-to-medium effect on anxiety symptoms and nonsignificant-to-small effects on depressive symptoms (Beard et al., 2012; Cristea, Kok, et al., 2015; Cristea, Mogoaşe, et al., 2015; Hakamata et al., 2010; Hallion & Ruscio, 2011; Heeren, Mogoaşe, Philippot, & McNally, 2015; Linetzky et al., 2015; Mogoaşe et al., 2014).

Effects on Attentional Bias

Meta-analytic reports on the effects of ABM on attentional bias have varied widely from small (Cristea, Kok, et al., 2015; Cristea, Mogoaşe, et al., 2015; Hallion & Ruscio, 2011; Heeren, Mogoaşe, Philippot, et al., 2015; Mogoaşe et al., 2014), medium (Linetzky et al., 2015), or large (Beard et al., 2012; Hakamata et al., 2010). Collectively, this research suggests that across studies, ABM exerts the hypothesized changes in attentional bias; however, variability in the inclusion/exclusion criteria used between these studies as well as variability in training methods within these reports makes it difficult to draw conclusions from meta-analytic data regarding which types of tasks in which disorders in which age groups under which conditions consistently change bias.

Relationship Between Symptom Reduction and Bias Change

Recent reviews have called for increased attention regarding the theoretical underpinnings of ABM; that is, that symptom change is affected through changes in attentional bias (Clarke, Notebaert, & MacLeod, 2014; Kuckertz & Amir, 2015; MacLeod & Clarke, 2015). Meta-analytic studies are one way of examining this relationship if such relationships are linear. However, if the relationship between bias change and symptom change is categorical in nature (i.e., studies that show change in bias also show change in symptoms and studies that do not show change in bias also do not show change in symptoms), then it is more appropriate to simply count the degrees of agreement or use a chi-square test or Cramér's V (Cramér, 1946). Based on 30 studies included in a recent review of ABM that assessed both change in attentional bias and symptoms (Clarke et al., 2014), we calculated a Cramér's V of .73 ($P<.001$), consistent with the notion that bias change and symptom change are categorically and strongly related. Conducting the more traditional correlational analysis, Hakamata et al. (2010) also showed a strong, marginally significant relationship between change in bias and symptoms, $r = .75$, $P = .052$. In a larger, later meta-analysis, Mogoașe et al. (2014) similarly reported a relationship between changes in bias and symptoms, $r = .42$, $P = .048$.

Theory of Intervention: How May ABM Modify Clinically Relevant Symptoms?

ABM is designed to reduce selective attentional processing of threat and/or increase attentional processing of neutral information (Beard, 2011). Such attentional biases have been thought to occur at an early, automatic level of processing (Bar-Haim, 2010). However, research suggests that ABM may also modify attentional control more generally (Heeren, Mogoașe, McNally, Schmitz A. and Philippot, 2015; Klumpp & Amir, 2010; McNally, Enock, Tsai, & Tousian, 2013). Dual process attentional models conceptualize attention as (1) goal-directed, strategic attention (i.e., top-down) and (2) stimulus-driven attention (i.e., bottom-up) (Corbetta & Shulman, 2002). According to attentional control theory (Eysenck, Derakshan, Santos, & Calvo, 2007), anxiety affects the balance between these attentional systems such that the bottom-up stimuli processing is given priority while weakening the top-down strategic control system. Moreover, increased processing of bottom-up stimuli (particularly when threat relevant) may further contribute to the maintenance of anxiety. This theory further states that anxiety is characterized by difficulty modulating attention in response to task-irrelevant internal or external stimuli.

Indeed, processes such as attentional bias toward threat and attentional control have direct clinical correlates in anxiety. For example, generalized anxiety disorder (GAD) is defined by difficulty controlling worry and difficulty concentrating (American Psychiatric Association, 2013). That is, individuals with GAD may have difficulty shifting their focus of attention from negative content (e.g., worries) to more benign or task-relevant content. It is possible that ABM may exert its effects in GAD by allowing anxious individuals to more easily shift their focus of attention from negative to neutral stimuli, thereby also rendering individuals more control over the content of their worries.

Issues and Controversies

Results of recent meta-analyses demonstrating nonsignificant-to-small effects of ABM have led to growing skepticism regarding the clinical efficacy of ABM (Cristea, Kok, et al., 2015; Cristea, Mogoaşe, et al., 2015). However, overall small clinical effects reported in some reviews may be driven by several factors (often confounded with one another) that merit further discussion.

Mechanisms

ABM is predicated on the notion that individuals with psychopathology possess disorder-relevant attentional biases that are modified through training. In the face of failures to replicate the promising clinical effects of early ABM studies, an increasingly greater emphasis has been placed on this theoretical model (Clarke et al., 2014; Kuckertz & Amir, 2015; MacLeod & Clarke, 2015). As authors of these reviews point out, ABM programs that have failed to produce symptom change have also failed to produce changes in attentional bias.

The discrepancy between the inconsistent ability of ABM to modify attentional bias versus the consistent link between changes in bias with changes in symptoms highlights an important area of future research. This issue has been emphasized by funding agencies, such as the National Institute of Mental Health, who are now asking for two-stage grant mechanism in which investigators must first demonstrate the ability of their intervention to consistently modulate the targeted mechanism (RFA-MH-15-300). Only after demonstration of the link between intervention and mechanism does the grant allow for continued research examining the link between degree of "target engagement" (i.e., manipulation of mechanism) and symptom reduction (http://grants.nih.gov/grants/guide/rfa-files/RFA-MH-15-300.html).

On the surface, change in attentional bias as a mechanism of symptom change is an easily testable theoretical model. Indeed, an overwhelming amount of research demonstrates that various forms of psychopathology are associated with deficits in attentional systems, and that ABM paradigms modify various attentional processes. However, questions regarding the nature of attentional biases left unanswered from the 1990s to 2000s may have hampered progress in the ABM field. For example, questions, such as the time course of attentional bias (Mogg, Bradley, Miles, & Dixon, 2004), facilitated disengagement versus difficulty disengaging (Amir et al., 2003), presence of bias for threat versus lack of neutral or positive bias (e.g., Pishyar, Harris, & Menzies, 2004; Taylor, Bomyea, & Amir, 2011), effects of state versus trait anxiety on bias (Amir et al., 1996; Garner, Mogg, & Bradley, 2006; Mansell, Ehlers, Clark, & Chen, 2002), and emotion-specific selective attentional capture versus general deficits in attentional control (Cisler & Koster, 2010; Heeren, Reese, McNally, & Philippot, 2012; Klumpp & Amir, 2010) are some of the relevant issues that need to be addressed when examining attentional bias. To add yet another layer of complexity, the answers to each of these questions may vary by factors such as disorder or age group (Carmona et al., 2015; Schneier et al., 2016). Given that each ABM study makes different decisions about training protocol based on widely varying assumptions about the nature of attentional bias, it is not surprising that the clinical efficacy of these varied procedures based on different theories is mixed.

Reliability of Assessment and Training Tasks

The paradigm most commonly used in ABM research is the probe detection task (Linetzky et al., 2015). A number of studies reported the efficacy of this task for manipulating both bias and symptoms (first meta-analysis: Hakamata et al., 2010). However, other research examining the reliability of bias assessment in this task showed inconsistencies (Schmukle, 2005; Staugaard, 2009). Despite the growing popularity of the probe detection task as an assessment and training instrument in clinical populations, few studies had systemically examined its reliability in clinical populations. Price et al. (2015) examined the test—retest reliability of the probe detection task across two adult social anxiety disorder samples and a pediatric healthy control sample. Moreover, Price et al. reported the effects on reliability that decisions such as cut off points for defining response latency outliers and other cleaning procedure had on bias measures. Across three studies, definition of outliers based on absolute cutpoints and standard deviation resulted in poor reliability. This was improved but still overall low when a data-driven approach (Winsorizing) was used to define outliers and only dot-bottom trials were used rather than collapsing across trials in which the probe appeared on the top versus bottom of the screen in vertically presented stimuli pairs.

Findings such as these, along with studies reporting poor internal consistency estimates for the probe detection task (Kappenman et al., 2014), have led some to conclude that, "after decades of research we still lack a measure of attentional bias to threat in the dot-probe task that can reliably index individual differences in anxiety" (Kappenman et al., 2014). It is correct that most studies using a priori discretionary cutpoints (to the extent reported in their method sections) have reported validity effects (i.e., correlations between symptoms and bias) using a seemingly unreliable bias calculation method. This raises serious questions regarding whether previously observed probe detection task findings were spurious.

Although an extended discussion of this issue is beyond the scope of this chapter, it is worth noting that reliability and measurement precision are distinct constructs that commonly, but not always, suggest similar conclusions about the quality of a measure (Singer & Willett, 2003). In short, under conditions in which there is little variability in the true change rates within a population, reliability may be poor despite high measurement precision. Much work needs to be done to better understand the psychometric properties of the probe detection task; however, this work may be facilitated by a clearer differentiation between the criteria being used to evaluate this measure (i.e., precision vs reliability) and consideration of the underlying assumptions being made about the construct of interest when discussing issues of reliability and precision.

Recently, Iacoviello et al. (2014) suggested that the traditional method of calculating bias via subtraction of response latency types averaged across a given session may not optimally capture the nature of attentional deficits in anxiety (see also Kuckertz et al., 2014; Zvielli, Bernstein, & Koster, 2015 for similar arguments). Instead, these authors argued that anxiety may be characterized by fluctuations in attentional bias within session, or attention bias variability (ABV), rather than a stable attentional bias trait per se. This concept is akin to attentional control deficits (Eysenck et al., 2007) but places particular emphasis on the role of attentional capture by disorder-relevant stimuli. This measure has demonstrated markedly improved reliability across sessions in comparison with traditional measures of bias in the context of the probe detection task (Price et al., 2015).

Fortunately, hypotheses regarding the methods to improve the psychometric properties of traditional measures of bias, as well as newer methods of measuring bias, can be easily tested with little additional data collection or resources. Indeed, using subject level data so that uniform decisions can be applied for probe detection task analysis should be obligatory in future studies. We suggest that investigators collaborate in reanalyzing previously determined unreliable probe detection datasets to determine whether alternate calculation formulas or outlier handling improve both the reliability and validity of this task.

In the context of seemingly poor reliability of reaction time measures, we (Kuckertz & Amir, 2014) and others have advocated for examining bias via neurobiological/physiological tools [e.g., event-related potentials (ERPs), Kappenman et al., 2014; fMRI, Britton et al., 2013; eyetracking, Price et al., 2015]. However, it is worth noting that these fields share similar issues regarding inconsistent findings and unknown reliability. For example, fMRI has been criticized as an arbitrary and imprecise measure of neurobiological functioning (Hardcastle & Stewart, 2002; Logothetis, 2008), and ERPs similarly frequently lack standardization regarding task parameters used to elicit ERPs, definition of time window, and even measurement (e.g., mean amplitude vs peak amplitude) (Clayson, Baldwin, & Larson, 2013; Luck, 2014). Furthermore under optimal measurement parameters, the test–retest reliability of ABV for characterizing attentional bias far exceeds that of eyetracking measures (Price et al., 2015). Although we strongly urge informed, procedurally sound assessment of bias using (neuro)physiological tools, we suggest that it may be premature to abandon response latency measurement of bias.

Quality of ABM Studies

Several recent meta-analyses have highlighted the role that the quality of individual ABM studies has had on findings (Cristea, Kok, et al., 2015; Cristea, Mogoaşe, et al., 2015; Heeren, Mogoaşe, Philippot, et al., 2015). This represents a critical and underemphasized area in ABM research. The authors of these reviews emphasized that higher quality studies were less likely to find significant results compared to lower quality studies and, somewhat paradoxically, that studies published in higher impact journals tended to produce significant results (Cristea, Kok, et al., 2015; Cristea, Mogoaşe, et al., 2015; Heeren, Mogoaşe, Philippot, et al., 2015). Quality was defined according to six criteria outlined by the Cochrane Collaboration (Higgins & Green, 2011): random sequence generation, allocation concealment, blinding of participants and assessors, blinding of outcome assessment, incomplete outcome data, and selective outcome reporting. As pointed out by Heeren, Mogoaşe, Philippot, and colleagues (2015), many of the studies included in the meta-analysis did not provide adequate information to determine if these quality criteria were met; such studies were coded as not meeting quality criteria based on absence of information. However, it is also important to note that not providing such data are not equivalent to not conducting the procedure. Thus, future meta-analyses should attempt to address this issue directly.

Moreover, to focus exclusively on the Cochrane criteria as an assessment of quality in ABM studies represents a failure to consider factors critical to quality delivery of ABM specifically. To illustrate this point, we consider an example where investigators are interested in treatment outcome differences between supportive psychotherapy and cognitive behavioral therapy (CBT). Suppose the authors met all Cochrane quality criteria. However, in the CBT condition, therapists were simply told to ask participants if their thoughts were realistic each week, and to ask participants how their behavior related to anxiety. The authors did not check to see what exactly happened in therapy sessions, whether exposure exercises occurred, and whether participants actually experienced changes in anxiety-related thoughts or behavior. This study may have low risk of bias (Higgins & Green, 2011), but it would be hard to argue that it is methodologically high quality because of its limited focus on the mechanisms of treatment. Similarly, in the rampant increase in popularity of ABM within recent years, many investigators have shifted their research interests to include ABM. Few studies report who programed the training task and their programing experience, whether the stimuli indeed represented the intended condition, how condition was determined when performing analyses (i.e., from a spreadsheet or from looking at reaction time data to see what participants actually did), and examination of training data to differentiate participants who completed the task as intended versus participants who did not (i.e., clicked through at 50% accuracy). Were outliers determined on the basis of examination of the data distribution, or on a priori cutoffs? Were stimuli and task procedures designed to maximize the likelihood of bias change? These issues represent open questions in the ABM field and likely can be advanced incrementally (e.g., addressing reliability of task first). But, just as researchers in the 1970s (Smith & Glass, 1977) continued to refine treatments such as CBT, current methodological quality questions should also include quality questions specific to working with computerized reaction time data. Clarke et al. (2014) best summarized these issues through the title of their recent article—absence of evidence is not evidence of absence.

Developmental Perspective

Research primarily based on adult samples suggests that anxious individuals have been characterized by an attentional bias for threat-related stimuli (for reviews, see Bar-Haim et al., 2007; Cisler & Koster,

2010). However, several studies suggest that the pattern of attentional bias throughout development may fit a U-shaped curve. For example, Carmona et al. (2015) found that younger clinically anxious youth (8−10 years) significantly differed from older clinically anxious youth (11−17 years) such that older youths demonstrated a significant attentional bias away from threat. Similar age-related patterns have also been demonstrated in nonclinical youth samples (Lonigan & Vasey, 2009; Reinholdt-Dunne, Mogg, Esbjorn, & Bradley, 2011). As ABM is designed to reduce attentional bias toward threat, this training may be most effective in younger children and adults, relative to adolescents. Thus, researchers should identify the optimum dose and method of delivery of ABM informed by stages of development.

Summary of ABM Research

ABM appears to exert its effects on both symptoms and bias across a wide range of psychological conditions. However, the size of these effects varies across disorders and population types. Eight meta-analyses of ABM suggest wide variability in methods, with little consistency regarding the optimal method of training attention. This inconsistency may be the result of poor reliability of training and assessment tasks. Recently, researchers have placed greater emphasis on reliability of these measures focusing not only on lamenting the lack of reliability in tools such as the probe detection task, but also on ways to improve reliability within the large number of datasets in which this tool has already been used (Price et al., 2015). This indeed represents an important endeavor, as research suggests that studies that do not succeed in changing attentional bias also fail to change symptoms (Clarke et al., 2014; Kuckertz & Amir, 2015; Kuckertz et al., 2014; MacLeod & Clarke, 2015). Finally, important strides have been made in facilitating a discussion of methodological quality in ABM studies (Cristea, Kok, et al., 2015; Cristea, Mogoaşe, et al., 2015; Heeren, Mogoaşe, Philippot, et al., 2015). This discussion should be expanded to include a discussion on quality issues specific to programming training tasks, analyzing reaction time data, and optimizing mechanisms of ABM.

INTERPRETATION BIAS MODIFICATION

Description

Interpretation biases are defined as "the tendency to selectively impose negative resolutions on ambiguous information" (MacLeod & Clarke, 2013, p. 541). These interpretation biases have been demonstrated in anxiety disorders (Amir, Prouvost, & Kuckertz, 2012; Butler & Mathews, 1983), depression (Mogg, Bradbury, & Bradley, 2006), and obsessive–compulsive disorder (Jelinek, Hottenrott, & Moritz, 2009). Interpretation bias tasks aim to increase the extent to which individuals interpret ambiguous situations as benign and/or decrease the extent to which individuals interpret such situations as threatening. As reviewed elsewhere (Menne-Lothmann et al., 2014), the primary training tasks include the ambiguous situations paradigm, homograph disambiguation tasks, and the word–sentence association paradigm (WSAP). For explanatory purposes, we present prominent examples of studies that have used each of these tasks and then discuss IBM findings.

Ambiguous Scenarios Task

In this task, participants are typically presented with short paragraphs describing an ambiguous situation. This scenario may end with either a positive, a neutral, or a negative resolution. In IBM conditions, participants are consistently trained toward a benign (i.e., positive or neutral) interpretation of the ambiguous scenario. For example, Blackwell and Holmes (2010) presented adults with major depressive disorder a series of short paragraphs in which the emotional resolution of the paragraph was not revealed until the end of the paragraph; for example, "'You ask a friend to look over some work you have done. They come back with some comments, which are *all very positive*' (resolution in italics)" (p. 341). Some studies using the ambiguous scenarios task prompt participants to select one of multiple benign or negative resolutions, and provide positive feedback (i.e., "correct") when a benign resolution is selected or negative feedback (i.e., "incorrect") when a negative resolution is selected (e.g., Mathews, Ridgeway, Cook, & Yiend, 2007).

Homographs Task

Homographs are words with the same spelling but different meanings (e.g., "strain" can either refer to something that causes stress or to the variety of a plant or animal). Using this feature of these words, researchers have developed homograph disambiguation tasks. For example, participants may view a homograph cue followed by a word fragment that is related to either the negative (e.g., "str_ss") or the benign (e.g., "var_ety") meaning of the cue. In one such study, Hayes, Hirsch, Krebs and Mathews (2010) presented individuals with GAD with homograph cues and asked them to solve a word fragment related to either a negative or benign meaning of a homograph. Participants were instructed to press a key when they knew what word the word fragment represented. They then typed the missing letters into the word fragment. In order to manipulate interpretation bias in the IBM condition, these researchers built a contingency between the homograph and the benign meaning by always presenting the word fragment associated with that interpretation of the homograph. In the control group, participants saw benign and negative word fragments with equal (i.e., 50%) frequency.

Word–Sentence Association Paradigm

In the WSAP participants, see either a threat word (e.g., "embarrassing") or a benign word (e.g., "funny") followed by an ambiguous sentence that could be interpreted as related to the previously presented word [e.g., "People laugh after something you said" (Beard & Amir, 2009)]. Participants are asked to indicate whether the word and sentence are related by pressing a button corresponding to a yes or no answer. Similar to the homograph tasks, in the training version of WSAP participants received the feedback "You are correct!" when they indicated either that (1) the benign word and sentence were related or (2) the threat word and sentence were unrelated, and received the feedback "You are incorrect" when they indicated either that (1) the benign word and sentence were unrelated or (2) the threat words and sentence were related. In the control condition, participants were equally likely to receive either feedback type regardless of their response.

Findings

Clinical Efficacy

Only one meta-analysis has focused specifically on IBM (Menne-Lothmann et al., 2014). In this review including 2526 adult participants, the authors reported a small but significant effect of benign IBM on increasing positive mood and decreasing negative mood. Similar results have been demonstrated in youth samples. In a combined reanalysis of six IBM studies with 387 healthy youth, Lau and Pile (2015) demonstrated that over one session of training, benign IBM significantly reduced negative mood, whereas control IBM conditions did not. When examining positive mood, Lau and Pile found that all groups experienced reductions in positive mood from pre- to posttraining; however, this decrease was smallest in the benign IBM group.

Several meta-analyses have included a focus on IBM research in the context of CBM more broadly (Cristea, Kok, et al., 2015; Cristea, Mogoaşe, et al., 2015; Hallion & Ruscio, 2011). These mixed meta-analyses have generally yielded less favorable results for the clinical efficacy of IBM. For example, Cristea et al. (2015) reported that, among youth, the effect of IBM was small and nonsignificant when collapsing a variety of symptom outcome measures across a wide range of populations. However, the authors also reported a moderate amount of heterogeneity among studies included in their analyses. This suggests that meta-analyses addressing more focused questions about the efficacy of IBM may be more informative than asking broadly whether IBM works under all conditions (e.g., diagnostic group, age group, delivery setting).

Effects of IBM on Interpretation Bias

Across meta-analyses including IBM, training has a significant effect on change in interpretations. For example, despite finding small and nonsignificant effects on symptom outcomes, Cristea, Mogoaşe, and colleagues (2015) report that, among youth, IBM had a moderate effect on posttraining interpretation bias. Similarly, Lau and Pile (2015) reported fewer negative interpretations and greater positive interpretations at posttraining for adolescents completing benign IBM relative to control conditions. Effects of benign IBM in adult populations also suggest consistent manipulation of interpretation bias. Menne-Lothmann et al. (2014) found that, at posttreatment, 91% of adults who completed benign IBM more strongly endorsed positive interpretations of ambiguous stimuli than negative interpretations, and that this effect for benign IBM was significantly stronger than control conditions.

The majority of youth IBM studies conducted to date (including all six studies reviewed by Lau & Pile, 2015) have been conducted using a single session of training in healthy youth. Therefore, it is possible that although benign IBM may represent a strong experimental manipulation of interpretation biases, ceiling and/or floor effects on positive and negative mood may preclude an influence on symptoms that could be expected in clinically affected populations. However, among adults completing benign IBM, mental health status of participants (i.e., healthy vs high symptom) moderated strength of effect on posttraining interpretation bias but not changes in mood state (Menne-Lothmann et al., 2014).

Relationship Between Symptom Reduction and Interpretation Bias

Similar to ABM, IBM is a theory-driven treatment that proposes that interpretation biases are causally involved in the etiology and maintenance of anxiety and mood disorders (Mathews & MacLeod, 2005; Mathews, 2012), and that through bias modification, anxiety and mood symptoms may subsequently decrease. Therefore, researchers have examined this hypothesis. In one recent meta-analysis, Menne-Lothmann and colleagues (2014) demonstrated significant correlation ($r = .58$) between change in interpretation bias and decrease in negative mood/anxiety symptoms across a variety of IBM studies with adults. Moreover, individual studies with clinically diagnosed populations have demonstrated the hypothesized relationship between bias change and symptom change in formal mediation analyses. For example, Williams et al. (2013) demonstrated that changes in interpretation bias mediated the effects of benign IBM on changes in depressive symptoms in a sample of clinically depressed adults after completing 7 days of IBM. Similarly, Amir and Taylor (2012) examined mechanisms of change in a 12-session IBM protocol for social anxiety disorder. These authors found that changes in threat interpretations for social situations mediated the relationship between group (benign IBM vs control condition) and changes in social anxiety symptoms. Moreover, these data suggest that IBM only affects symptoms to the extent that it effects changes in interpretation bias.

Theory of Intervention: How May IBM Modify Clinically Relevant Symptoms?

IBM and techniques such as cognitive restructuring in the context of cognitive CBT are both based on a wide variety of theoretical (Clark & Wells, 1995; Rapee & Heimberg, 1997) and empirical (Amir et al., 2012; Amir, Foa, & Coles, 1998; Beard & Amir, 2009; Huppert, Pasupuleti, Foa, & Mathews, 2007) support for the tendency for anxious individuals to perceive ambiguous situations as overly threatening. In cognitive restructuring, patients engage in an effortful process of finding evidence for or against negative versus more benign interpretations of ambiguous stimuli (for discussion, see Nowakowski, Antony, & Koerner, 2015). IBM more directly and automatically modifies interpretation biases through associative learning principles, whereby ambiguous situations are associated with neutral interpretations via repeated presentation and reinforcement (Lau & Pile, 2015). Therefore, it is possible that both IBM and cognitive restructuring techniques target the same interpretation biases thought to underlie the presence of anxiety. In support of this hypothesis, Mobini et al. (2014) found that both IBM and a CBT intervention (with cognitive restructuring component) resulted in modification of interpretation biases and reductions in social anxiety symptoms.

Issues and Controversies

Mechanisms

Although studies generally support the notion that IBM affects interpretation bias as well as mood, questions remain regarding the mechanisms of action best targeted through IBM. Here we discuss several mechanistic issues, calling for greater theory-driven investigations of IBM.

Lack of Benign Bias or Presence of Bias Toward Threat?

It is unclear whether interpretation biases are best described as a failure to favor benign interpretations, tendency to adopt threat interpretations, or a combination of both these biases (Amir et al., 2012; Huppert, Foa, Furr, Filip, & Mathews, 2003). It may be the case that although healthy individuals typically interpret ambiguous situations as benign, anxious individuals fail to do so (lack of benign bias). Conversely, it may be the case that faced with ambiguous situations, anxious individuals consistently interpret those situations as threatening. These differing perspectives on bias may have implications for the maintenance of anxiety and depression. For example, making threat interpretations of ambiguous social situations may be associated with avoidance of those situations, whereas failure to make benign interpretations may result in reduced positive affect (or increased depression) in those situations. However, the majority of interpretation bias assessment paradigms do not allow disentangling a tendency to interpret ambiguous situations as benign from a tendency to interpret an ambiguous situation as threatening. This is because the two measurements of biases are perfectly and inversely related. In the homographs paradigm, for a given item participants endorse either a threat or a benign interpretation. Similarly, in many ambiguous scenarios tasks, participants select either a threatening or benign resolution to an ambiguous scenario. However, Beard and Amir (2009) introduced the WSAP, which asks participants to endorse or reject the relationship between benign interpretations and ambiguous sentences, and separately to endorse or reject the relationship between threat interpretations and ambiguous sentences. The studies using the WSAP suggest different patterns related to different forms of psychopathology. For example, Amir et al. (2012) found that individuals with social anxiety disorder endorsed more threat interpretations and fewer benign interpretations of ambiguous situations relative to nonanxious controls, whereas Kuckertz, Amir, Tobin, and Najmi (2013) showed that individuals high in obsessive–compulsive symptoms differed from nonanxious controls in endorsement of threat interpretations but not in endorsement of benign interpretations. Such findings have implications for training emphasis in IBM.

Disambiguating "Benign": Train Toward Neutral or Positive?

Another theory-driven question underlying IBM concerns the relative advantages of training individuals to endorse positive rather than emotionally neutral interpretations of ambiguous situations (Holmes, Mathews, Dalgleish, & Mackintosh, 2006). For example, Beard and Amir (2008) trained socially anxious participants to endorse benign interpretations and reject negative interpretations by providing feed-back based on participants' response (e.g., "You are correct!" vs "You are incorrect"). However, these scenarios included training to endorse positive interpretations (e.g., "funny"—"Someone laughs at something you said") as well as neutral interpretations (e.g., "distracted"—"A friend does not respond when you say hello"). As IBM assumes that biased interpretations away from benign and/or toward threat contribute to the maintenance of anxiety, it may be useful for IBM researchers to use techniques used in cognitive restructuring in the context of CBT. Explicit in many CBT manuals is an emphasis that cognitive restructuring is not designed to promote "positive thinking" but, rather, to examine the logic of a given thought and promote more realistic interpretations (Heimberg & Becker, 2002). Oftentimes, the conclusion is a neutral rather than positive interpretation. Although few IBM studies have systematically investigated the differences between training toward neutral versus positive (cf. Holmes et al., 2006), it is possible that training toward neutral or mixed neutral/positive interpretations will result in more sustainable changes in cognition relative to promoting purely positive interpretations of ambiguity.

Are IBM Studies Targeting Automatic or Strategic Interpretation Biases?

Several studies have posited that IBM offers a complement to CBT in that it targets more automatic aspects of interpretation (Beard, 2011; Lau & Pile, 2015; Williams et al., 2013). However, the definition of the term "automatic" in the CBM literature is not clear (McNally, 1995). Indeed, IBM procedures differ from methods of interpretation modification in traditional cognitive restructuring during CBT. In CBT, patients' interpretations are examined using a variety of questions to analyze the logic for and against a given interpretation, and subsequently generate a "rationale response" (Heimberg & Becker, 2002). In contrast, in most IBM paradigms endorsement of benign interpretations is explicitly encouraged with little rationale for this decision. For example, Blackwell and Holmes (2010) tested an IBM program for depression in which patients simply listened to a variety of ambiguous situations, and were then given a benign interpretation as a resolution. In IBM studies using the WSAP (Beard & Amir, 2008; Taylor & Amir, 2012), participants are explicitly told, "You are correct!" when they state that a benign word is related to an ambiguous situation, or "You are incorrect" when they state that a threat word is related to an ambiguous situation. Although these training tasks do not explicitly state that the purpose of the task is to change automatic cognitions, endorsement rates of benign versus threat interpretations in this is clearly consciously available to all participants. Thus, using the definition of automatic in the sense of "capacity-free, unconscious, involuntary" (McNally, 1995), these paradigm would not meet the criteria of unconscious or involuntary as making a choice implies clear volition. To determine the extent to which IBM is working on an automatic level, it may be more informative to assess responses via response latency measures or electrophysiological measures (e.g., late positive potential; Moser, Hartwig, Moran, Jendrusina, & Kross, 2014). For example, the WSAP measures not only endorsement rates for benign and threat interpretations but also assesses speed of making those endorsements/rejections of word—sentence relationships. Thus, it may be possible to determine the extent to which various emotional disorders are associated with strategic (i.e., endorsement rates) versus automatic (i.e., response latencies) interpretation biases and to thereby design more targeted training paradigms.

Using the WSAP, preliminary data suggest that IBM does index strategic as well as more automatic aspects of interpretation bias. For example, Amir et al. (2012) demonstrated that individuals with social anxiety disorder endorsed significantly more threat interpretations and fewer benign interpretations of ambiguous social situations relative to nonanxious individuals. In addition, compared to nonanxious controls, individuals with social anxiety disorder were much slower to endorse benign interpretations of ambiguous situations relative to their speed in rejecting them.

Imagery in IBM

There is evidence that the efficacy of IBM is augmented when participants are asked to imagine the ambiguous situations presented. Imagery in the context of IBM refers to instructions to imagine oneself in the ambiguous situation rather than simply thinking about the situation (Holmes & Mathews, 2005). In a meta-analysis IBM studies, use of imagery instructions significantly enhanced effects of benign IBM on both interpretation bias as well as changes in symptoms compared to no-imagery benign IBM (Menne-Lothmann et al., 2014). As production of mental imagery is a strategic, effortful process in these studies, these findings lend support to the notion that IBM may operate on more than simply an automatic level of processing.

The utility of imagery techniques is less clear for youth, as few studies have directly compared imagery versus verbal instruction in IBM. Lau and Pile's (2015) meta-analysis found effects of benign IBM on interpretation bias and mood change. However, all of the studies used imagery instructions, thus precluding comparisons to verbal instructions. One notable exception is a study conducted by Vassilopoulos, Blackwell, Moberly, and Karahaliou (2012), in which the authors directly examined the effect of benign IBM with imagery versus verbal instructions in socially anxious youth. Vassilopoulos and colleagues found that children in the imagery condition demonstrated inferior outcomes relative to the verbal instructions condition in reduction in negative interpretation bias and social anxiety. Thus, an important area of research is to clarify the role of imagery in benign IBM for youth, including the use of pictures and sounds to facilitate production of mental images.

Developmental Perspective

Neurobiological and cognitive developmental research suggests periods of development during which IBM may be particularly effective. For example, research in cognitive vulnerabilities for depression suggests relative continuity of cognitive processing styles throughout childhood into adolescence; however, variability decreases substantially in late adolescence such that these processes become trait-like and more closely related to psychopathology (Hankin et al., 2009). Moreover, childhood and adolescence represent a period of rapid, nonlinear neural changes such that gray matter density in the frontal cortex does not stabilize until late adolescence or early adulthood (Gogtay et al., 2004). These developmental patterns may explain research demonstrating greater threat interpretation biases in anxious adolescents compared to their nonanxious peers, whereas differences between anxious and nonanxious children ages 7−10 were not found (Waite, Codd, & Creswell, 2015). Lau and colleagues (Lau & Pile, 2015; Lau, 2013) have argued that these developmental patterns suggest that interpretation biases may be most effectively targeted in mid- to late-adolescence, as this developmental period represents greater stability in cognitive processing styles and neural architecture relative to younger children and adolescents. Alternatively, a preventive approach would suggest that it is best to deliver IBM before the crystallization of trait-like processing styles in at risk children (e.g., family history of depression/anxiety, early subclinical symptoms) before adolescence. The greater variability in cognitive vulnerabilities in younger youth populations suggests that cognitive biases may be more malleable and hence more amenable to change in this period.

Two reviews have quantitatively examined age as a moderator of training-related effects of IBM. Lau and Pile (2015) reanalyzed data from six studies of IBM in nonsymptomatic youths ages 11−17 years. These authors divided their sample into early adolescence (11−14 years), mid-adolescence (15−16 years), or late adolescence (17−18 years). Consistent with their hypotheses, IBM was effective in modifying cognitive styles, with weak but significant changes in mood states Training effectiveness differed by age as well as gender within each developmental period. Specifically, for females completing IBM, the most effective period for change in interpretations was early and late adolescence. For males the most effective age for changing interpretations was mid-adolescence. However, changes in mood state were moderated by neither age nor gender, likely due to overall weak effects of training on mood in this nonsymptomatic sample. In contrast to youth, a meta-analysis of IBM in adults (Menne-Lothmann et al., 2014) did not find a moderating effect of age on any training-related outcomes, although training was more effective in women compared to men. Together, these reviews suggest the need for continued research and theory regarding the role of development and gender in training effectiveness.

Summary of IBM Research

Although there are fewer studies of IBM than ABM, the extant studies suggest that IBM shows promise as a method of manipulating interpretation bias and reducing anxiety and depressive symptoms. Similar to ABM, the clinical efficacy of IBM is small but significant across both adult (Menne-Lothmann et al., 2014) and youth (Lau & Pile, 2015) samples. Symptom changes are mechanistically driven by changes in interpretation bias (Amir & Taylor, 2012; Menne-Lothmann et al., 2014; Williams et al., 2013). Critical questions remain regarding how best to manipulate the mechanisms of action in IBM, which may be expected to increase the subsequent clinical impact of IBM. In addition, questions of reliability examined in the ABM literature are also of relevance to IBM. Interpretation bias in the context of IBM research has been assessed via a variety of paper-and-pencil as well as computerized paradigms, and it is unclear how best to validly and reliably assess interpretation bias, and target-specific aspects of interpretation bias (e.g., automatic and strategic, threat or benign).

OVERALL DISCUSSION

Meta-analytic data and a review of the literature suggest that CBM may offer promise as a clinical intervention tool. Potential practical benefits of CBM—transportability, augmentation effects with CBT, and cost-effectiveness (for review, see Beard, 2011)—are among the reasons for the enthusiasm for this approach. The mixed findings in the various meta-analyses suggest using any CBM intervention with any parameters may not be an effective treatment for all disorders for all individuals under all circumstances. To parse apart the complicated interactions that may arise, several issues common across CBM programs require increased attention.

First, an increased focus on mechanisms is needed. As argued elsewhere in the context of ABM (Clarke et al., 2014; Kuckertz & Amir, 2015; MacLeod & Clarke, 2015), one would not expect clinical outcome effects without a corresponding change in bias. Thus, failure to see clinical effects in the absence of bias change does not indicate that the mechanism is unrelated to outcome but, rather, that the experimental method was insufficient to produce mechanistic change. Nonetheless, null findings are ambiguous in that they do not provide information regarding whether researchers were indeed targeting a bias thought to maintain psychopathology. Although studies that change attentional bias have consistently yielded reductions in symptoms in the context of ABM (Clarke et al., 2014), a few exceptions in both the ABM and IBM literatures have demonstrated expected group differences in bias in the absence of expected group differences on symptoms or behavior (e.g., Clerkin, Beard, Fisher, & Schofield, 2015; Reese, McNally, Najmi, & Amir, 2010; Van Bockstaele et al., 2011).

The mechanisms are only as good as the quality of the measurement we use to assess them. To illustrate, since the introduction of the probe detection paradigm in 1986 (MacLeod et al., 1986), 30 years of accumulated research suggests that this task is a valid instrument in differentiating anxious and nonanxious participants (for reviews, see Bar-Haim et al., 2007; Van Bockstaele et al., 2014); yet, reliability of the task is at best moderate (Price et al., 2015). This seemingly defies a basic psychometric tenant—that reliability of an assessment instrument is a pre-requisite for its validity. To reconcile these differences, researchers should more clearly consider the statistical limitations associated with the measures they use (i.e., difference scores between response latencies to two types of stimuli), as well as alternate explanations for the apparent discrepancy between reliability-validity findings (for discussion of this issue, see Iacoviello et al., 2014; Price et al., 2015; Sipos, Bar-Haim, Abend, Adler, & Bliese, 2014). Although several measurement alternatives have been proposed to reconcile these differences and advance the measurement of attentional bias (Iacoviello et al., 2014; Zvielli et al., 2015), these alternatives await further validation to determine whether they represent an improvement over current measures of attentional bias.

Theory is critically important in order to advance the field and avoiding "ad hoc storytelling" (Treat & Weersing, 2005). Data from various ABM trials are available and can be used to replicate and validate any new measures of attentional bias. Such efforts demand a concerted effort and sharing of raw response latencies among investigators in order to advance the field.

In summary, it may be time to examine basic questions about the nature of cognitive biases, their relationship to symptoms, their psychometric properties, and the robustness of our experimental manipulations. In so doing, we must also insist on quality control that is focused not only on issues such an minimizing experimenter bias (Cristea, Kok, et al., 2015; Cristea, Mogoaşe, et al., 2015; Heeren, Mogoaşe, Philippot, et al., 2015), but also on issues related to proper delivery of active ingredient of the intervention. Accumulation of individual findings is important, but any one study can only advance the field so far. Real advancement is likely to come from accumulation of data across multiple studies, as is now becoming common in other areas (e.g., fMRI). It is also important to consider the nascent field of ABM in relation to the larger body of intervention research. In his classic paper entitled *In defense of external invalidity*, Mook (1983) described the importance of distinguishing between "'What Can' versus 'What Does'" happen in the context of experimental research, while appreciating the importance of research regarding "what can" happen. CBM research to date has demonstrated that brief, computerized interventions *can* have an effect on cognitive biases and subsequent emotional symptoms. Yet, meta-analyses suggest that this is not always what *does* happen in the context of CBM programs across a variety of situations using a variety of methods. Given the lack of the access to empirically supported treatments such as CBT (Gunter & Whittal, 2010), the fact that therapist-free, low-cost, and computerized interventions such as CBM *can* have an effect of mechanisms and symptoms suggests the potential benefit of future research in the CBM field regarding the parameters around which these effects occur.

References

Schneier, F. R., Kimeldorf, M. B., Choo, T. H., Steinglass, J. E., Wall, M. M., Fyer, A. J., & Simpson, H. B. (2016). Attention bias in adults with anorexia nervosa, obsessive-compulsive disorder, and social anxiety disorder. *Journal of Psychiatric Research, 79*, 61–69. Available from http://dx.doi.org/10.1016/j.jpsychires.2016.04.009.

American Psychiatric Association (2013). *Diagnostic and statistical manual of mental disorders* (5th ed.). Arlington, VA: American Psychiatric Publishing, Inc.

Amir, N., Beard, C., Burns, M., & Bomyea, J. (2009). Attention modification program in individuals with generalized anxiety disorder. *Journal of Abnormal Psychology, 118*(1), 28–33. Available from http://dx.doi.org/10.1037/a0012589.

Amir, N., Beard, C., Taylor, C. T., Klumpp, H., Elias, J., Burns, M., & Chen, X. (2009). Attention training in individuals with generalized social phobia: A randomized controlled trial. *Journal of Consulting and Clinical Psychology, 77*(5), 961–973. Available from http://dx.doi.org/10.1037/a0016685.

Amir, N., Elias, J., Klumpp, H., & Przeworski, A. (2003). Attentional bias to threat in social phobia: Facilitated processing of threat or difficulty disengaging attention from threat? *Behaviour Research and Therapy, 41*(11), 1325–1335. Retrieved from http://www.ncbi.nlm.nih.gov/pubmed/14527531.

Amir, N., Foa, E. B., & Coles, M. E. (1998). Automatic activation and strategic avoidance of threat-relevant information in social phobia. *Journal of Abnormal Psychology, 107*(2), 285–290. Available from http://dx.doi.org/10.1037/0021-843X.107.2.285.

Amir, N., Mcnally, R. J., Riemann, B. C., Burns, J., Lorenz, M., & Mullen, J. T. (1996). Suppression of the emotional Stroop effect by increased anxiety in patients with social phobia. *Behaviour Research and Therapy, 34*(11), 945–948. Available from http://dx.doi.org/10.1016/S0005-7967(96)00054-X.

Amir, N., Prouvost, C., & Kuckertz, J. M. (2012). Lack of a benign interpretation bias in social anxiety disorder. *Cognitive Behaviour Therapy, 41*(2), 119–129. Available from http://dx.doi.org/10.1080/16506073.2012.662655.

Amir, N., & Taylor, C. T. (2012). Interpretation training in individuals with generalized social anxiety disorder: A randomized controlled trial. *Journal of Consulting and Clinical Psychology, 80*(3), 497–511. Available from http://dx.doi.org/10.1037/a0026928.

Bar-Haim, Y. (2010). Research review: Attention bias modification (ABM): A novel treatment for anxiety disorders. *Journal of Child Psychology and Psychiatry, and Allied Disciplines, 51*(8), 859–870. Available from http://dx.doi.org/10.1111/j.1469-7610.2010.02251.x.

Bar-Haim, Y., Lamy, D., Pergamin, L., Bakermans-Kranenburg, M. J., & van IJzendoorn, M. H. (2007). Threat-related attentional bias in anxious and nonanxious individuals: A meta-analytic study. *Psychological Bulletin, 133*(1), 1–24. Available from http://dx.doi.org/10.1037/0033-2909.133.1.1.

Bar-Haim, Y., Morag, I., & Glickman, S. (2011). Training anxious children to disengage attention from threat: A randomized controlled trial. *Journal of Child Psychology and Psychiatry, and Allied Disciplines, 52*(8), 861–869. Available from http://dx.doi.org/10.1111/j.1469-7610.2011.02368.x.

Beard, C. (2011). Cognitive bias modification for anxiety: Current evidence and future directions. *Expert Review of Neurotherapeutics, 11*(2), 299–311. Available from http://dx.doi.org/10.1586/ern.10.194.

Beard, C., & Amir, N. (2008). A multi-session interpretation modification program: Changes in interpretation and social anxiety symptoms. *Behaviour Research and Therapy, 46*(10), 1135–1141. Available from http://dx.doi.org/10.1016/j.brat.2008.05.012.

Beard, C., & Amir, N. (2009). Interpretation in social anxiety: When meaning precedes ambiguity. *Cognitive Therapy and Research, 33*(4), 406–415. Available from http://dx.doi.org/10.1007/s10608-009-9235-0.

Beard, C., Sawyer, A. T., & Hofmann, S. G. (2012). Efficacy of attention bias modification using threat and appetitive stimuli: A meta-analytic review. *Behavior Therapy, 43*(4), 724–740. Available from http://dx.doi.org/10.1016/j.beth.2012.01.002.

Blackwell, S. E., & Holmes, E. A. (2010). Modifying interpretation and imagination in clinical depression: A single case series using cognitive bias modification. *Applied Cognitive Psychology, 24*(3), 338–350. Available from http://dx.doi.org/10.1002/acp.1680.

Bomyea, J., & Amir, N. (2011). The effect of an executive functioning training program on working memory capacity and intrusive thoughts. *Cognitive Therapy and Research, 35*(6), 529–535. Available from http://dx.doi.org/10.1007/s10608-011-9369-8.

Boutelle, K. N., Kuckertz, J. M., Carlson, J., & Amir, N. (2014). A pilot study evaluating a one-session attention modification training to decrease overeating in obese children. *Appetite, 76*, 180–185. Available from http://dx.doi.org/10.1016/j.appet.2014.01.075.

Britton, J. C., Bar-Haim, Y., Clementi, M. A., Sankin, L. S., Chen, G., Shechner, T., & Pine, D. S. (2013). Training-associated changes and stability of attention bias in youth: Implications for Attention Bias Modification Treatment for pediatric anxiety. *Developmental Cognitive Neuroscience, 4*, 52–64. Available from http://dx.doi.org/10.1016/j.dcn.2012.11.001.

Butler, G., & Mathews, A. (1983). Cognitive processes in anxiety. *Advances in Behaviour Research and Therapy, 5*(1), 51–62. Available from http://dx.doi.org/10.1016/0146-6402(83)90015-2.

Carmona, A. R., Kuckertz, J. M., Suway, J., Amir, N., Piacentini, J., & Chang, S. W. (2015). Attentional bias in youth with clinical anxiety: The moderating effect of age. *Journal of*

Cognitive Psychotherapy, 29(3), 185–196. Available from http://dx.doi.org/10.1891/0889-8391.29.3.185.

Cisler, J. M., & Koster, E. H. W. (2010). Mechanisms of attentional biases towards threat in anxiety disorders: An integrative review. *Clinical Psychology Review*, 30(2), 203–216. Available from http://dx.doi.org/10.1016/j.cpr.2009.11.003.

Clark, D. M., & Wells, A. (1995). A cognitive model of social phobia. In R. G. Heimberg, M. R. Liebowitz, D. A. Hope, & F. R. Schneier (Eds.), *Social phobia: Diagnosis, assessment, and treatment* (pp. 69–93). New York: The Guilford Press.

Clarke, P. J. F., Notebaert, L., & MacLeod, C. (2014). Absence of evidence or evidence of absence: Reflecting on therapeutic implementations of attentional bias modification. *BMC Psychiatry*, 14, 8. Available from http://dx.doi.org/10.1186/1471-244X-14-8.

Clayson, P. E., Baldwin, S. A., & Larson, M. J. (2013). How does noise affect amplitude and latency measurement of event-related potentials (ERPs)? A methodological critique and simulation study. *Psychophysiology*, 50(2), 174–186. Available from http://dx.doi.org/10.1111/psyp.12001.

Clerkin, E. M., Beard, C., Fisher, C. R., & Schofield, C. A. (2015). An attempt to target anxiety sensitivity via cognitive bias modification. *PLoS ONE*, . Available from http://journals.plos.org/plosone/article?id=10.1371/journal.pone.0114578.

Corbetta, M., & Shulman, G. L. (2002). Control of goal-directed and stimulus-driven attention in the brain. *Nature Reviews Neuroscience*, 3(3), 215–229. Available from http://dx.doi.org/10.1038/nrn755.

Cramér, H. (1946). *Mathematical methods of statistics*. Princeton: Princeton University Press.

Cristea, I., Mogoașe, C., David, D., & Cuijpers, P. (2015). Practitioner review: Cognitive bias modification for mental health problems in children and adolescents: A meta-analysis. *Journal of Child Psychology and Psychiatry*, 56(7), 723–734.

Cristea, I. A., Kok, R. N., & Cuijpers, P. (2015). Efficacy of cognitive bias modification interventions in anxiety and depression: Meta-analysis. *The British Journal of Psychiatry: The Journal of Mental Science*, 206(1), 7–16. Available from http://dx.doi.org/10.1192/bjp.bp.114.146761.

Dandeneau, S. D., Baldwin, M. W., Baccus, J. R., Sakellaropoulo, M., & Pruessner, J. C. (2007). Cutting stress off at the pass: Reducing vigilance and responsiveness to social threat by manipulating attention. *Journal of Personality and Social Psychology*, 93(4), 651–666. Available from http://dx.doi.org/10.1037/0022-3514.93.4.651.

De Voogd, E. L., Wiers, R. W., Prins, P. J. M., & Salemink, E. (2014). Visual search attentional bias modification reduced social phobia in adolescents. *Journal of Behavior Therapy and Experimental Psychiatry*, 45(2), 252–259. Available from http://dx.doi.org/10.1016/j.jbtep.2013.11.006.

Eldar, S., Apter, A., Lotan, D., Edgar, K. P., Naim, R., Fox, N. A., & Bar-Haim, Y. (2012). Attention bias modification treatment for pediatric anxiety disorders: A randomized controlled trial. *The American Journal of Psychiatry*, 169(2), 213–220. Available from http://dx.doi.org/10.1176/appi.ajp.2011.11060886.

Eysenck, M. W., Derakshan, N., Santos, R., & Calvo, M. G. (2007). Anxiety and cognitive performance: Attentional control theory. *Emotion*, 7(2), 336–353. Available from http://dx.doi.org/10.1037/1528-3542.7.2.336.

Garner, M., Mogg, K., & Bradley, B. P. (2006). Orienting and maintenance of gaze to facial expressions in social anxiety. *Journal of Abnormal Psychology*, 115(4), 760–770. Available from http://dx.doi.org/10.1037/0021-843X.115.4.760.

Gilboa-Schechtman, E., Foa, E. B., & Amir, N. (1999). Attentional biases for facial expressions in social phobia: The face-in-the-crowd paradigm. *Cognition and Emotion*, 13(3), 305–318. Available from http://dx.doi.org/10.1080/026999399379294.

Gogtay, N., Giedd, J. N., Lusk, L., Hayashi, K. M., Greenstein, D., Vaituzis, A. C., & Ungerleider, L. G. (2004). Dynamic mapping of human cortical development during childhood through early adulthood. *Proceedings of the National Academy of Sciences of the United States of America, 101*(21), 8174−8179. Available from http://www.jstor.org.

Gunter, R. W., & Whittal, M. L. (2010). Dissemination of cognitive-behavioral treatments for anxiety disorders: Overcoming barriers and improving patient access. *Clinical Psychology Review, 30*(2), 194−202. Available from http://www.ncbi.nlm.nih.gov/pubmed/19942331.

Hakamata, Y., Lissek, S., Bar-Haim, Y., Britton, J. C., Fox, N. A., Leibenluft, E., & Pine, D. S. (2010). Attention bias modification treatment: A meta-analysis toward the establishment of novel treatment for anxiety. *Biological Psychiatry, 68*(11), 982−990. Available from http://dx.doi.org/10.1016/j.biopsych.2010.07.021.

Hallion, L. S., & Ruscio, A. M. (2011). A meta-analysis of the effect of cognitive bias modification on anxiety and depression. *Psychological Bulletin, 137*(6), 940−958. Available from http://dx.doi.org/10.1037/a0024355.

Hankin, B. L., Oppenheimer, C., Jenness, J., Barrocas, A., Shapero, B. G., & Goldband, J. (2009). Developmental origins of cognitive vulnerabilities to depression: Review of processes contributing to stability and change across time. *Journal of Clinical Psychology, 65*(12), 1327−1338. Available from http://dx.doi.org/10.1002/jclp.20625.

Hardcastle, V. G., & Stewart, C. M. (2002). What do brain data really show? *Philosophy of Science, 69*(S3), S72−S82. Available from http://dx.doi.org/10.1086/341769.

Hayes, S., Hirsch, C. R., Krebs, G., & Mathews, A. (2010). The effects of modifying interpretation bias on worry in generalized anxiety disorder. *Behaviour Research and Therapy, 48*(3), 171−178.

Heeren, A., Mogoaşe, C., McNally, R. J., Schmitz, A., & Philippot, P. (2015). Does attention bias modification improve attentional control? A double-blind randomized experiment with individuals with social anxiety disorder. *Journal of Anxiety Disorders, 29*, 35−42. Available from http://dx.doi.org/10.1016/j.janxdis.2014.10.007.

Heeren, A., Mogoaşe, C., Philippot, P., & McNally, R. J. (2015). Attention bias modification for social anxiety: A systematic review and meta-analysis. *Clinical Psychology Review, 40*, 76−90. Available from http://dx.doi.org/10.1016/j.cpr.2015.06.001.

Heeren, A., Reese, H. E., McNally, R. J., & Philippot, P. (2012). Attention training toward and away from threat in social phobia: Effects on subjective, behavioral, and physiological measures of anxiety. *Behaviour Research and Therapy, 50*(1), 30−39. Available from http://dx.doi.org/10.1016/j.brat.2011.10.005.

Heimberg, R. G., & Becker, R. E. (2002). *Cognitive-behavioral group therapy for social phobia: Basic mechanisms and clinical strategies.* New York: Guilford Press.

Higgins, J. P. T., & Green, S. (2011). Cochrane handbook for systematic reviews of interventions version 5.1.0. [updated March 2011]. The Cochrane Collaboration, 2011.

Holmes, E. A., & Mathews, A. (2005). Mental imagery and emotion: A special relationship? *Emotion, 5*(4), 489−497. Available from http://dx.doi.org/10.1037/1528-3542.5.4.489.

Holmes, E. A., Mathews, A., Dalgleish, T., & Mackintosh, B. (2006). Positive interpretation training: Effects of mental imagery versus verbal training on positive mood. *Behavior Therapy, 37*(3), 237−247. Available from http://dx.doi.org/10.1016/j.beth.2006.02.002.

Huppert, J. D., Foa, E. B., Furr, J. M., Filip, J. C., & Mathews, A. (2003). Interpretation bias in social anxiety: A dimensional perspective. *Cognitive Therapy and Research, 27*(5), 569−577.

Huppert, J. D., Pasupuleti, R. V., Foa, E. B., & Mathews, A. (2007). Interpretation biases in social anxiety: Response generation, response selection, and self-appraisals. *Behaviour Research and Therapy, 45*(7), 1505−1515. Available from http://dx.doi.org/10.1016/j.brat.2007.01.006.

Iacoviello, B. M., Wu, G., Abend, R., Murrough, J. W., Feder, A., Fruchter, E., & Charney, D. S. (2014). Attention bias variability and symptoms of posttraumatic stress disorder.

Journal of Traumatic Stress, 27(2), 232–239. Available from http://dx.doi.org/10.1002/jts.21899.

Jelinek, L., Hottenrott, B., & Moritz, S. (2009). When cancer is associated with illness but no longer with animal or zodiac sign: Investigation of biased semantic networks in obsessive-compulsive disorder (OCD). *Journal of Anxiety Disorders*, 23(8), 1031–1036. Available from http://dx.doi.org/10.1016/j.janxdis.2009.07.003.

Kappenman, E.S., Farrens, J.L., Luck, S.J., Proudfit, G.H., Pfabigan, D.M., & Grubert, A. (2014). Behavioral and ERP measures of attentional bias to threat in the dot-probe task: Poor reliability and lack of correlation with anxiety. Available from http://dx.doi.org/10.3389/fpsyg.2014.01368.

Kemps, E., Tiggemann, M., & Hollitt, S. (2014). Biased attentional processing of food cues and modification in obese individuals. *Health Psychology: Official Journal of the Division of Health Psychology, American Psychological Association*, 33(11), 1391–1401. Available from http://dx.doi.org/10.1037/hea0000069.

Klumpp, H., & Amir, N. (2010). Preliminary study of attention training to threat and neutral faces on anxious reactivity to a social stressor in social anxiety. *Cognitive Therapy and Research*, 34(3), 263–271. Available from http://dx.doi.org/10.1007/s10608-009-9251-0.

Kuckertz, J. M., & Amir, N. (2014). *Cognitive biases in social anxiety disorder*. Social anxiety (pp. 483–510). Elsevier. Available from http://dx.doi.org/10.1016/B978-0-12-394427-6.00016-9.

Kuckertz, J. M., & Amir, N. (2015). Attention bias modification for anxiety and phobias: Current status and future directions. *Current Psychiatry Reports*, 17(2), 9. Available from http://dx.doi.org/10.1007/s11920-014-0545-x.

Kuckertz, J. M., Amir, N., Boffa, J. W., Warren, C. K., Rindt, S. E. M., Norman, S., & McLay, R. (2014). The effectiveness of an attention bias modification program as an adjunctive treatment for Post-Traumatic Stress Disorder. *Behaviour Research and Therapy*, 63, 25–35. Available from http://dx.doi.org/10.1016/j.brat.2014.09.002.

Kuckertz, J. M., Amir, N., Tobin, A. C., & Najmi, S. (2013). Interpretation of ambiguity in individuals with obsessive-compulsive symptoms. *Cognitive Therapy and Research*, 37(2), 232–241. Available from http://dx.doi.org/10.1007/s10608-012-9478-z.

Lau, J. Y. F. (2013). Cognitive bias modification of interpretations: A viable treatment for child and adolescent anxiety? *Behaviour Research and Therapy*, 51(10), 614–622. Available from http://dx.doi.org/10.1016/j.brat.2013.07.001.

Lau, J. Y. F., & Pile, V. (2015). Can cognitive bias modification of interpretations training alter mood states in children and adolescents? A reanalysis of data from six studies. *Clinical Psychological Science*, 3(1), 112–125. Available from http://dx.doi.org/10.1177/2167702614549596.

Linetzky, M., Pergamin-Hight, L., Pine, D. S., & Bar-Haim, Y. (2015). Quantitative evaluation of the clinical efficacy of attention bias modification treatment for anxiety disorders. *Depression and Anxiety*, 32(6), 383–391. Available from http://dx.doi.org/10.1002/da.22344.

Logothetis, N. K. (2008). What we can do and what we cannot do with fMRI. *Nature*, 453 (7197), 869–878. Available from http://dx.doi.org/10.1038/nature06976.

Lonigan, C. J., & Vasey, M. W. (2009). Negative affectivity, effortful control, and attention to threat-relevant stimuli. *Journal of Abnormal Child Psychology*, 37(3), 387–399. Available from http://dx.doi.org/10.1007/s10802-008-9284-y.

Luck, S. J. (2014). *An introduction to the event-related potential technique* (2nd ed.). Cambridge, MA: MIT Press.

MacLeod, C., & Clarke, P. J. F. (2013). Cognitive bias modification: A new frontier in cognition and emotion research. In M. D. Robinson, E. R. Watkins, & E. Harmon-Jones (Eds.), *Handbook of cognition and emotion* (pp. 540–562). New York: Guilford Press.

MacLeod, C., & Clarke, P. J. F. (2015). The attentional bias modification approach to anxiety intervention. *Clinical Psychological Science, 3*(1), 58–78. Available from http://dx.doi.org/10.1177/2167702614560749.

MacLeod, C., Mathews, A., & Tata, P. (1986). Attentional bias in emotional disorders. *Journal of Abnormal Psychology, 95*(1), 15–20. Available from http://dx.doi.org/10.1037/0021-843X.95.1.15.

Mansell, W., Ehlers, A., Clark, D., & Chen, Y.-P. (2002). Attention to positive and negative social-evaluative words: Investigating the effects of social anxiety, trait anxiety and social threat. *Anxiety, Stress, and Coping, 15*(1), 19–29. Available from http://dx.doi.org/10.1080/10615800290007263.

Mathews, A. (2012). Effects of modifying the interpretation of emotional ambiguity. *Journal of Cognitive Psychology, 24*(1), 92–105. Available from http://dx.doi.org/10.1080/20445911.2011.584527.

Mathews, A., & MacLeod, C. (2005). Cognitive vulnerability to emotional disorders. *Annual Review of Clinical Psychology, 1*(1), 167–195. Available from http://dx.doi.org/10.1146/annurev.clinpsy.1.102803.143916.

Mathews, A., Ridgeway, V., Cook, E., & Yiend, J. (2007). Inducing a benign interpretational bias reduces trait anxiety. *Journal of Behavior Therapy and Experimental Psychiatry, 38*(2), 225–236. Available from http://dx.doi.org/10.1016/j.jbtep.2006.10.011.

MacLeod, C., Rutherford, E., Campbell, L., Ebsworthy, G., & Holker, L. (2002). Selective attention and emotional vulnerability: Assessing the causal basis of their association through the experimental manipulation of attentional bias. *Journal of Abnormal Psychology, 111*, 107–123.

McHugh, R. K., Murray, H. W., Hearon, B. A., Calkins, A. W., & Otto, M. W. (2010). Attentional bias and craving in smokers: The impact of a single attentional training session. *Nicotine and Tobacco Research: Official Journal of the Society for Research on Nicotine and Tobacco, 12*(12), 1261–1264. Available from http://dx.doi.org/10.1093/ntr/ntq171.

McNally, R. J. (1995). Automaticity and the anxiety disorders. *Behaviour Research and Therapy, 33*(7), 747–754. Available from http://dx.doi.org/10.1016/0005-7967(95)00015-P.

McNally, R. J., Enock, P. M., Tsai, C., & Tousian, M. (2013). Attention bias modification for reducing speech anxiety. *Behaviour Research and Therapy, 51*(12), 882–888. Available from http://dx.doi.org/10.1016/j.brat.2013.10.001.

Menne-Lothmann, C., Viechtbauer, W., Höhn, P., Kasanova, Z., Haller, S. P., Drukker, M., & Lau, J. Y. F. (2014). How to boost positive interpretations? A meta-analysis of the effectiveness of cognitive bias modification for interpretation. *PLoS ONE, 9*(6), e100925. Available from http://dx.doi.org/10.1371/journal.pone.0100925.

Mobini, S., Mackintosh, B., Illingworth, J., Gega, L., Langdon, P., & Hoppitt, L. (2014). Effects of standard and explicit cognitive bias modification and computer-administered cognitive-behaviour therapy on cognitive biases and social anxiety. *Journal of Behavior Therapy and Experimental Psychiatry, 45*(2), 272–279. Available from http://dx.doi.org/10.1016/j.jbtep.2013.12.002.

Mogg, K., Bradbury, K. E., & Bradley, B. P. (2006). Interpretation of ambiguous information in clinical depression. *Behaviour Research and Therapy, 44*(10), 1411–1419. Available from http://dx.doi.org/10.1016/j.brat.2005.10.008.

Mogg, K., Bradley, B., Miles, F., & Dixon, R. (2004). Time course of attentional bias for threat scenes: Testing the vigilance-avoidance hypothesis. *Cognition and Emotion, 18*(5), 689–700. Available from http://dx.doi.org/10.1080/02699930341000158.

Mogoaşe, C., David, D., & Koster, E. H. W. (2014). Clinical efficacy of attentional bias modification procedures: An updated meta-analysis. *Journal of Clinical Psychology,* . Available from http://dx.doi.org/10.1002/jclp.22081.

Mook, D. G. (1983). In defense of external invalidity. *American Psychologist, 38*(4), 379–387. Available from http://dx.doi.org/10.1037/0003-066X.38.4.379.

Moser, J. S., Hartwig, R., Moran, T. P., Jendrusina, A. A., & Kross, E. (2014). Neural markers of positive reappraisal and their associations with trait reappraisal and worry. *Journal of Abnormal Psychology, 123*, 91−105. Available from http://dx.doi.org/10.1037/a0035817.

Nowakowski, M. E., Antony, M. M., & Koerner, N. (2015). Modifying interpretation biases: Effects on symptomatology, behavior, and physiological reactivity in social anxiety. *Journal of Behavior Therapy and Experimental Psychiatry, 49*, 44−52. Available from http://dx.doi.org/10.1016/j.jbtep.2015.04.004.

Pishyar, R., Harris, L. M., & Menzies, R. G. (2004). Attentional bias for words and faces in social anxiety. *Anxiety, Stress, and Coping, 17*(1), 23−36. Available from http://dx.doi.org/10.1080/10615800310001601458.

Posner, M. I. (1980). Orienting of attention. *The Quarterly Journal of Experimental Psychology, 32*(1), 3−25. Available from http://www.ncbi.nlm.nih.gov/pubmed/7367577.

Price, R. B., Kuckertz, J. M., Siegle, G. J., Ladouceur, C. D., Silk, J. S., Ryan, N. D., & Amir, N. (2015). Empirical recommendations for improving the stability of the dot-probe task in clinical research. *Psychological Assessment, 27*(2), 365−376. Available from http://dx.doi.org/10.1037/pas0000036.

Rapee, R. M., & Heimberg, R. G. (1997). A cognitive-behavioral model of anxiety in social phobia. *Behaviour Research and Therapy, 35*(8), 741−756. Available from http://dx.doi.org/10.1016/S0005-7967(97)00022-3..

Reese, H. E., McNally, R. J., Najmi, S., & Amir, N. (2010). Attention training for reducing spider fear in spider-fearful individuals. *Journal of Anxiety Disorders, 24*(7), 657−662. Available from http://dx.doi.org/10.1016/j.janxdis.2010.04.006.

Reinholdt-Dunne, M. L., Mogg, K., Esbjorn, B. H., & Bradley, B. P. (2011). Effects of age and anxiety on processing threat cues in healthy children. *Journal of Experimental Psychopathology*. Available from http://dx.doi.org/10.5127/jep.019611.

Riemann, B. C., Kuckertz, J. M., Rozenman, M., Weersing, V. R., & Amir, N. (2013). Augmentation of youth cognitive behavioral and pharmacological interventions with attention modification: A preliminary investigation. *Depression and Anxiety, 30*(9), 822−828. Available from http://dx.doi.org/10.1002/da.22127.

Rinck, M., Becker, E. S., Kellermann, J., & Roth, W. T. (2003). Selective attention in anxiety: Distraction and enhancement in visual search. *Depression and Anxiety, 18*(1), 18−28. Available from http://dx.doi.org/10.1002/da.10105.

Schmidt, N. B., Richey, J. A., Buckner, J. D., & Timpano, K. R. (2009). Attention training for generalized social anxiety disorder. *Journal of Abnormal Psychology, 118*(1), 5−14. Available from http://dx.doi.org/10.1037/a0013643.

Schmukle, S. C. (2005). Unreliability of the dot probe task. *European Journal of Personality, 19*(7), 595−605. Available from http://dx.doi.org/10.1002/per.554.

Schoenmakers, T. M., de Bruin, M., Lux, I. F. M., Goertz, A. G., Van Kerkhof, D. H. A. T., & Wiers, R. W. (2010). Clinical effectiveness of attentional bias modification training in abstinent alcoholic patients. *Drug and Alcohol Dependence, 109*(1−3), 30−36. Available from http://dx.doi.org/10.1016/j.drugalcdep.2009.11.022.

Singer, J. D., & Willett, J. B. (2003). *Applied longitudinal data analysis: Modeling change and event occurrence.* New York, NY: Oxford University Press.

Sipos, M. L., Bar-Haim, Y., Abend, R., Adler, A. B., & Bliese, P. D. (2014). Postdeplument threat-related attention bias interacts with combat exposure to account for PTSD and anxiety symptoms in soldiers. *Depression and Anxiety, 31*(2), 124−129. Available from http://dx.doi.org/10.1002/da.22157.

Smith, M. L., & Glass, G. V. (1977). Meta-analysis of psychotherapy outcome studies. *American Psychologist, 32*(9), 752−760. Available from http://dx.doi.org/10.1037/0003-066X.32.9.752.

Staugaard, S. R. (2009). Reliability of two versions of the dot-probe task using photographic faces. *Psychology Science Quarterly, 51*(3), 339−350.

Taylor, C. T., & Amir, N. (2012). Modifying automatic approach action tendencies in individuals with elevated social anxiety symptoms. *Behaviour Research and Therapy, 50*(9), 529–536.

Taylor, C. T., Bomyea, J., & Amir, N. (2011). Malleability of attentional bias for positive emotional information and anxiety vulnerability. *Emotion, 11*(1), 127–138. Available from http://dx.doi.org/10.1037/a0021301.

Treat, T. A., & Weersing, V. R. (2005). Clinical psychology. In B. S. Everitt, & D. C. Howell (Eds.), *Encyclopedia of statistics in behavioral science*. New York: John Wiley & Sons, Ltd. Available from http://dx.doi.org/10.1002/9781118445112.stat06732.

Van Bockstaele, B., Verschuere, B., Koster, E. H. W., Tibboel, H., De Houwer, J., & Crombez, G. (2011). Effects of attention training on self-reported, implicit, physiological and behavioural measures of spider fear. *Journal of Behavior Therapy and Experimental Psychiatry, 42*(2), 211–218. Available from http://dx.doi.org/10.1016/j.jbtep.2010.12.004.

Van Bockstaele, B., Verschuere, B., Tibboel, H., De Houwer, J., Crombez, G., & Koster, E. H. W. (2014). A review of current evidence for the causal impact of attentional bias on fear and anxiety. *Psychological Bulletin, 140*(3), 682–721. Available from http://dx.doi.org/10.1037/a0034834.

Vassilopoulos, S. P., Blackwell, S. E., Moberly, N. J., & Karahaliou, E. (2012). Comparing imagery and verbal instructions for the experimental modification of interpretation and judgmental bias in children. *Journal of Behavior Therapy and Experimental Psychiatry, 43*(1), 594–601.

Waite, P., Codd, J., & Creswell, C. (2015). Interpretation of ambiguity: Differences between children and adolescents with and without an anxiety disorder. *Journal of Affective Disorders, 188*, 194–201. Available from http://dx.doi.org/10.1016/j.jad.2015.08.022.

Wanmaker, S., Geraerts, E., & Franken, I. H. A. (2015). A working memory training to decrease rumination in depressed and anxious individuals: A double-blind randomized controlled trial. *Journal of Affective Disorders, 175*, 310–319. Available from http://dx.doi.org/10.1016/j.jad.2014.12.027.

Waters, A. M., Pittaway, M., Mogg, K., Bradley, B. P., & Pine, D. S. (2013). Attention training towards positive stimuli in clinically anxious children. *Developmental Cognitive Neuroscience, 4*, 77–84. Available from http://dx.doi.org/10.1016/j.dcn.2012.09.004.

Wiers, R. W., Houben, K., Fadardi, J. S., van Beek, P., Rhemtulla, M., & Cox, W. M. (2015). Alcohol cognitive bias modification training for problem drinkers over the web. *Addictive Behaviors, 40*, 21–26. Available from http://dx.doi.org/10.1016/j.addbeh.2014.08.010.

Williams, A. D., Blackwell, S. E., Mackenzie, A., Holmes, E. A., & Andrews, G. (2013). Combining imagination and reason in the treatment of depression: A randomized controlled trial of internet-based cognitive-bias modification and internet-CBT for depression. *Journal of Consulting and Clinical Psychology, 81*(5), 793–799. Available from http://dx.doi.org/10.1037/a0033247.

Yiend, J., & Mathews, A. (2001). Anxiety and attention to threatening pictures. *The Quarterly Journal of Experimental Psychology A, 54*(3), 665–681. Available from http://dx.doi.org/10.1080/02724980042000462.

Yiend, J., Parnes, C., Shepherd, K., Roche, M.-K., & Cooper, M. J. (2014). Negative self-beliefs in eating disorders: A cognitive-bias-modification study. *Clinical Psychological Science, 2*(6), 756–766. Available from http://dx.doi.org/10.1177/2167702614528163.

Zvielli, A., Bernstein, A., & Koster, E. H. W. (2015). Temporal dynamics of attentional bias. *Clinical Psychological Science, 3*(5), 772–788. Available from http://dx.doi.org/10.1177/2167702614551572.

20

Cognitive Training in Schizophrenia

Kristen M. Haut[1], Vijay A. Mittal[2],
Stewart A. Shankman[3] and Christine I. Hooker[1]

[1]Rush University Medical Center, Chicago, IL, United States
[2]Northwestern University, Evanston, IL, United States [3]University of
Illinois at Chicago, Philadelphia, IL, United States

INTRODUCTION

Schizophrenia is a chronic, severe mental illness afflicting approximately 1% of the population characterized by hallucinations, delusions, disorganized speech and thought, grossly disorganized behavior or catatonia, and reductions in emotional expression and motivation (Tandon et al., 2013). The healthcare burden of schizophrenia in the United States alone was over $62 billion in 2002 (McEvoy, 2007), which reflects the costs of treatment as well as the high costs of unemployment, poor social functioning and difficulties in independent living. It is now abundantly clear that cognitive deficits are a central feature of the illness and a primary cause of these poor functional outcomes, yet antipsychotic medications do not adequately address these deficits (Green, 1996). Thus, identifying effective cognitive treatments is imperative to addressing the full psychological and social burden of schizophrenia spectrum disorders. While novel pharmacologic agents have been tested with limited success (Goff, Hill, & Barch, 2011), neuroscience-informed behavioral interventions may prove more effective. Recent research indicates that cognitive training approaches may be a promising technique for addressing cognitive deficits in people with schizophrenia (Fisher, Herman, Stephens, & Vinogradov, 2016).

The Science of Cognitive Behavioral Therapy.
DOI: http://dx.doi.org/10.1016/B978-0-12-803457-6.00020-9

This chapter reviews the development of behavioral interventions for cognitive deficits in schizophrenia with an emphasis on contemporary approaches that incorporate a current understanding of systems neuroscience and learning-induced neuroplasticity. Long-standing awareness of cognitive deficits in schizophrenia and the pressing need to treat them has produced extensive research over the past 20 years that provides a substantial body of work for understanding cognitive training treatment effects and their potential underlying mechanisms. However, with accumulating evidence that cognitive deficits are associated with a broad range of psychiatric disorders, there is growing interest in applying new cognitive training approaches to other populations as well. Here, we review the extant research on cognitive training in schizophrenia, including different methodological approaches, observed effects, theoretical potential, and gaps in current knowledge, as a model framework for applying cognitive training approaches to psychiatric disorders more broadly.

THE NATURE AND ROLE OF COGNITIVE DEFICITS IN SCHIZOPHRENIA—SPECTRUM PATHOLOGY

Individuals with schizophrenia exhibit broad cognitive deficits and reduced intellectual functioning relative to expected abilities (Kahn & Keefe, 2013). Multiple cognitive domains are affected, including processing speed, attention, working and episodic memory, and executive functions like cognitive control (Haut et al., 2015; Keefe, 2008). In addition, social cognition, broadly defined as the perception, interpretation and processing of social information, is particularly salient as individuals with schizophrenia show impairments in the perception of facial and vocal emotions (Pinkham, Penn, & Perkins, 2007) and social cues (Haut & MacDonald, 2010) as well as impairments in theory of mind and empathy, indicating deficits in the ability to infer another person's mental state and react to those mental states appropriately (Lee, Zaki, Harvey, Ochsner, & Green, 2011). People with schizophrenia also have problems accurately attributing the source of internal and external stimuli, leading to difficulty distinguishing information coming from self or others (Brune, Abdel-Hamid, Lehmkamper, & Sonntag, 2007). On the whole, individuals with schizophrenia consistently show cognitive and social cognitive functioning a full standard deviation below that of healthy controls (Schaefer, Giangrande, Weinberger, & Dickinson, 2013).

Cognitive deficits in schizophrenia are especially relevant when considering the functional and social disability associated with the disorder. Cognitive impairments are actually more predictive of long-term outcome than severity of psychosis symptoms such as hallucinations or delusions (Green, Kern, & Heaton, 2004) as they affect the individual's ability to perform critical daily living skills, also known as their functional capacity. Social cognition most directly impacts overall community functioning (Green, Horan, & Lee, 2015). The ability to navigate the social environment is essential to well-being and social status and impairments contribute to difficulties in day-to-day social interactions and predict marital status, size of social network, and available social support (Fett et al., 2011). Thus, cognitive deficits have broad clinical implications, affecting independent living skills, quality of life, and community functioning and are the strongest predictors of every day functioning, highlighting the need for new treatment approaches.

Treatments targeting cognitive deficits are also an important avenue for early intervention and prevention in people at risk for psychosis. Treatment in the early phases of schizophrenia may produce larger gains than treatment provided in more chronic phases, highlighting the importance of early identification of individuals who may be developing schizophrenia. Individuals at *clinical high risk (CHR) for psychosis*, which generally includes adolescents and young adults who are experiencing attenuated positive symptoms that indicate disturbances in perception or thought but do not reach the severity of fully psychotic positive symptoms, have an approximately 30% risk of developing a psychotic episode within the next 2–3 years (Fusar-Poli et al., 2013). Despite the focus on psychosis-like symptoms in identifying CHR individuals, cognitive dysfunction is likely more proximal to the neurodevelopmental origins of schizophrenia (Haut, Schvarcz, Cannon, & Bearden, 2016). Deficits in cognition precede the onset of psychotic symptoms among individuals who ultimately develop schizophrenia (Seidman et al., 2013) and metaanalysis of CHR studies found that CHR individuals are impaired across a broad array of cognitive domains, with more severe deficits in verbal fluency and memory in those who subsequently transit to a psychotic disorder (Fusar-Poli et al., 2012). Cognitive deficits are also found in those with genetic vulnerability for schizophrenia, such as first degree relatives (Snitz, MacDonald, & Carter, 2006) suggesting they may be an endophenotype that represents genetic risk and are a treatment target that more directly impacts the underlying neural abnormalities that ultimately produce the symptoms of schizophrenia.

Unfortunately, cognitive deficits and the resulting functional disabilities are not adequately treated by standard antipsychotic medications, which primarily are limited to reducing the level of psychotic symptomatology (Harvey, 2010). Moreover, treatment of CHR individuals with antipsychotics is not always recommended as they have not been shown to substantially reduce rates of conversion to psychosis, do not substantially impact cognitive functioning, and may have negative neural and metabolic side effects (Adkins et al., 2011). As this chapter discusses, behavioral interventions that target cognitive functioning through cognitive training provide a potential alternative treatment that is less likely to introduce negative side effects yet also more directly targets some of these early cognitive signs of psychosis risk. Evidence from first-episode and CHR individuals shows that more significant cognitive deficits at or prior to psychosis onset are related to worse clinical and functional outcome, which again supports the assertion that cognition is a particularly important target for early intervention (Carrión et al., 2011). Given the profound functional consequences of cognitive deficits over the course of psychotic illness, interventions that improve cognition in the early stages of illness could have life changing benefits. However, in order to develop cognitive training programs that target the most relevant neurocognitive systems, it is necessary to identify the neural sources of cognitive deficits in schizophrenia.

NEURAL BASIS OF COGNITIVE DEFICITS IN SCHIZOPHRENIA

The cognitive difficulties observed in schizophrenia are a reflection of these underlying structural and functional neural abnormalities. For cognitive training interventions to be most effective, it is essential to understand how these neural systems support cognitive performance under normal circumstances—i.e., in healthy human development—as well as how internal and external factors enhance or degrade neural system function in schizophrenia. While an extensive review of these mechanisms is beyond the scope of this chapter, the following sections provide a brief overview of key neural systems implicated in the cognitive deficits found in schizophrenia.

Basic Neural Systems Supporting Cognition

Historically, much of the understanding of how cognition is represented in the brain used a modular paradigm, in which particular cognitive functions are localized within discrete regions of the brain. More recently, however, cognitive neuroscience has shifted to focus more on large-scale networks of brain regions that work in tandem to support cognitive functions (Bressler & Menon, 2010). Functional networks that may be particularly useful as targets for cognitive training in schizophrenia are the central executive network (CEN), episodic memory network (EMN), salience/emotion processing network (SEN), and the social brain/default mode network (DMN). The CEN is comprised primarily of prefrontal cortex, especially the dorsolateral prefrontal cortex (DLPFC), and lateral posterior parietal cortex (Seeley et al., 2007). Many higher order executive functions that require consciously directed and focused attention depend on the activity and connectivity of the CEN (Fox, Corbetta, Snyder, Vincent, & Raichle, 2006; Tandon et al., 2013), including working memory, planning, and decision-making (McEvoy, 2007; Sridharan, Levitin, & Menon, 2008), suggesting this neural network is essential for conscious, "top-down" cognitive functions. The EMN is more explicitly tied to the encoding and retrieval of accurate episodic memories and is largely comprised of the hippocampal–entorhinal complex in the medial temporal lobe and connections in the inferior parietal cortex (Green, 1996; Vincent et al., 2006). Strong connectivity and integration within this network is associated with better episodic memory performance and is necessary for precise recall of events and experiences (Geib, Stanley, Dennis, Woldorff, & Cabeza, 2017; Goff et al., 2011).

Other functional networks play a more prominent role in emotional and social cognitive processes. The DMN was first identified as a "task-negative" brain network including the medial prefrontal cortex (mPFC) and posterior cingulate cortex (PCC) that deactivated during most cognitively demanding tasks (Fisher et al., 2016; Raichle et al., 2001). However, this network is also highly engaged during tasks that require theory of mind and/or self-referential processing (Harrison et al., 2008; Kahn & Keefe, 2013), suggesting that neural systems supporting social cognition about self and others are typically activated at rest (Gusnard, Akbudak, Shulman, & Raichle, 2001; Haut et al., 2015; Keefe, 2008). Finally, the SEN is a network that includes subcortical structures, such as the amygdala and thalamus, as well as the insula and anterior cingulate cortex (ACC) (Pinkham et al., 2007; Seeley et al., 2007). This network is engaged in autonomic reactivity and serves to process external stimuli, detect salient features of the environment, and shift attention of those stimuli, which often have emotional resonance or other personally relevant content (Bressler & Menon, 2010; Haut & MacDonald, 2010). In particular, the SEN plays a role in switching between "task-positive" networks like the CEN and "task-negative" networks like the DMN in order to mediate attentional focus between external and internal events (Lee et al., 2011; Menon & Uddin, 2010).

Neural Abnormalities in Schizophrenia

There is substantial evidence that cognitive neural networks are disrupted in individuals with schizophrenia (Brüne et al., 2007;

Karlsgodt et al., 2008). People with schizophrenia show broadly decreased cortical network efficiency (Alexander-Bloch et al., 2012; Schaefer et al., 2013) and structural correlates have been demonstrated using diffusion tensor imaging (DTI), which allows for the measurement of the integrity of white matter, in tracts connecting the frontal lobe with the thalamus, cingulate gyrus, hippocampus, temporal and occipital lobe (Ellison-Wright & Bullmore, 2009; Green et al., 2004). Altered neural connectivity patterns have direct functional implications for cognitive functioning and clinical symptom severity (Cole, Anticevic, Repovs, & Barch, 2011; Green et al., 2015) including in recent onset, antipsychotic naïve individuals with schizophrenia (Fett et al., 2011; Lui et al., 2009).

The CEN shows substantial structural and functional alterations in individuals with schizophrenia (Chen et al., 2016; Fusar-Poli et al., 2013) as well as those at risk for psychosis (Haut et al., 2016; Jukuri et al., 2015). Individuals with schizophrenia show volumetric reductions in prefrontal cortex (Bora et al., 2011; Seidman et al., 2013) and many of the cognitive deficits in schizophrenia can be linked to altered functional activation of the prefrontal lobe (Fusar-Poli et al., 2012; Minzenberg, Laird, Thelen, Carter, & Glahn, 2009). DLPFC function in particular may be compromised early in the developmental course of psychosis (Brahmbhatt, Haut, Csernansky, & Barch, 2006; Snitz et al., 2006). In addition, medial temporal lobe regions key to the EMN network are also particularly impacted in psychotic disorders. The hippocampus and entorhinal cortex show structural differences between people with schizophrenia and healthy controls (Bora et al., 2011; Harvey, 2010) and episodic memory performance that relies on this network is impaired in schizophrenia (Adkins et al., 2011; Haut et al., 2015). People with schizophrenia demonstrate reduced functional activation and altered patterns of EMN connectivity during memory tasks (Carrión et al., 2011; Haut et al., 2014) and the morphological abnormalities present in CHR individuals who develop psychosis suggest that prefrontal and temporal lobe regions are particularly vulnerable to the disease process (Bressler & Menon, 2010; Cannon et al., 2014).

Deficits in social cognition implicate a neural network particularly utilized for engaging in complex social behaviors (Adolphs, 2009; Seeley et al., 2007) that overlaps with the DMN. Altered activation in regions critically involved in the perception and processing of social information have been found in individuals with schizophrenia, including the superior temporal sulcus (STS), mPFC, and anterior insula (Germine, Garrido, Bruce, & Hooker, 2011). Theory of mind deficits is linked to the temporoparietal junction, posterior cingulate, and mPFC (Hooker, Bruce, Lincoln, Fisher, & Vinogradov, 2011) and abnormal functioning in these regions is associated with self-reported and clinician-rated measures of social functioning and social interest (Tully, Lincoln, & Hooker, 2014). Altered connectivity within the DMN has been found in individuals with schizophrenia (Pankow et al., 2015) and those at risk for psychosis (Jukuri et al., 2013) and those with more severely disrupted connectivity have less social enjoyment and worse social functioning (Dodell-Feder, DeLisi, & Hooker, 2014).

Finally, the SEN is impacted in schizophrenia in relation to both salience processing and emotion functions. The insula and ACC show significant abnormalities in schizophrenia, suggesting that abberant salience processing may be a principal feature of the disorder (Palaniyappan & Liddle, 2012). In addition, this network is thought to be crucial in shifting between the CEN and the DMN and altered interactions with and between these networks may play a role in cognitive difficulties and symptomatology in schizophrenia (Chen et al., 2016). Individuals with schizophrenia show abnormal activation in the amygdala and medial orbitofrontal cortex while experiencing emotions as well as processing emotional facial expression in others (Gur et al., 2002). In addition, thalamic—cortical connectivity at rest suggests heightened connectivity with sensorimotor regions and reduced connectivity with prefrontal regions in people with schizophrenia (Anticevic et al., 2014) and CHR individuals (Anticevic et al., 2015).

Despite this evidence for substantial disruption in the functional and structural neural systems underlying cognition and social functioning in schizophrenia, individuals with schizophrenia do engage the same fundamental networks as healthy adults to perform a task. For example, when performing tasks that require executive functioning such as cognitive control or working memory, individuals with schizophrenia utilize regions that are also used by controls but with reduced activation, suggesting that they do not fully engage the network (Minzenberg et al., 2009). Studies of social cognition, such as facial emotion processing, indicate a similar pattern of results in that people with schizophrenia show reduced utilization of similar prefrontal and limbic system regions (Delvecchio, Sugranyes, & Frangou, 2013). These neuroimaging results suggest that individuals with schizophrenia are capable of engaging the networks required to execute these cognitive tasks and that treatments targeted toward actively engaging the underlying networks, particularly promoting increased activity, efficiency or plasticity, may be a particularly fruitful avenue for addressing these pernicious and clinically relevant symptoms. Cognitive interventions have thus been developed that target these critical networks, with the goal of improving the functioning of the underlying systems in order to enact behavioral changes.

GOALS AND APPROACHES OF COGNITIVE TRAINING IN SCHIZOPHRENIA

Cognitive training is "a behavioral training based intervention that aims to improve cognitive processes (attention, memory, executive function, social cognition, or metacognition) with the goal of durability and generalization" (Cognitive Remediation Experts Workshop (CREW), Florence, April 2010). This encompasses a broad array of techniques that aim to improve cognitive in a way that generalizes to real-world psychosocial functioning. Despite these common goals, there are significant differences in how programs try to achieve them, including both implicit and explicit differences in rationale, design, and techniques. Changes in cognition and function can be achieved by developing compensatory skills that circumvent impaired abilities or by restoring function within disrupted neural networks. Compensatory approaches work around the neurocognitive dysfunction using external cues or strategies, such as making lists or posting visible reminders, to aid behavior and/or by engaging other, presumably intact neural circuits to perform the target behavior. These modes of cognitive training seek to utilize other, more intact, cognitive capabilities to compensate for the cognitive deficits (Medalia & Saperstein, 2013). While these methods have been utilized in addressing cognitive dysfunction in schizophrenia, this chapter focuses more on attempts to restore cognitive abilities.

Restoration of function relied on the underlying neural architecture to be largely intact but weakened due to the underlying pathophysiology of the disorder. Cognitive training therapies provide exercises that attempt to improve cognitive and psychosocial function by engaging neuroplasticity within structures of the brain that are required to perform those tasks (Merzenich, Van Vleet, & Nahum, 2014). Training on fundamental cognitive abilities that are called for in a variety of situations can then improve the functioning and recruitment of those more basic skills in everyday activities. These neuroplasticity-based approaches show particular promise to improve cognitive and social impairment in schizophrenia by enhancing the function of underlying neural systems, yet historically, cognitive training has been applied to schizophrenia using a broad array of methods.

BACKGROUND AND DEVELOPMENT OF COGNITIVE TRAINING PROGRAMS IN SCHIZOPHRENIA

Early behavioral studies in individuals with schizophrenia demonstrated performance improvements following cognitive training

(Twamley, Jeste, & Bellack, 2003), indicating the potential for effective training-based interventions. Metaanalyses covering an array of these studies have shown a consistent, moderate effect size on global improvement of cognition (Grynszpan et al., 2011; McGurk, Twamley, Sitzer, McHugo, & Mueser, 2007; Wykes, Huddy, Cellard, McGurk, & Czobor, 2011). In McGurk et al. (2007), 1151 individuals with schizophrenia were combined to demonstrate a moderate improvement in cognitive functioning (effect size = 0.41) as well as improved psychosocial functioning (effect size = 0.36) and symptom reduction (effect size = 0.28). Wykes et al. (2011) showed similar results in 2104 participants with global cognition showing significant improvement (effect size = 0.45) that remained significant at follow-up (effect size = 0.43) and showed significant changes in symptoms and functioning. Grynszpan et al. (2011) specifically investigated studies that utilized computer-assisted cognitive remediation and also found significant changes across a number of domains, with effect sizes ranging from 0.29 to 0.64 across 805 subjects.

These metaanalyses encompass a number of cognitive training methods. In many, a "top-down" or consciously driven approach is used that emphasizes engaging higher order processes like cognitive control and planning to produce improved functioning. Training emphasizes learning information processing strategies, such as way to organize information, that are designed to aid in cognitive performance and subjects are provided with explicit practice and instruction on how to engage strategies in everyday life (Wykes et al., 2007). Top-down techniques assume individuals with schizophrenia have the capacity to engage in appropriate cognitive strategies and that self-initiation of cognitive strategies is impaired (Brahmbhatt et al., 2006). For example, individuals with schizophrenia show significant reduction in semantic organization for verbal information that impairs their subsequent recall (Brébion, David, Jones, & Pilowsky, 2004; Gsottschneider et al., 2011). However, even a brief training session on the use of semantic encoding strategies was shown to significantly improve performance on a task that measures self-initiated semantic encoding strategies (Guimond & Lepage, 2015). This shows that, while individuals with schizophrenia may not naturally engage in the most appropriate cognitive strategies, they are capable of utilizing them when explicitly trained. Other cognitive rehabilitation programs use mass-market educational software to engage subjects in problem-solving and other "top-down" abilities (Medalia, Dorn, & Watras-Gans, 2000). These individual training within a group format and place greater emphasis on learning style and individual goals in order to maintain interest and engagement. This combination of software with individualized training expectations has been shown to result in improved verbal comprehension and problem solving as well as reduced symptoms (Medalia, Revheim, & Casey, 2002).

Training strategies have also been employed in treatments designed to improve social cognition in individuals with schizophrenia like Social Cognitive Interaction Training (SCIT) (Penn et al., 2005) and Social Cognitive Skills Training (SCST) (Horan et al., 2009). The goal of these methods is to aid individuals with schizophrenia in understanding other's social and emotional cues and to teach the component skills necessary to engage in complex social situations appropriately. SCIT/ SCST provides manualized training regarding strategies and practice on improving emotion perception, theory of mind and counteracting cognitive biases in social interactions and improves social functioning in outpatients (Horan et al., 2009) and especially in inpatients (Combs et al., 2007).

Top-down and strategy based approaches are often administered in an individual or small group format which requires trained personnel to provide direct instruction. This limits the scalability of the approach as they require substantial investment of time and resources and utilization of these strategies in everyday life requires engagements of executive functions that are known to be impaired in individuals with schizophrenia. Alternative cognitive training methods employ a "bottom-up" approach that targets particular domains of cognitive abilities in order to improve the foundation for cognitive functioning. By engaging in hierarchical training that strengthens domains such as attention and memory before directly addressing problem solving or social skills, these methods strengthen the underlying architecture required for cognitive functioning, with the intention to improve real-world functioning in similar situations, which then encourages individuals to cognitively engage further.

A number of computer packages have specifically been developed to engage different cognitive domains such as attention, visuomotor skills, memory, reaction time, language and/or executive functioning (e.g., CogRehab (Bracy, 1995) and CogPack (Marker, n.d.). Modules are presented based upon the training goals for the treatments and domains are trained using repeated practice that provides increasing complexity and difficulty as training proceeds (McGurk et al., 2007). A combination of these "bottom-up" computerized training packages with more "top-down" therapist-led groups were used by many early cognitive training methods in schizophrenia, including Neurocognitive Enhancement Therapy (NET) (Bell, Bryson, Greig, Corcoran, & Wexler, 2001) and Cognitive Enhancement Therapy (CET) (Hogarty & Flesher, 1999). NET, which combines computerized training on cognitive functions like attention, memory and executive function with a weekly processing group and work or vocational therapy, improved performance on working memory and executive functioning tasks to a greater degree than the work/vocational therapy alone (Bell et al., 2001) and remained improved at least 6 months after treatment (Bell, Bryson, & Wexler, 2003). CET combines computer-based neurocognitive training with group-based social cognition training and shows greater improvements in neurocognition as well as in social adjustment and symptom reduction compared to supportive therapy (Hogarty et al., 2004).

Cognitive training interventions have also been tested in CHR individuals prior to conversion to a psychotic disorder. In particular, an integrated intervention that included cognitive training along with psychoeducation, individual and group therapy was found to significantly reduce the rate of progression to psychosis in a group of CHR individuals (Bechdolf et al., 2012). While the specific contribution of cognitive training is unclear, these results are more promising than cognitive therapy alone and suggest that more focused training may be useful in preventing the progression to psychosis (Morrison et al., 2012).

Despite the promising results demonstrated by these studies of cognitive training, there are significant limitations to their application and scalability. Treatments like CET or SCIT are experimental, therapist-delivered approaches that typically focus on building skills over the course of multiple individual or small-group sessions (Bartholomeusz & Allott, 2012). Despite their promise, they are rarely offered, in part due to the need for therapist training and the number of visits required; however, more recent researches have shifted toward enhancing the computerized training portion of these treatments using neuroscience-informed targeted cognitive training (TCT) that specifically engages neuroplasticity.

NEUROSCIENCE-INFORMED COGNITIVE TRAINING APPROACHES

Neuroplasticity-based TCT targets the underlying neural cause of cognitive deficiencies in schizophrenia to promote neuroplasticity that leads to behavioral changes, rather than focusing initially on the external behavior (Fisher et al., 2016). For example, given the DLPFC's role in executive function deficits in schizophrenia, this might be a promising target for a neuroplasticity-based TCT program. Utilizing tasks that engage the DLPFC, this protocol would encourage activation-dependent plasticity as well as refine connectivity with other regions in the CEN (Fisher, Holland, Subramaniam, & Vinogradov, 2010). In addition to targeting impaired neural systems, these methods are often more amenable to automation and individualization, for example, being performed primarily via online sessions, allowing for home-based TCT that is more flexible and cost-effective (Ventura, Wilson, Wood, & Hellemann, 2013). Neuroplasticity refers to the inherent property of the brain to produce long-term changes to neural structure and function in response to learning and experience. This encompasses both individual cell level synaptic plasticity that can produce or fine-tune synaptic connections and larger scale changes where the functions of cortical areas are altered. Most of these neuroplastic changes are activity dependent (Ganguly & Poo, 2013) and so neuroplasticity-based treatments utilize the natural capacity of the brain to change neuronal function by providing specific experiences to target the desired neural systems and shape neuronal response (Nahum, Lee, & Merzenich, 2013).

A neuroplasticity-focused approach may be particularly useful in schizophrenia as they may be vulnerable to neural processes that impair neuroplasticity under typical conditions and show altered patterns of expected neural development. Volumetric changes are attributed to reduced dendritic spine density rather than neuronal loss (Glantz & Lewis, 2000) and there is disruption in typical cortical development of the specific connections necessary for proper functional networks (Sultan, Brown, & Shi, 2013). Progressive gray matter reductions in first-episode individuals with schizophrenia (Asami et al., 2012) also suggests accelerated rates of synaptic pruning in key regions during adolescence (Cannon et al., 2014).

Late adolescence/early adulthood is the peak period of risk for onset of psychosis symptoms, suggesting that developmental processes during adolescence may play a role in the pathogenesis of schizophrenia (McGorry, 2011). One particular salient developmental process is the refinement of neural connections via synaptic pruning and the myelination of axonal connections (Petanjek et al., 2011). Progressive anatomical changes found in individuals at clinical high risk who subsequently convert to psychosis (Sun et al., 2009) reflect overly aggressive synaptic pruning or normal processes that interact with previously existing brain vulnerability. Given this dynamic neural state, neuroscience-informed TCT may be especially effective for harnessing inherent neuroplasticity mechanisms to normalize the affected developmental processes and prevent further cognitive decline.

Neuroplasticity focused TCT explicitly utilizes a number of principles to promote neuroplastic change most effectively. First, multiple levels of processing must be engaged in order to effect the most lasting and transferable changes in the brain. Working memory, for example, requires *both* "top-down" cognitive control mechanisms but also efficient "bottom-up" perceptual processing, so training engage both of these networks may be necessary (Gazzaley, 2011). TCT induces neuroplasticity in both directions of processing by providing intensive and adaptive training that is continuously modified individually for each subject to ensure that the task demands test their neurocognitive capacity. In addition, tasks are engaging and reward accurate performance in order to maintain individual motivation to continue training. Reward is associated with higher rates of neuroplasticity and higher long-term impact on neural changes (Adcock, Thangavel, Whitfield-Gabrieli, Knutson, & Gabrieli, 2006).

Behavioral Evidence Supporting Neuroscience-Informed Cognitive Training

Neuroplasticity focused TCT starts with tasks that emphasize "bottom-up" processes (such as starting with basic auditory and visual processing) in order to fine tune information processing. Individuals with schizophrenia have impairments in auditory processing that influence general cognitive deficits and particularly verbal learning deficits, memory and psychosocial functioning (Dale et al., 2010). Thus, TCT that emphasizes improving the accuracy and speed of auditory differentiation, as well as improving memory for sequential auditory sounds, was tested in individuals with schizophrenia and those who completed the training showed improvements on the auditory tasks and also on verbal working memory, verbal learning and cognition over all when compared to a control group of individuals with schizophrenia who participated in a computer game control condition (Fisher, Holland, Merzenich, & Vinogradov, 2009). Effect sizes for improvement following this training were higher ($d = 0.86$) than suggested by the metaanalyses for cognitive training overall and the highest improvements in cognition translated to the greatest improvements in quality of life at a 6-month follow-up (Fisher et al., 2010).

This auditory TCT not only normalized auditory sensory deficits but also produced greater improvements in verbal memory than previously developed drill and practice based training of memory itself (Popov et al., 2011). However, while neuroplasticity-based auditory processing training improved general neurocognition, it alone did not impact social cognition (Fisher et al., 2009). When it was combined with computerized social cognition training, subjects did show improvements on an emotional intelligence task (Sacks et al., 2013). Social cognition can also be a direct focus for TCT and one domain that has received a great deal of research is facial emotion recognition. Rapid, accurate facial emotion recognition is an important component of social interaction, as it provides contextual cues regarding others emotional states and receptiveness to social interactions and has been shown to predict functioning in individuals with schizophrenia over and above general cognitive functioning (Hooker & Park, 2002). Several computer-aided interventions have been found to significantly improve performance in individuals with schizophrenia, to the point where it is similar to that of healthy controls. This training also generalized beyond just improving facial affect recognition as individuals who received training also showed improved prosody recognition, theory of mind and social competence compared to individuals receiving general neurocognition training (Wölwer & Frommann, 2011). In addition, while the small sample size ($N = 20$ for affective training, $N = 18$ for neurocognitive training) limited determination of overall functional changes, there was a trend toward improved global social functioning.

One specific tool developed to improve facial emotion recognition is the Micro Expression and Subtle Expressions Training Tool (METT), which trains individuals to better recognize small or rapid changes in facial expression. Individuals with schizophrenia benefit from this training, with even a single session of METT leading to performance of the task at a level similar to that of healthy controls (Russell, Chu, & Phillips, 2006). Importantly, this improvement in accurate emotion recognition performance appears to be due to the specific training nature of METT as individuals with schizophrenia in a "repeated exposure" condition that shows the simulated video training without sound or feedback were not as successful at improving emotion recognition accuracy (Marsh, Luckett, Russell, Coltheart, & Green, 2012).

While neuroscience-based TCT has primarily been tested in individuals with schizophrenia, initial evidence suggests that heightened plasticity in the CHR phase may enhance positive response to cognitive training interventions (Fisher, Loewy, Hardy, Schlosser, & Vinogradov, 2013). A four-week TCT on attention, memory and executive functioning in both CHR individuals, and similarly aged individuals with schizophrenia showed that, while all improved cognitively following training, CHR showed greater improvement on verbal memory (Rauchensteiner et al., 2011). Similarly, 40 hours of TCT with added computerized social cognitive training demonstrated significant behavioral improvements in processing speed, visual learning and memory and overall global cognition in a group of CHR individuals (Nahum et al., 2014) and also demonstrated the feasibility of administering home-based, online TCT. A double-blind randomized controlled trial of CHR individuals showed that TCT on verbal learning and memory resulted in significant improvements compared to CHR individuals performing a computer game control (Loewy et al., 2016).

Neuroscience Evidence for Training-Induced Neuroplasticity

The development of neuroplasticity-based, TCT interventions requires an iterative process by which the understanding of the key elements to cognitive functioning and their relation to real-world functioning are combined with the determination of what neural systems are most malleable to refinement. Cognitive and social cognitive neuroscience research can help to identify the networks that underlie the core elements of broader adaptive functioning that are compromised in individuals with schizophrenia as well as identifying tasks that train each element essential to a particular skill in order to engage learning-based neuroplasticity. As research in this field has progressed, a number of potential targets have been developed in key systems that have been found to exhibit potential for neuroplasticity-based change in individuals with schizophrenia. Direct evidence of neuroplasticity has been demonstrated in animals, showing that auditory training can engage both synaptic and cortical map remodeling (Buonomano & Merzenich, 1998). While this cannot currently be demonstrated in humans at the cellular level, neuroimaging methods have been used to assess broader neural changes and clearly demonstrate neuroplasticity associated with learning and cognitive training (Caeyenberghs, Verhelst, Clemente, & Wilson, 2016).

In a study focused on improving working memory performance in particular, 9 individuals with schizophrenia completed 25 hours of a computerized cognitive training program that combined verbal working memory training on a series of N-back tasks with CogPack programs that focused on engaging attention and working memory. These individuals demonstrated improved performance on both the trained verbal working memory task and an untrained visual working memory task compared to nine demographically matched individuals with schizophrenia who participated in small-group manualized cognitive behavioral social skills training (CBSST). Cognitive training increased activation in regions of the CEN including the dlPFC, frontopolar cortex and ACC and greater increases in the left frontopolar cortex and left DLPFC were associated with greater improvements in behavioral performance (Haut, Lim, & MacDonald, 2010) (Fig. 20.1). A similar study comparing 15 individuals with schizophrenia who received 48 hours of training on working memory with 12 individuals who participated in a computer skills group found increased left DLPFC activity from baseline to posttreatment in the cognitive training group that was associated with behavioral improvement on a working memory n-back task. (Ramsay, Nienow, Marggraf, & MacDonald, 2017). In addition, this drill and practice based cognitive remediation program was associated with increased connectivity between the thalamus and the prefrontal cortex (Ramsay, Nienow, & MacDonald, 2016). Similar results have been found for spatial working memory, where eight individuals received 28 hours of training on the Rehacom suite of computerized exercises training attention, working memory, logical thinking, and executive functions. Cognitive training resulted in significantly increased activation

(A)

(B)

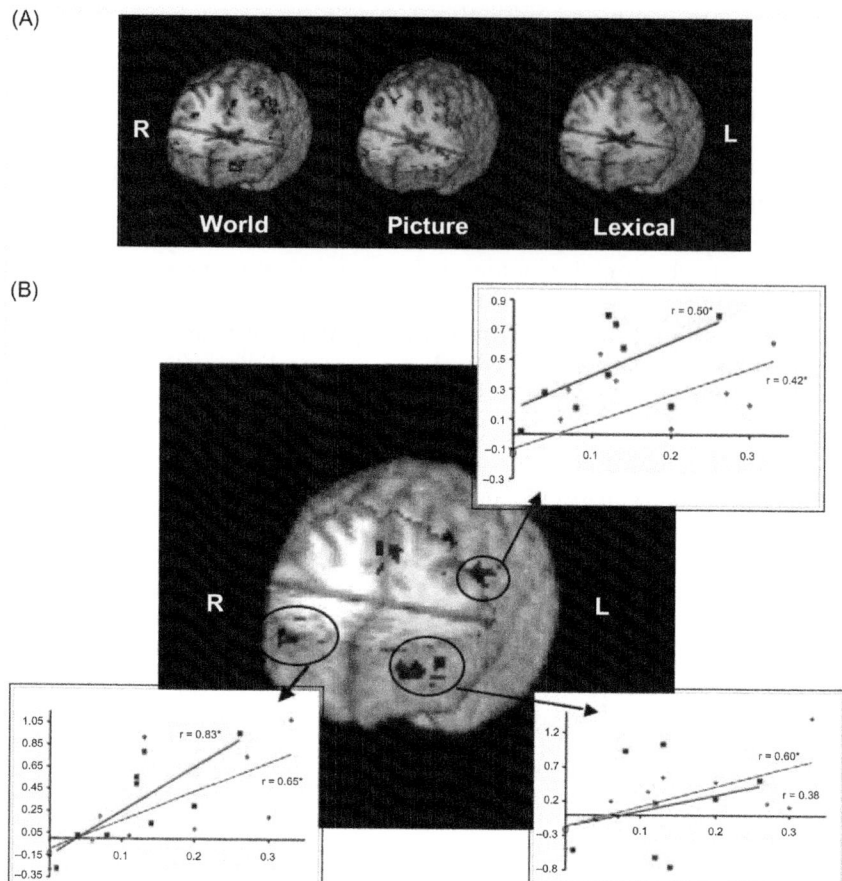

FIGURE 20.1 (A) Regions showing significantly greater posttest activity than pretest activity for the participants with schizophrenia in the cognitive remediation group compared with the participants with schizophrenia in the cognitive behavioral social skills training group or the healthy control group in the trained word 2-back task and the untrained picture 2-back task, demonstrating transfer of training effects to similar tasks. No significant group differences between pre- and posttest activity were found in a lexical decision task that does not utilize the trained domain of working memory and was thus not expected to exhibit changes in activation with training. (B) Significant correlations between improved behavioral performance and increased functional activation for both word working memory task (red, black in print version) and picture working memory task (blue, gray in print version). *Source: From Haut, K., Lim, K. & MacDonald, A. (2010). Prefrontal cortical changes following cognitive training in patients with chronic schizophrenia: Effects of practice, generalization, and specificity.* Neuropsychopharmacology, 35(9), 1850–1859.

in the left inferior frontal gyrus, cingulate gyrus, and inferior parietal lobe on an untrained spatial n-back working memory task and improved cognitive performance on attention and reasoning tasks overall compared to nine individuals with schizophrenia who received treatment as usual (Bor et al., 2011).

These results demonstrate that the prefrontal cortex is capable of functional plasticity when presented with a specifically targeted, intensive and adaptive working memory training program. While they primarily utilized computer-based training programs that are commercially available, each of these programs were delivered in a psychologist-led treatment group where subjects attended sessions at a treatment facility multiple times a week. Thus, the feasibility of these programs and the amount of training that can be performed in a given week is limited by the need for supervision. Neuroplasticity-focused TCT, however, uses intensive online computerized training protocol that allows for more regular, self-directed training sessions and has also been shown to produce neural changes and behavioral improvements following working memory training. Fifteen individuals with schizophrenia completed a TCT program available from Posit Science for an hour a day over 16 weeks, leading to 80 hours of training. Fifteen individuals with schizophrenia were also included as control subjects and they played commercially available computer games (e.g., hangman, solitaire) for an equivalent amount of time. Individuals in the TCT group first trained 50 hours of "bottom-up" adaptive basic auditory/verbal processing exercises that require the individual to make increasingly fine-grained distinctions between stimuli while also increasing working memory load, then received 30 hours of training combining similar tasks of visual discrimination (45 minutes per day) with training specifically on emotion identification (15 minutes per day). The TCT group demonstrated significant behavioral improvements on an untrained working memory task that working memory performance no longer differed from that of healthy controls whereas the control group did not. These behavioral improvements were associated with increased function in the medial and inferior frontal gyrus. Importantly, working memory improvements were sustained during a 6-month follow-up period without any further training were associated with improved occupational functioning at follow-up. This subsequent improvement in occupational functioning, only *after* cognitive improvements were present, suggests that TCT can show generalization not only to related cognitive tasks but that, given time, can lead to gains in real-world functioning (Subramaniam et al., 2014).

Neural changes have also been demonstrated in tasks that engage the EMN and DMN. Schizophrenia subjects participating in a randomized controlled trial of TCT that included the auditory and visual exercises (described in the previous paragraph) as well as social cognition training performed an untrained reality-monitoring task that requires the subject to identify the source of information as being self-generated or externally generated (Subramaniam et al., 2012). Individuals who participated in TCT demonstrated improved performance as well as task-associated activation in the mPFC that was similar to brain-behavior associations found in healthy controls. Improvement on this task demonstrates transfer of skills and evidence of neuroplasticity in the circuit that underlies this task despite training engaging the circuit using different tasks. Importantly, those in TCT who showed the largest performance and brain-activation related improvements also demonstrated improved social functioning at 6-month follow-up, again demonstrating that sustained neurocognitive improvements subsequently produce real-world functional improvements (Subramaniam et al., 2012).

A similarly designed intervention, in which 11 individuals with schizophrenia received 50 hours of auditory processing based TCT along with facial emotion recognition training, showed that those who received training were better able to recognize positive emotions than those in a placebo group who played computer games. TCT was associated with greater activation in regions of the SEN associated with emotion processing, including the superior temporal cortex and right postcentral gyrus (Hooker et al., 2012). Increased neural activation in the postcentral gyrus in particularly was associated with behavioral improvements in the TCT group on the MSCEIT Perceiving Emotions test, an untrained, standardized test of emotion perception. A follow-up study utilized the same training paradigm and also included 11 TCT subjects and 11 computer game controls but acquired fMRI on more sensitive emotion recognition task. Increased activation in the putamen, mPFC, and amygdala were demonstrated following TCT in individuals with schizophrenia and associated with improvements on the MSCEIT Perceiving Emotions test. In addition, increased amygdala activation specifically predicted improved performance on emotion perception measures (Hooker et al., 2013) (Fig. 20.2).

Facial emotion training alone in individuals with schizophrenia has also been associated with changes in networks and activity associated with face processing (Popova et al., 2014). Behavioral improvements following training in accurate recognition of emotions are associated with increased activation in brain regions utilized in bilateral inferior frontal cortex, right parietal cortex, and left middle and superior occipital lobe (Regenbogen et al., 2015), showing that training improves emotion recognition in individuals with schizophrenia via neuroplasticity within the neural network involved in the visual, attention, and emotional evaluation of affective facial expressions.

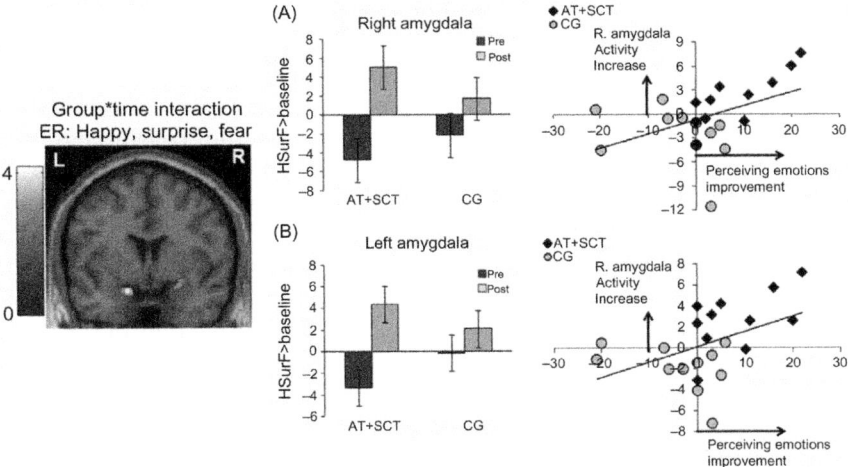

FIGURE 20.2 Group × Time interaction effects for emotion recognition (ER) of Happy, Surprise, Fear (HSurF). Color scale represent *t*-values. (A) right amygdale; and (B) left amygdala. Bar plots show amygdale activity (percent signal change) of the contrast HSurf > baseline for each group and time point. Scatter plots show correlations between change in amygdale activity (Post−Pre) and change in MSCEIT Perceiving Emotions (Post−Pre) across all participants. The correlation between neural activity increase and behavioral improvement was significant in right amygdale, $r = 0.45$, $p < 0.05$ and a trend in left amygdala, $r = 0.39$, $p < 0.10$. *Source: From: Hooker, C.I., Bruce, L., Fisher, M., Verosky, S.C., Miyakawa, A., D'Esposito, M., et al. (2013). The influence of combined cognitive plus social-cognitive training on amygdala response during face emotion recognition in schizophrenia.* Psychiatry Research: Neuroimaging, 213, 99−107.

There is also evidence that training can produce structural changes in the brain at the volumetric and synaptic level by inducing experience-dependent structural plasticity (Lövdén, Wenger, Mårtensson, Lindenberger, & Bäckman, 2013). Voxel-based morphometry, which measures volumetric structural changes, was used to examine structural MRI changes in a group of 31 individuals with recent-onset schizophrenia who received 2 years of CET compared to 27 who received enriched supportive therapy. CET reduced the rate of gray matter loss in individuals medial temporal lobe structures such as the hippocampus, parahippocampal gyrus, and amygdala and was also associated with general improvements in social cognition and functioning (Eack et al., 2010). CET has also been associated with increased dlPFC activity and decreased frontocingulate connectivity during performance of a cognitive control task (Keshavan, Eack, Prasad, Haller, & Cho, 2016) as well as preservation of resting state dlPFC-DMN functional connectivity and increased insula-DMN connectivity that are associated with improved regulation and perception, respectively (Eack, Newhill, & Keshavan, 2016). CET differs from the previously described working memory training and TCT in that is consists of weekly hour-long sessions over the course of 2 years cumulating in 60 sessions of computer-based neurocognitive training and 45 social-cognitive group sessions as well as weekly homework and individual coaching with an emphasis of generating strategies to generalization training to real-world settings. Strategy-training based cognitive remediation has also been shown to increase white matter integrity in the corpus callosum compared to a psychoeducational social skills training group (Penadés, Pujol, Catalán, & Massana, 2013).

As discussed earlier, intervention with individuals with CHR for psychosis may help to preserve cognitive function during the critical neurodevelopmental period of late adolescence/early adulthood. In a pilot study, 18 CHR individuals received TCT consisting of 45 minutes of cognitive training using the online program Lumosity and 15 minutes of social cognitive training using the Posit Science SocialVille program and their performance was compared to that of healthy controls. TCT was found to improve cognitive functioning significantly on measures of processing speed and visual learning as well as global cognition (Fig. 20.3) (Hooker et al., 2014). In addition, neuroimaging during a working memory task and an emotion recognition task demonstrated training-induced neuroplastic changes in the activity and connectivity of the CEN and SEN, respectively. Moreover, neural changes in these networks following training brought the level of activity and connectivity more toward that of controls, suggesting that training served to normalize function in these neural networks (unpublished data).

GAPS IN THE LITERATURE AND FUTURE DIRECTIONS

Identifying Effective Training Features

One priority going forward is identifying and maximizing the "active ingredients" in cognitive training protocols to produce the largest impact on an individual's functioning. There are substantial differences in methodology, dosage, mode of administration and targeted deficits across different training paradigms and no single treatment has been widely adopted or approved for insurance reimbursement. For example, the "dose" of cognitive training recommended by most programs is 45 minutes to 1 hour, 4–5 times per week for at least 40 hours but this is not been empirically validated. Interestingly, in a pilot study of TCT among CHR individuals, the majority of cognitive improvement occurred during the first 10 hours of training. In addition, the learning curve of performance on training exercises predicted the extent of cognitive improvement immediately after training as well as functional

(A)

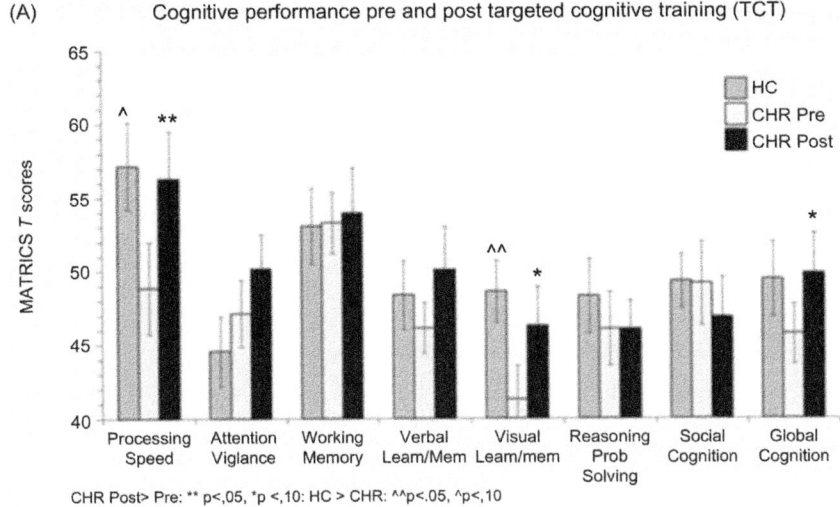

Cognitive performance pre and post targeted cognitive training (TCT)

CHR Post> Pre: ** p<,05, *p <,10: HC > CHR: ^^p<.05, ^p<,10

(B)

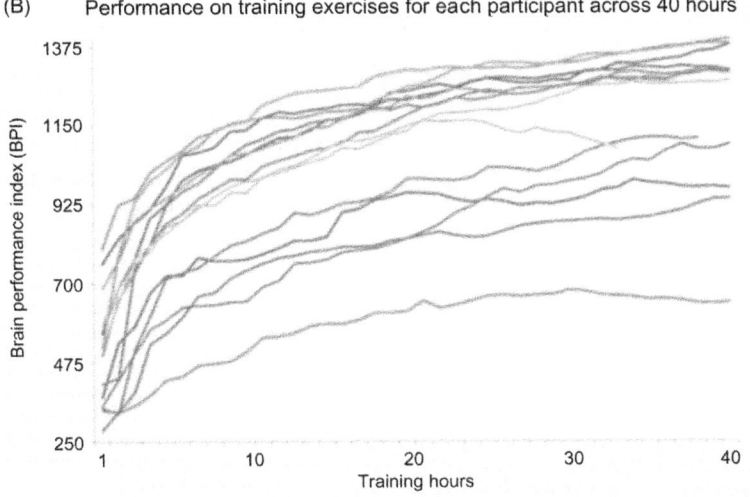

Performance on training exercises for each participant across 40 hours

FIGURE 20.3 (A) Cognitive performance (*T* scores) for each domain in the MATRICS Consensus Cognitive Battery. Error bars represent standard error of the mean. (B) Training performance on Lumosity exercises is charted for each participant over the entire TCT intervention. Performance on Lumosity games is measured with the "Brain Performance Index" (BPI) which is a standardized measure (normalized on Lumosity users system-wide) and has values ranging from 0 to 1700. *Source: From Hooker, C.I., Carol, E.E., Eisenstein, T.J., Yin, H., Lincoln, S.H., Tully, L.M., et al. (2014). A pilot study of cognitive training in clinical high risk for psychosis: Initial evidence of cognitive benefit. Schizophrenia Research, 157(2014), 314–316.*

improvement 1 month later; specifically, CHR individuals with steeper learning curves, showing greater gains in training performance over the first 10 hours, had a greater degree of improvement in cognition and functioning (Fig. 20.3B) (Hooker et al., 2014). This not only suggests substantial benefit of a relatively small dose of training, but also that initial response to training can be an early indicator of potential treatment benefit. Many questions remain regarding all training components, and, as this study indicates, detailed analysis of performance and other factors can provide valuable information to move the field forward.

Individual Differences in Treatment Response

Adaptive, individualized computer-based TCT is successful in targeting impaired neural circuits; however, there remains heterogeneity in the individual response to treatment and there is little known about factors that influence treatment response. Variability in response may be impacted by intrinsic motivation, as TCT requires active engagement and attention. The neuropsychological and educational approach to remediation (NEAR) emphasizes individualized goals for daily living to provide motivation via personal context as well as tailoring training to each individual's learning style (Medalia & Saperstein, 2011). However, similar to CET and SCIT, NEAR requires intensive involvement of therapists and is thus difficult to scale to the larger clinical population. A challenge for self-directed computerized TCT is to foster motivation with less clinician direction.

Genetic profiles may also impact an individual's response to treatment as many of the genes thought to confer susceptibility to schizophrenia likely also affect cognitive functioning more broadly (Zai, Robbins, Sahakian, & Kennedy, 2017). For example, single nucleotide polymorphisms in the COMT gene were associated with differing overall cognitive improvement following TCT in a group of subjects with schizophrenia (Panizzutti, Hamilton, & Vinogradov, 2013). Cognitive functioning prior to training can also help to predict response to treatment, with individuals with schizophrenia who have more preserved baseline cognitive functioning and more gray matter volume showing more capacity to improve with training (Keshavan et al., 2011).

Improving Transfer and Generalization

Cognitive training has been critiqued for a lack of evidence that training generalizes to untrained tasks in everyday life (Simons et al., 2016). Thus, randomized controlled trials must assess the transfer of performance improvements to overall social and role functioning as well as to control for generalized effects. Cognitive stimulation in general can produce generalized and individuals participating in these programs often receive more frequent supportive interactions with study personnel than provided by treatment as usual. A recent meta-analysis, specifically focusing on randomized controlled trials of cognitive remediation in schizophrenia found that there were only mild improvement on cognitive functioning in the control conditions whereas individuals receiving cognitive training showed greater improvements (Radhakrishnan, Kiluk, & Tsai, 2016). However, similar results across hours of training, characteristics of participants and domains trained suggest that many of the mechanisms of action may be nonspecific. Similarly, a metaanalysis combining neuroimaging results across a variety of training modalities found consistent increases in prefrontal, insular and thalamic regions in successful cognitive training in individuals with schizophrenia, especially with regards to the involvement of regions that predict skill transfer (Ramsay & MacDonald, 2015). Many cognitive training methods include direct efforts to improve the transfer of skills to real-world situations that can be key in translating cognitive gains into functional outcomes. Metaanalyses of cognitive remediation show more significant gains in functional outcomes for those individuals who received additional psychosocial intervention and strategy training compared to those who received cognitive remediation alone (McGurk et al., 2007; Wykes et al., 2011).

A particularly promising feature of TCT is that it can be implemented using computer-based platforms that provide the potential for low-cost, scalable, self-directed training. However, while studies frequently show improvement on auditory processing tasks overall, not all subjects seems to engage in or respond to the treatment and evidence for the transfer of these improvements to verbal memory and real-world functioning is mixed (Murthy et al., 2012). Thus, it must be demonstrated that these primarily computer based treatments translate to functional improvements in daily life.

Training Additional Social Cognitive Domains

Development of TCT to address other domains of social cognition will focus on a number of areas where underlying neural deficits may be amenable to treatment. Cognitive control, essential for generating strategies and problem solving, is also necessary for controlling the influence of emotion on behavior (Ochsner, Silvers, & Buhle, 2012). Impaired cognitive control of emotions is common in schizophrenia and arises from neural dysfunction in regions including that lateral prefrontal cortex (Tully et al., 2014) that could provide a target for interventions that train the individual to pay less explicit and implicit attention to negative emotional stimuli, thus improving social interaction (Hooker et al., 2014).

There is also evidence that training in the automatic inhibitory control of emotion can improve overall emotion regulation. In healthy controls, training on a working memory task utilizing emotional faces were shown to recruit cognitive control more efficiently on an emotional reappraisal task, altering function in the lateral prefrontal cortex (Schweizer, Grahn, Hampshire, Mobbs, & Dalgleish, 2013). Similarly, in healthy controls, compassion training has been found to alter activation in the networks supporting theory of mind and to increase prosocial behavior on an economic decision-making task (Klimecki, Leiberg, Ricard, & Singer, 2014). However, these methods of cognitive training have not yet been applied to individuals with schizophrenia.

Application to Other Psychiatric Disorders

Although individuals with depression do not evidence the level of cognitive impairment found in schizophrenia, they do exhibit impairments in attention, executive functions, and memory (McDermott & Ebmeier, 2009) that are trait-like (Sarapas, Shankman, Harrow, & Goldberg, 2012) and continue into remission. Computerized cognitive training (CCT) may therefore be helpful adjunctive and perhaps standalone interventions for individuals with depression. A 2016 metaanalysis (Motter et al., 2016) reviewed nine studies and found that CCT yield significant and large effects at improving attention (Hedge's $g = 0.67$) and working memory (Hedge's $g = 0.72$), but not executive functioning and verbal memory (Hedge's $g = 0.20$ and 0.09, respectively). CCT also improved measures of depression symptom severity (Hedge's $g = 0.43$) although results were mixed. CCTs may have larger effects on particular components of depression. For example, CCTs that target the ability to inhibit particular responses (an important component of cognitive control) decrease ruminative thinking, given that rumination is a repetitive cognitive process long associated with deficits in cognitive inhibition (see Joormann & Tran, 2009 for review). Indeed, several RCTs for CCT have shown promising results at targeting rumination specifically (Calkins, McMorran, Siegle, & Otto, 2015; Siegle, Price, & Jones, 2014).

Cognitive Bias Modification

Computerized interventions that target "hot" cognitive processes, in particular biases in how individuals cognitively process emotional stimuli, attempt to directly manipulate a cognitive bias by repeatedly exposing the individual to task contingencies that favor a less biased pattern of emotional processing (Cristea, Kok, & Cuijpers, 2015). There is a wide array of cognitive bias modification interventions that target different cognitive biases, but *attention bias modification (ABM)* is particularly relevant as it is consistent with a neuroscience-informed TCT approach. A hallmark characteristic of those with and at risk for anxiety and depression is an attentional bias favoring negative and/or threatening stimuli (Bar-Haim, Lamy, Pergamin, Bakermans-Kranenburg, & van IJzendoorn, 2007) and ABM attempts to ameliorate this cognitive bias by utilizing prolonged variants of tasks that encourage or "train" the participant to exhibit a desired allocation of attention. For example, a widely used measure attentional bias is the dot-probe task in which attention to dots (i.e., probes) that follow threatening stimuli are compared to the attention to dots that follow nonthreatening stimuli (with greater attention to threat preceding dots reflecting greater attention to threat (Bar-Haim et al., 2007)). The ABM version of the task typically consists of presenting dots that are consistently NOT associated with the threatening stimuli, thus training the individual to decrease their attention to the threatening stimuli (although this varies across ABM studies; see Mogoaşe, David, & Koster, 2014). Metaanalyses of randomized controlled trials of ABM demonstrate significant effects on attentional bias and on overall symptoms of anxiety and depression post-treatment (e.g., Cohen's $d = 0.42$; (Cristea et al., 2015)). ABM exhibits similar neural effects reported by other anxiolytic treatments (e.g., reduced bilateral amygdala, insula, and subgenual anterior cingulate) as well as increased activity in several regions of the prefrontal cortex, suggesting that ABM increases one's ability to engage top-down brain processes to regulate anxiety (Taylor et al., 2014). Other computerized cognitive bias modification interventions are being developed and evaluated (e.g., positive imagery; savoring of positive affective experiences; Blackwell et al. (2015)) highlighting the increased interest in attempts to directly target and modify "hot" cognitive biases.

POTENTIATION/AUGMENTATION OF COGNITIVE TRAINING EFFECTS

Despite the demonstrated effectiveness of cognitive training to improve function in individuals with schizophrenia, these effect sizes are overall modest and the transfer of cognitive improvements to real-world functioning is not always consistent (Simons et al., 2016). Metaanalyses have found that individuals who received some type of adjunctive therapy tend to improve to a greater degree than those that employ just a drill and practice method of training alone. These adjunctive therapies range widely, from social skills training to supported employment or other vocational rehabilitation, yet all were based on additional social or psychological support (McGurk et al., 2007; Wykes et al., 2011). TCT seeks to engage neuroscience-informed neuroplasticity however, there may be additional biological mechanisms that can be engaged as well. Thus, a growing area of research aims to determine what mechanisms might be engaged to potentiate learning and especially to enhance neuroplastic effects of training.

Exercise and Cognition

Consistent aerobic activity (e.g., at least 30 minutes per session, several times a week) preserves and promotes cognitive function through several processes including fostering neurogenesis (Pereira et al., 2007), slowing apoptosis (programmed cell death) (Austin, Ploughman, Glynn, & Corbett, 2014), driving beneficial epigenetic expression (promoting stress coping and increased neuronal activity) (Radom-Aizik, Zaldivar, Leu, Galassetti, & Cooper, 2007) and promoting neurotrophic factors (e.g., BDNF, IGF-1, VEGF) (Griffin et al., 2011). Exercise also is central for reducing inflammation, which can limit the positive effects of neurotrophic factors on synaptic plasticity (Handschin & Spiegelman, 2008) and has been found to increase gray matter volume in brain regions associated with cognitive control, memory processing, motor behavior, and reward (Erickson, Leckie, & Weinstein, 2014).

In the area of schizophrenia, preliminary evidence suggests exercise-based improvements of important cognitive domains. For example, Pajonk and colleagues found that after a brief cardiovascular exercise trial (12 weeks) individuals with schizophrenia showed a significant increase in hippocampal volume (12%) and increases in verbal memory when compared to a control group of individuals with schizophrenia in a nonaerobic activity (1%) (Pajonk, Wobrock, Gruber, & Scherk, 2010). Exercise may also enhance the benefits cognitive training by stimulating factors supporting synaptic plasticity. One study included a short 6-week intervention in which individuals with schizophrenia showed increased cognitive performance in visual learning, working memory and processing speed, as well as an increase in subjective quality of life following a combined trial (Oertel-Knöchel et al., 2014). An enriched environment paradigm of bicycle ergometer and cognitive remediation training over 3 months (Malchow et al., 2015) found long-term memory improvements in both healthy volunteers and individuals with schizophrenia who experience multiple episodes of psychosis. These individuals specifically also showed an improvement in global functioning and improvements in negative symptoms, cognitive flexibility, short and long-term verbal memory. Another recent pilot study on first-episode onset found significantly greater cognitive improvement in the cognitive training plus exercise group than in the cognitive training group alone (Nuechterlein et al., 2016).

CONCLUSION

In conclusion, this chapter outlined the development of novel behavioral treatments for the cognitive and social deficits associated with schizophrenia. Impaired cognitive functioning and especially impaired social cognition have a tremendous impact on the daily living skills and social interactions of individuals with schizophrenia, making them a primary cause of disability and poor quality of life. While these deficits are associated with clear abnormalities in a number of functional neural networks, current pharmacological treatments do not have a positive treatment effect. As a result, researchers have begun to explore cognitive training techniques in an attempt to develop effective mechanisms to restore cognitive function and to prevent cognitive decline in individuals at risk for psychosis.

A number of cognitive training protocols have been developed and tested in individuals with schizophrenia. Most demonstrate at least some improvements on cognitive abilities, though active ingredients and transfer of improved skills to real-world functioning have been less clear. However, the most recent class of treatments developed show more promise. These computer-based targeted cognitive training programs specifically utilize knowledge of cognitive neuroscience to target affected functional networks and more effectively induce neuroplasticity. Research suggests that these methods can induce functional changes in the brain that translate to behavioral improvement and, given time, to improvements in social and role functioning. Further research is necessary to optimize these treatments as well as to extend them to additional cognitive domains.

References

Adcock, R. A., Thangavel, A., Whitfield-Gabrieli, S., Knutson, B., & Gabrieli, J. D. E. (2006). Reward-motivated learning: Mesolimbic activation precedes memory formation. *Neuron*, *50*(3), 507–517. Available from http://dx.doi.org/10.1016/j.neuron.2006.03.036.

Adkins, D. E., Åberg, K., McClay, J. L., Bukszár, J., Zhao, Z., Jia, P., et al. (2011). Genomewide pharmacogenomic study of metabolic side effects to antipsychotic drugs. *Molecular Psychiatry*, *16*(3), 321–332. Available from http://dx.doi.org/10.1038/mp.2010.14.

Adolphs, R. (2009). The social brain: Neural basis of social knowledge. *Annual Review of Psychology*.

Alexander-Bloch, A., Lambiotte, R., Roberts, B., Giedd, J., Gogtay, N., & Bullmore, E. (2012). The discovery of population differences in network community structure: New methods and applications to brain functional networks in schizophrenia. *Neuroimage*, *59*(4), 3889–3900. Available from http://dx.doi.org/10.1016/j.neuroimage.2011.11.035.

Anticevic, A., Cole, M. W., Repovs, G., Murray, J. D., Brumbaugh, M. S., Winkler, A. M., et al. (2014). Characterizing thalamo-cortical disturbances in schizophrenia and bipolar illness. *Cerebral Cortex, 24*(12), 3116–3130. Available from http://dx.doi.org/10.1093/cercor/bht165.

Anticevic, A., Haut, K., Murray, J. D., Repovs, G., Yang, G. J., Diehl, C., et al. (2015). Association of thalamic dysconnectivity and conversion to psychosis in youth and young adults at elevated clinical risk. *JAMA Psychiatry, 72*(9), 882–891. Available from http://dx.doi.org/10.1001/jamapsychiatry.2015.0566.

Asami, T., Bouix, S., Whitford, T. J., Shenton, M. E., Salisbury, D. F., & McCarley, R. W. (2012). Longitudinal loss of gray matter volume in patients with first-episode schizophrenia: DARTEL automated analysis and ROI validation. *Neuroimage, 59*(2), 986–996. Available from http://dx.doi.org/10.1016/j.neuroimage.2011.08.066.

Austin, M. W., Ploughman, M., Glynn, L., & Corbett, D. (2014). Aerobic exercise effects on neuroprotection and brain repair following stroke: A systematic review and perspective. *Neuroscience Research, 87*, 8–15. Available from http://dx.doi.org/10.1016/j.neures.2014.06.007.

Bar-Haim, Y., Lamy, D., Pergamin, L., Bakermans-Kranenburg, M. J., & van IJzendoorn, M. H. (2007). Threat-related attentional bias in anxious and nonanxious individuals: A meta-analytic study. *Psychological Bulletin, 133*(1), 1–24. Available from http://dx.doi.org/10.1037/0033-2909.133.1.1.

Bartholomeusz, C. F., & Allott, K. (2012). Neurocognitive and social cognitive approaches for improving functional outcome in early psychosis: Theoretical considerations and current state of evidence. *Schizophrenia Research and Treatment, 2012*, 815315. Available from http://dx.doi.org/10.1155/2012/815315.

Bechdolf, A., Wagner, M., Ruhrmann, S., Harrigan, S., Putzfeld, V., Pukrop, R., et al. (2012). Preventing progression to first-episode psychosis in early initial prodromal states. *The British Journal of Psychiatry, 200*(1), 22–29. Available from http://dx.doi.org/10.1192/bjp.bp.109.066357.

Bell, M., Bryson, G., Greig, T., Corcoran, C., & Wexler, B. E. (2001). Neurocognitive enhancement therapy with work therapy. *Archives of General Psychiatry, 58*(8), 763. Available from http://dx.doi.org/10.1001/archpsyc.58.8.763.

Bell, M., Bryson, G., & Wexler, B. E. (2003). Cognitive remediation of working memory deficits: Durability of training effects in severely impaired and less severely impaired schizophrenia. *Acta Psychiatrica Scandinavica, 108*(2), 101–109. Available from http://dx.doi.org/10.1034/j.1600-0447.2003.00090.x.

Blackwell, S. E., Browning, M., Mathews, A., Pictet, A., Welch, J., Davies, J., et al. (2015). Positive imagery-based cognitive bias modification as a web-based treatment tool for depressed adults: A randomized controlled trial. *Clinical Psychological Science: A Journal of the Association for Psychological Science, 3*(1), 91–111. Available from http://dx.doi.org/10.1177/2167702614560746.

Bor, J., Brunelin, J., d'Amato, T., Costes, N., Suaud-Chagny, M.-F., Saoud, M., & Poulet, E. (2011). Psychiatry research: Neuroimaging. *Psychiatry Research: Neuroimaging, 192*(3), 160–166. Available from http://dx.doi.org/10.1016/j.pscychresns.2010.12.004.

Bora, E., Fornito, A., Radua, J., Walterfang, M., Seal, M., Wood, S. J., et al. (2011). Neuroanatomical abnormalities in schizophrenia: A multimodal voxelwise meta-analysis and meta-regression analysis. *Schizophrenia Research, 127*(1–3), 46–57. Available from http://dx.doi.org/10.1016/j.schres.2010.12.020.

Bracy, O. (1995). *CogReHab software*. Indianapolis (IN): Psychological Software Services.

Brahmbhatt, S. B., Haut, K., Csernansky, J. G., & Barch, D. M. (2006). Neural correlates of verbal and nonverbal working memory deficits in individuals with schizophrenia and their high-risk siblings. *Schizophrenia Research, 87*(1–3), 191–204. Available from http://dx.doi.org/10.1016/j.schres.2006.05.019.

Bressler, S. L., & Menon, V. (2010). Large-scale brain networks in cognition: Emerging methods and principles. *Trends in Cognitive Sciences, 14*(6), 277–290. Available from http://dx.doi.org/10.1016/j.tics.2010.04.004.

Brébion, G., David, A. S., Jones, H., & Pilowsky, L. S. (2004). Semantic organization and verbal memory efficiency in patients with schizophrenia. *Neuropsychology*, *18*(2), 378–383. Available from http://dx.doi.org/10.1037/0894-4105.18.2.378.

Brüne, M., Abdel-Hamid, M., Lehmkämper, C., & Sonntag, C. (2007). Mental state attribution, neurocognitive functioning, and psychopathology: What predicts poor social competence in schizophrenia best? *Schizophrenia Research*, *92*(1–3), 151–159. Available from http://dx.doi.org/10.1016/j.schres.2007.01.006.

Buonomano, D. V., & Merzenich, M. M. (1998). Cortical plasticity: From synapses to maps. *Annual Review of Neuroscience*, *21*, 149–186. Available from http://dx.doi.org/10.1146/annurev.neuro.21.1.149.

Caeyenberghs, K., Verhelst, H., Clemente, A., & Wilson, P. H. (2016). Mapping the functional connectome in traumatic brain injury: What can graph metrics tell us? *Neuroimage*. Available from http://dx.doi.org/10.1016/j.neuroimage.2016.12.003.

Calkins, A. W., McMorran, K. E., Siegle, G. J., & Otto, M. W. (2015). The effects of computerized cognitive control training on community adults with depressed mood. *Behavioural and Cognitive Psychotherapy*, *43*(5), 578–589. Available from http://dx.doi.org/10.1017/S1352465814000046.

Cannon, T. D., Chung, Y., He, G., Sun, D., Jacobson, A., van Erp, T. G. M., et al. (2014). Progressive reduction in cortical thickness as psychosis develops: A multisite longitudinal neuroimaging study of youth at elevated clinical risk. *Biological Psychiatry*, *77*(2), 147–157. Available from http://dx.doi.org/10.1016/j.biopsych.2014.05.023.

Carrión, R. E., Goldberg, T. E., McLaughlin, D., Auther, A. M., Correll, C. U., & Cornblatt, B. A. (2011). Impact of neurocognition on social and role functioning in individuals at clinical high risk for psychosis. *American Journal of Psychiatry*, *168*(8), 806–813. Available from http://dx.doi.org/10.1176/appi.ajp.2011.10081209.

Chen, Q., Chen, X., He, X., Wang, L., Wang, K., & Qiu, B. (2016). Aberrant structural and functional connectivity in the salience network and central executive network circuit in schizophrenia. *Neuroscience Letters*, *627*, 178–184. Available from http://dx.doi.org/10.1016/j.neulet.2016.05.035.

Cole, M. W., Anticevic, A., Repovs, G., & Barch, D. (2011). Variable global dysconnectivity and individual differences in schizophrenia. *Biological Psychiatry*, *70*(1), 43–50. Available from http://dx.doi.org/10.1016/j.biopsych.2011.02.010.

Combs, D. R., Adams, S. D., Penn, D. L., Roberts, D., Tiegreen, J., & Stem, P. (2007). Social cognition and interaction training (SCIT) for inpatients with schizophrenia spectrum disorders: Preliminary findings. *Schizophrenia Research*, *91*(1–3), 112–116. Available from http://dx.doi.org/10.1016/j.schres.2006.12.010.

Cristea, I. A., Kok, R. N., & Cuijpers, P. (2015). Efficacy of cognitive bias modification interventions in anxiety and depression: Meta-analysis. *British Journal of Psychiatry*, *206*(1), 7–16. Available from http://dx.doi.org/10.1192/bjp.bp.114.146761.

Dale, C. L., Findlay, A. M., Adcock, R. A., Vertinski, M., Fisher, M., Genevsky, A., et al. (2010). Timing is everything: Neural response dynamics during syllable processing and its relation to higher-order cognition in schizophrenia and healthy comparison subjects. *International Journal of Psychophysiology: Official Journal of the International Organization of Psychophysiology*, *75*(2), 183–193. Available from http://dx.doi.org/10.1016/j.ijpsycho.2009.10.009.

Delvecchio, G., Sugranyes, G., & Frangou, S. (2013). Evidence of diagnostic specificity in the neural correlates of facial affect processing in bipolar disorder and schizophrenia: A meta-analysis of functional imaging studies. *Psychological Medicine*, *43*(3), 553–569. Available from http://dx.doi.org/10.1017/S0033291712001432.

Dodell-Feder, D., DeLisi, L. E., & Hooker, C. I. (2014). The relationship between default mode network connectivity and social functioning in individuals at familial high-risk for schizophrenia. *Schizophrenia Research*, *156*(1), 87–95.

Eack, S. M., Hogarty, G. E., Cho, R. Y., Prasad, K. M. R., Greenwald, D. P., Hogarty, S. S., & Keshavan, M. S. (2010). Neuroprotective effects of cognitive enhancement therapy against gray matter loss in early schizophrenia: Results from a 2-year randomized controlled trial. *Archives of General Psychiatry, 67*(7), 674–682. Available from http://dx.doi.org/10.1001/archgenpsychiatry.2010.63.

Eack, S. M., Newhill, C. E., & Keshavan, M. S. (2016). Cognitive enhancement therapy improves resting-state functional connectivity in early course schizophrenia. *Journal of the Society for Social Work and Research, 7*(2), 211–230. Available from http://dx.doi.org/10.1086/686538.

Ellison-Wright, I., & Bullmore, E. (2009). Meta-analysis of diffusion tensor imaging studies in schizophrenia. *Schizophrenia Research, 108*(1–3), 3–10. Available from http://dx.doi.org/10.1016/j.schres.2008.11.021.

Erickson, K. I., Leckie, R. L., & Weinstein, A. M. (2014). Physical activity, fitness, and gray matter volume. *Neurobiology of Aging, 35*(Suppl. 2), S20–S28. Available from http://dx.doi.org/10.1016/j.neurobiolaging.2014.03.034.

Fett, A.-K. J., Viechtbauer, W., Dominguez, M.-D.-G., Penn, D. L., van Os, J., & Krabbendam, L. (2011). The relationship between neurocognition and social cognition with functional outcomes in schizophrenia: A meta-analysis. *Neuroscience and Biobehavioral Reviews, 35*(3), 573–588. Available from http://dx.doi.org/10.1016/j.neubiorev.2010.07.001.

Fisher, M., Herman, A., Stephens, D. B., & Vinogradov, S. (2016). Neuroscience-informed computer-assisted cognitive training in schizophrenia. *Annals of the New York Academy of Sciences, 1366*(1), 90–114. Available from http://dx.doi.org/10.1111/nyas.13042.

Fisher, M., Holland, C., Subramaniam, K., & Vinogradov, S. (2010). Neuroplasticity-based cognitive training in schizophrenia: An interim report on the effects 6 months later. *Schizophrenia Bulletin, 36*(4), 869–879. Available from http://dx.doi.org/10.1093/schbul/sbn170.

Fisher, M., Holland, C., Merzenich, M. M., & Vinogradov, S., M.D. (2009). Using neuroplasticity-based auditory training to improve verbal memory in schizophrenia. *American Journal of Psychiatry, 166*(7), 805–811. Available from http://dx.doi.org/10.1176/appi.ajp.2009.08050757.

Fisher, M., Loewy, R., Hardy, K., Schlosser, D., & Vinogradov, S. (2013). Cognitive interventions targeting brain plasticity in the prodromal and early phases of schizophrenia. *Annual Review of Clinical Psychology, 9*, 435–463. Available from http://dx.doi.org/10.1146/annurev-clinpsy-032511-143134.

Fox, M. D., Corbetta, M., Snyder, A. Z., Vincent, J. L., & Raichle, M. E. (2006). Spontaneous neuronal activity distinguishes human dorsal and ventral attention systems. *Proceedings of the National Academy of Sciences, 103*(26), 10046–10051. Available from http://dx.doi.org/10.1073/pnas.0604187103.

Fusar-Poli, P., Borgwardt, S., Bechdolf, A., Addington, J., Riecher-Rössler, A., Schultze-Lutter, F., et al. (2013). The psychosis high-risk state. *JAMA Psychiatry, 70*(1), 107–120. Available from http://dx.doi.org/10.1001/jamapsychiatry.2013.269.

Fusar-Poli, P., Deste, G., Smieskova, R., Barlati, S., Yung, A. R., Howes, O., et al. (2012). Cognitive functioning in prodromal psychosis: A meta-analysis. *Archives of General Psychiatry, 69*(6), 562–571. Available from http://dx.doi.org/10.1001/archgenpsychiatry.2011.1592.

Ganguly, K., & Poo, M.-M. (2013). Activity-dependent neural plasticity from bench to bedside. *Neuron, 80*(3), 729–741. Available from http://dx.doi.org/10.1016/j.neuron.2013.10.028.

Gazzaley, A. (2011). Influence of early attentional modulation on working memory. *Neuropsychologia, 49*(6), 1410–1424. Available from http://dx.doi.org/10.1016/j.neuropsychologia.2010.12.022.

Geib, B. R., Stanley, M. L., Dennis, N. A., Woldorff, M. G., & Cabeza, R. (2017). From hippocampus to whole-brain: The role of integrative processing in episodic memory retrieval. *Human Brain Mapping*. Available from http://dx.doi.org/10.1002/hbm.23518.

Germine, L. T., Garrido, L., Bruce, L., & Hooker, C. (2011). Social anhedonia is associated with neural abnormalities during face emotion processing. *Neuroimage*, *58*(3), 935–945. Available from http://dx.doi.org/10.1016/j.neuroimage.2011.06.059.

Glantz, L. A., & Lewis, D. A. (2000). Decreased dendritic spine density on prefrontal cortical pyramidal neurons in schizophrenia [see comments]. *Archives of General Psychiatry*, *57*(1), 65–73.

Goff, D. C., Hill, M., & Barch, D. (2011). The treatment of cognitive impairment in schizophrenia. *Pharmacology, Biochemistry, and Behavior*, *99*(2), 245–253. Available from http://dx.doi.org/10.1016/j.pbb.2010.11.009.

Green, M. F. (1996). What are the functional consequences of neurocognitive deficits in schizophrenia? *American Journal of Psychiatry*, *153*, 321–330.

Green, M. F., Horan, W. P., & Lee, J. (2015). Social cognition in schizophrenia. *Nature Reviews Neuroscience*, *16*(10), 620–631. Available from http://dx.doi.org/10.1038/nrn4005.

Green, M. F., Kern, R. S., & Heaton, R. K. (2004). Longitudinal studies of cognition and functional outcome in schizophrenia: Implications for MATRICS. *Schizophrenia Research*, *72*(1), 41–51. Available from http://dx.doi.org/10.1016/j.schres.2004.09.009.

Griffin, É. W., Mullally, S., Foley, C., Warmington, S. A., O'Mara, S. M., & Kelly, Á. M. (2011). Physiology & behavior. *Physiology & Behavior*, *104*(5), 934–941. Available from http://dx.doi.org/10.1016/j.physbeh.2011.06.005.

Grynszpan, O., Perbal, S., Pelissolo, A., Fossati, P., Jouvent, R., Dubal, S., & Perez-Diaz, F. (2011). Efficacy and specificity of computer-assisted cognitive remediation in schizophrenia: A meta-analytical study. *Psychological Medicine*, *41*(1), 163–173. Available from http://dx.doi.org/10.1017/S0033291710000607.

Gsottschneider, A., Keller, Z., Pitschel Walz, G., Fröböse, T., Bäuml, J., & Jahn, T. (2011). The role of encoding strategies in the verbal memory performance in patients with schizophrenia. *Journal of Neuropsychology*, *5*(1), 56–72. Available from http://dx.doi.org/10.1348/174866410X497382.

Guimond, S., & Lepage, M. (2015). Cognitive training of self-initiation of semantic encoding strategies in schizophrenia: A pilot study. *Neuropsychological Rehabilitation*, *26*(3), 464–479. Available from http://dx.doi.org/10.1080/09602011.2015.1045526.

Gur, R. E., McGrath, C., Chan, R. M., Schroeder, L., Turner, T., Turetsky, B. I., et al. (2002). An fMRI study of facial emotion processing in patients with schizophrenia. *American Journal of Psychiatry*, *159*, 1992–1999.

Gusnard, D. A., Akbudak, E., Shulman, G. L., & Raichle, M. E. (2001). Medial prefrontal cortex and self-referential mental activity: Relation to a default mode of brain function. *Proceedings of the National Academy of Sciences of the United States of America*, *98*(7), 4259–4264.

Handschin, C., & Spiegelman, B. M. (2008). The role of exercise and PGC1α in inflammation and chronic disease. *Nature*, *454*(7203), 463–469. Available from http://dx.doi.org/10.1038/nature07206.

Harrison, B. J., Pujol, J., López-Solà, M., Hernández-Ribas, R., Deus, J., Ortiz, H., et al. (2008). Consistency and functional specialization in the default mode brain network. *PNAS*, *105*(28), 9781–9786. Available from http://dx.doi.org/10.1073/pnas.0711791105.

Harvey, P. D. (2010). Cognitive functioning and disability in schizophrenia. *Current Directions in Psychological Science*, *19*(4), 249–254. Available from http://dx.doi.org/10.1177/0963721410378033.

Haut, K. M., & MacDonald, A. W. (2010). Persecutory delusions and the perception of trustworthiness in unfamiliar faces in schizophrenia. *Psychiatry Research*, *178*(3), 456–460. Available from http://dx.doi.org/10.1016/j.psychres.2010.04.015.

Haut, K. M., Karlsgodt, K. H., Bilder, R. M., Congdon, E., Freimer, N. B., London, E. D., et al. (2015). Memory systems in schizophrenia: Modularity is preserved but deficits are generalized. *Schizophrenia Research, 168*(1–2), 223–230. Available from http://dx. doi.org/10.1016/j.schres.2015.08.014.

Haut, K. M., Lim, K. O., & MacDonald, A. (2010). Prefrontal cortical changes following cognitive training in patients with chronic schizophrenia: Effects of practice, generalization, and specificity. *Neuropsychopharmacology, 35*(9), 1850–1859. Available from http://dx.doi.org/10.1038/npp.2010.52.

Haut, K. M., Schvarcz, A., Cannon, T. D., & Bearden, C. E. (2016). *Neurodevelopmental theories of schizophrenia: Twenty-first century perspectives* (pp. 1–46). Hoboken, NJ, USA: John Wiley & Sons, Inc. Available from http://doi.org/10.1002/9781119125556.devpsy223.

Haut, K. M., van Erp, T. G. M., Knowlton, B., Bearden, C. E., Subotnik, K., Ventura, J., et al. (2014). Contributions of feature binding during encoding and functional connectivity of the medial temporal lobe structures to episodic memory deficits across the prodromal and first-episode phases of schizophrenia. *Clinical Psychological Science.* Available from http://dx.doi.org/10.1177/2167702614533949.

Hogarty, G. E., & Flesher, S. (1999). Practice principles of cognitive enhancement therapy for schizophrenia. *Schizophrenia Bulletin, 25*(4), 693–708.

Hogarty, G. E., Flesher, S., Ulrich, R. F., Carter, M., Greenwald, D., Pogue-Geile, M. F., et al. (2004). Cognitive enhancement therapy for schizophrenia: Effects of a 2-year randomized trial on cognition and behavior. *Arch Gen Psychiatry, 61*, 866–876.

Hooker, C. I., Bruce, L., Fisher, M., Verosky, S. C., Miyakawa, A., D'Esposito, M., et al. (2013). The influence of combined cognitive plus social-cognitive training on amygdala response during face emotion recognition in schizophrenia. *Psychiatry Research, 213*(2), 99–107. Available from http://dx.doi.org/10.1016/j.pscychresns. 2013.04.001.

Hooker, C. I., Bruce, L., Fisher, M., Verosky, S. C., Miyakawa, A., & Vinogradov, S. (2012). Neural activity during emotion recognition after combined cognitive plus social cognitive training in schizophrenia. *Schizophrenia Research, 139*(1–3), 53–59. Available from http://dx.doi.org/10.1016/j.schres.2012.05.009.

Hooker, C. I., Bruce, L., Lincoln, S. H., Fisher, M., & Vinogradov, S. (2011). Theory of mind skills are related to gray matter volume in the ventromedial prefrontal cortex in schizophrenia. *Biological Psychiatry, 70*(12), 1169–1178.

Hooker, C. I., Carol, E. E., Eisenstein, T. J., Yin, H., Lincoln, S. H., Tully, L. M., et al. (2014). A pilot study of cognitive training in clinical high risk for psychosis: Initial evidence of cognitive benefit. *Schizophrenia Research, 157*(1–3), 314–316. Available from http://dx.doi.org/10.1016/j.schres.2014.05.034.

Hooker, C., & Park, S. (2002). Emotion processing and its relationship to social functioning in schizophrenia patients. *Psychiatry Research, 112*(1), 41–50.

Horan, W. P., Kern, R. S., Shokat-Fadai, K., Sergi, M. J., Wynn, J. K., & Green, M. F. (2009). Social cognitive skills training in schizophrenia: An initial efficacy study of stabilized outpatients. *Schizophrenia Research, 107*(1), 47–54. Available from http://dx.doi.org/ 10.1016/j.schres.2008.09.006.

Joormann, J., & Tran, T. B. (2009). Rumination and intentional forgetting of emotional material. *Cognition and Emotion, 23*(6), 1233–1246. Available from http://dx.doi.org/ 10.1080/02699930802416735.

Jukuri, T., Kiviniemi, V., Nikkinen, J., Miettunen, J., Mäki, P., Jääskeläinen, E., et al. (2013). Default mode network in young people with familial risk for psychosis – The Oulu brain and mind study. *Schizophrenia Research, 143*(2–3), 239–245. Available from http://dx.doi.org/10.1016/j.schres.2012.11.020.

Jukuri, T., Kiviniemi, V., Nikkinen, J., Miettunen, J., Mäki, P., Mukkala, S., et al. (2015). Central executive network in young people with familial risk for psychosis – The

Oulu brain and mind study. *Schizophrenia Research, 161*(2−3), 177−183. Available from http://dx.doi.org/10.1016/j.schres.2014.11.003.

Kahn, R. S., & Keefe, R. S. (2013). Schizophrenia is a cognitive illness: Time for a change in focus. *JAMA Psychiatry, 70*(10), 1107−1112. Available from http://dx.doi.org/10.1001/jamapsychiatry.2013.155.

Karlsgodt, K. H., Sun, D., Jimenez, A. M., Lutkenhoff, E. S., Willhite, R., van Erp, T. G. M., & Cannon, T. D. (2008). Developmental disruptions in neural connectivity in the pathophysiology of schizophrenia. *Development and Psychopathology, 20*(04), 1297−1327. Available from http://dx.doi.org/10.1017/S095457940800062X.

Keefe, R. S. E. (2008). Should cognitive impairment be included in the diagnostic criteria for schizophrenia? *World Psychiatry, 7*(1), 22−28.

Keshavan, M. S., Eack, S. M., Prasad, K. M., Haller, C. S., & Cho, R. Y. (2016). Longitudinal functional brain imaging study in early course schizophrenia before and after cognitive enhancement therapy. *Neuroimage.* Available from http://dx.doi.org/10.1016/j.neuroimage.2016.11.060.

Keshavan, M. S., Eack, S. M., Wojtalik, J. A., Prasad, K. M. R., Francis, A. N., Bhojraj, T. S., et al. (2011). A broad cortical reserve accelerates response to cognitive enhancement therapy in early course schizophrenia. *Schizophrenia Research, 130*(1−3), 123−129. Available from http://dx.doi.org/10.1016/j.schres.2011.05.001.

Klimecki, O. M., Leiberg, S., Ricard, M., & Singer, T. (2014). Differential pattern of functional brain plasticity after compassion and empathy training. *Social Cognitive and Affective Neuroscience, 9*(6), 873−879. Available from http://dx.doi.org/10.1093/scan/nst060.

Lee, J., Zaki, J., Harvey, P. O., Ochsner, K., & Green, M. F. (2011). Schizophrenia patients are impaired in empathic accuracy. *Psychological Medicine, 41*(11), 2297−2304. Available from http://dx.doi.org/10.1017/S0033291711000614.

Loewy, R., Fisher, M., Schlosser, D. A., Biagianti, B., Stuart, B., Mathalon, D. H., & Vinogradov, S. (2016). Intensive auditory cognitive training improves verbal memory in adolescents and young adults at clinical high risk for psychosis. *Schizophrenia Bulletin.* Available from http://doi.org/10.1093/schbul/sbw009.

Lövdén, M., Wenger, E., Mårtensson, J., Lindenberger, U., & Bäckman, L. (2013). Structural brain plasticity in adult learning and development. *Neuroscience and Biobehavioral Reviews, 37*(9 Pt B), 2296−2310. Available from http://dx.doi.org/10.1016/j.neubiorev.2013.02.014.

Lui, S., Deng, W., Huang, X., Jiang, L., Ma, X., Chen, H., et al. (2009). Association of cerebral deficits with clinical symptoms in antipsychotic-naive first-episode schizophrenia: An optimized voxel-based morphometry and resting state functional connectivity study. *American Journal of Psychiatry, 166*(2), 196−205. Available from http://dx.doi.org/10.1176/appi.ajp.2008.08020183.

Malchow, B., Keller, K., Hasan, A., Dörfler, S., Schneider-Axmann, T., Hillmer-Vogel, U., et al. (2015). Effects of endurance training combined with cognitive remediation on everyday functioning, symptoms, and cognition in multiepisode schizophrenia patients. *Schizophrenia Bulletin, 41*(4), 847−858. Available from http://dx.doi.org/10.1093/schbul/sbv020.

Marker, K. (n.d.). Cogpack. Ladenburg, Germany: Marker Software.

Marsh, P. J., Luckett, G., Russell, T., Coltheart, M., & Green, M. J. (2012). Effects of facial emotion recognition remediation on visual scanning of novel face stimuli. *Schizophrenia Research, 141*(2−3), 234−240. Available from http://dx.doi.org/10.1016/j.schres.2012.08.006.

McDermott, L. M., & Ebmeier, K. P. (2009). A meta-analysis of depression severity and cognitive function. *Journal of Affective Disorders, 119*(1−3), 1−8. Available from http://dx.doi.org/10.1016/j.jad.2009.04.022.

McEvoy, J. P. (2007). The costs of schizophrenia. *Journal of Clinical Psychiatry, 68*(Suppl. 14), 4–7.

McGorry, P. (2011). Transition to adulthood: The critical period for pre-emptive, disease-modifying care for schizophrenia and related disorders. *Schizophrenia Bulletin, 37*(3), 524–530. Available from http://dx.doi.org/10.1093/schbul/sbr027.

McGurk, S., Twamley, E. W., Sitzer, D. I., McHugo, G. J., & Mueser, K. T. (2007). A meta-analysis of cognitive remediation in schizophrenia. *American Journal of Psychiatry, 164*, 1791–1802.

Medalia, A., & Saperstein, A. (2011). The role of motivation for treatment success. *Schizophrenia Bulletin, 37*(Suppl. 2), S122–S128. Available from http://dx.doi.org/10.1093/schbul/sbr063.

Medalia, A., & Saperstein, A. M. (2013). Does cognitive remediation for schizophrenia improve functional outcomes? *Current Opinion in Psychiatry, 26*(2), 151–157. Available from http://dx.doi.org/10.1097/YCO.0b013e32835dcbd4.

Medalia, A., Dorn, H., & Watras-Gans, S. (2000). Treating problem solving deficits on an acute psychiatric inpatient unit. *Psychiatry Research, 97*, 79–88.

Medalia, A., Revheim, N., & Casey, M. (2002). Remediation of problem-solving skills in schizophrenia: Evidence of a persistent effect. *Schizophrenia Research, 57*(2–3), 165–171.

Menon, V., & Uddin, L. Q. (2010). Saliency, switching, attention and control: A network model of insula function. *Brain Structure and Function, 214*(5–6), 655–667. Available from http://dx.doi.org/10.1007/s00429-010-0262-0.

Merzenich, M. M., Van Vleet, T. M., & Nahum, M. (2014). Brain plasticity-based therapeutics. *Frontiers in Human Neuroscience, 8*, 385. Available from http://dx.doi.org/10.3389/fnhum.2014.00385.

Minzenberg, M. J., Laird, A. R., Thelen, S., Carter, C. S., & Glahn, D. C. (2009). Meta-analysis of 41 functional neuroimaging studies of executive function in schizophrenia. *Archives of General Psychiatry, 66*(8), 811–822. Available from http://dx.doi.org/10.1001/archgenpsychiatry.2009.91.

Mogoaşe, C., David, D., & Koster, E. H. W. (2014). Clinical efficacy of attentional bias modification procedures: An updated meta-analysis. *Journal of Clinical Psychology, 70*(12), 1133–1157. Available from http://dx.doi.org/10.1002/jclp.22081.

Morrison, A. P., Hutton, P., Wardle, M., Spencer, H., Barratt, S., Brabban, A., et al. (2012). Cognitive therapy for people with a schizophrenia spectrum diagnosis not taking antipsychotic medication: An exploratory trial. *Psychological Medicine, 42*(5), 1049–1056. Available from http://dx.doi.org/10.1017/S0033291711001899.

Motter, J. N., Pimontel, M. A., Rindskopf, D., Devanand, D. P., RMeeusen, K. M. E., & Sneed, J. R. (2016). Computerized cognitive training and functional recovery in major depressive disorder: A meta-analysis. *Journal of Affective Disorders, 189*, 184–191. Available from http://dx.doi.org/10.1016/j.jad.2015.09.022.

Murthy, N. V., Mahncke, H., Wexler, B. E., Maruff, P., Inamdar, A., Zucchetto, M., et al. (2012). Computerized cognitive remediation training for schizophrenia: An open label, multi-site, multinational methodology study. *Schizophrenia Research, 139*(1–3), 87–91. Available from http://dx.doi.org/10.1016/j.schres.2012.01.042.

Nahum, M., Fisher, M., Loewy, R., Poelke, G., Ventura, J., Nuechterlein, K. H., et al. (2014). A novel, online social cognitive training program for young adults with schizophrenia: A pilot study. *Schizophrenia Research. Cognition, 1*(1), e11–e19. Available from http://dx.doi.org/10.1016/j.scog.2014.01.003.

Nahum, M., Lee, H., & Merzenich, M. M. (2013). Principles of neuroplasticity-based rehabilitation. *Progress in Brain Research, 207*, 141–171. Available from http://dx.doi.org/10.1016/B978-0-444-63327-9.00009-6.

Nuechterlein, K. H., Ventura, J., McEwen, S. C., Gretchen-Doorly, D., Vinogradov, S., & Subotnik, K. L. (2016). Enhancing cognitive training through aerobic exercise after a first schizophrenia episode: Theoretical conception and pilot study. *Schizophrenia Bulletin, 42*(suppl 1), S44−S52. Available from http://dx.doi.org/10.1093/schbul/sbw007.

Ochsner, K. N., Silvers, J. A., & Buhle, J. T. (2012). Functional imaging studies of emotion regulation: A synthetic review and evolving model of the cognitive control of emotion. *Annals of the New York Academy of Sciences, 1251*, E1−24. Available from http://dx.doi.org/10.1111/j.1749-6632.2012.06751.x.

Oertel-Knöchel, V., Mehler, P., Thiel, C., Steinbrecher, K., Malchow, B., Tesky, V., et al. (2014). Effects of aerobic exercise on cognitive performance and individual psychopathology in depressive and schizophrenia patients. *European Archives of Psychiatry & Clinical Neuroscience, 264*(7), 589−604. Available from http://dx.doi.org/10.1007/s00406-014-0485-9.

Pajonk, F. G., Wobrock, T., Gruber, O., & Scherk, H. (2010). JAMA network | Archives of General Psychiatry | Hippocampal Plasticity in Response to Exercise in Schizophrenia. *Archives of General.*

Palaniyappan, L., & Liddle, P. F. (2012). Does the salience network play a cardinal role in psychosis? An emerging hypothesis of insular dysfunction. *Journal of Psychiatry & Neuroscience, 37*(1), 17−27. Available from http://dx.doi.org/10.1503/jpn.100176.

Panizzutti, R., Hamilton, S. P., & Vinogradov, S. (2013). Genetic correlate of cognitive training response in schizophrenia. *Neuropharmacology, 64*, 264−267. Available from http://dx.doi.org/10.1016/j.neuropharm.2012.07.048.

Pankow, A., Deserno, L., Walter, M., Fydrich, T., Bermpohl, F., Schlagenhauf, F., & Heinz, A. (2015). Reduced default mode network connectivity in schizophrenia patients. *Schizophrenia Research, 165*(1), 90−93. Available from http://dx.doi.org/10.1016/j.schres.2015.03.027.

Penadés, R., Pujol, N., Catalán, R., & Massana, G. (2013). Brain effects of cognitive remediation therapy in schizophrenia: A structural and functional neuroimaging study. *Biological Psychiatry, 73*(10), 1015−1023.

Penn, D., Roberts, D. L., Munt, E. D., Silverstein, E., Jones, N., & Sheitman, B. B. (2005). A pilot study of social cognition and interaction training (SCIT) for schizophrenia. *Schizophrenia Research, 80*, 357−359.

Pereira, A. C., Huddleston, D. E., Brickman, A. M., Sosunov, A. A., Hen, R., McKhann, G. M., et al. (2007). An in vivo correlate of exercise-induced neurogenesis in the adult dentate gyrus. *Proceedings of the National Academy of Sciences USA, 104*(13), 5638−5643. Available from http://dx.doi.org/10.1073/pnas.0611721104.

Petanjek, Z., Judaš, M., Šimić, G., Rašin, M. R., Uylings, H. B., Rakic, P., & Kostović, I. (2011). Extraordinary neoteny of synaptic spines in the human prefrontal cortex. *Proceedings of the National Academy of Sciences USA, 108*(32), 13281−13286.

Pinkham, A. E., Penn, D. L., Perkins, D. O., Graham, K. A., & Siegel, M. (2007). Emotion perception and social skill over the course of psychosis: A comparison of individuals "at-risk" for psychosis and individuals with early and chronic schizophrenia spectrum illness. *Cognitive Neuropsychiatry, 12*(3), 198−212. Available from http://dx.doi.org/10.1080/13546800600985557.

Popov, T., Jordanov, T., Rockstroh, B., Elbert, T., Merzenich, M. M., & Miller, G. A. (2011). Specific cognitive training normalizes auditory sensory gating in schizophrenia: A randomized trial. *Biological Psychiatry, 69*(5), 465−471. Available from http://dx.doi.org/10.1016/j.biopsych.2010.09.028.

Popova, P., Popov, T. G., Wienbruch, C., Carolus, A. M., Miller, G. A., & Rockstroh, B. S. (2014). Changing facial affect recognition in schizophrenia: Effects of training on brain dynamics. *NeuroImage: Clinical, 6*, 156−165. Available from http://dx.doi.org/10.1016/j.nicl.2014.08.026.

Radhakrishnan, R., Kiluk, B. D., & Tsai, J. (2016). A meta-analytic review of non-specific effects in randomized controlled trials of cognitive remediation for schizophrenia.

The Psychiatric Quarterly, 87(1), 57—62. Available from http://dx.doi.org/10.1007/s11126-015-9362-6.

Radom-Aizik, S., Zaldivar, F., Leu, S. Y., Galassetti, P., & Cooper, D. M. (2007). Effects of 30 min of aerobic exercise on gene expression in human neutrophils. *Journal of Applied Physiology, 104*(1), 236—243. Available from http://dx.doi.org/10.1152/japplphysiol.00872.2007.

Raichle, M. E., MacLeod, A. M., Snyder, A. Z., Powers, W. J., Gusnard, D. A., & Shulman, G. L. (2001). A default mode of brain function. *Proceeding of the National Academy of Sciences USA, 98*(2), 676—682. Available from http://dx.doi.org/10.1073/pnas.98.2.676.

Ramsay, I. S., & MacDonald, A. W. (2015). Brain correlates of cognitive remediation in schizophrenia: Activation likelihood analysis shows preliminary evidence of neural target engagement. *Schizophrenia Bulletin.*

Ramsay, I. S., Nienow, T. M., & MacDonald, A. W. (2016). Increases in intrinsic thalamocortical connectivity and overall cognition following cognitive remediation in chronic schizophrenia. *Biological Psychiatry: Cognitive Neuroscience and Neuroimaging.*

Ramsay, I. S., Nienow, T. M., Marggraf, M. P., & MacDonald, A. W. (2017). Neuroplastic changes in patients with schizophrenia undergoing cognitive remediation: Triple-blind trial. *The British Journal of Psychiatry, 115,* 171496. Available from http://dx.doi.org/10.1192/bjp.bp.115.171496.

Rauchensteiner, S., Kawohl, W., Ozgürdal, S., Littmann, E., Gudlowski, Y., Witthaus, H., et al. (2011). Test-performance after cognitive training in persons at risk mental state of schizophrenia and patients with schizophrenia. *Psychiatry Research, 185*(3), 334—339. Available from http://dx.doi.org/10.1016/j.psychres.2009.09.003.

Regenbogen, C., Kellermann, T., Seubert, J., Schneider, D. A., Gur, R. E., Derntl, B., et al. (2015). Neural responses to dynamic multimodal stimuli and pathology-specific impairments of social cognition in schizophrenia and depression. *The British Journal of Psychiatry, 206*(3), 198—205. Available from http://dx.doi.org/10.1192/bjp.bp.113.143040.

Russell, T. A., Chu, E., & Phillips, M. L. (2006). A pilot study to investigate the effectiveness of emotion recognition remediation in schizophrenia using the micro-expression training tool. *British Journal of Clinical Psychology, 45*(4), 579—583. Available from http://dx.doi.org/10.1348/014466505X90866.

Sacks, S., Fisher, M., Garrett, C., Alexander, P., Holland, C., Rose, D., et al. (2013). Combining computerized social cognitive training with neuroplasticity-based auditory training in schizophrenia. *Clinical Schizophrenia & Related Psychoses, 7*(2), 78—86A. Available from http://dx.doi.org/10.3371/CSRP.SAFI.012513.

Sarapas, C., Shankman, S. A., Harrow, M., & Goldberg, J. F. (2012). Parsing trait and state effects of depression severity on neurocognition: Evidence from a 26-year longitudinal study. *Journal of Abnormal Psychology, 121*(4), 830—837. Available from http://dx.doi.org/10.1037/a0028141.

Schaefer, J., Giangrande, E., Weinberger, D. R., & Dickinson, D. (2013). The global cognitive impairment in schizophrenia: Consistent over decades and around the world. *Schizophrenia Research, 150*(1), 42—50. Available from http://dx.doi.org/10.1016/j.schres.2013.07.009.

Schweizer, S., Grahn, J., Hampshire, A., Mobbs, D., & Dalgleish, T. (2013). Training the emotional brain: Improving affective control through emotional working memory training. *Journal of Neuroscience, 33*(12), 5301—5311. Available from http://dx.doi.org/10.1523/JNEUROSCI.2593-12.2013.

Seeley, W., Menon, V., Schatzberg, A., Keller, J., Glover, G., Kenna, H., et al. (2007). Dissociable intrinsic conectivity networks for salience processing and executive control. *Journal of Neuroscience, 27*(9), 2349—2356.

Seidman, L. J., Cherkerzian, S., Goldstein, J. M., Agnew-Blais, J., Tsuang, M. T., & Buka, S. L. (2013). Neuropsychological performance and family history in children at age 7 who develop adult schizophrenia or bipolar psychosis in the New England Family Studies. *Psychological Medicine*, 43(01), 119—131. Available from http://dx.doi.org/10.1017/S0033291712000773.

Siegle, G. J., Price, R. B., & Jones, N. P. (2014). You gotta work at it: Pupillary indices of task focus are prognostic for response to a neurocognitive intervention for rumination in depression. *Clinical Psychological Science*, 2(4), 455—471.

Simons, D. J., Boot, W. R., Charness, N., Gathercole, S. E., Chabris, C. F., Hambrick, D. Z., & Stine-Morrow, E. A. L. (2016). Do "brain-training" programs work? *Psychological Science in the Public Interest*, 17(3), 103—186. Available from http://dx.doi.org/10.1177/1529100616661983.

Snitz, B. E., MacDonald, A. W., & Carter, C. S. (2006). Cognitive deficits in unaffected first-degree relatives of schizophrenia patients: A meta-analytic review of putative endophenotypes. *Schizophrenia Bulletin*, 32(1), 179—194. Available from http://dx.doi.org/10.1093/schbul/sbi048.

Sridharan, D., Levitin, D. J., & Menon, V. (2008). A critical role for the right fronto-insular cortex in switching between central-executive and default-mode networks. *Proceedings of the National Academy of Sciences*, 105(34), 12569—12574. Available from http://dx.doi.org/10.1073/pnas.0800005105.

Subramaniam, K., Luks, T. L., Fisher, M., Simpson, G. V., Nagarajan, S., & Vinogradov, S. (2012). Computerized cognitive training restores neural activity within the reality monitoring network in schizophrenia. *Neuron*, 73(4), 842—853. Available from http://dx.doi.org/10.1016/j.neuron.2011.12.024.

Subramaniam, K., Luks, T. L., Garrett, C., Chung, C., Fisher, M., Nagarajan, S., & Vinogradov, S. (2014). Intensive cognitive training in schizophrenia enhances working memory and associated prefrontal cortical efficiency in a manner that drives long-term functional gains. *Neuroimage*, 99, 281—292. Available from http://dx.doi.org/10.1016/j.neuroimage.2014.05.057.

Sultan, K. T., Brown, K. N., & Shi, S.-H. (2013). Production and organization of neocortical interneurons. *Frontiers in Cellular Neuroscience*, 7, 221. Available from http://dx.doi.org/10.3389/fncel.2013.00221.

Sun, D., Phillips, L., Velakoulis, D., Yung, A., McGorry, P. D., Wood, S. J., et al. (2009). Progressive brain structural changes mapped as psychosis develops in "at risk" individuals. *Schizophrenia Research*, 108(1—3), 85—92. Available from http://dx.doi.org/10.1016/j.schres.2008.11.026.

Tandon, R., Gaebel, W., Barch, D. M., Bustillo, J., Gur, R. E., Heckers, S., et al. (2013). Definition and description of schizophrenia in the DSM-5. *Schizophrenia Research*, 150(1), 3—10. Available from http://dx.doi.org/10.1016/j.schres.2013.05.028.

Taylor, C. T., Aupperle, R. L., Flagan, T., Simmons, A. N., Amir, N., Stein, M. B., & Paulus, M. P. (2014). Neural correlates of a computerized attention modification program in anxious subjects. *Social Cognitive and Affective Neuroscience*, 9(9), 1379—1387. Available from http://dx.doi.org/10.1093/scan/nst128.

Tully, L. M., Lincoln, S. H., & Hooker, C. I. (2014). Lateral prefrontal cortex activity during cognitive control of emotion predicts response to social stress in schizophrenia. *NeuroImage: Clinical*, 6, 43—53. Available from http://dx.doi.org/10.1016/j.nicl.2014.08.012.

Twamley, E. W., Jeste, D. V., & Bellack, A. S. (2003). A review of cognitive training in schizophrenia. *Schizophr Bull*, 29(2), 359—382.

Ventura, J., Wilson, S. A., Wood, R. C., & Hellemann, G. S. (2013). Cognitive training at home in schizophrenia is feasible. *Schizophrenia Research*, 143(2—3), 397—398. Available from http://dx.doi.org/10.1016/j.schres.2012.11.033.

Vincent, J. L., Snyder, A. Z., Fox, M. D., Shannon, B. J., Andrews, J. R., Raichle, M. E., & Buckner, R. L. (2006). Coherent spontaneous activity identifies a hippocampal-parietal memory network. *Journal of Neurophysiology, 96*(6), 3517−3531. Available from http://dx.doi.org/10.1152/jn.00048.2006.

Wölwer, W., & Frommann, N. (2011). Social-cognitive remediation in schizophrenia: Generalization of effects of the Training of Affect Recognition (TAR). *Schizophrenia Bulletin, 37*(Suppl. 2), S63−S70. Available from http://dx.doi.org/10.1093/schbul/sbr071.

Wykes, T., Huddy, V., Cellard, C., McGurk, S. R., & Czobor, P. (2011). A meta-analysis of cognitive remediation for schizophrenia: Methodology and effect sizes. *American Journal of Psychiatry, 168*(5), 472−485.

Wykes, T., Reeder, C., Landau, S., Everitt, B., Knapp, M., Patel, A., & Romeo, R. (2007). Cognitive remediation therapy in schizophrenia: Randomised controlled trial. *The British Journal of Psychiatry, 190,* 421−427.

Zai, G., Robbins, T. W., Sahakian, B. J., & Kennedy, J. L. (2017). A review of molecular genetic studies of neurocognitive deficits in schizophrenia. *Neuroscience and Biobehavioral Reviews, 72,* 50−67. Available from http://dx.doi.org/10.1016/j.neubiorev.2016.10.024.

Internet-Based Cognitive Behavior Therapy

*Gerhard Andersson[1,2], Per Carlbring[3]
and Heather D. Hadjistavropoulos[4]*

[1]Linköping University, Linköping, Sweden [2]Karolinska Institute,
Stockholm, Sweden [3]Stockholm University, Stockholm, Sweden
[4]University of Regina, Regina, Canada

BACKGROUND

Although modern information technology is still relatively novel, there are now more than 150 controlled trials using this technology to either complement or deliver cognitive behavior therapy (CBT). The introduction of the internet in society in particular has led to a rapid expansion of research (Andersson, Carlbring, & Lindefors, 2016). Somewhat challenging in reviewing this literature on technology and CBT is that there is a lack of standard nomenclature in the area. Similar interventions are described under different names, but also different interventions are called the same term. For example, web-based CBT and internet-delivered CBT often mean exactly the same thing, whereas a term like computerized CBT can mean a treatment delivered via CD-ROM or an internet-based treatment. In this chapter, we will adhere to the term internet-based CBT (abbreviated ICBT) to refer to treatment programs that are delivered mainly via the internet, although from different platforms such as computers, tablets, and modern mobile phones (smartphones). These ICBT programs always include text, but increasingly also streamed video, audio files, animations and pictures, and interactive features (Andersson, 2015). In this chapter, we will first briefly describe how ICBT is commonly delivered and then move on to a review of the

The Science of Cognitive Behavioral Therapy.
DOI: http://dx.doi.org/10.1016/B978-0-12-803457-6.00021-0

evidence on the use of ICBT for the treatment of anxiety, depression, and somatic disorders. We will comment on innovations in the field as well as the literature on mechanisms of change, including a brief discussion on moderators and mediators of treatment outcome. Finally, we will draw attention to some challenges related to delivering ICBT.

HOW IT IS DONE

As with CBT, in general there is no single way to deliver ICBT and different approaches exist (Andersson, 2015). The presentation here will be based on an approach that has been tested in many controlled trials and also implemented in regular health care. We will, however, also comment on alternative approaches when relevant.

First, ICBT is preceded by a variety of assessment procedures that also partly rely on modern information technology. Validated self-report questionnaires are commonly used in research and clinical practice to monitor process and outcomes of CBT. In ICBT, questionnaires are completely computerized, and research has established that completing self-report measures via the internet is as good (or even better) as paper-and-pencil administration (van Ballegooijen, Riper, Cuijpers, van Oppen, & Smit, 2016). In many protocols, structured diagnostic interviews either in vivo or via telephone are included as part of the assessment procedure as self-report questionnaires are insufficient for the purpose of generating a probable diagnosis. Although it is possible to use web cameras for interviews, in our experience, telephone interviews generate sufficient clinically relevant information, for example, by using the Mini-International Neuropsychiatric Interview (Sheehan et al., 1998) to make a probable diagnosis. In addition to diagnostic information, interviews are commonly used to collect additional information regarding treatment motivation, availability for treatment, risk for suicide, additional problems that were not mentioned in an online screening (e.g., drug and alcohol problems), and also additional information about concurrent and past treatment (e.g., face-to-face treatment, psychotropic medication) history. It should be noted that protocols exist in which diagnostic interviews or diagnostic information is never collected, for example, in association with the program MoodGym (O'Kearney, Kang, Christensen, & Griffiths, 2009) or when treatment is offered as a lower intensity service (e.g., Hadjistavropoulos et al., 2016). Studies suggest that a clinical interview can boost outcome (Johansson & Andersson, 2012), but there are also examples in which diagnostic interviews have not yielded better results (Boettcher, Berger, & Renneberg, 2012a).

Second, ICBT consists of treatment contents, often derived from self-help texts and face-to-face manuals, but also material unique for the treatment format such as streamed videos, audio files, and interactive features within a program. Programs tend to be paced like face-to-face sessions with one "module" (sometime referred to as lesson) per week, with homework assignments between the weeks and a total length resembling face-to-face manuals but sometimes a bit shorter (5–15 weeks). In practice, this often means book length of material but divided into pedagogical sections. Some clients prefer to read text on paper and hence that can be offered as an option. All homework assignments, including registration sheets, are embedded within one system and do not require printing and uploading. In terms of program structure, elements like rationale, psychoeducation, case examples, instructions on how to identify and challenge thoughts, do exposure, and so forth are included depending on the condition at hand. For example, in the treatment of posttraumatic stress, instructions on how to write a trauma narrative are included (Ivarsson et al., 2014). All programs tend to end with a summary and advice on how to maintain gains and prevent relapse. It should be mentioned that there are other approaches, such as psychodynamically informed internet treatment, bias modification training, and even physical exercise programs developed and tested in trials (Andersson, 2016), but most programs are based on CBT and related approaches such as acceptance and commitment therapy.

Third, in guided ICBT there is an identified therapist who is in regular contact with the client most commonly by email but also at times by telephone. Email contact is contained in a secure online environment (Vlaescu, Carlbring, Lunner, & Andersson, 2015), resembling internet banking, with encrypted communication and a double-authentication procedure at login (at least in the Swedish systems). A typical therapist spends 5–15 min each week per client reading and responding to emails. In emails to clients, therapists typically provide feedback on homework assignments and answer client questions. Content analysis of therapist emails to clients shows a variety of therapist behaviors are present, such as alliance bolstering, task reinforcement, task prompting, psychoeducation, empathic utterances, and self-efficacy shaping (e.g., Paxling et al., 2013; Schneider et al., 2016). Although there is likely some variability in how guidance is provided in different settings, there is recent evidence showing considerable consistency in therapist assistance across different programs in different countries (Schneider, Hadjistavropoulos, & Faller, 2016). Although more research is needed showing causal relationships between therapist behaviors and client outcomes, it appears that some therapist behaviors are less effective, or at least correlated with less progress (e.g., deadline flexibility), whereas other behaviors (e.g., task reinforcement) are positively correlated with improvement (Paxling et al., 2013). Certain therapist behaviors, such as task reinforcement and questionnaire feedback, also appear to be related to client satisfaction (Schneider et al., 2016). Here it is important to note that some studies suggest that support can be provided from mainly a technical and not necessarily psychotherapeutic perspective (Titov et al., 2010).

In sum, ICBT in the therapist-guided format consists of several components. The unique contribution of careful assessment (e.g., diagnostic interviews), differences in how the treatment is set up, including the theoretical emphasis (behavioral versus cognitive versus acceptance-based), and the role of therapist behaviors are not well known. However, most studies suggest that therapist guidance boosts outcome compared with having no therapeutic guidance. Somewhat surprising, there is not much evidence suggesting that an attractive graphical design makes much difference in outcomes, but our clinical experience is that functionality is important and that clients are likely to drop out if the system crashes.

TREATMENT EFFECTS IN ANXIETY DISORDERS

ICBT studies have been conducted on clients presenting with most major disorders involving anxiety, including specific phobia, panic disorder, social anxiety disorder (SAD), generalized anxiety disorder (GAD), posttraumatic stress disorder (PTSD), obsessive—compulsive disorder (OCD), and health anxiety (formerly known as hypochondriasis), as well as on clients presenting with mixed anxiety and depression. The evidence-base varies for these conditions from small and few studies (specific phobia) to large and numerous trials (SAD). There are several reviews of this literature (Olthuis, Watt, Bailey, Hayden, & Stewart, 2015), and also comparative studies in which participants have been randomized to either guided ICBT or face-to-face therapy (Andersson, Cuijpers, Carlbring, Riper, & Hedman, 2014). In this section, we will comment on each of the disorders involving anxiety for which there is evidence and provide examples of studies.

Starting with specific phobia, there are few controlled studies on ICBT. One example of a small controlled ICBT trial ($N = 30$) focused on snake phobia (Andersson, Waara, et al., 2013). One-session live exposure treatment was compared against guided ICBT with four weekly text modules presented in an online treatment platform. Also included in the ICBT condition was a video in which exposure was modeled, and support provided via internet. Results on the behavioral approach test (BAT) at posttreatment showed that 61.5% of the ICBT group and 84.6% of the one-session live exposure group achieved a clinically significant improvement. At follow-up, the corresponding figures were 90% for the ICBT group and 100% for the exposure group. In contrast to most studies comparing ICBT against face-to-face treatment, this study and a related study on spider phobia (Andersson, Waara, et al., 2009) showed a slight advantage for the face-to-face treatment. There is a need for more and larger studies on ICBT for specific phobias. Of interest, as technology is improving, work is in progress to blend virtual reality treatment with ICBT (Miloff et al., 2016).

Panic disorder was one of the first conditions for which ICBT research was conducted in the form of randomized controlled trials (Carlbring, Westling, Ljungstrand, Ekselius, & Andersson, 2001). One example is a waitlist control study from Australia which included 59 individuals with diagnosed panic disorder with agoraphobia (Wims, Titov, Andrews, & Choi, 2010). The ICBT treatment consisted of six online lessons (including homework), guidance from a therapist, and participation in a moderated discussion forum. Results on the Panic Disorder Severity Scale showed a moderate between-group effect size at posttreatment ($d = 0.59$) and sustained effects at 1-month follow-up. Most other studies have reported slightly larger between-group effects (Olthuis et al., 2015), and three studies comparing ICBT against face-to-face CBT showed equivalent findings (Andersson et al., 2014). However, a recent trial from the Netherlands on panic symptoms found substantially higher dropout rates than previous studies of panic disorder, but the participants who actually completed the study improved in line with previous studies (van Ballegooijen et al., 2013). The evidence for panic disorder and panic symptoms is mixed, and only a few research groups have done studies. In contrast to some other conditions, like depression, there are no long-term follow-up studies (above 1 year after treatment). On the other hand, effectiveness data have been published showing that ICBT for panic disorder can be effective in routine care (Hedman et al., 2013).

SAD has been the topic of several controlled ICBT trials following the first study from Sweden (Andersson et al., 2006). The initial findings have been replicated by at least five different research groups, and one example of a trial was a study conducted in Romania with a program that was translated and culturally adapted from the Swedish ICBT program (Tulbure et al., 2015). The waitlist control study included 76 participants with diagnosed SAD. ICBT consisted of nine weekly modules with homework assignment and support from a therapist. Consistent with previous trials, the between-group effect size at posttreatment for the self-reported Liebowitz Social Anxiety Scale was large ($d = 1.19$). ICBT has also been compared against face-to-face group CBT with slightly superior outcome for ICBT (Hedman, Andersson, Ljótsson, Andersson, Rück, Mörtberg, et al., 2011), and effectiveness data have also been published (El Alaoui et al., 2015). Long-term follow-up data have been published on ICBT for SAD, with clients continuing to demonstrate improvement 5 years after treatment completion (Hedman, Furmark, et al., 2011). SAD is thus the most studied anxiety disorder when it comes to ICBT and, interestingly, trials on internet-delivered bias modification suggest that the outcome of ICBT is specific as bias modification has had poor outcomes in most studies (Boettcher, Berger, & Renneberg, 2012b). The challenge now is to investigate moderators of outcome and to widely disseminate ICBT for SAD in clinical practice.

Fewer trials have been conducted on GAD, but one controlled trial from Australia (Titov et al., 2009) and one from the Swedish group (Paxling et al., 2011), including 3-year follow-up data, showed promising large effects. An example of a controlled trial on GAD was a trial comparing the difference between support provided by a clinician and support from a more practical and technical perspective (Robinson et al., 2010). The study included 150 participants with diagnosed GAD allocated to three groups: Clinician-assisted versus technician-assisted versus delayed treatment. The ICBT treatment consisted of six online lessons, weekly homework assignments, and weekly supportive contact over a treatment period of 10 weeks. Both forms of support were equally effective when compared against the control condition on the Penn State Worry Questionnaire ($d = 1.06$). Given the comorbidity associated with GAD, it is not surprising that transdiagnostic ICBT has been tested (Johnston, Titov, Andrews, Spence, & Dear, 2011). There is also one controlled trial on acceptance-based ICBT (Dahlin et al., 2016). However, apart from the initial 3-year follow-up, little is known about the long-term effects, and there are no comparative studies against face-to-face CBT. Data on how well ICBT for GAD works in regular practice have been published, with medium-to-large effect sizes among the treatment completers (Mewton, Wong, & Andrews, 2012).

For PTSD and symptoms of posttraumatic stress, the first controlled trial was on a Dutch program called Interapy (Lange et al., 2003). There are further studies in which symptoms of PTSD have been the target, but also studies on diagnosed PTSD. One example is a trial from Sweden in which 62 persons with PTSD were randomly allocated to treatment or attention control (Ivarsson et al., 2014). The ICBT treatment consisted of eight weekly modules containing psychoeducation, breathing retraining, imaginal and in vivo exposure, cognitive restructuring, and relapse prevention. Therapist support and feedback on homework assignments were given weekly via an online contact handling system. The study also included a 1-year follow-up. Results on the Impact of Events Scale-Revised showed a large between group effect size of Cohen's $d = 1.25$. One-year follow-up data showed that treatment gains were maintained. Promising findings have also been observed in trials on immigrants (Knaevelsrud, Brand, Lange, Ruwaard, & Wagner, 2015). There are no direct comparisons against face-to-face CBT, but overall findings indicate that ICBT for PTSD can be effective.

It took some years for the first controlled study on ICBT for OCD to be published by the Swedish group (Andersson et al., 2012). Shortly thereafter, a trial from Australia was published (Wootton, Dear, Johnston, Terides, & Titov, 2013). One example of a trial tested technician-administered ICBT against treatment as usual in 67 clients with diagnosed OCD (Mahoney, Mackenzie, Williams, Smith, & Andrews, 2014). The treatment consisted of six online lessons completed over 10 weeks, including scheduled guidance and automated messages. Results at posttreatment on the Dimensional Obsessive-Compulsive Scale showed a between-group effect size of $d = 0.78$, and results were maintained at a 3-month follow-up.

When it comes to severe health anxiety (formerly known as hypochondriasis), there are only two controlled trials (Hedman, Andersson, Ljótsson, Andersson, Rück, Asmundson, et al., 2011; Hedman, Axelsson, et al., 2014). The latter study compared guided ICBT with a focus on exposure against behavioral stress management as a credible control condition. The treatments included 12 modules presented over 12 weeks. A total of 158 participants with severe health anxiety were included in the trial, and the outcome on the Health Anxiety Inventory showed that both treatments were highly effective but that ICBT was slightly superior ($d = 0.26$), and the time $\times$ condition interaction was statistically significant. Results were maintained at a 6-month follow-up. ICBT has not been compared against face-to-face CBT for severe health anxiety, and there is a need for more studies including replication of the findings.

Another condition, for which there is only one controlled trial, is body dysmorphic disorder (BDD). In the trial, 94 individuals with BDD were randomized to either 12 weeks of guided ICBT with eight modules or to online supportive therapy for 12 weeks (Enander et al., 2016). Results at posttreatment showed a between-group effect size of $d = 0.97$ on the main outcome (Yale–Brown obsessive compulsive scale for BDD). Apart from the studies and programs for specific disorders, there are programs that are transdiagnostic in nature or tailored according to client characteristics and symptomatic profile (Andersson & Titov, 2014). Often these approaches target the overlap between anxiety and depression, but also other comorbid problems such as stress, insomnia, and perfectionism. One study of this nature compared transdiagnostic ICBT against disorder-specific ICBT for GAD among 338 participants with diagnosed GAD (Dear et al., 2015). In addition, they contrasted guided versus unguided ICBT. Results showed large improvements in symptoms of GAD as assessed by the GAD-7 (within group Cohen's

$d = 1.51$ for transdiagnostic ICBT), with small differences between the conditions. Results were maintained at a 24 month follow-up. Both guided and unguided treatment resulted in similar outcomes.

In sum, the evidence base for ICBT is strong for some conditions involving anxiety and somewhat more limited for some conditions, such as OCD and severe health anxiety.

TREATMENT EFFECTS IN MOOD DISORDERS

There are a large number of trials on ICBT for depressive symptoms and major depression (Cuijpers, Riper, & Andersson, 2015). Fewer studies exist on relapse prevention, and there is only preliminary research on ICBT for bipolar disorder. Here we will focus on guided ICBT as there are several studies on unguided ICBT, mostly for depressive symptoms, showing weak results and large dropout rates (Christensen, Griffiths, Groves, & Korten, 2006). Finally, we will also comment on transdiagnostic and tailored ICBT. Some studies have directly compared guided ICBT against face-to-face therapy. In a meta-analytic comparative review including five studies that directly compared ICBT against face-to-face treatments, there was no difference between the two formats (Andersson, Topooco, Havik, & Nordgreen, 2016). The effect size was Hedge's $g = 0.12$ in favor of ICBT based on a total of 429 participants. Long-term effects of guided ICBT for depression have been documented up to 3 years after treatment (Andersson, Hesser, et al., 2013), and in in one trial ICBT was found to prevent relapse for participants with partially remitted depression (Holländare et al., 2011). There are a large number of ICBT programs for depression (Andersson, Wagner, & Cuijpers, 2016). Transdiagnostic ICBT has also been tested for depression and comorbid disorders (Titov et al., 2011), and there are examples of studies in which programs have been translated and culturally adapted from one language into another (Choi et al., 2012). There are also examples of ICBT being used outside of North America and Europe, including a Japanese program that includes manga pictures (Imamura et al., 2014).

We select one ICBT for depression study here to illustrate the potential of tailoring (Johansson et al., 2012). The study included 121 participants with major depression and comorbid symptoms who were randomized to three groups, including an active control group (monitored online discussion group), a tailored ICBT group (a prescribed set of modules targeting depression as well as comorbid problems tailored specifically to the individual client), and a standardized ICBT for depression group. Both active ICBT treatments were in the form of guided self-help lasting 10 weeks and lead to improvements on measures of depression, anxiety, and quality of life that were maintained at a 6-month follow-up. Interestingly, subgroup analyses showed that tailored ICBT was more effective than the standard ICBT for participants with higher levels of depression at baseline and more comorbidity.

Among the many studies on ICBT for depression are several effectiveness studies (Hedman, Ljótsson, et al., 2014) and comparisons of different forms of support (Titov et al., 2010), including no support at all (Berger, Hämmerli, Gubser, Andersson, & Caspar, 2011). Overall, studies suggest that ICBT for depression works and that unguided treatments in most studies have very small effects (de Graaf et al., 2009), but in some studies larger effects (Titov et al., 2013). There is need for more research to understand under what circumstances unguided ICBT programs obtain large effects (e.g., use of automated emails, quality of ICBT materials, on boarding prior to ICBT).

TREATMENT EFFECTS IN SOMATIC DISORDERS

ICBT has been developed and tested for a range of somatic problems (Beatty & Lambert, 2013), including, for example, chronic pain, headache, irritable bowel syndrome (IBS), tinnitus, diabetes, erectile dysfunction, and secondary psychological problems after cancer diagnosis. For some conditions, there are separate systematic reviews and meta-analyses. For example, the effect of ICBT for tinnitus distress was the subject of a small review paper that included six controlled studies with nine different comparisons and three studies in which ICBT was compared against group treatment (Andersson, 2015). Results showed a moderate effect size (Hedges's $g = 0.58$) against no-treatment control, and a minor difference when ICBT was compared against face-to-face group treatments (Hedges's $g = 0.13$). Another systematic review focused on chronic pain and headache and included 22 trials (Buhrman, Gordh, & Andersson, 2016). Most studies were on chronic pain in adults, but two were on children and five on headache and/or migraine. Small-to-moderate effects were found on measures of pain interference/disability (Hedge's $g = -0.39$), pain intensity (Hedge's $g = -0.33$), and pain catastrophizing (Hedge's $g = -0.49$). Some recent ICBT studies on somatic conditions have endorsed components of acceptance and commitment therapy in the programs, for example, on tinnitus (Hesser et al., 2012) and chronic pain (Buhrman et al., 2013). To date, effects do not appear to be better than programs that are more in line with regular CBT and applied relaxation. Few studies have directly compared ICBT against a credible control condition, but one example is a study on IBS in which the treatment program was tested against internet-based stress management. The trial included 195 participants diagnosed with IBS. Results showed a superior result for ICBT on measures of IBS symptoms (Ljótsson et al., 2011). Overall, ICBT studies on somatic problems show no sign of being inferior to face-to-face CBT, but, nevertheless, effects tend to be smaller than for anxiety and mood disorders.

OTHER CONDITIONS

There are a growing number of programs and studies on other conditions in addition to those mentioned previously. First, there are several controlled studies on ICBT for eating disorders, showing promising results (Loucas et al., 2014). Second, there are studies on stress management, showing moderate-to-large effects (Zetterqvist, Maanmies, Ström, & Andersson, 2003). Third, there are published studies on problems such as procrastination (Rozental, Forsell, Svensson, Andersson, & Carlbring, 2015) and perfectionism, all showing moderate-to-large between-group effects (Arpin-Cribbie, Irvine, & Ritvo, 2012). There are more examples of ICBT for various specific problems such as infertility distress (Haemmerli, Znoj, & Berger, 2010), pathological gambling (Carlbring & Smit, 2008), and ongoing work on interpersonal violence. In sum, new programs and studies are being produced at a fast rate. These programs and studies have the potential to inform face-to-face CBT as well as facilitate recruitment of larger samples and reduced costs compared to face-to-face studies.

INNOVATIONS AND THE SEARCH FOR PREDICTORS AND CHANGE MECHANISMS

In this chapter, we can only briefly comment on recent innovative work in the field of ICBT and research on predictors and mediators. Studies using modern brain imaging methodology to assess neural changes related to ICBT show promising outcomes (Månsson et al., 2013) and, in a recent study using machine learning, results of neuroimagining appeared to be of particular value in predicting treatment outcome, even more so than behavioral and demographic predictors (Månsson et al., 2015). Studies on genetic markers as predictors of outcome have been less promising (Hedman et al., 2012). As alluded to previously, the findings on bias modification procedures are mixed (Clarke, Notebaert, & MacLeod, 2014), with some studies showing additive effects in combination with ICBT (Williams, Blackwell, Mackenzie, Holmes, & Andrews, 2013), but there are also studies with no effects at all when attention training is a stand-alone intervention delivered via the internet (Boettcher et al., 2012b). In one study, the added effect of D-cycloserine in the treatment of OCD with ICBT was tested, showing that the effect may depend on concurrent antidepressant medication (Andersson et al., 2015). Overall, the prospect of conducting combined medication plus ICBT studies has the potential to answer outstanding questions regarding combined treatment effects.

Several studies have investigated the role of therapeutic alliance in ICBT, showing that clients usually rate the alliance as high with the online therapist, but that early alliance ratings rarely and only weakly are related to treatment outcome (Hadjistavropoulos, Pugh, Hesser, & Andersson, in press; Sucala et al., 2012). There are a few studies on cognitive function as a predictor of outcome, but in the largest dataset there was no association between scores on the Wisconsin Card Sorting Test at screening and treatment effects (Lindner et al., 2016). Innovative work is being conducted on the impact of ICBT on alternative outcome measures such as personality (Johansson, Lyssarides, Andersson, & Rousseau, 2013) and, as mentioned earlier in this chapter, knowledge about treatment and the condition treated (Andersson, Carlbring, Furmark, & on behalf of the SOFIE Research Group, 2012). This could be important as most studies have relied on self-reported disease-oriented measures and, to some extent, quality of life measures.

Although it is important to know if and for whom a treatment works, it is also important to investigate what mechanisms change occur. There are studies emerging on mediators of treatment outcome using repeated measures of theoretically relevant process measures (Ljótsson et al., 2013). Although this can be demanding for clients to report on a weekly basis, it is critical in order to identify temporal patterns in the data rather than having pre- and post-measures only. Other recent developments include the emerging work on blended treatments in which ICBT and face-to-face sessions are integrated. This can be a way forward for regular therapists to take advantage of modern information technology while still maintaining their clinical services (Bengtsson, Nordin, & Carlbring, 2015). It can also be a way to reduce the number of sessions while still generating the same outcome (Ly et al., 2015).

LIMITATIONS

As with all treatments, there are pros and cons. Recently, the possibility of negative unwanted effects of ICBT (e.g., deterioration) has been studied and a consensus statement was produced recommending that negative effects, while rare, need to be systematically reported (Rozental et al., 2014). A second limitation concerns negative attitudes among practitioners, in particular in the field of child and adolescent psychiatry

(Vigerland et al., 2014), who may be skeptical toward ICBT, but more in favor of blended ICBT and face-to-face interventions. A third limitation of the research, as noted above, is a lack of good intervention-specific theories as the usual psychotherapy theories (e.g., focus on therapist competence and the therapeutic alliance) do not apply or at least must be adapted. In the future, much more attention needs to be given to theories behind ICBT, which date are not well developed. Usually the theoretical underpinnings behind the treatment programs are derived directly from various forms of evidence-based face-to-face CBT treatments (e.g., CBT and acceptance and commitment therapy). ICBT, however, should also be described using a theoretical framework for the specific form of treatment delivery. Research on mechanisms of therapy can be informative for understanding ICBT (Andersson, Carlbring, Berger, Almlöv, & Cuijpers, 2009) as can research on how humans interact with computers and websites (Ritterband, Thorndike, Cox, Kovatchev, & Gonder-Frederick, 2009). Knowledge acquisition theories from education that focus on what clients actually learn and remember from their treatments also should be considered (Harvey et al., 2014). In ICBT, knowledge acquisition and how clients move from learning about techniques to actually implementing strategies makes it plausible to view ICBT as a form of distance learning, as clients are not seen by the therapist in session and the format resembles online education. Theories from basic cognitive psychology could be e helpful for understanding ICBT outcomes (Hattie & Yates, 2014), but, to date, rarely have been considered in ICBT research and or in face-to-face CBT either.

CONCLUSIONS

Although still relatively novel, ICBT can now be regarded as an established method of delivering CBT. There are problems and client categories (e.g., personality disorders and psychotic disorders) for which very little research has been conducted, and clients for which ICBT is unsuitable; yet, there is now sufficient evidence to support implementation of ICBT as a complement to other regular services. Supporting this conclusion, although not addressed in this chapter, there are clear results from cost-effectiveness studies showing the provision if ICBT reduces costs for society (Donker et al., 2015). Emerging research on translation and cultural adaption of ICBT programs across borders and use of ICBT with children adolescents and older persons represent important avenues for research. In conclusion, ICBT is here to stay and will continue to evolve as technology changes.

References

Andersson, E., Enander, J., Andrén, P., Hedman, E., Ljótsson, B., Hursti, T., & Rück, C. (2012). Internet-based cognitive behaviour therapy for obsessive-compulsive disorder: A randomised controlled trial. *Psychological Medicine*, *42*, 2193−2203. Available from http://dx.doi.org/10.1017/S0033291712000244.

Andersson, E., Hedman, E., Enander, J., Radu Djurfeldt, D., Ljótsson, B., Cervenka, S., & Rück, C. (2015). D-Cycloserine vs placebo as adjunct to cognitive behavioral therapy for obsessive-compulsive disorder and interaction with antidepressants. A randomized clinical trial. *JAMA Psychiatry*, *72*, 659−667. Available from http://dx.doi.org/10.1001/jamapsychiatry.2015.0546.

Andersson, G. (2015). *The internet and CBT: A clinical guide*. Boca Raton, FL: CRC Press.

Andersson, G. (2015). Clinician-supported internet-delivered psychological treatment of tinnitus. *American Journal of Audiology*, *24*, 299−301. Available from http://dx.doi.org/10.1044/2015_AJA-14-0080.

Andersson, G. (2016). Internet-delivered psychological treatments. *Annual Review of Clinical Psychology*, *12*, 157−179. Available from http://dx.doi.org/10.1146/annurev-clinpsy-021815-093006.

Andersson, G., Carlbring, P., Berger, T., Almlöv, J., & Cuijpers, P. (2009). What makes Internet therapy work? *Cognitive Behaviour Therapy*, *38*(S1), 55−60. Available from http://dx.doi.org/10.1080/16506070902916400.

Andersson, G., Carlbring, P., Furmark, T., & on behalf of the SOFIE Research Group (2012). Therapist experience and knowledge acquisition in Internet-delivered CBT for social anxiety disorder: A randomized controlled trial. *PloS ONE*, *7*(5), e37411. Available from http://dx.doi.org/10.1371/journal.pone.0037411.

Andersson, G., Carlbring, P., Holmström, A., Sparthan, E., Furmark, T., Nilsson-Ihrfelt, E., & Ekselius, L. (2006). Internet-based self-help with therapist feedback and in-vivo group exposure for social phobia: A randomized controlled trial. *Journal of Consulting and Clinical Psychology*, *74*, 677−686. Available from http://dx.doi.org/10.1037/0022-006X.74.4.677.

Andersson, G., Carlbring, P., & Lindefors, N. (2016). History and current status of ICBT. In N. Lindefors, & G. Andersson (Eds.), *Guided internet-based treatments in psychiatry* (pp. 1−16). Switzerland: Springer.

Andersson, G., Cuijpers, P., Carlbring, P., Riper, H., & Hedman, E. (2014). Internet-based vs. face-to-face cognitive behaviour therapy for psychiatric and somatic disorders: A systematic review and meta-analysis. *World Psychiatry*, *13*, 288−295. Available from http://dx.doi.org/10.1002/wps.20151.

Andersson, G., Hesser, H., Veilord, A., Svedling, L., Andersson, F., Sleman, O., & Carlbring, P. (2013). Randomized controlled non-inferiority trial with 3-year follow-up of internet-delivered versus face-to-face group cognitive behavioural therapy for depression. *Journal of Affective Disorders*, *151*, 986−994. Available from http://dx.doi.org/10.1016/j.jad.2013.08.022.

Andersson, G., & Titov, N. (2014). Advantages and limitations of Internet-based interventions for common mental disorders. *World Psychiatry*, *13*, 4−11. Available from http://dx.doi.org/10.1002/wps.20083.

Andersson, G., Topooco, N., Havik, O. E., & Nordgreen, T. (2016). Internet-supported versus face-to-face cognitive behavior therapy for depression. *Expert Review of Neurotherapeutics*, *16*, 55−60. Available from http://dx.doi.org/10.1586/14737175.2015.1125783.

Andersson, G., Waara, J., Jonsson, U., Malmaeus, F., Carlbring, P., & Öst, L.-G. (2009). Internet-based self-help vs. one-session exposure in the treatment of spider phobia: A randomized controlled trial. *Cognitive Behaviour Therapy*, *38*, 114−120. Available from http://dx.doi.org/10.1080/16506070902931326.

Andersson, G., Waara, J., Jonsson, U., Malmaeus, F., Carlbring, P., & Öst, L.-G. (2013). Internet-based vs. one-session exposure treatment of snake phobia: A randomized controlled trial. *Cognitive Behaviour Therapy, 42*, 284−291. Available from http://dx.doi.org/10.1080/16506073.2013.844202.

Andersson, G., Wagner, B., & Cuijpers, P. (2016). ICBT for depression. In N. Lindefors, & G. Andersson (Eds.), *Guided internet-based treatments in psychiatry* (pp. 17−32). Switzerland: Springer.

Arpin-Cribbie, C., Irvine, J., & Ritvo, P. (2012). Web-based cognitive-behavioral therapy for perfectionism: A randomized controlled trial. *Psychotherapy Research, 22*(2), 194−207. Available from http://dx.doi.org/10.1080/10503307.2011.637242.

Beatty, L., & Lambert, S. (2013). A systematic review of internet-based self-help therapeutic interventions to improve distress and disease-control among adults with chronic health conditions. *Clinical Psychology Review, 33*, 609−622. Available from http://dx.doi.org/10.1016/j.cpr.2013.03.004.

Bengtsson, J., Nordin, S., & Carlbring, P. (2015). Therapists' experiences of conducting cognitive behavioural therapy online vis-a-vis face-to-face. *Cognitive Behaviour Therapy, 44*, 470−479. Available from http://dx.doi.org/10.1080/16506073.2015.1053408.

Berger, T., Hämmerli, K., Gubser, N., Andersson, G., & Caspar, F. (2011). Internet-based treatment of depression: A randomized controlled trial comparing guided with unguided self-help. *Cognitive Behaviour Therapy, 40*, 251−266. Available from http://dx.doi.org/10.1080/16506073.2011.616531.

Boettcher, J., Berger, T., & Renneberg, B. (2012a). Does a pre-treatment diagnostic interview affect the outcome of Internet-based self-help for social anxiety disorder? A randomized controlled trial. *Behavioural and Cognitive Psychotherapy, 40*, 513−528. Available from http://dx.doi.org/10.1017/S1352465812000501.

Boettcher, J., Berger, T., & Renneberg, B. (2012b). Internet-based attention training for social anxiety: A randomized controlled trial. *Cognitive Therapy and Research, 36*, 522−536. Available from http://dx.doi.org/10.1007/s10608-011-9374-y.

Buhrman, M., Gordh, T., & Andersson, G. (2016). Internet interventions for chronic pain including headache: A systematic review. *Internet Interventions, 4*, 17−34. Available from http://dx.doi.org/10.1016/j.invent.2015.12.001.

Buhrman, M., Skoglund, A., Husell, J., Bergström, K., Gordh, T., Hursti, T., & Andersson, G. (2013). Guided Internet-delivered acceptance and commitment therapy for chronic pain patients: A randomized controlled trial. *Behaviour Research and Therapy, 51*, 307−315. Available from http://dx.doi.org/10.1016/j.brat.2013.02.010.

Carlbring, P., & Smit, F. (2008). Randomized trial of Internet-delivered self-help with telephone support for pathological gamblers. *Journal of Consulting and Clinical Psychology, 76*, 1090−1094. Available from http://dx.doi.org/10.1037/a0013603.

Carlbring, P., Westling, B. E., Ljungstrand, P., Ekselius, L., & Andersson, G. (2001). Treatment of panic disorder via the Internet—A randomized trial of a self-help program. *Behavior Therapy, 32*, 751−764. Available from http://dx.doi.org/10.1016/S0005-7894(01)80019-8.

Choi, I., Zou, J., Titov, N., Dear, B. F., Li, S., Johnston, L., & Hunt, C. (2012). Culturally attuned Internet treatment for depression amongst Chinese Australians: A randomised controlled trial. *Journal of Affective Disorders, 136*, 459−468. Available from http://dx.doi.org/10.1016/j.jad.2011.11.003.

Christensen, H., Griffiths, K., Groves, C., & Korten, A. (2006). Free range users and one hit wonders: Community users of an Internet-based cognitive behaviour therapy program. *Australian and New Zealand Journal of Psychiatry, 40*, 59−62. Available from http://dx.doi.org/10.1111/j.1440-1614.2006.01743.x.

Clarke, P. J., Notebaert, L., & MacLeod, C. (2014). Absence of evidence or evidence of absence: Reflecting on therapeutic implementations of attentional bias modification. *BMC Psychiatry, 14*, 8. Available from http://dx.doi.org/10.1186/1471-244x-14-8.

Cuijpers, P., Riper, H., & Andersson, G. (2015). Internet-based treatment of depression. *Current Opinion in Psychology*, 4, 131−135. Available from http://dx.doi.org/10.1016/j.copsyc.2014.12.026.

Dahlin, M., Andersson, G., Magnusson, K., Johansson, T., Sjögren, J., Håkansson, A., & Carlbring, P. (2016). Internet-delivered acceptance-based behaviour therapy for generalized anxiety disorder: A randomized controlled trial. *Behaviour Research and Therapy*, 77, 86−95. Available from http://dx.doi.org/10.1016/j.brat.2015.12.007.

Dear, B. F., Staples, L. G., Terides, M. D., Karin, E., Zou, J., Johnston, L., & Titov, N. (2015). Transdiagnostic versus disorder-specific and clinician-guided versus self-guided internet-delivered treatment for generalized anxiety disorder and comorbid disorders: A randomized controlled trial. *Journal of Anxiety Disorders*, 36, 63−77. Available from http://dx.doi.org/10.1016/j.janxdis.2015.09.003.

de Graaf, L. E., Gerhards, S. A., Arntz, A., Riper, H., Metsemakers, J. F., Evers, S. M., & Huibers, M. J. (2009). Clinical effectiveness of online computerised cognitive-behavioural therapy without support for depression in primary care: Randomised trial. *British Journal of Psychiatry*, 195, 73−80. Available from http://dx.doi.org/10.1192/bjp.bp.108.054429.

Donker, T., Blankers, M., Hedman, E., Ljótsson, B., Petrie, K., & Christensen, H. (2015). Economic evaluations of Internet interventions for mental health: A systematic review. *Psychological Medicine*, 45, 3357−3376. Available from http://dx.doi.org/10.1017/s0033291715001427.

El Alaoui, S., Hedman, E., Kaldo, V., Hesser, H., Kraepelien, M., Andersson, E., & Lindefors, N. (2015). Effectiveness of internet-based cognitive behavior therapy for social anxiety disorder in clinical psychiatry. *Journal of Consulting and Clinical Psychology*, 83, 902−914. Available from http://dx.doi.org/10.1037/a0039198.

Enander, J., Andersson, E., Mataix-Cols, D., Lichtenstein, L., Alström, K., Andersson, G., & Rück, C. (2016). Therapist guided internet based cognitive behavioural therapy for body dysmorphic disorder: Single blind randomised controlled trial. *British Medical Journal*, 352, i241. Available from http://dx.doi.org/10.1136/bmj.i241.

Hadjistavropoulos, H. D., Nugent, M. M., Alberts, N. M., Staples, L., Dear, B. F., & Titov, N. (2016). Transdiagnostic Internet-delivered cognitive behaviour therapy in Canada: An open trial comparing results of a specialized online clinic and nonspecialized community clinics. *Journal of Anxiety Disorders*, 42, 19−29. Available from http://dx.doi.org/10.1016/j.janxdis.2016.05.006.

Hadjistavropoulos, H.D., Pugh, N.E., Hesser, H., & Andersson, G. (In press). Therapeutic alliance in Internet-delivered cognitive behaviour therapy for depression and generalized anxiety. *Clinical Psychology & Psychotherapy*.

Haemmerli, K., Znoj, H., & Berger, T. (2010). Internet-based support for infertile patients: A randomized controlled study. *Journal of Behavioral Medicine*, 33, 135−146. Available from http://dx.doi.org/10.1007/s10865-009-9243-2.

Harvey, A. G., Lee, J., Williams, J., Hollon, S. D., Walker, M. P., Thompson, M. A., & Smith, R. (2014). Improving outcome of psychosocial treatments by enhancing memory and learning. *Perspectives on Psychological Science*, 9, 161−179. Available from http://dx.doi.org/10.1177/1745691614521781.

Hattie, J., & Yates, G. (2014). *Visible learning and the science of how we learn*. London: Routledge.

Hedman, E., Andersson, E., Ljótsson, B., Andersson, G., Andersson, E. M., Schalling, M., & Rück, C. (2012). Clinical and genetic outcome determinants of Internet- and group-based cognitive behavior therapy for social anxiety disorder. *Acta Psychiatrica Scandinavica*, 126, 126−136. Available from http://dx.doi.org/10.1111/j.1600-0447.2012.01834.x.

Hedman, E., Andersson, G., Ljótsson, B., Andersson, E., Rück, C., Asmundson, G. J. G., & Lindefors, N. (2011). Internet-based cognitive-behavioural therapy for severe health anxiety: Randomised controlled trial. *British Journal of Psychiatry, 198*, 230–236. Available from http://dx.doi.org/10.1192/bjp.bp.110.086843.

Hedman, E., Andersson, G., Ljótsson, B., Andersson, E., Rück, C., Mörtberg, E., & Lindefors, N. (2011). Internet-based cognitive behavior therapy vs. cognitive behavioral group therapy for social anxiety disorder: A randomized controlled non-inferiority trial. *PLoS ONE, 6*(3), e18001. Available from http://dx.doi.org/10.1371/journal.pone.0018001.

Hedman, E., Axelsson, E., Gorling, A., Ritzman, C., Ronnheden, M., El Alaoui, S., & Ljotsson, B. (2014). Internet-delivered exposure-based cognitive-behavioural therapy and behavioural stress management for severe health anxiety: Randomised controlled trial. *British Journal of Psychiatry, 205*, 307–314. Available from http://dx.doi.org/10.1192/bjp.bp.113.140913.

Hedman, E., Furmark, T., Carlbring, P., Ljótsson, B., Rück, C., Lindefors, N., & Andersson, G. (2011). Five-year follow-up of internet-based cognitive behaviour therapy for social anxiety disorder. *Journal of Medical Internet Research, 13*(2), e39. Available from http://dx.doi.org/10.2196/jmir.1776.

Hedman, E., Ljótsson, B., Kaldo, V., Hesser, H., El Alaoui, S., Kraepelin, M., & Lindefors, N. (2014). Effectiveness of Internet-based cognitive behaviour therapy for depression in routine psychiatric care. *Journal of Affective Disorders, 155*, 49–58. Available from http://dx.doi.org/10.1016/j.jad.2013.10.023.

Hedman, E., Ljótsson, B., Rück, C., Bergström, J., Andersson, G., Kaldo, V., & Lindefors, N. (2013). Effectiveness of Internet-based cognitive behaviour therapy for panic disorder in routine psychiatric care. *Acta Psychiatrica Scandinavica, 128*, 457–467. Available from http://dx.doi.org/10.1111/acps.12079.

Hesser, H., Gustafsson, T., Lundén, C., Henriksson, O., Fattahi, K., Johnsson, E., & Andersson, G. (2012). A randomized controlled trial of Internet-delivered cognitive behavior therapy and acceptance and commitment therapy in the treatment of tinnitus. *Journal of Consulting and Clinical Psychology, 80*, 649–661. Available from http://dx.doi.org/10.1037/a0027021.

Holländare, F., Johnsson, S., Randestad, M., Tillfors, M., Carlbring, P., Andersson, G., & Engström, I. (2011). Randomized trial of internet-based relapse prevention for partially remitted depression. *Acta Psychiatrica Scandinavica, 124*, 285–294. Available from http://dx.doi.org/10.1111/j.1600-0447.2011.01698.x.

Imamura, K., Kawakami, N., Furukawa, T. A., Matsuyama, Y., Shimazu, A., Umanodan, R., & Kasai, K. (2014). Effects of an Internet-based cognitive behavioral therapy (iCBT) program in Manga format on improving subthreshold depressive symptoms among healthy workers: A randomized controlled trial. *PLoS ONE, 9*(5), e97167. Available from http://dx.doi.org/10.1371/journal.pone.0097167.

Ivarsson, D., Blom, M., Hesser, H., Carlbring, P., Enderby, P., Nordberg, R., & Andersson, G. (2014). Guided internet-delivered cognitive behaviour therapy for post-traumatic stress disorder: A randomized controlled trial. *Internet Interventions, 1*, 33–40. Available from http://dx.doi.org/10.1016/j.invent.2014.03.002.

Johansson, R., & Andersson, G. (2012). Internet-based psychological treatments for depression. *Expert Review of Neurotherapeutics, 12*, 861–870. Available from http://dx.doi.org/10.1586/ern.12.63.

Johansson, R., Lyssarides, C., Andersson, G., & Rousseau, A. (2013). Personality change after Internet-delivered cognitive behavior therapy for depression. *PeerJ, 1*, e39. Available from http://dx.doi.org/10.7717/peerj.39.

Johansson, R., Sjöberg, E., Sjögren, M., Johnsson, E., Carlbring, P., Andersson, T., & Andersson, G. (2012). Tailored vs. standardized Internet-based cognitive behavior therapy for depression and comorbid symptoms: A randomized controlled trial. *PLoS ONE, 7*(5), e36905. Available from http://dx.doi.org/10.1371/journal.pone.0036905.

Johnston, L., Titov, N., Andrews, G., Spence, J., & Dear, B. F. (2011). A RCT of a transdiagnostic internet-delivered treatment for three anxiety disorders: Examination of support roles and disorder-specific outcomes. *PLoS ONE, 6*, e28079. Available from http://dx. doi.org/10.1371/journal.pone.0028079.

Knaevelsrud, C., Brand, J., Lange, A., Ruwaard, J., & Wagner, B. (2015). Web-based psychotherapy for posttraumatic stress disorder in war-traumatized Arab patients: Randomized controlled trial. *Journal of Medical Internet Research, 17*, e71. Available from http://dx.doi.org/10.2196/jmir.3582.

Lange, A., Rietdijk, D., Hudcovicova, M., van den Ven, J.-P., Schrieken, B., & Emmelkamp, P. M. G. (2003). Interapy: A controlled randomized trial of the standardized treatment of posttraumatic stress through the Internet. *Journal of Consulting and Clinical Psychology, 71*, 901−909. Available from http://dx.doi.org/10.1037/0022-006X.71.5.901.

Lindner, P., Carlbring, P., Flodman, E., Hebert, A., Poysti, S., Hagkvist, F., & Andersson, G. (2016). Does cognitive flexibility predict treatment gains in Internet-delivered psychological treatment of social anxiety disorder, depression, or tinnitus? *PeerJ, 4*, e1934. Available from http://dx.doi.org/10.7717/peerj.1934.

Ljótsson, B., Hedman, E., Andersson, E., Hesser, H., Lindfors, P., Hursti, T., & Andersson, G. (2011). Internet-delivered exposure based treatment vs. stress management for irritable bowel syndrome: A randomized trial. *American Journal of Gastroenterology, 106*, 1481−1491. Available from http://dx.doi.org/10.1038/ajg.2011.139.

Ljótsson, B., Hesser, H., Andersson, E., Lindfors, P.-J., Hursti, T., Rück, C., & Hedman, E. (2013). Mechanisms of change in exposure-based internet-treatment for irritable bowel syndrome. *Journal of Consulting and Clinical Psychology, 81*, 1113−1126.

Loucas, C. E., Fairburn, C. G., Whittington, C., Pennant, M. E., Stockton, S., & Kendall, T. (2014). E-therapy in the treatment and prevention of eating disorders: A systematic review and meta-analysis. *Behaviour Research and Therapy, 63C*, 122−131. Available from http://dx.doi.org/10.1016/j.brat.2014.09.011.

Ly, K. H., Topooco, N., Cederlund, H., Wallin, A., Bergström, J., Molander, O., & Andersson, G. (2015). Smartphone-supported versus full behavioural activation for depression: A randomised controlled trial. *PLoS ONE, 10*, e0126559. Available from http://dx.doi.org/10.1371/journal.pone.0126559.

Mahoney, A. E., Mackenzie, A., Williams, A. D., Smith, J., & Andrews, G. (2014). Internet cognitive behavioural treatment for obsessive compulsive disorder: A randomised controlled trial. *Behaviour Research and Therapy, 63C*, 99−106. Available from http://dx.doi. org/10.1016/j.brat.2014.09.012.

Månsson, K. N. T., Carlbring, P., Frick, A., Engman, A., Olsson, C. J., Bodlund, O., & Andersson, G. (2013). Altered neural correlates of affective processing after internet-delivered cognitive behavior therapy for social anxiety disorder. *Psychiatry Research: Neuroimaging, 214*, 229−237. Available from http://dx.doi.org/10.1016/j. pscychresns.2013.08.012.

Månsson, K. N. T., Frick, A., Boraxbekk, C.-J., Marquand, A. F., Williams, S. C. R., Carlbring, P., & Furmark, T. (2015). Predicting long-term outcome of Internet-delivered cognitive behavior therapy for social anxiety disorder using fMRI and support vector machine learning. *Translational Psychiatry, 5*, e530. Available from http://dx.doi.org/ 10.1038/tp.2015.22.

Mewton, L., Wong, N., & Andrews, G. (2012). The effectiveness of internet cognitive behavioural therapy for generalized anxiety disorder in clinical practice. *Depression and Anxiety, 29*(10), 843−849. Available from http://dx.doi.org/10.1002/da.21995.

Miloff, A., Lindner, P., Hamilton, W., Reutersköld, L., Andersson, G., & Carlbring, P. (2016). Single-session gamified virtual reality exposure therapy for spider phobia vs. traditional exposure therapy: Study protocol for a randomized-controlled trial. *Trials, 17*, 60. Available from http://dx.doi.org/10.1186/s13063-016-1171-1.

O'Kearney, R., Kang, K., Christensen, H., & Griffiths, K. (2009). A controlled trial of a school-based Internet program for reducing depressive symptoms in adolescent girls. *Depression and Anxiety*, 26(1), 65−72. Available from http://dx.doi.org/10.1002/da.20507.

Olthuis, J. V., Watt, M. C., Bailey, K., Hayden, J. A., & Stewart, S. H. (2015). Therapist-supported Internet cognitive behavioural therapy for anxiety disorders in adults. *Cochrane Database for Systematic Reviews*, 3, CD011565. Available from http://dx.doi.org/10.1002/14651858.cd011565.

Paxling, B., Almlöv, J., Dahlin, M., Carlbring, P., Breitholtz, E., Eriksson, T., & Andersson, G. (2011). Guided internet-delivered cognitive behavior therapy for generalized anxiety disorder: A randomized controlled trial. *Cognitive Behaviour Therapy*, 40, 159−173. Available from http://dx.doi.org/10.1080/16506073.2011.576699.

Paxling, B., Lundgren, S., Norman, A., Almlöv, J., Carlbring, P., Cuijpers, P., & Andersson, G. (2013). Therapist behaviours in Internet-delivered cognitive behaviour therapy: Analyses of e-mail correspondence in the treatment of generalized anxiety disorder. *Behavioural and Cognitive Psychotherapy*, 41, 280−289. Available from http://dx.doi.org/10.1017/S1352465812000240.

Ritterband, L. M., Thorndike, F. P., Cox, D. J., Kovatchev, B. P., & Gonder-Frederick, L. A. (2009). A behavior change model for internet interventions. *Annals of Behavioral Medicine*, 38, 18−27. Available from http://dx.doi.org/10.1007/s12160-009-9133-4.

Robinson, E., Titov, N., Andrews, G., McIntyre, K., Schwencke, G., & Solley, K. (2010). Internet treatment for generalized anxiety disorder: A randomized controlled trial comparing clinician vs. technician assistance. *PLoS ONE*, 5, e10942. Available from http://dx.doi.org/10.1371/journal.pone.0010942.

Rozental, A., Andersson, G., Boettcher, J., Ebert, D., Cuijpers, P., Knaevelsrud, C., & Carlbring, P. (2014). Consensus statement on defining and measuring negative effects of Internet interventions. *Internet Interventions*, 1, 12−19. Available from http://dx.doi.org/10.1016/j.invent.2014.02.001.

Rozental, A., Forsell, E., Svensson, A., Andersson, G., & Carlbring, P. (2015). Internet-based cognitive behavior therapy for procrastination: A randomized controlled trial. *Journal of Consulting and Clinical Psychology*, 83, 808−824. Available from http://dx.doi.org/10.1037/ccp0000023.

Schneider, L. H., Hadjistavropoulos, H. D., & Faller, Y. N. (2016). Internet-delivered cognitive behaviour therapy for depressive symptoms: An exploratory eamination of therapist behaviours and their relationship to outcome and therapeutic alliance. *Behavioural and Cognitive Psychotherapy*. http://dx.doi.org/10.1017/s1352465816000254.

Sheehan, D. V., Lecrubier, Y., Sheehan, K. H., Amorim, P., Janavs, J., Weiller, E., & Dunbar, G. C. (1998). The Mini-International Neuropsychiatric Interview (M.I.N.I.): The development and validation of a structured diagnostic psychiatric interview for DSM-IV and ICD-10. *The Journal of Clinical Psychiatry*, 59(Suppl 20), 22−33.

Sucala, M., Schnur, J. B., Constantino, M. J., Miller, S. J., Brackman, E. H., & Montgomery, G. H. (2012). The therapeutic relationship in e-therapy for mental health: A systematic review. *Journal of Medical Internet Research*, 14(4), e110. Available from http://dx.doi.org/10.2196/jmir.2084.

Titov, N., Andrews, G., Davies, M., McIntyre, K., Robinson, E., & Solley, K. (2010). Internet treatment for depression: A randomized controlled trial comparing clinician vs. technician assistance. *PLoS ONE*, 5, e10939. Available from http://dx.doi.org/10.1371/journal.pone.0010939.

Titov, N., Andrews, G., Robinson, E., Schwencke, G., Johnston, L., Solley, K., & Choi, I. (2009). Clinician-assisted Internet-based treatment is effective for generalized anxiety disorder: Randomized controlled trial. *Australian and New Zealand Journal of Psychiatry*, 43, 905−912. Available from http://dx.doi.org/10.1080/00048670903179269.

Titov, N., Dear, B. F., Johnston, L., Lorian, C., Zou, J., Wootton, B., & Rapee, R. M. (2013). Improving adherence and clinical outcomes in self-guided internet treatment for anxiety and depression: Randomised controlled trial. *PLoS ONE, 8,* e62873. Available from http://dx.doi.org/10.1371/journal.pone.0062873.

Titov, N., Dear, B. F., Schwencke, G., Andrews, G., Johnston, L., Craske, M. G., & McEvoy, P. (2011). Transdiagnostic internet treatment for anxiety and depression: A randomised controlled trial. *Behaviour Research and Therapy, 49,* 441–452. Available from http://dx.doi.org/10.1016/j.brat.2011.03.007.

Tulbure, B. T., Szentagotai, A., David, O., Stefan, S., Månsson, K. N. T., David, D., & Andersson, G. (2015). Internet-delivered cognitive-behavioral therapy for social anxiety disorder in Romania: A randomized controlled trial. *PLoS ONE, 10,* e0123997. Available from http://dx.doi.org/10.1371/journal.pone.01239.

van Ballegooijen, W., Riper, H., Cuijpers, P., van Oppen, P., & Smit, J. H. (2016). Validation of online psychometric instruments for common mental health disorders: A systematic review. *BMC Psychiatry, 16,* 45. Available from http://dx.doi.org/10.1186/s12888-016-0735-7.

van Ballegooijen, W., Riper, H., Klein, B., Ebert, D. D., Kramer, J., Meulenbeek, P., & Cuijpers, P. (2013). An Internet-based guided self-help intervention for panic symptoms: Randomized controlled trial. *Journal of Medical Internet Research, 15*(7), e154. Available from http://dx.doi.org/10.2196/jmir.2362.

Vigerland, S., Ljótsson, B., Bergdahl, F., Hagert, S., Thulin, U., Andersson, G., & Serlachius, E. (2014). Attitudes towards the use of computerized cognitive behavior therapy (cCBT) with children and adolescents: A survey among Swedish mental health professionals. *Internet Interventions, 1,* 111–117. Available from http://dx.doi.org/10.1016/j.invent.2014.06.002.

Vlaescu, G., Carlbring, P., Lunner, T., & Andersson, G. (2015). An e-platform for rehabilitation of persons with hearing problems. *American Journal of Audiology, 24,* 271–275. Available from http://dx.doi.org/10.1044/2015_AJA-14-0083.

Williams, A. D., Blackwell, S. E., Mackenzie, A., Holmes, E. A., & Andrews, G. (2013). Combining imagination and reason in the treatment of depression: A randomized controlled trial of internet-based cognitive-bias modification and internet-CBT for depression. *Journal of Consulting and Clinical Psychology, 81,* 793–799. Available from http://dx.doi.org/10.1037/a0033247.

Wims, E., Titov, N., Andrews, G., & Choi, I. (2010). Clinician-assisted internet-based treatment is effective for panic: A randomized controlled trial. *Australian and New Zealand Journal of Psychiatry, 44*(7), 599–607. Available from http://dx.doi.org/10.3109/00048671003614171.

Wootton, B. M., Dear, B. F., Johnston, L., Terides, M. D., & Titov, N. (2013). Remote treatment of obsessive-compulsive disorder: A randomized controlled trial. *Journal of Obsessive-Compulsive and Related Disorders, 2,* 375–384. Available from http://dx.doi.org/10.1016/j.jocrd.2013.07.002.

Zetterqvist, K., Maanmies, J., Ström, L., & Andersson, G. (2003). Randomized controlled trial of internet-based stress management. *Cognitive Behaviour Therapy, 3,* 151–160. Available from http://dx.doi.org/10.1080/16506070302316.

Virtual Reality and Other Realities

Cristina Botella[1], Rosa M. Baños[2],
Azucena García-Palacios[1] and Soledad Quero[1]
[1]Universitat Jaume I, Castellón, Spain
[2]Universitat de Valencia, Valencia, Spain

INTRODUCTION

Virtual reality or virtual realities (VRs) are multisensory computer-generated environments that allow the user to interact in these simulated worlds. Using different technological devices, VRs may artificially create sensory experiences in the user. These environments can be almost indistinguishable from real ones, trying to create lifelike experiences (e.g., VRs for pilot training) or fantastic imagined worlds that are completely different from reality (e.g., in video games or interactive stories).

A key idea behind VRs is the ancient human desire to use media to escape the boundaries imposed by the *real world* and experience *physical transcendence* (Biocca, King, & Levy, 1995), in other words, to go beyond the laws of time and space and move beyond the limits of the body and sensory channels. Is it possible to go back to the 13th century and travel with Marco Polo and enjoy his experiences at the court of Kublai Khan? Is it possible to move back in time and experience the Big Bang moment? Is it possible to communicate and interact with someone located light years away in a distant galaxy, or move to a microscopic quantum world?

VRs are a step forward in our *communication channels to reality* (Sekuler & Blake, 1994). A further milestone in humans' long journey of discovery and conquest is the use of tools, which has always been seen

The Science of Cognitive Behavioral Therapy.
DOI: http://dx.doi.org/10.1016/B978-0-12-803457-6.00022-2

551

as a fundamental characteristic of the human being. In fact, it is considered a significant factor in the evolution and development of the human species (Stringer & Andrews, 1988): from the first "Old woman stone tools" (Semaw et al., 2003) to contemporary Information and Communication Technologies (ICTs), such as the Internet, Google, Wikipedia, or the powerful Facebook, Twitter, and Instagram social networks (Botella et al., 2012).

In the case of VRs, important steps were taken by people such as Edward Link, who in 1929 created the *Link Trainer*, the first commercial flight simulator, mainly used during World War II to train pilots. In 1950 Morton Heilig developed the *Sensorama* to create a cinematographic experience that stimulates all the senses and fully immerses the person in the film, and he also developed the first Head Mounted Display. In 1965 Ivan Sutherland published *The Ultimate Display*, where he described a virtual world generated by a computer and kept in real time. Shortly after that, in 1968, Sutherland and his student Bob Sproull created the first VR Head Mounted Display connected to a computer and not to a camera. It was so heavy that it had to be suspended from the ceiling, leading to its name, *Sword of Damocles*. A few years later, Jaron Lanier called the new tool Virtual Reality, giving a name to the new field. Finally, the Matrix Film in 1999 showed the possibility of living in fully simulated worlds without really being aware. In fact, Tart (1991) stated that we already live in a variety of internally generated virtual realities. *"We each live 'inside' a world simulation machine. We almost always forget that our perception is a simulation, not reality itself, and we almost always forget that we have anything to do with the particulars of how the simulation works . . . . The structure of our nervous system, as programmed by our personal psychology, constitutes our stereo headphones and 'eyephones,' our 'touchphones,' 'tastephones,' and 'smellphones' (p. 227).* This idea is related to Marshall McLuhan's proposal (McLuhan, 1966) about media as extensions of ourselves; *media are extensions of the senses.*

As noted above, VR refers to the use of technology to create virtual worlds that simulate reality and only exist in the computer memory. That is, VRs aim to create the illusion of being present in worlds where we really are not. It is mainly a mental experience that makes the user believe that *he/she is there, present in the virtual world, and that this experience is real.* The user stops being a mere observer and becomes an active participant, entering the virtual adventure where it is possible to interact with objects and beings existing in the virtual world. This feeling *of being there, of judging this experience as something real and nonmediated,* immersed in a world that responds to our actions, experiencing the physical and emotional impact of perceptive clues we recognize and find believable, has been called *sense of presence* (Botella, Perpiñá, Baños, & García-Palacios, 1998; Lombard & Ditton, 1997; Riva et al., 2015; Riva,

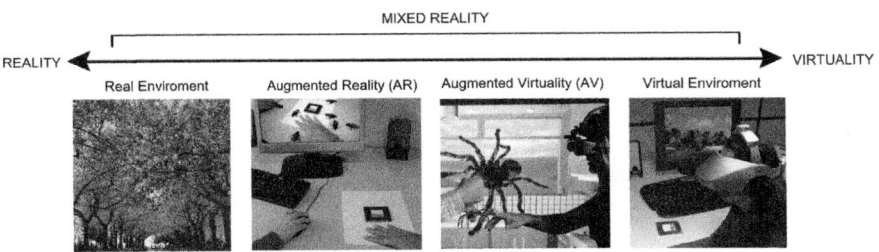

FIGURE 22.1   Reality-virtuality continuum.

2005). This term usually refers to a widely reported sensation experienced during the use of VRs, but also during the use of other media. "Users experiencing presence report having a compelling sense of being in a mediated space other than where their physical body is located" (Slater & Usoh, 1993).

Milgram and Kishino (1994) proposed the Mixed Reality concept, which involves the merging of real and virtual worlds somewhere along the *virtuality continuum* that connects completely real environments to completely virtual ones. As illustrated in Fig. 22.1, this concept relates to the mixture of classes of objects presented in any particular display situation, where real environments are shown at one end of the continuum, and virtual environments are shown at the opposite extreme. The left part of the continuum defines environments consisting solely of real objects in the real world (such as, the therapist's office). The right part defines environments consisting solely of virtual environments and virtual objects that completely replace the real world, for instance, a VR application for the treatment of panic disorder and agoraphobia that includes different relevant environments such as a mall, a bus, and a subway (Botella et al., 2004). In the middle, we find Augmented Reality: A real environment is *augmented* by means of virtual (computer graphic) objects, adding relevant information to the real world. For instance, an Augmented Reality system for the treatment of small animal phobia allows the patient to interact with the feared objects (virtual spiders or cockroaches) in the real world (Botella et al., 2005; Botella, Bretón, Quero, Baños, & García-Palacios, 2010). Finally, in Augmented Virtuality, a virtual world is being augmented and connected by sensors to the real world. An example would be a tactile augmentation that includes a toy spider that the patient can touch while immersed in the virtual Spider World for the treatment of spider phobia (Hoffman, García-Palacios, Carlin, Furness, & Botella, 2003).

This field of research has been significantly developed during the past 20 years in many domains. This chapter describes some of the most important achievements and discusses possible directions and perspectives for future developments in the Clinical and Health Psychology fields.

VR AS A STIMULATING, SAFE, AND CONTROLLED THERAPEUTIC CONTEXT

VRs are not a new form of therapy, but rather a set of technological developments within the current Clinical and Health Psychology fields (especially cognitive behavioral therapy—CBT—approaches) that can help the clinician to conduct the interventions in a more ecological and effective manner (David, Matu, & David, 2013). The many possible combinations of these *mixed realities* offer different benefits/advantages.

1. VRs are important communication media that are able to generate useful experiences in patients in order to provide them with new knowledge and meanings related to their problems. For instance, VRs can help therapists to show patients that the world and the self they perceive right now may not exactly match the reality (e.g., the extremely dangerous world an agoraphobic patient may perceive does not correspond exactly to the real world). A key element of VRs is the possibility that they help us open the patient's eyes to other new potential realities. Philip K. Dick defends this idea (Philip, 1988) when he explains what science fiction is and what makes *good* science fiction:

   > "We have a fictitious world; that is the first step: it is a society that does not in fact exist, but is predicated on our known society; that is, our known society acts as a jumping-off point for it; the society advances out of our own in some way..., our world transformed into that which is not or not yet;—this is the essence of science fiction, the **conceptual dislocation** within the society so that as a result new society is generated in the author's mind ..." and "in **good** science fiction the conceptual dislocation—the new idea—must be truly new ... stimulating, and, probably most important of all, it sets off a chain-reaction of ramification-ideas in the mind of the reader"...

   As occurs in science fiction, VRs allow us to work with patients in these stimulating and therapeutic environments to help them see that there are other possible ways of perceiving the world and the self, helping them to discover their strengths and promoting their positive functioning (Botella et al., 2012; Riva, Baños, Botella, Wiederhold, & Gaggioli, 2012).

2. VRs make it possible to go beyond reality. It is possible to design and develop new *virtual* situations, context or vital moments where the patient can start working in another way. For instance, the patient who suffers from fear of public speaking can practice before

the feared conference using significant variations (the difficulty and length of the talk, the quality of the performance, the receptiveness of the audience). In the same way, in our VR software for claustrophobia, the walls of a room or a lift can start to move, making a terrible noise, and shutting the patient up in a very small room.

3. VRs can be excellent sources of information about self-efficacy. Of all the possible sources of self-efficacy information proposed by Bandura (1977), performance accomplishments are especially influential because they are based on personal mastery experiences. VRs allow the therapist, without leaving the consultation room, to design different environments to assure the patient's success in each of his/her *virtual adventures*. It is possible to include some difficulties, challenges or occasional failures, which, later on can be overcome by the patient. Bandura's theory also predicts that, once established, self-efficacy is generalized to other situations. Therefore, we can use different graded/structured VR environments to achieve efficacy expectations of the highest magnitude, generality and strength (Botella et al., 1998; Botella, Baños, Perpiñá, & Ballester, 1988). A fundamental point here is that what is learned in VRs can be generalized to real life, which encourages the use of VRs to enhance the classic exposure technique (David et al., 2013; Opriş et al., 2012).

4. This ability of VRs is also important based on the inhibitory learning paradigm recently defended by Craske, Treanor, Conway, Zbozinek, and Vervliet (2014). VRs can be used to appeal to strategies such as expectancy violation or variability rather than to long exposure periods. In recent studies, VR environments were used in the treatment of spider phobia to examine whether exposure to the phobic stimulus in different contexts and/or with different stimuli reduces the recurrence of fear (Dunsmoor, Zielinski, & LaBar, 2014; Shiban, Pauli, & Mühlberger, 2013; Shiban, Schelhorn, Pauli, & Mühlberger, 2015). Results showed that exposure to multiple virtual stimuli produced a positive effect in terms of fear reinstatement and generalization of results.

5. VRs allow complete control over the situation, offering a controlled and sheltered environment where the patient can begin to explore, experience and act without feeling threatened (by the external world or by oneself) (Botella et al., 1988). Depending on the patient's needs, the therapist can introduce the feared situation in a more or less difficult or threatening way (e.g., number of people at the shopping mall; worse or better weather on the flight; number and size of spiders or cockroaches, and holding a positive or negative image of the self in the mind during a speech). Then, the patient can confront

the situation that he/she has always considered threatening without any risk, because nothing that the patient fears can actually happen. The claustrophobic patient can take a lift in a virtual world simulating the lift at the Empire State building, making sure the elevator will not be trapped between floors. A patient suffering from fear of flying will not experience turbulence or bad weather. In the case of a patient with fear of public speaking, nobody from the audience will laugh at him/her. This controlled and sheltered environment can be considered a *secure base* (Bowlby, 1973) where the patient can freely explore, experience, live, or revive current or past feelings and thoughts.

6. Within the general CBT framework, VRs may be used to implement different techniques more ecologically (David et al., 2013) designing controlled feared environments; applying problem-solving techniques (e.g., social skills training), whereas the patient is immersed in the relevant social environments; or applying coping strategies or cognitive restructuring whereas the patient is exposed to critical activating virtual stimuli (Szentagotai, Opris, & David, 2011).

7. Regarding the use of the imaginal exposure technique, VRs also have advantages for patients who have trouble imagining (Difede & Hoffman, 2002). Using the painting metaphor about imagery rescripting in CBT (Holmes, Arntz, & Smucker, 2007), VRs could be considered useful *imagery-interactive* techniques to view the *canvas* in a different way (repainting it), helping the patient to recognize that a negative image is merely a mental representation, and not reality per se. VR's flexibility makes it possible to modify the images in some of the ways proposed by Rachman (2007), replacing them with other more benign images, by reshaping, rescripting, or shrinking them to tiny dimensions. In sum, VRs can be a useful adjunct in applying this kind of experiential work in CBT.

8. VRs offer complete privacy and confidentiality, which is important from an ethical point of view. Different techniques (including exposure) can be applied through VRs, without leaving the therapist's office. VRs become an important therapeutic tool that both patient and therapist can use to start interacting and become familiar with the situation and the feared context, an intermediate step between the therapist's office and the real world, and a first step that may be crucial in the patient's decision to confront the real world.

9. All these VR characteristics make it possible to increase the self-training possibilities. The patient can work in a safe way on a given situation until he/she achieves a certain degree of control over it, thus strengthening the treatment outcomes. Moreover, given the

flexibility of VRs, all this therapeutic work can be done at the time and rhythm the patient wants or needs (Botella et al., 1998).

Considering all these possibilities, it is not surprising that the data indicate that VR exposure is well accepted, both among subclinical (García-Palacios, Hoffman, Kwong See, Tsai, & Botella, 2001) and clinical populations (García-Palacios, Botella, Hoffman, & Fabregat, 2007).

VR EFFICACY AS A PSYCHOLOGICAL TREATMENT TOOL

VRs have been used for the treatment of several disorders. Meta-analyses and systematic review studies conducted so far on the efficacy of VRs for the treatment of anxiety disorders, stress related disorders, psychosis, eating disorders, and health conditions (like pain management) are presented in Table 22.1.

In this section, we will briefly comment on the main conclusions derived from these review studies. Other studies not included in the reviews that provide initial support in some disorders will be briefly described.

Anxiety Disorders

As Table 22.1 shows, many of the meta-analyses (Opriş et al., 2012; Parsons & Rizzo, 2008; Powers & Emmelkamp, 2008) and systematic reviews (Gregg & Tarrier, 2007; McCann et al., 2014; Meyerbroker & Emmelkamp, 2010) include a mixture of several anxiety disorders (specific phobias, social phobia, panic disorder, agoraphobia, generalized anxiety disorder), and they also include posttraumatic stress disorder, as the majority of studies were conducted before the DSM-5 (American Psychiatric Association, 2013) was published.

Table 22.1 also shows other broader review studies which, in addition to anxiety disorders, also include other mental disorders (e.g., addiction) and other conditions (e.g., pain management or traumatic brain injury) (Turner & Casey, 2014) or subclinical anxiety (Diemer, Mühlberger, Pauli, & Zwanzger, 2014). Finally, one meta-analysis (Morina, Ijntema, Meyerbröker, & Emmelkamp, 2015) and one systematic review (Chicchi-Giglioli, Pallavicini, Pedroli, Serino, & Riva, 2015) focus on one anxiety disorder, specific phobias. Next, the main results and conclusions obtained for each anxiety disorder will be described. The efficacy in the case of posttraumatic stress disorder will be addressed later in this section.

TABLE 22.1 Meta-Analyses and Systematic Reviews Related to the Efficacy of VR/AR for Anxiety Disorders, Posttraumatic Stress Disorder, Psychosis, Eating Disorders and Obesity, and Pain Management

Disorders	Review Type	Paper	Included Studies	Sample	Studies Type	Standard Quality (Yes/No)	Results	Conclusions
Anxiety disorders Arach., Acro., FF, SP/SAD, Ag, PTSD	Meta-analysis	Parsons and Rizzo (2008)	21	Clinical and nonclinical (N = 300)	Clinical trials, between-groups design	No	VRs as an exposure technique had statistically large effects on all affective domains, as well as all anxiety/phobia groupings evaluated	VRs appears effective from a clinical psychology standpoint. Future studies are needed that report uniform and detailed information regarding presence, immersion, anxiety and/or phobia duration, and demographics
Anxiety disorders SPs, SP/SAD, PD, PTSD	Meta-analysis	Powers and Emmelkamp (2008)	13	Clinical (N = 397)	Well-controlled trials with random or matched assignment	No	A large mean effect size for VRs as an exposure technique compared to control conditions, Cohen's $d = 1.11$ (S.E. = 0.15, 95% CI: 0.82–1.39). In vivo treatment was not significantly more effective than VR exposure. There was a small effect size favoring VRs exposure over in vivo conditions, Cohen's $d = 0.35$ (S.E. = 0.15, 95% CI: 0.05–0.65)	VRs as an exposure technique are highly effective in treating phobias and more so than inactive (waiting list and attention control) and active (relaxation, bibliotherapy) control conditions. Also, VRs exposure is slightly but significantly more effective than exposure in vivo, the gold standard in the field

Anxiety disorders FF, Arach., Acro., SP/SAD, PD/Ag, PTSD	Meta-analysis	Opriş, Pintea, García-Palacios, Botella, Szamosközi, and David (2012)	23	Clinical (N = 608)	RCT	No	VRs exposure does far better than the waitlist control, and similar efficacy is found between the behavioral and the cognitive behavioral interventions incorporating a VRs exposure component vs. the classical evidence-based interventions. VRs have a powerful real-life impact, similar to that of the classical evidence-based treatments, and good stability in results over time. There is no difference in the dropout rate between VRs exposure and in vivo exposure	Results should be regarded with certain caution, given the relatively small number of studies and subjects involved. Similarly, the results cannot be generalized to the whole spectrum of anxiety disorders, given the limited availability of studies for certain anxiety disorders. Even in the case of the disorders for which some RCT exist, we have to note that the number of subjects and the number of studies are still rather small
Anxiety disorders SPs, SAD, PD, PTSD, AdD, PG **Other MD** Sch., Add. **Others** PM, IDD, CP, MS, TBI, D	Meta-analysis	Turner and Casey (2014)	30	Clinical and subclinical (N = 1485)	RCT	Yes	Random effects meta-analysis found an overall moderate effect size for VR interventions. Individual meta-analyses found an overall large effect size compared to nonintervention wait-lists, and an overall moderate effect size compared to active interventions. No correlation was found between treatment outcomes and methodological rigor	Limitations may include limited study numbers, the use of a single coder, a need for more in-depth analyses of variation in the form of VR intervention, and omission of presence as a moderating factor. The current review supports VR interventions as efficacious, promising forms of psychological treatment

(Continued)

TABLE 22.1 (Continued)

Disorders	Review Type	Paper	Included Studies	Sample	Studies Type	Standard Quality (Yes/No)	Results	Conclusions
Specific phobias Acro., Arach.	Meta-analysis	Morina et al. (2015)	14	Clinical (N = 479)	Clinical trials, between groups design	No	Patients undergoing VR did significantly better on behavioral assessments following treatment than before treatment, with an aggregated uncontrolled effect size of g 1/4 1.23. Also, they performed better on behavioral assessments at post-treatment than patients on wait-list (g 1/4 1.41). Results of behavioral assessment at post-treatment and at follow-up revealed no significant differences between VR exposure and in vivo exposure (g 1/4 _0.09 and 0.53, respectively).	Results demonstrate that VR exposure can produce significant behavior change in real-life situations and support its application in treating specific phobias. With regard to other disorders, future research needs to apply behavioral assessments in real-life as a means of measuring the efficacy of VR exposure. In general, more methodologically strong RCT with adequate power are needed to draw firmer conclusions
Anxiety disorders Acro., FF, DP, Arach., SP/SAD, PD & Ag, PTSD, BID	Systematic review	Gregg and Tarrier (2007)	17	Students and clinical (N = 731)	Between groups design	No	More than 50 studies using VRs were identified (the majority were case studies). Seventeen employed a between-groups design. VR-based therapy appears to be superior to no treatment; however, the effectiveness of VR therapy over traditional approaches is not supported by the research currently available	There is a lack of good quality research on the effectiveness of VR therapy. Greater emphasis must be placed on controlled trials with clinically identified populations

Disorder	Type	Study	N	Sample	Design	Controlled	Results	Conclusions
Anxiety disorders FF, Acro., SP/SAD, PD, PTSD	Systematic review	Meyerbroker and Emmelkamp (2010)	20	Clinical (N = 760)	Between groups design	No	Only in two specific phobias has more or less systematic research been done to state that VRs as an exposure technique is effective in comparison with the state-of-the-art CBT treatment, controlling for the effect of time. In more complex anxiety disorders, results of VRs as an exposure technique are promising	In outcome research on VRs as an exposure technique, often multiple components are merged in treatment protocols. These combined treatments are not always based on the state-of-the-art treatment for these specific disorders. Furthermore, it is necessary to dismantle the research methodology to separate the contribution of the various components
Anxiety disorders FF, Acro., Arach., PS/SA, SchP, PD & Ag, GAD, PTSD, MSRD	Systematic review	McCann et al. (2014)	27	Clinical (N = 1080)	RCT	Yes	VR exposure was found to have a small effect size advantage over active comparison groups and a large effect size advantage over inactive comparison groups, regardless of quality. Adherence to the study quality criteria was generally low, and this quality did not predict effect size	VR exposure may be an effective method of treatment, but caution should be exercised in interpreting the existing body of literature supporting VRs as an exposure technique relative to existing standards of care
Anxiety disorders FF, Acro., Arach., DP, SP/SAD, PD & Ag, PTSD **Subclinical** SA, FT, FH, FPS	Systematic review	Diemer et al. (2014)	38	Clinical, subclinical and healthy (N = 1267)	Case studies, quasi-experimental, randomized, crossover, observational counterbalanced	No	VRs exposure does provoke psychophysiological arousal, especially in terms of electrodermal activity. Results on psychophysiological habituation in VR are inconclusive. Study design and methodological rigor vary widely	Despite several limitations, this review provides evidence that VR exposure elicits psychophysiological fear reactions in patients and healthy subjects, rendering VRs a promising treatment for anxiety disorders, and a potent research tool for future investigations of psychophysiological processes and their significance during exposure treatment

(Continued)

TABLE 22.1 (Continued)

Disorders	Review Type	Paper	Included Studies	Sample	Studies Type	Standard Quality (Yes/No)	Results	Conclusions
Healthy								
ST, PS, VP, T/D, PA, H, H/I								AR seems to be a promising and useful tool for intervention in the treatment of specific phobias. Nevertheless, the small sample of subjects examined and the lack of a control group and randomized controlled studies show the need for more RCT to explore AR efficacy in clinical treatments
SPs SAP (cockroach & spider)	Systematic review	Chicchi-Giglioli et al. (2015)	13	Clinical (N = 689) and healthy (N = 74)	Case studies, multiple baseline design, experimental studies	No	To date AR has been mainly used in the evaluation and treatment of specific phobias such as phobias for small animals (cockroaches and spiders) and acrophobia. All these studies show that AR elicits anxiety as soon as the stimulus appears that decreases during the time of exposure	
PTSD	Systematic review	Goncalves, Pedrozo, Coutinho, Figueira, and Ventura (2012)	10	Clinical (N = 184)	6 controlled studies, 4 uncontrolled studies	Yes		VRs as an exposure technique proved to be as efficacious as traditional exposure therapy for different types of trauma. VRs exposure can be particularly useful in the treatment of PTSD that is resistant to traditional exposure

PTSD	Systematic review	Motraghi et al. (2014)	9	Clinical (N = 113)	Controlled studies	Yes	Preliminary findings suggest some positive results for VRs as an exposure technique for PTSD. However, the CONSORT appraisal revealed that the methodological quality of the studies was variable. The authors recommend additional research using well-specified randomization procedures, assessor blinding, and monitoring of treatment adherence
PTSD	Systematic review	Botella et al. (2015)	12	Clinical (N = 338)	Controlled studies	Yes	VRs as an exposure technique are effective for PTSD. Need for more controlled studies, standardization of treatment protocols, and including assessment of acceptability
Psychosis	Meta-analysis	Välimäki et al. (2014)	3	Clinical (N = 156)	Controlled studies	Yes	VRs had little effect on compliance, cognitive functioning, social skills, or acceptability of the intervention. Satisfaction with the intervention was better for the VR group

(Continued)

TABLE 22.1 (Continued)

Disorders	Review Type	Paper	Included Studies	Sample	Studies Type	Standard Quality (Yes/No)	Results	Conclusions
Psychosis	Systematic review	Veling et al. (2014)	4	Clinical (N = 257)	Uncontrolled and controlled studies	Yes		Small but expanding literature on VR interventions for delusions, hallucinations, neurocognition, social cognition, and social skills; Preliminary results are promising. VR appear to have a great potential for increasing our understanding of psychosis and expanding the therapeutic toolbox
Eating disorders and obesity	Systematic review	Ferrer-García and Gutierrez-Maldonado (2012)	12	Clinical (N = 86) Non clinical (N = 223)	Case studies, uncontrolled and controlled studies	Yes		Findings suggest that VR-based therapy is an effective intervention for treating body image disturbances. However, the review points out the lack of controlled studies and some methodological limitations that need to be addressed in future research
Eating disorders and obesity	Systematic review	Ferrer-García et al. (2013)	17	Clinical samples (N = 549)	Case studies, uncontrolled and controlled studies	Yes		Evidence of the efficacy of VR-based treatments for ED and obesity. The VR component seems to be especially suitable for reducing body image disturbances and for increasing self-esteem and self-efficacy

Pain	Systematic review	Morris, Louw, and Grimmer-Somers (2009)	9	Clinical samples (N = 152)	Case studies and controlled studies	Yes	VR distraction combined with pharmacologic analgesics significantly reduced pain during wound dressing changes and physiotherapy in burn injury patients
Pain	Systematic review	Malloy and Milling (2010)	11	Clinical (N = 261) Non clinical (N = 218)	Controlled studies	Yes	VR distraction was effective for reducing experimental pain, as well as the discomfort associated with burn injury care. Studies of needle-related pain provided less consistent findings. Overall, VR distraction may be useful for pain control with a variety of pain problems
Pain	Systematic review	Triberti et al. (2014)	11	Clinical (N = 212) Non clinical (N = 169)	Controlled studies	Yes	Results suggest that different psychological variables influenced VR analgesia. Sense of presence influenced the effectiveness of VR as a distraction tool. Anxiety as well as positive emotions directly affect the experience of pain

(Continued)

TABLE 22.1 (Continued)

Disorders	Review Type	Paper	Included Studies	Sample	Studies Type	Standard Quality (Yes/No)	Results	Conclusions
Pain	Systematic review	Garrett et al. (2014)	17	Clinical (N = 337)	Case studies and controlled studies	Yes		VR distraction showed evidence of short-term pain reduction. The short-term effects on physical function were moderate. Little evidence exists for longer-term benefits. The authors recommend further high-quality studies for the conclusive judgment of its effectiveness in acute pain, to establish potential benefits for chronic pain, and for safety

Note: Arach., arachnophobia; *Acro.,* acrophobia; *FF,* flying phobia; *SP/SAD,* Social Phobia/Social Anxiety Disorder; *Ag,* agoraphobia; *PD,* panic disorder; *SPs,* specific phobias; *PTSD:* posttraumatic stress disorder; *AdD,* adjustment disorders; *PG,* pathological guilt; *MD,* mental disorders; *Sch.,* schizophrenia; *Add.,* addition; *PM,* pain management; *IDD,* intellectual and developmental disabilities; *CP,* cerebral palsy; *MS,* multiple sclerosis; *TBI,* traumatic brain injury; *D,* dementia; *DP,* driving phobia; *BID,* body image disturbance; *PS/SA,* public speaking/social anxiety; *SchP,* school phobia: *GAD,* generalized anxiety disorder; *MSRD,* mixed stress-related disorders: *FT,* fear of tunnels; *FH,* fear of heights; *FPS,* fear of public speaking; *ST,* stress test; *VP,* visual pit; *T/D,* tunnel/darkness; *PA,* performance anxiety; *H,* height; *H/I,* hospital/injection; *SAP,* small animal phobia.

Specific Phobias

There is clear evidence about the efficacy of VRs for the treatment of specific phobias. Overall, results obtained in the four meta-analytic studies and the four systematic review studies show that VR is an effective exposure technique to treat anxiety disorders, with stronger evidence for specific phobias (acrophobia and fear of flying). In fact, a large number of studies included in these reviews were designed for the treatment of specific phobias (mainly arachnophobia, acrophobia, and fear of flying). Additionally, one meta-analysis specifically conducted for this disorder (Morina et al., 2015) demonstrates that gains from VR as an exposure technique can be generalized to real life. Moreover, a systematic review on the use of Augmented Reality as an exposure technique for small animal phobias shows that is a promising alternative for this problem (Chicchi et al., 2015). In addition, the first Randomized Controlled Trial assessing the efficacy of an Augmented Reality system compared to in vivo exposure for cockroach and spider phobias (Botella, Pérez-Ara, et al., 2016) shows that all participants improved after treatment, and the gains were maintained at follow-ups. Although in vivo exposure was more effective at post-treatment on some outcome measures, these differences disappeared at follow-ups. Along the same lines, the meta-analysis by Wolitzky-Taylor, Horowitz, Powers, and Telch (2008), comparing in vivo exposure versus other exposure modalities (imaginal, virtual), showed that, while in vivo exposure may be more efficacious in the short-term, this advantage is no longer present at follow-up.

Social Anxiety Disorder and Panic Disorder and Agoraphobia

From the existing meta-analyses and systematic review studies, we can conclude that there is some initial evidence, but it is not definitive (e.g., Meyerbroker & Emmelkamp, 2010; Powers & Emmelkamp, 2008). Moreover, as highlighted by most studies, and specifically by McCann et al. (2014) and Turner and Casey (2014), the quality of future research must be improved. In the specific case of *social anxiety disorder*, a systematic review on the use of VRs and Internet for the treatment of this problem is also available (García-García, Rosa-Alcázar, & Olivares-Olivares, 2011). The authors conclude that the inclusion of VRs and Internet in psychological treatments is very promising for the treatment of social anxiety disorder, with one of the most relevant limitations being the small number of participants used in the studies. In the case of *panic disorder and agoraphobia*, a controlled study exists, not included in the review studies analyzed above, that examines the contribution of VRs in applying the interoceptive exposure component for panic disorder and agoraphobia treatment (Pérez-Ara et al., 2010). The results showed that the efficacy of VRs in exposing patients to their feared sensations was similar to that of the traditional interoceptive exposure procedures (e.g., hyperventilation and running in place). Good acceptability of VRs in applying interoceptive exposure was also reported by patients (Quero et al., 2013).

Generalized Anxiety Disorder

The potential efficacy of VRs in this problem remains to be demonstrated. Due to the wide variety of topics that can trigger and fuel patients' worries, VRs in the treatment of this problem addressed the control of anxiety in general. Only one systematic review (McCann et al., 2014) included a study conducted by Riva's group (Gorini et al., 2010) showing the possibility of using VRs in the treatment of generalized anxiety disorder, but an important limitation was the small sample size. In a later study addressing a different aspect of this clinical trial, Repetto et al. (2011) assessed the possibility of using an ubiquitous approach, based on a virtual environment uploaded on a mobile phone. Even if the small sample means this study is considered a pilot study, results confirm the possibility of using VRs in the treatment of generalized anxiety disorder, and they support the clinical use of a mobile phone to reexperience and anchor the contexts of the VR sessions at home.

Obsessive–Compulsive Disorder

As Kim, Kim, Kim, Roh, and Kim (2009) point out, the number of VR tools addressing *obsessive–compulsive disorder* is still lacking, perhaps due to the heterogeneous symptoms of this problem. Preliminary data (e.g., Kim et al., 2010, 2012) show that checking in virtual situations can specifically elicit the expected response in people suffering from obsessive–compulsive disorder. However, to date no controlled study has been conducted to test the efficacy of VR for this problem.

Additionally, broader review studies on the application of ICTs in general (including VRs) for mental health are available in the literature (Aboujaoude, Salame, & Naim, 2015; Mohr, Burns, Schueller, Clarke, & Klinkman, 2013; Newman, Szkodny, Llera, & Przeworski, 2011). The conclusions are similar to those obtained in the meta-analyses and systematic reviews. VRs have shown good efficacy for anxiety (mainly for specific phobias), but more controlled studies are needed for other anxiety disorders (panic disorder, social phobia). Related to this, Turner and Casey (2014) assessed the relationship between treatment outcomes and methodological rigor, finding no correlation. In a similar way, McCann et al. (2014) found that adherence to the study quality was generally low; however, study quality did not predict the effect sizes obtained.

In sum, the use of VRs as a treatment tool to apply exposure therapy in the treatment of anxiety disorders is the most highly developed line of research, and there is a large amount of empirical evidence about its efficacy. However, as all the review studies presented in Table 22.1 conclude, more well-designed randomized controlled studies are needed. As Turner and Casey (2014) stated, the use of reporting guidelines such as the CONSORT and CONSORT-EHEALTH statements should promote a greater emphasis on methodological rigor, providing a firm foundation for the further development of clinical VR applications.

Stress-Related Disorder

According to DSM-5 criteria, stress-related disorders include Posttraumatic Stress Disorder and Adjustment Disorders (American Psychiatric Association, 2013). VRs have been used in this field mainly as an alternative way of delivering exposure therapy in the treatment of Posttraumatic Stress Disorder. One of the most effective evidence-based interventions for this disorder is prolonged exposure (Chambless et al., 1998; Foa, Gillihan, & Bryant, 2013; National Institute for Clinical Excellence, 2005), which includes in vivo and imaginal exposure to the stimuli related to the traumatic experience. Imaginal exposure has some limitations, such as difficulties in imagining the traumatic event, or the resistance to becoming emotionally engaged with the memory of the traumatic event (Foa et al., 2013). VRs can help to overcome the limitations of relying solely on the individual's memory and imagination to recall and process the traumatic experience. VRs offer sensory simulations of the events, which can help to augment the individual's imaginative capacities and prevent cognitive avoidance, enhancing emotional engagement, an essential issue in the efficacy of exposure.

Since the first case study to use VR for the treatment of Posttraumatic Stress Disorder (Rothbaum et al., 1999), a growing number of studies have addressed the efficacy and effectiveness of VRs in the treatment of this disorder. Several meta-analyses and systematic reviews (Botella, Serrano, Baños, & Garcia-Palacios, 2015; Gonçalves, Pedrozo, Coutinho, Figueira, & Ventura, 2012; Motraghi, Seim, Meyer, & Morissete, 2014) report that VRs have been used for various trauma victims, such as war veterans, victims of terrorist attacks, motor-vehicle accident victims, and criminal and domestic violence victims. The virtual environments used are mostly realistic replications of the traumatic events, although there are also more flexible virtual environments (adaptive displays) that can be customized to different traumatic events (i.e., Botella, García-Palacios, et al., 2010). VRs have been shown to be equally efficacious as traditional treatments, and outcomes are maintained in the long-term. An interesting result is that VRs could be particularly useful in patients who show resistance to traditional exposure, indicating that it could be an alternative to imaginal exposure in those cases where this way of delivering exposure is not effective. Regarding the limitations of VR exposure research, the available evidence indicates that the methodological quality of the studies is variable (for example when performing a CONSORT appraisal, Motraghi et al., 2014), and additional research is recommended using standardized treatment protocols, randomization procedures, assessor blinding, monitoring of treatment adherence, and assessment of acceptability.

VRs have also been used in the treatment of adjustment disorders. There is only one team working in this field. This VR world is a flexible environment where the stressful event can be represented with symbols (using music, pictures, sounds, videos, etc.) in order to work on and process it (Baños et al., 2009). This world has been successfully tested in the treatment of adjustment disorders (Andreu-Mateu, Botella, Quero, Guillén, & Baños, 2012; Baños et al., 2011; Quero et al., in press).

Psychosis

There are also some VR protocols used in the psychological treatment of psychosis. In this field, VR has been used to promote treatment compliance and as an adjunct to interventions for delusions, hallucinations, neurocognition, and social skills. An interesting contribution of VR in psychosis is the use of avatars. For example, Leff, Williams, Huckvale, Arbuthnot, and Leff (2013) developed a VR system where the patients can create an avatar of their persecutor and engage in a therapeutic dialogue with it with the support of the therapist.

This research is still in an early stage, but a meta-analysis and a systematic review have already been carried out. Regarding promotion of treatment compliance, Välimäki et al. (2014) performed a meta-analysis that included 3 controlled studies and 156 patients. The results indicated no clear evidence for or against the use of VR. VR has little effect on compliance, cognitive functioning, social skills, or acceptability of the intervention. An interesting result was that satisfaction with the intervention was better for the VR group.

The systematic review by Veling, Moritz, and van der Gaag (2014) found 4 studies with a total of 257 patients that explored the use of VR for different treatment targets in psychosis: hallucinations, delusions, social cognition, neurocognition, and social skills. The authors conclude that the research is still scarce, but expanding, and that the preliminary results are promising, indicating a high potential of VR as an adjunct to traditional psychotherapy in the treatment of psychosis.

Eating Disorders and Obesity

VRs have also been used in the field of eating disorders and obesity, mainly for the treatment of body image disturbances. VRs offer the possibility of capturing the complex features of the body image and make it easier to work on its modification and correction (Perpiñá, Botella, & Baños, 2003). VRs are also used for exposure, problem solving and practicing coping skills in difficult situations (eating/emotional/relational management). Two systematic reviews have already been conducted in this field. Ferrer-García and Gutierrez-Maldonado (2012) focused on VR for body image disturbances in eating disorders and found 12 studies (including controlled and uncontrolled studies) with nonclinical and clinical samples. The results of the review indicated that VRs are effective tools for treating body-image disturbances. The authors also recommend improving the methodological quality of the research in future studies.

Ferrer-García, Gutierrez-Maldonado, and Riva (2013) performed a second systematic review, but now including 17 studies with clinical samples suffering eating disorders and obesity and other applications of VR beyond the treatment of body image disturbances (eating/emotional/relational management). Again, they found evidence for the efficacy of VRs for eating disorders and obesity. The VR component was especially suitable for reducing body image disturbances and increasing self-efficacy and self-esteem.

Pain Management

One extended use of VR is for acute pain management. In this field, VRs have mainly been used as a distraction strategy for treating pain associated with medical procedures like wound care, physical therapy, and needle-related pain. The pioneer work in this field was conducted by Hoffman's team, testing the efficacy of VR as a distraction technique for burn patients (Hoffman, Patterson, Carrougher, & Sharar, 2001).

There are already four systematic reviews (Garrett et al., 2014; Morris, Louw, & Grimmer-Somers, 2009; Malloy & Milling, 2010; Triberti, Repetto, & Riva, 2014) addressing the efficacy and utility of VR distraction in nonclinical and clinical populations. These reviews indicate the efficacy of VR for reducing experimental pain and clinical pain. A more detailed analysis of the results showed that studies have demonstrated short-term pain reduction, but little evidence exists for longer term benefits. Triberti et al. (2014) explored the influence of several psychological variables in VR analgesia, finding that the sense of presence influenced the effectiveness of VR as a distraction tool. In addition, both anxiety and positive emotions directly affected the experience of pain.

The use of VR in the field of chronic pain is quite recent. Chronic pain is a more complex condition. The multidimensional perspective includes psychological programs as a promising treatment for chronic pain. Technology, including VR to support the interventions, could help to improve psychological treatments for chronic pain. Keefe et al. (2012) reviewed the possibilities of using VR, indicating some advantages, such as its use to standardize the presentation of therapeutic instructions in important treatment components like exposure. VR could help patients to gain control over pain in a VR environment, which would foster motivation to practice the strategies learned in their daily lives. There are some preliminary studies exploring the combination of VR with other interventions like mindfulness and relaxation for persistent pain (Botella et al., 2013). There is already a small clinical trial comparing VR versus treatment as usual to test the efficacy and acceptability of an activity-pacing component in combination with VR for fibromyalgia (García-Palacios et al., 2015). Participants in the VR condition achieved significant improvements in disability, perceived quality of life, and some coping strategies, and they reported high satisfaction with the VR component. These results show the potential of VR as a useful tool in combination with key therapeutic ingredients for the psychological treatment of chronic pain.

In sum, although the available evidence about the effectiveness of VR is uneven, depending on the problems addressed, the data so far are consistent enough to recommend further progress in this field.

VRs AS ECOLOGICAL ASSESSMENT SETTINGS

VRs have been proposed as an ecological form of assessment in psychology. Most of the assessment instruments used in clinical psychology are self-report measures. In developing these instruments, there are good standards of quality, and we have reliable and valid instruments available that can be used to measure complex constructs like catastrophization (Pain Catastrophization Scale: Sullivan, Bishop, & Pivik, 1995) or emotion dysregulation (Difficulties in Emotion Regulation Scale, Gratz & Roemer, 2004). Despite their utility, self-reports present limitations mainly related to ecological validity, which are overcome by using more ecological measures such as behavioral observations and rating scales of performance in natural settings. However, these methods are usually more difficult to administer and more expensive than paper and pencil self-report questionnaires. VRs could help in the task of developing more ecological measures that would be easier to deliver at a lower cost.

As mentioned above, VRs allow the presentation and control of different stimuli within dynamic and flexible environments, as well as offering methods for capturing and quantifying users' behavioral responses. One of the key features of VR is its capacity to generate simulated environments that mimic the outside world and use them to immerse patients in simulations that support different assessment procedures (Rizzo, Parsons, Kenny, & Buckwalter, 2012).

David et al. (2013) have proposed a new paradigm of evidence-based VR assessment tools in order to complement the existing psychological assessment instruments by obtaining more ecologically valid clinical information. In their review, David et al. state that this paradigm is only beginning, but the results so far are promising. Here we will present the most important advances in this field.

Pugnetti and colleagues (Pugnetti et al., 1995, 1998) developed a VR scenario that resembles the Wisconsin Card Sorting Test. It consists of a virtual building where users are required to use environmental cues to select appropriate doorways to go from room to room. This VR scenario was tested, and the results indicated that the VR system was more accurate than the Wisconsin Card Sorting Test in identifying executive function deficits (Elkind, Rubin, Rosenthal, Skoff, & Prather, 2001; Mendozzi, Motta, Barbieri, Alpini, & Pugnetti, 1998).

Rizzo et al. (2006) conducted a pioneer study in this area, developing the *Virtual Classroom*. It is a VR scenario for the assessment of attentional processes in children. It consisted of a simulated classroom in which children's attention performance was assessed while a series of common classroom distractors were systematically controlled and manipulated. The data obtained from testing the *Virtual Classroom* for the assessment of Attention Deficit Hyperactivity Disorder show that it provides controlled performance assessment within an ecologically valid environment. In a similar direction, other researchers have created virtual worlds designed to assess cognitive and functional performance in order to test and train children suffering from developmental disorders on activities relevant to them, such as fire safety (Rizzo, Strickland, & Bouchard, 2004) or street-crossing (Bart, Katz, Weiss, & Josman, 2008; Strickland, Marcus, Mesibov, & Hogan, 1996).

VR assessment tools have also been developed in the field of body image disturbances and eating disorders. Riva and colleagues developed the Body Image Virtual Reality Scale, an assessment tool designed to assess cognitive and affective components of body image. The Body Image Virtual Reality Scale includes seven female and seven male schematic figures that range from underweight to overweight to obtain precisely graduated increments between adjacent sizes. Perpiñá et al. (1999) developed virtual environments containing a 3D figure whose body parts can be enlarged or reduced. It is possible to conduct behavioral tests, and several discrepancy indices related to weight and figure can be combined. Ferrer-Garcia and Gutierrez-Maldonado (2008), Ferrer-Garcia, Gutierrez-Maldonado, Caqueo-Uritzar, and Moreno (2009) developed VR environments that are able to produce similar responses to those observed in the real world, and they have been shown to be useful for studying within-subject variability in body image disturbances. Purvis, Jones, Bailey, Bailenson, and Taylor (2015) explored the use of VR to elicit and detect changes in body image disturbances using high or low levels of body salience and social presence. The VR environments were different social settings (i.e., party, beach) and included the presence of thin, normal weight, and overweight avatars. The study tested the utility of these VRs environments in college students with high and low body concerns, and found that this type of assessment was useful.

In summary, VRs can help to develop measures to capture important and complex psychological variables in a more ecological way. This line of research is promising, and it is important to progress in exploring the clinical utility of these innovative assessment tools.

VR AS A REALISTIC LABORATORY SETTING FOR PSYCHOPATHOLOGY

The uses of VRs are not only limited to assessment and treatment, but they also include experimental research. VRs are proving to be a valuable methodology for developing an understanding of several psychopathological phenomena. VRs offer *highly realistic* simulations of the world where the person *can feel* like he/she is there and that the environment is real. They can be conceived as a laboratory setting where the researcher can control a large number of variables, while reliably registering a large number of responses (neurological, physiological, self-reports, etc.), but without having to sacrifice external validity to promote the internal validity of the experiments. In other words, because the person *is immersed* in a *realistic* world, simulating the environment and the tasks he/she performs in the *real* world, the generalizability of the results is significantly enhanced (Baños, Botella, & Perpiñá, 1999).

This specific range of VRs possibilities is only beginning to be explored, but the literature already contains some relevant examples of how this realistic laboratory can help us to understand some psychological and psychopathological phenomena. For instance, VRs have been used to study psychotic disorders. In this area, the work done by Freeman stands out. According to this author, *VR holds great promise in furthering the understanding and treatment of psychosis* (Freeman, 2008, p. 605), and he has proposed seven different applications of VRs to psychosis: symptom assessment, identification of symptom markers, establishment of predictive factors, tests of putative causal factors, investigation of the differential prediction of symptoms, determination of toxic elements in the environment, and treatment development. Moreover, VRs make it possible to control social environments, one of the key variables in understanding psychosis, thus providing many very relevant and exciting applications for research and treatment. Specifically, Freeman and colleagues (Freeman et al., 2005, 2007, 2008; Freeman, Pugh, Vorontsova, Antley, & Slater, 2010) have used VRs to study the occurrence of paranoid delusions and assessed whether individuals misinterpret the virtual avatars (computer characters representing people in virtual environments) as being hostile. Results have shown that patients with persecutory delusions had higher levels of paranoia in VR scenarios than individuals with high nonclinical paranoia, who in turn had higher levels of paranoia in VRs than individuals with low levels of paranoia. Thanks to the work of Freeman and others, we now know that use of VRs is feasible and safe in psychotic patients, and that psychotic symptoms and VR experiences are correlated to a degree that supports validity (Veling et al., 2014). Although most studies to date have been small, the preliminary results are promising and suggest that VRs may develop into an important tool for understanding psychotic disorders.

VRs can also be very useful in improving some experimental paradigms used in psychopathology research. For instance, VRs could be designed as *Mood induction procedures* (MIPs) to evoke emotional responses in participants in an experimental situation (Martin, 1990). These procedures have been used in many studies with different purposes, mainly to better understand the emotional processes and their influence on other psychological processes (Kucera & Havieger, 2012). Our group has developed MIPs using VRs (VR-MIPs) to induce different moods (sadness, joy, anxiety, and relaxation). They have been tested in several studies (e.g., Baños, Botella, Liaño, et al., 2004; Baños et al., 2006, 2012), and data have shown that VR-MIPs were able to induce the target moods in participants, and even change this induced mood to the opposite emotion.

Another use of VRs is the study of cognitive biases. So far, several experimental paradigms have been used in this field: the dot probe task, the emotional Stroop task, and other variants. Results using these paradigms in the traditional way have shown that emotionally disordered individuals preferentially process emotionally aversive information (e.g., Williams, Watts, MacLeod, & Mathews, 1988). In these tasks, words, pictures, or photographs with different emotional valences are presented to the participants. As mentioned, VRs make it possible to present more complex stimuli in *real and changing contexts*, as in real life, and then the ecological validity can be enhanced, increasing the generalizability of the outcomes. So far, few studies have applied VRs to the cognitive biases field (e.g., Baños, Botella, Quero, & Salvador, 2004). Recently, Urech, Krieger, Chesham, Mast, and Berger (2015) demonstrated the feasibility of a complex (e.g., body tracking and motor task) VR-based modified dot-probe paradigm in participants with high social anxiety.

Furthermore, as mentioned earlier, in the context of phobias, some authors have emphasized the capability of VRs to model acquisition, extinction, spontaneous recovery, and generalization of fear. Dunsmoor et al. (2014) recently published the first study investigating conditioning with social stimuli in VR, and Shiban et al. (2015) translated an animal model for social fear conditioning to a human sample using an operant social fear conditioning paradigm in VR. These authors point out that using VRs and virtual human agents has several advantages in research. They can simulate a social interaction that is more difficult to implement in a computer, the use of movement in VRs increases ecological validity, and participants' attention will be focused on the experiment, as they are not distracted by the laboratory or the examiner.

Related to the use of *virtual avatars*, VRs have also been proposed to study the self and the embodiment processes. One of the most interesting lines of research to emerge in recent years in the VR field is the inclusion of the (virtual) self in virtual worlds. In this field, different lines of research stand out. Baileson and his group (e.g., Aymerich-Franch, Kizilcec, & Bailenson, 2014; Bailenson, 2012; Fox, Bailenson, & Tricase, 2013) are interested in understanding the dynamics and implications of interactions among people. They consider VRs to be a basic research tool that can create a powerful and persuasive stimulus: the virtual self. Basically, they create avatars with a striking resemblance to the self, and they manipulate them in ways that would be difficult or even impossible in the real world. These virtual self-models are used to manipulate social cognitive constructs, such as identification, self-efficacy, and vicarious reinforcement, and then to encourage the imitation of particular behaviors (e.g., Fox & Bailenson, 2010; Fox, Bailenson, & Binney, 2009). These authors have also studied the implications of having a virtual avatar that represents the person, and the ties that individuals have to them (e.g., Ahn, Fox, & Bailenson, 2012). In a similar way, Slater and colleagues focused on how individuals come to embody their virtual representations of themselves, and they used VRs to alter the participant's sense of body ownership and agency (Kilteni, Norman, Sanchez-Vives, & Slater, 2012). For example, they demonstrated that male participants experienced a body transfer illusion, even when their virtual avatars were female (Slater, Spanlang, Sanchez-Vives, & Blanke,

2010), and that participants successfully embodied avatars that were shaped differently from them (with longer arms) (Kilteni et al., 2012).

These virtual embodiment experiences are being used to promote positive behaviors and human strengths. For instance, Falconer et al. (2014) analyzed the effects of identification with a virtual body to promote self-compassion and overcome excessive self-criticism. In a similar direction, Bailenson and colleagues examined the potential of using experiences of embodied avatars to increase prosocial behavior in the physical world (Rosenberg, Baughman, & Bailenson, 2013) and to elicit greater self-other merging, favorable attitudes, and helping behaviors toward people with disabilities (Ahn, Le, & Bailenson, 2013). Overall, these results show that the knowledge obtained in the virtual experience of being others in a virtual environment can be transferred to the physical world, converting it into an actual helping behavior, even when the other person is a stranger. These are only some examples of the latest VR developments in the field of basic and experimental research that can be very useful in helping us to better understand many psychological problems.

In addition to the advantages and possibilities already mentioned, VR is also a useful way to carry out research that would be ethically difficult to conduct in a real world environment. For instance, Slater and colleagues proposed that VRs could be useful in any social and psychological research where, for ethical or safety reasons, it is not possible to immerse experimental participants in the actual phenomenon to be studied. To demonstrate this, Slater et al. (2006) used VRs to reproduce Stanley Milgram's classic experiment on obedience to authority figures. Slater's aim was not the study of obedience itself, but rather the extent to which individuals would respond to such an extreme social situation as if it were real, in spite of knowing it was virtual. Results showed that, even though all the participants knew that neither the avatar nor the shocks were real, they tended to respond to the situation at the subjective, behavioral, and physiological levels as if they were.

In conclusion, VR applications for experimental research are still in their infancy, but they appear to be very useful tools and have a great potential for increasing our understanding of several psychological and psychopathological phenomena.

FUTURE PERSPECTIVES, EXPANDING, AND MERGING VRs WITH OTHER ICTs

As described in previous sections, the use of VRs to improve mental and physical health fields has been well established in the past two decades. However, VR applications in Clinical and Health Psychology are still in their infancy, and greater growth of VRs apps is expected in the coming years. This growth will come from different sources.

First, more evidence will be found about how VRs can be used to administer effective treatments, expanding the therapeutic toolbox for a broader group of mental disorders and other health problems (increasing complexity and heterogeneity), and allowing a more personalized and contextual diagnostic assessment and treatment. To achieve this goal, better-designed, randomized, controlled studies are needed to prove the utility of VRs.

The future of VR in these fields is also strongly tied to developments in technology. Future VR systems will be cheaper, more user-friendly, and more sophisticated. Currently, major technology companies dedicate a substantial amount of resources to VRs, developing affordable mobile VR headsets (e.g., Facebook: Oculus, Google: Cardboard, HTC: Vive, Samsung: Gear, Sony: PlayStation VR) (Oh et al., in press). These products are cheaper and lighter than their predecessors.

The rise of VRs will be connected to the smartphone industry as well. On the one hand, the impressive growth of smartphone devices has reduced the cost of displays and tracking components required for new VR headsets. On the other hand, a rise in smartphone VR apps is expected, offering visual and audio cues and using lower-cost technologies (Riley et al., 2011). Currently, new headsets like the Oculus Rift or Samsung's Gear VR are able to transform specially adapted smartphone apps into VR experiences. All these features will make VR more widely available in the near future.

In the coming years, VRs are also expected to merge with the Internet-based treatment approach to providing CBT (Andersson, 2009). These advances will make it possible to offer massive patient and therapist access to these treatments, providing the opportunity to reach more people in need and people who have no diagnosable disorder but want to promote their wellbeing. Currently, Internet-based treatments have been found to be effective for different disorders and problems in over 100 controlled studies (Andersson, 2016), and the forecast is that the impact of this field of research on regular mental health care will be even greater in the future (Cuijpers, Riper, & Andersson, 2015). Both fields (the Internet and VR) are expected to be mixed in order to offer more sophisticated treatments. These *Internet-based* VR applications could even offer effective treatment in the absence of a *real* therapist, offering self-guided treatments, or even treatments guided by artificial intelligence agents.

Another source of expansion will come from the combined use of VRs and wearable sensors, in order to monitor different responses (heart rate, galvanic skin response, kinetic information for eye gaze, EEG, fMRI for brain activation patterns, body movements, and so on).

Sensorization in VRs offers a unique opportunity to unobtrusively record and measure human responses, and even respond to them in virtual environments, opening up the possibilities of multiple applications in health-related fields and remote care.

In addition, when automated sensors are combined with electronic devices and mobile devices, the final solutions will make it possible to effectively, economically and continuously collect information in contexts representative of people's everyday lives (Kaplan & Stone, 2013; Nilsen & Pavel, 2013). Good current examples are the experience sampling method (ESM) and ecological momentary assessment, techniques that use immediate reporting of experience in respondents' everyday lives, providing greater data accuracy (Csikszentmihalyi & Larson, 1987; Heron & Smyth, 2010; Shiffman, Stone, & Hufford, 2008). However, as Veling et al. (2014) point out, current ESM procedures do not provide detailed information about the social environment because daily social environments are highly complex, changing, and influenced by the individual's behavior. VRs could help to map interactions between patients, and controlled virtual social environments could be designed in relation to specific symptom domains, physiological responses, and behaviors, leading to a more personalized and contextualized assessment.

Important advances have also been made in the use of interactive VRs since the introduction of Web 2.0, such as SecondLife or ActiveWorlds, where multiple users can interact in simulated environments that merge the physical and virtual world, creating a hybrid-augmented experience and increasing the experience of social presence (Gorini, Gaggioli, Vigna, & Riva, 2008). These authors also suggest that in these 3D interactive virtual worlds, it is possible to convey strong feelings of social presence (the belief that the other people in the virtual environment are real and are there) and enhance the feeling of togetherness among different remote users (even creating virtual communities of patients). These advances raise new possibilities for the health-related fields: Clinicians and patients may interact in VRs together, or the patient can interact with other patients or other support groups.

These socially interactive experiences can also be enhanced using avatars (Bente, Rüggenberg, & Krämer, 2005; Schroeder, 2002). Existing avatars are still standardized, schematic, and limited in their ability to interact, but future developments of more sophisticated, interactive, and personalized "virtual persons" can be foreseen. Research is still in its early stages, but it is clear that there is an enormous potential for avatars and intelligent agents to have many applications in health care.

Many other lines of growth can be envisioned, VRs could be combined with gamification's possibilities. Gamification is the act of using the elements of game design and applying it to other fields. Currently, there are some attempts to use gamification and computer games in psychological treatments (e.g., Merry et al., 2012; Walshe, Lewis, Kim, O'Sullivan, & Wiederhold, 2003), and VRs could be an excellent tool to blend the two fields. For instance, more options for interaction could be added, storylines in the environments could be based on the patient's actions, or the level of difficulty could be automatically adapted to different responses (e.g., arousal) (Veling et al., 2014).

So far, all these areas of work have been developed, separated, and tested in different fields with little or no communication among them. However, there is a consensus about a clear need for *tying it all together*, to create a *knowledge commons* (Spruijt-Metz et al., 2015). All these technologies can help us to improve the health-related fields in order to effectively offer treatment to change the behaviors of thousands of people in need, simultaneously measure many parameters in a nonobtrusive way in real time, and store all this useful information (physiological, behavioral, and contextual signals) for the future of all these people. These data can also help to understand human behavior, using emerging methodologies such as system modeling. The final objective is to harness ICTs to develop new, dynamic, adaptable, contextualized models of health behavior and behavior change in real contexts in the real world (Spruijt-Metz et al., 2015).

In conclusion, although VR applications and other ICTs are not a panacea, they have a promising future. The creation of applications combining different technologies is only a question of talent, time, and resources. An exciting future that surpasses science fiction is coming, and well-utilized VRs and other ICT tools will improve many aspects of human existence, including Clinical and Health Psychology. Definitely, all these technological advances present crucial opportunities to enhance disease prevention and management by extending health interventions beyond the reach of traditional care (Estrin & Sim, 2010). It is our responsibility to initiate, maintain and strengthen this path of interdisciplinary collaboration, which will make it possible to achieve all these advances (Emmelkamp et al., 2014). We really can do better (Schroder, 2007).

SUMMARY, CONCLUSIONS, DIFFICULTIES, AND ETHICAL CAUTIONS

In this chapter, we have tried to show that VRs are useful in the Clinical and Health Psychology field. We have described these mixed realities, and highlighted the role they can play in different areas. For psychological treatments, VRs can be considered stimulating, safe, and controlled therapeutic contexts because these technologies offer a series of advantages and/or possibilities to help both the patient and the therapist in the process of change. We have also described their potential contribution to the psychological assessment area as an ecological and controlled setting. Moreover, VRs may be very useful as a realistic laboratory for psychopathology, allowing a high level of control of several variables to test research questions that would be very difficult or impossible to address in a traditional laboratory setting.

The majority of the reviewed studies have used VRs as exposure techniques. This is not surprising, considering their ability to present the feared stimuli/situations in a controlled manner and, at the same time, assess and register a large number variables. Moreover, VRs can be a useful tool that facilitates the application of different CBT techniques. In the same way, they offer the possibility of preparing virtual adventures with different difficulty levels to fit the user's needs, making this tool an important source of personal efficacy.

The greatest development has been observed in the anxiety disorder field, using VR as an exposure technique. However, VRs have also been used for other problems, such as body image in eating disorders and obesity or pain management, where VRs become a *transformative experience* that can change our experience of the body and space. This leads to important possibilities for simulating and manipulating our internal reality, the way we perceive our body in different contexts and situations.

Data obtained in 5 meta-analyses and 14 systematic reviews support the use of VRs in the treatment of anxiety disorders (mainly specific phobias), stress-related disorders, eating disorders, obesity and pain management. In other disorders (generalized anxiety disorder, obsessive—compulsive disorder, psychosis), some data point to some evidence, but to date there are not enough studies with sufficient methodological quality to draw any conclusions. In any case, the available evidence indicates that it is worthwhile to advance in this direction in order to define which VRs can be more useful to whom, and how and when they should be applied, to improve health and wellbeing in both clinical and nonclinical populations.

However, there are still several problems to be solved to achieve these objectives. The first is to advance in the dissemination of VRs and other ICTs, keeping in mind that they are not a new therapy, but rather technological adjuncts that can be useful in the Clinical and Health Psychology fields. Second, one of the most important difficulties in the use of these is to get professionals to use and implement them in the existing services and in their daily routine. One way to solve this barrier in the coming years could be to include these subjects in the current postgraduate and doctorate courses, so that future professionals become familiar with these advances. Third, more research is needed using experimental designs with appropriate methodological quality to provide more consistent data. In the same way, it will also be necessary to conduct additional research on the utility of VRs in many areas in which, for the moment, there is only some promising evidence. Finally, it will be also necessary to continue paying attention to ethical issues because, although many of the problems highlighted 20 year ago have been solved (possible adverse side effects of VR or treating more severe disorders like personality disorders, bipolar or psychosis), caution is still required. The use of technology always involves the consideration of ethical issues, and these technologies are powerful enough that the necessary care must be taken. In any case, these warnings must not make us forget the potential that these new forms of experience have in providing care to everyone in need and in responding to many problems that still exist in psychopathology.

References

Aboujaoude, E., Salame, W., & Naim, L. (2015). Telemental health: A status update. *World Psychiatry*, 14, 223–230.

Ahn, S. J., Fox, J., & Bailenson, J. N. (2012). Avatars. In W. S. Bainbridge (Ed.), *Leadership in science and technology: A reference handbook*. Los Angeles: SAGE Publications.

Ahn, S. J., Le, A. M., & Bailenson, J. (2013). The effect of embodied experiences on self-other merging, attitude, and helping behavior. *Media Psychology*, 16(1), 7–38.

American Psychiatric Association.? (2013). *Diagnostic and statistical manual of mental disorders*. Washington: American Psychiatric Association.

Andersson, G. (2009). Using the Internet to provide cognitive behaviour therapy. *Behavior Research and Therapy*, 47, 175–180. Available from http://dx.doi.org/10.1016/j.brat.2009.01.010.

Andersson, G. (2016). Internet-delivered psychological treatments. *Annual Review of Clinical Psychology*, 12(1). Available from http://dx.doi.org/10.1146/annurev-clinpsy-021815-093006.

Andreu-Mateu, S., Botella, C., Quero, S., Guillén, V., & Baños, R. M. (2012). La utilización de la realidad virtual y estrategias de psicología positiva en el tratamiento de los trastornos adaptativos. *Behavioral Psychology/ Psicología Conductual*, 20, 323–348.

Aymerich-Franch, L., Kizilcec, R. F., & Bailenson, J. N. (2014). The relationship between virtual self-similarity and social anxiety. *Frontiers in Human Neuroscience*, 8, article number 944.

Bailenson, J. N. (2012). Doppelgangers: A new form of self. *The Psychologist*, 25(1), 36–39.

Bandura, A. (1977). Self-efficacy—Toward a unifying theory of behavioral change. *Psychological Review*, 84, 191–215.

Baños, R. M., Botella, C., Guillen, V., Garcia-Palacios, A., Quero, S., Breton-Lopez, J., & Alcañiz, M. (2009). An adaptive display to treat stress-related disorders: EMMA's World. *British Journal of Guidance and Counselling*, 3, 347–356.

Baños, R. M., Botella, C., Liaño, V., Guerrero, B., Rey, B., & Alcañiz, M. (2004). Sense of presence in emotional virtual environments. *Proceedings of Presence*, 156–159.

Baños, R. M., Botella, C., & Perpiñá, C. (1999). Virtual reality and psychopathology. *CyberPsychology & Behavior*, 2, 283–292. Available from http://dx.doi.org/10.1089/cpb.1999.2.283.

Baños, R.M., Botella, C. Quero, S., & Salvador, S. (2004): Assessing attentional biases in spiders and cockroaches phobics using virtual environments. *Poster presented at 38th Annual Convention of Association for Advancement of Behavior Therapy*. New Orleans.

Baños, R. M., Etchemendy, E., Castilla, D., García-Palacios, A., Quero, S., & Botella, C. (2012). Positive mood induction procedures for virtual environments designed for elderly people. *Interacting with Computers, 24*(3), 131−138.

Baños, R. M., Guillén, V., Quero, S., García-Palacios, A., Alcañiz, M., & Botella, C. (2011). A virtual reality system for the treatment of stress-related disorders: A preliminary analysis of efficacy compared to a standard cognitive behavioral program. *International Journal of Human-Computer Studies, 69*, 602−613.

Baños, R. M., Liaño, V., Botella, C., Alcañiz, M., Guerrero, B., & Rey, B. (2006). Changing induced moods via virtual reality. In W. IJsselsteijn, Y. de Kort, C. Midden, B. Eggen, & E. van den Hoven (Eds.), *Persuasive technology* (pp. 7−15). Berlin: Springer.

Bart, O., Katz, N., Weiss, P. T., & Josman, N. (2008). Street crossing by typically developed children in real and virtual environments. *OTJR: Occupation, Participation and Health, 28* (2), 89−96.

Bente, G., Rüggenberg, S., & Krämer, N. C. (2005). Virtual encounters. Creating social presence in net-based collaborations. In M. Slater (Ed.), *8th annual international workshop on presence* (pp. 97−102). London: University College London.

Biocca, F., Kim, T., & Levy, M. (1995). The vision of virtual reality. In F. Biocca, & M. Levy (Eds.), *Communication in the age of virtual reality* (pp. 3−14). Hillsdale: Lawrence Erlbaum Associates, Inc.

Botella, C., Baños, R., Perpiñá, C., & Ballester, R. (1988). Realidad Virtual y tratamientos psicológicos. *Análisis y Modificación de Conducta, 24*, 5−26.

Botella, C., Bretón, J. M., Quero, S., Baños, R. M., & García-Palacios, A. (2010). Treating cockroach phobia with augmented reality. *Behavior Therapy, 41*(3), 401−413. Available from http://dx.doi.org/10.1016/j.beth.2009.07.002.

Botella, C., García-Palacios, A., Guillen, V., Baños, R. M., Quero, S., & Alcañiz, M. (2010). An adaptive display for the treatment of diverse trauma PTSD victims. *CyberPsychology, Behavior, and Social Networking, 13*(1), 67−71.

Botella, C., García-Palacios, A., Vizcaíno, Y., Herrero, R., Baños, R. M., & Belmonte, M. A. (2013). Virtual reality in the treatment of fibromyalgia: A pilot study. *CyberPsychology, Behavior, and Social Networking, 16*, 215−223.

Botella, C., Juan, C., Baños, R. M., Alcañiz, M., Guillén, V., & Rey, B. (2005). Mixing Realities? An application of augmented reality for the treatment of cockroach phobia. *CyberPsychology & Behavior, 8*(2), 161−171.

Botella, C., Pérez-Ara, M. A., Bretón-López, J., Quero, S., García-Palacios, A., & Baños, R. M. (2016). In vivo versus Augmented Reality exposure in the treatment of small animal phobia: A randomized controlled trial. *PLoS ONE, 11*(2), e0148237.

Botella, C., Perpiñá, C., Baños, R. M., & García-Palacios, A. (1998). Virtual reality: A new clinical setting lab. *Studies in Health Technology and Informatics, 58*, 73−81.

Botella, C., Riva, G., Gaggioli, A., Wiederhold, B. K., Alcañiz, M., & Baños, R. M. (2012). The present and future of positive technologies. *CyberPsychology, Behavior, and Social Networking, 15*(2), 78−84. Available from http://dx.doi.org/10.1089/cyber.2011.0140.

Botella, C., Serrano, B., Baños, R. M., & Garcia-Palacios, A. (2015). Virtual reality exposure-based therapy for the treatment of post-traumatic stress disorder: A review of its efficacy, the adequacy of the treatment protocol, and its acceptability. *Neuropsychiatric Disease and Treatment, 11*, 2533−2545.

Botella, C., Villa, H., García-Palacios, A., Baños, R. M., Perpiñá, C., & Alcañiz, M. (2004). Clinically significant virtual environments for the treatment of panic disorder and ago-raphobia. *CyberPsychology & Behavior, 7*(5), 527−535.

Bowlby, J. (1973). *Attachment and loss. Separation* (Vol. 2). New York: Basic Books.

Chambless, D. L., Baker, M. J., Baucom, D. H., Beutler, L. E., Calhoum, K. S., & Crits-Christoph, P. (1998). Update on empirically validated therapies, II. *The Clinical Psychologist*, *51*, 3–16.

Chicchi-Giglioli, I. A., Pallavicini, F., Pedroli, E., Serino, S., & Riva, G. (2015). Augmented reality: A brand new challenge for the assessment and treatment of psychological disorders. *Computational and Mathematical Methods in Medicine*, Article ID: 862942.

Craske, M. G., Treanor, M., Conway, C. C., Zbozinek, T., & Vervliet, B. (2014). Maximizing exposure therapy: An inhibitory learning approach. *Behavior Research and Therapy*, *58*, 10–23.

Csikszentmihalyi, M., & Larson, R. (1987). Validity and reliability of the Experience-Sampling Method. *Journal of Nervous Mental Disorders*, *175*, 526–536.

Cuijpers, P., Riper, H., & Andersson, G. (2015). Internet-based treatment of depression. *Current Opinion in Psychology*, *4*, 131–135.

David, D., Matu, S. A., & David, O. A. (2013). New directions in virtual reality-based therapy for anxiety disorders. *International Journal of Cognitive Therapy*, *6*(2), 114–137.

Diemer, J., Mühlberger, A., Pauli, P., & Zwanzger, P. (2014). Virtual reality exposure in anxiety disorders: Impact on psychophysiological reactivity. *World Journal of Biological Psychiatry*, *15*(6), 427–442. Available from http://dx.doi.org/10.3109/15622975.2014.892632.

Difede, J., & Hoffman, H. G. (2002). Virtual reality exposure therapy for World Trade Center post-traumatic stress disorder: A case report. *CyberPsychology and Behavior*, *5*, 529–535.

Dunsmoor, J. E., Zielinski, D. J., & LaBar, K. S. (2014). Extinction in multiple virtual reality contexts diminishes fear reinstatement in humans. *Neurobiology of Learning and Memory*, *113*, 157–164.

Elkind, J. S., Rubin, E., Rosenthal, S., Skoff, B., & Prather, P. (2001). A simulated reality scenario compared with the computerized Wisconsin card-sorting test: An analysis of preliminary results. *CyberPsychology & Behavior*, *4*, 489–496.

Emmelkamp, P. M., David, D., Beckers, T., Muris, P., Cuijpers, P., Lutz, W., . . . Vervliet, B. (2014). Advancing psychotherapy and evidence based psychological interventions. *International Journal of Methods in Psychiatric Research*, *23*(S1), 58–91. Available from http://dx.doi.org/10.1002/mpr.1411.

Estrin, D., & Sim, I. (2010). Open mHealth architecture: An engine for healthcare innovation. *Science*, *330*(6005), 759.

Falconer, C. J., Slater, M., Rovira, A., King, J. A., Gilbert, P., Antley, A., & Brewin, C. R. (2014). Embodying compassion: A virtual reality paradigm for overcoming excessive self-criticism. *PLoS ONE*, *9*(11), e111933. Available from http://dx.doi.org/10.1371/journal.pone.0111933.

Ferrer-García, M., & Gutiérrez-Maldonado, J. (2008). Body image assessment software: Psychometric data. *Behavior Research Methods*, *40*(2), 394–407.

Ferrer-García, M., & Gutiérrez-Maldonado, J. (2012). The use of virtual reality in the study, assessment, and treatment of body image in eating disorders and nonclinical samples: A review of the literature. *Body Image*, *9*(1), 1–11.

Ferrer-García, M., Gutiérrez-Maldonado, J., Caqueo-Urízar, A., & Moreno, E. (2009). The validity of virtual environments for eliciting emotional responses in patients with eating disorders and in controls. *Behavior Modification*, *33*(6), 830–854.

Ferrer-García, M., Gutiérrez-Maldonado, J., & Riva, G. (2013). Virtual reality based treatments in eating disorders and obesity: A review. *Journal of Contemporary Psychology*, *43*(4), 207–221.

Foa, E. B., Gillihan, S. J., & Bryant, R. A. (2013). Challenges and successes in dissemination of evidence-based treatments for posttraumatic stress: Lessons learned for prolonged exposure therapy for PTSD. *Psychological Science in the Public Interest*, *14*, 65–111, Supplement.

Fox, J., & Bailenson, J. N. (2010). The use of doppelgängers to promote health behavior change. *CyberTherapy & Rehabilitation, 3*(2), 16−17.

Fox, J., Bailenson, J. N., & Binney, J. (2009). Virtual experiences, physical behaviors: The effect of presence on imitation of an eating avatar. *PRESENCE: Teleoperators & Virtual Environments, 18*(4), 294−303.

Fox, J., Bailenson, J. N., & Tricase, L. (2013). The embodiment of sexualized virtual selves: The Proteus effect and experiences of self-objectification via avatars. *Computers in Human Behavior, 29,* 930−938.

Freeman, D. (2008). Studying and treating schizophrenia using virtual reality: A new paradigm. *Schizophrenia Bulletin, 34*(4), 605−610.

Freeman, D., Garety, P. A., Bebbington, P., Slater, M., Kuipers, E., Fowler, D., & Dunn, G. (2005). The psychology of persecutory ideation II: A virtual reality experimental study. *The Journal of Nervous and Mental Disease, 193*(5), 309−315.

Freeman, D., Pugh, K., Antley, A., Slater, M., Bebbington, P., Gittins, M., & Garety, P. (2008). Virtual reality study of paranoid thinking in the general population. *The British Journal of Psychiatry, 192*(4), 258−263.

Freeman, D., Pugh, K., Green, C., Valmaggia, L., Dunn, G., & Garety, P. (2007). A measure of state persecutory ideation for experimental studies. *The Journal of Nervous and Mental Disease, 195*(9), 781−784.

Freeman, D., Pugh, K., Vorontsova, N., Antley, A., & Slater, M. (2010). Testing the continuum of delusional beliefs: An experimental study using virtual reality. *Journal of Abnormal Psychology, 119*(1), 83.

García-García, E. S., Rosa-Alcázar, A. I., & Olivares-Olivares, P. J. (2011). Terapia de exposición mediante realidad virtual e internet en el trastorno de ansiedad/fobia social: Una revisión cualitativa. *Terapia Psicológica, 29,* 233−243.

García-Palacios, A., Botella, C., Hoffman, H., & Fabregat, S. (2007). Comparing acceptance and refusal rates of virtual reality exposure vs. in vivo exposure by patients with specific phobias. *CyberPsychology and Behavior, 10*(5), 722−734.

García-Palacios, A., Herrero, R., Vizcaíno, Y., Belmonte, M. A., Castilla, D., Molinari, G., & Botella, C. (2015). Integrating Virtual Reality with activity management for the treatment of fibromyalgia: Acceptability and preliminary efficacy. *Clinical Journal of Pain, 31,* 564−572.

García-Palacios, A., Hoffman, H. G., Kwong See, S., Tsai, A., & Botella, C. (2001). Redefining therapeutic success with virtual reality exposure therapy. *CyberPsychology & Behavior, 4*(3), 341−348.

Garrett, B., Taverner, T., Masinde, W., Gromala, D., Shaw, C., & Negraeff, M. (2014). A rapid evidence assessment of immersive virtual reality as an adjunct therapy in acute pain management in clinical practice. *Clinical Journal of Pain, 30*(12), 1089−1098.

Gonçalves, R., Pedrozo, A. L., Coutinho, E. S., Figueira, I., & Ventura, P. (2012). Efficacy of virtual reality exposure therapy in the treatment of PTSD: A systematic review. *PLoS One, 7*(12), e48469.

Gorini, A., Gaggioli, A., Vigna, C., & Riva, G. (2008). A second life for eHealth: Prospects for the use of 3-D virtual worlds in clinical psychology. *Journal of Medical Internet Research, 10*(3), e21.

Gorini, A., Pallavicini, F., Algeri, D., Repetto, C., Gaggioli, A., & Riva, G. (2010). Virtual reality in the treatment of generalized anxiety disorders. *Studies in Health Technology and Informatics, 154,* 39−43.

Gratz, K. L., & Roemer, L. (2004). Multidimensional assessment of emotion regulation and dysregulation: Development, factor structure, and initial validation of the difficulties in emotion regulation scale. *Journal of Psychopathology & Behavioral Assessment, 26*(1), 41−54.

Gregg, L., & Tarrier, N. (2007). Virtual reality in mental health. A review of the literature. *Social and Psychiatry Epidemiology*, *42*, 343–354. Available from http://dx.doi.org/10.1007/s00127-007-0173-4.

Heron, K. E., & Smyth, J. M. (2010). Ecological momentary interventions: Incorporating mobile technology into psychosocial and health behavior treatments. *British Journal of Health Psychology*, *15*, 1–39.

Hoffman, H. G., García-Palacios, A., Carlin, A., Furness, T., & Botella, C. (2003). Interfaces that heal: Coupling real and virtual objects to cure spider phobia. *International Journal of Human-Computer Interaction*, *16*, 283–300. Available from http://dx.doi.org/10.1207/S15327590IJHC1602_08.

Hoffman, H. G., Patterson, D. R., Carrougher, G. J., & Sharar, S. R. (2001). Effectiveness of virtual reality-based pain control with multiple treatments. *The Clinical Journal of Pain*, *17*, 229–235.

Holmes, E. A., Arntz, A., & Smucker, M. R. (2007). Imagery rescripting in cognitive behaviour therapy: Images treatment techniques and outcomes. *Journal of Behavior Therapy*, *38*, 297–305.

Kaplan, R. M., & Stone, A. A. (2013). Bringing the laboratory and clinic to the community: Mobile technologies for health promotion and disease prevention. *Annual Review of Psychology*, *64*, 471–498.

Keefe, F. J., Huling, D. A., Coggins, M. J., Keefe, D. F., Rosenthal, M. Z., Herr, N. R., & Hoffman, H. G. (2012). Virtual reality for persistent pain: A new direction for behavioural pain management. *Pain*, *153*, 2163–2166.

Kilteni, K., Normand, J. M., Sanchez-Vives, M. V., & Slater, M. (2012). Extending body space in immersive virtual reality: A very long arm illusion. *PLoS ONE*, *7*(7), e40867.

Kim, K., Kim, C., Kim, S., Roh, D., & Kim., S. I. (2009). Virtual reality for obsessive–compulsive disorder: Past and the future. *Psychiatry Invest*, *6*, 115–121. Available from http://dx.doi.org/10.4306/pi.2009.6.3.115.

Kim, K., Kim, C. H., Cha, K. R., Park, J., Rosenthal, M. Z., Kim, J., & Kim, C. (2010). Development of a computer-based behavioral assessment of checking behavior in obsessive–compulsive disorder. *Comprehensive Psychiatry*, *51*, 86–93.

Kim, K., Roh, D., Kim, C. H., Cha, K. R., Rosenthal, M. Z., & Kim, S. I. (2012). Comparison of checking behavior in adults with or without checking symptoms of obsessive–compulsive disorder using a novel computer-based measure. *Computer Methods and Programs in Medicine*, *108*, 434–441.

Kučera, D., & Haviger, J. (2012). Using mood induction procedures in psychological research. *Procedia-Social and Behavioral Sciences*, *69*, 31–40.

Leff, J., Williams, G., Huckvale, M. A., Arbuthnot, M., & Leff, A. P. (2013). Computer-assisted therapy for medication-resistant auditory hallucinations: Proof-of-concept study. *The British Journal of Psychiatry*, *202*, 428–433.

Lombard, M., & Ditton, T. (1997). At the heart of it all: The concept of presence. *Journal of Computer-Mediated Communication*, *3*, 0. Available from http://dx.doi.org/10.1111/j.1083-6101.1997.tb00072.x.

Malloy, K. M., & Milling, L. S. (2010). The effectiveness of virtual reality distraction for pain reduction: A systematic review. *Clinical Psychology Review*, *30*(8), 1011–1018.

Martin, M. (1990). On the induction of mood. *Clinical Psychology Review*, *10*(6), 669–697.

McCann, R. A., Armstrong, C. M., Skopp, N. A., Edwards-Stewart, A., Smolenski, D. J., June, J. D., & Reger, G. M. (2014). Virtual reality exposure therapy for the treatment of anxiety disorders: An evaluation of research quality. *Journal of Anxiety Disorders*, *28*(6), 625–631. Available from http://dx.doi.org/10.1016/j.janxdis.2014.05.010.

McLuhan, M. (1966). *Understanding media*. New York: Signet.

Mendozzi, L., Motta, A., Barbieri, E., Alpini, D., & Pugnetti, L. (1998). The application of virtual reality to document coping deficits after a stroke: Report of a case. *CyberPsychology and Behavior, 1,* 79−91.

Merry, S. N., Stasiak, K., Shepherd, M., Frampton, C., Fleming, T., & Lucassen, M. F. (2012). The effectiveness of SPARX, a computerised self-help intervention for adolescents seeking help for depression: Randomised controlled non-inferiority trial. *British Medical Journal, 344,* e2598. Available from http://dx.doi.org/10.1136/bmj.e2598.

Meyerbröker, K., & Emmelkamp, P. M. (0030). Virtual reality exposure therapy in anxiety disorders: A systematic review of process-and-outcome studies. *Depression and Anxiety,* 27(10), 933−9944.

Milgram, P., & Kishino, F. (1994). A taxonomy of mixed reality visual displays. *IEICE Transactions on Information Systems, 12,* 1321−1329.

Mohr, D. C., Burns, M. N., Schueller, S. M., Clarke, G., & Klinkman, M. (2013). Behavioral intervention technologies: Evidence review and recommendations for future research in mental health. *General Hospital Psychiatry, 35,* 332−338.

Morina, N., Ijntema, H., Meyerbröker, K., & Emmelkamp, P. M. (2015). Can virtual reality exposure therapy gains be generalized to real-life? A meta-analysis of studies applying behavioral assessments. *Behavior Research and Therapy, 74,* 18−24. Available from http://dx.doi.org/10.1016/j.brat.2015.08.010.

Morris, L. D., Louw, Q. A., & Grimmer-Somers, K. (2009). The effectiveness of virtual reality on reducing pain and anxiety in burn injury patients: A systematic review. *Clinical Journal of Pain, 25*(9), 815−826.

Motraghi, T. E., Seim, R. W., Meyer, E. C., & Morissette, S. B. (2014). Virtual reality exposure therapy for the treatment of posttraumatic stress disorder: A methodological review using CONSORT. *International Journal of Clinical Psychology, 70,* 197−208.

National Institute for Clinical Excellence (2005). *Post-traumatic stress disorder (PTSD): The management of PTSD in adults and children in primary and secondary care (clinical guideline 26).* London: National Institute for Clinical Excellence.

Newman, M. G., Szkodny, L. E., Llera, S. J., & Przeworski, A. (2011). A review of technology-assisted self-help and minimal contact therapies for anxiety and depression: Is human contact necessary for therapeutic efficacy? *Clinical Psychology Review,* 31, 89−103.

Nilsen, W. J., & Pavel, M. (2013). Moving behavioral theories into the 21st century: Technological advancements for improving quality of life. *Pulse, IEEE, 4,* 25. Available from http://dx.doi.org/10.1109/MPUL.2013.2271682.

Oh, S.Y., Shriram, K., Laha, B., Baughman, S., Ogle, E., & Bailenson, J. (in press). Immersion at scale: Researcher's guide to ecologically valid mobile experiments. *Proceedings of IEEE Virtual Reality (VR).*

Opriş, D., Pintea, S., García-Palacios, A., Botella, C., Szamosközi, S., & David, D. (0032). Virtual reality exposure therapy in anxiety disorders: A quantitative meta-analysis. *Depression and Anxiety, 29*(2), 85−893.

Parsons, T. D., & Rizzo, A. A. (2008). Affective outcomes of virtual reality exposure therapy for anxiety and specific phobias: A meta-analysis. *Journal of Behavior Therapy and Experimental Psychiatry, 39*(3), 250−261. Available from http://dx.doi.org/10.1016/j.jbtep.2007.07.007.

Pérez-Ara, M., Quero, S., Botella, C., Baños, R. M., Andreu-Mateu, S., García-Palacios, A., & Bretón López, J. (2010). Virtual reality interoceptive exposure for the treatment of panic disorder and agoraphobia. In B. Wiederhold, G. Riva, & S. Kim (Eds.), *Annual review of cybertherapy and telemedicine* (pp. 61−64). San Diego: Interactive Media Institute.

Perpiñá, C., Botella, C., & Baños, R. M. (2003). Virtual reality in eating disorders. *European Eating Disorders Review, 11*(3), 261−278. Available from http://dx.doi.org/10.1002/erv.520.

Perpiñá, C., Botella, C., Baños, R., Marco, J. H., Alcañiz, M., & Quero, S. (1999). Body image and virtual reality in eating disorders: Exposure by virtual reality is more effective than the classical body image treatment. *CyberPsychology and Behavior*, 2, 149–159.

Philip, K. D. (1988). *Beyond lies the hub. The collected stories of Philip K. Dick. (Vol. 1,*. Preface). London: Víctor González.

Powers, M. B., & Emmelkamp, P. M. (2008). Virtual reality exposure therapy for anxiety disorders: A meta-analysis. *Journal of Anxiety Disorders*, 22(3), 561–569. Available from http://dx.doi.org/10.1016/j.janxdis.2007.04.006.

Pugnetti, L., Mendozzi, L., Attree, E., Barbieri, E., Brooks, B. M., Cazzullo, C. L., & Rose, F. D. (1998). Probing memory and executive functions with virtual reality: Past and present studies. *CyberPsychology and Behavior*, 1, 151–162.

Pugnetti, L., Mendozzi, L., Motta, A., Cattaneo, A., Barbieri, E., & Brancotti, S. (1995). Evaluation and retraining of adults' cognitive impairments: Which role for virtual reality technology? *Computers in Biology and Medicine*, 25, 213–227.

Purvis, C. K., Jones, M., Bailey, J. O., Bailenson, J., & Taylor, C. (2015). Developing a novel measure of body satisfaction using virtual reality. *PLoS ONE*, 10(10), e0140158.

Quero, S., Andreu-Mateu, S., Moragrega, I., Baños, R.M., Molés, M., Nebot, S., & Botella, C. (in press). Un programa cognitivo-conductual que utiliza la realidad virtual para el tratamiento de los trastornos adaptativos: Una serie de casos. *Revista Argentina de Psicología Clínica*.

Quero, S., Pérez-Ara, M., Bretón-López, J., García-Palacios, A., Baños, R. M., & Botella, C. (2013). Acceptability of virtual reality interceptive exposure component for the treatment of panic disorder with agoraphobia. *British Journal of Guidance & Counselling*, 42 (2), 123–137.

Rachman, S. (2007). Unwanted intrusive images in obsessive–compulsive disorders. *Journal of Behavior Therapy and Experimental Psychiatry*, 38, 402–410.

Repetto, C., Gaggioli, A., Pallavicini, F., Cipresso, P., Raspelli, S., & Riva, G. (2011). Virtual reality and mobile phones in the treatment of generalized anxiety disorders: A phase-2 clinical trial. *Personal and Ubiquitous Computing*, 17(2), 253–260.

Riley, W. T., Rivera, D. E., Atienza, A. A., Nilsen, W., Allison, S. M., & Mermelstein, R. (2011). Health behavior models in the age of mobile interventions: Are our theories up to the task? *Translational Behavioral Medicine*, 1(1), 53–71. Available from http://dx.doi.org/10.1007/s13142-011-0021-7.

Riva, G. (2005). Virtual reality in psychotherapy: Review. *CyberPsychology & Behavior*, 8, 220–230.

Riva, G., Baños, R. M., Botella, C., Widerhold, B., & Gaggioli, A. (2012). Positive technologies: Using interactive technologies to promote positive functioning. *CyberPsychology, Behavior, and Social Networking*, 15(2), 69–77. Available from http://dx.doi.org/10.1089/cyber.2011.0139.

Riva, G., Botella, C., Baños, R., Mantovani, F., García-Palacios, A., & Gaggioli, A. (2015). Presence-inducing media for mental health applications. In L. M. Biocca, F. Freeman, J. Ijsselsteijn, & W. Schaevitz (Eds.), *Immersed in media* (pp. 283–332). New York: Springer International Publishing.

Rizzo, A. A., Bowerly, T., Buckwater, J. G., Klimehuk, D., Mitura, R., & Parsons, R. D. (2006). A virtual reality scenario for all seasons: The virtual classroom. *CNS Spectums*, 11, 35–44.

Rizzo, A. A., Strickland, D., & Bouchard, S. (2004). Issues and challenges for using virtual environments in tele rehabilitation. *Telemedicine Journal and e-Health*, 10, 184–195.

Rizzo, A. S., Parsons, T. D., Kenny, P., & Galen-Buckwalter, J. (2012). Using virtual reality for clinical assessment and intervention. In L. L'Abate, & D. A. Kaiser (Eds.), *Handbook of technology in psychology, psychiatry, and neurology: Theory, research, and practice* (pp. 277–318). EEUU: Nova Science Publishers.

Rosenberg, R. S., Baughman, S. L., & Bailenson, J. N. (2013). Virtual superheroes: Using superpowers in virtual reality to encourage prosocial behavior. *PLoS ONE, 8*(1), e55003.

Rothbaum, B. O., Hodges, L., Alarcon, R. D., Ready, D., Shahar, F., Graap, K., & Baltzell, D. (1999). Virtual reality exposure therapy for Vietnam veterans with posttraumatic stress disorder. *Journal of Traumatic Stress, 12*, 263–271.

Schroeder, R. (2002). *The social life of avatars.* New York: Springer.

Schroder, S. A. (2007). We can do better improving the health of the American People. *New England Journal of Medicine, 357*, 1221–1228.

Sekuler, R., & Blake, R. (1994). *Perception* (3rd ed.). New York: McGraw Hill.

Semaw, S., Rogers, M. J., Quade, J., Renne, P. R., Butler, R. F., Dominguez-Rodrigo, M., & Simpson, S. W. (2003). 2.6-Million-year-old stone tools and associated bones from OGS-6 and OGS-7, Gona, Afar, Ethiopia. *Journal of Human Evolution, 45*(2), 169–177. Available from http://dx.doi.org/10.1016/S0047-2484(03)00093-9.

Shiban, Y., Pauli, P., & Mühlberger, A. (2013). Effect of multiple context exposure on renewal in spider phobia. *Behavior Research & Therapy, 51*(2), 68–74. Available from http://dx.doi.org/10.1016/j.brat.2012.10.007.

Shiban, Y., Schelhorn, I., Pauli, P., & Mühlberger, A. (2015). Effect of combined multiple contexts and multiple stimuli exposure in spider phobia: A randomized clinical trial in virtual reality. *Behavior Research & Therapy, 71*, 45–53. Available from http://dx.doi.org/10.1016/j.brat.2015.05.014.

Shiffman, S., Stone, A. A., & Hufford, M. R. (2008). Ecological momentary assessment. *Annual Review of Clinical Psychology, 4*, 1–32.

Slater, M., Antley, A., Davison, A., Swapp, D., Guger, C., Barker, C., & Sanchez-Vives, M. V. (2006). A virtual reprise of the Stanley Milgram obedience experiments. *PLoS ONE, 1*(1), e39.

Slater, M., Spanlang, B., Sanchez-Vives, M. V., & Blanke, O. (2010). First person experience of body transfer in virtual reality. *PLoS ONE, 5*(5), e10564. Available from http://dx.doi.org/10.1371/journal.pone.0010564.

Slater, M., & Usoh, M. (1993). Representations systems, perceptual position, and presence in immersive virtual environments. *Presence, 2*(3), 221–233.

Spruijt-Metz, D., Hekler, E., Saranummi, N., Intille, S., Korhonen, I., Nilsen, W., & Pavel, M. (2015). Building new computational models to support health behavior change and maintenance: New opportunities in behavioral research. *TBM, 5*, 335–346. Available from http://dx.doi.org/10.1007/s13142-015-0324-1.

Strickland, D., Marcus, L. M., Mesibov, G. B., & Hogan, K. (1996). Brief report: Two case studies using virtual reality as a learning tool for autistic children. *Journal of Autism and Developmental Disorder, 26*(6), 651–659.

Stringer, C. B., & Andrews, P. (1988). Genetic and fossil evidence for the origin of modern humans. *Science, 239*, 126–128.

Sullivan, M. J., Bishop, S. R., & Pivik, J. (1995). The pain catastrophizing scale: Development and validation. *Psychological Assessment, 7*(4), 524–532.

Szentagotai, A., Opriş, D., & David, D. (2011). Virtual reality in evidence-based psychotherapy. In J. Kim (Ed.), *Virtual reality* (pp. 445–468). InTech. Available from http://www.intechopen.com/books/virtual-reality.

Tart, C. T. (1991). Multiple personality, altered states and virtual reality: The world simulation process approach. *Dissociation, 3*, 222–233.

Triberti, S., Repetto, C., & Riva, G. (2014). Psychological factors influencing the effectiveness of virtual reality-based analgesia: A systematic review. *CyberPsychology, Behavior and Social Networking, 16*, 335–345.

Turner, W. A., & Casey, L. M. (2014). Outcomes associated with virtual reality in psychological interventions: Where are we now? *Clinical Psychology Review, 34*, 634–644. Available from http://dx.doi.org/10.1016/j.cpr.2014.10.003.

Urech, A., Krieger, T., Chesham, A., Mast, F. W., & Berger, T. (2015). Virtual reality-based attention bias modification training for social anxiety: A feasibility and proof of concept study. *Frontiers in Psychiatry*, 6. Available from http://dx.doi.org/10.3389/fpsyt.2015.00154.

Välimäki, M., Hätönen, H. M., Lahti, M. E., Kurki, M., Hottinen, A., Metsäranta, K., & Adams, C. E. (2014). Virtual reality for treatment compliance for people with serious mental illness. *Cochrane Database of Systematic Reviews*, 10, 10.1002/14651858.CD009928.pub2.

Veling, W., Moritz, S., & van der Gaag, M. (2014). Brave new worlds-review and update on virtual reality assessment and treatment in psychosis. *Schizophrenia Bulletin*, 40(6), 1194–1197. Available from http://dx.doi.org/10.1093/schbul/sbu125.

Walshe, D. G., Lewis, E. J., Kim, S. I., O'Sullivan, K., & Wiederhold, B. K. (2003). Exploring the use of computer games and virtual reality exposure therapy for fear of driving following a motor vehicle accident. *CyberPsychology and Behavior*, 6, 329–334.

Williams, J. M., Watts, F. N., MacLeod, C., & Mathews, A. (1988). *Cognitive psychology and emotional disorders*. New York: John Wiley & Sons.

Wolitzky-Taylor, K. B., Horowitz, J. D., Powers, M. B., & Telch, M. J. (2008). Psychological approaches in the treatment of specific phobias: A meta-analysis. *Clinical Psychology Review*, 28, 1021–1037.

Further Reading

Botella, C., Guillén, V., Baños, R. M., García-Palacios, A., Gallego, M. J., & Alcañiz, M. (2007). Telepsychology and self-help: Treatment of fear of public speaking. *Cognitive and Behavioral Practice*, 14, 46–57. Available from http://dx.doi.org/10.1016/j.cbpra.2006.01.007.

Larson, R., & Csikszentmihalyi, M. (1983). The experience sampling method. *New Directions for Methodology of Social and Behavioral Science*, 15, 41–56.

Sutherland, I. (1965). *The ultimate display. Information processing 1965. Proceedings of the IFIP Congress* (pp. 506–508). Washington DC: Spartan Books.

Index

Note: Page numbers followed by *"f"* and *"t"* refer to figures and tables, respectively.

CPI Antony Rowe
Eastbourne, UK
May 07, 2020